European Warfare, 1350

MW00827677

The period 1350 to 1750 saw major developments in European warfare, which not only had a huge impact on the way wars were fought, but are also critical to long-standing controversies about state development, the global ascendancy of the West, and the nature of 'military revolutions' past and present. However, the military history of this period is usually written from either medieval or early-modern, and either western or eastern European, perspectives. These chronological and geographical limits have produced substantial confusion about how the conduct of war changed. The chapters in this book provide a comprehensive overview of land and sea warfare across Europe throughout this period of momentous political, religious, technological, intellectual, and military change. Written by leading experts in their fields, it not only summarises existing scholarship, but also presents new findings and new ideas, casting new light on the art of war, the rise of the state, and European expansion.

FRANK TALLETT is Head of the School of Humanities at the University of Reading, and Co-director of its Centre for the Advanced Study of French History. His previous publications include *War and Society in Early Modern Europe, 1495–1715* (1992, 2nd edn 2002), *Priests, Prelates and People: A History of European Catholicism from 1750 to the Present* (with Nicholas Atkin, 2003), and, as co-editor, *The Right in France: From Revolution to Le Pen* (2003).

D. J. B. TRIM is Research Fellow at the Department of History at the University of Reading. His previous publications as editor and co-editor include *The Chivalric Ethos and the Development of Military Professionalism* (2003), *Cross, Crown and Community: Religion, Government and Culture in Early Modern England 1400–1800* (2004), *Amphibious Warfare 1000–1700: Commerce, State Formation and European Expansion* (with M. C. Fissel, 2006), and *Persecution and Pluralism: Calvinists and Religious Minorities in Early-Modern Europe, 1550–1700* (2006).

European Warfare, 1350–1750

Edited by
Frank Tallett and D. J. B. Trim

CAMBRIDGE
UNIVERSITY PRESS

CAMBRIDGE UNIVERSITY PRESS
Cambridge, New York, Melbourne, Madrid, Cape Town, Singapore,
São Paulo, Delhi, Dubai, Tokyo

Cambridge University Press
The Edinburgh Building, Cambridge CB2 8RU, UK

Published in the United States of America by Cambridge University Press,
New York

www.cambridge.org
Information on this title: www.cambridge.org/9780521713894

First published 2010

Printed in the United Kingdom at the University Press, Cambridge

A catalogue record for this publication is available from the British Library

Library of Congress Cataloguing in Publication data
European warfare, 1350–1750 / [edited by] Frank Tallett, D. J. B. Trim.
    p.   cm.
  Includes bibliographical references and index.
  ISBN 978-0-521-88628-4 (hbk.) – ISBN 978-0-521-71389-4 (pbk.)
  1. Military art and science–Europe–History–To 1500.   2. Military art
  and science–Europe–History–16th century.   3. Military art and
  science–Europe–History–17th century.   4. Military art and
  science–Europe–History–18th century.   5. Europe–History, Military.
  6. Europe–History, Military–1492–1648.   7. Europe–History,
  Military–1648–1789.   8. Europe–Politics and government.
  9. State, The–History.   10. Revolutions–Europe–History.
  I. Tallett, Frank.   II. Trim, D. J. B. (David J. B.)   III. Title.
  U37.E94 2010
  355.02094′0903–dc22

ISBN 978-0-521-88628-4 Hardback
ISBN 978-0-521-71389-4 Paperback

For Evie, Debbie, and Joanna

Contents

Figures

Maps

Tables

Notes on contributors

GÁBOR ÁGOSTON is Associate Professor in the Department of History, Georgetown University in Washington, DC. His field of research includes Ottoman military, economic, and social history, and the comparative study of the Ottoman and Habsburg Empires in the early-modern era. He is the author of *Guns for the Sultan: Military Power and the Weapons Industry in the Ottoman Empire* (2005), and co-editor with Bruce Masters of the *Encyclopedia of the Ottoman Empire* (2008). He has also published four Hungarian-language books and many scholarly articles and chapters in Hungarian, English, and Turkish. His current research concerns Habsburg–Ottoman rivalry in the sixteenth and seventeenth centuries.

RONALD G. ASCH has held posts at the German Historical Institute in London and the University of Münster in Germany, the chair of early-modern history at the University of Osnabrück, and is now teaching at the University of Freiburg. He is the editor of *Politics, Patronage and the Nobility: The Court at the Beginning of the Modern Age* (1991) and the author of *Der Hof Karls I. Politik, Provinz und Patronage 1625–1640* (1993), *The Thirty Years' War: The Holy Roman Empire and Europe, 1618–1648* (1997), and *Europäischer Adel in der Frühen Neuzeit* (2008). He is now working on a comparative history of the French and the English monarchies in the seventeenth century.

MATTHEW BENNETT is Senior Lecturer at the Royal Military Academy Sandhurst, where he has taught for twenty-five years. His research interests are the ethos and practice of medieval warfare with a focus on chivalry and the crusades. His publications include *The Cambridge Illustrated Atlas of Warfare: The Middle Ages, 732–1487* (1996), *Dictionary of Ancient and Medieval Warfare* (1998), *Campaigns of the Norman Conquest* (2001), and *Agincourt 1415* (1991), as well as two dozen academic articles. He co-edits the 'Warfare in History' book series for Boydell Press and is a Fellow of the Royal Historical Society.

KELLY DEVRIES is Professor of History at Loyola University Maryland. His numerous works on medieval military history and technology include *The Artillery of the Dukes of Burgundy, 1363–1477*, co-authored with Robert Douglas Smith (2005); *Joan of Arc: A Military Leader* (1999); *The Norwegian Invasion of England in 1066* (1999); *Infantry Warfare in the Early Fourteenth Century: Discipline, Tactics, and Technology* (1996); and *A Cumulative Bibliography of Medieval Military History and Technology* (and updates) (2001–8). He is editor of the monograph series 'History of Warfare' for Brill, and is currently writing *The World's Battlefield: Warfare in the Eastern Mediterranean from Troy to Iraq*.

JAN GLETE was, until 2008, Professor of History at Stockholm University; he died of cancer in 2009. He had published extensively on nineteenth- and twentieth-century Swedish industrial and financial history, before turning later in his career to Swedish military and naval history, European naval history, and the formation of early-modern European fiscal-military states. His work on state formation was exceptionally influential. His publications in English include *Navies and Nations: Warships, Navies and State Building in Europe and America, 1500–1860* (1993), *Warfare at Sea, 1500–1650: Maritime Conflicts and the Transformation of Europe* (2000), and *War and the State in Early Modern Europe: Spain, the Dutch Republic and Sweden as Fiscal-Military States, 1500–1660* (2002).

STEVEN GUNN is Fellow and Tutor in History at Merton College, Oxford, and a Fellow of the Royal Historical Society. He is the author of *Charles Brandon, Duke of Suffolk, c. 1484–1545* (1988), *Early Tudor Government, 1485–1558* (1995) and, with David Grummitt and Hans Cools, *War, State, and Society in England and the Netherlands, 1477–1559* (2007). He has edited *Cardinal Wolsey: Church, State and Art* (1991) with P. G. Lindley, *Authority and Consent in Tudor England* (2002) with G. W. Bernard, and *The Court as a Stage: England and the Low Countries in the Later Middle Ages* (2006) with Antheun Janse. He is currently writing a book on the councillors of Henry VII.

RHOADS MURPHEY is Reader in Ottoman Studies based at the Centre of Byzantine, Ottoman, and Modern Greek Studies in the College of Arts and Law, University of Birmingham. His research interests include the fields of Ottoman social and economic history (sixteenth to seventeenth centuries), Ottoman historians and historiography, and Ottoman political philosophy and sovereignty concepts. A study of Ottoman military institutions, *Ottoman Warfare, 1500–1700*, was published in 1999. His latest book, *Exploring Ottoman Sovereignty*, was published in 2008.

OLAF VAN NIMWEGEN has held posts at the Universities of Utrecht and Amsterdam, the Netherlands Defence Academy in Breda, and is now based at the University of Groningen. His publications include three major books on Dutch military history: *De subsistentie van het leger* (1995); *De Republiek der Verenigde Nederlanden als grote mogendheid 1713–1756* (2002); and '*Deser landen crijchsvolck': Het Staatse leger en de militaire revoluties (1588–1688)* (2006); an English edition of the latter is forthcoming as *The Dutch Army and the Military Revolutions (1588–1688)*. He is currently writing a military history of the Dutch army from 1550 to 1814.

DAVID PARROTT is College Fellow and University Lecturer at New College, Oxford. His research interests lie in seventeenth-century French political, military, and administrative history, and in early-modern European warfare; and in addition to publishing numerous scholarly papers he is the author of *Richelieu's Army: War, Government and Society in France, 1624–1642* (2001). A Fellow of the Royal Historical Society, he co-edits the 'Warfare in History' series for Boydell Press, and gave the 2004 Lees Knowles lectures on military history at the University of Cambridge. He is at present completing a book on privatised military organisation and the early-modern state.

SIMON PEPPER recently retired as Professor of Architecture at the University of Liverpool. An architect with a Ph.D. in Art History (Essex University), he is the author (with Nicholas Adams) of *Firearms and Fortifications: Military Architecture and Siege Warfare in Sixteenth-Century Siena* (1986) and (again with Nicholas Adams) contributed much of the fortification material to *The Architectural Drawings of Antonio da Sangallo the Younger and His Circle* (3 vols., 1993–4). He has published widely in the fields of nineteenth- and twentieth-century social housing and cultural buildings. He is now widening the scope of his military history interests beyond the confines of early-modern military architecture and siege warfare.

CLIFFORD J. ROGERS is Professor of History at the United States Military Academy at West Point. He is the author of *Soldiers' Lives through History: The Middle Ages* (2007); *War Cruel and Sharp: English Strategy under Edward III, 1327–1360* (2000); and *Essays on Medieval Military History: Strategy, Military Revolutions, and the Hundred Years War* (2010). He is also editor or co-editor of *The Journal of Medieval*

Military History, as well as *The Military Revolution Debate* (1995), two other books and the three-volume *Oxford Encyclopedia of Medieval Warfare and Military Technology*. His current projects include a two-volume *Encyclopedia of Medieval Warfare and Military Technology*, and an edition and translation of the fourteenth-century St Omer Chronicle.

LOUIS SICKING is Lecturer in the Department of History at the University of Leiden, and a Fellow of the Netherlands Institute for Advanced Study. His publications on maritime history and the history of European expansion include *Zeemacht en onmacht: Maritieme politiek in de Nederlanden, 1488–1558* (1998), *Neptune and the Netherlands: State, Economy, and War at Sea in the Renaissance* (2004), *Colonial Borderlands: France and the Netherlands in the Atlantic in the Nineteenth Century* (2008), and most recently, as co-editor, *Beyond the Catch: Fisheries of the North Atlantic, the North Sea and the Baltic, 900–1850* (2009). He is currently researching risk management in the maritime trade of the sixteenth-century Low Countries.

FRANK TALLETT is Head of the School of Humanities at the University of Reading. He is the author of *War and Society in Early Modern Europe, 1495–1715* (1992, 2nd edn 2002), co-author (with Nicholas Atkin) of *Priests, Prelates and People: A History of European Catholicism from 1750 to the Present* (2003), and co-editor (again with Nicholas Atkin) of *Religion, Society and Politics in France* (1991), *Catholicism in Britain and France 1789–1996* (1996) and *The Right in France: From Revolution to Le Pen* (1998; 2nd edn, 2002). He co-edits the book series 'Warfare, Society and Culture' for Pickering and Chatto, is a contributing editor to Wiley–Blackwell's *Encyclopedia of War*, and is a Fellow of the Royal Historical Society.

DAVID J. B. TRIM is Visiting Fellow in the Department of History, at the University of Reading.. A Fellow of the Royal Historical Society, he is editor of the *Journal of the Society for Army Historical Research* and co-editor of the Pickering and Chatto series 'Warfare, Society and Culture'. His research interests are English and European military, religious, and cultural history, on which his publications include, as editor or co-editor, *Amphibious Warfare 1000–1700; Commerce, State Formation and European Expansion* (with M. C. Fissel, 2006), *The Chivalric Ethos and the Development of Military Professionalism* (2003), and four other books.

LÁSZLÓ VESZPRÉMY is Director of the Hungarian Institute of Military History, and Visiting Professor of History at Central European

University, both in Budapest. His scholarly publications include *A Millennium of Hungarian Military History* co-edited with Béla Király (2002), and critical editions of the two medieval histories of Hungary, the *Gesta Hungarorum* of 'the anonymous notary of King Béla' (1991) and Simon of Kéza's *Gesta Hungarorum* (1999). He edits the Budapest Institute of Military History's monograph series, and co-edits the Columbia University Press series 'Atlantic Studies on Society and Change'.

Acknowledgements

This book had its origins in the perception of a group of academics at the University of Reading that, for progress to be made in the great debates about military history in the pre-industrial era, historians needed to cross the chronological divide that has tended to separate scholars of the Middle Ages from historians of the early-modern world. The initial concept was to stage a conference on medieval and early-modern military history that would bring together specialists from across the period 1350–1750 to discuss common issues. We are indebted to two colleagues who have since left Reading, Anne Curry and Clare Dale, for their encouragement and contribution to discussions at the formative stage.

As the concept developed, the editors came to feel that what was really desirable was a volume that would tackle the major themes in the history of warfare in late-medieval and early-modern Europe. We identified those themes and the leading experts on them, and enlisted a group of prominent scholars to write on them. We are grateful to all our contributors for providing us, in timely fashion, with authoritative and stimulating essays that summarise current scholarship and present new research and ideas. We are additionally obliged to Gábor Ágoston and Simon Pepper for their help with maps. We are very grateful to Michael Watson, history Editor at Cambridge University Press, for his interest in and enthusiastic support for this book, from its concept through to press. We also thank Helen Waterhouse for overseeing the passage of the book into production, and Sarah Price and Robert Whitelock for their superb work in production and copy-editing.

Having worked out the concept of the book, its table of contents, and the contributing authors, we still wanted to go ahead with a conference: both to serve the original purpose, of bringing historians of different periods together; and as a way of enhancing the quality of the chapters in the book, by presenting drafts to an audience of experts, whose comments and criticism would be integrated into the final texts. The conference (entitled *Crossing the Divide: Continuity and Change in*

Late-Medieval and Early-Modern Warfare) was held at the University of Reading in September 2007, and has been an important and integral part of the process of producing this book. The discussions between scholars working on different periods, different regions in Europe, and different types of history were extremely productive and exciting. Each chapter that follows has been improved by the comments and criticisms raised during discussion sessions (and by comments over tea, coffee, and dinner). The contributors to this volume were particularly notable participants in discussions at the conference, but important contributions were made by many other scholars. Thus, while the chapters that follow are the work of particular scholars and bear their individual imprint, the volume as a whole is a collaborative work in more ways than one.

We are therefore grateful to everyone who participated in the conference and helped to stage it. We thank the forty-one scholars from twelve countries (Belgium, Canada, France, Germany, Hungary, Japan, the Netherlands, Norway, South Korea, Sweden, the UK, and the USA) who attended for crossing chronological, geographical, and disciplinary divides, and so helping make this a better volume: Ronald Asch, Jim Beach, Adrian Bell, Matthew Bennett, Alan Bryson, Adam Chapman, Alan Cromartie, Kelly DeVries, John Dillon, Gary Evans, Joel Félix, Caroline Finkel, Mark Fissel, Robert Frost, Bernard Ganly, Jan Glete, Roeland Goorts, Rosa Groen, Steve Gunn, Simon Healy, Margaret Houlbrooke, Ralph Houlbrooke, Alan James, Michiel de Jong, Andy King, Gunnar Knutsen, Rhoads Murphey, Olaf van Nimwegen, David Parrott, Simon Pepper, Rebecca Rist, Nick Rodger, Cliff Rogers, Shinsuke Satsuma, Alaric Searle, D. H. Seo, Louis Sicking, Oliver Teige, László Veszprémy, Andrew Wheatcroft, and David Whetham. We are particularly beholden to those who served as chairs of sessions. The conference could not have taken place without the exceptional efficiency of the support team comprising Nina Aitken, who made most of the logistical arrangements, and Natasha Madgwick.

We are especially pleased to acknowledge the generous award of a grant by the British Academy, and the funding provided by the School of Humanities and Department of History at the University of Reading, without which the conference could never have occurred. We are also grateful to the Royal Historical Society for funding, which made it possible to allow post-graduate students to attend at a discounted rate.

We are saddened that, while the book was in production, Jan Glete died of cancer. We are indebted to him for several insightful interventions at the original conference, as well as for his incisive chapter; and we thank his assistant Mats Hellenberg for his assistance with queries and with the proofs.

The draft of the introduction was completed during the autumn of 2007, when Frank Tallett had a term of sabbatical leave. The editing process was completed during the spring and summer of 2008, when David Trim held the Walter C. Utt Visiting Chair in History at Pacific Union College. We are grateful to the University of Reading for the research leave granted to Frank Tallett, and to Pacific Union College and the Walter C. Utt Endowment, for David Trim's appointment to the Utt Chair, both of which greatly facilitated completion of the volume.

Sometimes academic historians are more focused on teaching, research and administration than they, or their children, would like. The editors are exceptionally grateful to their daughters, Deborah and Joanna Tallett and Genevieve Trim, for forbearance and patience when dad was at work, or at home but 'busy' – this work is dedicated to them.

Note on the text

In order to keep this book to a reasonable length, references and supporting examples have been curtailed by contributors, and the editors have supplied one comprehensive bibliography, rather than separate bibliographies for each chapter. All works are cited in the notes by author and short title; full bibliographical details will be found in the bibliography at the end of the volume. This is divided into printed primary works and secondary works, but otherwise is alphabetised. Where more than one chapter from a collection of essays is cited, the book is listed separately, by editors' surnames, as well as by the authors of the various chapters. It is cited in full the first time it appears, but thereafter by short title.

Abbreviations

AHR	*American Historical Review*
AoH	*Acta orientalia academiae scientiarum Hungaricae*
ASF	Archivio di Stato, Florence
BN, MS Fr.	Bibliothèque Nationale de France, Manuscrits Français
EHR	*English Historical Review*
Hk	*Hadtörténelmi közlemények* [Hungarian *Quarterly of Military History*]
HZ	*Historische Zeitschrift*
JMH	*Journal of Military History*
NAN	Het Nationaal Archief, The Hague, Netherlands
NAUK	The National Archives, Kew, United Kingdom
RAZH	Rijksarchief in Zuid-Holland, The Hague, Netherlands
SCJ	*Sixteenth Century Journal*
TRHS	*Transactions of the Royal Historical Society*
UA	Het Utrechts Archief, Utrecht, Netherlands
ZfO	*Zeitschrift für Ostforschung*

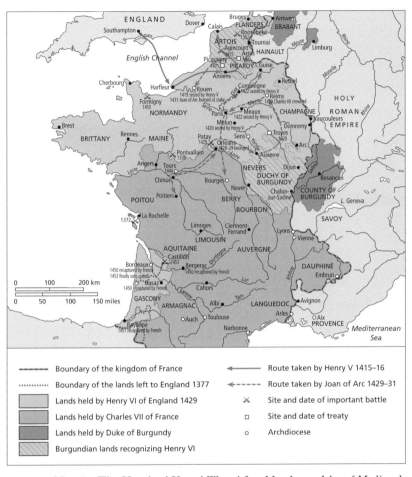

Map 1   The Hundred Years' War. After Matthew, *Atlas of Medieval Europe*, 196.

Map 2   Battles, sieges, and fortresses in the Low Countries and northern France, *c.* 1400–1750. After Tallett, *War and Society*, xi.

Map 3 Central Europe, *c.* 1480. After Magocsi, *Historical Atlas of Central Europe*, 32.

Map 4   The Italian wars. After Black, *Cambridge Atlas of Warfare*, 49.

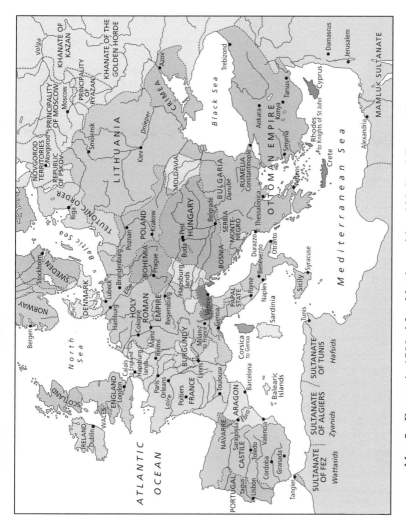

Map 5 Europe in 1500. After Matthew, *Atlas of Medieval Europe*, 19.

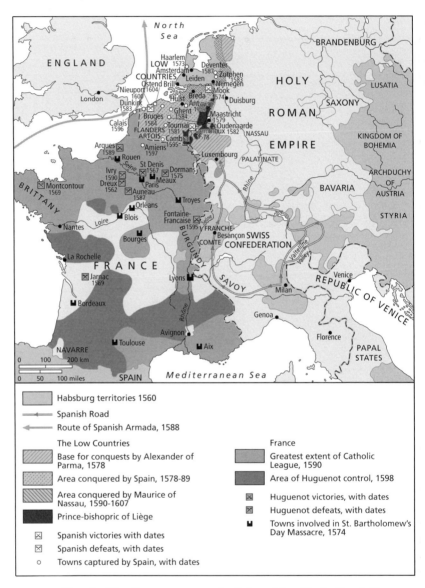

Map 6   The European wars of religion. After Black, *Cambridge Atlas of Warfare*, 57.

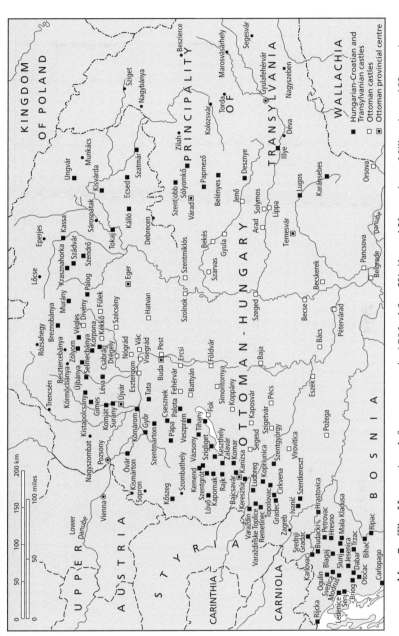

Map 7 The Hungarian defence system in 1582. After Király and Veszprémy, *Millennium of Hungarian Military History*, 722.

xxix

North Sea

DUTCH
REPUBLIC

BREMEN-
VERDEN

WESTPHALIA

The Hague
Breda
1624–5
Bergen
1622

's Hertogenbosch
1629

Osnabrück

Stadtlohn
1623

CLEVES

Wesel
1629

Brussels
SPANISH
NETHERLANDS

Maastricht
1632

BERG

MARK

Jülich
1622

Ehrenbreitstein
1632

Lens
1648

Koblenz
1634

COLOGNE
Höchst
1622

Le Chatelet
1636   1636
Corbie
1636   La Chapelle
Roye
1636

Rocroi
1643

LUXEMBURG

Trier
1635

Mainz
1636–7

Meuse

METZ

LOWER 1622
Frankenthal
PALATINATE

Mannheim
1622

Heidelberg
1622

Wiesloch
1622

FRANCE

PFALZ-
ZWEIBRÜCKEN

Wimpfen
1622

TOUL

Moselle

Philippsburg
1632

Rhine

1638
Breisach

Freiburg
1644

Tuttlingen
1643

L. Constance

ALSACE

FRANCHE-
Dole
1636   COMTÉ

Rheinfelden

Einsiedeln
1638   Bregenz
1646

SWISS
CONFEDERATION

L. Geneva

GREY
LEAGUE

Valtelline

L. Como

SAVOY

MILAN

MONTFERRAT
Casale
1628–9

PARMA

Genoa
1625

⚔ — Boundary of the Holy Roman Empire
✕   Battles
♜   Sieges
●   Other towns

Map 8   The Thirty Years' War. After Parker, *Thirty Years' War*,
210–11.

Map 8   (continued)

Map 9   Central Europe in 1648. After Magocsi, *Historical Atlas of Central Europe*, 58.

1　'Then was then and now is now': an overview of change and continuity in late-medieval and early-modern warfare

Frank Tallett and D. J. B. Trim

This book examines how European warfare changed in the 400 years from the mid fourteenth to the mid eighteenth century. Military change and its effects in this period have emerged as of critical importance in European and global history. Some scholars have argued that dramatic changes in technology and the art of war, amounting to nothing less than a 'military revolution', were responsible for the development of strong central states within Europe and their subsequent domination of the rest of the globe. At the heart of several global historical and sociological grand narratives is the issue of what changed and what remained the same in the organisation, administration, and conduct of warfare, and its wider repercussions, especially for power relationships within polities.

However, European warfare in this period has generally been approached either from a late-medieval or from an early-modern perspective, leading to substantial confusion over whether change occurred, the nature of changes (if any) and when changes occurred (if they did). Geographically, as well as chronologically, historians have generally adopted a narrow focus, concentrating either upon western or upon eastern Europe; historical inquiry is generally restricted to specific national case-studies, and is focused disproportionately on western European nations, particularly France, Germany, Scandinavia, Spain, and England. These have been assumed, rather than proven, to be typical; many scholars have ignored the considerable military power of Poland and the Ottoman Empire. In addition, military historians have created their own specialisms; in consequence, late-medieval and early-modern sieges and battles are often treated in isolation from each other and the campaigns of which they were part, while the implications of war at sea for the wider history of conflict are rarely elucidated. Furthermore (and with some honourable exceptions), historians of technology, historians of the art of war, and historians of the state and of society have tended to talk amongst themselves rather than engaging in dialogue with other types of historians; and far too often historians do not talk at all with political scientists and sociologists.

This book crosses the chronological divide between medieval and early-modern history, the geographical divide between western and eastern Europe, and the artificial boundaries between different types of history, so that the extent and nature of continuity and change can be identified. The book takes as its starting point the fact that armies and fleets were for fighting – at its heart is a concern with combat and the conduct of military operations, and with how societies, states and polities organised themselves for conflict. This reflects the fact that academic history in recent years has primarily concerned itself with the social and institutional contexts of war, rather than the business for which armies and fleets were created.[1] The result has been a rich and nuanced historiography of the relationship between war and society; but it comes at the price of an impoverished understanding of how and why wars were actually waged, of the reasons for military success and failure, and of the consequences. Yet such an understanding is crucial, because the fate of nations could be decided by their ability to wage warfare effectively. In this period, Bulgaria, Cyprus, Hungary, Novgorod, Portugal, Serbia, Siena, Wallachia, and arguably Scotland, were all conquered or absorbed by other polities as a result of catastrophic failures in military campaigns; whereas military and naval success established the Ottoman Empire as first a European and then a global power, and turned the Grand Duchy of Muscovy into the Russian Empire, the Swedish component of the Union of Kalmar into a separate kingdom and (briefly) a great power, the northern provinces of the Habsburg Netherlands into the independent Dutch republic, and the territories of the Hohenzollern Electors of Brandenburg into the kingdom of Prussia. The social history of armies and navies should not distract attention from their primary function: campaigning. This book, then, is a history of warfare, rather than of war.

This volume is not structured as a chronological narrative. Instead, fourteen leading historians have each examined a particular aspect of European warfare over several centuries. All share a common concern to identify what changed, how, and why – and what remained the same. Collectively the chapters deal with warfare across the whole of Europe, over the whole of the period, drawing on evidence from a wide geographical range, and integrating campaigns both at sea and on land. Maritime technology and naval tactics are the specific focus of one chapter, but naval strategy, particular naval and amphibious campaigns, and the economic implications of war at sea are integrated into

---

[1] See Lynn, 'Embattled Future', 782–4; Citino, 'Military Histories', 1070–1.

other chapters. This book thus provides a comprehensive picture of European warfare from 1350 to 1750.

This periodisation was chosen deliberately and reflects three issues. The first is that warfare changed in this period. This was recognised by contemporaries. A military treatise written by the Englishman Robert Barret in 1598 is constructed as a dialogue between a country gentleman and a veteran of the Eighty Years' War; in it the former asks whether there is any need for 'great change' in the armament of English soldiers, whose ancestors had won wars with bows and bills. The experienced soldier simply replies: 'Then was then, and now is now. The wars are much altered since the fierie weapons came up.'[2] As this implies, developments in technology (the introduction of gunpowder) were an important part of the reason for change; however, as chapters in this volume show, incremental improvements in metallurgy, as well as in weapon design and in production techniques, were at least as important as the application of gunpowder to missile technology in stimulating changes to the conduct and organisation of war. When one compares, for example, the War of the Eight Saints (1375–8) with the War of the Austrian Succession (1740–8), the weaponry, battlefield tactics, and even more, the strategy and national management of war, stand in stark contrast to each other. This is not of course to suggest that the armies of the seventeenth or eighteenth centuries were necessarily superior to their medieval counterparts, either in their fighting qualities or in generalship, but that the manner of waging warfare had changed.

Second is the fact that, traditionally, scholars have seen the military changes of the sixteenth and seventeenth centuries as of critical importance in shaping European history – a point to which we shall return below. However, the exact period of the alleged 'military revolution' has been the subject of heated debate. As a result, dates for its genesis and terminus have been extended far beyond the original periodisation; indeed, many scholars now contest the very existence of a military revolution. The only way to assess the significance and extent of changes in warfare is to cover the whole epoch in which 'revolutionary' change has been perceived.

Third, sociologists and political scientists have described this 400-year period as critical to the emergence of the modern international state system, which reached its apogee in the nineteenth and early twentieth centuries. Whether or not this period truly witnessed the birth of the *modern* state, there were significant changes in political realities. In the mid fourteenth century powerful monarchies emerged,

[2] Barret, *Moderne Warres*, 2.

in which systems or central institutions existed through which part of royal/princely power was exercised – systems or institutions that, if they survived long enough, could take on a life of their own. In addition, in these monarchies, subjects had a nascent sense of self-identity. These monarchies were becoming polities, in which there existed, or there was the prospect of, an exercise of power that could continue efficiently beyond the lifetime of a particular prince and so could be effective, to some extent, regardless of the personality of the ruler. Although these polities were still focused on the person of the prince or dynasty, they nevertheless had the potential to transcend them.

That potential was realised in various places and at various times throughout the period; but by the middle of the eighteenth century it had been widely realised across Europe. This is reflected in the increasing use of the term 'state' by contemporaries in the seventeenth and eighteenth centuries. Institutions or systems that had been established or had emerged in the fourteenth century had rarely survived across 400 years; but they provided some basis for subsequent institutions or systems that became permanent. At the same time, for reasons that remain much debated by scholars and in ways that are not clearly understood, the collective identity of the governed had become more closely aligned with the polity than with the prince (despite the enduring importance of dynastic loyalty into the nineteenth century). In consequence, by the early eighteenth century, some polities had acquired such a sense of identity, and such well-established, influential, and authoritative institutions, that the power of the polity was no longer only a function of the personality of the prince or the gene pool of the ruling family.

For example, in France, Spain, the Dutch republic, Brandenburg-Prussia, and Austria, the sovereign's ability either as commander in the field, or as war leader more generally, remained important, but not decisive. Each of these states was a power and a force to be reckoned with in European international politics throughout the first half of the eighteenth century, even when the head of state was mediocre or downright ineffective as a war leader. Spain and the Netherlands were in decline in this period, but still disposed of formidable military power, at least potentially, and this bore little relationship to the identity of the head of state. Louis XV's France was not as bellicose as Louis XIV's, but France throughout the eighteenth century was still arguably Europe's leading land power, even though neither Louis XV nor XVI had the same predilection for military uniform or participating on the battlefield as the Sun King. Austria emerged as a great power after 1648, despite a sequence of rulers who were indifferent war leaders.

Although Denmark accepted the status of a regional power from the second half of the seventeenth century on, it was able to maintain this status and preserve its core territories, while engaged in a series of wars, despite having no great royal military leaders.

By contrast, Sweden had a sequence of kings who were talented field commanders; their fondness for war led to an extreme case of over-extension and the collapse of the Swedish Empire; yet while this again demonstrates that the military ability of the sovereign was no longer decisive in the fates of nations, the existence of institutions, systems, and a sense of national identity ensured that Sweden maintained the status of a regional – albeit no longer a European – power. To be sure, the Ottoman Empire may seem to constitute an exception, since personal ability to lead armies on campaign was an essential ingredient for military success, which was in turn vital if the sultan was to establish and maintain his personal authority. Nevertheless, the Turks did have permanent institutions and systems – such as those that produced the *timari* cavalry, Janissary regular infantry and *kadi* administrators – which enabled the Sublime Porte to wage large-scale, long-term wars throughout the seventeenth and early eighteenth centuries, despite the personal ineptitude of a whole series of sultans after Murad IV (1612–40), the last Turkish ruler who was also a capable battlefield leader. In all these nations, leadership in war was no longer inextricably intertwined with command in the field, whereas, up to the fourteenth century, princes who successfully waged war were invariably also capable battlefield leaders.

The late-medieval and early-modern period thus saw the development of polities whose power was not dependent on the monarch – the emergence of what can reasonably be termed great powers, rather than great princes. In the fourteenth century and earlier, the ability to wage long wars of attrition had been a hallmark of great princes; by the middle years of the eighteenth century, it was also a hallmark of great powers.

Central to this pivotal development had been changes in and associated with warfare. The permanent institutions or systems associated with the state had largely been founded in response to the demands of warfare. They were by no means always more effective than their medieval forerunners, but their permanence meant that they had the potential to develop institutional memory and corporate identity; this in turn gave rise to greater authority and allowed, as a spin-off, the development of military and naval professionalism, which ultimately did help give rise to enhanced efficiency. As this happened, they also enhanced the power of the centre over peripheries, and of rulers over the ruled. Furthermore, the waging of long-term wars, associated with the polity, not just the prince, acted as a stimulus to nascent national identities, which also helped to bind polities together, so that, again, there was a willingness to sacrifice for the polity, even if not the prince. To be sure, scepticism about the rightness of war had emerged in the sixteenth century, expressed by humanists such as Erasmus and by radical Protestants such as the Anabaptists; and in the eighteenth century, some, like the Abbé St Pierre in France, argued that war was actually unnatural. Yet for the most part war continued to be perceived as part of the divinely ordained order, and was regarded as the ultimate test – albeit now not just of the prince and his cause, but also of the polity.

Of course, state development did not end in the eighteenth century. The early-modern state was to be transformed into the nation-state after the emergence of revolutionary political ideology in North America and France. Yet however much the nation-state – the fundamental political unit of the modern world – owes to the rhetoric of the 1790s and 1840s, modern nation-states developed out of the polities that first emerged in the period 1350–1750.

For all these reasons, then, warfare in this period is critical to an understanding of the emergence of Europe's nation-states in the nineteenth century – their governance and government were shaped more by the exigencies of waging warfare than by any other single factor. However, this has a relevance that transcends European history, because Europe's great powers proceeded to dominate the globe – a process that was begun in the sixteenth century. Between 1500 and 1800 Europeans gained control of more than 35 per cent of the globe; by 1914 the figure was 84 per cent. If the dramatic expansion of the final hundred years has attracted most scholarly attention, it was nonetheless founded on the extraordinary early acquisition of more than a third of the world's surface that began with the expansion of Spain into the Americas and of Portugal into the African and Indian Ocean littoral in the late fifteenth century.

Explanations of how this was accomplished have frequently juxtaposed modern, forward-looking, technologically superior Europeans against static, tradition-bound, primitive peoples. Primacy has been given to the use of force: well-armed, disciplined, and trained Europeans purportedly cut a swathe through poorly armed, badly led and ill-trained local levies. It must be recognised that, as a number of revisionist historians have begun to point out, this model oversimplifies what was a complex phenomenon. Non-military factors, such as disease and diplomacy, were often crucial to the success of Europeans; and Indian, Moroccan, Persian, and Japanese military technological development – at least until the late sixteenth century – matched or sometimes surpassed that of western Europeans.[3]

Nonetheless, the ability of Europeans to globally utilise means for the conduct of warfare forged in Europe and adapted to local circumstances clearly is a significant factor in the expansion of Europe overseas. European warfare between 1350 and 1750 is thus vitally important for an understanding of world – as well as European – history. Because theories about the global dominance of the West are premised upon purported changes within Europe, the focus of this book is on these, rather than on developments in Asia or Africa, fascinating as the latter have proved to some historians of warfare. While they help to explain why Europeans did not enjoy unvarying military success in the sixteenth and seventeenth centuries,[4] they add nothing to our understanding of what changed and what remained the same in the European art of war. They do not, therefore, form any part of the consideration of this volume.

Overseas expansion, like state development, has been linked to theories of a 'military revolution'. First advanced in the 1950s by an historian of seventeenth-century Sweden, Michael Roberts, it was adapted in the 1970s by an historian of the Spanish Monarchy, Geoffrey Parker, to include a greater emphasis on the introduction of artillery fortresses (of the so-called *trace italienne* style) in the sixteenth century; later, in the 1980s, Parker ascribed the global dominance of the West to this model of the military revolution. The Parker–Roberts thesis has since been heavily modified and attacked outright. Jeremy Black and Clifford Rogers, for example, have argued for a sustained period of military evolution, rather than of revolution, potentially beginning in the late fourteenth century and not concluding until the eighteenth century; others have rejected the entire concept of a 'military revolution'. The military revolution debate has now lasted for decades and has spawned an extraordinary number of publications, for both academic and popular readerships, but at times it has been remarkably fierce and it still generates historiographical controversy.[5] Yet while the geographic area encompassed has expanded, the conceptual frame of reference is still much the same.

---

[3] E.g. Chase, *Firearms*; Black, *European Warfare 1494–1660*, *European Warfare 1660–1815*, and other works.

[4] Cf. e.g. Black, 'Introduction', 7, and *European Warfare 1494–1660*, 207–11.

[5] For the classic statements on the military revolution, see Roberts, 'Military Revolution'; Parker, *Military Revolution*; Black, *Military Revolution?*; and the essays in Rogers, *Military Revolution Debate*. Recent contributions by key protagonists: Parker, 'Military Revolutions', 'Gunpowder Revolution', and '"Military Revolution", 1955–2005'; Black, *European Warfare 1494–1660*, 'On Diversity', 'Military Revolutions', and 'Was There a Military Revolution?'.

Rehearsing the details of the military revolution debate runs the risk of sterility, especially because this volume is a wider study of European warfare, rather than only of the military revolution thesis. While the chapters that follow are not intended to be the last word in this controversy, they do authoritatively indicate where significant changes in the art of war and the state management of war did – and did not – occur. They suggest that no simple model of a military revolution, especially one that puts undue emphasis on technological developments as the driver of change, is going to be adequate. Moreover, they reinforce the judgement that any discussion of broad social, political, and economic changes must include military developments both as part of the explanatory model and as part of the outcome.

Certainly, while the military revolution thesis has not gained universal acceptance amongst historians of warfare, it has been widely adopted by sociologists, such as Charles Tilly and Michael Mann; by authors of general histories; and by economic historians, such as John Brewer and Jan Glete; all of whom see significant military *change*, if not revolution, as integral to the development of the state and to wider political developments. Brewer used Peter Dickson's theory of a financial revolution in state affairs to explain the formation in Britain of what he termed a 'fiscal-military state',[6] which Glete has expanded into a broad explanatory model for the emergence of great powers in Europe.[7]

Furthermore, the model of a 'military revolution' was the basis for the concept of the 'revolution in military affairs (RMA)' – the term used to describe the marriage of hi-tech 'systems that collect, process and communicate information with those that apply military force'. Because only the United States or, in some cases, its allies have access to 'stealth, "smart", space and computer weaponry', this 'RMA' has resulted (or so it is claimed) in the ability of the United States, untrammelled by constraints of 'time and space', to attack targets across the globe with great precision, the minimum use of manpower and the maximum deployment of technology.[8] However, the conceptualisation of a revolutionary change as reliant on technology was a direct borrowing from the apparent emphasis in Roberts and Parker's work on technological innovation as the driver of tactical, operational, and institutional change.[9] Military theorists based in the United States identify technology as the best source for radical new ways to project power, partly

[6] Brewer, *Sinews of Power*.
[7] He discusses them further in Chapter 14 in this volume.
[8] See Knox and Murray, *Dynamics of Military Revolution*; Freedman, 'Britain', 111; Smith and Uttley, 'Military Power', 3, 8; Black, 'Introduction', 5.
[9] Knox and Murray, 'Thinking', esp. 2, 13.

because of the unwillingness of late twentieth-century US politicians to accept casualties, partly because of an enduring presumption that political objectives can be secured primarily or only through military force, but also because this is what the historiography of the early-modern 'military revolution' seems to suggest.

Thus, in a number of respects, late-medieval and early-modern European warfare is central to current and ongoing debates about the nature of power, both in the past and in the present. Particularly critical are the issues of how warfare changed and how it remained the same, and the reasons for both continuity and change.

For example, warfare, as the following chapters show, was important not just in the formation of states, but also in their decline and even fragmentation. If, as has been argued by some scholars, notably Jeremy Black, the motor for military change (and hence for European state development and expansion in Africa, Asia, and the Americas) was not technological developments but rather changes in culture and organisational ability,[10] this has potentially profound implications for theorists of the technologically based 'Revolution in military affairs'. Similarly, Paul Kennedy's theory that links economic change and military conflict and holds that powers naturally tend to over-reach themselves, if substantiated by the historical record, has potentially worrisome implications for the nations of Europe and North America.[11] European warfare between 1350 and 1750 is therefore of more than purely historical interest.

The chapters that follow do not attempt to consider every aspect of late-medieval and early-modern warfare. Rather, they focus on the key issues: How and why did warfare change in the period roughly spanning 1350 to 1750, and what effect(s) did changes have?

Chapter 2 analyses the purpose, role, or function of warfare in medieval and early-modern international relations, dealing with *strategy* (or grand strategy) rather than the conduct of military operations, which is dealt with in Chapter 9. Polities are examined in Chapter 2 from an international perspective; Chapters 3 to 6 address the role and power of the state within polities, but in the context of actual campaigning and combat capabilities, rather than from a purely institutional perspective. Each of these four chapters has a slightly different chronological focus, reflecting the lack of uniformity in developments across Europe and across the period, but collectively they provide comprehensive geographical and chronological coverage. The subject matter of these chapters includes

---

[10] E.g. Black, *European Warfare 1660–1815*, 3 and *European Warfare 1494–1660*, 1–3, 51–3, 213–14; Wills, 'Maritime Asia', 89–90, 93–4, 105.

[11] Kennedy, *Great Powers*.

finance, logistics, and recruiting from the state perspective; however, these issues also need to be addressed from the perspective of military organisation. Thus, Chapters 3 to 6 deal with how recruits and supplies were *obtained* by regimes. How they were *processed* and *organised* by militaries is the specific concern of Chapters 7 and 8 (and is considered in several other chapters). Chapter 7 focuses on military organisation in the Ottoman Empire – the most significant eastern power; Chapter 8 considers military organisation in the West, using the Netherlands (often called 'the cockpit of Europe' for the frequency with which wars were fought there) as a microcosm.

Thus, Chapters 3 to 8 examine the development, evolution, and efficiency of military institutions and hierarchies, and explore the relationship between state development and military organisation. Their concern is with how states and military organisations waged war, and how effectively their armies and navies fought. They cover most of Europe and the whole of the period, and are based on scholarship in a wide range of languages, including several rarely utilised by historians writing in English.

The book moves from issues relating to the state and administration, to explicit consideration of issues concerning the 'art of war'. Chapter 9 examines what some writers have termed *strategy* but modern military studies refer to as the *operational*, rather than *strategic*, level of war: the conduct of warfare at the level of the campaign, rather than of the battlefield. While the history of military campaigns has all too often been considered only in terms of battles, in this period sieges were of exceptional importance, and Chapter 9 is written by a pre-eminent historian of siege warfare. He focuses on often overlooked yet vitally important aspects of the conduct of operations: 'developments in the nature of military command and its tools of communication; the heavy weapons available to commanders in the field and in siege warfare; and what was known in all of Europe's principal languages as "small war"'.

Explicit attention to tactics (Chapter 10) is essential, rather than considering them as part of a wider 'art of war on land', because the extent to which there was continuity or change on the battlefield is subject to quite different statements by different schools of history, and is fundamental to the 'military revolution' thesis; and yet tactics are rarely addressed by academic historians. In general, arguments for substantive change in tactics, linked to arguments for a military revolution, have been made by early-modernists, and have tended to be based on a superficial knowledge of combat in general, and medieval combat in particular. However, Chapter 10 is written by a leading expert on medieval warfare and combat.

Chapter 11 explores naval warfare at the operational and tactical levels (the place of naval warfare in grand strategy is raised in Chapter 2 and the place of naval institutions is addressed in Chapter 3). Far too often, maritime and naval historians have considered practices and developments in the Mediterranean basin, the Atlantic, and the Northern Seas, in isolation from each other; Chapter 11 explores the impact of technological developments, both in weaponry and in ship design and construction, across the whole European littoral, and assesses whether there was a 'naval revolution'.

The last part of the book considers how ideas and economic structures affected the ways warfare was conceived and waged, and the wider consequences of war. Chapter 12 examines the circumstances in which war was regarded as legitimate, and the forms of behaviour regarded as permissible in its conduct. Chapter 13 examines the ways in which religious belief variously acted as restraint, license, and inspiration for both princes and soldiers. Chapter 14 analyses the extent to which changes in the way states organised for war were shaped by economic and financial imperatives, and the socio-economic significance of those changes; it is significant in drawing substantially on social science methodology, which is married with historical analysis. Finally, Chapter 15 highlights and compares the principal conclusions about warfare in this period drawn by the separate authors and reaches some conclusions about war and state development.

Every effort has been made to avoid overlap and redundancy between chapters; when chapters touch on subjects that are treated in more detail in another chapter, this is indicated by footnotes. There are no glaring inconsistencies of interpretation amongst the various chapters; there are some differences of opinion or emphasis, reflecting the fact that there *are* different schools of thought on many of the issues discussed in this book. Ultimately this is a contribution to an ongoing debate, rather than the last word; but while the chapters that follow accurately reflect the current state of knowledge, they do more. Each in its own right is a significant contribution to the history of late-medieval and early-modern warfare.

Despite the differences in authorial approach, a number of common themes emerge from these contributions. First is the importance of the existence everywhere across Europe, both east and west, of an elite group in society whose socio-cultural identity was bound up with military endeavour.

In western and central Europe, this group was the nobility, which might comprise up to 4 per cent of the population in most of western Europe and double that in parts of eastern Europe. In England and

Wales, where, unusually, only the eldest son inherited noble status, the term 'nobility' was reserved for the holders of titles, or peers, but what in English was known as 'the gentry' was part of the nobility – even English writers of the period write of the *nobilitas maior* and *nobilitas minor*. To be sure, a declining proportion of an expanding noble population actually fought on the battlefield as the period went on. Nevertheless, the nobility continued to justify its privileges by reference to their military function. These privileges were both financial and political. Financially, for example, nobles were generally exempt from taxation because they paid, or were liable to pay, their dues in blood (what in France was known as the *impôt de sang*) rather than in coin. Politically, it was maintained that nobles had a right to offer counsel to a ruler, which in practice meant that the highest offices in government were reserved for them; and they had a disproportionate presence and voice in the representative institutions that, until at least the seventeenth century, flourished in most western European polities.

In eastern Europe the situation was more complex. In the Ottoman Empire, there was in theory no hereditary nobility. Nevertheless, there existed an elite focused on war and owing its status to its military function. The *timar* system linked land use to military service; those who were assigned land by the sultan formed a social and political elite, and though originally 'retention of their land assignments was contingent on military services provided to the state', the seventeenth century witnessed the growing 'financial and military independence of the provincial elites'.[12] In what became the Russian Empire, the boyars (roughly the equivalent of the western nobility, though in reality the descendants of independent princes who had been gobbled up by Muscovy) proved disloyal, unreliable, and a political threat in the sixteenth century; the boyars refused to acknowledge the son of Ivan IV (1530–84) as his heir when Ivan thought he was dying. He therefore attempted to sideline them; *pomestie* land was granted to retainers of the Tsar in return for military service. Ivan IV in particular made use of *pomeschiki* (holders of *pomestie* land), both in his military campaigns and as administrators. Ivan also took more direct measures against the boyars, expelling some from their land and killing others. However, although *pomestie* land, like the medieval fief, was not meant to become hereditary, in practice this was what happened; and *pomeschiki* owed their status to military service. Thus, despite certain differences between East and West, there were significant similarities.

---

[12] Below, Murphy, Chapter 6, p. 139; Ágoston, Chapter 7, p. 130.

It was not only that nobles intrinsically were warriors and therefore derived certain privileges from war. Nobles were also presumed to be innately superior in military matters. While early-modern theorists accepted the principle that some members of the lower orders might demonstrate courage, reliability, and capacity for leadership, in doing so they were demonstrating noble characteristics, which would be rewarded with elevation to aristocratic status. But such men were also presumed to be very much the minority. Princes, who were themselves noble, fully accepted that military ability was the product of noble breeding.

Indeed, as Simon Pepper highlights in Chapter 9, 'For all of our period and beyond – and certainly well into the Napoleonic era – rulers continued to lead their armies in battle in person.' Numerous kings and sovereign princes commanded armies on campaign and in combat in this period after their accession to power – some with disastrous results, others with spectacular success. An incomplete list includes John II, Charles VIII, Louis XII, Francis I, Henry II, Henry IV, Louis XIII, and Louis XIV of France; Henry V, Edward IV, Richard III, Henry VII, Henry VIII, Charles I, William III, and George II of England; James IV and James V of Scotland; Sebastian I of Portugal; Ferdinand I of Aragon; Ferdinand II of Naples; Matthias Corvinus and Louis II of Hungary; John II Casimir and John III Sobieski of Poland; Christian IV of Denmark; Gustavus Adolphus, Charles XI, and Charles XII of Sweden; Frederick William I and Frederick II 'the Great' of Prussia; three consecutive princes of Orange: William I, Maurice, and Frederick Henry; Elector Frederick II of the Palatinate and Elector Frederick William I of Brandenburg; the Holy Roman Emperors Sigismund, Maximilian I, and Charles V; the Russian tsars Ivan IV 'the Terrible' and Peter I 'the Great'; and the Ottoman sultans Murad II, Mehmed II, Selim I, Süleyman I 'the Magnificent', and Murad IV. The roll-call is neither comprehensive; nor does it include those who had experienced combat as princes, but not after succession to the crown (notable examples included Philip II of Spain, Henry III of France, and Charles II of England). War was the sport of kings and princes as well as of nobles. All shared a common value system in which military prowess was prized.

The identification of the aristocratic socio-cultural elite with military endeavour continued until the eighteenth century, in a way not true later. Although the aristocracy remained a military service caste into the twentieth century, nevertheless in many European countries aristocratic identity ceased to be conceived of wholly or primarily in military terms, because a range of other career paths were increasingly available, both in cultural and economic terms.[13] This also reflected the fact that the nobility's role had, in the latter part of our period, increasingly become service in general, rather than military service in particular. And this meant that increasingly service was acceptable in an administrative or bureaucratic capacity, rather than necessarily in an army or navy. The transformation of nobles from personal followers of a prince into servants of the state was only to be completed in the nineteenth century, but had begun 300 years earlier.

The nobility were crucial to the formation of military forces. They provided the leadership and expertise, which contemporary society presumed was innate and almost unique to them. They also provided troops. In Islamic Europe, up to the early sixteenth century, most mounted troops (*akinci*) were followers of lords and not controlled by the sultan; even thereafter, the *timari*, the elite who owed their status to the fact of their service on campaigns, were expected to supply followers as well as to serve in person. Much the same was true of the *pomeschiki* cavalry of Muscovy, whose lands were similarly held on condition of military service.[14] In Latin Christendom, up to the seventeenth century, nobles often possessed their own standing military forces (or retinues), which formed the basis for many medieval and early-modern armies. Even nobles without retinues – and they became much less common in the late seventeenth century – frequently supplied troops to royal armies by mobilising their tenants and dependents; this remained the case in the era of great powers, for in the mid eighteenth century, Prussian nobles and Scottish landowners raised substantial forces in this way. Finally, although nobles often did not pay taxes, in effect they subsidised the war efforts of princes and republics because they generally contributed to the raising and support of troops out of their own pockets, frequently being reimbursed only partially, if at all.

This leads to the second theme, which is the tension between rulers' desire to wage wars that would increase their wealth and power, and their inability to do so without the cooperation of their social and political elites – especially the nobility but also financiers, urban elites, and religious leaders (whether Catholic, Orthodox, Protestant, or Islamic). The often unruly and semi-autonomous warrior class, with its predisposition to violence and capacity to raise forces, posed a particularly significant challenge to any centralising tendencies in polities; yet rulers could not wage war without its cooperation. Other social elites were

---

[13] Storrs and Scott, 'Military Revolution'.
[14] Cf. Ágoston, Chapter 6 and Murphey, Chapter 7, below; and Davies, 'Russian Military Power', 147, 162.

only rarely a violent threat to central authority, yet their involvement in the financing, recruiting, movement, and supply of armies and navies was equally essential to the effective prosecution of warfare. The story of the evolution of polities into states is therefore less one of the triumph of state power, imposed from above, than one of cooperation, compromise, and concession between rulers and the ruled. Thus, as Jan Glete stresses in Chapter 14, 'explanations emphasising "lack of resources" as limits of medieval and early-modern warfare are political rather than economic'. And as David Parrott observes in Chapter 4, polities, if they were to wage war effectively, required a working 'relationship between rulers and political elites, whether of traditional nobilities, provincial aristocracies, administrative, legal, or financial corporations, or fiscal-mercantile interest-groups'.

The necessity for rulers to negotiate with their elites in order to wage war had direct military consequences. The decision to go to war, the operational and strategic objectives of campaigns, the way they were conducted, and the conclusion of peace, might be shaped by the demands and imperatives of aristocratic participants in conflict. These could balance and sometimes count for more than the designs and desires of princes. For example, leading boyars of Muscovy deserted Grand Duke Basil II in 1433, leading to his capture by a rival claimant; Henry III of France was pushed into the Third War of Religion (1577) by the insistence of the Catholic-dominated States-General; Christian IV's failure to obtain the support of the Danish nobility condemned his intervention in the Thirty Years' War to disaster.

The tension between rulers' desire to control and their inability to mobilise armies without the involvement of their elites, especially the nobility, is particularly evident in the commercialisation of recruitment and command, which is characteristic of medieval and early-modern warfare in both East and West. Throughout the period, military and naval forces under the direct control of the state were routinely less numerous and less significant than those raised by contract, although the balance began to shift in the late seventeenth century – again, in both Christian and Islamic Europe.

Medieval forces were raised by contract and by semi-feudal forms of obligation. Even when captains supplied troops by contract (by indenture as it was known in England), they often did so simply by mobilising their household servants and retainers. This continued to be the case in the sixteenth and seventeenth centuries, but by then rulers were also having increasing resort to military entrepreneurs. These men – and there were over 300 of them operating in their Thirty Years' War heyday

(1618–48)[15] – raised and equipped forces on their own initiative, using their own money or credit networks. Their troops were then available to the highest bidder. For such men, contracting and sub-contracting was a business, rather than a mechanism through which their personal followers, tenants, and dependents were mobilised for the service of their prince. These *entrepreneurs de guerre*, or military enterprisers, often sub-contracted with other, lesser captains, who in turn either drew on their personal affinities, or instead recruited by public appeal solely on a cash basis. Army units were owned by the enterprisers who raised them; *proprietorship* as well as *entrepreneurship* thereby became significant in warfare. A whole army, such as those led by Albrecht von Wallenstein and Bernhard of Saxe-Weimar in the Thirty Years' War, thus represented the accumulation of venture capital on an enormous scale.

The virtues of this system were that it allowed rulers to obtain large, trained, and experienced forces quickly, and that it obviated, to some degree, the need to negotiate with elites in society. However, military entrepreneurship by its very nature represented an affront to a prince's sovereignty, and military enterprisers had the potential to act autonomously and against their employer's wishes. For example, Sir Francis Drake obtained Elizabeth I's sanction for an amphibious assault on Lisbon in 1589 on the basis that it would destroy the Spanish fleet; but he obtained the necessary funding from commercial backers by promising plunder; and ultimately, commercial imperatives prevailed over the sovereign's strategic vision.[16] Rulers accordingly began to phase out the use of military enterprisers from the late seventeenth century.

Yet the commercialisation of warfare continued, in two respects. First, small principalities, notably in central and western Germany, began to hire out their forces en masse to larger powers, although these forces were now recruited and officered by the state rather than by entrepreneurs.[17] Furthermore, they formed a declining proportion of armies, the balance of which was raised and paid for by state authorities. Second, as David Parrott argues in Chapter 4, proprietorship remained a prominent feature of such armies, since the officers purchased their positions through the system known as venality (after the early-modern French term *vénalité*). In theory things had changed, because, in principle, officers enjoyed ownership only of their military office, rather than of the troops they commanded (unlike in the sixteenth and seventeenth centuries); however, in practice, they were still

[15] Redlich, *German Military Enterpriser*.
[16] See Wernham, 'Amphibious Operations'.
[17] E.g. Ingrao, *Hessian Mercenary State*; Wilson, *German Armies*.

expected to invest in their command by using their personal resources to recruit, equip, and feed their men. Right to the end of the eighteenth century, wealthy individuals who raised a regiment for the Austrian and British armies would often be rewarded with its colonelcy as a result. The regiment was under state control; but proprietorship and entrepreneurship endured.

A similar picture obtains at sea. Naval warfare was, to a great extent, carried out by privateers. Some were opportunistic sea captains but many were the agents of venture capitalists, who might not go to sea themselves but financed vessels, their armaments, and crew. Such naval entrepreneurs anticipated and often obtained substantial financial rewards from the operation of what was often called *guerre de course*. Larger-scale, state-directed naval operations were only the monopoly of state-financed and state-owned specialist warships from the second half of the seventeenth century; up until then, fleets were put together by mobilising a large range of types of vessels, many of which came from and returned to private ownership on completion of a campaign.

It may be that one reason for the move away from the employment of military entrepreneurs, both on land and on sea, was a greater ability of states to finance their bellicose ambitions themselves, rather than relying on outsourcing. Chapter 14 describes 'a critical threshold' of resource control that, when passed by a state, made its military power 'stronger than any conceivable combination of domestic power-holders'. To be sure, from medieval Hungary to the newly emerging 'great powers', expenditure on warfare exceeded income everywhere in Europe, throughout this period. But in the use of credit, the sale of civic and military offices, direct imposition of taxation (in some polities), and exploitation of Church resources (in Christian countries), we see a range of fiscal devices: some new, others old but implemented more efficiently, that allowed governments to increase the size of their military infrastructure. In addition, tax yields were generally higher, both because Europe's population was increasing and because of expanded commerce and industry. Moreover, some states may even have reached the point in a resource extraction–coercion cycle at which a state's military power allowed it to raise resources without negotiation or cooperation, a development never ascribed to earlier than the fifteenth century – and thus a definite example of change, rather than continuity.[18]

To be sure, in Portugal the wealth derived from overseas expansion allowed the House of Aviz unusual domination over 'domestic power

---

[18] Cf. Mann, *Sources*; Tilly, *Formation*.

holders'; in the Ottoman Empire occupying forces levied tribute directly upon the subject populations throughout the period; in Brandenburg-Prussia, higher tax revenues were obtained in the last hundred years of this period partly because an expanded military was used by the state to collect taxation. However, the Portuguese, Turkish, and Prussian experiences were exceptional; and, as Gábor Ágoston demonstrates in Chapter 6, the Ottomans became less exceptional, with central administration gradually losing control over revenues. Even if a dynasty or republican elite became 'stronger than any conceivable combination' of domestic rivals, rulers frequently still could not 'extract resources' from the ruled unchecked, not least because bureaucratic institutions of this period lacked the necessary efficiency. Furthermore, in an age of 'multiple monarchies', military power might suffice to dominate only one component part of a polity, as Sigismund II, King of Hungary and Holy Roman Emperor, found in the fifteenth century; as the Spanish Habsburgs and the Tudors found in the sixteenth century; and as the Austrian and Spanish Habsburgs and the Stuarts found in the seventeenth century. But in addition, even insurrections that were unlikely or unable to overturn the existing order could create such financial and social disorder that regimes sought to avoid them. After all, even when a dynasty or regime continued, rulers could be replaced (sometimes precisely because they carried out policies regardless of the possibility of insurrection), as happened to Basil II of Muscovy in 1433 and 1446, the Lord Protector Somerset in England after the great peasant rebellions of 1547, and several seventeenth-century Ottoman sultans.

In any case, unchecked 'resource extraction' and the exercise of unbridled power offended notions of counsel, consent, and mutual obligation between rulers and ruled, and traditions of justice and ethics. These existed across Christian Europe and were articulated by well-established representative institutions, such as the Castilian *Cortes*, the Catalonian *Corts general*, the French *Etats généraux*, the *Staten-Generaal* of the Netherlands (and the *Staten* of Holland), the *Reichstag* of the Holy Roman Empire, the Swedish *Riksdag*, the Hungarian *Diéta* and *Rendek*, and the Polish *Sejm*; and by judicial institutions, such as the French *parlements* and the imperial *Reichshofrat* and *Reichskammergericht*. Even in so-called absolutist France, under Louis XIV and Louis XV, the nobility were willing accomplices in the assertion of royal authority.[19] Across Europe, princes and their elites perceived, albeit falteringly, that there was generally more to be gained through cooperation than through conflict.

---

[19] Rowlands, 'Aristocratic Power' and 'Monopolisation'.

Thus, as the chapters that follow demonstrate, in late-medieval and early-modern Europe a range of complex models emerged that allowed warfare to be resourced successfully, though none of these models worked without strains in the body politic. Sometimes, elites (in Jan Glete's words) evolved 'new type[s] of organisation of resources for protection and violence'. But they often met with opposition, so that, as László Veszprémy shows of late-medieval Hungary, reforms were only half carried out; or traditional, so-called 'backward-looking' models, such as entrepreneurship, were adapted and proved, as David Parrott shows of seventeenth-century western Europe, more robust and successful than teleological readings of history have accepted. The top-down, state-centred extractive system that was to emerge as predominant in the nineteenth century was neither the only nor the inevitable model for earlier polities, which could effectively resource war by mobilising from the bottom up.

This brings us to a further common theme. The modern tendency to reduce warfare merely to a question of cost–benefit analysis would not have made any sense to contemporaries in the late-medieval and early-modern periods. Prestige and honour – what the Spanish referred to as *reputación* and the French as *gloire* – were 'both an object, and an instrument, of policy'.[20] Such issues, along with questions of dynastic rights and religious faith, were often equally important as, or more important than, strategic and economic concerns in the decision to make war or peace, at least until the eighteenth century when the latter began to figure more prominently in the calculations of statesmen and sovereigns.

Territorial disputes, at least in western and central Europe, were usually underpinned by dynastic claims until the French Revolutionary Wars (1792–9). However, there *were* changes between the mid fourteenth and the mid eighteenth centuries. In the early part of the period rulers often felt obliged to pursue dynastic claims irrespective of the strategic or economic value of the territories they claimed. Whereas in the second half of this period, as Kelly DeVries argues in Chapter 2, there was increasingly a degree of calculation involved when rulers and statesmen decided on issues of war and peace – dynastic claims would now be weighed for the advantages they might yield to the state, or even be invented to allow occupation of desirable territory. If some English kings of the Hundred Years' War seem to have made pragmatic calculations about the desirability of asserting their inherited 'right' to the French crown, these were short-term strategies and their entitlement to the French throne was maintained in the face of the increasing

---

[20] Elliott, 'Question of Reputation?', 477.

improbability of securing it. Charles VIII, Louis XII, and Francis I of France pursued, at times recklessly, dynastic claims in southern and northern Italy that were never likely to succeed, offered no strategic benefits to the French nation, and would cost far more in blood and treasure than could ever be worthwhile – except in terms of the prestige of the sovereign and his dynasty. Likewise, Philip II of Spain in 1580 felt obliged to assert a dynastic claim to the throne of Portugal in order to maintain his own and his house's *reputación*, even though he knew this would probably cause hostilities between Spain and France and divert Spanish resources away from the war in the Netherlands. Ultimately, whatever the economic benefits that accrued to Spain by the acquisition of Portugal, these were more than outweighed by the costs of defending the Portuguese Empire. It was not only sovereigns for whom reputation, prestige, and honour were bound up in the waging of war and the upholding of dynastic claims. These were the virtues and values of the nobility from which rulers sprang; all noble families were concerned with genealogy and dynastic inheritance. Wars for dynastic claims were typically supported enthusiastically by the warrior elites – of Muslim, as much as of Christian, Europe.

In contrast, although Louis XIV engaged in the War of the Spanish Succession (1701–13/14) as much for personal and dynastic *gloire* as for strategic reasons, he manufactured dynastic entitlements to justify his seizure of territories on France's northern and eastern frontiers during the War of Devolution (1667–8). In even more blatant fashion, Frederick the Great's claims in the 1740s to Austria's demographically and economically valuable Silesian territories were completely contrived. Inherited rights continued to be part of the rhetoric of territorial claims but were increasingly divorced from the reality of why states went to war. This constituted a significant change in the period covered by this book.

The importance attaching to personal and dynastic honour meant that princes were frequently careless of the resources at their disposal and acted recklessly in their pursuit of prestige. However, in this regard there was some change to be discerned over the course of the four centuries under review. The internationalisation of conflict, a theme of Chapter 2, developed largely because princes and republics realised that alliances were a further way of mobilising greater resources. As DeVries observes, 'an alliance almost always defeated a single principality', and so there was a quest for allies to enhance the chances of victory. Whereas monarchs from the first half of this period were often willing to fight alone against great international combinations where they felt their honour was at stake, this generally was not the case later.

Furthermore, the growth of the Atlantic trade in the late seventeenth and eighteenth centuries led statesmen to accord a higher priority to economic issues when deciding whether to go to war. And from the early eighteenth century, there were attempts in most major conflicts to destroy the enemy's economy as well as their military forces.

Dynastic claims had been a cause of war not merely because the renown of kings and ruling houses would be severely damaged if such claims were not maintained. In Christendom, where God was believed to be immanent and to guide the affairs of men and of kingdoms, dynastic claims to territory arose out of circumstances that were understood to be divinely ordained, such as the extinction of one royal house and the emergence of another. No human agency could have predicted that Henry II of France (d. 1559), who had four sons and a daughter, would have no legitimate grandchildren and that the Valois dynasty would thus come to an end. Similarly, the deaths of Louis II Jagiellon of Hungary in battle with the Turks in 1526, leaving no legitimate heir, and of Sebastian I of Portugal on an ill-advised 'crusade' in the Maghreb in 1578, leaving only an elderly cardinal as heir to the Portuguese throne, seemed to sixteenth-century eyes to be the work of providence. Failing to pursue a dynastic claim could be tantamount to a rejection of divine will.

The need to conform to divine will was a significant cause of war in other ways, and this was true across Europe for much of the period, as D. J. B. Trim shows in Chapter 13. The crusading impulse remained powerful in Christendom at least until the sixteenth century. It helped, for example, to push Castilians into Granada, North Africa, and further afield, and produced a steady stream of recruits and financial aid to the armies of eastern princes, from Cyprus to Poland. It was given renewed impetus by the expansion of the Ottoman Turks into Europe in the late fourteenth century and into the central Mediterranean from the late fifteenth century, and by their drive north and west into Latin Christendom in the sixteenth century. Then the fracturing of Catholic Europe by the Protestant Reformation made the religious identity of polities a deciding factor in shaping alliances and enmities. Confessional identity might turn long-established relationships upside down. France had been England's traditional enemy and Spain its traditional ally; but under Elizabeth I, England fought against Spain, at times in alliance with France. Even if princes sought to avoid wars against religious rivals, they often faced severe rebellions or civil wars arising out of religious animosities, and these internal conflicts could acquire international dimensions, as was the case with the revolts in Scotland (1560), the Netherlands (1568–1648), Granada (1568–71), and Bohemia (1618–20). Even where religion was not the main cause of war, it might internationalise local conflicts, extend, and embitter them.

As a consequence of ideological and cultural – as well as commercial, economic, and strategic – imperatives, warfare was a universal constant in Europe throughout the period. War was accepted as integral to the conduct of relationships between polities; *all* polities faced a struggle to maintain their relative position in what was a cut-throat environment. This did not mean that anything was acceptable in conflict – on the contrary, as Matthew Bennett shows in Chapter 12, medieval and early-modern contemporaries had clear, if evolving, notions of what was legal and legitimate in warfare. But the fact that there were constraints on military conduct helped, perhaps paradoxically, to make war acceptable. War was thus also waged simply because it was a natural mechanism for resolving disputes.

Because war was a constant it was natural that rulers looked to maintain at least some forces on a permanent basis. Eventually, to be sure, standing armies and navies became common, but it is important to recognise that, from the late fourteenth century, princes sought, often successfully, to have forces available on an ongoing basis, rather than having to raise them afresh for each campaign. A permanent presence is different, if not inevitably superior, to ongoing availability – this is an important point. However, it is also important to recognise that permanence has implications for more than war-making capability; it also has implications for the relationship between princes and the ruled, and the state and its various communities.

What emerges from the chapters that follow is that, right across Europe, the mid fifteenth century was a crucial period for 'standing armies': permanent forces were established in France, Burgundy, the Low Countries, Hungary, Spain, and the Ottoman Empire. Although they were typically developments of previous experiments, these permanent forces all were to survive. Thus, the standing armies of modern Europe can be traced to the mid-to-late fifteenth century. The emergence of permanent forces was a crucial change, as David Parrot and Jan Glete suggest in Chapters 4 and 14. Permanent forces could transform internal relations within polities. However, what also emerges from the following chapters is that they did not, in themselves, transform international relations because, contrary to the views of some scholars, large standing armies were not in and of themselves a cause of war.

The emergence of recognisable standing armies and navies in the late seventeenth century appears to go hand in hand with the emergence of great powers. However, this seems to have been coincidental rather than causative. It was not standing armies and navies that differentiated great powers from the rest – standing armies were maintained by small and relatively insignificant states across central and southern Europe. What mattered was size and staying power. These were a function of a range of factors, including the existence of a resource base and the capacity to exploit it. Permanent state institutions could help in exploiting resources but could not alone determine war-making capability.

What is also clear from the following chapters is that, similarly, in this period technology was not a determinant either of great power status or, indeed, of the outcomes of European conflicts. This is not to say that technology was unimportant; as a number of chapters indicate, it caused very significant changes in the art of war both on land and at sea. However, technology was almost always shared and did not remain the preserve of any one society. Furthermore, what counted was the ability to use technology.

To be sure, technological differences were a factor in determining the result of some campaigns. For example, the French re-conquest of Normandy and Gascony in the 1440s and 1450s was aided by their use of relatively mobile artillery trains; the Turks captured Constantinople in 1453 with powerful siege artillery; the fall of the Moorish kingdom of Granada (1492) resulted from the ability of the Catholic kings of Spain to deploy modern artillery weapons against medieval fortifications; Charles VIII's initial success in Italy in 1494 owed much to the perception that the powerful French artillery train had rendered all medieval Italian fortifications obsolescent (though Simon Pepper notes in Chapter 9 that reality did not invariably match expectation); and Ivan IV's large siege train played a key role in the Russian conquest of Kazan in 1551. In all these cases, however, one side had a substantial technological advantage. Once artillery technology spread, which it quickly did in the early fifteenth century, the counter-technology of the artillery fortress was developed and siege trains no longer had the capacity radically to affect campaigns. Technology changed the techniques of siege warfare and this in turn influenced campaigning, but technology was not the decisive factor in military success and failure.

What typically mattered in warfare was not simply the possession of a certain type of technology. Just as important were the capability to supply and maintain it, and the ability to deploy it to good effect. For example, what was critical to the Ottomans' extraordinary military success in this period was not their possession of advanced technology per se, but rather their ability to sustain long campaigns by very large armies; and this, as Rhoads Murphey shows in Chapter 7, was due to their having developed by around 1520 effective systems for central 'management of resources and ... re-distribution of those resources to achieve the state's war aims', which, until their breakdown in the early eighteenth century, allowed the Ottomans to arm, rearm, and provision large, amply equipped armies.[21] In contrast, as László Veszprémy argues in Chapter 5, the presence of extensive modern fortifications in Hungary in the 1520s did little good, for they were unstocked. Without an effective logistical system, new technologies might be of little consequence in campaigns. The Ottoman army had more troops with firearms at the battle of Mohács (1526) and their decisive victory has often been attributed to that fact; however, as Veszprémy shows, the Hungarians also had infantry with firearms and considerable artillery, albeit considerably outweighed by that of the Turks, as Ágoston notes in Chapter 6. The Turkish triumph, which destroyed the independent and once-powerful Hungarian kingdom, changing the balance of power in eastern Europe for centuries, was thus not the victory of a technologically advanced power over a backward one, but of a power that more effectively supplied and utilised the technology both used.

It resulted, moreover, not just from the Ottoman adoption of gunpowder weapons, but also from their tactical system (particularly as put into practice by the Janissaries), which utilised firearms effectively. Indeed, as Clifford Rogers compellingly demonstrates in Chapter 10, gunpowder weapons were most effective when combined with other weapons-systems, rather than when used in isolation. At sea, too, as Louis Sicking argues in Chapter 11, while the introduction of cannon on board ships would eventually transform the nature of naval warfare, this was a gradual process, not fully realised until the development of specialist, purpose-built, cannon-carrying warships. Fleets composed of such ships rendered obsolescent fleets that included sizeable numbers of merchantmen, or ships of mixed martial and mercantile design; they also decisively outclassed galley fleets in the Mediterranean. However, this was the result of a long evolution of an optimal delivery platform, not simply of the introduction of gunpowder weapons to war at sea.

Furthermore, the optimal use of technology depended on cultural considerations. The Ottomans led Europe in the widespread use of

---

[21] These drew on the sizeable indigenous arms industry, briefly discussed by Ágoston, Chapter 6, below.

gunpowder weaponry, yet into the seventeenth century they continued also to make extensive use of composite bows in both their armies and fleets, reflecting Turkish traditions and values; bow, cannon, and musket were integrated into effective tactical systems for nearly 300 years. However, Ágoston attributes the Ottomans' eventual military decline to their intellectual culture, which was unreceptive to the Renaissance and scientific revolution; as a result, the theorisation of the art of war and application of scientific principles to combat and logistics that were commonplace in western Europe (to the benefit of the Habsburg armies!), and were copied in eighteenth-century Russia, were unknown in the Ottoman Empire. The English, like the Turks, continued to use the longbow alongside the arquebus and musket, both on land and at sea, until late in the sixteenth century; the government finally mandated the end of archery in the 1590s, but only after a long and bitter public debate, which reflected the pre-eminent place of the longbow in English culture and national myth. The Swedes continued to use pikemen in the early eighteenth century, when all other western European armies had abandoned them, because Swedish military culture prized the use of cold steel.

As we suggested at the start of this chapter, technological development was not simply a matter of gunpowder. The introduction of gunpowder probably triggered a number of other technological and tactical innovations, as contemporaries believed – notably Robert Barret, whose view we quoted earlier. But gunpowder itself could not have been applied nearly as successfully to battles and sieges without significant strides in metallurgy. As Rogers shows in Chapter 10, it was because new, much harder, arrow-proof armour was produced in the sixteenth century that armies made widespread use of arquebusiers and musketeers, discarding the traditional archers and crossbowmen. Gunpowder weapons would have been used in any case for sieges, but gunpowder's widespread introduction in man-portable form was a direct consequence of metallurgical advances. Furthermore, without the ability to cast substantial numbers of reliable cannon and without advances in techniques for mounting and moving heavy guns, there could have been no large artillery trains and no fleets of purpose-built battleships. Military historians have too often written of the influence of gunpowder while ignoring the broader technological advances on which its effective use depended. Technological change did enable significant changes in the art of war, but did so in ways that were complex, and mediated through social and cultural filters.

It is of course a truism that all periods are times of change. Yet the elements of change and continuity in the 400 years examined in this book emerge as being of particular significance, both for the history of war and warfare, as well as for broader political and societal developments. It is hoped that the contributions to this volume help to reveal more clearly the contours of what will be ongoing debates about the nature and significance of late-medieval and early-modern European warfare.

2   Warfare and the international state system

Kelly DeVries

On 28 May 1453 the walls of Constantinople were finally breached by gunpowder weapons, allowing the Ottoman Turks entry into the city. Streaming through the breaches, the elite Janissaries quickly opened the gates, then they and other Ottoman soldiers spread through the large city. The Janissaries proved extremely respectful of the Constantinopolitans. Disciplined and well trained, they did not rape, ravage, or pillage, nor kill anyone unarmed or begging for their lives. The same could not be said for the irregular forces, who were given three days of pillage, the period allowed by the Qur'an according to Ottoman religious leaders. Yet even then Mehmed had set limits: Hagia Sophia would be his, the world's greatest Christian church becoming a monument to an epoch-making Islamic victory. The sultan meant it, too. He personally cut off the head of an irregular soldier whom he found attacking the icons in the Hagia Sophia with a sword. Neither was the Church of the Holy Apostles to be violated, remaining a place of worship (albeit the only one) for the Christians who would continue to live in the city. As Runciman notes, 'the Greeks, as the second people in his Empire, could keep the second great church'.[1]

The reason for Mehmed's restrictions was simple. Long before his attack on Constantinople, he had decided to make the city his imperial capital. Conquerors are different from invaders. Invaders steal all they can carry; immediate profit is their goal, and anyone who stands in the way, even if they do not pose a military threat, is to be disposed of quickly. Often the invaded lands will remain under the control of the invaders, generally because there is no one left to re-take them. The lands provide profit, serve as a monument to success, or as examples to others of the results of non-submission. Conquerors, on the other hand, expect to rule over the lands and people they conquer. They

---

[1] Runciman, *Fall of Constantinople*, 153, 199–200, 204. This remains the seminal work on the fall of Constantinople, but see also DeVries, 'Gunpowder Weaponry at Constantinople'; Crowley, *Constantinople*.

may rape and pillage but only up to a point, otherwise the value of the conquered territories and their inhabitants will be adversely affected. Constantinople provides the ideal example.

Thus, when he conquered Constantinople, Mehmed (r. 1444–6, 1451–81) was thinking of Empire-building, and the Empire built by Mehmed and his successors was vast: by the death of his great-grandson, Süleyman I 'the Magnificent' (r. 1520–66), it stretched from the Danube to the Euphrates and controlled the entire eastern Mediterranean littoral from Italy to Algeria.[2] In addition to Ottoman armies, the sultans also sent a large number of ambassadors through-out the world. Ostensibly charged with making peace, they also spread the threat of war. Their very presence in a country often implied that it was regarded by the sultans as a target for future conquest. Ottoman diplomacy and war-making went hand in hand and advanced a set of coherent and consistently maintained goals.

The military and diplomatic policies of Mehmed II and his succes-sors for the next century-and-a-half fulfilled all the characteristics of a 'grand strategy', as recently defined by Geoffrey Parker.[3] Mehmed and his successors based their decisions on what they thought were the 'overall security' needs of their state: 'the threats [they] perceive, the ways [they] confront them, and the steps [they] take to match ends and means'. While this often involved war, it might imply a restriction of conflict, limiting war. Above all, their forecasts for the future con-cerned 'the state's overall political, economic and military aims, both in peace and war, to preserve long-term interests, including the manage-ment of ends and means, diplomacy and national morale and political culture in both the military and civilian spheres'.[4]

In historical terms the Ottoman capture of Constantinople symbol-ically marked the end of the Middle Ages when goals of war were often more immediate and geographically close than they were long-term and international, and announced the beginning of the early-modern period, when states rose and were sustained by both war and diplomacy in an international theatre, or fell because they could not endure against

---

[2] Discussed in more detail by Ágoston, Chapter 6, below.

[3] Parker, *Grand Strategy*. His definition is in turn based on those of Liddell Hart, *Strategy*; Luttwak, *Grand Strategy*; and Wheeler, 'Methodological Limits'. Although Hess does not describe it as a 'grand strategy', he arrives at the same conclusions in his seminal 'Ottoman Seaborne Empire'; and Ágoston, 'Limits of Imperial Policy', expli-citly uses the term 'Ottoman grand strategy'.

[4] Parker, *Grand Strategy*, 1. The latter part of his quotation is taken from Wheeler, 'Methodological Limits', 10, who quotes from Kennedy, 'Grand Strategy', 4–5. Such repetition must be seen to give status to the definition.

others whose leaders had a more international and grand-strategic view.

The grand strategy of the Ottoman sultans reflected what is best termed the internationalisation of power-politics.[5] Military squabbles increasingly were not based on who wore what crowns or who owed allegiance to whom, but instead were fought over land, which was valued above all for its economic and strategic potential. Dynastic factors continued to be important, but gradually became less significant than economic and strategic factors. From the sixteenth century, wars would also be fought over religion (as discussed in Chapter 13). Wars were more and more characterised by a growth in size and scope, with respect to geography, casualties, cost, and, especially, ruthlessness. Moreover, they tended to be fought between alliances as polities combined, often on quite flimsy pretexts, in order to confront opposing alliances.

The Italian wars both evidenced this trend and gave it further impetus. For eight centuries after the fall of the Roman Empire, Italy was invaded and fought over by outside powers, to a greater degree than its prestige or wealth justified. During the fourteenth and fifteenth centuries Italians fought each other, using mercenary bands: the *condottieri*. Venice fought with Milan; Venice fought with Verona; Venice fought with Genoa; Venice fought with Piacenza; Venice fought with Padua; Venice fought with Florence; Venice fought with Ferrara; Milan fought with Pisa; Milan fought with Bologna; Milan fought with Ferrara; Milan fought with Florence; Florence fought with Pisa; Florence fought with Lucca; Florence fought with Pistoia; Florence fought with Siena; Florence fought with Volterra; and Florence fought with the Papacy, who it seemed paid everyone to fight each other.[6] Although alliances and truces were frequently made during the period, none lasted for very long.

Yet despite their bellicose pedigrees, the Italian states were shocked by French military power when Charles VIII invaded Italy in 1494 to exert his claim to the Neapolitan throne. Machiavelli, Guicciardini, and Cellini all expressed amazement at the French king's military feat, while Pope Alexander VI, on hearing of his approach to Rome, fled through a secret passage from the Vatican to the Castel Sant' Angelo.[7]

---

[5] The terms 'globalisation' and 'imperialism' can also be used to describe these developments, but both tend to have been politicised more than 'internationalisation'.

[6] The best study of the military history of Italy during this period remains Mallett, *Mercenaries*.

[7] The best studies on the 1494 French invasion of Italy are in Abulafia, *French Descent*. Machiavelli refers to it, in both *Prince* and *Art of War*; Guicciardini in his *History of Italy*; and Cellini in his classic *Autobiography*. On Alexander VI, see Mallett, *Borgias*.

Ironically, Charles' expedition turned out to be almost completely fruitless from a French perspective, with most of his men dying of disease or at the battle of Fornovo (6 July 1495).[8] But his invasion opened the flood-gates of European conflict in the Italian peninsula, which were not closed until the middle of the sixteenth century. This was probably because none of the Italian city-states felt that they could face such a large and powerful army as the French in battle. Indeed, some of the larger polities – Milan, Florence, and the Papal States – chose to ally with the French, although others, including Venice and Naples, chose to oppose them. The Venetians and Neapolitans accordingly made their own alliances with Maximilian I of the Holy Roman Empire; Ferdinand II, king of Aragon; and his wife, Isabella, queen of Castile. The small Italian states learned how dangerous it was both to oppose and to ally with larger competitors. Charles VIII left Italy after Fornovo, abandoning his former allies to fare as best they could. It took little time for Spanish forces under General Gonzalo Fernández de Córdoba to enter Naples and eject its small French garrison. The Milanese, led by Duke Ludovico Sforza, quickly sued for peace and negotiated an alliance of their own with the Spanish and Germans.

Warfare persisted for the next half-century. Following the deaths of the Holy Roman Emperor Maximilian I, and Ferdinand II of Aragon, in 1519 and 1516 respectively, their grandson Charles V continued the fighting against France and its allies in Italy. When he abdicated the throne in 1555–6 and divided his lands between his brother, Ferdinand I (the Holy Roman Empire and Austrian territories), and son, Philip II (Spain and the Low Countries), they too continued the wars. When Charles VIII of France died in 1498, his bellicose legacy was continued first by Louis XII (r. 1498–1515), then by Francis I until 1547, and then by Henry II (r. 1547–59). By the time of Henry's death the conflicts in Italy had come to be wholly subsumed into the bigger rivalry between the Habsburgs and France. Italian allies were adopted by the Germans, Spanish, and French, of course, but the wars transcended their peninsular disputes. Even the relatively large and wealthy Italian polities, Milan, Florence, Venice, and Naples, were forced to sit on the sidelines as larger and more technologically advanced European armies strove for mastery.[9] France won a victory at Ravenna (1512) but lost at Novara (1513) and then returned with a triumph at Marignano

---

[8] Nicolle, *Fornovo*, is a good study.
[9] On the condition (and impotence) of the Italian states during these wars, see Covini, 'Liens', and 'Bonds'.

(1515).[10] Habsburg forces dealt heavy blows to French military prestige with impressive tactical performances at Bicocca in 1522 and Pavia in 1525, but then tarnished their reputation – in effect suffering a strategic reversal – by sacking Rome in 1527.[11] In the Italian wars fought from 1527 to 1529 the Habsburgs won only a marginal victory but did recover Burgundy. Between 1536 and 1538 France secured victory and also had the upper hand in the fighting of 1543 and 1544, albeit only marginally. In the final stage of this round of conflict, 1551 to 1559, the Habsburgs emerged the winners.[12] By the middle decades of the sixteenth century the wars had spread outside Italy, though this continued to host the majority of engagements; and other major European states had joined in. England, under Henry VIII and Mary, took to the field, gaining Boulogne from France in 1544, only to lose that and Calais in between 1557 and 1558.[13]

Most of these later Italian wars ended in treaties – Cambrai in 1529, Nice in 1538, and Crépy in 1544 – which actually turned out to be only short-lived truces. Yet when both sides met and signed the Peace of Cateau-Cambrésis on 3 April 1559 the wars that had been ongoing for sixty-five years came to an end. The treaty was sensible: Henry gave Savoy and Piedmont to Emmanuel-Philibert of Savoy, an ally of Spain but someone he could tolerate and work with; he returned Corsica to Genoa; and he gave up rights to Milan. The Holy Roman Empire and Spain had to cede Turin, Saluzzo, Pinerolo, and two other fortified locations to France, which also retained control over the bishoprics of Toul, Metz, and Verdun, won from Charles V, and Calais, taken from Mary Tudor.[14] Yet taken overall, the terms of the Peace of Cateau-Cambrésis were no better or worse than those in previous agreements. So, why did the Peace of Cateau-Cambrésis endure?

Historians have usually provided two answers. The first is the shift from 'dynastic' to 'religious' wars in Europe. The Italian wars (and those fought elsewhere in Europe at the same time) were between rival dynasties – in this case Valois and Habsburg – competing above all for prestige as well as for the land that they claimed by right of dynastic

---

[10] In general on the wars of Italy see Taylor, *Art of War*; Tracy, *Emperor Charles V*; and the articles in Balsamo, *Passer les monts*; Boillet and Piejus, *Guerres d'Italie*; and Shaw, *Italy*.

[11] The battle of Bicocca has received limited interest and can be accessed only in the general works above. For Pavia see Giono, *Battle of Pavia*, and Konstam, *Pavia*. On the Sack of Rome see Chastel, *Sack of Rome*, and Hook, *Sack of Rome*.

[12] Troso, *Italia!*, is a little-known but excellent work on this period.

[13] See Fissel, *English Warfare*, 1–20.

[14] The standard treatment of the peace conference and treaty of Cateau-Cambrésis is Russell, *Peacemaking*.

succession. The religious wars, notably those in the second half of the sixteenth and first half of the seventeenth century, while not completely without dynastic motivation, nonetheless emphasised the ability to secure religious control over peoples who were already under political suzerainty: the civil wars in France, the wars between principalities in the Holy Roman Empire, the wars between cantons in Switzerland, and the Spanish wars in the Netherlands would be good examples. Cateau-Cambrésis, it is said, allowed for the shift from one type of war to another.[15] But it is more complex than that. France was thrown into an inheritance crisis by the death of Henry II in a freak tournament accident and it was this, as well as confessional differences, that triggered almost forty years of religious wars, from 1562 until Henry IV's 'Paris is well worth the price of a mass' conversion enabled him to win over both Catholics and Protestants and, in 1598, to end the *guerres de religion*.[16] Dynastic accident as well as religious civil war made France a cipher on the international scene and prevented her challenging the terms of Cateau-Cambrésis.

However, there is another for the success of the Peace of Cateau-Cambrésis, albeit one that is rarely recognised: internationalisation. By this I mean that the states involved in the peace conference and signatories to the two treaties that arose from it became more interested in the larger geographical world and their places in it than they did in parochial conflicts with their neighbours.[17] The proximity of Ottoman armies to the south-eastern frontier was of greater concern to the new Emperor, Ferdinand I, than they had been to his brother, Charles V.[18] Under Charles, imperial armies had stopped Süleyman the Magnificent from capturing Vienna in 1529, but thereafter they had done little to keep Ottoman forces from threatening the borders. After Güns was captured in 1532, following a dramatic defence of the town by its garrison and militia, who numbered fewer than 700 men but received little help from imperial forces, a permanent Ottoman military presence

---

[15] This is usually the progression made in broad chronological military histories; for example, Ropp, *War in the Modern World*; Howard, *War in European History*; Jones, *Art of War*; and Archer *et al.*, *World History of Warfare*.

[16] Knecht, *French Religious Wars* is a concise introduction; his *French Civil Wars* is a more detailed work; Holt, *French Wars of Religion* is the best overview history. On the conversion of Henry IV see Wolfe, *Conversion*.

[17] Because France dissolved into civil and religious wars for the rest of the century, its internationalisation is not immediately apparent, and difficult to link to the Peace of Cateau-Cambrésis. As such it is not included in this discussion of the signatories of the 1559 treaties.

[18] The Holy Roman Empire was not an actual signatory of the treaties of Cateau-Cambrésis, but as they also ended imperial conflict with France in Italy, allowing Emperor Ferdinand effectively to change his foreign policy, it is included here.

was stationed less than 100 kilometres from Vienna. Subsequent conquests of important Hungarian towns in 1543 and 1544 rendered the Ottoman imperial border even more insecure. Nor did the peace treaty between the two powers negotiated in 1547 bring stability: it lasted a mere four years.[19] Apart from the defence of Vienna and raids (both successful and unsuccessful) on the Ottoman-ruled North African littoral,[20] Charles V had thus done little to oppose Ottoman power in Europe or along the Mediterranean. The actions of Ferdinand I after Cateau-Cambrésis in shifting the military emphasis to the Ottoman frontier reflected dissatisfaction amongst some in the imperial court – probably including Ferdinand himself – with Charles V's military priorities. Ferdinand had greater personal knowledge of Ottoman military capabilities than his brother: it had been Ferdinand's decision to send troops into Transylvania in 1551 that had prompted the breaking of the Peace of 1547, and that led to Turkish victories at Szeged, Fülek (Fil'akov), and Temesvár in 1552. Peace with France in 1559 allowed Ferdinand to make the Ottoman threat his chief military priority.

As for Spain, the treaties of Cateau-Cambrésis also enabled Philip II to broaden his military perspective. This was especially important because his New World holdings, which had recently begun to pay huge economic dividends, and the religious problems of the Low Countries required attention. Philip could now redirect his gaze and his resources beyond the immediate problems with France – easier to do after victories at Saint-Quentin (1557) and Gravelines (1558) and a favourable peace in 1559 – to the potential financial rewards from the Americas[21] and to the looming fight with Protestantism in the Netherlands.[22] Military and economic threats from Portugal and Morocco as well as Ottoman expansion into the western Mediterranean also required consideration; while England, under his step-sister-in-law, Elizabeth, was a potential enemy.

Within the generation after Cateau-Cambrésis, Philip would be at war with his Dutch subjects, Portugal, and England. It took fewer than five years for Philip to stir up the Low Countries, and only four more before Spanish troops were in Brussels.[23] By 1568 the government of the Low Countries

---

[19] Black, *Cambridge Atlas of Warfare*, 25–6, and Turnbull, *Ottoman Empire*, 52–3.

[20] See Tracy, *Charles V's Crusades*, which is given context in his *Emperor Charles V*.

[21] Parker's *Grand Strategy* defines this as part of the 'grand strategy' of Philip. See also his *World Is Not Enough*.

[22] Even before the Treaty of Cateau-Cambrésis, Philip had begun making demands on the religious diversity of the Low Countries. See Israel, *Dutch Republic*, 129–37.

[23] The chronology of the Dutch Revolt can be followed in numerous historical works. The best modern account is Parker, *Dutch Revolt*, although there is still great value in the classics of Geyl, *Revolt*, and Motley, *United Netherlands*.

had been radically reformed, to the anger of many Netherlanders, and the leading Protestant nobles were in exile. It is difficult not to see Philip's confessionally shaped grand strategy at work here, although he undoubtedly believed that any military action would be short and end in easy victory. Of course, the Eighty Years' War (1568–1648) and the establishment of a sovereign state in the northern Netherlands proved him wrong, but this outcome was inconceivable in 1559–67 when this aspect of Philip's policy of internationalisation was initially implemented.

The situation with Portugal was settled more smoothly. For centuries, relations between the various Iberian kingdoms had been turbulent. While the medieval military history of Spain usually focuses on the *reconquista* of Muslim sultanates, it could as easily be perceived as a series of civil wars between Christian principalities, punctuated with periods of Christian–Muslim conflict.[24] The disunity of much of Christian Iberia was ended by the marriage of Ferdinand of Aragon and Isabella of Castile in 1469 and the subsequent accession to their thrones by their grandson, Charles V, in 1516, but Portugal continued to remain independent. Although Portugal in the fifteenth and early sixteenth centuries had conducted military operations against its Iberian neighbours as well as more distant foes, while Philip II was king there was peace, with Philip exhibiting a patience that some historians have judged to be uncharacteristic but was also undoubtedly part of his grand strategy.[25] Ultimately, patience brought Philip greater rewards than he would probably have gained from launching a war against Portugal. Her young king, Sebastian I, was killed by the Moroccans at the battle of Alcazarquivir on 4 August 1578.[26] His successor and great-uncle, Cardinal Henry, ruled for only two years and died childless: as a cleric he could in any event have had no legitimate heirs. At this point Philip, as a cousin, put forward his claim to the vacant throne. There were other claimants, including other European royalty, but Philip had the wealth, army, and ecclesiastical support to back his claim, and in April 1581 he was formally named King of Portugal at the *Cortes* of Thomar. His overseas Empire now included Brazil and several trading posts in Africa, the southern Arabian peninsula, India, the East Indies, Macao, and Nagasaki.

---

[24] Hillgarth makes exactly this point in his seminal *Spanish Kingdoms*. But the *Reconquista* still holds sway for many medieval military historians, as in O'Callaghan, *Reconquest and Crusade*; Lomax, *Reconquest*; and Reilly, *Contest*. Interestingly, many Spanish historians prefer Hillgarth's approach and believe that Anglo-American historians of medieval Spain have overemphasised the importance of the *Reconquista*.

[25] Unfortunately, in *Grand Strategy*, Parker does not deal with Portugal. On the relationship between Portugal and Spain see Elliott, *Imperial Spain*, 264–73.

[26] Alcazarquivir is the most frequent anglicisation of the Arabic place name.

By the mid sixteenth century the Spanish overseas territories were not only extensive but had also begun to pay huge economic dividends. The first fifty years of Spanish conquests in the Americas had produced meagre benefits, insufficient even to cover the military costs. Nevertheless, this in no way diminished the wish of the conquerors, impelled by military adventurism and a sense of 'manifest destiny', to acquire more lands, especially as it seemed easy to do. Hispaniola was captured in 1492, Panama and Nicaragua in 1510–24, Puerto Rico in 1511, Cuba in 1511–13, Mexico in 1519–21, Guatemala in 1523–42, Tumbres in 1526, Cartagena in 1532, Lima in 1535, Honduras in 1536–8, New Granada (Columbia) in 1536–9, Asunción in 1537, Valparaiso and Buenos Aires in 1536, Campeche in 1540, the Central Andes in 1540–58, Santiago in 1541, Potosí (Bolivia) in 1545, La Paz in 1548, Valdivia in 1552, Florida in 1565, and Caracas in 1567.[27] Some gold and silver had trickled into Spain between 1500 and 1545, but the discovery of silver mines at Potosí in that year heightened interest in the wealth of the Americas, and when silver mines in Zacatecas (in Mexico) were added three years later the resulting economic benefits began to change Spanish governmental policies. Significantly, Spanish grand strategy became even more internationalised.

Charles V had shown little recognition of these potential riches. But Philip II was aware that shipments of treasure from the New World increased steadily throughout his reign, and brought enormous wealth.[28] Because Cateau-Cambrésis had freed Philip from many of his European military concerns, he was able to devote a large proportion of his fleet to the transportation and protection of the American treasure, and by the mid 1560s a system was in place to secure this. The timing was determined by the hurricane season. Each year, a first fleet, the *flota*, was sent to Vera Cruz in Mexico in May, and a second fleet, the *galeones*, to Nombre de Dios in Panama in August.[29] Both fleets numbered sixty to seventy ships and the trip to and from the Americas took approximately ten to twelve weeks. The schedule made it easy to coordinate logistics on both sides of the Atlantic, but it also meant that the Spanish were not the only ones to know the chronology of the shipments, although, at least initially, secrecy

---

[27] Although there are many substantial studies of the Spanish conquest of the New World, the basic names, dates, and places can be found in Black, *Cambridge Atlas of Warfare*, 12–14, and Seed, 'Conquest'.

[28] Elliott, *Europe Divided*, 61 has a short but extremely impressive chart of the silver that was brought into Spain between 1560 and 1600, ultimately totalling several hundred million ducats. For greater detail, see Hamilton, 'Imports'.

[29] I owe the suggestion that this was determined by the Caribbean hurricane season to my Loyola University colleague, Bill M. Donovan, for whose assistance in this essay I am very grateful.

was not much of an issue as the fleets were so well protected that only the most suicidal captains would risk an attack.[30]

Nevertheless, a few felt the risk was worthwhile. Early threats to the treasure fleets came from French 'pirates', soon joined by English privateers. Ultimately, Elizabeth I's government would torture and burn English Catholics (some with ties to Spain) while welcoming Protestant exiles from the Low Countries; she would support the Dutch rebels and the Spanish Moriscos.[31] Conversely, Philip would later seek to dethrone Elizabeth and send armadas against England. But in 1559 Spain and England were on the same side, with France as the common enemy. Religion and geo-political issues drove the two kingdoms apart. Religion was the expressed reason for English intercession on the side of the Protestants in the Dutch Revolt. English involvement was initially covert and difficult to trace back to any official military policy.[32] It became overt with the signature of the Treaty of Nonsuch (1585) and the despatch of Robert Dudley, the earl of Leicester, to the Netherlands with an English army. Most historians suggest that this change of course was a reaction to the assassination of William of Orange on 10 July 1584, an event that many in Protestant Europe worried would mean an end to the Dutch Revolt. William had not only been fighting in defence of Protestantism but also keeping the Spanish occupied.[33] England entered into a war that had become a stalemate, but that threatened to eventuate in a Spanish victory in the Low Countries, which would have given them dominance over the Channel, thereby immediately allowing them realistically to threaten England with invasion. Although Leicester's campaign in the Low Countries was largely unsuccessful in operational terms,[34] it bolstered the rebel cause, and all was forgiven with the defeat of the Armada, sent by Spain to protect an invasion force that had been assembled in the southern Low Countries to attack England.[35]

---

[30] On the Spanish sailing pattern see Elliott, *Europe Divided*, 54–5. On the ships used to make these open sea voyages see Phillips, *Six Galleons*, and Konstam, *Spanish Galleon*.

[31] For relations between Spain and England see Parker, *Philip II*. But note that Kamen, *Philip of Spain*, disagrees with Parker on many interpretations, including his idea of Philip's grand strategy.

[32] Elliott, *Europe Divided*, 303–6; Doran, *Elizabeth I*; Trim, 'Fighting', Chapters 3–5, pp. 95–198.

[33] Jardine, *Awful End*.

[34] Fissel, *English Warfare*, 142–6.

[35] The literature on the defeat of the Spanish Armada is vast and does not need to be repeated here. Mattingly's *Defeat* remains authoritative and there are valuable articles in Gallagher and Cruickshank, *God's Obvious Design*, and Rodríguez-Salgado, *Armada*.

Apart from William's assassination, other events, some more than an ocean away, prompted Elizabeth's decision to extend her open opposition to Spain in the Netherlands. In 1568 the English rejected a naval alliance with Spain when a Spanish fleet attacked a squadron under John Hawkins, who had been trading slaves with the Spanish colonies, at San Juan de Ulua in the Caribbean.[36] In response Elizabeth actively sought English ships to act as privateers; no fewer than thirteen expeditions sailed to the Caribbean between 1570 and 1577.[37] They would also increase in numbers and intensity over the next half-century. Perhaps surprisingly, such pirate raids were generally successful, costing the Spanish large amounts of gold and silver. Thus by the time the English officially entered the Dutch Revolt, their conflict with the Spanish and consequently their grand strategy had already become international.

The internationalisation of policy by the Austrian Habsburgs, Spain, and England after the Peace of Cateau-Cambrésis was novel. But it was not without precedent and neither were these the most successful late-medieval and early-modern states to do this. Between the end of the fourteenth and middle of the eighteenth centuries a number of polities recognised the value of internationalising their foreign and military policies and thereby augmenting their position, while some that had been dominant during the Middle Ages did not pursue a grand strategy of internationalisation, and experienced a concomitant fall in authority. Two polities – Portugal and the Ottoman Empire – exemplify the benefits of internationalisation; while two– the Timurid Khanate and Venice – reveal the opposite.

In 1415, a Portuguese expedition had captured the North African port town of Ceuta.[38] In spite of this success, a further incursion into Morocco was not made until 1458, but from then until 1525 raids continued until the entire coastline from Ceuta to Santa Cruz was occupied. Several fortified Portuguese outposts were established, creating a hold on both the Atlantic and the Mediterranean coasts of Morocco.[39] The incursion into Morocco, Portugal's first international conquest, aimed to establish an overseas presence in order to further trade, proselytise for the Catholic faith, and promote exploration. A similar grand strategy influenced all Portuguese maritime expeditions. By 1419–20 the African coastal island of Madeira, discovered

[36] Kelsey, *Hawkins*, 70–93.
[37] Lenman, *England's Colonial Wars*, 83; Andrews, *Trade, Plunder and Settlement*, 128–9.
[38] Cook, *War for Morocco*, 84–8.
[39] *Ibid.*, 89–240.

with the Azores Islands during the previous century, had been colonised. In the following decade, Portuguese sailors also explored and settled on the Canaries and Azores Islands, giving their ships friendly ports to visit on their voyages to and from the African coast, which began in the 1430s. In the 1440s, Portuguese mariners discovered the Cape Verde Islands, reached the mouth of the Senegal River, and sent back the first shipments of gold and slaves to Portugal. In 1455–6 and 1458–60, Alvise Cadamosto and Diogo Gomes, respectively, sailed up the Senegal and Gambia rivers and down the coast as far as Sierra Leone. In 1483, Diogo Cão reached the mouth of the Congo River. In 1488, Bartholomew Diaz discovered the Cape of Good Hope and rounded the southern tip of Africa. And in 1498, Vasco da Gama journeyed to Calicut, India.[40] He had reached Asia, the goal of Columbus and other explorers. The rich trading possibilities of India could now be accessed, and those of China and Japan were at hand. The Portuguese government spared no expense in pursuing these possibilities, which were initially risky but soon became extremely profitable. Even as they were establishing trading-post fortresses in India, the Portuguese were sailing up the eastern coast of Africa and into the East Indies. By 1514 fortifications had been built at Sofala, Kilwa, and Mozambique in East Africa; on Socotra Island at the mouth of the Red Sea; and at Ormuz at the mouth of the Persian Gulf; at Cochin, Cannanore, and Goa on the coast of west India; and at Malacca. The Molucca Islands were reached, with trading posts established, at Macao (1521), on the coast of China (1557) and Nagasaki in Japan (1570).[41]

Early in the sixteenth century the Portuguese fought very few conflicts but generally defeated their opponents. Their ships were superior and generally outgunned their enemies.[42] However, in 1509 both the Portuguese fleet and its Mamluk Egyptian opponent were equally well armed, which may be why they traded victories. Nor did the Portuguese ships outgun the Ottoman fleet, yet they defeated Ottoman squadrons at Diu in 1538 and at Ormuz in 1507 and 1554.[43]

---

[40] See, for example, Russell-Wood, *World*; Diffie and Winius, *Foundations*; Disney, 'Portuguese Expansion'; the articles in Bethencourt and Chaudhuri, *História*, I; and the essays of Scammell collected in *Ships, Oceans, and Empire* and *Seafaring, Sailors and Trade*. For the chronology above I have followed Phillips, *Medieval Expansion*, 214–15.

[41] See Russell-Wood, *World*; Diffie and Winius, *Foundations*. See also Black, *Cambridge Atlas of Warfare*, 15–16, who provides the basic chronology and geography; and Pearson, 'Indian Ocean'.

[42] See DeVries, 'Effectiveness', 393; Newitt, 'Amphibious Warfare', 111–17, 120–1; Konstam, 'Naval Tactics', 19, 22.

[43] Black, *Cambridge Atlas of Warfare*, 15–16; Newitt, 'Amphibious Warfare', 113, 117, 121.

Yet if the Portuguese were successful in distant lands and on distant seas, closer to home in Morocco they suffered significant military setbacks. Here, as elsewhere, their policy was to establish fortified settlements along the coast, using local traders to transport goods to and from the interior.[44] Hardly any of the hinterland was directly controlled by them and none was fortified, and this ultimately proved to be their Achilles heel. Between 1541 and 1550 the Moroccan Sa'adis regained almost all their settlements, leaving only Ceuta, Tangier, and Mazagano in Portuguese hands.[45] Compared to the rest of their trading Empire, Morocco had brought little profit, one reason why Portugal spent little in defence of its acquisitions; yet the coastal enclaves in Morocco were a vital link in the chain connecting Portugal to its eastern Empire. Only in 1574 did Sebastian I take a large army into the region around Tangier. Faced with little resistance, he secured the defence of the important town. Satisfied for the moment, he returned four years later with another force, but this time he was opposed by an army that greatly outnumbered his and, at the battle of Alcazarquivir, he was defeated and killed.[46]

As noted earlier, the result of his death was the acquisition of Portugal by Philip II. He and his successors (Spain controlled Portugal until 1640) have been condemned by historians for draining off Portuguese resources for their own more Spanish projects,[47] notably the invasion of England, the war in the Netherlands, and the conquest of the Americas, whose gold and silver were more lucrative than spices and silk. But it should be noted that the enormity of the new Spanish Empire, which stretched from Europe into South America, Africa, the Arabian subcontinent, the Indian Ocean, and eastern Asia, meant that resources would be spread thinly. Priorities had to be set and understandably this meant that Portuguese grand strategy was relegated to a lower spot on the agenda. Accordingly, Portuguese holdings in Asia soon began to shrink, the Dutch especially profiting from their decline. They replaced the Portuguese in the Moluccas in 1605, Malacca in 1641, and Sri Lanka in 1638–58, and along the south-western Indian coast in 1663. The Dutch also moved against Portuguese South America, beginning in 1624, and at first enjoyed great success; but there the Spanish took more of an interest in defending their holdings, and finally, in 1654, the Dutch

---

[44] DeVries, 'Fortifications', 105.
[45] Elbl, 'Portuguese Fortifications', 352; DeVries, 'Fortifications', 106.
[46] Cook, *War for Morocco*, 241–72; Trim, 'Campaign of Alcazarquivir'; Bovill, *Battle of Alcazar*.
[47] Black, *War and the World*, 47–8.

were forced to retreat, leaving them with the overseas colonies they retained into the twentieth century.[48]

This necessarily brief overview of Portuguese expansion into East Africa, the Arabian Peninsula, and Indian Ocean, might suggest that Ottoman opposition to them was limited and unsuccessful. Yet such a conclusion would unfairly diminish the stature of the Ottomans as the most significant international world power of the late-medieval and early-modern periods. The Ottomans were founded and named after a central Turkish dynast from Asia Minor, Ghazi Osman, who used mainly familial forces to defeat a much larger Byzantine army at the battle of Baphaeum in 1301, and to capture Nicaea in 1304.[49] Over the next century, Osman's successors conquered almost all of modern Turkey (Constantinople and Trebizond excepted) and much of south-eastern Europe. Most of the Byzantine Empire, Bulgaria, Macedonia, Greece, Montenegro, Bosnia, and Serbia was overrun, and in two major battles – at Kosovo (1389) and Nicopolis (1396) – Ottoman armies also crushed western opponents. In the former they defeated a large Serbian force led by the ruler, Prince Lazar; in the latter they destroyed a crusading force drawn from across Europe. Only twice did the Ottomans lose significant military engagements during this period, at Rovine in 1395 – when a Hungarian and Wallachian army defeated them in battle but were unable to stop their Balkan campaign – and at Ankara in 1402, when Tamerlane and his Mongols trounced their army and captured the sultan, Bayezid I, who committed suicide afterwards.

A succession crisis between Bayezid I's sons, Süleyman and Musa, halted Ottoman expansion for several years, but under Murad II (r. 1421–44 and 1446–51) advances recommenced, primarily in the remains of the Byzantine Empire and south-eastern Europe. His capture of Smyrna (1424), Salonika (1430), and Albania (1432), and his defeat of the Hungarians on the Upper Danube (1428) prompted Pope Eugenius IV to call for a crusade against the Turks in 1440. Although the numbers recruited from the West proved small and insignificant, the call to crusade invigorated those who were defending lands against the Turks. In 1441, Vladislav of Poland and Hungary raised the siege of Belgrade, the next year the Hungarian János Hunyadi defeated the Ottomans invading Transylvania, in 1443 the Albanians revolted and regained their independence, and in 1444 Hunyadi won the battle of Mount Kunovica. However, when Murad II demolished a crusading

---

[48] Black, *Cambridge Atlas of Warfare*, 17; *War and the World*, 64–5.
[49] On the rise of the Ottomans, see İnalcık, *Ottoman Empire*, and Imber, *Ottoman Empire*, but for a strictly military focus see also Turnbull, *Ottoman Empire*.

army at the battle of Varna (1444) and defeated Hunyadi at the second battle of Kosovo (1448), the Turks recovered control of the Balkans except for Albania and put an end to further ideas of stopping the Turks in south-eastern Europe or Byzantium.[50] On 3 February 1451, Murad died and was replaced by his son, Mehmed II. The latter's greatest achievement, the conquest of Constantinople in 1453, was recounted earlier, but Mehmed's other victories merit recognition: Athens (1456), Serbia (1459), the Morea (1460), Trebizond (1461), Herzegovina (1467), Kaffa (1475), and Albania (1478). There were defeats – against Hunyadi at Belgrade in 1456; Hunyadi's son, Matthias Corvinus, at Jaysca in 1463 and Savacz in 1475; and against the Knights Hospitaller at Rhodes in 1480. But while they temporarily delayed the Ottoman advance, none rolled it back or even obstructed it indefinitely.

Mehmed's grandson, Selim I (r. 1512–20), also expanded the Ottoman Empire, although his interest lay in the Middle East rather than south-eastern Europe, capturing Aleppo, Damascus, Cairo, Syria, Israel, and Egypt in between 1516 and 1517.[51] But his conquests paled in comparison to those of his son, Süleyman I (r. 1520–66), who added so much territory to his Empire that he earned the cognomen 'the Magnificent' from his enemies (his own subjects called him 'the Lawgiver'): Belgrade (1521); Rhodes (1522); much of Hungary and Dubrovnik (1526); Obrovac and Udbina (1527); Jajce and Banja Luca (1528); Güns (1532); Baghdad and Iraq (1534); Klis (1537); the Red Sea coast, Aden, Karpathos, the northern Sporades, Castelnuovo, and Jedisan in Moldavia (1538); Monemvasia and Naupalia (1540); Pécs, Székesfehérvár, and Gran (Esztergom) in 1543; Visegrád (1544); Samos (1550); Temesvár (1552); Chios (1556); and Naxos (1566). Yet Süleyman's armies were not invincible. They could not capture Vienna in 1529, Corfu in 1537, Reggio in 1543, Erlau (Eger) in 1552, Malta in 1565, or Szigeth (Szigetvar) in 1566 (where Süleyman died).[52] He was willing to do almost anything to avoid defeat. Indeed, at times his soldiers' lives appeared almost inconsequential to him; by his own testimony it cost him more than 103,000 men to capture Rhodes, for example.[53]

---

[50] Invaluable in understanding the Crusade of Varna are the original sources in Imber, *Crusade of Varna*.

[51] Hess, 'Ottoman Conquest', 55–76.

[52] Kunt and Woodhead, *Süleyman*, nicely covers the military endeavours of Süleyman. See also Guilmartin, *Gunpowder and Galleys* (2003 edn).

[53] This appears not to be an exaggeration, as contemporary accounts of the siege by Hospitallers reveal an incredible death toll in capturing the city, and also the willingness of the sultan, who was present at the siege, to send troops day after day to certain death in charging walls so well protected by heavy defensive gunfire. See Smith and DeVries, *Sieges of Rhodes*, and Brockman, *Two Sieges*.

Mehmed II, Selim I, and Süleyman had the same grand strategy, which had long been integral to Ottoman political and military thought, perhaps from as early as Osman's time, certainly from the reign of Bayezid I. Their goals were to enlarge their Empire, to protect its central core, to retain contact with potential enemies by means of diplomacy and espionage, and to prepare constantly for future conquests even if these would be carried out by their successors. Of course, what they could not know was whether these successors would have the political and military acumen and tenacity successfully to pursue their grand strategy. For example, Süleyman's son, Selim II, had none of the political or military leadership qualities of his father, nor was he well respected by his people, perhaps best indicated by the nickname they gave him, 'the Sot'. Yet even this weakest of sultans of the early-modern period achieved some major military victories, for example capturing Cyprus in 1570–1 despite a valiant and desperate Venetian attempt to retain control of the island, and Tunis in 1574 thus ending its two-year occupation by the Spanish. More importantly, large numbers of troops were garrisoned along the borders of the Ottoman Empire; and in the Red Sea, Persian Gulf, Mediterranean Sea, and Indian Ocean there was a heavy Ottoman naval presence.[54]

However, it was the failure at Lepanto in 1571, when an allied force defeated the large Ottoman fleet off the Balkan coast, that forever tarnished Selim's reputation. Contemporaries in the West were encouraged by the victory at Lepanto, which seemingly pointed to a vulnerability in the Ottoman war machine; but recent historians have exaggerated the battle's significance in the European struggle to keep the Turks at bay. Defeat at Lepanto was quickly followed by the successful capture of Tunis in 1574; later successes, such as the victory over imperial forces at the battle of Kerestes and the capture of Erlau in 1596, the defeat of the Poles and Lithuanians at the battle of Cecora in 1620, and the conquest of Crete in 1645–69, all reasserted the Ottomans' claim to be the dominant power in the eastern Mediterranean. The Turks even had enough strength and confidence to besiege Vienna again in 1683, although some have seen their ultimate defeat there after losing to the relief army of imperial and Polish troops as the proverbial 'beginning of the end', especially as it was followed in fairly quick succession by the loss of Buda (1686), defeat at the second battle of Mohács (1687), the loss of Belgrade (1690 – although it was recaptured in 1717), the surrender of Hungary to the Austrians in 1718, and the loss of over 100 smaller fortified sites. In fact, the military situation became so depressing for

---

[54] Turnbull, *Ottoman Empire*, 57–60.

the army that in 1730 the Janissaries overthrew the hereditary line of sultans who had held the throne since Osman, and usurped their power. Still, this provided little relief for an Empire that would eventually become 'the sick man of Europe'.[55]

Observers, both contemporary and modern, frequently praise Ottoman military administration, strategy, tactics, and equipment, which often stood in contrast to those of their European enemies.[56] This was undoubtedly crucial to Ottoman military success. But so too was the grand strategy of the Empire. Both worked together to produce a long series of victories against Byzantine, European, Persian, Middle Eastern, or North African forces. From the Black Sea to the Tunisian peninsula, from the Danube River to the Indian Ocean, from Indonesia to East Africa, the international size, scope, and influence of the Ottoman Empire and its grand strategy was, for more than three centuries, matched only by that of the trans-oceanic Spanish Empire.

If the Ottoman Empire was the prime example of a state that began to follow more international grand strategies during the late-medieval and early-modern periods, there were others that continued to be limited in their foreign and military policies, choosing either simply to defend themselves or to wage war only on their neighbours. Examples include the Timurid Khanate and Venice, which will be considered in turn.

The history of the thirteenth-century Mongol conquests falls outside the chronology of this volume. Suffice it to say that the vastness of those conquests has never been replicated since. The original Empire had fragmented by 1315 into many smaller states. These individual Khanates nevertheless retained formidable powers, and excited both fear and interest in their neighbours and further afield. The Timurid Khanate was probably the most feared of the Empire's successor states. Located in western and central Asia, at its height it stretched from the Persian Gulf in the south to the Black, Caspian, and Ural seas in the north, and from Asia Minor in the west to India in the east, and covered what would become Kazakhstan, Kyrgyzstan, Turkmenistan, Tajikistan, Uzbekistan, Afghanistan, Iran, Georgia, Armenia, and Azerbaijan, and parts of Iraq, Syria, Pakistan, India, and Russia. It was also essentially the creation of one man, Timur 'the lame', or Tamerlane, and with his death it largely disappeared.[57] A self-described descendant of Genghis Khan who married

---

[55] Black, *Cambridge Atlas of Warfare*, 94–7. For general histories of the decline of the Ottoman Empire see Quataert, *Ottoman Empire*; Finkel, *Osman's Dream*, 289–554.
[56] See Chapters 6 and 7, by Àgoston and Murphey, below.
[57] Manz, *Rise and Rule* is the scholarly biography of choice for Tamerlane, although Marozzi's *Tamerlane* is also good.

a more direct descendant of Genghis – not a rare occurrence in Asia at the time – Tamerlane gained fame and a fearsome reputation as a cavalry leader fighting in the confusing Mongol wars of the mid fourteenth century. In 1369, he was proclaimed ruler of the Chagatai Khanate and established his capital at Samarkand. From then until his death in 1405 he waged war, first to consolidate his power in Chagatai, and then against his neighbours, successfully invading Persia, the lands of the rival Mongol Khanate of the Golden Horde in Central Asia, and northern India. His notorious massacres of urban populations gave him an international reputation for ruthlessness. At the sack of Delhi in December 1398, according to his own account, his army killed more than 110,000 people.

From 1399 to 1402 Tamerlane turned his military might west, against Syria and Iraq. Timurid armies quickly overran Aleppo and, after destroying a Mamluk army, they conquered Damascus, following each sacking with their by-now common massacre of the inhabitants. Baghdad suffered the same fate in June 1401, with over 20,000 people killed. This led him into confrontation with the Ottomans. On 20 July 1402, having been declared an 'enemy of Islam', Tamerlane's forces faced those of Sultan Bayezid I at the battle of Ankara. Both generals were buoyed by a confidence based on recent military success, but at the end of the day it was the Ottomans who fled the field, leaving their sultan in the hands of Tamerlane facing humiliation and eventual suicide.

Two-and-a-half years later, while on yet another campaign, this time aimed at Mongolia although his army never reached there, Tamerlane died. One might think that the possessor of such a military résumé would command praise from historians. Yet he does not, for he left an uncertain legacy. Where was Tamerlane's grand strategy, where was his 'vision for the future'? Many rulers who gained or sustained power by military means, such as Mehmed II or Philip II, wanted to build an enduring legacy for themselves and for their people. Accordingly, they *conquered* rather than *invaded*, building a nexus of trade and taxation in their newly acquired lands that ensured stability, protection, and strength for the future. Tamerlane left little or nothing behind him. He devastated rather than conquered, destroying the agricultural, industrial, and mercantile economies – as well as the populations – of any region he invaded. True, he gained huge immediate rewards – it is said that nine elephants were required just to carry the jewels and gems from India back to Samarkand – but nothing of an international legacy. Consequently his successors could not hold on to Tamerlane's Empire, and within a century it had disappeared.[58]

[58] See Manz, *Power, Politics and Religion.*

Venice, too, seems to have an impressive late-medieval–early-modern military record. Indeed, some modern historians of Venice, including Frederick Lane, John Julius Norwich, and Gary Wills, are so captivated by the beauty and wealth of the city that they have difficulty isolating the achievements of the High and Late Middle Ages and transpose them on to subsequent periods.[59] To do so ignores, for example, the history of Venice during the Italian wars of 1494 to 1559, when the land and naval power of the republic was contingent upon alliances with more significant states to the north, and came at the cost of hiring large numbers of expensive mercenaries.[60] Such a view also ignores the example of the wars fought between the Venetians and the Ottomans between 1685 and 1699, and between 1714 and 1718. Although their opponents had been weakened by losses in Austria and Hungary, the Venetians made little headway even against those Ottomans across the Adriatic Sea; the Venetians acquired the northern coast but the southern coast was left in Turkish hands and Ottoman piracy accordingly continued unabated.[61]

Moreover, although the Venetians were consistent members of the Holy Leagues formed by the Papacy to oppose the Ottomans, and were occasionally the most active proponents of the League, as in 1538 and 1572, their actual participation usually was at best half-hearted and partial. Taken in the long term, Venice preferred to try to fend off Turkish attacks by negotiation (though in the long run this merely postponed the inevitable and, as we will see, the Turks eventually stripped Venice of its maritime Empire).[62] For example, treaty agreements to protect Cyprus and Crete always included provisions keeping the Venetians from releasing Christian captives. They did not allow provisions or reinforcements for the besieged city of Rhodes in 1522 to sail through or from Crete and Cyprus; indeed, the great military engineer Gabriel Tadini di Martinengo, whose presence had been requested by the Grand Master of the Hospitallers, Philippe de l'Isle Adam, had to sneak over to Rhodes when the Venetian officials

---

[59] Lane, *Venice: A Maritime Republic*; Norwich, *History of Venice*; and Wills, *Venice*. Even Mallett and Hale, *Military Organisation*, are not completely immune to this, often downplaying the losses suffered by Venice against the Ottomans and ignoring some of the agreements into which Venice was forced to try and hold on to her eastern Mediterranean islands.

[60] Finlay, 'Immortal Republic'.

[61] Black, *Cambridge Atlas of Warfare*, 96–7. For the 1685–99 war see also Topping, 'Last Imperial Venture'.

[62] See especially Setton, *Papacy and the Levant*, III and IV, for a discussion of Venice's dealings with the Ottomans in a vain attempt to preserve Cyprus and Crete; on Turco-Venetian relations, see Hocquet, 'Venice and the Turks'.

denied his request to go there.[63] Nor did Venetian attempts to retain their holdings in the eastern Mediterranean succeed. When a sultan decided he wanted one of the Venetian possessions, he simply took it, as exemplified when Cyprus was conquered in 1570. True, Crete held out for more than two decades (1645–69) but this was attributable to the tenacious resistance of local inhabitants and owed little to Venetian assistance.[64] Additionally, Ottoman ships continued to prey upon Venetian vessels throughout this period, even those guarded by fleets of galleys and warships, as evidenced by the large number of Venetian bronze cannon that still fill the museums and city squares of modern Turkey.[65] Such unhindered piracy severely affected the economy of Venice, which lost its previous glory and economic prosperity.

As the world became larger for states such as Spain, Portugal, England, the Ottoman Empire, and France, it became smaller for the Venetians. The vaunted republic had at one time exercised an economic and military dominance over the whole of the eastern Mediterranean. From the eleventh to the thirteenth centuries, it had made monopolistic deals to supply the crusaders in the Holy Land; it had manipulated a large army of crusaders to destroy a cross-Adriatic Croatian rival Zadar (Zara) and then to invade and conquer Constantinople after Byzantines made the decision to trade solely with Genoa; it had sent merchants and missionaries to Mongolia, India, and China; and it had hired large numbers of mercenaries. Yet by the mid seventeenth century the republic had shrunk economically and militarily almost to insignificance. Its grand strategy never developed beyond a narrow focus on neighbouring Italian city-states and the eastern Mediterranean, and was reduced to a local concern with survival.[66]

The internationalisation of power-politics generally involved the use of military force at some point. Yet we should not exaggerate the significance of armies and navies in determining outcomes. Wars at the end of the medieval and beginning of the early-modern periods were increasingly expensive, both in terms of money and men, and they were risky. The powerful leaders discussed above all tried to make their armies

---

[63] This is reported by both the eyewitness chroniclers of the siege, Jean de Bourbon and Jacobus Fontanus, who marvelled at the Venetians' 'heresy' in siding with the Ottomans over the Knights Hospitallers. See Smith and DeVries, *Sieges of Rhodes*.

[64] This war is covered almost as a sideshow throughout Setton's *Venice, Austria, and the Turks*; the Cretans did receive some assistance from France and the Knights of Malta: Rowlands, 'French Amphibious Warfare', 268, 288, 303–4, 307.

[65] Robert D. Smith and Ruth Rhynas Brown have made an extensive inventory of these guns and plan to publish a study of them in the near future.

[66] See, amongst others, Setton, *Venice, Austria, and the Turks*; Rapp, *Industry*; and Tenenti, *Piracy*.

unbeatable. This generally meant recruiting substantial forces, and arming their troops with the best new military technologies available.[67] However, numbers did not inevitably guarantee victory. For example, a huge Ottoman army besieged Rhodes in 1480. It numbered between 70,000 and 170,000 according to contemporary sources (modern historians incline to the former) and faced a force of Hospitaller Knights, other soldiers, and militia totalling fewer than 4,000, yet the Ottomans were forced to withdraw in defeat.[68] Moreover, if a single polity was able to combine with others, it could offset disadvantages of size: other things being equal, an alliance almost always defeated a single principality. Finally, as states became more internationalised their armies and navies were spread more thinly, and keeping an enemy from taking advantage of smaller home forces and more thinly garrisoned borders accordingly increased in importance. Diplomacy thus became increasingly significant, certainly when compared to the Middle Ages. It provided intelligence of military movements, innovations, and intentions; it was key to negotiated alliances and treaties; and it relayed economic information about the host territory.

Ambassadors had been around since ancient times, of course, and they had always attempted to act as spies and negotiators, and sometimes to convey threats and propaganda. When acting as negotiators or offering threats their meetings were frequently recorded by at least one of the parties. Thus Herodotus' *The Persian Wars* is filled with multiple examples of ambassadors moving between Greek cities to negotiate alliances, and going from the Persians to the Greeks to deliver threats and demand surrender.[69] Priscus' account of his participation in the eastern Roman imperial embassy to Attila adds enormously to our knowledge of the leader of the Huns and his people.[70] And negotiations for peace between Richard the Lionheart and Saladin also announced an end to the Third Crusade and the effective defeat of the English king by the Ayyubid sultan. Unsurprisingly, there are fewer accounts of ambassadors acting as spies.

Yet ancient and medieval ambassadors were often hampered by differences in status, office, or religious loyalties. When an ambassador did not recognise a foreign leader as his equal in social or political skills, if he felt that his mission was religiously sanctioned, or when

---

[67] For an overview of the changes being made in military technology during this time, see DeVries, 'Sites'.
[68] Smith and DeVries, *Sieges of Rhodes*.
[69] E.g., Herodotus, *The Persian Wars*, viii.132–44; ix.6–11.
[70] The most accessible version is at http://ccat.sas.upenn.edu/jod/texts/priscus.html (trans. J. M. Bury).

he simply knew the status of any treaty or agreement was temporary, diplomatic results were limited. No better example of this can be found than in the writings of Luitprand of Cremona who, when sent to the Byzantine Empire in 968–9 as an ambassador from Berengar II of Italy, so disdained the Byzantines that his embassy failed miserably.[71] Moreover, embassies were rarely retained in a foreign land for any length of time with the authority to seek diplomatic measures on their own.[72]

Diplomacy in its modern definition was born from the international struggles of the fifteenth to the seventeenth centuries. As Garrett Mattingly has noted: 'Perhaps the extension of the resident ambassadors is as good a test as any of "modernity", with the moment of its adoption by any Western power marking the emergence of that power from what we call the "Middle Ages" into the modern state system. It is clear that by 1648 the system was virtually complete.'[73] During this period all political powers of any significance maintained extensive diplomatic ties with other polities, whether (potential) friends or (potential) enemies, as part of their grand strategies. As noted earlier, the Ottomans sent embassies and diplomats to every state that would accept them.[74] Despite fervent papal hostility that began with Pope Pius II (1458–64), who, as Cardinal Aeneas Silvius Piccolomini, had tried to raise crusading ardour against the Ottomans,[75] most western European powers welcomed these diplomatic approaches. They proffered some prospect of accord with this most vicious and successful enemy. Even recent military foes of the Ottomans – such as the Hospitallers in 1481, only a year after their successful defence of Rhodes – agreed to house and protect the new sultan, Bayezid II's brother, Cem (who had also claimed the throne), in return for peace. Cem stayed with them until 1494, when Pope Alexander VI and his sons, Don Juan and Cesare Borgia, took him into the Vatican, and never during that time were Rhodes or any other Hospitaller possessions threatened.[76]

European states reciprocated by sending their own diplomats to Constantinople. Venetian ambassadors were there almost immediately after Mehmed II's conquest, even sending a number of painters to

---

[71] Henderson, *Select Historical Documents*, 476.
[72] The best book on medieval diplomacy remains Queller, *Office*.
[73] Mattingly, 'First Resident Embassies', 423. This remains his opinion in the seminal *Renaissance Diplomacy*.
[74] Yurdusev, *Ottoman Diplomacy*.
[75] DeVries, 'Lack of Response'.
[76] The very interesting story of Cem (also written as Jem or Djem) can be found in Vatin, *Sultan Djem*, and Freely, *Jem Sultan*.

the sultan's court, including Gentile Bellini, whose famous portrait of Mehmed now hangs in the National Gallery in London.[77] The French, too, despite not sharing the same fears of direct military engagement as the Venetians, sent ambassadors to the Ottomans in an attempt to form a military alliance during the Italian wars, even while Francis I was promising the Papacy to lead an anti-Turkish league.[78]

By the mid sixteenth century, permanent embassies could be found in all European states. They had become so numerous in Philip II's court, with up to fourteen embassies present at a single time, that the king claimed he 'wasted his day' listening to their entreaties. He, of course, sent diplomats to all of these ambassadors' lands.[79] It was the same story in France, England, Scotland, Portugal, the Netherlands, the Holy Roman Empire, and Italy.[80]

In the periodisation of history, knowing when to divide the Middle Ages from the early-modern period is difficult. An exact date will remain elusive, but in military terms there seems to be no question that for a medieval state to remain powerful into the early-modern period its leaders needed to devise a grand strategy, one that took into account that technological changes in ship construction and weapons had made travel and conquest throughout the entire world possible. This marks one of the key changes over the period from 1350 to 1750.

---

[77] Campbell and Chong, *Bellini and the East*. On Venice's diplomatic connections with the Ottoman Turks see Hocquet, 'Venice and the Turks'.

[78] Jensen, 'Ottoman Turks'.

[79] Parker, *Grand Strategy*, 19, 56.

[80] Mattingly, *Renaissance Diplomacy*, 105–78.

3 War and the emergence of the state: western Europe, 1350–1600

Steven Gunn

The role of war in the development of later medieval and early-modern western European states has been hotly debated and yet remains curiously out of focus. At one extreme stand those historians and historical sociologists who have argued that military competition between states was the main driver of state development. At the other stand those who think war hindered or perverted processes of state formation based on the rule of law, the realisation of an ideal model of sovereignty, or the construction of social coalitions based on religious or moral interests. Yet neither group has found the means to engage very directly with the other's arguments, proceeding mostly by assertion and counter-assertion. What measurable evidence has been produced for the importance of one force or another has tended to be of the sort that can only be weighed on one side of the argument or the other, such as the increasing size of armed forces or the increasing volume of litigation.[1]

Detailed study of the impact of war on individual countries, meanwhile, has served to demonstrate the immense variety of experience between and even within different polities. This has tended to make historians sceptical of the models built by sociologists to classify polities by social structure, political tradition, and military engagement, and thus explain their different constitutional trajectories.[2] Michael Roberts' 'military revolution', once a convenient link between changes in military technology and organisation and the changes in government needed to sustain and exploit them, has mutated under intensive scrutiny either into a series of smaller military revolutions or into one so long-lasting and multi-faceted that it is hard to link to specific political changes.[3] It has also been studied mostly by military historians, interested in the military inputs rather than the political outputs of Roberts' equation. And where recent investigations have examined

---

[1] Gunn, Grummitt, and Cools, 'War and the State'.
[2] Tilly, *Coercion*; Downing, *Military Revolution*; Ertman, *Birth of the Leviathan*.
[3] Rogers, *Military Revolution Debate*.

the relationship between military change and wider state development, they have asked more why some states became more effective military competitors than others, than how war modified states in general.[4]

Beneath these debates lie fundamental issues about the driving forces in history and the nature of human society. Do our institutions rest at base on the associative and collaborative characteristics of human nature, or on the competitive and violent? Do they change as the underlying modes of production and class relations change, or as political actors confront day-to-day problems or make outward reality of inward political ideals? These questions are certainly too large to address, let alone resolve, in a chapter such as this, yet they help to explain why the effects of war on the state have been viewed so differently by different authors that it is hard to speak of a unified debate on the subject. Rather than review the existing controversy in all its ramifications, then, perhaps we should examine the various ways in which war might have affected the relations between rulers and their subjects in this period and ask what changes and variations are evident across the period from the Black Death to the Thirty Years' War, and across Europe from the Atlantic to the Oder, and how they might be explained.

The terms for the modern debate on war and state formation were largely set around 1900 by Max Weber and Otto Hintze. They and their successors, from Joseph Schumpeter, Norbert Elias, and Gerhard Oestreich to Charles Tilly, Michael Mann, and others, have defined a number of characteristics of the ideal modern state linked to its war-making capacity. It had permanent armed forces, under the direct control of the central authorities, comprising paid, professional soldiers and sailors, and equipped with the best available military technology. For some scholars such forces were in themselves the token of state-hood: as Oestreich put it, 'The institution of a standing army and its incorporation into the activities of the state was what first created the early modern state with its concentration of power at the centre.'[5] These forces permitted the conquest of new territories, thus expanding the human and economic resources at the state's disposal, but also pacifying the areas already under the state's jurisdiction, thereby enforcing the monopoly on the use of legitimate force that was a vital characteristic of state power, and offering protection to the state's subjects as they went about their economically productive business. They also facilitated the coercion of subject populations necessary for the extraction of the resources needed to sustain military effort, all the more vital

[4] Glete, *War and the State*; Frost, *Northern Wars*.
[5] Oestreich, *Neostoicism*, 50.

as armies grew ever larger. This extraction changed the state from a 'domain state' to a 'tax-state', supported by the ruler's levies on the income and possessions of his subjects, rather than on his landholdings and other rights: a 'tax-state' capable, through further elaboration of credit arrangements, of development into a 'fiscal state'.

It was not only the functions of these military and fiscal institutions that mattered, but also their characteristics. They were regulated bureaucratically, and the individuals in them, holding their positions by official appointment rather than social privilege, were subject to forms of discipline that modelled the wider relationship between dutiful subjects and the sovereign. In this they pointed to the widest impact of war on the state's relations with its subjects, the way in which it validated the leadership of the ruler and justified his assertion of extreme powers to direct their lives at times of emergency; these powers might survive into peacetime or serve as the model for other profound interventions in the lives of subjects, shaping not just warfare states but welfare states.[6]

By contrasting two great armies we can see why many of these characteristics have been thought to have their origins in the period we are considering. The French army at Agincourt in 1415, numbering perhaps 12,000, rested on the innovations of the thirteenth and fourteenth centuries in which rulers had developed durable institutions for negotiating with their subjects over the taxation necessary to field armies of paid troops. Yet it still bore clearly the lineaments of the unpaid feudal armies and dependence on demesne revenues of French kings two or three centuries earlier. It was gathered by calling together the household servants and other followers of the realm's great noblemen, some of whom hesitated over whether to comply, and combining them with urban militia contingents and irregularly sized groups of knights and esquires collected by local royal bailiffs in response to a general summons to the nobility. It was led by a bickering collection of the high-born, was equipped with whatever weapons individuals happened to possess, and could be held together only for the duration of the campaign. It was supported by direct taxes that were intermittent, indirect taxes that would be cancelled in the wake of defeat, and minimal arrangements for state credit.[7]

In contrast, the Spanish Army of Flanders in the 1580s and 1590s, numbering over 60,000, was built around a core of veterans in

---

[6] Weber, *Economy and Society*; Hintze, 'Formation' and 'Military Organisation'; Elias, *Civilising Process*; Tilly, *Coercion*; Tilly, *Formation*; Mann, *Sources*, I; Bonney, 'Introduction', 12–14.

[7] Curry, *Agincourt*, 96–7, 102–6, 179–87; Genet, 'Which State Rises?'; Henneman, 'France in the Middle Ages', 103–4, 116–18.

permanent companies and *tercios* of notionally fixed size; recruited by captains bearing royal commissions; mustered under the supervision of royal officials; provisioned by an elaborate system of staples on their lines of march; supplied with bread, clothing, arms, mounts, even free medical care, by the government. It was heir to the successful tactical exploitation of pikes, infantry firearms, light cavalry, artillery, and fortifications by several generations of Spanish commanders on the battlefields of Italy, Germany, and France, and it was officered by men arranged in clear hierarchies, many of whom wrote expert treatises on the art of war and argued for the importance of promotion on merit, not birth. It was sustained by permanent direct and indirect taxes levied on Castile, Naples, and the loyal parts of the Netherlands, by the issue of government bonds secured upon them, and by vast credit operations organised by the bankers of Genoa. Even its tendency to mutiny and negotiate collectively for the means to support itself, rather than simply to dissolve when money ran short, made it more 'modern' than its equivalent at Agincourt.[8]

Such selective contrasts support a narrative of linear modernising change, but the wider picture is more complex, suggesting that many features of the modern military-fiscal model might appear precociously only to fade again, as states passed through cycles of centralisation and decentralisation in their military arrangements. Several decades before Agincourt Charles V of France had deployed thousands of men in regularly mustered companies of standard size under permanently retained captains, funding them from regular direct taxation.[9] Not long after Agincourt the English occupied Normandy with a tax-funded army of permanent garrisons, manned by 5,000 or more experienced soldiers, mustered, reviewed, and paid by officials in a system so bureaucratic that John, Lord Talbot, terror of the French, was refused full payment for the men under his command until he could prove that three of them really were each called John Browne.[10] In the sixteenth century, however, England had the smallest standing forces and the most demesne-dependent fiscal arrangements of any major western state.[11] After the 1590s even the Spanish system buckled into a decentralising shift from direct government *administración* to *asiento*, the procurement of military services on contract.[12]

[8] Parker, *Army*, 32–8, 88–101, 139–57, 161–73, 271, 274–7; González de León, 'Spanish Military Power'; Muto, 'Spanish System'; Calabria, *Cost of Empire*, 37–103.
[9] Contamine, *Guerre, état et société*, 135–204.
[10] Curry, 'English Armies'; Ormrod, 'England', 27–47.
[11] O'Brien and Hunt, 'England', 58–61, 75–85.
[12] Thompson, *War and Government*, 256–73.

The implementation and perpetuation of change was contingent not only upon political and economic circumstances – the competence of royal leadership; the compliance of social elites; the absence of the famines, plagues, and other problems afflicting Spain in the 1590s – but also on geo-politics. An England occupying Normandy in the fifteenth century had different requirements from an England mounting occasional *chevauchées* across France in the fourteenth. A Venice on the defensive in its land and sea empires in the sixteenth century had different requirements from a Venice conquering its way across the north Italian mainland in the fifteenth, and used garrisons and militias more than the large standing cavalry forces of the age of expansion.[13] A Spanish monarchy aiming to sustain its power far from Spain amongst potentially hostile populations by maintaining large garrisons and a field army sufficient to overwhelm individual sites of resistance had more need of a force like the Army of Flanders than any other state.[14]

These qualifications notwithstanding, standing forces did come into being in many polities in the fifteenth century, and many shared to some degree the professionalism and bureaucracy of the Weberian model. Most consisted not of infantry but primarily of cavalry, in companies totalling several thousand men each in Milan, Venice, Naples, France, the Burgundian–Habsburg Netherlands, and Castile, and a few hundred in Austria.[15] There were technical reasons for this: improvements in armour and equipment made heavy cavalrymen – who could, through regular pay, afford them and the strong horses to match – unusually effective in the decades after 1430.[16] But there were also social and political reasons that kept standing companies of men-at-arms in the employ of many states long after they ceased to be a battle-winning force. The Venetian *lanze spezzate* were increasingly recruited from the republic's mainland territories – 90 per cent by 1587 – and captained by nobles from the same areas or even from the city itself.[17] The *compagnies d'ordonnance* introduced in France in 1445 and Burgundy in 1471 likewise succeeded, after some teething problems, in drawing significant sections of the nobility into paid state service under the leadership of the great nobles who captained the companies and were in many cases also the local patrons of the men-at-arms

---

[13] Mallett and Hale, *Military Organisation*, 4–5.
[14] Adams, 'Tactics or Politics?', 261–4.
[15] Contamine, *War and Composition between States*, 168–72; Mallett, *Mercenaries*, 110–14; Wiesflecker, *Maximilian*, V, 554–6.
[16] Vale, *War and Chivalry*, 105–28.
[17] Mallett and Hale, *Military Organisation*, 186–9, 205, 367–75.

they recruited.[18] When the nobility split apart in times of civil war this could be problematic: in 1465 several French companies followed their captains or local princes against Louis XI, and by the 1580s some were fighting for the crown, some for the Huguenots and some for the Catholic League.[19] But under normal circumstances it made the standing army a tool of the ruler's powers of patronage as well as a military instrument: as Charles V's ambassador Eustace Chapuys put it in 1535, if Henry VIII used his new taxation on the Church to raise an *ordonnance* of a thousand men-at-arms, it would be 'both to gain the heart of the nobles and in case of any mutiny'.[20] The same was true of the permanent companies of guards, sometimes numbering over a thousand, that developed in fifteenth-century princely households throughout Europe. Their higher-ranking members were, in Philippe Contamine's phrase, 'courtiers in their military guise', serving for the contacts their place gave them with the prince as well as for their wages of war: likewise the English gentlemen pensioners under Elizabeth, or the urban aristocrats drawn to the companies of men-at-arms attached to the Italian courts of the later sixteenth century, at Ferrara, Mantua, and Florence.[21]

Other standing forces were less obviously part of the political matrices of the state. Artillery arsenals were built up by many rulers from the later fifteenth century at the nodes of military and political coordination of their territories, single or multiple: Mechelen for the Habsburg Netherlands, Paris for France, London and Calais for England, Innsbruck and half-a-dozen lesser centres for the Emperor Maximilian's Austrian lands. They held expensive and sophisticated weaponry ready for campaigns that might come suddenly, and they retained the permanent staff needed to operate it, small in number compared with the cavalry – fewer than 200 at Mechelen, around 300 at Paris – but high in expertise. Besides deploying cannon and shot, they proclaimed the magnificence of the rulers who created and maintained them, as they commissioned lovingly detailed inventories of their contents and issued grandiose ordinances in the vain attempt to standardise gun calibres. They might also smooth the relations between those rulers and the

---

[18] Contamine, *Guerre, état et société*, 278–8, 399–487; Potter, *War and Government*, 161–3; Carroll, *Noble Power*, 69–76; Gunn, Grummitt, and Cools, *War, State, and Society*, 142–4.

[19] Lassalmonie, 'L'abbé Le Grand', 80–3; Commynes, *Memoirs*, 69; Carroll, *Noble Power*, 70.

[20] Brewer *et al.*, *Letters and Papers*, VII, no. 121.

[21] Contamine, *War*, 165–7; Contamine, *Histoire militaire*, I, 220; Tighe, 'Gentlemen Pensioners'; Hanlon, *Twilight*, 332.

towns that housed them, especially when the local economy was as dependent on the arms industry as Mechelen's.[22]

Permanent infantry forces for deployment in the field were as yet rare, the Spanish *tercios* being the exception until the French crown began to maintain regiments between bouts of civil war in the 1560s, but the increasing fortification of the frontiers of the major states led to a proliferation of garrisons.[23] England had perhaps 2,000 infantrymen in garrisons in the 1550s, Venice nearly 6,000, France and Spain around 7,000 each, and the Netherlands conceivably 10,000, but we should not estimate their military effectiveness too highly. Major garrison forces like those of Metz or Calais were doubtless formidable, but many garrison soldiers were aged veterans or even invalids, and garrison towns from Valois Abbeville to Habsburg Mariembourg and the Venetian *terraferma* bred reports of troops sent out to gather the harvest on their captains' estates, doubling up as shopkeepers, or selling their clothes to make ends meet. While their captaincies provided a further fund of patronage for noblemen, garrisons also had negative political effects when they fell out with townsfolk or irritated urban authorities in arguments over excise exemptions and the control of town gates. Here geo-politics again came into play, as states garrisoning thinly populated borders or coastlines found their troops less provocative to civilian sensibilities than those who had to place garrisons in large population centres.[24]

The growing scale of garrison forces is also a reminder of the questionable nature of two tempting assumptions about standing forces. First, while the possession of standing troops might be thought to make a state more disposed to prey aggressively upon its neighbours, this argument would hold better for mobile forces than for garrisons. In practice the largest standing armies were maintained not just by expansionist states like France between 1445 and 1559, but also by those like sixteenth-century Venice, more concerned with retention than acquisition of territory. A system of repeated contracting to raise troops for profitable warfare by politically influential domestic noblemen – the English system of the fourteenth and fifteenth centuries – would

---

[22] Roosens, 'Arsenaal'; Roosens, 'Keizerlijke artillerie'; Grummitt, 'Defence'; Wood, *King's Army*, 51–2, 153–64; Wiesflecker, *Maximilian*, V, 559–62.

[23] Wood, *King's Army*, 106–10.

[24] *Ibid.*, 47–51, 92–5; Gunn, Grummitt, and Cools, *War, State, and Society*, 22, 75–8; Mallett and Hale, *Military Organisation*, 389–93, 452; Thompson, *War and Government*, 297; Grummitt, *Calais Garrison*; Berckmans, 'Mariembourg et Philippeville', 125; Wellens, 'Le procès', 37; Potter, *War and Government*, 169; Hale, *War and Society*, 135.

actually seem more likely to generate aggression than the maintenance of professional standing forces.[25] Second, while standing forces ought in theory to have increased the internal coercive power of the state and assisted towards its realisation of a monopoly of violence, evidence that they were so used is patchy. Against sedition they had a role, the French quartering their *ordonnances* on Brittany in the immediate aftermath of its submission, the Habsburgs keeping garrisons in newly assimilated provinces like Utrecht and Friesland even when external threats declined. But only small parts of the Venetian forces were used against crime and banditry, it is not clear how far the military and judicial arms of most states cooperated, and on balance soldiers caused at least as much disruption as they solved.[26]

However novel or significant these standing forces were, they never sufficed to yield whole armies, especially as the forces raised for major campaigns tended to grow larger. The two main sources of further recruitment – temporary companies of native troops and contracted non-native mercenaries – had rather different political connotations, at least in their purest forms, but were both used by almost all states. The Spanish *tercios* were only ever a minority in the Army of Flanders and, even in the heyday and heartland of mercenary service, the German princes in the war of the League of Schmalkalden were calling out thousands of native soldiers.[27] Native troops were generally raised by an appeal to local power-holders, whether noblemen or urban authorities. Cavalry in particular were best obtained through the clientage networks of the nobility; in England this remained true even after infantry recruitment had shifted in the mid sixteenth century from a 'quasi-feudal' to a 'national' system, under which local commissioners were asked for drafts of men from the county militias. Nobles and towns alike bargained for the best terms they could get for acting as the ruler's recruiting agents, while using the recruitment process to strengthen their own hold over their followers or the townsmen under their control.[28] Rulers might choose them as recruiting agents in preference to foreign mercenary contractors as cheaper, more convenient, more easily exploited by under-payment, and more readily inspired by

---

[25] Ayton, 'English Armies'.
[26] Contamine, *Guerre, état et société*, 315–16; Gunn, Grummitt, and Cools, *War, State, and Society*, 22, 273–80; Mallett and Hale, *Military Organisation*, 218–20, 377–8; Potter, 'Rigueur de justice'.
[27] Parker, *Army*, 25–35, 271; Oestreich, *Neostoicism*, 224–6.
[28] Potter, *War and Government*, 166–73; Gunn, Grummitt, and Cools, *War, State, and Society*, 51–60, 138–42, 144–7; Goring, 'Social Change'; Boynton, *Elizabethan Militia*, 76–88; Adams, 'Puritan Crusade?'.

patriotic duty or the quest for royally endorsed honour. But in doing so they ran the risks that their troops could not be expected to leave the country if disbanded in a disorderly state and that noble captains disgruntled by defeat, financial strain, or sudden unemployment – York in England in the 1450s, Egmond in the Netherlands in the 1560s – might prove disruptive in domestic politics.[29]

Such companies' relationship to the militias maintained almost everywhere for local defence varied widely, from the attempts of English noblemen to keep their most militarily competent followers out of the militia so that they might be available to serve in their own companies, to the efforts of Dutch town councils to keep their companies of *schutters* at home to defend the town and maintain social order.[30] Trained militias, selecting out the ablest men from general musters of all adult males, were much in vogue in the sixteenth century, not only because they appealed to the contemporary obsession with classical precedents, but also because they promised the benefits of standing infantry forces without the cost. Ideas of training and selection were not new. English villagers and townsfolk had been under orders to do regular archery practice since 1363 and were periodically mustered in the fifteenth century; Silesia, Bavaria, and Austria had legislated for select militias under threat from the Hussites around 1430; France had introduced the *francs-archers* at the same time as the *bandes d'ordonnance*.[31] But the demands of pike drill and shooting practice with firearms made the need for trained militias more urgent, and most states sought to develop them.

Military historians' verdict on the effectiveness of these forces has generally been poor, especially where the grander schemes to base whole field armies on them are concerned: Machiavelli's Florentine militia of 1505–6, the French *légions* of 1534, the English trained bands of 1573.[32] Yet they were in some ways more important than standing armies for the relationship between war and state formation. The most successful seem to have been those where the government's plans fitted best with local traditions of self-defence, such as the Tyrol, or where arming large sections of the populace with firearms was a token of the state's confidence in the unforced loyalty of its subjects, as in the

---

[29] Jones, 'Somerset, York and Wars'; Troeyer, *Lamoraal van Egmont*.
[30] Boynton, *Elizabethan Militia*, 31–3, 161–2, 186–7; Knevel, *Burgers, passim*.
[31] Strickland and Hardy, *Great Warbow* (Stroud edn), 199; Goodman, *Wars of the Roses*, 141–5, 149; Schnitter, *Volk und Landesdefension*, 42; Contamine, *Guerre, état et société*, 334–66.
[32] Hale, *War and Society*, 199–200; Potter, *War and Government*, 174–7; Boynton, *Elizabethan Militia*, 90–125.

Venetian *terraferma*.[33] Both characteristics combined with the use of an unusually well-informed and well-coordinated corps of local royal officials in recruitment to produce the militia army best equipped for external warfare, that of Vasa Sweden.[34] The more sophisticated trained militias, such as those introduced around 1600 by John VII of Nassau and Maurice of Hesse, incorporated many of the disciplinary and organisational features of the Dutch and Huguenot armies. Even the less organised schemes called out large sections of the male population for regular musters organised by local authorities, constrained them to buy weapons if they did not possess those thought suitable for their level of wealth, and subjected them to harangues about their duty to the fatherland and the sole right of their prince to command their military service. Many combined coercion with negotiation by trading privileges or tax reductions for enlistment.[35]

In the military literature inspired by Machiavelli and his ancient models, patriotic militiamen were directly contrasted with fickle mercenaries. The differences were of course overdrawn. Mercenaries like the Swiss functioned as militiamen when it came to defending their village, canton, or federation, and indeed owed their cohesion in battle even when in mercenary service to the very local basis of their recruitment.[36] *Landsknechte* in Habsburg service were thought to be susceptible to appeals to defend the 'honour of the German nation' and the Spanish kings preferred to recruit their landsknechts from the lands of their Austrian cousins.[37] But rulers clearly did face choices over the balance to strike between shaping their subjects to meet their military aims and hiring non-native mercenaries; and rulers of comparable states reached different conclusions. Here a range of factors came into play. Economic and fiscal differences generated a spectrum of states: from those with tax income so small that even most native troops served without pay, and the hiring of any but a few experts (say artillerymen) was out of the question; through those able to raise sufficient tax revenue or borrow sufficient cash on an occasional basis to pay their native troops and hire significant bodies of mercenaries (say pikemen and heavy cavalry) to make up deficiencies in their native forces for major campaigns; to

[33] Schnitter, *Volk und Landesdefension*, 46–8; Mallett and Hale, *Military Organisation*, 364–6.

[34] Glete, *War and the State*, 184–6, 189–91, 194–5, 201–6.

[35] Schnitter, *Volk und Landesdefension*, 43–6, 74–98, 110–26; Knevel, *Burgers*, 44–8; Boynton, *Elizabethan Militia*, 13–30; Glete, *War and the State*, 195; Galasso, *Regno di Napoli*, 737–78; Potter, *War and Government*, 176.

[36] McCormack, *Mercenaries*, 11–14, 24–34, 74–5.

[37] Möller, *Regiment der Landsknechte*, 68–70; Parker, *Army*, 29.

those with a tax and credit base sufficient to compose three-quarters of their field army of hired foreigners: Scotland, England, and France were examples of each type.[38] Denmark and Sweden present a similar contrast, one equipped through dues on Baltic trade to hire mercenary forces afresh for each war, the other able to hire some foreigners but for most purposes forced to develop a durable system of conscription of the native peasantry.[39]

National military cultures also played a part in such choices. Just as particular groups of mercenaries were hired by various states for their expertise with particular weapons or tactics – Genoese crossbowmen, English longbowmen, Bohemian users of the *Wagenburg*, German or Dutch artillerymen, Swiss or German pikemen, Albanian *stradiot* light cavalry, German *Reiter* pistoleers – so rulers with native soldiers famed for a particular speciality had no need to hire foreigners, and rulers of composite territories brought expert troops from one part to serve in another. The local standard of living was also a factor: booming Brabant and Holland attracted military and other labour in the sixteenth century, while Venice had always to hire a wide range of infantry because its *terraferma* possessions were too prosperous to generate enough recruits.[40] Lastly and most intriguingly there is the possibility that rulers chose to employ mercenaries because they did not trust, or wished to coerce, their own subjects.[41] Machiavelli suspected this of the kings of France: 'The king [of France] has disarmed his own people so as to command them more easily.'[42] Certainly foreign troops were thought most reliable in dealing with popular disturbances such as those in England in 1549 and Antwerp in 1554, and were correspondingly unpopular, a fact that may have encouraged national solidarity amongst those repressed by foreign mercenaries, if not affection for the rulers who sent them.[43]

Yet it would be wrong to think of mercenaries as a simple commodity of military force, available for purchase by any state with sufficient fiscal strength. In any polity that used mercenaries regularly, generals and diplomats built up relations with mercenary contractors mirroring those between noblemen and their clients within the domestic political

---

[38] Phillips, *Anglo-Scots Wars*, 42–87; Wood, *King's Army*, 38–42.

[39] Krüger, 'Kriegsfinanzierung', 277–84; Frost, *Northern Wars*, 30–7; Glete, *War and the State*, 202–3.

[40] Gunn, Grummitt, and Cools, *War, State, and Society*, 22–3, 297; Mallett and Hale, *Military Organisation*, 315.

[41] Kiernan, 'Foreign Mercenaries'.

[42] Machiavelli, *Art of War*, ed. Lynch, 23.

[43] Gunn, Grummitt, and Cools, *War, State, and Society*, 299–302.

system. The mercenaries were themselves drawn into that system by frequent service, the payment of pensions to retain their service from one year to the next, the need to retain political favour in order to get past wages paid and good terms for their next engagement, sometimes by grants of land inside their employer's territories that promised to make them part of the domestic nobility. Often they lived in areas not far from the ill-defined borders of the great states that employed them: Cleves for the Netherlands, for example; the Grisons for Venice; the Tyrol or Trentino for Spanish Lombardy; Alsace or Lorraine for France. They could not be sure that some political or military reversal might not turn them from employees into subjects, as for example the French drive towards the Rhine in 1543 seemed to threaten. Even if it did not, the backing of a great prince or his influential generals might be helpful to them in their private feuds or family politics.[44] For the princes of Germany and Italy in particular, mercenary hire forged political relationships at both ends of the state-building process. Princes hired lesser noblemen to fight for them and thus built them steadily into their consolidating statelets; princes hired themselves out as captains with ready-made armies – the Gonzaga of Mantua, the Malatesta of Rimini, the Montefeltro of Urbino, Albrecht Alcibiades of Brandenburg-Kulmbach, Johann of Küstrin – and thus confirmed their position amongst the alliances of the great and strengthened the financial and political position of their own rule at home; sometimes commanders won whole principalities – Francesco Sforza at Milan, Albrecht of Saxony in Friesland – or, like Franz von Sickingen, tried in vain to do so.[45]

The rise of *trace italienne* fortifications, better able than their predecessors to resist artillery, has rightly played an important part in debates about the effects of war on the state, but again the issue is complex. They do seem to have encouraged larger expenditure on construction and the maintenance of larger numbers of garrison troops.[46] Yet it is not clear whether on balance they acted in favour of the elimination of smaller states, unable to afford their construction and defence; or their preservation, able to shelter behind them

---

[44] McCormack, *Mercenaries*, 50–1, 63–4, 76–7; Gunn, Grummitt, and Cools, *War, State, and Society*, 147–9; Mallett and Hale, *Military Organisation*, 42–3, 76–81, 313–30; Potter, 'International Mercenary Market'; Potter, *War and Government*, 178; Wagner, *Fürstenberg*, 75–6, 105–7; Redlich, *German Military Enterpriser*, I, 56–62; Edelmayer, *Söldner und Pensionäre*, 174–202, 256–9.

[45] Covini, 'Bonds', 28–33; Edelmayer, *Söldner und Pensionäre*, 138–40, 180–1; Redlich, *German Military Enterpriser*, I, 36–8, 48–9, 59–60; Wiesflecker, *Maximilian*, V, 94–9.

[46] Parker, *Military Revolution* (1988 edn), 6–63.

until their larger adversaries exhausted themselves.[47] The inability of noblemen or towns tempted to insubordination to afford fortifications capable of defying princely artillery has been a staple of the argument that rulers' siege trains enabled them to confront 'local entities' and 'force their submission to the increasingly more powerful state'.[48] Yet in civil war conditions the difficulty of deploying siege artillery against dissident strongholds became painfully evident.[49] Even in major wars, smaller and less sophisticated fortifications, such as those maintained by nobles or created by small towns adapting their medieval walls, could still play an important strategic role, holding up large armies long enough to frustrate whole campaigns.[50] The role of garrisoned urban citadels in controlling restive townsfolk seems less equivocal. Contemporaries clearly thought of them as 'like the bridle in the mouths of wild horses', as Francesco De Marchi put it. They prescribed them as a punishment and preservative against recurrence in the wake of revolts such as that at Ghent in 1539 and Siena in 1552, and avoided them when they wished, as Venice did, to proclaim their confidence in their subjects' unforced affection.[51]

We should also consider the process of construction of the new fortifications and their symbolic function. Their complexity and cost increased the state's role in fortification over that of urban authorities and individual noblemen, but urban fortification projects, even when ordered by kings and designed by their expert engineers, could strengthen civic control of the surrounding countryside and urban authorities' control of the townsfolk, ordered to perform forced labour on the new works and demolish their own houses if they got in the way.[52] The heavy demand for pioneers generated conscription measures and conditions of service worse than those for soldiers: when the authorities in the Habsburg Netherlands ran out of vagrants to enrol as pioneers they were to find anyone they could, 'constraining to this, if needs be, those amongst them who are unwilling'; French pioneers had to be dressed in uniform cassocks to make it easier to recapture those who ran away.[53] Yet

[47] Hook, 'Fortifications'; Arnold, 'Fortifications', 201–26.
[48] DeVries, 'Gunpowder Weaponry and the State'.
[49] Wood, *King's Army*, 153–83.
[50] Gunn, Grummitt, and Cools, *War, State, and Society*, 152–3; Pepper and Adams, *Firearms and Fortifications*, 93–116.
[51] Law, 'Significance of Citadels'; Pepper and Adams, *Firearms and Fortifications*, 27–8, 158; Gunn, Grummitt, and Cools, *War, State, and Society*, 303–4, 323–4; Mallett and Hale, *Military Organisation*, 420–3.
[52] Gunn, Grummitt, and Cools, *War, State, and Society*, 67–73, 97–101; Pepper and Adams, *Firearms and Fortifications*, 31, 71–8, 83.
[53] Gunn, Grummitt, and Cools, *War, State, and Society*, 243; Wood, *King's Army*, 165–6.

fortified borders and coastlines spoke of the ruler's concern to protect his subjects, and proclaimed his majesty through their decoration with badges, inscriptions, and triumphal gateways, and even through the names of the new fortress towns: Carlentini, Charlemont, Cosmopolis, Frederikstad, Mariembourg, Philippeville. Large schemes of coastal fortification like those in Henrician England or Spanish Naples visibly enclosed the state's territory, though the effect must have been somewhat spoilt if the forts fell into ruin within decades, as half of those in Naples had done by 1590.[54] Mapping projects, often related to fortifications or other strategic purposes, helped rulers and subjects visualise their realms as territorially bounded units.[55]

While older literature, perhaps betraying its Germanic focus, tended to concentrate on armies rather than navies, lately the rise of standing navies of galleys and gunned sailing ships has been stressed as another major innovation of this period and absorbed into the sociological literature as the first token of the 'permanent-war state'.[56] Navies, like armies, might be permanent at one moment and disappear the next, as did the French galley fleet based at Rouen and Harfleur in the fourteenth century or the Habsburg fleet at Veere in the sixteenth.[57] Their fate depended on strategic logic: the Lancastrian dual monarchy, ruling on both sides of the Channel, allowed Henry V's fleet to wither, while the Tudors, having lost their continental possessions, saw their fleet as the key to isolating and dominating the British archipelago; the policy-makers of Spanish Italy debated whether to meet the Islamic threat by coastal defence or a galley fleet; the Danes and the Swedes competed for Baltic dominance in the 1560s and 1570s before pausing in rough equilibrium.[58] Their creation or reconstruction often involved wearisome struggles between central policy-makers, upholders of local privilege in remote coastal areas, and powerful mercantile interests.[59] Yet their role in protecting commerce made it credible to earmark tolls on trade to pay for them, making naval developments the clearest examples of military expansion as protection-selling visible in the period.[60]

[54] Gunn, Grummitt, and Cools, *War, State, and Society*, 302–5; Checa Cremades, 'Monarchic Liturgies', 94–5; Hale, *War and Society*, 207; Duffy, *Siege Warfare*, 165; Galasso, *Regno di Napoli*, 483, 714–15.

[55] Buisseret, *Monarchs, Ministers and Maps*.

[56] Parker, *Military Revolution* (1988 edn), 82–114; Glete, *Navies and Nations*; Mann, *Sources*, I, 457.

[57] Contamine, *Histoire militaire*, 116–18, 154–69; Sicking, *Zeemacht*, 179–213.

[58] Rodger, *Safeguard*, 143–7, 196–8; Galasso, *Regno di Napoli*, 715–18; Glete, *Warfare*, 116–24.

[59] Sicking, *Zeemacht*, 239–47; James, *Navy and Government*, 32–76.

[60] Rodger, *Safeguard*, 125, 157; Sicking, *Zeemacht*, 182; Glete, *War and the State*, 80–2, 104–6, 110–16, 162–71, 200–1.

The physical demands of maintaining ships and supplying their crews tended to generate substantial supporting bureaucracies and physical infrastructure, making institutions like the Venetian Arsenal or the Tudor Council for Marine Causes more convincingly bureaucratic than those administering most contemporary armies, and naval bases like Le Havre, Portsmouth, and Finale nerve centres of royal authority.[61] The comparatively high cost of ships, the need to victual crews for lengthy periods at sea, and the rising numbers of guns on ships made navies a weighty feature in state budgets and one that, unlike fortifications, was hard to cut back without serious long-term damage. By the later sixteenth century, the navies of maritime states like England and Spain cost more in peacetime than their standing armies and, even in wartime, when the number of troops employed on land rose dramatically, they might account for between 25 and 50 per cent of all military expenditure; Venice's naval expenses in her wars against the Ottomans and Uskoks were similarly weighty.[62] Ships were also tokens of royal magnificence for those who saw them and were named and decorated appropriately: Henry VII's *Sovereign*, Henry VIII's *Henry Grâce à Dieu*, Philip II's *Argo*, painted with complex images and inscriptions linking Jason and the Argonauts to the Burgundian-Habsburg Golden Fleece, Magellan, and Columbus.[63] Yet here too there are problems with a straightforward narrative of military expansion and state growth. Decentralised structures for naval administration, like those of the nascent Dutch republic, might prove more effective at harnessing expertise and channelling resources than more apparently modern institutions.[64] Maritime communities, dependent on trade or fishing, might cooperate more productively with a ruler's war aims under conditions of maritime truce, devolved convoying, or licensed privateering than in the construction of a state navy.[65]

Such considerations emphasise the degree to which the state's ability to make war depended on a range of negotiated relationships, notably that between ruler and nobility.[66] Noble clientage networks permeated army recruitment and noble army command rested on the display of

---

[61] Loades, *Tudor Navy*, 53–5, 81–9, 106, 149–50, 166, 186; Lane, *Venice: A Maritime Republic*, 361–4; Knecht, *Renaissance Warrior*, 367–8; Hanlon, *Twilight*, 54.

[62] Rodger, *Safeguard*, 126; Loades, *Tudor Navy*, 137–8, 142, 155, 166–9, 254, 277; Thompson, 'Finance', 275, 284–5; Mallett and Hale, *Military Organisation*, 462, 479–84.

[63] Loades, *Tudor Navy*, 39–41, 62, 67; Tanner, *Last Descendant*, 7–9.

[64] Glete, *War and the State*, 162–71.

[65] Sicking, *Zeemacht*, 73–146, 214–47; Rodger, *Safeguard*, 182, 199–200, 280–1, 293–6.

[66] Glete, *War and the State*, 52–66.

social prestige in rich tents, generous hospitality, and the use of personal credit to pay troops when state funds were lacking. The martial honour of the nobility was increasingly channelled by monarchical orders of knighthood, princely regulation of heraldic display, and grants of titles of noble rank, but could be proclaimed through chivalrous funerals, armoured portraits, and admiring chronicles. Successful captains might also win grants of land and office, and the favour of the prince. Wages of war aided the cash liquidity of noblemen, especially in the wake of the Black Death when conditions were difficult for landlords. Nobles whose role in everyday jurisdiction was being reduced by the advance of centralising law courts, professional lawyers, and learned law found a judicial role in the discipline of armies. Provincial governorships and similar posts proved a means for rulers to harness noble influence to the cause of local defence and to advance the integration of newly won provinces as their local elites were recruited for military service elsewhere under the governor's leadership; meanwhile they enabled noblemen to appropriate royal authority to reinforce their own power.[67]

The relationship was not without its tensions. Any substantial army recruited through and led by the nobility gathered a significant slice of the national elite and thus became 'a forum for debate' in ways that might prove uncomfortable for kings.[68] Some polities, like Spanish Naples, would not trust the native nobility with commands at home, though they were welcome to serve overseas.[69] Some, republican Florence in particular, were so wary of noble political ambition that they consistently failed to harness noble military aptitude, with eventually fatal results.[70] Some, such as Bavaria and Brandenburg, found the nobility so resistant to the idea of arming the peasantry that their schemes for militia reform were obstructed or entirely stymied.[71] Some nobilities, like the French, apparently found it easier to absorb foreign-born commanders than others, like the English.[72] In states with well-developed judicial institutions, like England, nobles whose pursuit of private feuds by violent means met with princely disapproval might be sent abroad to wield their swords, but in those with a weaker judicial framework, like the Empire, the most disruptive feuders might move in and out of

---

[67] Zmora, *Monarchy, Aristocracy, and the State*, 8–21, 30–6, 55–68; Boulton, *Knights*; Gunn, Grummitt, and Cools, *War, State, and Society*, 155–64, 177–92, 200–31; Hanlon, *Twilight*, 261–72, 333–4; Potter, *War and Government*, 65–112; Harding, *Provincial Governors*.
[68] Ayton, 'Battle of Crécy', 21–2.
[69] Hanlon, *Twilight*, 49, 227–9.
[70] Mallett, *Mercenaries*, 92–3, 129–31, 220.
[71] Schnitter, *Volk und Landesdefension*, 108, 124–9.
[72] Contamine, *Guerre, état et société*, 419–21; Walker, 'Janico Dartasso'.

rulers' military employment with apparent impunity.[73] Noble power in military borderlands had sometimes to be given freer rein than in the heartlands of the state, but legally minded councillors like Mercurino de Gattinara or Thomas Cromwell found it hard to reconcile with their general insistence on the prince's justice and order. Issues such as the conclusion of private truces to protect noblemen's estates in wartime were particularly problematic.[74] In many areas the greatest lords were able to operate across cultural and political frontiers more effectively than were the more institutionalised forms of princely power, making the houses of Orange–Nassau, Guise, or Campbell, the last with their 5,000 or more armed Highlanders, galley fleet, and castles, a factor to be reckoned with in the politics of more than one polity.[75]

In the Weberian model the bureaucrats introduced to administer standing forces and increasing taxes were the antithesis of the nobility but, in practice, as historians have long pointed out, early-modern bureaucracies were far from the ideal. When they worked best it was often because, like the naval administrations of the mid-sixteenth-century Netherlands or Elizabethan England, they were shot through with bonds of clientage and kinship, and only rarely because, like the Venetian military administration, they harnessed ideals of public service in the context of a reasonably meritocratic *cursus honorum* for the elite.[76] When they worked worst they worked very badly indeed, and the larger the influence they wielded and the sums of money they dispensed, the more tempting they became to those who wished to become parasitic upon them. By the later sixteenth century the Spanish system was riddled with corruption, nepotism, and feuding between competing bodies.[77] The Elizabethan military bureaucracy in Ireland, considerably expanded from its early Tudor predecessor, was laughably unbureaucratic, with much absenteeism, delegation, and incompetence, minimal record-keeping, and virtually no check on individual captains' cheating of the crown, the soldiers, and the local population.[78] The late Elizabethan and Jacobean navy was not much better.[79] As long as bureaucracies were managed by rulers and ministers embedded in court-based patronage systems, the potential for dysfunction was high.

[73] Powell, *Kingship, Law and Society*, 220–2; Wiesflecker, *Maximilian*, I, 91–101.
[74] Ellis, *Tudor Frontiers*; Headley, 'Conflict', 49–80; Tracy, *Holland*, 85–7.
[75] Carroll, *Noble Power*, 48, 89–95,172–82, 188–92; Dawson, *Politics of Religion*, 51–6.
[76] Sicking, *Zeemacht*, 59–60, 209–10, 225–6; Loades, *Tudor Navy*, 182–3; Mallett and Hale, *Military Organisation*, 159–80, 203–5, 248–73.
[77] Thompson, *War and Government*, 42–66.
[78] Brady, 'Captains' Games', 148–51.
[79] Rodger, *Safeguard*, 364–78.

Negotiation, compromise, and distortion were also characteristic of the fiscal systems developed to sustain states at war.[80] Certainly state budgets expanded everywhere between the thirteenth century and the sixteenth, and did so most dramatically in wartime, though the calculation of per capita figures and those converted into silver or wheat equivalents to allow for population growth and inflation often makes the achievement look less startling than crude figures taken straight from government accounts would suggest. Certainly most states funded themselves increasingly through direct and indirect taxation of their subject populations rather than demesne resources. Certainly smaller states, such as the duchy of Guelders, were often dragged into fiscal change by the need to preserve their independence against their larger neighbours.[81] Certainly the political independence of individual towns was curtailed as rulers intervened to cope with the bankruptcies induced by taxation and local expenditure for war, especially civil war.[82] Yet this was not a simple victory for centralised state power. The fiscal changes of the thirteenth, fourteenth, and fifteenth centuries were based on bargains between rulers and subjects about the pursuit of the common good and the role of negotiation and representation – often, though not necessarily, through formal representative institutions – in ensuring that the ruler kept to it.[83] Such institutions may often have seemed a hindrance to sixteenth-century rulers bent on maximising their income, but they were the tip of an iceberg of compromise, without which fiscal extraction was impossible.

That compromise was mostly with the socially powerful. From the tax-exempt nobility of many states downwards, elites did their best to divert the burden of taxation onto the rural and urban middling sort and poor, provided only that the payment of state taxes should not interfere with their tenants' payment of rent. Generally their efforts were more successful than those of the many popular revolts against taxation, though these might win short-term concessions or divert rulers from more provocative to less provocative kinds of exaction. Another ready target, at least for lay elites, was clerical wealth, whether expropriated at the Reformation or relentlessly taxed as in Spain or France. Taxing the foreign consumers of trade under the state's control was of course the best solution of all when it could be made to work, but economic and strategic change meant that such boons as the English wool subsidy, the

---

[80] For the following three paragraphs see in general Bonney, *Fiscal State*, *passim*, and Bonney, *Economic Systems*.
[81] Shaïk, 'Taxation and State-Making'.
[82] Gunn, Grummitt, and Cools, *War, State, and Society*, 92–7.
[83] Genet, 'Which State Rises?'.

Danish Sound dues, or the Portuguese royal pepper monopoly could not last forever.

The way taxes were gathered built these compromises into the system. States' dependence on local elites, down to the level of leading villagers, to assess and collect direct taxation, equipped them to manipulate it in their own interest. The farming of indirect taxes distorted them to the benefit of the smaller or greater merchants able to supply government with the liquid cash to buy the farms. Where representative institutions could not be persuaded to grant realistic taxes on overseas trade, governments like that of the Habsburg Netherlands responded by banning trade with the enemy in wartime and then selling licences to evade the ban to the greatest traders, thus damaging their smaller rivals. Where tax bureaucracies did develop, they readily became venal, partly negating their modern or rational features.[84] Funded state debts too had distorting political or economic effects. In the Netherlands and Naples alike they drew the capital resources of local elites into supporting the state in the mid sixteenth century in return for favourable investment conditions, but in one they led those elites to take so much grip on fiscal policy that the ruler's freedom of manoeuvre was seriously cramped, and in the other they drew investment out of the local economy and thus weakened the state's long-term fiscal base.[85]

The third area of war's effects, beyond the development of military institutions and fiscalism, is the hardest to pin down and yet in some ways the most interesting. War-making enhanced the powers of rulers over their subjects in many ways. Controls on trade with the enemy, the promotion of military industries, and attempts to channel food to armies and deny it to invaders encouraged wide-ranging interventions in economic life. Orders to arrest enemy aliens and confiscate their goods, and treason prosecutions of those aiding the enemy, defecting to the enemy, or plotting to surrender towns, all enforced identification with the fatherland and loyalty to its ruler. All these of course, like the welfare measures demanded by the ill effects of war, might develop the powers of the local authorities implementing them as much as those of the ruler and central administration.[86] Wartime propaganda familiarised subjects with notions of the common good, patriotic duty, and the ruler's emergency powers, and denigrated the enemy, defining national identities by opposition to villains like the 'wicked

---

[84] Collins, *Fiscal Limits*; Schofield, 'Taxation'; Craeybeckx, *Grand commerce*, 207–49; Robisheaux, *Rural Society*, 179–86.

[85] Tracy, *Holland*, 116–35, 176–87; Calabria, *Cost of Empire*, 104–29.

[86] Hale, *War and Society*, 220–9; Goodman, *Power and Penury*, 88–141; Gunn, Grummitt, and Cools, *War, State, and Society*, 82–6, 252–6, 285–93, 308–12.

English, filled with pride' who attacked the French coast in 1543. In time printed pamphlets, blending into the sixteenth-century market for cheap printed news, were added to public proclamations and the exploitation of the Church's information network of announcements from the pulpit, intercessory processions, and fasts. Public celebration of military success was encouraged, though local opinion apparently had a say in whether it was victories or peace treaties that launched the biggest parties. For some rulers at least – Charles V being a prime example – military heroism was the main ingredient of their public image. All the arts of the Renaissance were bent to exalting their feats in defence of their people, and for those subjects unlikely to see a Titian painting or a luxurious tapestry there were triumphal arches at civic entries, cheap woodcut prints, and armour-clad portraits on coins.[87] Yet rulers clearly also bore some responsibility for the burdens that war placed upon their subjects. They had to be seen to seek peace when possible, to alleviate the suffering of those driven from their homes by war or wounded in their service. They had to discipline and pay their troops, not only for the sake of combat effectiveness, but to appease the civilian population on whom the soldiers would prey if not restrained. If they failed, then the anarchy visited on France by the free companies in the wake of Poitiers might not be far away.[88]

The teleological approach to the formation of national states in the Weberian tradition has perhaps distracted attention from a fourth way in which war impacted on the development of polities on the largest scale. As historians have been stressing for several decades, the characteristic early-modern polity was a composite or agglomerate state, made up either of a core and distinctive peripheries, or of multiple formerly independent and sometimes widely scattered units.[89] Early-modern rulers faced with practical problems of strategy and resource mobilisation therefore operated in a context very different from that of the model unitary centralising state. Peripheral regions in which major wars were fought with all the resources the state could muster from its core territories might be drawn rapidly into centralised political, military, and fiscal networks, as Valois Picardy was.[90] Peripheral regions in which conquest or pacification were pursued at minimum

[87] Jones, 'Church and Propaganda'; Seguin, *L'information en France*, quotation at 44–5; Gunn, Grummitt, and Cools, *War, State, and Society*, 247–52, 257–72, 283–4; Checa Cremades, *Carlos V*.

[88] Hale, *War and Society*, 168–70, 182–4, 189–91, 197–8; Gunn, Grummitt, and Cools, *War, State, and Society*, 244–7, 273–7; Sumption, *Hundred Years War*, II, 351–404.

[89] Elliott, 'Composite Monarchies'.

[90] Potter, *War and Government*.

cost, like Tudor Ireland, might fall prey either to the construction of power-bases by the local nobility so entrenched that central government could barely cope without them, or to a brand of private-enterprise colonialist warlordism unlikely to promote good order and the reconciliation of the native population to royal rule.[91] The attempt to maintain large strongholds at a distance from the main territory, such as English Calais or Portuguese Ceuta, forced rather different developments in domestic fiscal and administrative systems from those needed to serve a longer, but closer, militarised frontier.[92] In composite monarchies, meanwhile, the development of each part might be conditioned by the role it was called on to play in relation to its ruler's wider strategy and by the reaction of all his other dominions to the calls made upon them. In the case of Charles V, the Netherlands, Naples, and Castile were all put under pressure to develop their fiscal systems to support Charles as he set out in person on one great military campaign after another from 1529 to 1552, but through their responses the representative institutions of the Netherlands secured increasing local control of strategy and expenditure, those of Naples met Charles' needs more generously as local elites competed for his favour, and those of Castile were steadily drawn into cross-subsidising his ventures all over Europe.[93]

Lastly we should remember that wars helped to break states down as well as to build them up. The strains of war – heavy taxation, economic disruption, noble alienation from one another or from the king and his courtiers, disenchantment with monarchs unable to deliver the victory their propaganda promised as due by God's judgement on the rightness of their cause – interacted with other political, dynastic, and religious contingencies to produce serious political breakdowns such as the Wars of the Roses, the French Wars of Religion, and the Dutch Revolt. These exposed the way in which the capacity to fight external wars did not correspond in any uncomplicated sense to the ability to coerce internal dissidents: noble generals, militias, and even parts of standing armies might prove unreliable, mercenaries unpopular, and the greatest armies in Europe incapable of winning civil wars.[94] The mobilisation of armies to defy royal power also has much to tell us about the incomplete nature of military and political change. In some polities, such as the Netherlands, organising for dynastic war had consolidated

---

[91] Ellis, *Tudor Frontiers*; Brady, *Chief Governors*, 19–20, 29, 72, 109–10, 122–3, 169–208; Brady, 'Captains' Games', 139–59.
[92] Ormrod, *Political Life*, 102–5; Russell, *Prince Henry*, 59–76.
[93] Tracy, *Emperor Charles V.*
[94] Wood, *King's Army.*

administrative and political structures at provincial rather than central level, making it easier for a province such as Holland to pursue its own interests against the prince.[95] Populations had to be kept armed and local militias organised for self-defence during wars sanctioned by the state, but this enabled arms, experience, and even militia structures to be turned against the authorities in revolts like those in England in 1450 and 1536, and in Germany in 1525, and to defend towns such as Haarlem and La Rochelle in longer-lasting struggles.[96] Noble power had to be harnessed to army recruitment and command, but this equipped dissidents – the Percies, Nevilles, or Guises – to raise forces for private war and insurrection.[97] Naval ventures had to be made in cooperation with ports and their ship-owners, but this enabled the mobilisation of rebel forces at sea like those of the Huguenot Rochellais and the Sea-Beggars.[98] It is of course true that most states emerged strengthened from civil wars, as effective political leadership reconstructed the political, fiscal, and military systems developed before the breakdown, or incorporated new devices forged in civil conflict; but this was not always the case, especially when external rivals were able to take advantage of internal turmoil.

War, then, did not build the ideal modern state in any straightforward way in this period. Yet it clearly did stimulate the creation of military and fiscal institutions more like those of present-day states than those of high-medieval Europe had been, and it licensed the extension of rulers' powers over many other areas of their subjects' lives. The contribution made by such changes to the overall shaping of states in this period is hard to compare with that of other factors, though we can try. Analysis of state budgets suggests that military spending, even with the advent of standing forces, was not the single largest category in peacetime, competing with legal bureaucracies, princely households, building projects, and so on: the Venetian army took a fifth of the budget in 1508, the English navy a tenth in 1551–3. In wartime, however, military expenditure swamped all other categories, and as funded debts developed, so paying for previous wars by paying the interest on the debt became an ever heavier burden even in peacetime.[99] This is probably the clearest evidence we have for the role of

[95] Kokken, *Steden en staten*; Tracy, *Holland*.
[96] Bohna, 'Armed Force'; Bush, *Pilgrimage of Grace*, 56–8, 116–18, 224–5, 293, 345–52, 407–8; Schnitter, *Volk und Landesdefension*, 58–63; Knevel, *Burgers*, 66–111; Pablo, 'Contribution', 196–7.
[97] Griffiths, 'Local Rivalries'; Carroll, *Noble Power*, 70–1, 160, 202.
[98] James, *Navy and Government*, 11–23; Glete, *Warfare*, 152–4.
[99] Mallett and Hale, *Military Organisation*, 131, 461–84; Loades, *Tudor Navy*, 155; Körner, 'Expenditure', 402–9, 416; Thompson, 'Finance', 273–98.

war in state growth and it plays a central role in expositions of war's overriding importance.[100]

Analysis of regularly employed state servants, more equivocally, might suggest that those dedicated to war may have come in this period to out-number those dedicated to other matters, but only in those compara-tively few larger polities that developed substantial standing forces, and perhaps not even there. The estimated 12,000 French office-holders of 1505 were fewer than the 14,000 armed men kept on foot on average in the 1450s and 1460s and the 25,000 kept up in the 1480s and 1490s, but the 40,000 officials of the early seventeenth century outnumbered the 15,000 or so troops kept by Henry IV in peacetime, and were not far short of the real troop numbers raised in the 1620s. In England, less bureaucratised and less militarised, the entire permanent staff of the judicial, fiscal, naval, and military establishments in 1603 may well have been outnumbered by the 4,830 licensed preaching clergy of the Church of England.[101] Counting the size of armies, navies, and mili-tary bureaucracies is a way to demonstrate the importance of war as a driver in state formation, but the wider the perspective we take, the less decisive such calculations appear.

This brings us to perhaps the most important question of all, but the hardest to answer. In an average year, did the average subject – allow-ance made for wide differences between different social classes; town and countryside; the borders and the core regions of polities; and so on – have more contact with the military and fiscal agencies of the state or with others? Increasing rates of litigation in many states might sug-gest that on this test the judicial agencies of government would give the soldiers, recruiters, and tax collectors a run for their money, especially if we include the town and private jurisdictions increasingly built by proc-esses of appeal and legal codification into systems of justice with the prince at their head. Expanding systems of social welfare would also be a competitor in some areas, as would almost everywhere the increasingly entwined efforts of Church and state at moulding faithful, respectable, and obedient Christian subjects through preaching, catechism, and the strictures of moral courts. It remains open for those who place their whole stress on war to argue that all such measures were merely means to pacify or discipline the populace in order better to harness their mili-tary potential. For maximum impact, such an argument would have to

---

[100] Mann, *Sources*, I, 424–30, 451–6; Tilly, *Coercion*, 74–5; Parker, *Military Revolution* (1988 edn), 61–4.

[101] Schulze, 'Emergence and Consolidation', 268; Contamine, *Guerre, état et société*, 317; Contamine, *Histoire militaire*, 341, 346; Guenée, *States and Rulers*, 204; Williams, *Tudor Regime*, 107–8; Haigh, *English Reformations*, 275.

show both that significant numbers of contemporaries thought in these terms and that the provision of justice, welfare, and moral discipline was regularly pursued more strongly in polities engaged in intensive military competition than in those that were not. In the absence of such demonstration, the assertion of war's exclusive importance remains in the realm of general arguments about the fundamental nature of humanity, where mere historians should perhaps fear to tread.

4 From military enterprise to standing armies: war, state, and society in western Europe, 1600–1700

David Parrott

In 1633 the European conflict that had begun in 1619 was entering its fifteenth year. After the savagely fought battle of Lützen in November 1632, which had claimed the life of Gustavus Adolphus of Sweden but had failed to undermine Swedish military power in the Empire, the following campaign proved a lacklustre affair. Neither the imperial army under Albrecht Wallenstein nor the Swedish–German army wanted to risk another major encounter. The imperial army ended the 1633 campaign in winter quarters on the territories of its Habsburg overlord, Emperor Ferdinand II. Early in January 1634, forty-seven senior officers, each the colonel-proprietor of at least one regiment, assembled at Pilsen, south-west of Prague, to discuss orders from the court at Vienna.[1] The most significant instruction was to decamp into quarters in adjoining German territories, tantamount to fighting a winter campaign against the Swedish troops presently occupying these areas.[2] Following the repudiation of the court directives, dismissed as operationally impractical, the assembled officers each signed a document in which they subscribed to an oath of unconditional obedience to Wallenstein.[3]

At the time, and in the debates that have persisted ever since about Wallenstein's 'treason', the significance of this oath has been linked to the fact that Wallenstein had created the largest mercenary army ever seen in Europe. In early 1634 it had an effective strength of around 45,000, and at its peak in 1629 it had numbered over 100,000 soldiers on paper.[4] The traditional mercenary contract by which a colonel or captain

---

[1] Cechová et al., Documenta Bohemia bellum, 427–38 (regimental list for 1633), 444–54 (1634).

[2] Wallenstein to Ferdinand II, 17 December 1633, and Ferdinand II to Wallenstein, 24 December 1633, in ibid., 217–20; Mann, Wallenstein, 999–1008.

[3] Mann, Wallenstein, 1023–6; Srbik, Wallenstein's Ende, 104–6.

[4] Konze, Stärke, 35–51, suggests around 74,000 men in total at the end of the 1633 campaign; Löwe, Organisation, 6–8: the overall number of regiments was smaller in 1629, but each had a far higher effective strength; ibid., 13–18; Cechová et al., Documenta Bohemica bellum, 444–54; Pohl, 'Profiantirung', 23–32.

offered to raise a unit for a ruler in return for initial costs – recruitment, wages, and supplies – had been superseded by contracts with military enterprisers. The enterpriser met all the costs of raising and operating units against the offer of lump-sum reimbursements, usually made well into the campaign. The military contractor thus became a creditor rather than an employee, was militarily and politically far less subordinate to higher authorities, and developed his own priorities surrounding the preservation and deployment of his troops. If the ruler was negotiating with a general contractor to bring an army corps or an entire army into his service, the situation was further complicated as the contractors drew not on their own resources, but upon networks of credit. Further levels of interested parties were involved: sub-contracting colonels, financier networks, merchant consortia prepared to make contracts for the feeding or supply of the armies. Thus the commander presided over a group of stakeholders whose concern was to protect and secure their investment and ensure a suitable return.[5]

In January 1634 at Pilsen, Wallenstein's priorities were totally at odds with the Emperor's circle in Vienna, who interpreted his refusal to move the army onto non-Habsburg territory as defiance of imperial authority. As early as December 1633 Ferdinand II had decided to replace his insubordinate generalissimo, but the oath signed by the officer-proprietors convinced him that action was urgently needed; Wallenstein was convicted of *Reichsrebellion*, and on the night of 25 February 1634 he and his closest remaining supporters were murdered.[6]

Wallenstein's death can be presented as the end of an era in military history. It is placed within a traditional debate about state reliance on mercenaries. The parameters were already well-established when Machiavelli attacked the use of mercenaries in his *Arte della guerra* (1521), in terms that combined a humanist, moralising distaste for soldiers as hired wage-earners with supposedly empirical arguments for their ineffectiveness and unreliability.[7] Machiavelli's own heavily loaded rhetoric was adopted by theorists and historians, and a period from fourteenth-century Italian princes' reliance on mercenary bands to the Thirty Years' War has been unified in a simple, reductionist argument: any short-term benefits from employing mercenaries are outweighed by the dangers, unreliability, and military ineffectiveness of their service.[8] The enterpriser and the general contractor represent the final, most dangerous

---

[5] Ernstberger, *Hans de Witte*, 179–225; Kunisch, 'Wallenstein', 153–61.
[6] Srbik, *Wallenstein's Ende*, 110–23, 160–96; Kampmann, *Reichsrebellion*, 101–65.
[7] Anglo, *Machiavelli*, 537–8.
[8] Kiernan, 'Foreign Mercenaries', is a much cited yet banal evocation of this traditional theme.

evolution of mercenary forces, but European rulers finally got the point; from the later seventeenth century mercenaries were restricted to units incorporated into and subordinated to the military administration of state-raised armies, before their ultimate and complete elimination in the nineteenth century. This marginalisation of the mercenary is completed by the elaboration of an alternative military genealogy, which privileges the role played by state militias.[9] Early-modern experiments in setting up conscript militias are seen as the real precedent for standing armies, viewed in turn as the defining feature of the European absolutist state. What were in practice generally ill-conceived, half-hearted, and militarily insignificant initiatives to create and deploy militias have received disproportionate historical attention.[10]

Militias thus replace mercenaries as the foundation on which rulers supposedly built their state-raised, financed, and administered standing armies. In this context military entrepreneurship could be depicted as a dead-end, leading one historian of state-building to assert explicitly that Wallenstein was an irrelevant anachronism.[11] It might indeed appear that the armies of the later seventeenth century had moved away from the murky motivations and private enterprise of *condottieri* and general contractors, to be replaced by forces whose state-controlled organisational and operational characteristics would be recognisable into the twentieth century. Louis XIV's army is regularly presented as the paradigm of this transformation. Following his announcement in 1661 that he would henceforth rule in person, the king's highest priority was a reform of the French army to bring it under direct royal authority and to make it an effective instrument of government policy.[12] The results purportedly represent one of the great military success-stories of early-modern Europe. In 1667, 70,000 infantry and 35,000 cavalry swept aside the defences of the Spanish Netherlands, while between 1672 and 1678 the army, expanded up to an operational strength of 250,000, almost conquered the United Provinces in a single campaign, then held its own against a substantial European coalition for a further six years of war.[13] In 1690 the army reached an unprecedented wartime strength of 340,000 effectives, and continued to win victories

---

[9] A genealogy neatly encapsulated by a work such as Papke, *Von der Miliz zum stehenden Heer* ['From militia to standing army'].

[10] Hahlweg, *Heeresreform*; Schulze, 'Deutsche Landesdefensionen'; and see Nimwegen, Chapter 8 in this volume. Some scepticism about this approach can be found in Schulten, 'Nouvelle approche'.

[11] Porter, *War*, 70–1.

[12] Louis XIV, *Memoirs for the Dauphin*, 124–30.

[13] André, *Le Tellier et Louvois*, 178–9; Lynn, *Wars of Louis XIV*, 144–5. See Nimwegen, Chapter 8 in this volume.

in the field throughout the Nine Years' War even as the resources of the Allied coalition imposed overwhelming burdens on France.[14] The achievement of unprecedented expansion with the maintenance of tactical and operational effectiveness is represented as a direct product of far-reaching administrative-military reform.

Louis XIV's army provided a powerful stimulus to other rulers to reshape their own armed forces. Moreover, such directly controlled armies can be seen as a major step towards a state 'monopoly of violence'. Thus the military transition is linked to a wider process of growing central power. Indeed, army reform can be seen as a catalyst for wider political and social change, since the financial burden of an expanded army fell primarily upon the state, requiring changes to the allocation and collection of tax revenues, and leading to the development of an expanded civil administration. One attraction of Roberts' 'military revolution' thesis to non-military historians is this link between the administrative needs of 'new model armies' and the establishment of the 'well-ordered police state'.[15]

Yet for all its attractions, this scenario represents a fundamental misunderstanding of the wider issues of state power and society. Jan Glete notes the hazards of looking at this period in terms of the growth of a reified 'state', existing apart from the wider social context in which these military systems operated.[16] Much discussion of armies and state power pays insufficient attention to recent research into the character of early-modern central authority and its relationship to provincial and institutional elites. The creation or transformation of an army is not some act of will imposed by the ruler upon a passive body of subjects. Armies and military institutions represent the relationship between rulers and political elites, whether of traditional nobilities; provincial aristocracies; administrative, legal, or financial corporations; or fiscal-mercantile interest-groups. Like all aspects of political change in this period, the key issues are negotiation and compromise, building systems and institutions in which the aspirations of both ruler and all, or part, of the elites can be satisfied. For any military force, beyond the ruler's immediate household troops or retainers, to come into existence requires willingness by these elites to 'invest' – socially, financially, culturally – in military activity and institutions.[17]

---

[14] Lynn, *Giant*, 53.
[15] See, for example, Downing, *Military Revolution*, 56–83; Porter, *War*, 63–104; Roberts, 'Military Revolution'; and Glete, Chapter 14 in this volume.
[16] Glete, *War and the State*, especially Chapter 2.
[17] Lane's important concept that 'state-building' can be seen in terms of negotiation between the ruler and his subjects about the costs and extent of the protection that

The creation and operation of early-modern military force involves negotiations between the ruler and his elites with a direct impact on matters such as prioritisation of resources, levels of participation, mechanisms for funding and overseeing forces raised, and ultimately questions of ownership. In this context the assumed continuity between the older hiring of mercenaries and the later emergence of the military enterpriser, and the dismissal of both as an historical dead-end, needs to be re-examined. Whereas the traditional practice of hiring and funding mercenaries, often foreigners, under direct state contract, largely failed to generate a sense of shared interest and reciprocal benefit between elites and ruler, the enterprise system developed in the late sixteenth and first decades of the seventeenth century offered real possibilities for the negotiation of workable compromises. Moreover, once the military systems of the later seventeenth century are examined it is clear that many of the trade-offs and concessions that were characteristic of entrepreneurial warfare persisted in only slightly modified form in the armies of the later period. This sharing of interests is clear in the case of early-modern navies, where the integration of state and private funding and organisation was widespread and explicit.[18]

Why should early-modern elites wish to engage in military service? One set of reasons was essentially cultural. War and military command could demonstrate moral and physical qualities that a far wider European elite than just a traditional 'sword' nobility had been educated to esteem very highly.[19] The notion of military duty that could define an individual in an honourable relationship to the rest of society meshed, sometimes uneasily, with traditional chivalric ideals of individual prowess, performed under the eyes of the ruler.[20] The second group of reasons related to social aspirations. Early-modern states accorded highest levels of social esteem to nobility whose titles were derived from military service.[21] The *impôt du sang* was not merely an excuse for the avoidance of taxation but a justification for the assertion of noble privilege

---

the ruler should provide: *Profits from Power*, 12–65. This is discussed in Chapter 14, below.

[18] Parker, 'Dreadnought Revolution'; Wernham, 'Amphibious Operations'; Glete, *Navies and Nations*, 151–62; Glete, *Warfare at Sea*, 60–75; James, *Navy and Government*, 100–3, 110–15.

[19] Oestreich, *Neostoicism*, 76–89.

[20] Potter, 'Chivalry and Professionalism'; Fantoni, 'Il "Perfetto Capitano"'; Dewald, *Aristocratic Experience*, 45–68; vast numbers of treatises concerning the duties and appropriate behaviour of gentleman officers were published throughout the sixteenth and seventeenth centuries, many illustrating this tension between collective obligation and individual ambition.

[21] Even in the United Provinces, military virtues and noble status were associated, and the court assembled round the Orange princes made great play on the ennobling role

more generally, and for the exclusion or downgrading of those whose titles came from administrative service or simple purchase.[22]

Much elite military service undertaken for broadly cultural or social reasons involved substantial personal expense, and this might conflict with, or complement, the third major motivation, which was financial. A few great nobles and wealthy *anoblis* might pursue a military career simply to maintain social prestige, exercise a natural *métier*, or demonstrate the extent to which the family had moved up from its original administrative/fiscal/commercial base. But many officers who had entered military service primarily for cultural and social reasons still hoped at the same time to recoup some of their financial expenditure. Beyond this, moreover, was an area in which elites might engage in military activity for overt financial advantage. At the lowest level this was simply the hope, shared with the common soldiers, of profit from looting and ransoms.[23] In addition, however, were the relatively small numbers for whom war was an investment opportunity, offering returns on the efficient conduct and management of military resources. Direct involvement in the provision of military force presented greater opportunities for economic advantage. Even before the epoch of the military enterpriser, this can be seen in the funding and organisation of maritime privateering,[24] those Italian *condottiere* captains who had managed to establish a permanent contractual relationship with a particular Italian city or princely state, and those captains of *Landsknechte* and *Reiter* who relied upon their own reputation and that of their troops to build a remunerative career based on a succession of short-term service contracts.[25] Before the later sixteenth century, however, armies provided limited outlets for those whose primary motive for the raising and organisation of military force was financial return on an investment.

The evolution of privatised force in the military organisation of major European states in the later sixteenth and early seventeenth centuries can be seen as the opening up, enhancement, and diversification of the economic benefits from involvement in warfare, with a far-reaching impact on the relationships between rulers and a growing circle of their

---

of warfare; and the iconography of the Oranjezaal at the Huis ten Bosch was resolutely military: Trim, 'Army'; Israel, 'Courts'.

[22] Devyver, *Le sang épurée*, 88–108; Jouanna, 'Noblesse'.

[23] Redlich, *Praede Militari*, 41–53.

[24] Glete, *Naval History*, essays by Tracy, Baetens, and Stradling.

[25] Mallett, *Mercenaries*, on the successful *condottieri* in fourteenth- and fifteenth- century Italy. A classic example of such success would be the *Landsknecht*-commander, Georg von Frundsberg, though it is worth noting that the uncertainties of employment took their toll on the financial benefits of service; see Baumann, *Frundsberg, passim*, on the shortness of individual service contracts.

elites who were prepared and able to invest in the state's military system. The use of mercenaries was dramatically transformed by military developments from the late fifteenth century. The crushing successes of massive Swiss infantry pike-squares, and the fact that their only effective rivals on the battlefield were the comparably organised German *Landsknechte*, turned mercenaries from secondary force-enhancers such as Genoese crossbowmen, into the dominant weapons-system of the early sixteenth century. Mercenaries had always been more costly than troops raised by native elites because of their contractual stipulations about up-front money for recruitment, and advances of pay for what was envisaged as a short period of service.[26] The large pike-blocks of Swiss and German infantry had to be bought in an expensive sellers' market. Add to that burden the new style of German *Reiter* cavalry, able to deploy pistolier tactics such as the *caracole*, and a situation had been created by the 1540s in which well over 50 per cent of a major western army could consist of mercenary units. In 1558, German and Swiss troops comprised 70 per cent of the French royal army.[27]

Traditional military elites faced a double challenge: rulers were now spending a high proportion of their military budgets on contracts with hired troops rather than on traditional military service; and the nature of this warfare was squeezing these elites out of their traditional military functions largely in favour of infantry specialists whom they disdained to emulate, and whose economic calculations – based on offering short-term service – would not work financially or militarily outside their own world of easy access to underemployed but strongly cohesive peasant communities.[28]

In these circumstances of escalating commitment to expensive mercenary forces, what had saved rulers from financial disaster was the relative shortness of wars, which were rarely of more than two, or at most three campaigns. Extraordinary finance could be raised to cover the costs of these mercenary contingents in addition to the troops raised and funded from the rulers' subjects, with the possibility of financial retrenchment and repudiation of debts once peace had been negotiated. The turning point was the decade of the 1550s when the Habsburg–Valois conflict, begun in 1552, was waged untill 1559. The

---

[26] Swiss contracts with the French crown specified a lump sum of three months' pay in addition to recruitment costs: Burin de Roziers, *Capitulations*, 97 cites the capitulation that remained the model from 1553 to 1671.

[27] Wood, *King's Army*, 38–41; *Reiter* tactics are discussed by Rogers, Chapter 10 in this volume.

[28] Wohlfeil, 'Adel', 212–14, on the difficulty of getting German nobles to serve as *Landsknecht* officers.

French and Spanish crowns were forced to reschedule debt payments in 1557, precipitating financial crises and widespread default on military obligations. Both powers limped through one further campaign to the then inevitable Peace of Câteau-Cambrésis in 1559.[29]

Yet paradoxically the likelihood that wars might be fought over several campaigns, though it threatened the limited revenues and credit of the ruler, also opened up the possibilities for military entrepreneurship. The typical mercenary contract before the later sixteenth century had been based on the assumption that a short war would result in the rapid demobilisation of the unit, perhaps after a single campaign. Any colonel prepared to advance his own funds to meet recruitment or relocation on behalf of a ruler during a short war ran the high risk of default on repayment. However, once a unit had a potential life of five to ten years, the establishment costs became less significant, and the likelihood of reimbursement and profit greater.[30] Before the outbreak of the Thirty Years' War, lengthy campaigns in the Netherlands, France, and Hungary had led to the development of the contract system in ways that enhanced the financial and administrative responsibility of the proprietor-commander. That this also coincided with the end of the German–Swiss monopoly over infantry tactics, and the rise of mixed-weapon units in which cohesion came as much from fighting experience as from regional or communal solidarities, also facilitated the possibilities available to the military enterprisers.

The willingness of rulers to deal with regimental proprietors and general contractors did not necessarily imply the total abandonment of state-recruited, directly financed units of soldiers by the major European powers. Thus Spain's Army of Flanders used traditional state-administered units – the *tercios* of Spain and Italy – alongside soldiers who had been recruited by military enterprisers including Walloon and German colonels, who would raise and equip their soldiers in return for lump-sum payments, often extracted as military taxes or 'contributions' from the localities where they were garrisoned. Indeed, the ability to shift much of the financial burden of the larger military establishment onto the resources of military enterprisers may have made it easier to continue to maintain these *corps d'élite*.[31] The imperial army of Wallenstein, especially during his second generalship from 1632, was unusual in being composed entirely of unit-proprietors: this was more typical of independent general contractors like Christian of Halberstadt,

---

[29] Discussed by DeVries, Chapter 2, above.
[30] Redlich, *Military Enterpriser*, I, 225–6.
[31] Maffi, *Baluardo della corona*, 92–130.

Charles IV of Lorraine, or Bernhard of Saxe-Weimar, who had no initial allegiance to a ruler and whose private armies could maintain themselves in the particular circumstances of war in the Holy Roman Empire pending a formal contract with one of the major belligerents. In contrast, Swedish generals such as Banér and Torstensson were both employees of the Swedish crown, commanding units of Swedish soldiers in the pay of the state, but were also proprietor-colonels themselves and held authority within an army largely composed of German proprietor-colonels. This dual authority was important in making the system work, ensuring that a balance was struck between the military interests of the ruler and the corporate interests of proprietary officers. Regimental proprietorship also eroded the distinction, characteristic in sixteenth-century armies, between those composed notionally of 'subjects' and the foreign mercenaries hired to fight alongside them. Colonel-proprietors were selected from both subjects and non-subjects; the criterion for selection was economic capacity and military reputation. Moreover, the concern of the colonel recruiting a regiment for long-term service was to find experienced, high-quality soldiers; their origins were unimportant.[32]

Military enterprise transformed the economic relationship between ruler and officer-proprietor to the potential benefit of both sides. For the ruler, obviously, it represented a solution to problems that endured to the end of the *ancien régime*. First, given that most ordinary fiscal burdens rested overwhelmingly on the unprivileged mass of society, how was the ruler to persuade the elites to contribute some share of their much greater resources to state expenses? Second, how was the ruler, whose financial credit was poor, to find alternative sources to guarantee loans and borrowing?[33] In both cases military enterprise proved an effective way of mobilising the resources of the elites to finance the ruler's war effort. It would be mistaken to see this mobilisation of funds simply in terms of a few dozen colonel-proprietors advancing the costs of recruiting their regiments. Behind the colonels, who were often multiple proprietors of regiments, stood a network of financial backers and investors who provided the credit nexus that underpinned the financing of all these contract-armies. Moreover, the contract-army would have outsourced responsibility for food supply, armaments and equipment, munitions, and the construction of fortifications.[34] In the cases where naval squadrons operated under contract, supply and dockyard maintenance might be contracted out. Huge areas of military financing could

---

[32] Burschel, *Söldner*, 145–65.
[33] Hüther, 'Dreißigjährige Krieg'.
[34] Ernstberger, 'Wallenstein'; Zünckel, 'Rüstungshandel'; Zünckel, *Rüstungsgeschäfte*, 54–77.

be taken into the private sector.[35] This delegation of the state's fiscal activity brought with it immense potential profits (and losses) to enterprisers.[36] Capital was mobilised that would not have been obtained at all if it had depended upon the credit worthiness of the state. Without it, the Thirty Years' War would have ended far earlier because of the incapacity of the revenue-raising mechanisms of the belligerent states.[37]

Proprietorship was no less important for the elites who financed regiments and underwrote the costs of warfare. For some – both military commanders and their financial backers – it offered opportunities for substantial capital return in a context of economically disruptive warfare when other sources of investment were less attractive. A crucial aspect of this was undoubtedly the direct control of tax yields through the collection of contributions.[38] Rulers may have been reluctant to delegate this power to assess and collect taxes, but without it the entire enterprise system would have collapsed. The financing of war brought a militarised elite and their financial backers onto the centre stage of the state, and offered both the possibility of financial remuneration, and some security, via proprietorship, for the capital invested. At the same time, a substantial part of its appeal at the level of the enterpriser-commanders was that it had not negated the other motivations for military service: cultural and social validation or opportunities for upward mobility; political and social networking and opportunities for political advancement; association with a martial ethos and its values.[39]

Although the enterprise system brought confluence between the interests of the ruler and those elites involved directly and indirectly in the financing of military force, this still left unanswered the two traditional criticisms of the system. The first was that it was an ineffective way to wage war. Enterprise had come into being as a short-term solution to meeting the costs of raising and maintaining troops. But this meant that the military enterprisers who had raised the cheapest and poorest-quality recruits had no interest in pursuing tactical and strategic objectives; they aimed to batten on to territory and subject it to war taxes. Rulers who

[35] Ernstberger, *Hans de Witte*, 293–311; Schöningh, *Rehlinger*, 43–54, 92–7.
[36] For profits made by the Swedish and imperial commanders through the management of the army, see Lorentzen, *Schwedische Armee*, 15; see also Redlich, *Military Enterpriser*, I, 408–10.
[37] Hüther, 'Dreißigjährige Krieg', 61–7; Opel, 'Deutsche Finanznoth'; Kunisch, 'Wallenstein', 153–4.
[38] The costs of maintaining the imperial army in the Westphalian circle of the Empire between 1639 and 1650 came to at least fifteen million talers, of which all but a small fraction was raised through the direct collection of contributions; Salm, *Armeefinanzierung*, 168.
[39] Villiger, Steinauer, and Bitterli, *Chevauchées*, 7–9, 208–27.

had short-sightedly committed themselves to this system were unable to escape its clutches until the Peace of Westphalia allowed them finally to buy off the military enterprisers.[40] The second criticism was that the system carried an unacceptably high level of political risk. This reflected in part the belief that soldiers who served simply for financial gain were inherently untrustworthy. But focusing on the example of Wallenstein in 1634, the more specific argument was that the interests of a commander with a heavy financial stake in his army and a mass of powers and rights over his officers and troops will be at odds with those of a ruler who possesses sovereign authority over the army, but has little practical control or influence over its day-to-day operations.

Both concerns underestimate the success of military enterprise in giving the elites a powerful financial and political stake in the achievement of military victory. A cursory examination of the conduct of the Thirty Years' War makes it clear that this was not a struggle fought between apathetic military enterprisers, simply prepared to occupy territory, extract contributions, and wait for a peace settlement. At the very least, defeat would make it more difficult to pursue reimbursement of interest and capital. Both ruler and military enterprisers had a positive interest in achieving military goals that would strengthen their military and political bargaining position. And crucial to this was operational success: holding territory, and where possible destroying enemies' ability to maintain their own forces.[41] In this respect contract-armies were arguably more effective than armies run directly under state control. Contractors wished above all to preserve the army, in which they had a considerable financial interest. This did not mean that they were reluctant to pursue aggressive operational goals, but it did make them sensitive to the threat posed to their troops by inadequate logistical support. This concern to maintain adequate supply and high levels of mobility ensured, for example, that the operational strength of field armies was substantially reduced in the second half of the Thirty Years' War, while the proportion of cavalry was increased to well over 50 per cent.[42] And far from filling the ranks of bloated armies with cheap, poor-quality recruits, enterpriser-colonels were strongly motivated to use experienced veterans who could ensure that these small, highly mobile armies were hard-hitting and tactically flexible forces.[43] It also meant that the costing, collection, and transport of food and

---

[40] Oschmann, *Nürnberger Executionstag*, 75–80.
[41] Croxton, 'Territorial Imperative?', 266–72.
[42] Kapser, *Kriegsorganisation*, 221–49; Sörensson, 'Kriegswesen'.
[43] Kapser, *Kriegsorganisation*, 262–4 on the high proportion of experienced soldiers in the Bavarian army; Kroener, 'Soldat', 119.

munitions were more thoroughly planned, and delegated to financiers and merchants whose practical experience was matched by their financial interest in making the supply system work.[44] The military contractors commanding the imperial army in the 1640s drew resources from the Westphalian circle in the same way that the Swedes redeployed the resources of the north German states they occupied to pay and supply the army operating against the Emperor.[45] The main reason why the Thirty Years' War lasted so long was not military stagnation, but the deployment of effective, long-serving veteran armies, whose mobility and fighting effectiveness tended to prevent any power from gaining the upper hand militarily.[46]

The argument for the political unreliability of contract-armies is equally unconvincing, not least because large elements of the elites, whose primary motive for being drawn into military service may have been economic, were nonetheless loyal because they continued to prize the cultural and social benefits of military involvement. Such benefits would be nullified by a perceived willingness to act against the ruler in whose state they wished to enjoy these benefits. More importantly, and unlike a *condottiere* captain of two centuries earlier, the web of contracts and sub-contracts that every large-scale enterpriser incurred made treason or the transfer of allegiance extraordinarily difficult. There is no unambiguous evidence that Wallenstein intended to betray the Emperor; even the oath of January 1634 was rapidly followed by another, sworn by the officers still present at Pilsen, explicitly affirming the ultimate authority of the Emperor.[47] The refusal of Wallenstein and his officers to risk the army was not preservation for its own sake, but to ensure that it was in a fit state to start military operations by the summer of 1634. The result was a campaign in which the main Swedish army was annihilated at Nördlingen by combined imperial and Spanish forces.

The most striking seventeenth-century instance where military commanders posed a real threat to the survival of the state occurred where the government had been reluctant to move towards overt military enterprise, and where the tensions and resentments between commanders and central power were correspondingly far greater. The French crown, largely owing to the experience of the Wars of Religion, was determined

[44] Hildbrandt, *Quellen und Regesten*, II, 215–39: run of correspondence between Marx Conrad Rehlinger and Bernhard of Saxe-Weimar, 1638–9.
[45] Salm, *Armeefinanzierung*, 113–22; Böhme, 'Geld'.
[46] See the account of the campaigns of 1647 and 1648 in Höfer, *Ende des Dreißigjährigen Krieges*.
[47] Mann, *Wallenstein*, 1096–100.

not to enter into contractual relationships with its own subjects for raising and maintaining troops. Contracts were made only with foreign enterprisers, the largest of them with Bernhard of Saxe-Weimar in 1635.[48] However, the crown's reluctance to accord proprietary rights to its own elites was not matched by any restraint in exploiting their financial resources to contribute to the costs of levy and upkeep of the soldiers in units that they theoretically held as the direct appointees of the crown. Taking advantage of the cultural and social aspirations of French elites to hold military office, the crown was able to extort financial assistance from those who were either anxious to push themselves forward as candidates for command or, once *in situ*, were concerned that their unit would collapse or be disbanded around them, and that they would be dismissed before they had gained any benefits from association with military command.[49] The French crown refused to recognise economic motives for elite military involvement, treating military service as state employment, so that officers were in theory remunerated by the crown simply in return for service in a state-run army. The reality was very different; military expansion after 1635 rendered the state wholly incapable of meeting the costs of its armed forces.

Unit and general officers were pressured into larger, unsecured financial commitments on behalf of their troops as almost every aspect of state financing proved unequal to the scale of military activity. When French troops did establish a strong enough position across the frontiers to extract contributions, these were administered by the military bureaucracy, and not used directly to recompense the expenditure of the officers.[50] The system bred resentment, evident in endemic levels of corruption amongst the unit officers, unmitigated by any calculation that recruitment and muster fraud, by weakening the military effectiveness of the unit, would reduce its market value and the overall striking power of the army corps. Above all, there was no wider financial linkage between military officers and networks of financial investors, manufacturers, and merchants that characterised an army dominated by military enterprisers. Contractors were involved in the supply of the French army and navy, but they made their agreements centrally with the crown and its administrators; they had no direct interest in the success and failure of the armies since their chances of reimbursement were tied to the yield of provincial taxes or other assigned revenues.[51] Given

---

[48] Noailles, *Bernhard*, 481–6.
[49] Parrott, *Richelieu's Army*, 313–65.
[50] *Ibid.*, 267–70.
[51] *Ibid.*, 381–7.

the chronic over-extension of the state fiscal system, the failure to meet financial obligations was inevitable, and with it the collapse of centrally negotiated supply contracts. Army officers were outside this process, constrained to intervene at a local level in what were usually unfavourable circumstances when suppliers had reneged on contracts for which they had received a small fraction of promised civil tax revenues.

The *Fronde*, though seen as pivotal to French seventeenth-century history, remains curiously under-studied, not least in its military dimensions. In many ways the so-called *Fronde des princes* would be better termed the *Fronde des généraux*, and treated as a series of challenges to the French state via grandees who controlled military force. Whereas it might be supposed that the crown had ensured that these grandees could not obtain autonomous control of the armies they commanded, the truth was that much of the officer-corps depended on them. Many of the officers were indebted to their commanders, who had advanced them the money they used to keep their units operational. They had limited obligations to a virtually insolvent crown, and correspondingly larger ones to their commanders, whose patronage and political leverage would both keep them in service and ensure that they eventually left the army without heavy financial loss. Condé's army supported him throughout the revolt against the crown in Paris and Guyenne, and the majority of his officers and soldiers joined him in transferring allegiance to the Spanish crown from 1653.[52] The comte d'Harcourt had no difficulty persuading his troops to support his seizure of Breisach in 1653, while in late 1655 the maréchal d'Hocquincourt defected to the Condéen party taking many of his troops with him.[53]

If military organisation is seen not as some exclusive prerogative of would-be absolute monarchs, but as a sphere of negotiation between rulers and their greater subjects, military enterprise had much to commend it. It offered the possibility of establishing long-term sustainable military force, largely created from the considerably greater, more reliable, and cheaper financial and borrowing potential of sociopolitical elites. They received in return a combination of proprietary rights over their units and direct control of tax revenues through a military organisation that they in large part controlled. If vestiges of state-raised and -maintained forces continued to exist as a *corps d'élite*, these were incorporated into forces where the commander, a Spínola, a Tilly, or Banér, was himself a contractor, and whose approach to the subsistence, munitions supply, equipment, and transport of the army

[52] Inglis-Jones, *Grand Condé*, 45–90.
[53] Chéruel, *Histoire de France*, I, 66–7, 128–39; II, 314–21.

was based on the extension of enterprise and private contracts into all these fields. France, where the crown rejected the adoption of military enterprise, saw the establishment of a military system that, proportionate to French population and resources, operated a great deal less effectively than those of her enemies and allies. It also, paradoxically, resulted in exactly the danger that is frequently ascribed to supposedly self-interested armies of military enterprisers – a major military revolt against crown authority, which crippled France's military capacity throughout the 1650s.

What therefore changed in the second half of the seventeenth century, and why? The coming of peace after 1648 made it largely unacceptable to license military contractors to reimburse their own and their creditors' investment via the direct collection of heavy war taxes on home territory. Moreover, while sections of the elite benefited from military participation, others were the victims of this military system, and had no intention of tolerating its continuation beyond the end of the war.[54] For most of the German rulers in the immediate aftermath of the war the situation was straightforward: decades of state indebtedness and economic disruption, and the lack of self-financing opportunities, now required the demobilisation of all military forces. The formidable Bavarian army was reduced to a few companies of household troops.[55] In contrast, successful aggression had changed the situation for Sweden: the German territories gained through Westphalia needed to be defended and a military presence in the Empire sustained. But as this depended on maintaining a significant part of the large forces raised under contract, the problem of providing financial support in peacetime soon became intense. Domestic crisis was followed by the only real – though temporary – solution to this problem, the resumption of full-scale war in 1655.[56]

The return of international instability and war had a more general significance. Long-term political survival without military force looked increasingly risky, yet reconstructing armies using military entrepreneurs was not viable during an uncertain but, for the moment, sustainable peace.[57] In addition to these practical dilemmas, an ideological hostility to the delegation of military force remerged. It was hardly controversial to assert that delegating military organisation was incompatible

---

[54] Conrad Rehlinger neatly demonstrates the paradox of gain and loss, calculating both the costs and re-sale value of the military offices possessed by his sons in the Swedish army, and the damage to his property in Augsburg by the same army in the early 1630s: Hildbrandt, *Quellen und Regesten*, II, 173–4.

[55] Oschmann, *Nürnberger Executionstag*, 558–9; Wilson, *German Armies*, 28–9.

[56] Frost, *Northern Wars*, 200–5; Roberts, *Oxenstierna to Charles XII*, 111–15.

[57] Wilson, *German Armies*, 29–32.

with princely sovereignty. The point had been made repeatedly in the Spanish councils of war and finance from the 1580s, but had usually been overruled on the grounds that whereas state *administración* of the armies and navies was more worthy of the sovereign authority of the Spanish crown, *asiento* or contracts were cheaper and the only way that the great edifice of Spanish military power could be kept running.[58] The German and Italian princes, the Austrian Habsburgs, and the Scandinavian monarchies had been similarly pragmatic, but the Peace of Westphalia, with its strong emphasis on princely sovereignty, may have helped to increase the desire to create armies that were seen as more directly subject to the ruler's sovereign will. The presentation of Louis XIV's French army after 1661 as the triumph of royal and ministerial authority certainly encouraged other rulers to deploy the same rhetoric and aim to create armies that similarly appeared as instruments of the sovereign's will.[59]

Yet behind this rhetoric there lies a bigger issue that makes notions of a simple shift to direct 'state control' of armies unconvincing. Without elite participation through military entrepreneurship, rulers would have been unable to tap the wider resources of their societies and the earlier increases in the scale of military activity would have been unsustainable. If the creation of new standing armies was simply based upon the establishment of central control over armed forces and the reduction of the officer-corps to employees of an ever more powerful state apparatus, then it is hard to see how this feat would have been achieved with the resources available to an early-modern monarch. In the case of France the question is even more particular: by what means could the French crown renegotiate the relationship with its elites to make military service more attractive than had previously been the case, while apparently tightening the control of the crown over the mechanisms of operation and control?

As two recent studies have demonstrated in detail, the mechanism by which the army of Louis XIV was subjected to greater central and ministerial control while ensuring the willingness of the elites to commit to military service and, most crucially, to bear a high proportion of its costs, was a formalisation and institutionalisation of venality in military office.[60] While the official line throughout the seventeenth century was that the sale of military office was prohibited, it was widely

[58] Thompson, *War and Government*, 256–73; Thompson, 'Aspects'; Goodman, *Spanish Naval Power*, 29–32.
[59] Cornette, *Roi de Guerre*, 249–83.
[60] Rowlands, *Dynastic State*, 166–71; Drévillon, *L'impôt du sang*, 179–211.

known that almost all newly formed regiments were commissioned on the basis of the financial contribution of the colonels-to-be. It was also the case that in those *régiments entretenus* – the originally small number of regiments with a permanent existence – while officerships were not sold openly, considerable sums were paid informally by the incoming officer to compensate the outgoing officer or his relatives for the loss of the post and the expenses that he had incurred. Both of these practices had flourished in the army under Richelieu and Mazarin; the former lay at the root of the problems with the officer-corps, since the financial contributions remained unrecognised when regiments were disbanded or 'reformed', often after only a few months' service. Ministers turned a blind eye to the second style of 'internal venality' but, given the relatively smaller numbers of permanent units, it could have limited effect on the perceptions of the officer-corps as a whole.

Generations of historians writing about the post-1661 reforms of Le Tellier and Louvois have treated the persistence of military venality as an anomaly, totally out of keeping with the spirit of their modernising initiatives.[61] In fact, it stands at the very heart of the compromise that crown and ministers needed to establish with the elites. The initial, post-1659 demobilisation had reduced the French standing army to a permanent force of around 55,000 men – a level at which, at a fairly basic level, the crown might have been able to assume the great bulk of the operational costs and create an employee-army. However, king and war ministers had no doubt that an assertive foreign policy would again require large-scale military expansion. Tolerating – and expanding – 'internal venality' within the officer-corps was indeed a standing affront to ideals of thorough administrative and professional reform in the army: it was impossible, for example, for a long-serving lieutenant to acquire a company command without private funds to pay the outgoing captain. But a far more important consideration than this for the crown and ministers was that abolishing venality would discourage wealthy potential officers from investing in their units, thus depriving the crown of the financial means to make military expansion viable and sustainable. Venality provided a recognition of these financial commitments. It determined the price the unit would fetch if the commander wished to demit his office. Royal policy strengthened this in two ways. Characteristically of Louis XIV's regime, the price of these payments to acquire captaincies and colonelcies was officially prescribed, but the effect of this was simply to establish these official sums as the *minimum* price on assuming the office. No serious attempt was made to prevent posts in more prestigious or

---

[61] See, for example, Rousset, *Louvois*, I, 179–81; André, *Le Tellier et Louvois*, 315–17.

better-maintained regiments being sold for substantially higher prices.[62] Second, the size of the permanent, standing army leapt to 140,000 men in the lead-up to the Dutch war, and subsequently drifted upwards towards 180,000 during the 1680s. Thus, though a regiment established in wartime with funds provided by a newly commissioned colonel continued to carry a risk of disbandment without compensation, far more regiments were now part of a permanent military establishment in which internalised venality offered the officers some financial security for their own 'investment' in its upkeep. Even in the case of the 'impermanent' regiments, the situation was ameliorated by the greater willingness to keep these units in service for several campaigns, avoiding the capricious way that earlier administrations would disband regiments because it had been cheaper to persuade a new wave of officers to invest than to assemble the financial packages that would allow the reconstruction of existing ones. Furthermore, despite concerns about military effectiveness, aspiring colonels of new, wartime levies were allowed to form regiments containing significantly fewer companies and men than in the past.[63] If short-term service in the royal army was to continue to attract members of the elites, the investment needed to be more moderate than hitherto.

On the back of a venality that was positively encouraged in all but the units of the king's household, a new and more effective relationship was forged between the crown and those members of the French elites drawn into military service. Massive levels of private investment achieved a permanent army on a scale and quality far beyond the resources that the crown could afford. The relationship was quite different from that prevailing in the earlier century. For much of the first half of Louis XIV's reign, the crown was able to honour a reasonable proportion of its basic financial obligations to the army, and as military service increased in prestige during the reign so the demand for officerships continued to exceed supply well into the last wars of Louis' reign. For these reasons the notion of a more powerful system of external control, better discipline of the soldiers in garrisons, and more uniformity of arms and equipment, was not a myth. At the same time, this was an army that was based upon massive financial contributions from its officers, overseen by a ministry that actively sought to promote the wealthy into colonelcies and more senior posts, and accepted that colonels were de facto proprietors of their units.[64] In these circumstances,

---

[62] Chagniot, 'Rationalisation', 103–4; Corvisier, *Louvois*, 335–6.
[63] Drévillon, *L'impôt du sang*, 169–73.
[64] Chagniot, 'Rationalisation', 103 gives a typical example of a colonel spending 5,700 *livres* to have his family crest embroidered on the banners and clothing of his dragoon regiment.

the administration could have little real success in tackling endemic problems of insubordination and non-cooperation across an officer-corps where social status consistently trumped military rank based on experience and service.[65]

It is illuminating to note that where the crown did not consider that its claims to sovereignty entailed direct possession of military power, for example in the supply of the army with food and munitions, this was still overtly put out to contract. Equally significant in claiming that something like a modern bureaucracy had now taken control of the armed forces is that the great majority of the 'bureaucrats' – *commis-saires*, *contrôleurs*, and *trésoriers* – were venal office-holders owing their positions to the patronage of the Le Tellier and their allies, just as naval administrators were heavily drawn from clients of the Colbert clan.[66] The royal navy had been developed by Colbert on the basis of overt royal-ministerial control, but it depended in fact on the willingness of groups of the elites to provide financial support for fitting out and maintaining the fleet.[67] In 1693, faced with the inability of the state to maintain even partial funding of both army and navy, the latter was effectively dissolved. Individual captains were offered their ships and letters of marque and allowed to pursue their own financial interests via a *guerre de course* as long as the war lasted. The crown had to accept that the only workable solution to maintaining a navy was decentralisation and a return to full-scale contracting.[68]

This account of the French crown's compromises with elite interests in building its armed forces can equally be applied to other European 'reformed' armies of the later seventeenth century. If traditional, circular arguments about state-building, the growth of armies, and further state-building are brought into question, the matter of how to finance permanent armed force on an unprecedented scale remains.[69] It can only be answered by placing the elites back into the picture, and demonstrating that they had a convincing blend of motives not merely for military involvement, but for a willingness to underwrite a large part of the costs of their involvement.

In the new standing force of the Great Elector of Brandenburg-Prussia, and in many other German principalities, as well as in the Habsburg armies fighting on the Ottoman frontier, the officers were still

[65] *Ibid.*, 107–8; Chagniot, *Paris et l'armée*, 255–311.
[66] Rowlands, *Dynastic State*, 88–91; Dessert, *La Royale*, 46–59.
[67] Dessert, *La Royale*, 61–73.
[68] *Ibid.*, 77; Symcox, *Crisis*, 143–220.
[69] For a good example of this circularity see Sicken, 'Dreißigjährige Krieg', 581–98, especially 598.

straightforward creditors of the crown, lending money to feed, clothe, or pay the basic wages of their troops when central funds and provisioning proved inadequate. In the case of senior imperial officers operating in Hungary and further south, licences to recoup their debts through the direct collection of local customs and sales taxes were granted by the Emperor. Such 'contributions' were of course very widely readopted as soon as any formal hostilities were begun, and were either collected by the officers in the field as the enterprisers of the Thirty Years' War had done, or collected on behalf of the monarch and his administration, with the commanders adding a percentage for their own expenses. In 1676 the Brandenburg Elector warned the Emperor that his generals had extorted by way of contributions some 30,000 to 80,000 talers per head during the last two campaigns.[70]

This traditional ad hoc dependence on the financial resources of the senior officers, with its capacity to reassert the enterpriser's interests as creditor of the monarch, was matched by a series of developments that were akin to the French model of recognising a legitimate financial interest by the colonel-proprietor, recoverable on the transfer of the unit to another commander. As Fritz Redlich neatly defined the change, regiments were no longer large-scale business concerns in many European states after 1650, but they were certainly still investments from which the colonel would hope to recoup his capital with benefit. They did not offer opportunities to generate large profits over and above the initial and subsequent investment in upkeep, but they were a lot more than administrative appointments. They remained, moreover, highly prestigious, and in many armies senior officers continued to seek to hold the titular colonelcies of more than one regiment.[71] Part of the return on the investment was through variants on French-style 'internal venality': substantial sums paid to an outgoing colonel by his successor would amortise some of the expenses incurred in the unit's upkeep. In addition, the regimental commander, through a series of opportunities connected with 'administrative charges' – the sale of rights such as leaves of absence, and gratuities for internal appointments and promotions, as well as, in some armies, continued rights to supply equipment and clothing – could generate a significant annual income.[72]

Moreover, although the business opportunities from regimental command were being reduced, this was not to the benefit of an all-embracing state administration, but to the rank which became the organisational

[70] Redlich, *Military Enterpriser*, II, 61.   [71] Lund, *War*, 25–6.
[72] Redlich, *Military Enterpriser*, II, 56.

and entrepreneurial lynchpin of most *ancien régime* armies, the captain. The first half of the eighteenth century saw the flourishing of the *Kompaniewirtschaft*, with the captain as businessman-investor, whose activities – keeping the men clothed and the equipment in good order, and maintaining the company at its established strength – offered a traditional style of military proprietorship, in which capital investment and good management were a means to a decent profit over the life of the unit. Not all captains were serving heads of companies: every general, senior officer, and colonel had a company that he ran for profit, while appointing a lieutenant-captain to command in his place. The major profits from managing a company came from having direct control of recruitment – both of the ordinary soldiers, and the NCO's and subaltern officers. Profit and patronage came together in the hands of the landowner-captain, who used his influence and standing both to raise recruits more cheaply than on the open market and to reward local clients with junior officerships.

At one level this shift of enterprise down one rung of the command ladder might be seen as a step towards the state-controlled army: reducing the danger posed by independent proprietor-commanders by fragmenting their activities into smaller units. From another perspective, it can be seen as an efficient version of the French mechanism for maintaining and widening the extent of recognised investment by the elites in military service: now every officer from captain upwards was a direct financial stakeholder in the organisation and the effectiveness of the army.

The persistence of entrepreneurship across the armies of the later seventeenth century had the same benefits and costs as in the French case. The prestige and status of officer-service continued to grow, and with it the competition to obtain commands. The structure of all of these armies ensured that the vast majority of posts would be filled by those whose financial resources would be channelled into the upkeep of their units, offering in return official recognition of this commitment through marketability of the office and some potential for investment return. The main cost was that the much vaunted administrative initiatives and controls identified with these standing armies – the commissioners, inspectors, *intendants* – became limited agents of central authorities who recognised that the military officers were heavily engaged in the financing of the war machine, and that the administrators needed to tread carefully around issues of discipline, moderate levels of financial misappropriation, and proprietary interest. Above all, the system turned officer-corps across Europe into a distinct caste, increasingly professional, but acutely aware of points of social status within the hierarchy, and mirroring factional and dynastic rivalries through insubordinate, disruptive, and assertive behaviour.[73] The entire military system played to the social values of the surrounding societies, in which corporate and individual privilege and status were being reinforced in return for underpinning the otherwise unattainable ambitions of central power.

The legacy of military enterprise during the Thirty Years' War was the creation of what are anachronistically seen as 'state-armies' in the later seventeenth century. Military organisations have come adrift from more recent research about the social underpinnings of 'absolute' government. In this context the model of shared interests between ruler and elite embodied in military enterprise deserves more attention. The spirit of Wallenstein looms more heavily over the armies of Eugen, Vendôme, and Marlborough than has usually been allowed.

---

[73] *Ibid.*, II, 154–5.

5   The state and military affairs in east-central Europe, 1380–c. 1520s

László Veszprémy

The political setting

The fourteenth century has rightly been termed the *Blüte der Staaten*, or renaissance of old and new state formations in east-central Europe.[1] The small states of the region, such as Serbia, Wallachia, Bulgaria, whose fortunes waxed and waned over time, in the long run fell victim to their more powerful neighbours: the core states of Hungary, Poland, and Bohemia, which by the end of the fourteenth century were much strengthened politically and economically; and the Ottoman Empire, which gained control of the Balkans from the late fourteenth century onwards.[2] The Teutonic Knights and Lithuania exercised important roles for a time, but by the sixteenth century they had both become buttresses of the Polish crown.[3] Of the lands surrendered by the Teutonic Knights, some came to constitute East Prussia, while the western territories were integrated into the Polish kingdom. The Tartars and the territories they dominated were militarily significant, especially for the Poles, since they both served as allies of the Lithuanians and provided auxiliary troops to the Ottomans. In addition to the Polish and Hungarian hussars (and later the Cossacks), the Tartars were the only group that adhered to tactics based upon the deployment of light cavalry.[4]

An important factor in the reconfiguration of states in east-central Europe was the fact that several monarchs enjoyed long reigns, allowing them to implement a series of reforms. King Matthias Corvinus held

---

[1] Schneider, *Spätmittelalterliche Königtum*.
[2] See Szakály, 'Turco-Hungarian Warfare'; Fodor, 'Simburg and the Dragon'; Papp, 'Hungary'; Rázsó, 'Hungarian Strategy'.
[3] For the Polish developments, see Czamanska, 'Poland and Turkey'.
[4] By the end of the fifteenth century Venice also hired light cavalry troops against the Turks from its Balkan territories Durazzo, Zante, and Morea, and hired bowmen in Serbia; see Pedani, 'Turkish Raids', 287–91. The Hungarian hussars also adopted light cavalry tactics after the first light cavalry units arrived from the Balkans, retreating before the Turks.

the Hungarian throne for thirty-two years (Korvin Mátyás, 1458–90), while in Poland Jagiello (Jogaila, Wladislaw II) ruled for forty-nine years (1386–1434), and Casimir Jagiello for 46 years (Kazimierz IV JagielloÍczyk, 1447–92).[5] This was particularly important because, in both Poland and Hungary, the rulers were elected by the national assembly, or Diet, and the monarchs accordingly had limited opportunity to control the power of the barons. The state administration was largely under the control of the nobility, who manipulated it to their own advantage, and it lacked competent officials, especially experts in military affairs. The nobles were especially careful to hamper the establishment of a mobile mercenary army, not unsurprisingly since they harboured memories of its activities from the reigns of earlier, would-be absolutist rulers. In consequence, Casimir's attempts to create a mercenary army as well as a navy in the Baltic Sea met with little success even though he threatened severe punishment to those who refused to take up arms. In an unparalleled act of reprisal, King John Olbracht of Poland punished the 2,400 absentees who did not take part in his 1497 campaign against Wallachia by confiscating their estates.[6]

The geographical-historical context

East-central Europe was dominated by two huge states, Hungary and Poland. Bohemia was geographically far smaller, even with Moravia and Silesia, though it was economically and socially far more developed.[7] By the 1520s, Bohemia had an estimated population of 1 million; Moravia had 600,000 inhabitants with a population density of some $30\,km^{-2}$ in 1600, making it the most densely inhabited area in the region, with urban dwellers accounting for around 50 per cent of the total. In contrast, the Hungarian population density was around $13\,km^{-2}$ in 1500, with a quarter or fifth of the population living in the towns.

With an area of $320,000\,km^2$, late-medieval Hungary was larger than modern-day Italy and only just fell short of modern Germany. Thanks to both organised and spontaneous waves of immigration, the population of the country around 1500 was certainly some 3 million, or even between 4 and 4.5 million according to some estimates. Figures for

---

[5] For general overviews see Engel, *Realm*; Sedlar, *East Central Europe*; Rowell, *Lithuania*; Stone, *Polish–Lithuanian State*. For King Matthias see Kovács, *Mattia Corvino*; Kubinyi, *Matthias Rex*.

[6] Nadolski, *Uzbrojenie*, English summary, 465–81; Russocki, 'Zwischen Monarchie', 398–402.

[7] For the geographical-historical description see Fischer, *Handbuch*, III, 968–72 (for Bohemia), 1006–8 (for Hungary), 1064–9 (for Lithuania), and 1076–82 (for Poland).

Poland were even higher. Its geographical area was notably swollen after its union with Lithuania (1387) and it acquired strategically significant areas during its wars against the Teutonic Order. Admittedly, the union took many years to take real shape and only became firm after the Union of Lublin (1569). In the mid fifteenth century Poland's area was some 1.2 million km^2, though it shrank to 990,000 by the mid sixteenth century, but it remained sparsely populated compared to Hungary. Around 1370, its 240,000 km^2 held 2 million people (giving an average density of 8 km^{-2}), which increased to some 7 to 8 million by 1578, including 3 to 4 million in Lithuania. Both Lesser and Greater Poland had about 1.2 million inhabitants, with 21 people km^{-2}. By contrast, the population density in the Lithuanian, White Russian, and Ukrainian areas was around 5 to 6 km^{-2}. The proportion of the population living in urban centres was 25 per cent in Greater and Lesser Poland, 14 per cent in Masovia, and a mere 5 per cent in Lithuania. It is questionable whether the Polish kingdom actually increased its military strength and efficiency by acquiring enormous territories, since it scarcely proved capable of civilising and assimilating them and utilising their resources. It seems probable that the territorial increase did not boost state revenues proportionate to the increased burden of expenses attendant on defending long frontiers. The two states of Hungary and Poland thus rose to the status of regional powers without an appropriate economic basis, and each remained highly vulnerable throughout the course of its history.

Military consequences

Similar though they were in many respects, Poland and Hungary were in different strategic situations. Hungary had natural frontiers around the Carpathian Basin, which it had firmly held from the eleventh century. There was one major enlargement of the kingdom's territory when Croatia was acquired in 1095; it was retained until the end of the First World War, though Dalmatia and the Adriatic littoral, seized at the same time, were lost to Venice in 1403. The Hungarian kings realised the need to create a zone of allied and vassal provinces around them (western Austria, Galicia/Halic, Wallachia, South Slavs). Until 1301 (indeed in principle until 1918) the Hungarian kings bore the royal titles of eight neighbouring areas, but in practice they acquired a buffer zone only in the south, as far down as modern-day Bosnia, which they held until the advance of the Ottomans. The loss of the last of its buffer states, Serbia (1459) and Bosnia (1463) during Matthias' reign, brought the Ottomans close to the heartland of the country and the Hungarian army was no longer able to ward off attacks launched from the borders. The provinces of the Hungarian kingdom were ruled by high dignitaries. However, they turned against the central power only rarely and for brief periods of time, and in this regard the country's cohesion was unprecedented in the region. By contrast, Polish history was characterised by strong provincial sub-division and rivalry, by a constant struggle with neighbours for the possession of Silesia, Galicia/Halic, north Moravia, and areas of Lithuania and Prussia.

Decisive for the states of east-central Europe was the growing strength and expansion of the Ottoman Empire, which resulted in the break-up of the independent medieval Czech and Hungarian kingdoms by 1526, and the acceptance of the Habsburg personal union. Also of great importance was the Hussite struggle in Bohemia in the fifteenth century, which became one of the motors of military modernisation in the region. The Hussites managed to defeat German imperial troops for many years, and Hussites served as mercenaries in every country in the region. Indeed, in the war between the Teutonic Order and Poland, they even fought on opposite sides. The political consequences of the civil war started by Hussitism were the eventual enfeeblement of the Bohemian kingdom and ultimately its disintegration as an independent country.[8]

There were several parallel developments in fifteenth-century military affairs across Europe. Around 1450, attempts were made to set up a new model army in Hungary and in Poland by kings Matthias and Casimir Jagiello, while at the same time the evolution of a standing army, the *bandes d'ordonnance*, began in France.[9] French and Hungarian motivations were similar: the countries faced enemies against whom a permanent army, or at least a core of forces, had to be kept constantly in being. In traditional, offensive warfare it was accepted that armies would be mobilised for the occasion and return home after the campaign. Home defence, however, presupposed a standing army stationed in the marches even in peacetime, which put an unprecedented burden on the royal treasury. Besides, as a result of the static warfare on the Hungarian–Ottoman front lines, the spoils of war, which had maintained armies for centuries, could be counted on less and less, because eventually the border castles stood in the middle of something like deserts. The case of Belgrade, where a sultan's camp with all its associated wealth and arsenal was seized by the Christians in 1456,

---

[8] See Schmidtchen, 'Karrenbüchse'; Petrin, *Hussitenkrieg*, Appendix I, 23–31; Durdík, *Hussitisches Heerwesen*, 128–80; Tresp, *Söldner*. Cf. Trim, Chapter 13 in this volume.
[9] Discussed by Steven Gunn in Chapter 3, above.

represents an exception to the general rule.[10] Poland's first permanent mercenary army, deployed on the eastern border to counter the threat from the Tartars in 1479, had some 900 cavalry and 200 infantry, occasionally complemented by larger mobile mercenary units. From the 1430s, Hungary organised its defence line in the south. The permanent garrison troops, numbering almost 10,000 by the 1520s, were at the heart of the defensive system and on their own proved capable of defending the border castles and resisting attacks for several weeks or even months, as the case of Belgrade in the years 1440 and 1521 illustrates. However, the key to the defensive system was a well organised interplay between the local garrisons on the one hand and mobile royal troops with logistical support on the other. The standing garrisons were a successful initiative but proved to be a burden for the royal budget in Buda in the same way that Calais was for London from the 1370s.[11]

The motivation to create an up-to-date army, despite its associated financial and social costs, differed from kingdom to kingdom. In France, the military target – England – was obvious. In Hungary, resistance to the Ottomans also presented what appeared a similarly unambiguous goal. But King Matthias was too clever an army commander to confront the Ottoman Empire directly. Rather, he kept his mercenary army (labelled the 'Black Army' by posterity) in the conquered Silesian, Moravian, and Austrian areas for logistical and financial reasons, only leading them once against the Turks. In this expedition he achieved only limited success, although the Ottomans remained wary of attacking the country for some decades thereafter. However, it became clear to all concerned that this Western-type army was ill-suited to the demands of warfare in the zone of Hungarian–Ottoman fortress fighting. Matthias employed Czech soldiers who had fought in Upper Hungary and brought with them the best Hussite battle tactics, but he also complemented his army with Polish, Austrian, Hungarian, and Swiss soldiers. At the muster in Wiener Neustadt in 1487, his 'Black Army' of mercenaries numbered 20,000 cavalry and 8,000 infantry, of whom approximately 10,000 were in permanent employment. They comprised the mobile element of his forces; the garrison troops of the southern fortresses were additional. Innovative though this was there was nevertheless much continuity from former periods under Matthias, with typically archaic elements of the medieval royal administration being preserved. Thus

---

[10] For the siege of Belgrade, see Held, 'Defense'; Housley, 'Capistrano'; Bak, 'Hungary'; Nowakowska, 'Poland'.

[11] Cf. Sherborne, *War, Politics and Culture*, 18–19.

there is little evidence in Hungary for the development of an apparatus of competent and job-conscious bureaucrats, which was beginning to emerge in some other Renaissance states.[12] Matthias' mass employment of mercenaries was an ill-matched attempt to modernise the army, since he did not at the same time introduce concomitant reforms to state administration and finances.

To be sure, Hungarian forces achieved some significant victories. In 1479 a traditional army of the nobility defeated the Ottomans in the greatest battle of the age in the fields of Kenyérmező/Şibot (Transylvania). And in 1456 the Turkish sultan was ignominiously ejected from his camp outside Belgrade by an ad hoc contingent of forces while the well-equipped western troops were still on their way. However, contemporaries failed to realise that the Ottoman defeat was due to their faulty reconnaissance, which had described the Hungarian defences at Belgrade as poor. Consequently the sultan had not deemed it necessary hermetically to encircle Belgrade: without the mistakes made by the Ottoman high command, the city would probably have fallen in 1456. The Hungarian successes in 1456 and 1479 would lead to seven decades of almost undisturbed peace with the Ottomans. Agreed formally in 1495 but in practice dating from 1483, this lasted until 1520. The Hungarian–Ottoman peace proved unfortunate in some respects. It actually impeded further military and fiscal reform since it reinforced the mistaken notion that the country was already spending enough on defences and that there was no need for further changes. The Hungarian nobility was led to believe that it was possible to come to a lasting agreement with an aggressive great power and to preserve the earlier frontiers even from a subordinate position. As a consequence of this passive and paralysing situation, a declining proportion of Hungarian leaders had first-hand experience of open warfare with the Ottomans.[13] As a result, when Sultan Süleyman undertook his fateful invasion of Hungary in 1526, no experienced commander could be found for the Hungarian army. There was, moreover, hardly any opportunity to practise speedy mobilisation of the 'national' forces, since Hungary lived in peace with all its other neighbours in this same period. In a sense, therefore, seventy years of 'peace' helped to precipitate Hungarian defeat in the Ottoman campaigns of 1521 and 1526.[14]

---

[12] For the 'Black Army', see Rázsó, 'Military Reforms', and 'Mercenary Army'.

[13] Kubinyi, 'Battle'. The battle of Szávaszentdemeter–Nagyolaszi in 1523 was the last Hungarian victory against the Turks, and the Hungarian loss of some 700 cavalrymen was regarded by contemporaries as a 'catastrophe'.

[14] Kubinyi, 'Hungary's Factions'.

Polish war-making in the same period was an apparent success-story, although the lack of fundamental military reforms is analogous to the Hungarian development. In Poland, the measures to be taken were determined by the union with the Lithuanians. The creation of the Polish–Lithuanian Union first erased from Europe's map a huge non-Christian state (the last pagan state in Europe); while it secondly robbed the Teutonic Order of the ideological basis for its campaigns, and this gradually led to Polish military superiority over the Teutonic Knights.[15] After the Thirteen Years' War (1454–66), the Grand Master finally acknowledged the suzerainty of the Polish king and fully submitted to his sovereignty in 1525. Military victories led the Poles to believe that further significant foreign political and military successes could be achieved and the country enormously enriched without the need for essential domestic reforms and tax increases. This dangerous belief appeared confirmed by the result of the battle of Grunwald (Tannenberg), which ended the Polish–German Great War in 1410, when the feigned retreat of the auxiliary Lithuanian troops caused decisive confusion on the German side.[16]

In fact, finance would prove problematic for both Hungary and Poland. Hungarian tax revenues gradually decreased towards 1526, at a time when military expenditure kept increasing, concomitant with the maintenance of mercenaries and a standing army. National revenues amounted to 400,000 *forint*s under King Sigismund, rising to 800,000 under Matthias, but in the 1520s they were only around 200,000 to 250,000. On the expenditure side, some 170,000 to 180,000 *forint*s were spent on the maintenance of the southern frontier zone fortresses alone.[17] Military spending far exceeded royal income in Poland, too. Whereas the crown's annual revenue was some 20,000 *złoty*, the annual cost of the mounted mercenaries (1,000 strong) was 24,000 *złoty*; while the Thirteen Years' War alone cost some 2 million.[18]

The ultimate goal of the Hungarian military reforms, which achieved some success, was to force the aristocrats and prelates who fielded the troops to collect the war tax themselves, as they could do so more effectively than the central royal court. Largely incapable of gathering the tax itself, the court relinquished responsibility for its collection on

---

[15] Weise, 'Heidenkampf'.
[16] Ekdahl, 'Flucht'.
[17] The register of treasury payments to garrison soldiers of southern Hungary for 1513–14 shows a total strength of 7,817 (5,547 cavalry, 1,170 infantry, and 1,100 boatmen), which absorbed about half of the whole budget with the cost of maintenance: Kubinyi, 'Battle', 73–6.
[18] Nadolski, *Uzbrojenie*, English summary, 465–81.

condition that some part should still be spent on defences. Additionally, the counties acquired the right to collect a part of the war tax in order to hire mercenaries (typically drawn from the local, lesser nobility). In practice this arrangement functioned reasonably well, which explains why the system of mobilisation did not collapse despite dwindling central tax revenues. Other consequences of the weakness of royal authority were that its ability to control and punish were limited, and the efficiency of the system accordingly depended on the resolve of the landowners. In the final analysis, a strange mixture of paid army and the traditional feudal levy evolved. The national assembly that voted the money had little influence over this army's quality and the timing of its mobilisation.[19] Although there were promising attempts to introduce extraordinary regular annual taxation for defence against the Ottomans from 1397 onwards, this never developed into a routine part of the regular budget.[20]

A look at Map 3 confirms that the enormous expanse of the Hungarian and Polish–Lithuanian kingdoms, while it offered favourable possibilities, also involved an incredible logistical challenge. The mobilisation of troops in appropriate numbers and for the right time verged on the impossible and never really happened as planned. In the traditional historiography a delay in arriving at the battlefield was customarily ascribed to personal conflicts or political rivalry. In many cases, however, there was more to it. The enormous territory of Hungary and Poland was a barrier to concentrating forces at a single point, and the troops were in any case naturally slow to gather. This can clearly be seen in Hungary in 1456, 1521, and 1526. It is interesting that in both 1521 and 1526 the Hungarian royal army progressed from north to south (from Buda towards Belgrade) at the same speed, and engaged in battle when the majority of the auxiliaries were still on the way. In each case, the remaining forces coming from the north or north-west (with the exception of the Croatians) had no chance at all to join the army in time for battle. Problems associated with the assembly of forces and the timing of mobilisation were compounded by the fact that some troops were drawn by personal loyalty to sovereigns rather than attachment to the nascent Hungarian nation. In 1521, the Moravian Diet promised 7,220 well-equipped (heavy) infantry and 400 horsemen as well as 18 cannon, and the Poles sent to Hungary 500 cavalrymen

---

[19] The beginnings of the indentured retinues with the practice of sub-contracts go back to the reforms of King Sigismund, though we do not have a detailed picture of this system.

[20] For this aspect see Bak, 'Hungary', 117.

and 2,000 foot-soldiers, all of whom failed to arrive in time (though a Tartar incursion into Poland in the meantime was a factor in their tardiness).[21] Just as the Croatian cavalry contingent (450 strong) failed to reach the battlefield of Mohács in 1526, so the mercenary army of the Teutonic Order numbering several thousand did not manage to arrive at Grunwald in 1410.[22]

Difficulties of mobilisation were also aggravated by the fact that it was difficult to predict at which point on the 700 km southern border there would be an attack. It should be mentioned that the 4,000 Moravian and Polish infantrymen employed with papal money *did* arrive in time in 1526, probably because mercenaries were easier to mobilise than troops from the territorial nobility. It may also have been disadvantageous to mobilise too early, as the troops might disband before the battle. This fate befell the Teutonic Order in 1422, when the army was called to arms for four weeks. It did assemble, with provisions for that length of time, but after the four weeks the troops went home.[23] This nicely illustrates how, even when mobilisation was organised well in advance, mistakes could also be committed. In 1456, mobilisation was set for 1 August, half a year before the start of the campaign, but the Ottoman troops had already attacked the walls of Belgrade by 4 July, so the mobilisation date and the Hungarian war plans had to be modified in the meantime. At that time, the Hungarian royal court was poorly prepared to control mobilisation as it had no administrative apparatus to oversee military affairs. This is plainly proved by the delay in despatching the letters with the mobilisation orders and the fact that there were no officials to supervise the effectiveness of the measures that had been taken.[24]

In all the countries under review, there were scarcely any logistic routes or central stores. In Hungary the frontier castles maintained by the royal treasury were important, but in peacetime hardly any ammunition was stored in them and the stocks were only replenished before battles. To be sure, there were some positive examples of good practice. In 1525, 1,000 handgunners were brought to the fortress of Jajca in Bosnia, which was tantamount to mounting a small campaign. Fortress inventories also reveal that, in the 1500s, considerable reserves of firearms, cannon, and guns were maintained, but usually without the

---

[21] For the rate of march of the Hungarian royal army see Szabó, 'Mohácsi és "hadügyi forradalom"', Part II, 583–5.
[22] See Biskup, 'Problem'.
[23] See Ekdahl, 'Krieg', 637–8.
[24] Szabó, 'Mohácsi és "hadügyi forradalom"', Part II, 585–7; Szabó, *Mohácsi*, and *Mohács (1526)*.

necessary stone or metal bullets. Additionally, there is evidence of a royal cannon foundry in Buda, and of a central arsenal for firearms, for which the Danube proffered an ideal transport route. It was probably owing to the greater availability of storage (*Zeughaus*) and the existence of trained staff in urban centres that the king ordered a greater part of the cannon to be provided by the towns. The position of the Teutonic Order was exceptional in this regard: surviving inventories reveal enormous reserves that could easily equip any army. For example, in 1404, in Marienburg there were 465 helmets, 1,099 suits of armour, 118 bows, and 24,000 arrows, while Königsberg (today's Kaliningrad, Russia) had 321 helmets, 110 suits of armour, 742 bows, and 30,000 arrows in stock.[25]

Reforms on a limited scale

In earlier historiography, several scholars maintained that it was the lack of firearms that led to Hungary's defeat by the Turks.[26] That is partly true, but in the fifteenth century the central European states were comparable to both the West and the East in the adoption of gunpowder weaponry, though by the battle of Mohács in 1526 Ottoman gun-founding capacity wholly exceeded that of Hungary.[27] The dissemination of firearms can best be traced in town account books from the 1390s, which repeatedly mention the urban presence of artillery. An eloquent – though indirect – proof of the development of Hungarian artillery is that the decisive figure in mid-fifteenth-century Ottoman artillery was of Germanic origin: called Orbán (Urbán), he originated from Transylvania.[28] A proportion of the Hungarian noble troops had to be foot-soldiers equipped with firearms by 1518, and handgunners are even portrayed in miniature in 1514 grants of royal privileges,[29] indicating that the social prestige of firearms was also considerable.

Similarly noteworthy is the increasing proportion of infantry in the Hungarian royal army.[30] An ordinance of around 1516–18 stipulated that each grouping of 10,000 troops should be divided into 3,000 heavy

---

[25] There were 4,500 crossbows, and 1 million arrows stored as reserve in Königsberg at the beginning of the fifteenth century, with an unparalleled capacity for weaponry production in the workshops of the Order: Ekdahl, 'Horse'; Ekdahl, 'Pferd'.
[26] See Veszprémy, 'Bombardes'.
[27] Ágoston, *Guns*; Ágoston, 'Ottoman Artillery'; Veszprémy, 'Birth'; Veszprémy, 'Innovations', 287–91.
[28] For the activity of Master Orbán in 1453, see Paschalidou, 'Walls', 172–8; DeVries, 'Gunpowder Weaponry at Constantinople'; Melville-Jones, *Siege*.
[29] Hungarian National Archives, DL 67255, printed in Zay, *Lándorfejírvár*, 8.
[30] For the European beginnings see Stone, 'Technology'.

cavalry, 3,000 light cavalry, and 4,000 infantry. Half the foot-soldiers were to be equipped with handguns, the other half with lances and pikes. Infantry probably comprised around half the Hungarian army in the battle of Mohács. Both Poland and Hungary, which had roughly equal populations of approximately 3 million, could draft some 50,000 to 60,000 men for fighting. (Andrej Nadolski accepts as realistic the early fifteenth-century estimate of the Venetian Marino Sanuto, that 50,000 horsemen could be mobilised within the country and 25,000 outside the borders.)[31] In Hungary the number and quality of the troops of the leading magnates were decisive: there were 1,000 soldiers in the king's *banderium* (private army) and another 400 in each of the armies of the four highest court dignitaries (the Transylvanian *voivode*, the commander of the *Székelys*, the *banus* of the Temes district, and the *banus* of Croatia) totalling 1,600 men. Added to them were the troops of the prelates and of 40 nobles listed by name. The troops of the upper clergy, totalling some 7,000 soldiers, were easier to mobilise. In addition, there was a county army of 20,000 and the 20,000-strong contingent of the nobility, the traditional general levy. A mere 1,000 mercenaries could be expected from the royal towns, but they were more prepared to provide ammunition, guns, and wagons. Under the leadership of the Temes and the Croatian commanders, another 8,000 to 10,000 fighters served mostly in the castles and the Danube navy, as mercenaries.[32]

The construction and maintenance of the double defence line of castles in the south was an outstanding Hungarian military achievement during the reigns of kings Sigismund of Luxembourg and Matthias Corvinus.[33] The rows of fortresses and their hinterlands together with their associated mobile troops in the southern counties (Temes district, Transylvania, Croatia–Dalmatia–Slavonia), and the activity of Italian military engineers, successfully defended the kingdom up to 1521. The first defence line stretched from Szörény (Turnu Severin) through Orşova, Belgrade, Szabács (Šabac), Banja Luka, Jajca (Jajce), and Knin to Klissa on the Adriatic. The second, inner, line ran from Temesvár (Timişoara) through the Szerémség (Srim) and Bihács (Bihać) to Zengg (Senj) in Dalmatia. The castles in the first line were in the king's possession, but even the privately owned castles received subsidies from the central budget.

---

[31] Nadolski, *Uzbrojenie*, 475.

[32] Engel, 'Hunyadi'; Rázsó, 'Mercenary Army'; Szakály, 'Border Defense'; Kubinyi, 'Road'; and more recently see Rady, 'Rethinking'.

[33] The series of castles built in Hungary during the reign of Sigismund can be compared only to the efforts of Casimir the Great, who initiated almost forty castles in his kingdom of Poland: Szymczak, 'Construction'.

Conclusion

As we have seen, the military problems of east-central European polities did not lead to comprehensive reforms. In both Poland and Hungary the challenges were met with traditional responses and within the framework of the established system of mobilisation. The example of the east-central polities confirms the truth of Philippe Contamine's statement: 'There is an institutional link, a correspondence between the type of army and the State and the society which supports it and creates it.'[34] It is no accident that the two European countries with the highest proportion of nobles, possessing decisive influence upon the Diets, obstinately maintained a traditional defence organisation, even if some military innovations were introduced. Rather than tolerate a basically mercenary army in the hands of the government, they favoured an expensive but overcomplicated military system that, in times of acute danger, proved incapable of meeting the challenges it faced. Half-reforms were inadequate.

In late-medieval Hungary the Turkish advance had a positive impact on the military role of the royal power. Traditional legal practice expected the king to do no more than summon a general levy of the noblemen and lead it personally. As a consequence of the international situation, kings Sigismund of Luxembourg (1387–1437) and Matthias were the first Hungarian monarchs to transform the military system radically, thanks to their international perspectives and foreign advisors, combining military reforms with the centralisation of political power and financial resources necessary for a nationally based defence. In this process, the second half of the fifteenth century is noteworthy because the administration of the country, at least in some fields, became separated from the person of the king, and 'laws' were going to be regarded as generally accepted rules, and not only locally relevant privileges.[35]

However, from a military-historical point of view, four issues above all strained these structural changes: the mercenary system and the general professionalisation of warfare, the appearance of firearms and their adaptation to castle-building, the need for a permanent military staff to face more intensive campaigning, and the increasingly aggressive Turkish menace. Notwithstanding its advances, the Hungarian

---

[34] See Contamine, *Guerre au Moyen Age*, 296–306.
[35] Martyn Rady especially emphasises the positive outcomes of the Jagellonian rule in Hungary concerning the 'institutional growth, political discourse and ideology, the uses of history and the construction of a polity founded on the principles of dialogue and consent', as a consequence of the demands of war prompting rulers to consult more: Rady, 'Rethinking', 18.

military system as a whole failed to match the growing challenges of the fifteenth and sixteenth centuries. This failure, in turn, became the reason for accepting Habsburg rule and for integrating Hungarian warfare into the imperial border defence system.[36] The Hungarians had previously tried to find other ways of solving this problem, inviting Czech and Polish kings to the Hungarian throne, uniting their countries in the form of a personal union, but without any success.

The military reforms started after the well-known defeat of the Christians at Nicopolis (1396), and king Sigismund of Hungary really transformed and reshaped the mobilisation and border defence system, making them both more effective, and launching a process of organisational and technical modernisation. Sigismund increased the use of wagon camps and firearms in the army, reformed the practice of mobilisation, issued standard military regulations, and contracted enormous loans to undergird military expenditures; he also maintained the support of the warrior nobility through a kind of indirect pay. These reforms stopped the Turkish advance in the southern border regions from the Adriatic littoral up to the Romanian principalities, and, with the unexpectedly successful defence of Belgrade in 1456, turned the direction of the Turks towards the East (Persia and Egypt) and the Mediterranean (the sieges of Otranto and Rhodes in 1480). The military build-up was based on a double defence line of castles with Belgrade at the centre, where some 10,000 permanently paid soldiers were stationed; the spectacular adoption of firearms from a central arsenal in Buda, distributing firearms of smaller and larger calibre to the 500 largest castles all over the country; the recruitment of professional gun-masters in the royal cities; and new mobilisation methods. Because both kings financed this system from the public revenues, the nobles and commoners alike were dissatisfied, and after the death of the two kings they revolted against it. Without strong royal control, the consent of the political estates disappeared, and the state budget collapsed. The country, in spite of its immense territory and relative richness, became unable to finance the new and very expensive way of centrally organised warfare in the long run.

The historian Kelly DeVries is perhaps right to suggest that Hungarian military successes, such as that in 1456, created an illusion in the West by exaggerating the military capabilities of Hungary, and in this way hindered a rapid, general western military response to the Turkish expansion in east and central Europe.[37] On the other hand, military successes also fostered the illusion in Hungarian society

---

[36] Pálffy, 'Origins'.
[37] DeVries, 'Lack of Response'.

that, even without a sharing of the financial and administrative burdens and the political risk of the military budget, the king would be able to defend them, or that the outdated personal noble levies would save the country's independence. These illusions were dispelled by the fatal defeat at Mohács (1526), which disrupted the national defence system forever, and even more so by the subsequent permanent Ottoman occupation of the country. Charge of protecting western Europe's eastern marches passed to the Austrian Habsburgs; as Chapter 6 shows, they reorganised the region's obsolete defensive system, so that outdated crusading practice was gradually replaced by an early-modern state-managed system. However, this came at the expense of the Hungarian independence. The limits to Hungarian war-making had huge human, sociological, administrative, and financial costs.

Postscript

Based on a recently discovered contemporaneous Italian description, Antonin Kalous has published the array of the royal army on 20 July 1526 as it readied for the battle of Mohács (29 August).[38] It reveals that the military innovations of the age (mercenaries, infantry, camp of war wagons, artillery) were a significant part of the Hungarian army and suggests the presence of some 4,000 horsemen and 3,000 foot-soldiers. To every ten foot-soldiers a carriage with supplies was ordered, which could also serve as part of a wagon fortification (a Hussite innovation). The author not only described this in words but also made a drawing of the battle-array: in the middle was the king, preceded by the 2,500-strong light cavalry and the 600 heavy cavalry. On the wings were various infantry units: gunmen (*scopietieri*); footmen with large, long shields (pavises) of the Bohemian type; heavily equipped infantrymen with pikes (*armati benissimi con meze piche, longo ferro; armati con meza picha*); and the artillery with a large number of cannon of different size (altogether eighty-five Hungarian cannon were put into action at Mohács). All the modern military innovations of the age appeared in the army, yet decisive defeat occurred anyway. In the Hungarian case, state institutions and military organisation were as significant as technological and tactical innovations, for the latter could only take full effect if facilitated by the former.

[38] Kalous, 'Elfeledett források'; the original drawing survives in the Vatican Archives, Latinus MS 3924.

6 Empires and warfare in east-central Europe, 1550–1750: the Ottoman–Habsburg rivalry and military transformation

Gábor Ágoston

The period from the sixteenth to the mid eighteenth centuries in east-central and eastern Europe saw the emergence of three major land Empires: the Ottomans, the Austrian Habsburgs, and Romanov Russia. Military historians of east-central Europe have long been preoccupied with the profound changes in warfare observed during this period in certain parts of western Europe, commonly referred to as the 'European military revolution', and have tried to measure military developments in east-central Europe against those in western Europe.[1] However, while comparing military developments in east-central and western Europe may reveal interesting parallels and differences, comparing and contrasting military developments in the three eastern Empires helps better to assess the changing military capabilities of the Ottomans, Habsburgs, and Romanovs, and thus to understand the shifts in the military fortunes of these Empires. Since Russia emerged as an important military power and as the Ottomans' main rival only in the mid eighteenth century – that is, towards the end of the period covered in this volume – the chapter focuses on the Ottomans and their Austrian Habsburg rivals.[2]

The main thesis of this chapter is that Ottoman expansion and military superiority in the sixteenth century played an important role in Habsburg military, fiscal, and bureaucratic modernisation and in the creation of what came to be known as the Austrian Habsburg monarchy or 'Habsburg central Europe'. In order to match Ottoman military might, from the mid sixteenth century on the Habsburgs established a new border defence system in Hungary and Croatia, strengthened and

---

[1] On the military revolution debate, see above, Chapter 1 n. 4. On the Habsburg–Ottoman context see Kelenik, 'Military Revolution'; Ágoston, 'Habsburgs and Ottomans' and 'Disjointed Historiography'; and Börekçi, 'Contribution'.

[2] I am preparing an article to be published in a special volume on the subject in the Kritika Historical Studies book series (University of Pittsburgh Press) that assesses Ottoman military capabilities vis-à-vis that of the Romanovs in the eighteenth century. Virginia Aksan has tackled the problem in several of her studies, e.g., Aksan, 'Locating the Ottomans', and *Ottoman Wars*.

renovated their forts, and centralised and modernised their military, their finances, and their bureaucracies.

However, Habsburg centralisation and military reforms remained incomplete and slow to take root. This was due in part to the Habsburgs' multiple political and military commitments (rivalry with France, the Protestant challenge in the Holy Roman Empire and the Netherlands, and Ottoman–Habsburg rivalry in the Mediterranean), but also to the limits of Habsburg imperial authority caused by Vienna's dependence on the estates in military-resource mobilisation and war financing. Limits to Habsburg imperial authority existed in the Holy Roman Empire and the Habsburg hereditary lands, but were most obvious in Hungary, the very frontier challenged by ongoing Ottoman expansion, and the one that most needed the resources for military reforms. Although Hungary relied on Vienna for its defence against the Ottomans, the Hungarian nobility was reluctant to give up its centuries-old rights and privileges in the administration and financing of warfare (discussed in Chapter 5). The Hungarian estates (*rendek*) could and did challenge Vienna's policy not only in the Hungarian kingdom now under Habsburg rule, but also from Ottoman-ruled Hungary and the principality of Transylvania, an Ottoman vassal state established in eastern Hungary under Süleyman the Magnificent (r. 1520–66). Ottoman Hungary and Transylvania offered refuge for those Hungarians who challenged Vienna's centralising policy in repeated armed insurrections. Moreover, Transylvania, especially under its Protestant princes, Gábor Bethlen (r. 1613–29) and György Rákóczy I (r. 1630–48), challenged the Habsburgs during the Thirty Years' War in several campaigns (in 1619, 1623, 1626, and 1644) and provided the Hungarian estates with much-needed military and diplomatic support in their endeavour to protect or, when circumstances made it possible, expand their privileges at Vienna's expense.

Yet despite its multiple military commitments, its limited authority, and its deficient military, bureaucratic, and financial reforms, Vienna still managed considerably to strengthen its military capabilities vis-à-vis the Ottomans. By the end of the sixteenth century, Habsburg forces fighting in Hungary in the Long War of 1593–1606 achieved temporary tactical superiority over the Ottomans. By the end of the seventeenth century, in another long war of 1684–99, between the Ottomans and the members of the Holy League, the Habsburgs were able to match Ottoman military capabilities in terms of numbers of mobilised troops and military hardware, though even then only in alliance with the other members of the Holy League (Venice, Poland, and Russia). In the peace treaty of Karlowitz (1699), which ended the war, the Ottomans lost most of Hungary to the Habsburgs, who thus became the most powerful monarchy in central Europe. By re-conquering and integrating central Hungary, Transylvania, and by 1718 the Banat of Temes (the last Ottoman-controlled territory in southern Hungary) into the Habsburg Monarchy, Vienna considerably extended its pool of human and economic resources for mobilisation in future war efforts. These resources were now secured by a new military border or *Militargränze* based on the Danube River, the natural border between the Balkans and Hungary. Equally importantly, by acquiring Hungary and Transylvania, Vienna also removed the support bases of the Hungarian nobility, who in the sixteenth and seventeenth centuries had repeatedly challenged Vienna's authority and legitimacy, limited its access to military and economic resources, and compromised its strategy.

The Ottomans for their part took notice of Habsburg military reorganisations as early as the late sixteenth century. Many of the adjustments the Ottomans introduced in their military in the seventeenth century (which are discussed in Chapter 7) were in part responses to improved Habsburg military capabilities. However, Ottoman readjustment strategies led to military decentralisation, and weakened Istanbul's control over its armed forces and resources while augmenting its dependence on provincial elites and provincial military forces in war-making.

In trying to understand the decline of Ottoman military capabilities vis-à-vis the Habsburgs this chapter considers changing Ottoman and Habsburg military capabilities and border defence, as well as the role of military technology and weaponry. It argues that, by the late seventeenth century, Habsburg military, bureaucratic, and financial reforms, despite their many limitations, resulted in an army that was not only comparable in size to that of the Ottomans, but was better trained, as well equipped, and had a more efficient command structure. While advances in war-related sciences and military technology brought only modest advantages for the Ottomans' European enemies before the standardisation of weaponry and industrialisation of warfare in the nineteenth century, the role of war academies and ministries had more profound results.

Ottoman conquests and military strengths

By the sixteenth century the Ottomans had emerged as one of the most important Empires in Europe and in the territories known today as the Middle East. Theirs was an Empire only to be compared to the better-known Mediterranean Empires of the Romans and Byzantines, the similarly multi-ethnic neighbouring Habsburg and Romanov Empires, and the other great Islamic Empires of the Abbasids,

Timurids, Safavids, and Indian Mughals. In the Ottomans' emergence the turning point was the 1453 conquest of Constantinople, the capital of the thousand-year-old Byzantine Empire, by Sultan Mehmed II (r. 1444–6, 1451–81).[3] The Ottomans made Constantinople their capital and the logistical centre of their campaigns, and within fifty years had cemented their rule over the Balkans and turned the Black Sea into an 'Ottoman lake', although their control along its northern and north-western shores was never complete and was exposed to Cossack and Polish-Lithuanian attacks.[4] In 1516–17, Sultan Selim I (r. 1512–20), who had turned his attention eastwards, defeated the Mamluk Empire of Egypt and Syria, and in so doing almost doubled the Empire's territories from 883,000 km^2 in 1512 to 1.5 million km^2 in 1517. With his conquests, Selim also became the ruler of Mecca and Medina, 'the cradle of Islam', as well as of Damascus and Cairo, former seats of the Caliphs, the successors of the Prophet Muhammad. Selim and his successors duly assumed the title of 'Servant of the Two Noble Sanctuaries' (Mecca and Medina). With this title came the duty of organising and protecting the annual pilgrimage to Mecca, which gave the Ottomans unparalleled prestige and legitimacy in the Muslim world. The protection of the maritime lanes of communication between Ottoman Constantinople and Cairo thus became vital for the Ottomans. This in turn necessitated that they strengthen the Ottoman navy, thus giving the originally land-based Empire a maritime dimension. Selim's conquests also led to confrontation with the dominant Christian naval powers of the Mediterranean: Venice, Spain, and the Knights Hospitaller of Rhodes. Meanwhile, protecting the Red Sea littoral against Portuguese encroachment brought the Ottomans into conflict with the Portuguese. All of these conflicts were left to Selim's successor, Süleyman I (r. 1520–66) to resolve.

In 1521, Süleyman marched against Hungary and conquered Belgrade. The next year, his navy captured the island of Rhodes, driving the Knights Hospitaller to Malta. These swift conquests in the early years of Süleyman's reign, especially in light of previous Ottoman failures (Belgrade, 1456; Rhodes, 1480) under Mehmed II, established Süleyman's image in Europe as a mighty adversary. The sultan led his armies on thirteen campaigns, threatened the Habsburg capital Vienna twice (1529, 1532), and conquered Hungary (1526–41). His victories

---

[3] See DeVries, Chapter 2, above.
[4] The old view, proposed by Halil İnalcık, that the Ottomans had controlled the Black Sea littoral has recently been modified. See Ostapchuk, 'Human Landscape', and Kolodziejczyk, 'Inner Lake or Frontier?'.

at Rhodes (1522) and at Preveza in north-western Greece (1538) made the Ottomans masters of the eastern Mediterranean. In 1534–5, he conquered Iraq, including Baghdad, the former seat of the Abbasid caliphs. Iraq also served as a major frontier against the Safavid Empire of Persia (1501–1722), which followed Shia Islam and was the Ottomans' main rival in the east, both ideologically and militarily.

All these conquests would have been unthinkable without the Ottoman military machine and the efficient use of continuously expanding resources by the Ottoman central and provincial administration. Beyond sheer military might, however, we should not overlook the Ottomans' clever use of information gathering, ideology, propaganda, and political pragmatism, which were also of major significance. In their rivalry against the Habsburgs, Ottoman ideologues and strategists used religion, millenarianism, and universalist visions of Empire to strengthen the legitimacy of the sultan within the larger Muslim community. Similarly, Ottoman victories against Habsburg Catholicism and Safavid Shiism formed an integral part of Ottoman propaganda.[5] In the early years of Süleyman's reign, grand vizier Ibrahim Pasha consciously propagated the sultan's image as the new world conqueror, the successor of Alexander the Great, whereas in his latter years the sultan viewed himself as 'lawgiver', or 'law abider' (*kanuni*), a just ruler in whose realm justice and order reigned.[6] Yet as important as this kind of propaganda was, it was ultimately the Ottoman military machine through which the Ottomans conquered and ruled over the Balkans, Asia Minor, and the Arab lands.

The early-sixteenth-century Ottoman military was considered by European contemporaries to be the best and most efficient in the world. The bulk of the Ottoman army consisted of the fief-based provincial cavalry (*timar*-holding or timariot *sipahi*), whose remuneration was secured through military fiefs or prebends (*timar*). In return for the right to collect well-prescribed revenues from the assigned *timar* lands, the Ottoman provincial cavalryman was obliged to provide for his arms, armour, and horse, and to report for military service along with his armed retainer(s) when called upon by the sultan. The number of armed retainers whom the provincial cavalryman had to keep, arm, and bring with him on campaigns increased proportionately to his income from his fief. From perhaps as early as the reign of Bayezid I (r. 1389–1402), muster rolls were checked during campaigns against registers of *timar* lands in order to determine if all the cavalrymen from

---

[5] See Ágoston, 'Limits of Imperial Policy'.
[6] Fleischer, 'Lawgiver'.

a given region had reported for military duty and brought the required number of retainers and equipment. If the cavalryman did not report for service or failed to bring with him the required number of retainers, he lost his military fief, which then was assigned to someone else. The *timar* fiefs and the related bureaucratic surveillance system provided the Ottoman sultans through the late sixteenth century with a large standing cavalry army, while relieving the central Ottoman bureaucracy of the burden of revenue raising and paying military salaries.[7] In 1525 there were 10,668 *timar*-holding *sipahi*s in the European side of the Empire, and 17,200 in Asia Minor, Aleppo, and Damascus. Based on their income, they were capable of providing at least 22,000 to 23,000 armed retainers, although some estimate the number of possible retainers at as high as 61,000. In sum, the total potential force of the standing provincial cavalry can be estimated at a minimum of 50,000 men (and perhaps as many as 90,000 men).[8]

The other component of the army was formed by the 'slaves of the (Sublime) Porte' (*kapıkulu*), that is, the sultan's standing salaried army. It consisted of the sultan's elite infantry or Janissaries, gunners (*topçu*s), gun-carriage drivers (*top arabacı*s), armourers (*cebeci*s), and the six divisions of salaried palace cavalrymen (*sipahi*s, *silahdar*s, right- and left-wing *ulufeci*s and *gureba*s). Of these, the most important were the elite Janissaries, (from the Turkish term *yeni çeri* or 'new army'), established under Murad I (r. 1362–89). The corps was financed by the treasury and remained under the direct command of the sultan. The replacement of Janissaries was ensured by the *devşirme* (collection) system, introduced probably also during the reign of Murad I. Under this system Christian lads between eight and twenty years old – preferably between twelve and fourteen – were periodically collected and then Ottomanised. Subsequently, they became members of the salaried central corps or were trained for government service. Having their own standing army, the sultans thus could claim a monopoly over organised violence, and did not have to negotiate with local power-brokers when they wanted to deploy operationally effective armies. As can be seen from Table 6.1, the number of salaried troops was between 15,000 and 16,000 in the first half of the sixteenth century, but it increased by 75 per cent during the reign of Süleyman I.

---

[7] The system is aptly described in Káldy-Nagy, 'First Centuries', and Imber, *Ottoman Empire*, 193–206.

[8] Káldy-Nagy, 'First Centuries', 161–2. Murphey, *Ottoman Warfare*, 37–9, using the same source, estimated the number of potential retainers at 61,520, and that of the total potential *Timariot* cavalry force at 99,261, but his numbers seem too optimistic.

Table 6.1. *The number of salaried troops in the first half of the sixteenth century.*

	1514–15	1527–8	1567–8
Janissaries	10,156	7,886	12,798
Gunners	348	696	1,204
Gun-carriage drivers	372	943	678
Armourers	451	524	789
Palace cavalry	5,316	5,088	11,044
Total standing army	**16,643**	**15,137**	**26,513**

Data are from the Ottoman treasury balance sheets that give the number of troops paid from the treasury. See Özvar, 'Osmanlı Devletinin', 237; data for 1527–8 and 1567–8 were published by Káldy-Nagy, 'First Centuries', 167–9.

In addition to the provincial cavalry and the standing salaried army, two more groups, the *azab*s – a kind of peasant militia serving as foot-soldiers during campaigns, in fortresses and on ships – and the freelance light cavalry, the *akıncıs* or 'raiders', were also militarily significant, numbering several tens of thousands in the first decades of the sixteenth century.[9] In sum, Süleyman probably could count on an army whose strength on paper was close to 90,000 or 100,000 men, of which he routinely mobilised between 50,000 and 60,000 troops for his campaigns.

The Ottomans also showed genuine interest and great flexibility in adopting weaponry and tactics that originated in Christendom. They not only adopted firearms at an early stage of the development of their armed forces (in the latter part of the fourteenth century), but were also successful in integrating gunpowder weaponry into their military by establishing a separate artillery corps as part of the sultans' standing army in the early fifteenth century. In much of western Europe, by comparison, artillerymen remained a transitory category somewhere between soldiers and craftsmen well into the seventeenth century. The Ottomans also established cannon foundries and gunpowder works in Istanbul and the major provincial capitals throughout the Empire. In this way they became self-sufficient in weapons and ammunition production, which also enabled them to establish long-lasting firepower superiority in eastern Europe, the Mediterranean, and the Middle East. At Çaldıran (1514) on the eastern frontier the Ottomans had some 500

[9] During Süleyman's 1521 campaign against Belgrade the *akıncıs* numbered 20,000. See Káldy-Nagy, 'First Centuries', 170.

cannon, whereas the Safavids had none. At Mohács (1526) the Ottomans employed some 240 to 300 cannon, whereas the Hungarians used 85. By the mid fifteenth century, when Ottoman technological receptivity was coupled with mass-production capabilities, self-sufficiency in the manufacturing of weapons and ammunition, and top-quality Ottoman logistics, the sultans' armies gained superiority over their European opponents, which they were able to maintain until about the end of the seventeenth century.[10]

When Süleyman's forces captured Belgrade (1521) and the neighbouring forts, the Ottomans assumed control over the whole Danube region as far as Belgrade and effectively destroyed a major section of the medieval Hungarian defence system, established by King Sigismund of Luxembourg (r. 1387–1437) and his successors. The country now lay open for a major Ottoman invasion, which duly occurred in 1526. In the battle of Mohács (1526) Süleyman's army of between 60,000 and 70,000 men annihilated the much smaller Hungarian army (26,000 men) and killed King Louis Jagiellon (r. 1516–26).[11] Although the sultan marched to Hungary's capital Buda, he did not occupy the country, and did not annex it to his Empire. Instead it was the election of two kings, Ferdinand I of Habsburg (r. 1526–64) and the pro-Ottoman János Szapolyai (r. 1526–40), to the Hungarian throne by competing factions of the Hungarian nobility, and the ensuing civil war between them, that together with the presence of Ottoman armed forces in southern Hungary secured Ottoman control over Hungary for the time being.

With Szapolyai's death in 1540, Ferdinand launched a military campaign aimed at assuming control over Hungary. From the perspective of the Ottoman capital, this threatened to upset the balance of power in central Europe between the two Empires. It prompted Süleyman to conquer the strategically important central lands of Hungary together with its capital city Buda, which controlled the Danubian waterways into central Europe. The Ottoman-held parts of the country were soon transformed into two provinces, that of Buda (1541–1686) and Temesvár (R. Timişoara, 1552–1716).[12] Hungary's strategically less important eastern territories were left by the sultan in the hands of

---

[10] See Ágoston, *Guns*, and 'Turkish War Machine'; cf. Murphey, Chapter 7, below.
[11] Perjés, *Fall*; cf. Veszprémy, Chapter 5, above.
[12] Many of these places had several name forms. Unless the name has a widely accepted English form (such as Belgrade), I follow contemporary usage but also give present-day name forms for easier identification. Abbreviations used: Cr. = Croatian, G. = German, Gr. = Greek, Hu. = Hungarian, Ott. = Ottoman Turkish, Pol. = Polish, Serb. = Serbian, Sl. = Slovak, R. = Romanian.

Szapolyai's widow and infant son, and soon became the principality of Transylvania, an Ottoman vassal state.[13] Ferdinand's attempt in 1542 to expel the Ottomans from Buda ended in humiliation, and lack of adequate commitments of Habsburg resources in the 1540s led to the tripartite division of Hungary and turned the country into the main continental battleground between the two major Empires of the age, that of the Habsburgs and that of the Ottomans.

The Ottomans soon occupied and fortified the main forts of Hungary, and in the 1540s and 1550s deployed in them some 15,000 garrison soldiers, whose number reached between 18,000 and 20,000 by the 1570s and 1580s. With approximately 7,000 *timar*-holding *sipahi*s, who in Hungary also manned the border forts, the total number of Ottoman soldiers in Hungary probably reached 25,000 in the latter part of the sixteenth century.[14] The Habsburgs, who from 1526 were kings of Hungary and thus inherited from their predecessors on the Hungarian throne the burden of halting further Ottoman advances in central Europe, now faced this formidable Ottoman military machine.

The Habsburgs and the new Military Border in Hungary

Retaining only the western and northern parts of the Hungarian kingdom, Ferdinand and his Hungarian supporters faced the challenge of establishing a new border defence system that could contain further Ottoman inroads into central Europe and protect Ferdinand's hereditary lands and kingdoms; as well as the city of Vienna, the Habsburg capital, which was situated only some 220 km to the west of Buda, the centre of the newly created Ottoman province in Hungary.

Facing imminent Ottoman conquest, members of the Hungarian nobility and their kings tried to use all possible structures to defend their frontier. A new line of fortifications was established in the middle of Hungary, following the hills, mountains, and river systems of Transdanubia and northern Hungary – the only possible natural defence line that the topography of the region offered. However, these hasty constructions were insufficient in the face of Ottoman mastery of the art of siege warfare. Between 1521 and 1566 only thirteen castles were able to resist Ottoman firepower for more than ten days, and only nine for more than twenty days. In this period only four forts managed

---

[13] Fodor, 'Ottoman Policy towards Hungary'; Oborni, 'Die Herrschaft Ferdinands I. in Ungarn'.
[14] Hegyi, *A török hódoltság*, I, 156–66.

to repel Ottoman sieges (Kőszeg in 1532, Temesvár in 1551, Eger in 1552, and Szigetvár in 1556) and the latter three were all to be captured by the Ottomans before the end of the century.[15]

In view of these Ottoman successes, Vienna assumed a central role in organising and financing the defence of Hungary, especially after the establishment of the Aulic or Court War Council (*Wiener Hofkriegsrat*), the central administrative office of Habsburg military affairs in 1556.[16] The Habsburgs hired Italian military architects and engineers to direct and supervise the modernisation of the most important forts. In the case of the strategically most important forts, such as Győr, Komárom, (Sl. Komarno), Érsekújvár (Sl. Nové Zámky), Kassa (Sl. Košice), Nagyvárad (R. Oradea), and Szatmár (R. Satu Mare), the entire town was fortified, thus creating 'fortified towns' (*Festungstädte*) of the type well known in Italy, France, and the Netherlands.[17]

The new crescent-shaped defence line stretched some 1,000 km in length from the Adriatic Sea to northern and north-eastern Hungary (see Map 7), and comprised between 120 and 130 large and small forts and watchtowers in the late sixteenth century, and some 80 to 90 in the next century. The strategically more significant sections of the Hungarian border were heavily fortified. In 1607, the important section 400 km in length between the Muraköz region (between the rivers Drava and Mura in southern Hungary, now Međimurje in northern Croatia) and Murány (Muráň in modern Slovakia) was protected by 60 garrisons, which meant 15 forts per 100 km section, whereas the comparable ratio was 11.5 in the Spanish Netherlands and 8 in France and the Holy Roman Empire.[18] In the 1570s and 1580s, some 22,000 soldiers guarded the entire border, which was comparable in size to the Ottoman garrison forces deployed by Istanbul in Hungary.

The Habsburgs and the Hungarian estates: interdependence and compromise

The main office of Habsburg military administration was the Court War Council. Although responsible for the recruitment, armament, and supply of troops, as well as for the maintenance of arsenals, warehouses, and border forts, the Court War Council had limited financial authority. More importantly, in the sixteenth century the Habsburg

---

[15] Marosi, *XVI. századi váraink*, 32.
[16] On the development of the defence system see Pálffy, 'Origins'.
[17] Gecsényi, 'Ungarische Städte'.
[18] Cigány, *Reform*, 67–8.

monarchy was still in transition from a 'domain-state' to a 'tax-state'. Revenues came from two main sources: *camerale* and *contributionale*. The monarch's *camerale* or 'ordinary revenues' came from his shrinking domain lands, mines, and customs duties, and were supposed to cover the expenditures of the court. *Contributionale*, on the other hand, were considered 'extraordinary' subsidies to meet emergency military expenses, and had to be voted by the estates. While the Court War Council administered 'extraordinary' taxes, ordinary cameral revenues were administered by the Court Chamber (*Hofkammer*) or Treasury, set up by Ferdinand I in 1527.[19]

The Court Chamber in Vienna was the main administrative body of financial affairs in the Austrian Habsburgs' lands. However, its subordinate provincial chambers in Prague for Bohemia (from 1527), Breslau (Wrocław) for Silesia (from 1557), Pozsony (Sl. Bratislava) for Hungary (from 1528), and Kassa for Upper Hungary (from 1567) also administered cameral revenues in their respective parts of the monarchy. Two of the above-mentioned chambers, the Hungarian Chamber (*Camera hungarica*) in Pozsony and the Zipser Chamber (*Camera scepusiensis*) in Kassa, along with the Lower Austrian Chamber (*Niederösterreichische Kammer*) in Vienna, played a crucial role in administering revenues from Hungary and paying the garrisons in Hungary and Croatia.[20]

The tax base of the Habsburgs in Hungary was limited: Ferdinand usually managed to collect revenues only from about thirty-two or thirty-three of the seventy-two counties of pre-Mohács Hungary. He collected some 400,000 to 640,000 *forint*s from Hungary, which amounted to 25 to 30 percent of his total revenues from his kingdoms. Of his successors, Maximilian I's (r. 1564–76) revenues from Hungary totalled 642,000 *forint*s and those of his successor, Rudolf I (r. 1576–1608), about 550,000 *forint*s.[21] These revenues were insufficient to cover the salaries of the garrisons stationed in the Hungarian–Croatian border forts, which by the last years of Ferdinand's reign amounted to approximately 800,000 *forint*s (1 million Rhenish florins). Moreover, soldiers' pay was only one, albeit the most substantial, defence-related expense. The costs of rebuilding forts, maintaining the Danubian river flotillas in Komárom and Győr, and of military administration, intelligence, and communication have been estimated at about 400,000 to 500,000 *forint*s per year. Thus the total annual cost of the Hungarian–Croatian

---

[19] Schulze, 'Emergence and Consolidation'; Bonney, 'Revenue.' On the Austrian Habsburgs see Winkelbauer, 'Finanzgeschichte', 184–7.
[20] Kenyeres, 'Finanzen', and 'Einkünfte'.
[21] Kenyeres, 'Einkünfte', 145–6.

Military Border amounted to between 1.7 and 2.1 million *forints*, which equalled Ferdinand's total annual revenues from his kingdoms and provinces.[22]

The Habsburgs' non-Hungarian lands and the Holy Roman Empire were also required to contribute to the defence of Ferdinand's Hungarian kingdom. The imperial aid, however, was somewhat contingent because Hungary, unlike Bohemia, was not part of the Reich, and thus the imperial estates were obliged to finance the defences of this neighbouring country only if the Ottomans threatened the territory of the Empire or the city of Vienna, which after Charles V's abdication (1556) and Ferdinand's election as Emperor (1558) assumed the position of imperial capital (*Reichshaupstadt*). Although the Hungarian frontier was far from Speyer, Regensburg, or Augsburg, where the imperial Diet held its meetings, the 'Turkish Question' (*Türkenfrage*) and 'Turkish aid' (*Türkenhilfe*) were recurrent issues at the Diet's meetings. Between 1576 and 1606 the income from the *Türkenhilfe* amounted to 18.7 million Rhenish florins. When the Court War Council in 1613 stated that 'every province had to upkeep its respective confines in Hungary', it formulated a time-honoured practice.[23] The Croatian section of the border was maintained by the estates of Carniola and Carinthia, and the Slavonian section by the Styrian estates; the Inner Austrian lands spent more than 18 million Rhenish florins for the forts in Croatia and Slavonia in the sixteenth century. The Kanizsa border area (and, after Kanizsa's conquest by the Ottomans in 1600, the forts facing Kanizsa) was financed by the Styrian, Hungarian, and imperial estates; the Győr section by the estates of Lower Austria and the Reich; the mining town or Lower Hungarian border area by the Bohemian and Moravian estates; and the Upper Hungarian section by the Hungarian, Silesian, and imperial estates.[24]

Owing to their dependence on the Emperor-king's other kingdoms, the Hungarian estates eventually lost control over military and financial affairs. However, since they continued to administer substantial revenues through the two Hungarian Chambers, the Hungarian estates managed to retain some influence over defence policy. Equally importantly, it was the Hungarian nobility who provided a much-needed workforce for the strengthening and modernising of the border forts. The *gratuitus labor*, a new extraordinary tax introduced by Ferdinand, was in fact the uncompensated labour of the peasants, which was approved and administered by the estates. Similarly, without the *allodia*, or

---

[22] Pálffy, 'Preis für die Verteidigung', 32–3.
[23] *Ibid.*, p. 34.
[24] *Ibid.*, 34–9, 43; Czigány, *Reform*, 63.

freeholds of the Hungarian aristocracy, the provisioning of the garrison soldiers would have been unthinkable. The *allodia*'s contribution to the soldiers' pay was crucial, especially when the soldiers might go unpaid for months, which became increasingly the case in the seventeenth century, especially during the Thirty Years' War.

The interdependency of Vienna and the estates resulted in the dual nature of the administration of the border defence system. Two types of captain-generalcy were created, controlled respectively by the Viennese War Council and the Hungarian estates. The border defence was primarily the responsibility of the captain-generals of the borders (*Grenzobrist/Grenzoberst* or *supremus capitaneus confiniorum*). The country was divided into smaller border areas (*Grenzgebiete*) in which these captain-generals controlled the main forts, built, modernised and maintained by the central power. At the same time and in the same territories, so-called district captain-generals *(Kreisobrist/Kresoberst or supremus capitaneus partium regni Hungariae)* were in charge of smaller forts of secondary importance, as well as of the obsolete forces at their disposal, made up of noble, county, and town troops and a small force of several hundred cavalry and infantry paid by the Habsburg rulers. While the captain-generals of *Grenzgebiete* could be from neighbouring Habsburg lands or Hungarian lords acceptable to the Aulic War Council, the less important district captain-generals were almost exclusively native Hungarians.[25]

Growing Habsburg military power in Hungary: winning over the estates

The establishment and manning of the military border led to increased militarisation of Hungarian society. By the 1570s, a quasi-permanent military force made up of the Hungarian soldiers of the border forts had emerged; their number in the four captain-generalcies in Hungary proper was about 11,000 in the 1580s and about 14,000 to 15,000 in the mid seventeenth century. Although most of them were of peasant origin, in return for their military service they gained privileges similar to that of the nobility.[26] By the seventeenth century all the captain-generals, save those of the strategically most important Győr, came from Hungary's most influential landowning aristocrats. Thus the estates gained crucial control over the Hungarian soldiery deployed in royal forts.

[25] Pálffy, 'Origins', 39–49.
[26] Czigány, *Reform*, 102–3.

In addition to these garrison soldiers paid at least partly by Vienna, the Hungarian landowning aristocrats also had their own private armies. Estimates regarding the combined strength of the private armies of the Hungarian landowning magnates vary between 10,000 and 20,000 men in the seventeenth century. To this one should add at least 8,000 to 15,000 (or perhaps as many as 20,000 to 25,000) *hajdú* soldiers. Most of these were regular soldiers serving in royal forts or imperial regiments, while others were considered semi-regular reserve forces, often employed by the magnates or the princes of Transylvania.[27]

The ultimate dependence of the soldiers of the border forts, the *hajdús*, and the members of the serving lesser nobility (*servitor*) on their aristocrat employers (*dominus*) provided the large landowners with an effective military force and military-administrative personnel that could be used against the centralising policy of the Habsburgs. The Hungarian soldiers of the border forts along with the *hajdús* formed the bulk of the army of István Bocskai during his anti-Habsburg uprising of 1604–6. In 1605, in return for their military service, Bocskai, who by then was elected prince of Hungary and Transylvania, collectively ennobled some 10,000 *hajdú* soldiers, liberated them from their *corvée*, and settled them in his lands in eastern Hungary.[28]

The estates' position was further strengthened by the existence of Ottoman-held Hungary and the principality of Transylvania. Having strong personal, economic, and cultural ties with territories under Habsburg rule, these parts of the country not only offered refuge for the Hungarian rebels, but also effectively backed the estates' political demands both on the battlefields and in international diplomacy. Unlike in Bohemia, where the anti-Habsburg rebellion of the estates in 1618–20 was crushed ruthlessly, Vienna had to be more cautious in Hungary to avoid losing further territories to her arch-enemy, the Ottomans. Harsh absolutism provoked anti-Habsburg rebellions with the military backing of the Hungarian soldiers of the border forts, Transylvania, and even the Ottoman-held territories, and led to repeated loss of territories, either to the Ottoman vassal princes of Transylvania, or to the Ottomans. This is what happened when the princes of Transylvania, Gábor Bethlen and György Rákóczy I, led several successful campaigns against the Habsburgs during the Thirty Years' War, often with the agreement and backing of the Ottomans. In 1619 Bethlen, in support of his Bohemian fellow-Protestants, launched a campaign against Emperor Ferdinand II that conquered Kassa and Érsekújvár, two key forts of the Habsburg Military Border and seats of two

---

[27] Nagy, *"Megint fölszánt magyar"*, 81–96.
[28] Rácz, *Hajdúk*; Nagy, *Hajdúvitézek*.

general-captaincies; then, in 1620, the Hungarian nobles assembled at the Diet of Besztercebánya (Ger. Neusohl; Sl. Banská Bystrica), dethroned Ferdinand, and elected Bethlen as their king (1620). By the treaty of Nikolsberg (1622) Bethlen conceded his claim to St Steven's crown to Ferdinand, while Ferdinand ceded seven counties in Upper Hungary to Bethlen and guaranteed to continue financing their garrisons. The terms were renewed in 1624 and 1626 after subsequent campaigns by Bethlen in 1623 and 1626, and in 1645 after György Rákóczy I's campaign, though following Rákóczy's death in 1648 the Habsburgs regained five of these counties. Bethlen could have commanded 8,000 troops in 1619–20, 10,000 in 1623, and perhaps 20,000 in 1626, whereas Rákóczy's army is estimated at 15,000 men in 1644–5. The overwhelming majority of them (80 to 90 per cent) were *hajdús*.[29]

Nevertheless, despite persistent financial constraints and frictions between the ruler and his Hungarian estates, the interdependence of Vienna and the Hungarian estates in the face of constant Ottoman threat made the uneasy compromise work. Although individual fortresses, including the most up-to-date, fell to Ottoman artillery assaults despite costly modernisation, the Military Border as a defence system was able to defend the Habsburg hereditary lands and the remaining territories of the Hungarian kingdom.

More crucially, with the Habsburg takeover of Hungary and Transylvania after the re-conquest of Hungary from the Ottomans in the wars of 1684–99, the Hungarian estates lost the military and diplomatic support that they had previously enjoyed during their anti-Habsburg insurrections. In 1688, as a token of their gratitude for the dynasty that expelled the Ottomans from their country, the Hungarian estates gave up their centuries-old right to resist the dynasty (*ius resistendi et contradicendi*) along with their right freely to elect their kings, thus accepting the Habsburgs as their hereditary sovereigns. While on the surface the insurrection and anti-Habsburg war of Ferenc Rákóczy (1703–11) seemed yet another anti-Habsburg rebellion of the type of Bocskai, Bethlen, and György Rákóczy, in fact it took place in radically changed circumstances and with higher stakes. By 1703, both the principality of Transylvania and Ottoman-held Hungary, from where the insurgents had received military support and found refuge in the seventeenth century, were in Habsburg hands. What was at stake in the 1703–11 insurrection was the new administration of the country and the estates' role in it. The defeat of the estates' rebellion and the ensuing compromise further strengthened

---

[29] Nagy, *"Megint fölszánt magyar"*, 91, though he gives larger figures.

the sovereign's power vis-à-vis the Hungarian estates and his hold over the newly acquired country and its resources.

Habsburg military strength vis-à-vis the Ottomans

On the battlefield against the Ottomans, the Habsburgs employed troops that were at the cutting edge of European military technology and tactics as early as the late sixteenth century. As with the modernisation of defences, some of the changes the Habsburgs introduced in their field armies were also, at least partly, prompted by Ottoman firepower superiority. Lazarus Freiherr von Schwendi, the captain-general in Upper Hungary (1565–8), emphasised the importance of firearms as a counter to the arquebus-armed Janissaries. He advised his Emperor to enrol Spanish and Italian arquebusiers as well as horsemen equipped with this weapon.[30] Others seconded his views. At the 1577 military conference in Vienna, most experts were of the opinion that 'for the time being, hand firearms are the main advantage of Your Majesty's military over this enemy [i.e. the Ottomans]'.[31] From the 1570s onwards, the Austrian Habsburgs modernised the divisions of their military deployed in Hungary against the Ottomans. In so doing they made use of the experience gained by the Spanish armies fighting in Flanders, troops considered by historians to be at the cutting edge of contemporary military art. The proportion of Habsburg infantry soldiers carrying firearms fighting in the Long Hungarian War of 1593–1606 against the Ottomans is said to have been as high as in the army of Flanders.[32] Even though the sources – the *Bestallungen* or recruitment contracts – upon which such observations are based should be treated with greater scepticism, they signalled a significant change in the way Habsburg firepower was deployed. The Ottomans were quick to notice the Habsburgs' improved military capabilities. However, their responses not only failed to maintain their previous advantage, but also, in the long run – especially when exacerbated by a series of social and economic crises – were ruinous.

More importantly, after the Thirty Years' War, the Habsburgs managed to keep some of their regiments, and thus to establish their standing army. Again, estimates regarding the size of the Habsburg standing army in various years vary greatly, but Figure 6.1 should give the reader some sense as to its strength.

However modest these figures might be in comparison with French army strength, they marked a major change in Habsburg military and

---

[30] Parry, 'Manière de combattre', 225.
[31] Geőcze, 'Hadi tanácskozások', 658.
[32] Kelenik, 'Military Revolution', 154.

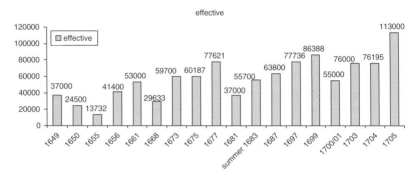

Figure 6.1 Effective strength of the Habsburg standing army.
Source: Hochedlinger, *Austria's Wars*, 104.

bureaucratic capabilities. For the first time in their long confrontation with the Ottomans, the Habsburgs were able to enlist, pay, and deploy armies that were comparable in size with that of the Ottomans, even if reductions usually followed the cessation of hostilities, for state finances and bureaucracies were still unable to upkeep such large numbers in the long run. But as we shall see, this was also the case in the Ottoman Empire. Moreover, these Habsburg troops were perceived by both parties as better trained and equipped.

The permanent army also required new forms of recruitment. The *Landrekrutenstellung* or 'provincial recruitment' system, which by the 1680s was the main method of raising substantial numbers of soldiers in wartime, still depended on the estates; however, reforms made the system more efficient and less expensive. From the mid seventeenth century on, and especially during and after the long war of 1684–99, the central government gradually assumed greater control over recruitment, financing, and supply. This was true even when we consider that Vienna did not achieve a measure of centralisation comparable to its European rivals over the administration of warfare until about 1740. Still, compared to the Ottomans, the control of the relevant Viennese central governmental bodies (Court War Council, Court Chamber, War Commissariat), gave substantially more oversight over war-making to the Emperor, his generals, and administrators than the sultans (or their grand viziers) of the late seventeenth and early eighteenth centuries enjoyed.

Ottoman military transformations

From the late sixteenth century on, the traditional Ottoman military, fiscal, and administrative systems went through major crises and transformations, owing partly to the changing nature of warfare and tactics in Europe, which the Ottomans faced for the first time during the Long Hungarian War of 1593–1606 while fighting the Habsburgs.[33] In a treatise composed soon after the battle of Mezőkeresztes in 1596, the single major field battle of the war, Hasan Kafi al-Akhisari complained that the imperialists used the most modern types of arquebus and cannon and showed a distinct advantage over the Ottomans.[34] Other contemporaneous Ottoman observers made similar remarks. The Ottoman chronicler Selaniki Mustafa Efendi contended that the Ottomans 'could not withstand the musketeers from Transylvania'. In 1602, the grand vizier reported from the Hungarian front to the sultan that 'in the field or during a siege we are in a distressed position, because the greater part of the enemy forces are infantry armed with muskets, while the majority of our forces are horsemen and we have very few specialists skilled in the musket'.[35] However, the temporary tactical superiority of the Habsburg forces did not materialise in strategic advantages. On the contrary, the peace treaty of Zsitvatorok (1606) that ended the war confirmed the Ottoman conquest of two key border provinces.

However, the Ottomans introduced military reforms in order to counterbalance increased Habsburg firepower and military efficiency, and their long-standing effects proved to be disastrous. First, the Ottoman government increased the numbers of Janissaries; second, it introduced newly established formations of arms-bearing infantry, hired from amongst the vagrants of the subject population, usually designated in the sources as *sekban* and *levend*. As a result of complex and not yet fully understood economic and social changes of the latter part of the sixteenth century, thousands of peasants became deprived of home and country, and many of these became outlaws possessing firearms – despite all efforts by Istanbul to ban the use of firearms amongst the subject population. During the long Iranian and Hungarian wars (1578–90 and 1593–1606) the government welcomed with open arms soldiers who knew how to use firearms and who could be recruited for a campaign or two and then discharged. However, these *sekban*s did not return to their villages after the campaigns. Instead, they joined the bandits or supported uprisings in Anatolia. The government used the Janissaries to put down the rebellions and, with this action, set the two main elements of the Empire's armed forces against one another.[36]

---

[33] İnalcık, 'Military and Fiscal Transformation'.

[34] İpşirli,' 'Hasan Kâfî el-Akhisarî', 268; also quoted from an older German translation by Parry, 'Manière de combattre', 228.

[35] Orhonlu, *Osmanlı tarihine*, 70–1; quoted in English by İnalcık, 'Socio-Political Effects', 199.

[36] İnalcık, 'Military and Fiscal Transformation', 283–337; Finkel, *Administration of Warfare*, 37–48; Griswold, *Rebellion*; Barkey, *Bandits and Bureaucrats*.

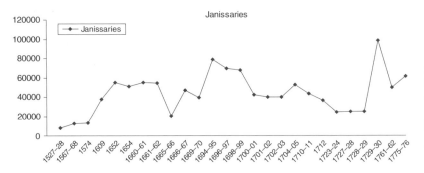

Figure 6.2 The number of Janissary troops, 1514–1776.

Source: Genc and Özvar, *Osmanlı Maliyesi*, I, 237–38.

The increase in the number of Janissaries also had several unwelcome consequences. Whereas the treasury had paid 12,800 Janissaries in the late 1560s, 37,600 Janissaries were on the payroll by 1609. Their number fluctuated between 51,000 and 55,000 in the 1650s and decreased considerably in the 1660s, only to reach its peak of almost 79,000 in 1694–5 during the 1684–99 war against the Holy League. It remained high (67,700 and 69,600) in the rest of the century, only to decrease again after the war. It was about 36,000 to 40,000 in the first decade of the eighteenth century, dropped even more in the 1720s, and rose again sharply in 1729–30 during the war against Iran. The number was still more than 61,000 after the Küçük Kaynarca peace treaty (1774) that ended the exhausting Russo-Ottoman war of 1768–74 (see Figure 6.2).

Although the number of Janissaries increased substantially, only a fraction of them were ever mobilised for campaigns. Many were deployed in frontier garrisons, with strategically important forts having Janissary garrisons of 1,000, 2,000, or 3,000 men.[37] In general, some 30 to 60 per cent of the Janissaries were on frontier duty in the 1650s and the 1710s. Even in 1691–2, during the war against the Holy League, the proportion of Janissaries in frontier garrisons was no less than 42 per cent. While those serving in forts close to the front could be, and sometimes were, mobilised for campaigns, the majority were charged with the defence of the Empire's borders (see Figure 6.3).

Not all Janissaries who stayed in Istanbul were mobilised for campaigns either. Many were pensioners or guards. In 1660–1, only 33 per cent (18,013 men); in 1697 about 30 per cent (21,000 men); in

---

[37] Ágoston, *Guns*, 27.

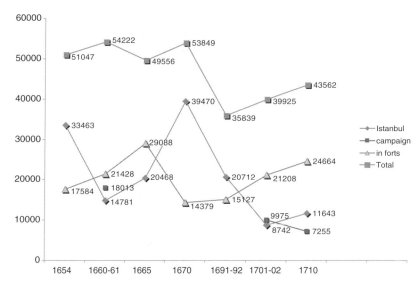

Figure 6.3 Janissaries in Istanbul and on frontier duty.
Source: Genc and Özvar, *Osmanlı Maliyesi*, II, 112–13, 224, 249, 287.

1701–2, 25 per cent (9,975 men); and in 1710, 17 per cent (7,255 men) of the totals participated in military campaigns.

The ratios of mobilised to total troops are similar if one looks at the sultans' standing army as a whole. In 1710, during the Russo-Ottoman war of 1710–11 for instance, out of the total number of 52,337 infantry in the standing army (Janissaries, gunners, gun-carriage drivers, armourers, and their pensioners), only 10,378 men – that is, less than 20 per cent – took part in the campaign.[38] While narrative sources give inflated figures regarding the strength of the Ottoman armed forces, in light of the above data it is clear that the troops mobilised by the sultans from their standing army no longer outmatched that of Habsburg Austria by the early eighteenth century.

What is more, even those who participated in the campaigns performed poorly. The increased demand for troops required widening the pool of recruitment, and also led to a decline in military skills and put an additional burden on the treasury, which faced recurring deficits from the early 1590s onwards. To ease the burden on the treasury, beginning in the seventeenth century the Janissaries were increasingly paid from *timar* revenues and allowed to engage in trade and craftsmanship. By the late seventeenth century, Janissary service had been radically transformed

[38] Genç and Özvar, *Osmanlı Maliyesi*, II, 289.

and many Janissaries had become craftsmen and shop owners, though still privileged with tax-exempt status as a reward for their supposed military service, for which they continued to draw pay.

The increase in the number of Janissaries was also related to the deterioration of the *timar* system and the provincial cavalry. New research dates the end of the 'classical' provincial administration and revenue management system to the 1610s. Revenues became administered by a gradually expanding body of beneficiaries and provincial elites, and most never made their way to the central government treasury. While in the sixteenth century the treasury administered some 58 per cent of revenues, this share shrank to 25 per cent in the next century. This in turn led to the financial and military independence of the provincial elites, whose attempts to appropriate ever larger shares of resources increased the burden on taxpayers, and thus added to the economic and social strains that led to revolts and rebellions amongst the peasant population. Since a good proportion of the emerging new elite came from the ranks of the Janissaries, their growing control over the local resources once distributed as *timar*s to the provincial *sipahi* cavalry led to competition and friction on the local level between Janissaries and *sipahi*s.[39] The latter were on the losing side, for the military value of the *sipahi* cavalry diminished greatly with increased use of firepower by the infantry. Although paper figures for the provincial cavalry rose spectacularly in the seventeenth century, only a small portion of the *timar*-holders could actually be mobilised at any given time. Their place was taken by the provincial forces maintained by provincial governors and local strongmen. The majority of such forces were recruited from the above-mentioned vagrant *levend*s, and the total mobilised strength of these provincial forces could reach 50,000 to 70,000 men in the early eighteenth century.[40]

Conclusion

The threat posed by Ottoman military superiority in the early sixteenth century was a crucial factor in Habsburg military, bureaucratic, and financial reforms. Owing in part to this Ottoman challenge, the Habsburgs assumed the burden of defending their newly acquired Hungarian kingdom. They established a new line of defence against the Ottomans that they modernised according to the latest standards of the age. However, until the latter part of the seventeenth century, Vienna remained dependent on the estates of the Austrian Hereditary Lands,

---

[39] Fodor, *Válallkozásra kényszerítve.*
[40] E.g. about 65,000 to 70,000 during the Prut campaign; Yıldız, *Haydi Osmanlı,* 133.

Bohemia and Hungary, for financing, manning, and supplying its forts. Beginning with the establishment of its standing field army in 1649 and through continuous military, financial, and bureaucratic reforms, Vienna gradually managed to assert ever greater control over its military capabilities, and by 1740 achieved considerable state centralisation of warfare.

The Ottomans, on the other hand, followed a reverse path. At the beginning of the period under investigation, the Ottoman sultans had substantially more control over their resources and armed forces than their Habsburg rivals. This is true even if we acknowledge that the Ottoman central administration also had to compromise and negotiate with its provincial elites and that Ottoman authority was never as omnipresent as former historiography has led us to believe.[41] However, by the early eighteenth century, provincial elites appropriated a good share of the Empire's resources, with which they established and maintained their own armies. Owing to the deterioration of the *timar* system and the provincial administration, the sultans became increasingly dependent on local elites and their troops in administering their Empire, maintaining law and order in the provinces, and, more importantly, raising armies for campaigns.[42]

Similar decentralisation can be observed with regard to the production of weapons and ammunition in the Ottoman Empire, which resulted in diminished production capabilities. While in the seventeenth century the Ottoman powder mills could annually manufacture some 761 to 1,037 tonnes of powder, this amount had fallen to 169 tonnes by the second half of the eighteenth century. Self-sufficiency in powder manufacturing ended around the mid eighteenth century. The history of weapons manufacturing is more complicated. The main producer of Ottoman cannon was the Istanbul Imperial Cannon Foundry, although the Ottoman government operated local foundries in many provincial capitals and mining centres. Ottoman stockpiles of weapons and ammunition greatly outnumbered the weapons and ammunition supplies of their Hungarian and Habsburg adversaries as late as the 1680s. During the Russo-Ottoman war of 1768–74 the Istanbul foundry, unlike the Empire's powder mills, was still operating at full steam, producing cannon in significant numbers, though contemporaries noted their poor quality.[43]

Throughout the fifteenth, sixteenth, and seventeenth centuries, the Ottomans were successful in copying, and even improving on, European

---

[41] See, for example, Ágoston, 'Flexible Empire'.
[42] Aksan, *Ottoman Wars*, 54–9.
[43] Ágoston, *Guns*, 128–89.

weapons, by using models or the knowledge of skilled gun-founders or blacksmiths. However, they missed the scientific and bureaucratic innovations that took place in Europe during the Renaissance with its associated scientific revolution. While the overall effects of these movements on warfare became crucial by the end of the eighteenth century, they were less obvious before that. Galileo's firing tables had little practical value in an age when cannon lacked standardisation (before the mid eighteenth century); even fortress design and the building of fortifications, a field where the usefulness of mathematics for the military engineer seems most obvious, required only 'a minimum of geometry and a maximum of sound engineering common sense'.[44] The most successful engineers, such as the French master of siege warfare, Sébastien le Prestre de Vauban (1633–1707), combined these skills. However, the aggregate effect of new knowledge and intellectual techniques, accumulated through experiments with new weapons and fortifications, and through the systematic study of the enemy's military strengths and weaknesses, was crucial in the long run.

The works written by Lazarus Freiherr von Schwendi (Emperor Maximilian II's captain-general in Hungary from 1565 to 1568), Giorgio Basta (Emperor Rudolf II's commander in Hungary and Transylvania from 1596 to 1606), Raimondo Montecuccoli (field marshal and commander-in-chief of the Habsburg armies from 1664 to 1680), and Miklós Zrínyi (Nikola Zrinski, a Hungarian/Croatian statesman and military leader, 1620–64) contained astute observations on the strengths and weaknesses of the Ottoman military and on how to defeat it. Luigi Ferdinando Marsigli, a Bolognese military engineer and polymath, who fought against the Ottomans in Habsburg service in the 1680s and 1690s, compiled the best concise description of the contemporary Ottoman army (*Stato militare dell'Imperio ottomano*, 1732).[45] Most of this knowledge was systematised and taught to the ever-growing number of military engineers and officers in newly established military academies.[46]

Military treatises such as those that Schwendi, Montecuccoli, or Marsigli wrote about the Ottoman army were wanting in the Ottoman Empire. That is to say, the Ottomans lacked works that would systematically describe the available resources, and military strengths and weaknesses of their opponents. Even more important was the lack of Ottoman war and naval academies and ministries. Starting under Richelieu (1585–1642), the French ministries of war and the marine had, by the mid seventeenth century, emerged as central bureaucratic

[44] Wolf, 'Commentary', 33.
[45] The best analysis of these works remains Parry, 'Manière de combattre'.
[46] See, for example, Hale, *Renaissance War Studies*, Chapters 8, 10.

organisations responsible for the planning and conduct of war. Other European states followed suit. The Engineering Academy was opened in Vienna in 1718 in order to train Habsburg subjects in military architecture, a field that had traditionally been dominated by foreign engineers from Italy, the Holy Roman Empire, and France. The Military Academy in Wiener Neustadt was opened in 1752, and the institution had 400 places by 1769.[47]

Staffed by administrators, clerks, soldiers, engineers, and map-makers (whose importance is discussed in Chapter 9), European war ministries were responsible for a wide array of tasks – from weapons improvement to clothing, and from training to the supply of weapons, food, and fodder. Improvements in weapons technology, organisation, and logistics owed much to the experiments of such ministries. They were instrumental in improving the effectiveness of European resource mobilisation, recruitment practices, and weapons and munitions industries. The new types of knowledge accumulated, taught, and systematised in the new European bureaucratic centres of war-making could not be transmitted easily. These academies also trained the new cadres of officers who were familiar with the latest improvements in military-related sciences and skills that Ottoman officers usually lacked. Moreover, as contemporary Ottoman observers recognised, the number of officers (including non-commissioned officers) and the ratio of officers to rank-and-file was substantially higher in the Habsburg armies than in their Ottoman counterparts. As a result, Habsburg commanders were better able to control their armies, which were organised into smaller and more agile units than the officers in the Ottoman army.[48]

Equally importantly, by the end of the seventeenth century the Ottomans seemed less capable of adjusting their military personnel and tactics to the changed nature of eighteenth-century warfare, which in east-central Europe was dominated by open battles rather than sieges. This failure to adjust was due partly to Ottoman military culture, but also partly to Ottoman successes in siege warfare – the dominant type of warfare throughout the 150-year period of Ottoman confrontation with the Habsburgs in Hungary. The Habsburg military, fiscal, and bureaucratic reforms of the sixteenth and seventeenth centuries, including the establishment of a standing army with related bureaucratic and fiscal institutions responsible for manning and supplying it, as well as actual

---

[47] Hochedlinger, *Austria's Wars*, 124, 306.
[48] Part of a process examined by Rogers, Chapter 10, below.

experience in pitched battles, ultimately brought about a shift in the balance of military power towards the Habsburgs.

The strength of the European armies and the weaknesses of the Ottoman military were also noticed by Ottoman observers. Ibrahim Müteferrika (1674–1754), the Hungarian renegade and founder of arabic letter printing in the Ottoman Empire, identified as early as 1732 those characteristics that, in his opinion, ensured the strength of the European armies, and argued that it was precisely the absence of these elements that weakened Ottoman military capabilities. He praised the structure of the Christian armies; the balanced proportions of infantry, cavalry, and dragoons; and the excellent cooperation between these groups. Other laudable qualities included: superior methods of training and drilling soldiers, discipline, the high proportion of officers (at least 25 per cent), the competency of the high command, the order and defence of the camps, military intelligence and counter-intelligence, 'geometric' troop formations, *la manière de combattre*, and the volley technique to maintain continuous fire.[49] His evaluation repeated many of the conclusions of contemporary European observers, including Luigi Ferdinando Marsigli or Maréchal de Saxe. In 1732, the latter had claimed that 'it is not valour, numbers or wealth that they [the Ottomans] lack; it is order, discipline and technique'.[50]

---

[49] Müteferrika, *Milletlerin Düzeninde*, 73–112.
[50] Quoted in Parker, *Military Revolution* (1999 edn), 128.

7   Ottoman military organisation in south-eastern Europe, *c.* 1420–1720

Rhoads Murphey

The main focus of this chapter's analysis of early-modern Ottoman military practice in the European sphere is the Empire's institutional development and the expansion of its capacity for waging war. A number of developments impacted on the Ottomans in the period between the mid fifteenth and early eighteenth centuries, resulting in changes to the bureaucratic structure and procedures supporting military operations. There were substantial shifts in the Empire's geo-political situation; the size and composition of the Ottomans' own armies altered, as did the manner of and methods for waging war; and there were significant changes in the pace of military change amongst the Empire's traditional adversaries, including the Austrians and Hungarians. In response, the bureaucratic structures and procedures supporting Ottoman military operations changed and developed. Because this was an ongoing process it is difficult to pinpoint a particular point of critical change from the experimental and immature phases of military organisational and institutional development, to the achievement of a fully developed institutional infrastructure capable of supporting mass recruitment and multi-seasonal wars, which became typical after *c.* 1600. It is therefore appropriate to consider the ways in which, in addition to maintaining parity with their European counterparts in terms of weapons technology and battlefield tactics, the Ottomans managed to generate a process of 'continuous military revolution' in the organisational, bureaucratic, and institutional aspects of the warfare that was sustained right up to the 1720s. For the Ottomans, the question was how best to confront multiple and ongoing hurdles and challenges, a prospect they addressed by seeking new solutions, by adopting a stance of bureaucratic flexibility, and by a willingness to adapt traditional procedures to new military realities. Stasis or stagnation in its military methods would have spelled doom for the Empire, but even more so would institutional stagnation or atrophy; and it is this latter aspect of Ottoman adjustment to the changing conditions in early-modern warfare that will be at the forefront of this assessment of the Ottomans' continuous military revolution.

While many have criticised the tactical performance of the Ottoman army during the 1683 siege of Vienna, from the standpoint of preparation, mobilisation of men, and provision of logistical support on an unprecedented scale, it was an unqualified success. Up to the first decades of the eighteenth century, the Ottomans surpassed their central European contemporaries in their ability to mobilise and support large armies in the field. Three broad phases of institutional and bureaucratic development bolstering the military preparedness of the Ottomans can be identified. In the first, lasting roughly from 1420 to 1520, control over the military was gradually wrested from the hands of military enterprisers such as the march lords who commanded a large reservoir of self-remunerating, self-regulating light cavalry raiders called the *akinci*. The second phase, from *c.* 1500 to 1570, witnessed the emergence of mechanisms for state control – eventually a near monopoly – over military provision through the development of an advanced financial and administrative apparatus, itself sustained by a period of monetary stability and budgetary surplus. In the final phase, between *c.* 1570 and 1720, bureaucratic norms and procedures were continuously adjusted to cope with the challenge of supporting burgeoning, cash-paid, standing armed forces during an era of budgetary constraints, endemic cash shortage, and revenue shortfall.

In all three periods there were challenges for a central authority attempting to rationalise and standardise procedures for waging war efficiently, but the need for efficiency maximisation was greatest in the last of these, characterised as it was by mounting financial pressures. Furthermore, it was at this stage that the Empire first faced rival military institutions comparable in scale with their own, in some cases developed in imitation of Ottoman military practice. The resulting competition for pre-eminence placed even greater pressure on the Ottomans to enhance and increase their own levels of efficiency to keep pace with the modernisation and expansion of capacity being achieved by formerly weaker competitors. In what follows, some greater attention will accordingly be devoted to this final, crucial phase of organisational development, and in particular to two related aspects of Ottoman military organisation: arrangements for feeding the army and methods of mobilising forces and maintaining discipline. The connection between diet and discipline on the one hand, and the physical and psychological well-being of soldiers on the other, had always been recognised by Ottoman military planners, and retaining their competitive edge in this sphere of military provision was something they worked hard to maintain from the fifteenth century onwards. The advance mobilisation, storage, and rapid and efficient distribution of supplies to active military fronts was a particular Ottoman strength and is probably the least appreciated aspect of Ottoman military proficiency.

In order to set developments in the period from 1570 to 1720 into context, it would be helpful at this juncture to compare the divergent trajectories of the Ottoman and Habsburg Empires in the process of centralisation and concentration of state power, and to provide an account of the first two phases of Ottoman military development.

Administrative cohesion and bureaucratic structures in the Habsburg and Ottoman Empires

Traditionally, the evaluation of military systems has accorded an undue weight, sometimes bordering on apotheosis, to the achievements and exploits of larger-than-life personalities who were perceived to have profoundly altered the course of historical events. The Ottomans and their European contemporaries are no exception to this general rule. In the anti-Ottoman wars of the fifteenth century, John Hunyadi acquired a legendary status in his own lifetime and became a subject of national myth after his death, largely because of his successful defence of Belgrade in 1456. Similarly, Eugene of Savoy, Belgrade's temporary liberator in 1717, also acquired legendary and later mythical status in traditional European historiography. Yet if the personal qualities of an exceptional commander were on occasions crucial to success in individual campaigns and battles, more important than these exceptional individuals – who were not reproducible and unlikely to emerge more than once a century – was the strength of the underlying military systems. After Eugene's brilliant successes against the Ottomans in back-to-back campaigns, one defensive (at Petrovaradin in 1716) and the other offensive (against Belgrade in 1717), his successors' failure twenty years later in the anti-Ottoman wars of 1737–9 to match his record can be attributed only in part to poor leadership. The problems besetting the early-eighteenth-century Austrian army were above all organisational, linked to the inadequacy of their military planning process and the ad hoc and unreliable systems for delivery of basic supplies to the army. The failures in Austria's military systems were cruelly exposed in the first and second Silesian wars of 1740–2 and 1744–5 respectively, which revealed unresolved problems arising from the related issues of institutional fragmentation, poor communications, and a lack of centralised planning. These resulted in serious military inefficiencies that undermined battlefield performance. In response, a reform agenda was announced in 1749 – the *Regulament und Ordnung des gesammten kaiserlich-königlichen Fuss-Volks* – though this is best regarded as a proclamation of intent, since many of the initiatives it promised only came into effect towards the end of Maria Theresa's long reign.[1] The transformation and rapid growth of the Austrian monarchy's capacity for war as judged from its army transport services in the period between the mid 1750s and 1780 was certainly impressive when compared to the situation during the War of the Spanish Succession (1701–13). Then, the Habsburg Empire's supply system had a well-deserved reputation as 'probably the worst in western Europe'.[2] During the Austro-Ottoman conflict of 1714–18, Eugene of Savoy, despite his brilliance on the battlefield, struggled largely unsuccessfully against the weight of custom and long-established practice to introduce an element of cohesion and rationality into the Austrian military system. In spite of his thirty-three-year term as president of the *Hofkriegsrat* (Aulic War Council) between 1703 and his death in 1736, the general left a chequered legacy characterised overall by institutional stagnation or even regression, and it is generally agreed that he was a much better fighter than he was an administrator. Real progress was made only after 1749, as part of broader centralising reforms.[3]

In the case of the Ottomans it was the *strength* of their underlying military systems, rather than individual leadership, that provides the main explanation for the sustainability of their presence in the northern Balkans, whether in the mid fifteenth or the early eighteenth century. In his account of the slow and incremental process of advance towards a Habsburg-style absolutist system in central Europe, Peter Wilson attributes key importance to the development of 'the bureaucratic (or institutional) infrastructure necessary to put executive authority into practice' as one of the key elements supporting political power; and he notes in particular 'the importance of written culture and methods of record keeping' as significant drivers of the capacity to exercise political (and by extension military) power.[4] As a state based on the circulation of paper and orders of various types emanating from the centre, the Ottomans developed an early and precocious capacity for the storage and circulation of information in written form, so that record-keeping and central control over the circulation of information were already well advanced in the Ottoman Empire by the middle decades of the fifteenth

---

[1] On the *Regulament* of 1749, see Duffy, *Army of Maria Theresa*, 76.
[2] McKay, *Prince Eugene*, 39.
[3] On Kaunitz's reforms, see Fichtner, *Habsburg Monarchy*, 75–6.
[4] Wilson, *Absolutism*, 36.

century.[5] This contrasts with the incompleteness of record-keeping procedures and habits elsewhere until much later. In the Austrian monarchy, for example, the establishment of the *Kriegsarchiv* in 1711, which provided a means for tracking, monitoring and enforcing compliance with state orders, was noted as an epoch-making event.[6]

A comparison of the performance and efficiency of Ottoman armies with their counterparts in western Europe raises the question as to why the Ottomans elected neither to offer financial incentives or develop profit-sharing mechanisms, nor to develop a fully fledged system of military entrepreneurship comparable to the western model. The short answer is that Ottoman Empire had achieved a concentration of resources and had developed administrative mechanisms for extracting them through its control over taxation and its ownership of land to a far more advanced degree than typically encountered in the monarchical systems of western Europe in the early-modern period. The Ottomans thus had no pressing need to devise new methods of securing the cooperation of a socially dominant class of landed nobility with hereditary status as encountered in most European social contexts. Ottoman military planners were relieved of the necessity of cajoling regional elites into cooperation with the state's military aims, or of convincing them of the mutual profitability to both state and private investors of confronting the dynasty's rivals and the monarch's enemies on the field of battle. Ottoman power-sharing arrangements with provincial elites were based more on political compromise than on a calculation of the mutual profits to be derived from cooperation. Furthermore, in many Ottoman provincial contexts, especially the core regions of the Empire where the *timar* system was in place, the backbone of society consisted of the state's own agents and administrative representatives – the *timar*-holding class of cavalrymen – whose retention of their land assignments was contingent on military services provided to the state.

In the Ottoman system, raising the appropriate mix of specialised military personnel divided between cavalry, infantry, and artillery, and even the auxiliary services such as transport and commissariat, was not organised on a profit-and-loss basis both as a matter of principle and for good practical reasons. The use of private contractors carried the risk that concerns over the profitability of the enterprise and the need to satisfy financial vested interests might dominate over other more fundamental requirements including flexibility and the ability to adapt to the contingencies thrown up by campaigns. Outsourcing of either

[5] See Ágoston, 'Information', on Ottoman knowledge of rivals.
[6] Henderson, *Prince Eugene*, 82.

service provision or army supply to private interests risked a dilution of authority and division or confusion of energies devoted to meeting military objectives. Moreover, a system driven by strict adherence to the logic of military efficiency had clear advantages on which the Ottomans were able to capitalise. Overall, they were able to reduce the marginal costs of warfare, particularly the costs associated with the army's food supply. Aspects of the so-called 'command' economy, which offered the Ottoman ruler the authority to requisition grain supplies for the army at controlled prices or as tax levies well in advance of campaign, played a key role in containing war expenditure. Consequently, the Empire enjoyed an enhanced capacity to survive the wars of attrition, mounted by determined international coalitions, with which it was regularly faced. Because the Ottoman military elite, the Janissary infantry forces, consisted of waged subordinates rather than a group of semi-independent agents hired by the state on a contractual basis, as encountered in the western entrepreneurial model, the Janissaries remained, if not always subservient to and compliant with the wishes of their political masters, still chiefly beholden, as well as directly answerable to them. While a complete fusion of identity and interest between the state and military providers was nowhere either achieved or achievable in the early-modern era, the Ottomans came closer to realising that fusion of interests than any other contemporary polity.

To be sure, dominance of the military over political authority appeared to manifest itself from time to time in the Ottoman polity with the involvement of the sultan's *kullar* (the military/administrative corps) in decisions about the selection (enthronement) and deselection (dethroning, forced abdication) of Ottoman rulers. Yet these episodes constituted a limited and time-specific form of involvement in politics. And the 'rebellions' of the *kullar*, particularly in the tumultuous years of the late seventeenth century, were less concerned with issues of governance or the assertion of a dominant voice in the determination of state policy than with localised issues such as the level of compensation packages. Outside their demands for better wages, the *kullar* neither asserted nor gained a wider involvement in or dominance over state policy and imperial politics. Thus in terms both of bureaucratic efficiency and the subservience and serviceability to state and dynastic interest of its military structures and organisation, the non-proprietary and non-entrepreneurial model of warfare adopted by the Ottomans was well suited to the demands and challenges posed by the large-scale mobilisation of resources (both human and material) that characterised the pattern of warfare, especially after the mid seventeenth century.

The development of Ottoman military capacity and bureaucratic support systems, *c.* 1420–1570

The first clashes between the medieval kingdom of Hungary and the Ottomans over the disputed vassal status of the Bulgarian bans along the Danube frontier occurred in the 1360s.[7] But it was not until *c.* 1430, after the restoration of political order and territorial integrity caused by Timur's invasion of Anatolia in 1402, that the battle-lines in the northern Balkans were clearly drawn and the Ottomans found themselves in a position to resume their programme of military expansion. Warfare during the middle decades of the fifteenth century was still dominated by dispersed raids carried out against an extended frontier zone mostly by the freelance *akinci* raiders who cooperated with the sultan without being fully controlled by him. The transition from an Ottoman military dominated by dispersed warrior hordes to centrally mobilised armies bound to the sultan's independent political will and financed by his own treasury occurred gradually during the sultanate of Murad II (1421–44 and 1446–51). Traces of the old system of army mobilisation under commanderies controlled by the semi-independent lords of the march were in evidence as late as the 1440s. But thereafter, the resources available to the state through land registration and control over the revenues deriving from land, coupled with a developing bureaucratic apparatus capable of effectively assessing and extracting the Empire's agricultural, mineral, and commercial wealth, provided the capacity to lessen dependency on military provision from private sources and to mobilise modestly proportioned armies by drawing on the state's own agents, both the seasonally mobilised timariots and permanent standing forces.

Fifteenth-century Byzantine observers of the Ottomans' developing capacity for waging war noted the storming of the Hexamilion walls guarding the Isthmus of Corinth in 1446 as a watershed event. Apart from the use of siege cannon to destroy the walled defences, it was the sultan's role in mobilising and commanding his own independent troops (i.e. Janissaries and other standing regiments attached to his household troops), thus supplanting the once dominant role of the *akinci* commanders, that attracted particular notice in the contemporary sources. Earlier attacks against the same target in 1423 and 1431, led by the march lord Turakhan Beg, had deployed a motley collection of skirmishers and raiders from various parts of the Thessalian frontier. But Murad II's winter campaign, undertaken only weeks after his

---

[7] Szakály, 'Turco-Hungarian Warfare', 69–70 and nn. 5–6.

resumption of the throne in Edirne in September 1446, demonstrated his political dominance and independent command over all the Empire's resources including both *akinci* freelancers and Janissary 'slaves', as well as his possession of the technology for casting cannon in the field, all of which allowed him to deploy overwhelming and unanswerable force against his adversaries. Having imprisoned Turakhan for insubordination and lack of cooperation during the Varna campaign two years earlier, the sultan now pointedly assumed Turakhan's place as leader and asserted his claim to command obedience whenever (even for an unseasonable campaign in November–December) and wherever (even along the frontiers of the Thessalian march regarded formerly as Turakhan's exclusive reserve) he might choose.[8]

Both technologically and politically Murad II's assertion of exclusive authority over the army marked an important turning point in early Ottoman military development, though the definitive crossing of the divide from what were in essence ad hoc arrangements to fully developed military institutions occurred later as the result of the centralising bureaucratic reforms carried through by his son and successor Mehmed II after the fall of Constantinople in 1453. To be sure, from a technological standpoint it is evident that while the Ottoman cannon and siege methods were capable of clearing away loosely defended and hastily constructed fortifications such as the walls of Hexamilion, they were not sufficiently developed to achieve decisive results against more artfully constructed and heavily defended Venetian fortresses such as Corinth. Its surrender to the Ottomans in 1458 after a four-month siege was only achieved by what still remained the most effective method: starving the garrison into submission.[9] Possession of advanced technology was less critical to the Ottoman military success in this period (and in later ones) than their ability to sustain prolonged sieges and campaigns by mobilising large numbers of men and through the development of effective systems for rearming and provisioning their armed forces. In the case of the Cretan war, for instance, a series of campaigns required consecutive seasons of mobilisation over a twenty-four year period between 1645 and 1669.

None of their rivals was capable of mobilising manpower so readily and reliably. Largely as a result of the development of Ottoman independence in military recruitment and the emergence of an embryonic

---

[8] On Turakhan Beg's first and second lightning raids in 1421 and 1431, and his easy subduing of the Hexamilion target using only his own limited resources consisting of no more than 25,000 (according to other sources only about 10,000) horsemen, see Zakythinos, *Despotat*, II, 196, 212.

[9] See *ibid.*, I, 259–60.

institutional and bureaucratic framework to support military activity, the balance of military power shifted in the Ottomans' favour during the Hunyadi era of the 1440s and 1450s. The existence of a significant military reserve capacity allowed them to recover quickly from temporary setbacks such as the retreat from Zlatitsa in 1443 and to regroup the following season, attacking the European coalition forces led by Hunyadi at the battle of Varna in November 1444 with devastating effect.[10] Some notion of the disproportionate (even asymmetric) size of the two armies at Varna can be gleaned from İnalcık's account of the battle.[11] He suggests that the crusaders set out with a force of 16,000 knights collected from Hunyadi's allies and his own cohorts. Drawing only on internal sources, the Ottomans mobilised 30,000 to 40,000 troops from Anatolia who were joined by a further 7,000 Rumelian troops following their crossing of the Gallipoli Straits into Rumelia. When the volunteer and self-mobilising *akinci* forces are included, it seems probable that an Ottoman force totalling nearly 60,000 took the field against the invading crusader army of 16,000. This disparity in army size, already apparent in the 1440s, remained characteristic of Balkan confrontations until the early decades of the eighteenth century. For example, in the summer of 1717 an Ottoman grand vizier, Halil Pasha, led a force of approximately 150,000 troops to attempt the rescue of the 7,000-strong garrison defending Belgrade. He encountered a besieging force led by Eugene of Savoy, that had began the campaign with a nominal strength of 80,000, but that had been so depleted by disease, desertion, and casualties by the later phases of the siege in early August that its numbers had shrunk to no more than 50,000. Yet important though it was, the size of forces alone did not guarantee success, as Eugene's victory in this campaign (considered later in this chapter) indicates. Other aspects of the Ottomans' developing capacity for war must also be considered as part of the explanation for the Ottomans' overall record of success in the Balkans during the course of more than two-and-a-half centuries of intermittent but recurrent encounters with the armies of neighbouring states. By the mid fifteenth century, the Ottomans held the advantage not only with regard to the capacity for mobilising troops, but also with respect to the preparations for conflict, ranging from finance and food supply to the organisation of transport

---

[10] In his commentary on the events of 1443–4 Szakály ('Turco-Hungarian Warfare', 89), remarks on the Ottomans' ability 'rapidly [to] make up for their losses in manpower' and contrasts this position with the crusader armies who 'having been so painstakingly assembled [were] dispersed after the campaign and everything had to be started anew for the next enterprise'.

[11] İnalcık, 'Crusade of Varna', 306 n. 87, 308.

systems capable of reliably delivering concentrations of supplies to battle fronts and zones of conflict well in advance of campaign.

The increasing Ottoman capacity for war was not, of course, achieved without some strain on resources. But the allocation of resources in a planned and evenly distributed manner was a particular Ottoman forte, both in the fifteenth century and in later periods. For instance, after Mehmed II's capture of Corinth in 1458 he required some of his standing troops and the bulk of the Anatolian timariots to forgo the normal winter demobilisation and to accompany him to Skopje in Macedonia, where he remained until at least November, supporting his grand vizier's efforts against the Danubian frontier. The campaign resulted in the final and definitive annexation of Serbia.[12] In recognition of the extension of service obligations and the extraordinary demands placed on his *timar* cavalrymen, Mehmed awarded them a permanent increase in the fixed assessments (in effect rents) collected from tenants on their land, raising the assessment by 50 per cent, from 22 silver *asper*s per landholding unit (roughly 6 to 8 hectares), to 33 *asper*s.[13] Historians and his contemporaries have commented on Mehmed II's command capabilities and instinctive flair for tactical matters; his organisational reform and expansion of the Ottomans' institutional capacity for war is less widely recognised. His expansion of the central treasury's revenue yield to accommodate a threefold increase in the size of the Janissary corps, from the 3,000 to 4,000 inherited from his father to a force of some 10,000 to 12,000 by the end of his reign,[14] is a further aspect of his development of the seemingly boundless Ottoman military and naval capacity, which awestruck and clearly envious European observers invariably highlighted.

Significant though Mehmed II's reign was to the growth of institutional structures, the Ottomans' bureaucratic capacity subsequently continued to develop, notably in response to the expansion of the Empire's territory (Egypt and Syria were conquered in 1517 for example), and to support the larger field armies that were deployed in the European theatre following the conquest of Buda in 1541. The logistical demands of Ottoman armies have received detailed scrutiny from experts including Gilles Veinstein, whose work provides a useful summary of the general situation. His calculations for Sultan Süleyman's Hungarian campaign in 1543 indicate that the army was provided with 55,500 tonnes of barley (as fodder for the animals) and

---

[12] *Ibid.*, 324–5; Tursun Beg, *History*, 42–3.
[13] See Kemal Paşazade, *Tarih*, VII, 164.
[14] See *Encyclopaedia of Islam*, XI, 323.

about 17,800 tonnes of wheat and flour for baking loaves for the stand-ing troops. Pre-positioning grain at forward-supply stations located on the army's route of march to the front was a critical dimension of military planning and involved close communication between the centre and the provinces in the months leading up to the active cam-paign season. Veinstein also shows that preparations for Kara Ahmed Pasha's Transylvanian campaign of 1552 included the mobilisation of 30,000 sheep from the trans-Danubian principalities and a further 75,000 from the European provinces, to serve as the army's travelling larder.[15]

Despite the relatively modest size of this army – Ahmed's own forces were augmented by only 2,000 Janissaries and 3,000 cavalrymen of the Porte – and the limited scale of its supply needs, the Transylvanian campaign of 1552 demonstrates unequivocally that the Ottomans by the mid sixteenth century possessed the organisational capacity to secure advance procurement of grains. They had developed storage outlets for grain along the Danube and the naval transport required to move it to huge repositories and collection points such as Belgrade, and could efficiently support armies in what was, at the time, still relatively new and unfamiliar imperial territory north of the Danube, more than 1,000 km distant from the Empire's political and administrative centre at Istanbul. Moreover, by the mid sixteenth century, the Ottoman war machine had become a year-round enterprise. Its most frenetic period of pre-campaign activity occurred in the winter months between late November and early March, when the stocks of grain and ammunition, and other vital supplies in major garrisons and supply dumps, had to be inspected, inventoried, and replenished from reserve stores supplied by inland districts and transferred in time to coincide with the com-mencement of the campaigning season in late spring or early summer. The general troop mobilisation in some districts began even earlier. On the European front, where mobilisation of supplies became a more or less annual event in the Empire's history from the 1540s to the 1570s, the Ottomans quickly became both adept and experienced at supply operations. The region's proximity to productive agricultural zones and easy access via established riverine transport links gave the Ottoman Empire still further advantage over its adversaries. In contrast, only on relatively rare occasions during the long centuries of conflict with its Ottoman rivals between *c.* 1365 and *c.* 1720 was the Habsburg court in Vienna able to orchestrate or enforce consistent and semi-continuous inter-regional sharing or transfer of surpluses (whether cash reserves or

---

[15] Veinstein, 'Provisioning', 178, 180. See also Finkel, *Administration of Warfare*.

other basic supplies) sufficient in both quantity and kind successfully to confront Ottoman military might.

The burden of military provisioning was readily sustainable during the era of budgetary surpluses and monetary stability that lasted for the whole of Sultan Süleyman's long reign (1520–66). Although his thirteen imperial campaigns ranged from Buda to Baghdad, the relatively modest size of his standing forces, compared to the armies of the seventeenth century, helped to contain the cost of conducting his wars. The impact of war on Ottoman economy and society in times of budget deficit and greater fiscal restraint has attracted considerable scholarly debate.[16] However, recently discovered data on the income and expenditure of the Ottoman central treasury over the 250-year span between 1510 and 1760[17] reveals that despite the steady and inexorable growth in the size of all military units, from Janissary infantry to *sipahi* cavalrymen, the proportion of regular state revenues devoted, for example, to military wages was kept at surprisingly stable levels. The Ottomans became adept at tapping new resources, identifying new streams of irregular revenue, restructuring contributions in kind, and introducing new forms of excise taxes. They thus ensured that the burdens of supporting military activity and maintaining a high level of preparedness for war were evenly distributed and could be sustained by the general population. The Ottomans' capacity to mobilise for war seems to have been little affected by the persistent inflation and general financial instability associated with the closing decades of the sixteenth century.

To be sure, the support of ever larger armies and the dogged pursuit of ultimately indecisive campaigns conducted over successive seasons, beginning with the conflict with Iran between 1578 and 1590 and continuing almost without respite with the Fifteen Years' War with the Habsburgs (1592–1606), caused considerable social disruption, especially in the eastern provinces of the Empire, which faced Iran. However, there was no sign that shortage of men, money, or materials weakened Ottoman resolve to engage the enemy on either front. Figures from the Ottoman treasury relating to the wages paid to the standing infantry force, the Janissaries, between the reigns of sultans Süleyman I and Ahmed III (1703–30) reveal considerable consistency and stability with regard to the fiscal impact of the long-term growth in troop numbers and salaries needed to maintain the Empire's military profile in the age of siege warfare after 1600.

Overall, the data in Table 7.1 show that while the proportion of the budget devoted to military salaries occupied an exaggerated place

---

[16] See for example Genç, 'L'économie ottomane'.
[17] See Genç and Özvar, *Osmanlı Maliyesi*.

Table 7.1. *Salary payments to the Janissaries as a percentage of overall state treasury expenditure, 1548–1710 (in millions of* akçe*).*

Budget date	Janissaries' salary payments	Overall annual income (*Irad*)	Percentage for Janissaries' pay
1548	19.2	198.9	9.7
1631	77.2	271.6	28.4
1667	132.8	553.4	24
1692	119.7	938.7	12.8
1702	140.7	1,182.3	11.9
1710	144	1,300.9	11.1

Figures for 1548 (reign of Süleyman I) are taken from Murphey, *Ottoman Warfare*, 44, Table 3.4. All others are from Genç and Özvar, *Bütçeler*: reign of Murad IV (1631), I, 326; reign of Mehmed IV (1667), II, 170; reign of Ahmed II (1692), II, 224; reign of Mustafa II (1702), II, 248; reign of Ahmed III (1710), II, 287.

during the middle decades of the seventeenth century, the introduction of new revenue sources towards the end of the century allowed a return to a more 'normal' distribution of treasury resources. The strength of the permanent standing infantry corps rose from 12,131 in 1548 to 39,925 in 1702, reaching 43,562 in 1710, but their share of the budget did not increase significantly.

Ottoman record-keeping practices and communications capabilities, and some comparisons with the bureaucratic structures in contemporary European states

To achieve a clearer picture of the systems underpinning Ottoman military power, it would be useful at this point to look in some detail at the Empire's administrative structures. From the earliest period of Ottoman imperial expansion, efficient management of resources had been linked to and was dependent on the growth of an administrative apparatus capable of communicating the wishes of the sovereign to the provinces and of processing incoming reports from the provinces concerning local supplies, material conditions, and the degree of local compliance with resource-sharing demands issuing from the centre. At the micro-administrative – that is, the municipal – level of imperial administration, it was the *kadi*'s court that served as a clearing house for the exchange of information and as a general communications nexus, and it is no accident that the standard accounts of Ottoman conquests in court chronicles habitually refer to the installation of a *kadi* as the first step towards the introduction of the Ottoman regime in a newly conquered province. Contemporary histories also accord a role equal to that of the *kadi* to security officials such as the commander of the local garrison (*dizdar*) and mobiliser of the district's timariot forces (*sancak bey*) in the stabilisation of such territories.[18] Throughout the Empire, central administration communicated with the localities using the same agents, the *kadi*, and did not have to contend with other intermediaries with strongly entrenched local influence. The standard term of appointment for *kadi* was under two years,[19] and grades, salary rates, and terms of employment were all strictly regulated. As a result, although the risks of corruption and subversion of state objectives could never be entirely eliminated, on the whole the centre could rely on swift compliance with its wishes at the local level thanks to this cadre of loyal and educated administrative agents. The production of paper evidence and standardised notarial procedures for verifying payments, registering guaranteed prices in local markets, and confirming safe delivery of military and civilian consignments, as well as a host of other data collection and verification services, were key areas of responsibility for a *kadi*. Without their input, the smooth running of military procurements, the balancing of civilian and military demands on regional food stocks, and the transfer and transport of available food surpluses for military use – all key tasks directly related to Ottoman military efficiency – would have been unachievable.

When normal procedures failed, the *kadi* was expected to step in and sort out the problem, and their use as all-purpose 'fixers' enhanced the government's ability to react swiftly and to manage local crises. All imperial edicts (*ferman*) were kept and often registered in duplicate copies (*suret*) logged into the *kadi*'s running register of court business (the *sicil*). The *kadi* played a key role in the dissemination of edicts issued by the imperial council in Istanbul to the relevant authorities at the sub-municipal levels of the village and wider suburban districts within his township's jurisdiction. Additionally, they were responsible for the inbound stage of the communications process, from locality to centre. Their feedback and assessments on the scale and pace of local progress in meeting the state's demands formed a key dimension of the efficient execution and conclusion of official business.

---

[18] See for example Tursun Beg, *History*, paragraphs 12 (p. 45), 14 (p. 46).
[19] The norm was twenty months: *Encyclopaedia of Islam*, IV, 375.

While the Ottoman judiciary played no direct role in military procurements as purchasing agents or suppliers to the military, its administrative assistance, particularly in the area of monitoring compliance with the terms of state supply contracts and applying fines and other punishments for non-compliance, was key to the overall success of the undertaking. Standardised forms for accounting and reporting were universal throughout the Ottomans' core central provinces, where direct taxation was applied, and their application to newly acquired territories made it possible to impose standard demands and expect standard levels of compliance across a wide territory without having to renegotiate terms or reinvent basic administrative structures. Multiple *suret* of standard requests for graduated taxes and provisions, calculated according to regular fixed rates imposed on each tax household (*hane*) within a given tax district, could be sent out easily to multiple recipients and communicated to both taxpayers and collectors easily and well in advance of the commencement of the campaign season. The standardisation of basic rates and methods for assessment and collection made the task of supplying grain to the army highly efficient. Moreover, the practice of fining those who failed to provide their allocated provisions, or commuting the balance to a cash payment, also made it easier to collect contributions. Paper reminders were issued in the event of incomplete or tardy payment, while those who met their obligations in full had this confirmed by a written receipt. Everyone involved in the process thus knew what was expected of them.

The paper trail that linked centre and locality and defined the mutual rights and responsibilities of the state and the individual was maintained by a system of standard accounting and accountability that was regularised, routinely accepted, and generally recognised by the taxpaying public in the central Ottoman lands from the mid sixteenth century onwards. More than the gunpowder revolution, it is this paper revolution that explains and typifies the dynamism of the Ottoman military system in its heyday. As we shall see, its application to roll-calls, troop musters, and salary distributions in the seventeenth and early eighteenth centuries, when the efficient use of resources became increasingly urgent, formed an important dimension of Ottoman military proficiency after 1570.

In contrast to the Ottomans, an advanced level of bureaucratic consolidation within the Habsburg imperial system occurred only from the middle decades of the eighteenth century. One indication of the Habsburgs' determination to achieve a degree of bureaucratic and fiscal centralism came with the decision in 1749 to maintain a permanent standing army force numbering 108,000, after the disastrous conclusion of the first and second Silesian wars.[20] Prior to that date, military funding came from irregular and unreliable sources, including loans, subsidies, and contributions, grudgingly awarded by a series of local provincial assemblies (*Stände*) dispersed throughout the Empire, that often proved uncollectable in practice. The organisation of military procurements, based on a decentralised system of private contracting, was even more chaotic. The same basic system that had prevailed during the Thirty Years' War (1618–48), whereby the proprietary regiment and its commanding officer, who was also its owner (*Inhaber*), was responsible for supply and provisioning, remained in place for the better part of a century after the conclusion of the war for want of a comprehensive alternative.[21] Regimental commanders accordingly became interested parties in the profits to be made from supplying their own troops with clothes, equipment, and food. Until the proclamation of the *Regulament* of 1749, this proprietorial system precluded the development of a rational and routine approach to army supply.

A regimental commander was above all concerned to recoup both the initial investment made to acquire the regiment and also his financial outlay on supplies. Such concerns overshadowed any commitment to more abstract notions such as *Dienst* or service to the ruler. Notions of loyalty or obligation to an entity as abstract and inchoate as 'the state' or even the dynasty were even less likely to dominate his thinking. Throughout Europe, war was still regarded as a legitimate means for gaining personal honour and profit at the time of Prince Eugene (d. 1736). He amassed a huge personal fortune during his lifetime and died one of the richest men in Europe. Such habits and practices, coupled with the fragmentation of jurisdiction and ownership, made it difficult for the state to audit or inspect its military units, enforce standard norms of discipline, or enhance military efficiency to any appreciable degree. Not only did the state or crown lack the bureaucratic capacity to intervene in internal regimental affairs, it even lacked the juridical right to do so.

With regard to the efficiency of revenue assessment and collection, seventeenth-century Austria had become a byword for ineptitude. During the near-continuous wars from 1689 to 1714, Austria was acknowledged as both the most debt-ridden and the least efficient resource extractor of all the major belligerents. She managed to collect only one-third of the income that existed on paper during the relative calm of peacetime; the record was even worse during the confusion of

---

[20] See Duffy, *Army of Maria Theresa*, 145; and Fichtner, *Habsburg Monarchy*, 68.
[21] Mears, 'Standing Army', 137.

war.[22] Field commanders frequently resorted to stopgap measures to secure the funds or food necessary for war, or had to stall and avoid engagement with the enemy. The territorial and jurisdictional complexity of the Habsburg Empire was undoubtedly part of the reason for delays and defaults, but the lack of institutional backup and management failures at the centre also contributed to the ramshackle state of army finances and provisioning.

A comparison of Ottoman military and bureaucratic efficiency in the seventeenth century with that which prevailed elsewhere in Europe thus reveals that it possessed significant advantages, particularly in the twin areas of food supply and provisioning on the one hand, and troop mobilisation and payment on the other. The Ottomans had an efficient central bureaucratic apparatus. Its ability to process and record requests for changes in the methods of assessment and forms of payment gave the Ottoman system great flexibility. Allowing taxpayers to switch (according to their ability to pay) between providing goods in kind, cash substitutes, or labour services (including transport) made the Ottoman campaign provisioning system more practicable and enforceable from the taxpayers' perspective; the same flexibility (and the record-keeping capacity that made it possible) gave the state the ability to compensate for deficiencies and deficits in one area by supplementary collections in another. After 1590, the increase in cash transactions and cash-in-lieu collections (*bedel*) for grain and other necessities of war made it possible further to rationalise and accelerate army supply by permitting on-the-spot grain purchases closer to active military fronts, drawing upon supplies put in place by advance bulk purchases made at low, state-supported prices, which prevailed at harvest time when supplies were plentiful.

Süleyman's European conquests during the first half of the sixteenth century gave an appearance of bureaucratic orderliness and economy. But his campaigning lacked the capacity for quick reaction to accommodate the changing demand profile of armies mobilised for prolonged stays in the field or multi-seasonal conflicts, which were necessitated by the new pattern of warfare and the extended geographical reach of the Empire in the high imperial era after the 1570s. The true test of Ottoman military efficiency was only truly confronted and met under the more challenging conditions of war and army provisioning characteristic of the expanded infantry armies associated with seventeenth-century warfare. Overcoming and accommodating budgetary gaps and cash-flow problems represent only one dimension, and not necessarily

---

[22] McKay, *Prince Eugene*, 16, 145.

the most important, of the many changes in organisation and approach needed to keep pace with the change in duration, intensity, scale, and geographical dispersion characteristic of war in the new period. To cope with these changes in the pattern of warfare after the 1570s, the Ottomans needed to achieve new levels of efficiency in two particular areas: management of the army's food supply, and management of troop mobilisation and payment. The remaining sections of the chapter will be devoted in large part to these two key areas.

Management of the army's food supply during the long seventeenth century, *c*. 1570–*c*. 1717

Published data on Ottoman campaign provisioning in the seventeenth century suggest an assessment and collection system that was responsive to place and circumstance. What is interesting in the context of this analysis is less the extent of contributions or the apportionment of these, but rather the high levels of taxpayer compliance and the Ottomans' success in the collection of the apportioned amounts. In the case of Ferhad Pasha's 1590 Caucasian campaign, for which 193,400 tax households were assessed, the requisition quotas were sufficient to meet five-sixths of the army's requirements during the campaign, supplies being delivered well in advance of the army's arrival to predetermined depots along the route of march.[23]

Although the sophistication and achievements of the Ottomans' military supply system should not be exaggerated, nonetheless by early-modern standards their soldiers were well provided for. In the case of the Danube front, the Ottomans' ability to pre-position quantities of grain sufficient to sustain large armies by advance shipments using both sea and river transport was unquestionably a key reason for their military success in this theatre. Their ability to stock and re-provision major fortresses along the Danube enabled them to withstand long sieges and to supply their field units during offensive campaigns. Their success in holding out for so long under sustained pressure by the coalition forces of the *Sacra Ligua* during the 1690s can also be attributed to this ability to deliver a virtually uninterrupted stream of supplies to their forces defending a wide front along the Danube.[24]

---

[23] See İnalcık and Quataert, *Ottoman Empire*, 534, Table II.18.
[24] On the advantage gained by the Ottomans from the relatively advanced state of their logistical systems by comparison with their Habsburg opponents during the reign of Mustafa II (1695–9), see Majer, '17. yüzyılın', in particular p. 193.

The special care paid by the Ottomans to the adequacy of the soldiers' diet was undoubtedly based on a calculation of the physical, spiritual, and material benefits to be derived from having a well-fed, well-clothed, and regularly paid soldiery. While cases of mass desertion and collective insubordination were not unknown, Ottoman sensitivity to the needs of their troops made such events rare. When military provisioning failed or was disrupted, the consequences for their forces were devastating. The Ottomans' military record over the course of their 150-year occupation of central Hungary was remarkably free from such disruptions; and when they did occur they were generally explicable by exceptional conditions that in the main had little to do with planning failures and more to do with operational circumstances, adverse weather, or other intangibles such as psychological stress or the breakdown in relations between army command and the rank-and-file. For example, the loss of Esztergom to a Habsburg army under Mansfeld in September 1595 resulted neither from the strength of the enemy's siegeworks nor from the exhaustion of the Ottoman garrison's food and water supply, but rather from the demoralisation and psychological fragility of the garrison defenders after more than two months of active siege and two failed relief efforts. Three years later, the campaign to recapture the key fortress of Varad (Oradea) in Transylvania failed because of the insecurity of regular supply routes, which were disrupted by attacks on supply convoys along the Danube and Tizsa rivers. This led to a catastrophic collapse of supply networks.[25] As a result, some Ottoman troops, retreating from Varad in the late autumn of 1598, were driven to disobedience and desertion, while others succumbed to disease, in particular gastric disorders such as dysentery, brought on by poor diet. Yet this example of military disaster caused by a collapse of the supply system remains unusual.

During the Polish–Turkish War of 1620–1, Osman II's campaign against Hotin, although well planned and prepared, unravelled because of the length of the Ottoman supply lines that extended far to the north in Polish–Ukrainian borderland north of Kamenetz-Podolsk. Unlike the case of Esztergom in 1595, it was the fear rather than the reality of shortages that undermined the army's morale. Afraid of a military collapse, the sultan assaulted the fortress before its defences had been sufficiently weakened. When these attacks failed, the pressure on the sultan to authorise immediate demobilisation proved irresistible; his army then suffered because of the exceptionally long retreat.

---

[25] Knolles, *Generall historie*, 1110; Soranzo, *Ottoman*, fo. 26b.

Similarly, faced with supply uncertainties during Eugene of Savoy's prolonged blockade and investment of Belgrade between 15 June and 24 August 1717, the Ottoman troops (both garrison defenders and relief forces) suffered something akin to panic. Throughout the course of the campaign the Ottoman forces had worries about their overall strategic position that extended far beyond the conflict zone around Belgrade. Part of Eugene's very effective strategy was to disable and disrupt Ottoman communications in the interior by carrying out foraging raids and attacks deep into Ottoman territory in northern and central Serbia, penetrating far to the south and seriously affecting the safe passage of men and supplies along the access route via the Morava River all the way north to Belgrade.[26] Insecurity is both a state of mind and an objectively verifiable condition, and although the contagion of fear was not commonly associated with Ottoman soldiers, especially the battle-hardened Janissaries, on this occasion it caused an Ottoman mass retreat from a position of apparent tactical advantage. Eugene's operations had proved the effectiveness of disrupting Ottoman supply lines. However, he had accomplished this by mobilising rapidly and then putting the Ottomans under pressure from the very start of the campaigning season, and such a feat was neither easily achievable nor frequently repeatable.

One method used by the Ottomans to prevent supply disruptions from affecting a campaign, which reveals the strength of their bureaucratic and institutional structures, was to provide at least part of the elite soldiers' diet from the high-calorific, nutritious food source provided by the sheep herds – the army's travelling larder – that accompanied their armies on campaign. Meat supplies were arranged via the regularly updated and seasonally adjusted provision of price supports (*zarar-i lehm*), and allowed the Janissaries in particular to receive a reliable daily meat ration of 60 *dirhem* (about 200 g), even though this added significantly to the campaign budgets.[27] Whether Ottoman troops fought more fiercely and determinedly and consistently maintained a higher morale than their opponents because of their superior diet may be debated, but this is clearly suggested by the available evidence.

Management of troop mobilisation and payment during the long seventeenth century, *c.* 1590–*c.* 1720

Alongside food supplies, pay and service conditions were significant factors in maintaining troop morale and ensuring good discipline and

---

[26] Raşid, *Tarih*, II, 182a, 183a.
[27] Petrosian, *Mebde*, fos. 67a–b; Murphey, *Ottoman Warfare*, 89–90; Genç and Özvar, *Osmanlı Maliyesi*, I, 328.

military performance. Guaranteeing that sufficient coin was on hand or readily deliverable to safe areas near the front to pay regular salaries as well as bonuses for exceptional acts of bravery was a further aspect of campaign planning. Money played a crucial role both in incentivising soldiers and in discouraging disruptive behaviour, and constituted one of the commander's main inducements for ensuring high levels of performance and dedication from his troops. Controlling how and when the money was distributed was a key aspect of a commander's role and leadership that could have a decisive impact on the outcome of battle. In paying the forces, military commanders relied upon the clerical services of a dedicated band of administrators who verified muster rolls, cross-checked the identity of each payee against centrally maintained registers, and carried out on-the-spot inspections. Unsurprisingly, the call-up of this body of officials constituted a primary aspect of pre-campaign preparations.

The elaborateness and efficiency of general Ottoman record-keeping procedures are clearly evident in the campaign of the grand vizier Silhadar Ali Pasha against the Venetian positions in Corinth, Nauplion, and other parts of the Morea in 1715.[28] Out of a total of 110,364 men, the infantry forces (87,520) outnumbered the mounted troops (22,844) by a factor of 4 to 1, which placed the Ottoman army squarely amongst its peers in early-modern Europe in terms of its composition.[29] Although seasonally mobilised provincial cavalry was no longer a numerically or tactically important part of the army, strict standards of discipline and timeliness in reporting for duty were still maintained. As punishment for his late attendance with insufficient troops, one senior figure in the Anatolian army, the governor of Karaman, was relieved of his command.[30] In this campaign, the maintenance of strict discipline and prevention of unnecessary or unsanctioned damage to civilian life or property were of high priority both during the march to the front and while on operations there. This was not invariably the case in Ottoman campaigns, but was regarded as especially important in 1715 since the Morean campaign was intended as a preliminary to the re-establishment

---

[28] As well as Ottoman records, the sources include the journal of Benjamin Brue, who served as interpreter to the French embassy in Istanbul between 1710 and 1740, published posthumously in Paris; Brue, *Journal*.

[29] In *c.* 1740 Maria Theresa's army was composed of a nominal force of 159,600 (with 108,000 effectives). Of these, infantry represented 75 per cent of the total force (119,600) and cavalry 25 per cent (40,000). See Duffy, *Army of Maria Theresa*, 145 and (for the nominal strength of the various regiments) 63, 91.

[30] Clearly considered dramatic events worthy of notice, such leadership changes occupied a prominent place in all accounts of the campaign; see Brue, *Journal*, 2–3; Agha, *Nusretname*, II.ii.332; Raşid, *Tarih*, II, 108b.

of Ottoman rule after hostilities concluded. The Ottomans claimed their government would be more just and less harsh than that of the Venetian regime, so it was important that any excesses or unsanctioned exactions by soldiers against the civilian population be kept to a minimum. The execution by a military tribunal of six timariots from the Anatolian districts of Menteshe and Hudavendigar together with their district commander (*alay beyi*) illustrates how the Ottomans enforced a strict code of military discipline by means of well-established procedures. Even more than the dismissal of officers noted above, military executions had a significant effect in modifying the behaviour of soldiers of all ranks.[31]

Standardisation of service conditions and the enforcement of performance expectations had been achieved by the Ottoman military system in earlier periods, when the Janissary corps formed a more manageable cohort of about 10,000 men. The challenge faced by the army in 1715 was how to ensure the preservation of these standards when this cohort had expanded to some 40,000. As noted above, one major means the commander had at his disposal for modifying soldiers' behaviour was pay. Development of accounting, auditing, and verification procedures that could operate effectively and efficiently on a mass scale posed a bureaucratic challenge that the Ottoman army successfully met in the time of Silahdar Ali Pasha. A complex system that, in outline, involved the verification of pay-entitlement certificates (*esame*) by a series of auditors, collators of pay records (*mukabeleci*), and the paymaster general's office (*sergi emaneti*), was established. But the commander too had to throw his weight against fraud and collusion in the acceptance of forged or altered pay documents. Ali Pasha's determination in this regard was confirmed by his summary execution of a highly placed official and former chief cavalry officer, Kara Osman, whom he had earlier appointed as military governor in Nauplion during his own absence in the south.[32]

The best means for ensuring maximum cooperation with mobilisation orders for cash-paid troops such as the Janissaries was to organise the distribution of the quarterly pay instalments (*kıst*) in a staggered and irregular way so that the Janissaries remained in rank until as near the conclusion of the campaign season as possible. Apart from posting guards on principal routes to prevent unauthorised departures,[33] the most effective method of encouraging attendance at roll-call was

---

[31] See Raşid, *Tarih*, II, 106a, 123a.
[32] Brue, *Journal*, 36; Raşid, *Tarih*, II, 128a.
[33] Brue, *Journal*, 37; Raşid, *Tarih*, II, 117b.

to delay the distribution of wages. In the 1715 Morean campaign, the first collective pay distribution took place only after the army had returned from the south to the plain of Nauplion on 21 September; and the second, a double *kıst* distribution of six months' pay arrears, was delayed until after the returning Ottoman force had re-crossed the straits and reached the plain of Larissa on 9 October.[34] Stringent accounting procedures ensured not just that those registered as absent (*na-mevcud*) were excluded from pay distributions, but that the pay certificates (*esame*) of persistent truants, particularly those belonging to the ranks of the standing cavalry, were permanently revoked. The issuing of receipts for grain allowances and pay, the validation of pay certificates, and the confirmation of attendance at the regular army inspections and roll-calls (*yoklama*) that fell between pay distributions all formed an important bureaucratic and record-keeping dimension of Ottoman military efficiency, which has been underestimated by scholars and deserves greater recognition.

Conclusion

Having now completed a full chronological circle, from the first crossing of the Corinth straits by the assembled forces of Murad II in 1446 and the siege of Corinth by his successor Mehmed in 1458, to the fully institutionalised, rationalised, and bureaucratised Ottoman army commanded by Ali Pasha against the same targets in 1715, it is appropriate to ask at what point the organisational, administrative, financial, and managerial revolution in Ottoman military practice achieved its fully evolved and mature form. The principles of central provision and bureaucratic management of resources, and the effective accumulation and re-distribution of those resources to achieve the state's war aims, were all fully operative by the reign of Sultan Süleyman, who was the first Ottoman sultan to manage the projection of Ottoman military power throughout the wider imperial space between the Tigris in the southeast and the Danube in the north-west. But rather than seeing the development of Ottoman military traditions and institutions as a static moment that crossed the divide between primitivism and modernism, or autonomy and state regulation, it is more useful to see the rationalising of Ottoman military provision as a continuous revolution whose final evolutionary phase was not reached until the era of large armies and multi-seasonal mobilisations typical of the mid-to-late seventeenth century.

[34] Brue, *Journal*, 59, 62; Raşid, *Tarih*, II, 130a, 133a.

The heightened scale and complexity of military organisation driven by technological developments in the age of siege warfare after the 1630s required a level of bureaucratic refinement and sophistication together with an enhanced efficiency in resource mobilisation that were not typical of the single-season, cavalry-dominated mobilisation pattern that prevailed during most of the sixteenth century. Ottoman military bureaucracy faced some of its most severe tests after 1630. Despite periodic setbacks and inevitable individual campaign failures, its organisational response to the challenges it faced kept it at the forefront of European military development until the early decades of the eighteenth century. At that stage, European states had caught up with the Ottomans, challenging them not only in terms of the scale of resources dedicated to the conduct of war, but also in the efficient management of those resources and in the effective enforcement of standards of service and troop discipline. The evolutionary trend that led to the increasing privatisation of military provision in the Ottoman Empire, evidenced by the fielding of recent recruits, and seasonally mobilised and paid 'mercenary' troops to fight in wars against Russia after 1768, was the opposite of the trend towards state-regulated, central military provision, which had by then become well advanced in contemporary European polities. The wheel had truly come full circle.

8 The transformation of army organisation in early-modern western Europe, c. 1500–1789

Olaf van Nimwegen

The framework: militia, mercenaries, and the standing army

The greatest problem facing the early-modern state was not fighting wars but maintaining and managing its armed forces. Especially in the fifteenth and sixteenth centuries, governments had to be wary of becoming hostages of the soldiers they had hired. As already noted in Chapters 3 and 4, the Florentine politician Niccolò Machiavelli (1469–1527) viewed mercenaries as a grave threat to the stable governance of a polity. In his *Arte della guerra* (1521), he argued that troops who depended for their livelihood on pay presented their employer with only three options: 'either [he] must keep them continually engaged in war, or must constantly keep them paid in peacetime, or must run the risk of their stripping him of his kingdom.'[1] Although his concerns were overstated, in the context of the Italian city-states they were understandable; there was a real risk of the *condottieri* turning against their political masters and seizing power for themselves. However, mercenaries were of course not a recent phenomenon.[2] Nor were infantry victories over noble heavy-cavalry-based armies, when the former were on the defensive; but in the fifteenth century, Swiss infantry successfully *attacked* mounted opponents in the open field. The Swiss did not need ditches, woods, brooks, or hedges to face a charge; armed with pikes and halberds they formed a living forest that could resist an attack from all sides.[3] The crushing victories won by the Swiss against the Burgundians and Habsburgs not only encouraged their employment as mercenaries by princes across Europe but also prompted Emperor Maximilian I (1459–1519) to imitate their organisation, weaponry,

---

[1] Machiavelli, *Art of War*, ed. and trans. Wood, 20.
[2] Cf. Chapters 3 to 5 in this volume.
[3] Verbruggen, *Krijgskunst*, 246, 291–306; Nicholson, *Medieval Warfare*, 49–50. Swiss tactics are discussed by Rogers in Chapter 10, below.

and tactical formation. The Italian states were amongst the first to feel the power of the 'new' infantry from the Holy Roman Empire: the *Landsknechte*. Impressed by the fighting strength of the Swiss and *Landsknechte*, Machiavelli championed the creation of a Florentine army also made up of infantry. However, because of the danger mercenaries posed to the political order, instead of hired soldiers he wanted to build his army on the citizens of Florence. Machiavelli believed that a militia would serve to ensure a close connection between the people and the state. Like ancient Rome, Florence's security should depend on its armed citizenry.[4]

Machiavelli's *Arte della guerra* was studied all over Europe, but his idea to substitute a militia for an army of mercenaries was deemed unfeasible and even unnecessary by his (near) contemporaries, hence the rise of the military enterprisers discussed in Chapter 4. Military authors such as the French theorist Raymond de Fourquevaux (1508–74) agreed that the *soldatesca* had many shortcomings, but instead of replacing them with armed citizens, he advocated a moral reform that would turn the unruly soldiers into disciplined troops. He admitted that this would not be easy, because most soldiers were more apt to do wrong than right. What mattered therefore was to compel the troops to do good, i.e., no looting or mutinies. This required that military laws govern the lives of the soldiers. In this way doing good would in the long run become second nature, because the soldiers could be forced to make changes, to which they would become accustomed, and then what had become customary would become natural and soldiers would serve the common good.[5]

In the 1580s the theme of a highly disciplined army was picked up by the Dutch humanist Justus Lipsius (1547–1606), who in 1589 published the *Politica*, of which Book V deals exclusively with armed forces.[6] To a large extent, Lipsius followed Machiavelli and Fourquevaux's train of thought. He was also greatly impressed by the Roman army and scorned the *soldatesca*. However, whereas Machiavelli wanted to do without them and Fourquevaux limited his goal to disciplining them so that they would no longer pose a threat to their employers and the populace, Lipsius sought to turn soldiers into one of the two pillars of the state – the other was bureaucracy. He saw this as the only way to put an end to the anarchy of the religious wars of his day.[7] In order to

[4] Wood, 'Introduction' to Machiavelli, *Art of War*, 27; Delbrück, *Geschichte*, IV, 25.
[5] Fourquevaux, *Instructions*, 94.
[6] Lipsius, *Politica* (citations throughout the chapter are to the 1590 Dutch translation).
[7] Oestreich, 'Lipsius', 58, 61–3; Oestreich, *Antiker Geist*, 21, 153; see also Oestreich, *Neostoicism*.

achieve his aim he envisaged an army composed of native front-line troops who were permanently under arms, and auxiliaries who were only to serve in times of war either in the field or in garrisons. Both the professional soldiers and the reserve were to be imbued with a sense of duty. This required moral education, regular drill, and bodily labour. The latter two would make soldiers pliant to follow orders, proficient in the use of their weapons and accustomed to hardships, and the first would mentally prepare them for this. Troops should practise sobriety in food and chastity, because 'the habit of voluptuousness robs a soldier of his strength and valour', Lipsius warned.[8] The foundation for Lipsius' ideas was the Roman Stoic philosophy with its emphasis on constancy in adversity and contempt for death.[9]

The influence of Lipsius was not limited to the intellectual sphere. The Nassau cousins, Maurice and William Louis, who together commanded the forces of the Dutch republic in the late sixteenth and early seventeenth centuries, applied his advocacy of discipline and drill with relish. However, Lipsius' plea for a standing army supported by a militia was too much ahead of its time. Until the second half of the seventeenth century, early-modern states were loath to be intimately involved in the maintenance of their troops. They regarded the upkeep of units as the private responsibility of the company commanders. The captains themselves were supposed to recruit, arm, clothe, and feed their soldiers; the government limited its activities to paying the troops. A standing army on the other hand required that the state take over many of the responsibilities of its officers. In order to understand this, it is necessary to define what a standing force is. I suggest the following definition: a standing army consists of professional troops, that is, their organisational- and command-structures remain in being in peacetime; officers and men alike are for their livelihood and career bound to a particular government.[10] When required, the companies could easily be augmented to a war footing without compromising unit cohesion and the necessary level of training. This development enabled states to field a powerful army within a matter of months. In this chapter, I argue that France under Louis XIV was the first state to realise the enormous advantages accruing from a nucleus army. True, the French *compagnies d'ordonnance*, founded in 1445, already constituted a permanent force, but even at full strength – approximately 9,000 men – its numbers

[8] Lipsius, *Politica*, 197–200, 208–10, 214 (quotation).
[9] Oestreich, *Antiker Geist*, 63–4, 66.
[10] See Trim, 'Introduction' to *Chivalric Ethos*, esp. 4–13; Nimwegen, *Crijchsvolck*, 11–12, 294–5.

were too small to meet the military requirements of the French kings.[11] Consequently, until the second half of the seventeenth century French monarchs had to rely on the nobles with their followers, newly raised mercenary companies, and hired Swiss regiments to fight their wars.[12] The Sun King demonstrated French military might in the Dutch war (1672–8) and the Nine Years' War (1688–97). By *c.* 1700 all European powers had standing armies.

The eighteenth century marks the highpoint of the standing army. In particular, the Prussians under Frederick the Great were the marvel of Europe. No other troops could compete with their level of discipline and training. As a result of the Prussian performance in the War of the Austrian Succession (1740–8) and the Seven Years' War (1756–63), all states tried to model their armies on the Prussian example. However, whereas at the outset draconian discipline was a means to an end, it increasingly became the goal itself. By punishing the slightest transgressions with inhumane severity, soldiers changed from fearsome warriors into mindless puppets.[13] This development fed the fear of critics of absolute monarchy that princes were intentionally transforming Lipsius' pillars of the state: from protectors against foreign enemies into instruments of internal oppression. The wheel had turned full circle again – the answer to the danger posed by paid standing armies seemed again to be citizen forces. The French Revolution (1789) and the dismal performance of the 'mindless' soldiers of the great powers against the French revolutionary armies led on the Continent to the reform of the standing armies into national armies of conscripts.

The remainder of my chapter is devoted to elaborating the above-mentioned issues. I will focus in particular on developments in the Dutch armed forces, which exemplify all the issues and trends mentioned.

Landsknechte: the era of the free soldier (sixteenth century)

Maximilian I of Habsburg is usually said to have been the founder of the *Landsknechte*. Through his marriage in 1477 with Mary of Burgundy he became ruler of the Burgundian possessions, which included the most wealthy provinces of the Netherlands. In order to ward off his many enemies he concluded contracts with military entrepreneurs to

---

[11] See Gunn, Chapter 3 in this volume, and sources cited there; cf. Fiedler, *Kriegswesen*, 27.

[12] Parrott, *Richelieu's Army*.

[13] Kunisch, *Fürst*, 178–80.

raise troops. Like all other early-modern rulers, Maximilian lacked the bureaucratic means to raise an entire army himself. He had at his disposal the *bandes d'ordonnance* founded by Charles the Bold in 1471, but the new way of fighting introduced by the Swiss required thousands of foot-soldiers. The *bandes* were modelled on the French *compagnies d'ordonnance*. Each *bande* was made up of 600 horse (men-at-arms and mounted archers), and 300 foot (archers, handgunners, and pikemen).[14]

The *Landsknechte* mirrored the Swiss in organisation, weaponry, and tactics, but were raised in the Holy Roman Empire. They were typically organised in regiments, usually of ten companies, each of between 300 and 400 men. Their weapons consisted of pikes, halberds, two-handed swords, and arquebuses, with the pikemen forming the backbone of the unit. Like the Swiss, they were drawn up in massive formations called *Gewalthaufen*, with a depth of forty to sixty men, and they copied Swiss tactics.[15] The close order, use of combined weapons, and discipline of the *Landsknechte* made them able to defeat numerically superior forces: in 1496 and 1498 they twice defeated Frisian armies that outnumbered them ten to one. The Frisian chronicler Worp van Thabor concluded that the Frisians lost both times because they put all their trust in numbers and an all out assault. '[The Frisians] went as a flock of sheep without a shepherd ... That is why they were defeated, because victory depends more on the art of fighting, than on strength or bravery.' What really mattered, Thabor continued, was that soldiers remain in formation and obey their superiors.[16]

Landsknechte were recruited by entrepreneurs for whom the running of a company or entire regiment was a means of living. Their contract stipulated the number of companies they had to raise and arm. Usually the entrepreneur himself took command over his troops as captain or as colonel if he had gathered an entire regiment. Recruiting took place in cities and towns; as a rule the captain set up his quarters in an inn and treated his potential employees to free beer. The conclusion of a contract was sealed by the payment of a bounty. The recruits then marched to a previously agreed town for muster. Until that moment the captain had to provide his men with food, because soldiers received their first pay only after their names had been added to the muster roll. The captains were compensated in part for their recruiting costs. In February

[14] Nicholson, *Medieval Warfare*, 51.
[15] See Rogers, Chapter 10 in this volume; Quaas, *Landsknechte*, 114–15, 120–1, 139, 168–9.
[16] Tyaerda van Rinsumageest, *Kronyken*, 237, 300 (quotation).

1567 the States of Utrecht paid an entrepreneur 700 guilders to raise 400 men in their province and adjoining territories.[17] The greater the distance of travel the higher the compensation offered. For example, if recruits for service in the Netherlands had to come from the County of Solms in the Holy Roman Empire, three guilders per man were paid.[18]

Becoming a *Landsknecht* meant leaving normal society and joining an organisation that, similarly to a monastic order, lived by its own rules. This does not of course mean that soldiers and monks lived a comparable life; on the contrary. Monks were supposed to be pious and chaste, whereas *Landsknechte* emphasised their manhood as expressed by their unruly behaviour and extravagant clothing. Drinking bouts were part of their daily life, and although uniforms were not introduced until the later seventeenth century, one could easily recognise *Landsknechte* by their colourful and baggy clothes. They could afford these because they were paid partly in cloth in lieu of ready money, which was always in short supply. Women and children accompanied the *Landsknechte*: wives with legitimate offspring and prostitutes with bastard children. The women washed and mended clothes, cooked food, and took care of the sick and wounded.

The *Landsknechte*, however, had another aspect. Their tactics on the battlefield required absolute obedience to their commanders if they wanted to stay alive. A lonely pikeman stood no change against an enemy armed with a sword or on horseback. Only when fighting as a group was he able to withstand an attack successfully. The *Landsknechte* consequently developed a very strong corporate identity. This made them redoubtable as a fighting-force, but also had the potential to make them a menace to their employers and the common people. Often disagreement arose regarding the length of service and the payment of arrears, and in these disputes the *Landsknechte* acted as a group as well. The accepted practice of supplementing pay with loot helped to meet their financial demands, but set an unhappy precedent for what they might do when those demands were not met – a precedent followed by troops of various nationalities, not only the *Landsknechte*.

The 'Sack of Rome' in 1527 by the German troops of Emperor Charles V left 8,000 to 10,000 civilians dead in the spiritual capital of Europe. In the 'Spanish Fury' at Antwerp in November 1576, the Spanish army of Flanders killed probably another 8,000 men, women, and children.[19]

---

[17] States of Utrecht to treasurer Jan van den Ham, 22 February 1567, UA, Staten van Utrecht Landsheerlijke Tijd 599.

[18] Contract with Count von Solms, 13 June 1585, NAN, Regeringsarchieven Geünieerde Provincies 152.

[19] Tracy, *Emperor Charles V*, 47; Parker, *Dutch Revolt*, 178.

The armies were in both cases owed large sums of money, although religious hatred also played a part in the brutality: many of the imperial soldiers who sacked Rome were Lutherans; and the Spaniards in Antwerp, the centre of radical Protestantism in Flanders, did not let slip the opportunity to slaughter heretics.

Of all sixteenth-century mercenaries, *Landsknechte* were especially difficult to control, because the troops themselves elected some of their officers and were directly involved in the administration of military justice. According to old wisdom those 'who want to gain honour with soldiers, must pay well and punish immediately'.[20] The *Artikelbrief* (Letter of Articles) regulated the command structure and disciplinary system of the *Landsknechte*. The oldest known *Artikelbrief* for the *Landsknechte* raised in the Netherlands dates from 1546.[21] The articles dealing with the management of the company stipulated the rate of pay – five guilders of twenty stivers per month of thirty days (art. I); the right of Charles V to appoint, without consulting the *gemeente* (community of common soldiers), the captains, ensigns, *veltweyfels* (sergeants), and the personal of military justice (sheriff and provost) (art. III); a prohibition on the unlawful assembly of the soldiers, i.e. that they gathered out of their own accord to make known their grievances (art. X); and finally that it was the duty of every soldier to carry out the orders of his superiors (art. XXXVI). Next to these four stipulations there were numerous articles that concerned penal offences, such as the looting of churches and farms; the destruction of images of saints and altars; the killing of townspeople, villagers, peasants, and clergy; and the raping of nuns and women.

The soldiers were verbally acquainted with the contents of the *Artikelbrief*. In case of a newly raised company, all troops then had to swear an oath of allegiance to their employer (for example the Emperor, the king of Spain or a Provincial States in the Low Countries). Next, the captain presented the officers to the soldiers and arranged the election of the 'common' offices. The staff of a company of *Landsknechte* was quite large. Besides the three 'great' officers (captain, lieutenant, and ensign), a sergeant, a *voerder* (first corporal), and two *gemene weyfels* (common corporals), it typically included a *fourier* (quartermaster-sergeant), a provost, a clerk, a surgeon, two or three drummers, one or two pipers, two bodyguards for the captain, three boy-servants – one for each of the great officers – and occasionally also a minister or priest, and a cook, all in all about twenty-two men.[22] The ensign

[20] Anon., *Der bussen meesterije*, 28.
[21] Groninger Archieven, Groningen, Netherlands, Familiearchief Van Ewsum 195.
[22] See for example Wijn, 'Noordhollandse regiment', 241.

was responsible for the colours, a large square piece of cloth painted in various hues and adorned with depictions. The colours were of significant practical use. During battle clouds of dust and powder obscured the vision of the soldiers, and the colours therefore served them as a rallying point. Its symbolic value was perhaps even greater. The colours embodied the company, and the ensign had to guard it therefore with his life.[23]

The responsibility of a *Landsknecht veltweyfel* was to assign to each soldier a place in the battle-array. This required that he be familiar with the experience, weapons, and equipment of each individual soldier. During a battle he was stationed behind the company and it was his duty to kill any soldier on the spot who fled. The *veltweyfel* was a great help to his captain, because, like no other, he knew the mood of the soldiers. His importance for the functioning of the company found expression in his rate of pay, which might be six times the pay of a common soldier. The office of lieutenant was still a novelty in the sixteenth century: the first ones were appointed around 1530. For a long time an ensign was considered of higher rank than a lieutenant, and paid accordingly, but because *Landsknecht* lieutenants were appointed by the captains it was they who were entrusted with running the captains' business during their absence, and so the lieutenant's status increased.

The *voerder* and *gemene weyfels* seconded the *veltweyfel*. However, their duties were not concerned with tactical matters only. Together with the quartermaster-sergeant they were entrusted with 'common' offices. All soldiers were eligible but in practice it was mostly the same persons that were re-elected for a new term of a month. The *voerder* had to have knowledge of legal matters, because during a criminal trial it was his duty to represent the accused soldier. The *Landsknechte* knew two forms of criminal justice: judgement by a court under the presidency of a military sheriff appointed by the colonel, and judgement by the common soldiers themselves. In the first instance a public trial was held in which the regimental provost acted as prosecutor. Appeal against the verdict was not possible. This meant in most cases that the convicted soldier was handed over to the executioner to be hanged or beheaded. The company clerk crossed out the soldier's name on the muster sheet and put a little gallows next to it. If a soldier, however, was accused of defiling the honour of the regiment, for example by murdering someone in a cowardly manner, he was handed over to the community to face a *spiesgericht*, a trial of pikes. All soldiers gathered in a circle and signified by show of hands whether they considered the accused guilty or not; if

---

[23] Nimwegen, *Crijchsvolck*, 34.

the former, he was sentenced to death. Often the rank-and-file troops formed a lane through which the accused had to go, and they stabbed him to death with their pikes.[24]

The *weyfels* looked after the interests of the soldiers when they had grievances. Usually this had to do with deductions for food, clothing, equipment, and weapons. Soldiers did not receive their pay directly but always through their captain, who was issued a monthly lump sum. The money was divided at his discretion amongst the soldiers, but only after deducting payment for the items he had advanced to them. Finally, it was the responsibility of the quartermaster-sergeant to assign each soldier a place to camp. This was a sensitive business, because all soldiers preferred the best spots, for example near a thicket for firewood or a well for water. Therefore, the office of quartermaster-sergeant was also an elected one to avoid accusations that some soldiers were always assigned the best locations.[25]

From free soldier to disciplined mercenary (late sixteenth century to first half of the seventeenth century)

The *Landsknecht* was the product both of medieval society with its division into estates and self-regulating guilds, and the myriad of principalities and city-states that made up the Holy Roman Empire. The German historian Hans Delbrück defined a *Landsknecht* as 'a free soldier who changed his place of employment [at will]'. *Landsknechte* limited their feelings of loyalty to the regiment in which they served, and did not concern themselves with the political and religious issues of the wars in which they fought: they served whoever paid them.[26] Consequently, they became unruly and mutinous as soon as their pay ceased. Wealthy employers such as Emperor Charles V or Philip II of Spain were not greatly worried by this. They sat out the unrest, and then either came to an agreement with the mutineers or quelled the revolt with loyal troops. For less powerful princes and small states, however, the highly autonomous *Landsknechte* posed an enormous threat, and even the wealthier monarchs were happy to reduce the autonomy of their mercenary infantry. When, in 1572, the majority of cities in Holland and Zeeland revolted against Philip II, they immediately discarded the regimental

---

[24] See Baumann, *Landsknechte*, 103, 106; Baumann, *Frundsberg*, 129–30; Möller, *Regiment der Landsknechte*, 96, 98; Swart, *Krijgsvolk*, 118.

[25] Baumann, *Landsknechte*, 99.

[26] Delbrück, *Geschichte*, IV, 9, 77.

structure of the *Landsknechte* and organised their troops at company level. A few years later, between 1575 and 1576, the States of Holland weakened the power of the soldiers further by abolishing the common offices of *voerder, gemene weyfel,* and *fourier,* and their equivalents, not only in companies of infantry raised in Germany and the Netherlands (*Landsknechte* proper), but also in units of other nationalities. The Hollanders in this followed the example of the French, English, and Spaniards. The troops lost the right to represent themselves; instead, they were put under the guardianship of their captain as if they were minor orphans. In Dutch service, as elsewhere in western Europe, companies were reorganised into sections, each under the command of a corporal appointed by the captain.[27]

The decision of the Hollanders to do without regiments was, however, unfavourable for the fighting ability of their troops. Soldiers with firearms could only operate in the open if a large unit of pikemen supported them. This required the joining of companies into regiments. The reputation of the Spaniards as superb troops partly rested on the *esprit de corps* of the celebrated *tercio*s – equivalent to very large regiments. Unlike the *Landsknechte,* they had never been self-governing, but they had a tremendous collective identity.

The tactical need for a regimental organisation placed the rebels in a serious dilemma. Circumstances left them with no other choice than to temporise. In 1576 all the Netherlands rose in revolt, which made it imperative that a field army be organised. No longer was the fighting limited to the polders of Holland; it spread to open country. The rebels tried to cope with the new reality in the following manner: they reintroduced regiments, but ordered the colonels to appoint only captains who were agreeable to the political leadership.[28] In the long term this solution worked out very well, but not before two other conditions had been met: the insurance of steady pay and the enforcement of strict discipline.

The army of the States-General was in disarray in the 1580s: internal divisions in the United Provinces led to unrest amongst the troops. Mutinies and the betrayal of towns to the Spaniards were the consequence. Financial reorganisation prevented the disintegration of the

---

[27] Wijn, 'Noordhollandse regiment', 241–2; Swart, *Krijgsvolk,* 265–8; muster rolls, September 1575 and 21 May 1576, NAN, Collectie Ortel 37; regimental contract, 1573, NAN, Derde Afdeling: Handschriften 478; Parker, *Army,* 274; Wood, *King's Army,* 88.

[28] Deputies of the Union of Utrecht, memo, 1 October 1580, Groninger Archieven, Familiearchief Van Ewsum 196; instructions for muster-commissioner Joriem Fruick, 3 November 1583, NAN, States-General 11090.

Dutch forces. In December 1586 Johan van Oldenbarnevelt, Advocate of Holland (which provided 64.25 per cent of the United Provinces' military budget) maintained that the size of the Dutch army should never exceed the funds that the provinces were ready to allot to it.[29] The Dutch took to heart the view of the ancient Greeks and Romans, who maintained that wars were not won by the largest army but by the one superior in discipline and training.[30] Two of the most ardent advocates of this view were the *stadholders* Maurice and William Louis of Nassau (mentioned earlier). Maurice of Nassau was greatly influenced by Lipsius, with whom he studied for a year (1583–4),[31] and William Louis was a serious student of the teachings of the Byzantine Emperor Leo VI (866–912) – who stressed the importance of drill and exercise – and other classical commentators.[32] From 1592 onwards Maurice and William Louis drilled and trained the Dutch troops to a very high standard indeed, as was shown to the world on 2 July 1600 in the battle of Nieuwpoort, where they famously defeated the previously indomitable Spanish *tercios*.

The discipline of the Dutch army was exemplary, but similarly to other armies across western Europe, the captains, as of old, continued to be responsible for the upkeep of their units. Although the Dutch were pioneering more effective tactical systems, they perpetuated traditional administrative and financial practices. Standard practice in virtually all western European armies was for muster commissioners to check whether the companies complied with regulations, and to deduct the pay of missing troops from the total amount paid to the captains. This seems reasonable, but its effect was negative. Captains were paid for the number of men in their unit, rather than the soldiers being paid directly, and so there was a strong incentive for the captains to defraud the government. The captains were obliged to replace any loss from their own pockets, regardless of whether soldiers were killed in action, died of disease or accident, or had deserted. Only after they had made good their losses were captains again entitled to full pay, but it could be months before a new muster had taken place, and the recruits had to be fed in the meantime. The company commanders therefore adopted the habit of leading the muster commissioners by the nose in order to create a fund for the replacement of losses. They did this by hiring people who pretended to belong to the unit during the muster: so-called *passevolants*.

---

[29] Nimwegen, *Crijchsvolck*, 70–1.
[30] E.g. Frontinus, *Strategemata*, 287, 289; Vegetius Renatus, *De re militari*, 75–6.
[31] Waszink, Introduction to Lipsius, *Politica*, 21.
[32] Hahlweg, *Heeresreform*, 41–2, 48–9.

Muster commissioners were fully aware of this fraudulent practice, but they often looked the other way so as not to frustrate military operations. Reductions in pay inevitably led to a reduction in army size, because many company commanders reacted to this by letting go of their most experienced and therefore most expensive soldiers. Maurice of Nassau estimated that fraud, together with illness and deaths caused by fighting, were responsible for a difference of one-quarter to one-third between paper and effective unit strengths. In June 1604, during the siege of Sluys, he observed: 'The army can never be in the field for three or four months without enfeebling a great part of it or one third or quarter of the troops as a result of illness, desertions, deaths, and injuries.'[33] For the Dutch army in its entirety (troops in garrisons and in the field) the difference between real and paper strength was roughly 25 per cent. Although a large gap existed between paper and effective strengths, the Dutch army still compared favourably to the French and Spanish armies. The difference between paper and real strength in the French case could be at least a third while in the case of Spain it could be a staggering 50 per cent.[34]

In his study of the early-seventeenth-century French army, David Parrott shows that the French crown deliberately ruined its captains in order to be relieved of paying arrears.[35] The French government could do this because it could easily find other candidates to replace the insolvent captains. The Dutch republic could not. France had 18 million inhabitants, the Seven Provinces 1.5 to 2 million. It is true that many officers and soldiers serving in the Dutch army came from abroad, but often the financial basis of foreign officers was less solid than that of native-born company commanders.[36] As previously noted, the Dutch regents were not prepared to give the captains financial compensation for losses in men and equipment, but they at least tried to pay their troops regularly. They were aided in this endeavour by an institution peculiar to the Dutch army, namely that of the *solliciteurs-militair*, or agents. These were businessmen who concluded contracts with the captains. In return for an agreed monthly sum, they advanced the pay to the company. Often the Provincial States were not able to make payment in full and in time. Thanks to the intermediary role of the *solliciteurs-militair* the soldiers were assured of their pay. This was of the utmost importance, because the troops had to buy food themselves.

---

[33] Maurice to Otto Roeck and Ferdinand Heman, 6 June 1604, NAN, States-General 4908.

[34] Parrott, *Richelieu's Army*, 220; Parker, *Military Revolution* (2nd edn), 45.

[35] Parrott, *Richelieu's Army*, 350–3; cf. Chapter 4 in this volume.

[36] See for example Trim, 'Fighting', Chapter 6.

The duties of a *solliciteur-militair* were not limited to advancing money; he also looked after the captain's interests. When for example there was a dispute with a muster commissioner over the 'closing' of a muster-role, orders for payment were issued only after a muster sheet had been approved, i.e. closed.[37]

The innovative *solliciteurs-militair* system gave the Dutch republic an important advantage over its enemies. However, in the 1630s and 1640s this financial arrangement nearly collapsed under the strain of army growth. The Dutch forces numbered in those years 80,000 men on paper, and 60,000 in effect. The state revenues were not up to this level of spending and the arrears in pay grew accordingly. Heavy borrowing on the money market and the credit advanced by the *solliciteurs-militair* kept the military machine going, but after the conquest of 's-Her-togenbosch in 1629 and Maastricht in 1632 the regents of Holland were getting more and more alarmed about the financial position of their province. In January 1643 Holland owed the troops in its pay more than 3 million guilders, and the seven provinces taken together were more than 5 million guilders in arrears. In order to prevent massive bankruptcies and mutinies the States of Holland forced Frederick Henry, who became Prince of Orange and commander-in-chief of the Dutch army after the death of his half-brother Maurice in 1625, to reduce the number of troops from 80,000 to 60,000. The Hollanders argued that this would not reduce fighting strength, since a quarter of the army existed only on paper, and in future the remaining 60,000 effective troops would be paid on time. The reduction took effect on 1 March 1643.[38]

The creation of the standing army of professional troops (second half of the seventeenth century to first half of the eighteenth century)

The second half of the Eighty Years' War (1621–48) compared very favourably to the 1570s and 1580s. Both the Spanish government in the southern Netherlands and the United Provinces, by abolishing common offices in the 1570s, closer tying of pay to musters, and vigorous drilling, had created relatively disciplined armies that no longer posed a threat to the polity and the population they were hired to serve. Both sides had

---

[37] Nimwegen, *Crijchsvolck*, 67–8.
[38] List of pay arrears to January 1643, and States of Holland, resolution, 8 May 1643, RAZH, Archief Staten van Holland 1293-II 76; 'Rapport van de heeren Gecommitteert', 11 October 1635, RAZH, Archief Jacob Cats 32.

learned, as the German historian Ronald Asch keenly observes, that 'the other side almost always had an opportunity to retaliate in kind if a village was burnt or civilians slaughtered'.[39] Unfortunately the same could not be said of the conduct of the Thirty Years' War (1618–48) and the French–Spanish war (1635–59), which were marked by extreme brutality. The Sack of Magdeburg on 20 May 1631 by the army of the Catholic League horrified Europe: appalled eyewitnesses alleged that Tilly's soldiers slaughtered 20,000 to 30,000 men, women, and children.[40] Some areas of the Holy Roman Empire became so desolate that military operations there were no longer feasible. This was particularly the case in the later years of the French–Spanish war, when France suffered at the same time from civil war during the *Frondes*.[41]

The experiences of the 1650s and the subsequent War of Devolution (1667–8), which Louis XIV waged against Spain for dominion over the Spanish Netherlands, had a profound influence on the organisation of the French army. In the 1660s the Sun King and his two secretaries of war, Le Tellier and his son Louvois, thoroughly reformed the French army. By meting out severe punishment to *passevolants* and by prosecuting the captains who engaged in this fraudulent practice, the Le Telliers succeeded in reducing the discrepancy between paper and real unit strengths to acceptable levels. Guy Rowlands shows that it dropped from between 30 and 40 per cent to just 10 to 20 percent. In addition, Inspector-General Jean Martinet vigorously imposed discipline on both men and officers: henceforward the latter had to obey commands given to them by superior officers regardless of their own social status. The effectiveness of the French army was further improved by the establishment of large depots containing bread for the men and fodder for the horses.[42]

Whereas in France every care was taken to improve the army, the opposite occurred in the Dutch republic. After the Peace of Münster (1648) the Dutch army was reduced to a peacetime strength of just 29,000 men. Unfortunately, fighting quality, as well as numerical strength, decreased. Less than a decade after 1648 the Dutch army was in a sorry state. The regiments had been fragmented and many experienced officers had either died or been discharged. The deaths of Frederick Henry in 1647 and William II in 1650 left the Dutch army without

---

[39] Asch, 'Military Violence', 307.
[40] Edzart Jacob Clant to Ernst Casimir, 5 June 1631, Koninklijk Huisarchief, The Hague, A23-VII-C-342.
[41] Discussed by Parrott, Chapter 4, above.
[42] Rowlands, *Dynastic State*, 171, 192–3, 259; Lynn, *Giant*, 244, 405–6; Martin, 'Army', 112, 115.

a Captain-General of the Union. Lacking a commander-in-chief, the United Provinces' army de facto fell apart into seven provincial armies. The regents accepted this militarily unsound solution, because recent events had made them consider soldiers as a political liability again. In the summer of 1650 William II had used the army for a coup d'état that probably would have succeeded in creating a Dutch monarchy, but for his sudden death in November. The States of Holland immediately abolished the *stadholder*-ship, and took effective control over the nomination of officers and the moving of troops in the pay of Holland, and most of the six other Provincial States followed suit. As a result, the Dutch army was relegated to a force fit only for garrison duty. This did not particularly worry most of the ruling merchant elites. After the Thirty Years' War the Austrian Habsburgs needed peace, and Spain posed a limited threat. In 1665, however, the bishop of Münster attacked the republic in conjunction with the English king, Charles II. The Dutch fleet performed well,[43] but the Dutch army could hardly take the field. Companies were under strength and the officers inexperienced. It took until the winter of 1665 before the Dutch army was sufficiently up to strength to begin a counter-offensive. In April 1666, the bishop of Münster made peace with the republic, but only because of his own financial weakness. To John Maurice of Nassau–Siegen, commander of the Dutch field army in the war with Münster, the lesson to be learned from 1665 was clear: he warned the regents that unless the offensive capabilities of the army were revived, the security of the republic could not be assured.[44] The truth of this became fully apparent in 1667, when Louis XIV marched into the Spanish Netherlands.

The War of Devolution between France and Spain sent a shockwave through the republic. In January 1668, the Grand Pensionary of Holland, John de Witt, forged a triple alliance with England and Sweden to stop France from devouring the entire Spanish Netherlands. However, the War of Devolution did not become a European war. On 2 May 1668 the peace of Aix-la-Chapelle was signed. Louis XIV seemed to be content with the conquests his armies had made so far. The regents immediately lost interest in implementing John Maurice's advice to organise the companies of horse and foot in permanent regiments and to hold annual manoeuvres with the greater part of the Dutch army. The general feeling was: 'It is peace, it is not so very urgent now.'[45] The States-General even decided to reduce their army to 33,000 men. However, it was

[43] See Sicking, Chapter 11 in this volume.
[44] Nimwegen, *Crijchsvolck*, 253–7, 270, 347–54.
[45] Dibbetz, Preface to *Groot militair woordenboek*.

already apparent in July 1669 that Louis XIV was preparing to invade the republic, and that the attack would begin as soon as the French army was ready.

The enormous scale of French military preparations alarmed the regents and made them aware that the decision to decrease the Dutch army had not been a wise one. Between December 1670 and June 1672 the Dutch army was increased to 100,000 men on paper, or about 80,000 effectives. Only 22,000 of these were available for field duty, because the greater part was tied up in garrisons. Louis XIV attacked the republic with forces totalling 80,000 men – possibly even 100,000 men.[46] To this very powerful army must be added the allied forces of the bishop of Münster and the Elector of Cologne. The discrepancy in numbers turned the French invasion into a triumphal march. In 1672, 'the year of disaster', Utrecht, Overijssel, and Gelderland were lost to the French and their allies, but Holland, Zeeland, the city of Groningen, and Friesland stood their ground. The struggle for survival compelled the Dutch to reform their army; they succeeded in doing this in an astonishingly short space of time – about two years.

The collapse of Dutch defences resulted in the restoration of the commandership-in-chief and *stadholder*-ship, to both of which the twenty-one-year-old William III Prince of Orange was successfully appointed. William III wanted to counter-attack as soon as possible, but the disheartened and weakened army was yet unable to accomplish this aim. Turning the French onslaught was only feasible if self-confidence could be re-established in the troops, regular pay ensured, and financial support afforded to the officers so that they could make good their losses. This last constituted a fundamental turn. Until then the Provincial States had adhered to the old custom that the company commanders themselves were responsible for maintaining their units at full strength. The disastrous circumstances prevailing in 1672 forced a change in attitude. During the winter of 1672 and spring of 1673 the States of Holland took a number of decisions that fundamentally altered the relationship between army and state. These decisions affected the Dutch army in its entirety. As a consequence of the French invasion, the Dutch army in effect became the Holland army.

During the winter of 1672 the Dutch troops lived from hand to mouth, especially the troops in the former pay of the three occupied provinces. The *solliciteurs-militair* were not keen on serving the company commanders of these units, because they could not give any security,

---

[46] Council of War, 5 June 1672, RAZH, Familiearchief Van Slingelandt De Vrij Temminck 22.

having lost all their property to the invaders. In 1643 the collapse of army finance had been prevented by a reduction in troop numbers. In the 'year of disaster' that same solution was unthinkable – every man was needed. Thus, a new payment system was devised. All the troops paid by Holland were divided into eight groups, congruent with regimental organisations, and then allocated to a director. Each group consisted on average of sixty-three companies of foot and fifteen of horse. The eight directors were obliged to service all captains, regardless of their credit status. In return they were given the monopoly on paying the troops, received an interest rate of 6.95 per cent per year for money advanced to the troops, and moreover were entitled to a steady monthly compensation for each company they served. It is not clear how long this system functioned, but it is certain that in 1676 thirty-three *solliciteurs-militair* were employed for advancing money to the troops in the pay of Holland. Apparently it had not been possible to limit their number to just eight, probably because of the enormous sums of money involved. The new situation was not disadvantageous for the troops, because the thirty-three *solliciteurs-militair* could not refuse a captain either.[47]

The States of Holland also helped the company commanders directly. In July 1673 two important measures were taken.[48] First, officers were reimbursed for expenses resulting from replacing troops killed in action. This was a very important development because, as already noted, until that time the captains had had to recruit losses out of their own pockets, forcing them to resort to fraud, and hampering military operations. Maurice and Frederick Henry had loathed fighting bloody battles, because great losses would ruin the captains. The arrangement recompensing losses changed this. Within six weeks an army could be ready for battle again. Whereas before that time the Dutch army had to retire to its garrisons after heavy fighting – as was the case after Nieuwpoort in 1600 – from 1673 onwards, the army could stay in the field and, after a short recovery period, risk another battle. The second important measure entailed that infantry captains whose companies were mustered at 90 per cent of paper strength were paid for the full complement. Soldiers who died of other causes than fighting (illness or accident) and deserters still had to be replaced by the captains out of their own pockets, but the States did not leave them to their fate in those cases either. The bonus system enabled the company commanders to create a fund out of which these replacements could be paid for.

[47] RAZH, Archief Gaspar Fagel 126, and Archief Gecommitteerde Raden van Holland 3026, resolution of 13 March 1676.
[48] States-General of the Netherlands, *Recueil van verscheide placaaten*, no. 9.

Captains whose companies were below 90 per cent strength, however, were not entitled to this bonus, and those whose companies mustered 75 per cent or less were not only heavily fined, but were moreover dismissed if they were negligent in repairing their losses within a specified period of time. Impressed by this system, near the end of the Dutch war, Louvois introduced a comparable bonus scheme in the French army to give infantry captains an incentive to maintain their companies at least at 80 per cent of full strength.[49]

The Dutch rank-and-file also fared well with the greater involvement of the government. Food and medical help were assured. The troops no longer had to buy their basic food, bread, from local bakers. Instead, they were provisioned by a firm that contracted with the government, bought rye on the Amsterdam grain market, stocked it in supply depots (magazines), and milled it. From the resulting flour their bakers produced loaves of six pounds each (sufficient for one man for four days) and carted them to the army. The bread price was fixed in the contract so that the troops were protected against rising food prices.[50] Wounded soldiers received first aid in field hospitals, and were only then sent to the nearest city, resulting in a decline in soldiers who died unnecessarily because of undressed wounds.[51]

What were the benefits of these expensive measures? The States of Holland had not acted out of altruism, of course. The financial aid for officers and the improvement of living conditions for the rank-and-file justified the vigorous prosecution of fraud, and the introduction of ruthless discipline. No one was exempt from harsh punishments any longer, not even colonels. In contrast to his ancestors William III did not turn a blind eye to fraud. Fraudulent officers were cashiered, heavily fined, and could even be beheaded. The 'High Council of War' also severely punished insubordination: officers could lose their rank and be obliged to serve as common soldiers; the rank and file had to run the gauntlet or were given lashes. Cowardice in the face of the enemy and looting of their own population were considered offences punishable by death. William III authorised the provost-general summarily to execute troops who were caught *in flagrante delicto*, and units that disgraced themselves on the battlefield were collectively punished by executing one soldier from each company.[52] Frederick Henry had always spoken of the Dutch troops as his children, and although William III was not

---

[49] Rowlands, *Dynastic State*, 202.
[50] Nimwegen, *Subsistentie*, 24, 26–39, and *Crijchsvolck*, 304–12.
[51] Kerkhoff, *Over de geneeskundige*, 56, 68–76.
[52] Major-General Godard van Reede-Ginkel to his father, Zedigem, 11 May 1677, UA, Huisarchief Amerongen 2732; *Hollantse Mercurius* (1677), 46; Adriaan van der Hoop,

indifferent to their plight, he was not as concerned for them as his forebears had been. On the contrary, for him troops were expendable because he knew he could make good the losses. The aforementioned financial arrangements and the continuous drill ensured this.

For Maurice, William Louis, and Frederick Henry, turning mercenaries into disciplined and outstandingly trained troops had been the goal of their efforts. That the exercise programme developed by them could be used to guarantee a steady influx of recruits for the army was not realised by them. After 1672 this was self-evident. An anonymous Dutch officer remarked at the start of the eighteenth century: 'It is a constant truth that in wartime or in times of recruitment, a fellow can learn to exercise in six to eight weeks and be turned into a good soldier.'[53]

The military reforms carried through in the winter of 1672 and the first half of 1673 yielded astounding results. The feeling of defeatism and despair was rooted out and replaced by one of defiance. In the summer of 1673 William III finally started his longed-for counter-offensive. In 1674, 30,000 Dutch troops were sent to the Spanish Netherlands, where they fought together with Spanish and imperialist forces. About the same number of troops served there from 1675 to 1678, approximating to 40 per cent of total Dutch forces, which can be estimated at 70,000 effective men. On paper the army of the States-General should have mustered around 80,000 men, so that the difference between official and effective strength amounted to just 15 per cent! This low percentage is comparable to that of the French army, which Rowlands, as already noted, estimates at 10 to 20 per cent.

After the return of peace in 1678 the Dutch army was reduced to a peace establishment of 40,000 men. In contrast to 1648, however, much care was now taken to ensure that regimental structures were left intact, and that the experience gained during the last war was preserved. The year 1678 saw the birth of the Dutch standing army. The companies exercised regularly on a regimental level, and were mustered frequently. Muster rolls show that the companies of foot had an effective strength of about 90 per cent.[54] In the subsequent Nine Years' War (1688–97) and the War of the Spanish Succession (1701–13) the Dutch, in alliance with England and the Habsburgs, succeeded first in containing and then almost in defeating France. During the Nine

memo to the Council of State re 'provoost-generaal van het leger', NAN, Collectie Van der Hoop 150.
[53] 'Memorie en reflectie artillery', NAN, Collectie Van der Hoop 106.
[54] 'Camp 1683', UA, Huisarchief Amerongen 3610; muster rolls, 1684, NAN, States-General 12548.488.4.

Years' War the bonus system for soldiers' pay again operated,[55] but from 1701 onwards Dutch captains had to maintain their companies on full strength at all times.[56] At the start of the eighteenth century the armies of the major European states were well matched in organization, discipline, tactics, weaponry, and food supply, many aspects of which were copied in whole or in part from those of the Dutch republic.[57] That is why the famous French soldier and author de Puységur considered the wars of his day as the most difficult. They are waged, he writes, with armies of 80,000 men and more, 'against others which will be of equal strength and which will also have their supply depots and their well-furnished artillery magazines'.[58]

The decline of the standing army

Until the second half of the eighteenth century the legacy of Louis XIV and William III determined how western European states waged their wars. When the War of the Austrian Succession began, the French, British, and Dutch viewed it as a continuation of the War of the Spanish Succession. Their armies mirrored the organisation and tactics of the late seventeenth century. Armies of again 80,000 to 100,000 men were pitched against each other and large siege operations were undertaken. From a military perspective, however, it was not the old type of warfare fought in the Netherlands that attracted European attention, but the daring strategy of the young Prussian king, Frederick II.

The foundations of Prussian military might had been laid during the reign (1713–40) of Frederick William I, the 'soldier king'. He had made society subservient to the army, so that Prussia could maintain an armed force on a war footing in times of peace. In fact, Prussia became a military camp. The failure of the French army in the Seven Years' War seemed to confirm that the best way to ensure military success was to copy as best as possible the organisation and drill of the Prussians. This view was not untested, however.

Machiavelli's argument for a citizens' militia, and the importance Lipsius attached to the moral moulding of the soldier, were revived by the adherents of the Enlightenment out of fear for despotism and unease at the harsh treatment of the soldiers. In France and the Dutch republic, the two states who had lost much of their military prestige

[55] Stapleton, 'Coalition army', 117.
[56] Dibbetz, *Groot militair woordenboek*, s.v. 'Compleethouding der compagni[e]ën'.
[57] For example, British captains received financial assitance in imitation of the Dutch 'sollicitors' or regimental agents; Guy, *Oeconomy and Discipline*, 59–61.
[58] Puységur, *Art, principes et règles*, II, 153 (quotation), 155.

after 1748, many worried about the widening gap between soldiers and civilians.[59] The Dutch 'Patriots', the opponents of William V (1748–1806), were disturbed by the republic's military weakness, yet at the same time distrustful of the *stadholder*'s management of the Dutch army. Was military effectiveness really served by requiring all soldiers to have a pigtail of two feet in length and to exercise in unnatural poses? Prussian soldiers were frightened into doing their duty by fear of the rod in the hands of their drillmasters, and deserted whenever an opportunity presented itself.[60] Would it not be better, the Patriots argued, if soldiers served willingly and fought bravely out of love for their country? Instead of an army of mindless puppets herded by cruel officers, the Patriots favoured an army made up of native volunteers supported by a militia. Patriotism should fire the zeal of both troops and militiamen. Similar opinions were advanced in France.[61]

It is true that, in observing very strict discipline, Frederick the Great followed the example set by William III, but whereas the *stadholder*-king had made use of exemplary punishment only at a moment when the survival of the Dutch republic was at stake – the Dutch war of 1672–8 – the Prussian king made excessive discipline an everyday practice.[62] To contemporaries, Prussian military service was synonymous with barbarism, and Prussian troops were mere robots.[63] However, there was more to the Prussian army than brutal discipline.

In Prussia each captain was allotted a number of 'hearths' or households where only he was permitted to recruit. They provided a reservoir from which he could bring his company to full strength when insufficient foreign recruits could be found. The famous *Kantonsystem* protected the company commanders against the uncertainties of the market for soldiers.[64] In the Dutch republic and France, however, the captains were not so fortunate; they had to compete with each other. In the course of the second half of the eighteenth century recruits became hard to find. Improvements in agriculture and the growth of the textile industry offered increasing numbers of young men an alternative to military service. Consequently the captains had to entice recruits by offering higher and higher bounties, which they had to pay for themselves, but the government was unwilling to compensate the captains for

---

[59] Gembruch, 'Verhältnis', 379–82; Kunisch, *Fürst*, 179–80.
[60] Sikora, 'Verzweiflung', 260.
[61] Klein, *Patriots*, 56, 167–82; Gembruch, 'Verhältnis', 382.
[62] Frederick II of Prussia, *Werke Friedrichs des Großen*, II, 398; Duffy, *Army of Frederick the Great*, 62; Nimwegen, *Crijchsvolck*, 290–2.
[63] Kunisch, *Fürst*, 178–80, 211.
[64] Duffy, *Army of Frederick the Great*, 54–7; Guddat, *Infanterie*, 35–6.

the ever-increasing costs of recruitment. Some Dutch officers warned the *stadholder* that all captains would be ruined unless the *Kantonsystem* was introduced in the republic, but other Dutch officers considered it incompatible with a civil society. William V also feared that if Dutch regiments were assigned steady garrisons in the provinces that paid them, the merchant elites in the cities would use that opportunity to get a hold on the captains and colonels. It would take a revolution to destroy the foundation of the standing army of mercenaries: one of the first acts of the Batavian republic (1795–1806) was the abolition of the private ownership of companies.[65]

In the late eighteenth century the harshly disciplined and low-paid soldiers were no longer feared or viewed with contempt by civilians, but pitied by them. Ironically, it was the idea of the people in arms brought forth by the French Revolution that would once again turn armies into a scourge.

[65] Amersfoort, 'Vaderland', 13.

9 Aspects of operational art: communications, cannon, and small war

Simon Pepper

Introduction

Operational art – as the term is used in this essay – falls somewhere between strategy and tactics, and concerns the business of war-fighting in most of its aspects save the purely political or logistical. The word 'strategy,' in the sense of grand strategy, probably did not enter European vocabulary until the end of the eighteenth century. However, as Hew Strachan recently pointed out, even if the practice did not have a label, it certainly existed long before the eighteenth century.[1] The term 'tactics' had ancient origins, of course, and was well understood in our period, even if the available weapons and types of soldiers using them were in some areas undergoing radical change. Even excluding grand strategy and the tactical handling of troop formations in combat, operational art is a formidably wide field and this essay's discussion is limited to three inter-related aspects: developments in the nature of military command and its tools of communication, the heavy weapons available to commanders in the field and in siege warfare, and what was known in all of Europe's principal languages as 'small war'.

Two of these topics relate to significant changes. Mapping techniques and other aspects of post-medieval communications transformed the ability of commanders to envisage the landscape of war. The development of gunpowder artillery produced a weapon that – literally – expanded the tactical landscape. In battles, guns brought into range distant targets; in sieges they stimulated the development of elaborate rampart and bastioned fortification systems, which eventually extended far beyond the lines of medieval walls. By contrast, our third topic, the small war of raids and skirmishes, demonstrates a surprising level of continuity in the experience of soldiers and others caught up in operations that only rarely involved the major battles that feature so prominently in traditional accounts.

---

[1] Strachan, Letter, responding to information that the term was from Joly de Maizeroy (1771).

181

Although traditional military history is dominated by battles, recent scholarship stresses the rarity of major field engagements and the relative dominance of the siege. Even in the so-called 'age of battles', battle was less common than often supposed. As Rory Muir observes, although

> one modern authority [Gunther Rothenberg] state[s] that there were no fewer than 713 battles in Europe in the thirty years 1790–1820 ... the great majority of these were partial combats between detached forces, advance and rearguards and the like, rather than pitched battles between the main bodies of opposing armies ... actual fighting was comparatively rare in the life of a Napoleonic soldier.[2]

Furthermore, the consequent emphasis on the slow pace of early-modern warfare can easily convey the message that conflict itself had become a slow-motion affair of forms, artifice, style, and convention rather than, as Jeremy Black succinctly put it, being waged 'for real'.[3] The high casualty figures in both battles and sieges, and the widespread destruction of life and property in the war zones, rebut any notion of early-modern war as an exercise in unreality.[4] Nor was the mayhem confined to battlefields or siege lines. In the lengthy intervals of campaigning between battles, in a broad swathe of territory surrounding all sieges, and across Europe's many contested frontiers, low-intensity warfare took place on a daily basis. Patrols skirmished; foragers seized provisions and animals; raiding parties burnt villages and crops to deny them to the enemy, whilst others destroyed them in reprisal for the failure to pay contributions. What was known universally as 'small war' was waged on a scale that was anything but small. Indeed, for many soldiers, for much of the time, small war almost certainly provided their primary experience of active service and combat. Yet the phenomenon of small war remains relatively unresearched, and one of the objectives of this paper is to examine whether it ever formed part of a broader scheme of operations.

The military revolution thesis – as most forcefully articulated by Geoffrey Parker – takes as its starting point the challenge posed by late-medieval gunpowder artillery and the rapid response of the fortification designers.[5] The development of the Italian bastion, which was both capable of resisting artillery and of accommodating defensive guns, is presented as a major factor in the near stalemate of siege-dominated

---

[2] Muir, *Tactics*, 7.
[3] Black, *European Warfare 1660–1815*, 70.
[4] Tallett, *War and Society*, 105–12, 148–68 for military and civilian casualties; Porter, *Destruction*, for property losses.
[5] Parker, *Military Revolution* (1st edn), 7–16.

warfare, becoming in turn the driver behind the engagement of ever larger numbers of troops in early-modern armies. The cannon that initiated this escalating cycle, however, are often forgotten. It is perhaps the time to review some of the recent research that sheds new light on the changing availability of artillery and the effect this may have exercised on its tactical employment. This is the second topic to be examined in the paper.

Operational command itself throws up questions too. One recent historian of British military leadership explained his choice of case studies from amongst those who had served after the English Civil War by arguing that he could not 'compare the deeds of a British general in 1815 or 1915 with Henry V or even Cromwell – figures who combined military with supreme political or dynastic power'.[6] It is worth reminding ourselves here that many early-modern campaigns were conducted by generals who served at the pleasure of royal masters, republics, or even parliamentary democracies; and that this relationship exercised a profound bearing on the way strategy was shaped and operations conducted. Any picture of senior command in war needs to take on board these factors. Taken literally it was a picture that some official artists attempted to capture in paint, in addition to the more conventional heroic battle scenes and graceful surrenders.

Communications, maps, and changing patterns of command

A fresco by Giorgio Vasari in the Florentine Palazzo Vecchio shows Cosimo I de' Medici, duke of Florence, planning the siege of Siena. The active phases of the war that resulted in the defeat and disappearance of one of the last independent republics in Italy lasted from 1553 to 1556. The fresco was painted in the late 1560s and shows Cosimo sitting hunched over his desk, dividers in hand, overlooked by allegorical figures of Prudence and Fortitude. On the desk there is a model of Siena, while the duke closely studies a plan of the fortifications. Although obviously a conceit, the picture has the ring of truth about it. Cosimo was one of the great interventionist rulers of the century and, if not in quite the same paper-generating, detail-obsessed league as Philip II of Spain, even so a formidable 'armchair warrior' who deluged his commanders in the field with advice, orders, and endless demands for information. His intelligence network was extensive, his appetite for correspondence insatiable. At times he received almost daily reports

[6] Urban, *Generals*, xii.

from the army besieging Siena, some thirty miles to the south, which has left a revealing run of despatches from the army commander, the Marquis of Marignano, as well as from Bartolomeo Concino (the civilian secretary to the Council of War, encouraged by the duke to give his own spin on events), and from Chiappino Vitelli (maestro di campo with the imperial army, who provided a second – often highly critical – 'professional' opinion). Marignano was not a likeable man, but one almost feels sorry for him when he responded angrily – perhaps desperately – to Cosimo's tactical suggestions. 'I must speak my mind freely', he protested, when Cosimo had again urged aggressive action close to Siena's walls in broken country that made it difficult for his troops to maintain contact with one another, 'these are drawing-room plans which do not work in practice ... If only you could see the ground, I know it would give you a better understanding.'[7]

Like Philip II of Spain, Cosimo regularly worked far into the night annotating despatches, often sending responses so quickly that they reached the camps outside Siena within twenty-four hours of the original despatch. Clearly, this speed of turnaround was only possible when the action was close to the central seat of government. Letters from Brussels in peacetime – Geoffrey Parker tells us – could reach Philip II in Spain via France in 'eleven, ten or (in at least one case) nine days' using relays of despatch riders, but a message sent in time of war by an alternative route that avoided French territory (via Besançon, Chambéry, Turin, and Genoa, and from there by sea to Barcelona) could take two months.[8] Highly sensitive material such as the duke of Parma's strategy for the invasion of England took the longer route.[9] The kind of 'dialogue' that developed between Cosimo and Marignano was hardly possible with a potential four-month gap between proposal and reply. The two monarchs, both attempting to fight wars by remote control, shared a common need for information about the overall physical context for strategy-making. Vasari captures this well. Models were certainly used when they could be made and moved.[10] Drawings and maps were much easier to make, to copy, and to transport. In the closing

---

[7] ASF, Mediceo del Principato 1853, 16 April 1554 and 22 April 1554, in Pepper and Adams, *Firearms and Fortifications*, 126. Compare with Turenne to Louvois, 14 November 1672: 'If you were here, you would laugh at that idea' (quoted in Lynn, *Wars of Louis XIV*, 118).

[8] Parker, 'Treaty of Lyon', 130.

[9] However, Parker, *Grand Strategy*, 54–5, 185 suggests that Parma's choice of the long route for his first plans in 1585 was actually a delaying tactic.

[10] Pope Clement VII had a cork model of the Florentine fortifications in 1529–30 smuggled out in sections at considerable risk. Venice started the first state collection of fortress models in 1550; Gerola, 'I plastici', 217–21.

stages of the siege of Siena in 1555, the architect and military engineer, Maestro Giorgio di Giovanni, was instructed to go up the tower of the City Hall to draw a plan of the city for the use of the republican regime, which was even then preparing to continue the fight after the surrender of their capital.[11] Both sides needed up-to-date maps.

Cartography fascinated the rulers of early-modern Europe. Baroque courts surrounded themselves with images of the world. The frescoed Vatican Map Gallery provided detailed topographical information as well as a message about the 'world of the church'.[12] The ducal apartments of the Florentine Palazzo Vecchio had similar decorative maps.[13] Seventy maps hung in the throne room of the Escorial palace in Spain.[14] King Philip II commissioned major mapping programmes for Spain and the Low Countries using the expertise in surveying that had flowered early in Holland and Venice, the two leaders of Europe in land reclamation and hydraulic engineering.[15] The early maps were hand-drawn and expensive to copy, and the models very much more so. Both opened up new military potential as well as problems: the demands of security having to be balanced against the propaganda value of the more public schemes (and later the *gloire* that attached to the spectacular exhibition of fortress models in the grand gallery of the Tuileries under Louis XIV).[16] Initially security was emphasised. When the pro-imperial regime in Siena embarked upon the construction of modern bastions in 1528, discreet efforts were made through diplomatic channels to give Antonio de Leyva, the imperial commander in Italy and governor of Milan, sight of the fortification drawings.[17] The regulations promulgated in 1550 for the safe-keeping of the Venetian fortress models required them to be kept under lock and key, with a register recording every occasion one was consulted, and the name of the officer who had access.[18] By making map-making a Spanish royal monopoly, however, Philip II's obsessive secrecy eventually denied his servants the ability to plan with them. As Parker concluded: 'A government that lacked the cartographic tools required to organize its resources or to project its power, and instead resorted to outdated general atlases for strategic planning, was no longer

---

[11] Pepper and Adams, *Firearms and Fortifications*, 228 n. 64.
[12] Gambi and Pinelli, *La galleria*.
[13] Fiorani, *Maps*, 171ff.
[14] Buisseret, *Mapmaker's Quest*, 60.
[15] Parker, 'Philip II, Maps and Power'.
[16] Roux, Faucherre and Monsaingeon, *Plans*.
[17] Letter from Fortunato Vecchi, Sienese ambassador in Milan, 9 October 1528, requesting this information for the Spaniard; Archivio di Stato Siena, Balia 583, no. 95.
[18] Concina, *Macchina territoriale*, 184–5.

a convincing imperial power.'[19] This is not the place for a potted history of maps, but it is perhaps worth noting that the development of *printed* maps – which allowed all parties in a strategic dialogue to share the same information – went hand in hand with the growth of positional warfare as the preferred operational mode.[20]

It is not suggested here that 'command by remote control' became the dominant mode in our period; but some of its features can be recognised as elements of change. Nor are our leading figures presented as prototypes of the soldier-diplomat in the Eisenhower mould, but here too there are some players who provide early indications of this tendency. Well into the Napoleonic era rulers continued to lead their armies into battle in person, sometimes gravely compromising the clarity of the command structure when alliances brought a number of monarchs to the field of battle on the same side. Those who led from the front, however, take centre stage. Henry V came of age at Agincourt; Henry VIII, pathetically anxious to imitate him, missed the greatest opportunity of his reign at Flodden whilst vainly seeking a battle in France. Louis II of Hungary and Bohemia was killed in battle with the Turks at Mohács in 1526. Mehmet II, Selim I, and Süleyman I (the victor of Mohács) personally led the Ottoman armies on an extraordinary wave of conquest in the late fifteenth and early sixteenth centuries. Charles VIII of France led his army into Italy in 1494; Francis I charged the Swiss at Marignano and was famously captured at Pavia, while the Emperor Charles V participated personally in operations at Mühlberg in 1547 and Metz in 1552 in the closing stages of his long rule.[21] Northern Europe saw inspirational battlefield commanders such as Gustavus Adolphus and Charles XII – both killed in action – and much later Frederick II of Prussia, all of whom exercised a notably personal style of leadership in battle, with little paperwork (at least at the time). Others, however, developed command styles much closer to those of Philip II or Cosimo de' Medici. Personally brave and fascinated by war in all of its aspects, Louis XIV is sometimes said to have favoured siege warfare over other forms because it allowed him to participate – with the celebrated engineer Vauban at his elbow – in a way that he

---

[19] Parker, 'Philip II, Maps and Power', 120–1.

[20] Bound atlases may not have been good for strategy, but (used with caution) clearly illustrate the spread of bastioned fortifications as well as places where they arrived surprisingly late: see Zeiller, *Topographia Galliae*; Braun and Hogenberg, *Civitates orbis*; and Fer, *Les forces*, with its focus on fortresses and fortified towns.

[21] Although Titian's famous picture of Charles V at Mühlberg has the Emperor on horseback, it is practically certain that he was carried on a litter because of a bad attack of gout. But he was there.

recognised would have been beyond him in a faster-moving battle. For much of his reign, however, the Sun King conducted his many wars and campaigns at a strategic level with his minister of war Louvois in close attendance. With France's armies in action in Flanders, the Rhineland, northern Italy, and sometimes also on the Spanish border, delegation became a necessity (albeit often seriously qualified by the exercise of the royal prerogative to intervene). John Lynn has categorised Louis XIV's style of command as *guerre du cabinet*.[22] It was not exclusive to France. Many features of *guerre du cabinet* can be recognised in the yearly cycle of Louis XIV's nemesis, Marlborough, who cannot possibly be seen as an armchair general but who nevertheless generated a prodigious correspondence from the field. Marlborough maintained it between campaigning seasons through the agency of his quartermaster-general, William Cadogan, who often remained on the continent all the year round, preparing options for the following season, and evolving into something very like a chief of staff in modern parlance. The general's winter was spent usefully in England 'schmoozing Conservative politicians' – Mark Urban's colourful phrase – as well as securing relationships with his wife and the queen.[23]

Guerre du cabinet demanded accurate geographical information. Philip II and his staff used it to find secure routes that would link Spain with its armies in the Low Countries.[24] To coordinate army movements in the field demanded yet more detail: on roads, villages, castles, rivers, fords, and bridges. The positional choreography that allowed Marlborough finally to penetrate the lines of *Ne Plus Ultra*, or to organise the preparation of food dumps at regular intervals along the planned route of the long march to Blenheim, would have been near to impossible without good maps. Louis XIV's persistent encroachments on his neighbours' territories fed on maps. The identification of potential invasion corridors and decisions about the fortification of defensible sites demanded detailed surveys and site evaluations, including background economic information on the availability of construction materials and labour. It was this infrastructural work that occupied so much of the time of Vauban and his engineer colleagues on their seemingly endless surveys of Louis XIV's expanding frontiers, and that loomed large in their correspondence with Louvois and the king, who – in this area of policy, as in others – wished himself to confirm key decisions.

---

[22] Lynn, *Wars of Louis XIV*, 71.
[23] This analysis is influenced by conversation with Professor Richard Holmes. See his *Marlborough*.
[24] Parker, 'Treaty of Lyon', 127–42.

It is difficult to escape the conclusion that an important contributory factor to the generally slow pace of warfare from the late sixteenth to the early eighteenth centuries was the increasing complexity of what might be termed 'military politics' (the closer involvement of rulers and governments as well as the generals) and the concomitant increase in paperwork. The growing bureaucratisation entailed by maintaining larger armies was a chief cause of the increase in administrative complexity. However, mapping should not be ignored in this calculation, for positional tactics – whether siege-based, or turning on the movement and manoeuvre of field armies – depended heavily upon military geography and its chief instrument, the accurate map.

Artillery: potential and problems

Artillery was another of the key instruments of early-modern operations. Although the development and growing effectiveness of gunpowder artillery was one of the most important factors driving change, both in siege warfare and field engagements, the impact of the new weapon is more difficult to chart than at first appears. Artillery supply and its effectiveness fluctuated wildly over time and in different theatres of operations, giving what is often a confusing picture of the impact of the improved weapons in both sieges and field engagements.

By the middle years of the fifteenth century artillery had developed to a point where it could be used to good effect in sieges, playing a crucial role in the French re-conquest of English Normandy in the 1450s and the fall of Constantinople to the Ottomans in 1453. Artillery played a key role in the Spanish re-conquest of Granada (1492) and, of course, in the first French invasion of Italy (1494–5).[25] If the last event did not actually initiate the development of the Italian bastion – which was already taking shape well before 1494 – it certainly contributed to the urgency with which the Italian states tackled the modernisation of their fortress and city walls, as well as the overhaul of their own artillery.[26] Alongside the sometimes hysterical treatment of this phase of the military revolution by contemporary Italian historians, however, runs a stream of conflicting evidence: on the one hand, accounts of impressively large siege trains delivering frighteningly destructive results; and, on the other, primary data recording persistent shortages of guns, gunners, trained draught animals, and ammunition. The

---

[25] Cook, 'Cannon Conquest'; Taylor, *Art of War*; and below for 1494–5.
[26] For the Italian bastion, see the seminal paper by Sir John Hale, 'Early Development'; for a narrower perspective, Pepper, 'Castles and Cannon', 286–9.

French bombardment of the Castelnuovo in the first siege of Naples in 1495 – one of the examples conventionally quoted as a striking success for the artillery – quickly exhausted the famous iron cannonballs of Charles VIII's siege train before the castle surrendered for other reasons.[27] Shortage of gunpowder led to the surrender of the Anglo-Dutch garrison of Sluys in 1587.[28] No doubt specialist scrutiny of other campaigns would tell the same story.

Numbers of guns need to be treated with caution. The French siege train that went to Naples in 1494–5 in the invasion that sparked the Italian wars is often said to have comprised thirty-six siege cannon. Closer analysis suggests a total of eight or nine full cannon and four culverins – with the rest of the total made up by much smaller guns. A prodigious siege train of some sixty heavy cannon was assembled for the League of Cambrai's siege of Padua in 1509; but its impact was much reduced by the fact that it only reached full strength towards the end of the siege, by combining the guns of the Emperor Maximilian (which had to be hauled over the mountains from Innsbruck), the king of France (hauled mainly from Milan where the French artillery had been augmented by the best of the weapons collected from captured Venetian fortresses), and the duke of Ferrara (who was the closest to Padua of the League's Italian allies to own a substantial stock of guns).[29]

By the middle years of the sixteenth century the picture was little clearer. For the imperial attempt to recapture Metz in 1552, Charles V used river barges to move guns from all over the Rhineland so as to concentrate as many as fifty siege pieces in his batteries, which then delivered formidable barrages against the strengthened fortifications (but not fast enough to destroy them before the defenders built a second rampart behind the breach).[30] Again, the heavy guns were delayed. Even so, this operation was an original attempt to concentrate forces quickly for a siege that had been launched late in the campaigning season. It took place in what could be described as the 'heartland of the military revolution' – a densely urbanised and industrialised region where gun manufacturers were not thin on the ground. In central Italy the story was different. Early in the war of Siena a battery of twelve siege pieces was concentrated to bombard Montalcino (1553), without success; and

---

[27] Pepper, 'Castles and Cannon', 281 n. 62. See below for similar problems in the Siena campaign.
[28] Fissel, *English Warfare*, 155.
[29] Pepper, 'Face of the Siege,' 41–5.
[30] Salignac, *Siège de Metz* (ed. Petitot), 335–44, and map in 1553 edition. See also Zeller, 'Siège de Metz'; and for the fortifications: Turrel, *Metz*; Thiriot, *Portes*.

towards the end of the protracted series of operations around Siena enormous efforts were made by the Florentine and imperial forces to assemble a battery of eighteen guns (and the same number of experienced gun-crews) for the surprise bombardment of a neglected section of the walls, in an effort to end the siege quickly. After bringing together guns and gunners from all over the theatre, including weapons from warships and the adjacent (theoretically neutral) Church States, probably around thirty *pezzi grossi* were assembled, but only nine of them went into action and the long-planned 'batteria' was a disappointing failure. Starvation and lack of hope of French relief forced the eventual surrender of Siena.[31]

Guilmartin's analysis of the Ottoman campaign against Malta in 1565, and its outcome, stressed the shortages of heavy artillery and ammunition experienced by both sides in what by any standards was a major confrontation.[32] Guilmartin was in fact the first to have identified a much wider sixteenth-century shortage of artillery with profound implications for his own field of Mediterranean naval tactics as well as siege warfare.[33]

Much the same picture shortly afterward emerges from France itself during the Wars of Religion. Here the first four civil wars saw the former European leader in artillery warfare lose its pre-eminence. 'By the time of the fifth civil war', as James Wood shows,

financial difficulties, supply shortages, casualties and the strain of continued operations far to the south of the only reliable and readily available artillery resources in the kingdom had finally, it seems, reduced the artillery service to a shadow of its former self. None of the siege operations in 1574–75 deployed more than about twenty heavy guns, that is, one-third to one-half fewer guns than the army had used at sieges during the first four civil wars.[34]

The provision of just six siege guns (admittedly with transport, powder, and shot) to the Huguenots by Elizabeth I of England in 1569 was regarded as highly significant.[35] Royalist–Catholic forces defeated the Huguenots in *battle* (a pyrrhic victory at Dreux in 1562, resoundingly at Moncontour in 1569) but were unable to capitalise on these victories by capturing the Protestant strongholds. After Moncontour – which initially seemed that rarity of the period, a decisive victory – the royal forces threw away their advantage by exhausting their troops

---

[31] Pepper and Adams, *Firearms and Fortifications*, 101–4, 131–7.
[32] Guilmartin, *Gunpowder and Galleys* (1974 edn), 180–4.
[33] *Ibid.*, 181: in the sixteenth century '... there simply wasn't that much artillery around'.
[34] Wood, *King's Army*, 182.
[35] Trim, 'Fighting', 102–4.

in an over-lengthy siege of the primitively fortified small town of Saint-Jean-d'Angély (1569). The crown proved unable to break the resistance of the Huguenot main base at La Rochelle in the first great siege of that city in 1573. In France, too, gunners were in short supply. 'Even when the crown managed to put together a 14-piece train for the duke of Guise's army in Champagne in late 1575', reports Wood, 'there were not enough personnel to sustain it and it spent the rest of the war rotting in scattered depots all over the northeastern part of the kingdom'.[36]

La Rochelle was finally overcome half a century later after a siege on which the French crown concentrated most of the military resources of the kingdom for almost twelve months from 1627 to 1628, but the surrender was negotiated. 'Although the French ministers and high command were preoccupied by siege warfare, this did not, paradoxically, lead to a development in the quality and quantity of artillery in the armies.'[37] Parrott cites the *états* of 1638 for the army of Italy indicating a strength of between 9,000 and 10,000 infantry, 3,000 cavalry, and a total of 5 artillery pieces. February 1640 saw the army of Italy with only four serviceable 'moyennes' – cannon firing a ball of ten to twelve pounds – contrasted with the ninety cannon of Gustavus Adophus' army in Bavaria in 1632, the eighty cannon reported for Banér's Swedish army in 1639, and the forty-two cannon with the imperial army invading Burgundy in 1636.[38] Many of these guns – particularly those of the Swedish armies – may well have been small- or medium-calibre field pieces. Even so, the disparity in numbers is striking. Parrott points to the threefold demand for guns from armies, fortresses, and navy – and concludes that the 'primary consumer of newly founded artillery was Richelieu's expanding Atlantic navy, while the extensive new fortifications at Le Havre, Brouage and Brest created a further heavy demand'.[39] Fortress commanders were reluctant to give up their guns with doubtful chances of replacement.[40] All of these factors meant that in Richelieu's time: 'Few of the French sieges of the period were brought to a conclusion because artillery bombardment had rendered the defences untenable.'[41]

If the deficiencies in the availability of artillery represented a limitation on successful siege operations, armies without guns were robbed of one of their main tactical advantages – the ability to force an enemy

---

[36] *Ibid.*, 183.
[37] Parrott, *Richelieu's Army*, 65.
[38] *Ibid.*, 66.
[39] *Ibid.*, 67.
[40] *Ibid.*, 67–8, citing Pepper and Adams, *Firearms and Fortifications*, 23–4.
[41] Parrott, *Richelieu's Army*, 70.

in a strong position to attack (thus losing the benefit of a prepared position) or to withdraw (always risky in the face of an enemy), or to suffer mounting casualties and potentially disastrous breakdowns in morale as an artillery bombardment ran its course against formations that stood their ground.[42] Solid shot of all calibres was effective at long range against 'soft targets' such as bodies of troops, and the relatively dense formations adopted by pike-armed infantry made particularly good targets (as did the squares later adopted by musket- and bayonet-carrying infantry when threatened by cavalry).[43] Horses could easily be panicked by bombardment. Artillery placed traditionally in front of the battle-line was likely to be lost or overrun (if only temporarily) in a general assault; but its main purpose in our period was often to provoke a battle that otherwise might well be denied. This, after all, was how the English longbow archery had been used initially at Agincourt (1415). The arrow storm provoked the French into an attack on a congested battlefield of Henry's choice. Without it the French could have held their position and let the starving English army risk an attack, or an equally difficult retreat from their prepared and staked position.[44] Artillery would carry up to 1,000 yards, and effectively more on hard ground, which caused the low-trajectory cannonballs to skip or bounce their way through troop formations causing casualties even at low velocity.[45] Artillery therefore had the potential to deplete infantry formations or break up cavalry at long range. In itself this was not a battle-winning tactic, but it could force an enemy into attack or withdrawal. In the absence of artillery it was much easier for an enemy to avoid battle with all of its uncertainties.

The shortage of French land-service artillery seems finally to have been resolved by the end of the seventeenth century. Jamel Ostwald's recent study of Vauban's legacy shows a significant increase in all types of artillery, as well as a greater reliance on firepower to shorten sieges. Ostwald also observes a flowering of what he calls 'martial vigor' – probably the same aggressive spirit that so impressed the Italians in 1494–5 – which could sometimes carry fortifications by a swarming escalade with scant regard for casualties (amongst the attackers) or for the scientific and casualty-averse approach to siege tactics advocated by Vauban – what Blomfield has called *grande*

---

[42] True also in later centuries: 'The standing to be cannonaded, and having nothing else to do, is about the most unpleasant thing that can happen to soldiers in an engagement.' Ensign Leeke on Waterloo, quoted in Muir, *Tactics*, 47.

[43] Cf. the discussion by Rogers, in the next chapter.

[44] Barker, *Agincourt*, 287–97.

[45] Hall, *Weapons*, 151–3.

finesse. Ostwald collected detailed artillery statistics for twenty-five sieges between 1697 and 1712. The dates mark the 'perfect siege' of Ath (Vauban's masterpiece in delivering a rapid result at remarkably light cost) and the fall of Bouchain, one of the keys to the *Ne Plus Ultra* lines. An astonishing 288 cannon were assembled for the assault on Douai (1710), but only 16 for the attack on Zoutleeuw (1705). If these two potentially distorting figures are excluded, an average of 64 cannon and 34 heavy mortars were employed by the attacking forces, not counting howitzers and the much lighter Coehoorn mortars.[46] These figures should be compared with those for the operations against La Rochelle in 1573, when the crown 'made a supreme effort, perhaps the greatest of the entire civil war period, assembling some 42 cannon and great culverins ... double the size of the field trains which had marched with the army in the first three civil wars'. However, 'None of the siege operations in 1574–75 deployed more than about twenty heavy guns.'[47]

The War of the Spanish Succession saw massed artillery beginning to play a more active role on the battlefield as well as in sieges.[48] Marlborough concentrated most of his own allied artillery into 'grand batteries', which at both Blenheim (1704) and Malplaquet (1709) amounted to some forty guns – capable of delivering an intense bombardment in the area he wanted to establish as the focus for battle – whilst reserving his cavalry for the decisive move elsewhere.[49] For Ramillies (1706) the Allies brought as many as 120 guns against 70 for the French.[50] Marlborough's grand batteries, of course, fell well short of the artillery strengths that would be marshalled for battles in the Seven Years' War, and when Frederick the Great learned how to use artillery and solved Prussia's procurement problems, 'grand batteries' were employed in ever increasing numbers.[51] Napoleon (himself originally a gunner) made progressively more use of artillery in his later campaigns: Leipzig (1813) saw Napoleon's 700 guns pitted against combined Allied artillery strengths of between 915 and 1,500 guns by different

---

[46] Ostwald, *Vauban*, Appendix F.
[47] Wood, *King's Army*, 161, 182.
[48] Although secondary campaigns were still starved of guns: Rowlands, 'Louis XIV and French Failures', notes effects at the siege of Montmélian in 1691.
[49] Weigley, *Age of Battles*, 85, 97; Chandler, *Marlborough*, 150. Barnett, *Marlborough*, 109 gives Marlborough a total of sixty-six cannon at Blenheim against ninety guns, giving the French the best of the initial exchanges of fire along the length of the line.
[50] Chandler, *Marlborough*, 149–50.
[51] For example 170 Prussian guns versus 210 Austrian pieces at Leithen (1757), while at Zorndorf (1758) Prussia mounted 60 guns in a single battery, 'an unheard of number'. Showalter, *Wars*, 202, 210, 214.

counts.[52] If the first artillery revolution of the fourteenth and fifteenth centuries introduced a powerful new weapon, one has to look some two centuries later for a *second* turning point in the ability of commanders to use artillery to decisive effect in both siege and field warfare.

This second artillery revolution turned on its manufacturing base. France experienced consistent shortages because its foundries were fragmented and dispersed all over the northern provinces in small units, poorly financed, and run as private enterprises with only limited state support. Although Richelieu indeed attempted to prioritise the navy, the navy itself remained chronically under-gunned. Ships coming into port often had their guns removed and reinstalled in ships about to put to sea, both extending their turnaround times and reducing the battle-worthy strength of the fleet to well below the number of sea-worthy vessels.[53] England and the Netherlands, by contrast, pioneered the use of centralised gun-casting (respectively, from the Ordnance Office in the Tower of London and the Mechelen arsenal) and the use of cast-iron (in place of the much more costly bronze) artillery.[54] The Burgundian Netherlands originally sourced iron ore from near Liège, but Protestant Holland later used state and private money to fund mines and foundries in Sweden, where iron was available in large quantities. Late-fifteenth- and sixteenth-century England initially exploited the iron industry of the Weald of Kent and Sussex, where (with the help of specialists from northern France and the Low Countries) the ore proved well suited to cannon-casting.[55] This was the first of the industrial developments that would give eighteenth-century England a strong lead in arms production.

New powers, however, often faced an uphill task in establishing an arms industry on the scale demanded by modern warfare. In the mid fifteenth century the Ottomans, later to be perhaps the most prodigious deployers of artillery in Europe, relied on experts from central Europe.[56] The Prussian arms industry was launched by Frederick

---

[52] Weigley, *Age of Battles*, 280; but see the suggestion that Napoleonic reliance on artillery was a function of progressive exhaustion, and depletion of infantry and cavalry; McConachy, 'Roots of Artillery Doctrine'.

[53] Private information from Professor N. A. M. Rodger, *Crossing the Divide* conference, Reading, September 2007. See also Kennett, *French Armies*, 99 and *passim* for an excellent survey of the 'military supply complex' in the eighteenth century, and Showalter, *Wars*, 172–3. See Nef, 'War', for France after Louis XIII.

[54] Gunn, Grummitt, and Cools, *War, State, and Society*, 23–6; Fissel, *English Warfare*, 43–7, 188–93.

[55] Schubert, 'First Cannon', and 'Superiority'. See also Awty, 'Continental Origins', and 'English Cannon Founding'. For cannon technology, see Guilmartin, *Gunpowder and Galleys* (1974 edn), 157–75. For gunpowder, see Hall, *Weapons*.

[56] As shown by Veszprémy, Chapter 5, above.

William I with a powder mill and arms factory at Spandau.[57] However, most of the raw materials had to be imported: iron from Sweden, tin and lead from England, components such as gun-locks from Holland. The private firm of Splitgerber and Daun was founded in 1712 and evolved into the main state provider, developing a primitive production line capable of turning out 300 muskets a week. Cannon-founding, however, proved endlessly problematic until in 1757 a Dutchman introduced the latest technology of casting the barrels solid – thus eliminating blow-holes and other weaknesses – and then boring them out to the desired calibre with water-powered drills.[58] Although Prussian arsenals produced some 1,500 artillery pieces between 1741 and 1762, Swedish guns were still imported in large numbers and efforts continued to be made – all without success – to discover the secrets of the Swedish manufacturing processes and so reduce the state's reliance on foreign expertise.

These fragments from the economic history of arms production provide a partial explanation for the persistent shortages of the heavy guns that transformed the early-modern art of war. When available in the right numbers and properly supported with men and munitions, their impact could be devastating. Only by the late seventeenth century, it seems, were these conditions satisfied regularly enough for massed artillery to feature prominently in battle-plans or to overwhelm properly designed and well-armed bastioned fortifications with offensive firepower. Another century was to pass before the battlefield killing potential of artillery was to escalate dramatically once again with the introduction of shrapnel. In its early centuries, however, artillery remained an unreliable asset – like modern close air support, enormously powerful and frequently highly effective, but all too often not there when it was most wanted.

'Small war' and its operational significance

'Small war' is becoming belatedly recognised as an integral component of early-modern warfare, with a role in siege-centred campaigns, the support of main bodies of troops, and the occupation and exploitation of enemy territory.[59] This last included counter-insurgency against rebels and those treated as rebels (as civilians bearing arms were so frequently

---

[57] Showalter, *Wars*, 95–101, provides the following background.
[58] *Ibid.*, 99.
[59] Satterfield, *Princes, Posts and Partisans*, 8, credits Lynn, *Giant*, 538, with first raising the issue of *petite guerre* as a substantive element in French seventeenth-century strategy, but see also Kunisch, *Kleine Krieg*.

regarded by regular soldiers).[60] Small war involved both infantry and cavalry; but it became a speciality of the light horse. For much of the Middle Ages, indeed, the mounted raiding expedition, or *chevauchée*, was the basic form of offensive military activity: yielding loot and ransoms, leaving destruction in its wake, but not amounting to an invasion in the modern sense of territory seized and occupied.[61]

This kind of operation continued in our period, sometimes on an ambitious scale and with a degree of mobility that forces us to re-examine our certainties about the slow pace of some early-modern campaigning. After the defeat of the Huguenots at Moncontour (1569), Admiral Coligny mounted the surviving Protestant infantry and with his cavalry embarked upon 'a remarkable nine-month perambulation through southern France, looting and burning along the Garonne, through Languedoc from Toulouse to Nîmes, and up the right bank of the Rhône to Chalon-sur-Sâone'.[62] It was this, along with the Catholic weakness in siege artillery noted earlier, which enabled the Huguenots to undo the apparently decisive effects of the defeat at Moncontour. A high-speed *course* was executed by Brigadier-General Feuquières in 1689, when he led a thirty-five-day cavalry raid over 800 km collecting contributions from Würzburg, Nuremberg, Ulm, Augsburg, and Pforzheim.[63] This was a form of war at which the Venetians had excelled during the fifteenth and sixteenth centuries, using their *stradiotti*, or irregular light cavalry, recruited in the republic's overseas colonies in Dalmatia, Albania, and Greece, where they often proved a match for Ottoman raiders. Austria inherited the mantle of acknowledged masters of small war during the seventeenth and eighteenth centuries with their Hussar light cavalry and *Grenzer* (borderer) companies. Often known as 'Croats' the *Grenzer* included Catholic Croatians, Orthodox Serbians, and even radical Protestants, who enjoyed a degree of autonomy and religious toleration for their readiness to serve in permanent militia communities on the long military frontier with the Ottoman Balkans.[64]

Small war embraced calculated moves against targets of high value, such as the demolition of dykes in the Low Countries campaigns, or

---

[60] McCullough, *Coercion*, deals with the revolt of the Camissards (peaked 1702–4) in Languedoc against the re-Catholicisation policies of Louis XIV.

[61] See Bennett, Chapter 12, below.

[62] Wood, *King's Army*, 27–8.

[63] Chandler, *Art of Warfare*, 52.

[64] Showalter, *Wars*, 52, notes that during the Silesian war following Mollwitz (1741), the Prussians (who had won the battle) suffered continuous reversals in their subsequent occupation because of Austrian tactics honed on the Hungarian frontier. See also Duffy, *Frederick the Great*, 32, and *Army of Frederick the Great*.

the mills and bridges that featured in Sienese defensive tactics as well as the economic warfare of their Florentine enemies.[65] Occasionally a 'surgical strike' could be locally decisive; such as the raid carried out in 1536 at the initiative of Blaise de Monluc to burn the mill of Auriol, in Provence, thereby destroying the flour and bread supplies of the imperial army besieging nearby Marseilles, and forcing the imperialists to raise the siege. The incident is described in detail in Monluc's *Memoirs*, which reveal the clear thinking that preceded the raid.[66] Such operations were an integral part of the art of war, though disdained by many earlier military historians.[67]

The attack and defence of unmodernised fortresses, or even temporarily strengthened country houses, was a regular feature of the French Wars of Religion and of the English Civil War, which saw a number of ad hoc defences evolve into minor siege epics, such as that of Basing House in 1643–5.[68] Much of the destruction mentioned earlier originated, not in major sieges – still less battles – but in the minor operations that accompanied both kinds of major operation and filled the long intervals between them. The results were equally disastrous. When the small town of Marlborough was sacked in 1643 the pamphlet denouncing the outrage was entitled *Marlborough's Miseries, or, England Turned Ireland* – and this title tells us as much about the regular nature of low-intensity conflict in Ireland as the misfortune of the English town.[69] The pillaging of villages and towns – we need to remind ourselves – was an integral part of both late-medieval and early-modern warfare. It was not only something undertaken by rogue units, but rather was part of a commander's 'operational art'. The celebrated and infamous 'harrowing of Bavaria' by Marlborough's army before Blenheim was ordered to 'press the Elector' to reconsider his recent alliance with the French, as well as to bring the latter to battle.[70] This was small war on a massive scale, and the devastation was something that could touch the consciences of those involved, including Marlborough himself and Prince Louis, Margrave of Baden, who 'found the whole business deeply distasteful, declaring that he wished to fight like a general, not like a hussar'.[71] Satterfield

---

[65] Pepper and Adams, *Firearms and Fortifications*, 86–7.
[66] It was one of the case-studies featured in Harari, *Special Operations*.
[67] Notably Oman, *History Sixteenth Century*.
[68] The siege of Basing House, Hampshire was one of the most celebrated operations of the English Civil War. See Godwin, *Civil War*; Warren, *Story of Basing House*; Emberton, 'Love Loyalty'.
[69] *Marlborough's Miseries, or, England Turned Ireland* ... (1643), title-page reprinted in Porter, *Destruction*, 35.
[70] Holmes, *Marlborough*, 277ff.
[71] *Ibid.*, 278.

identified the organised and centrally controlled conduct of partisan warfare (using the term in its original sense of war conducted by small parties of detached troops), as an evolving element in late-seventeenth-century French strategy whereby enemies would be worn down by the cumulative effects of numerous small actions – what much later would be codified as a strategy of attrition.[72]

What of partisan warfare by civilians? For much of our period the distinction between navies and merchant shipping was blurred.[73] Privateers played the role of 'civilians in arms' at sea, sometimes legitimised by letters of marque. In 1693–4 France effectively 'privatised' the royal navy and scaled up privateering enterprise correspondingly.[74] Land-based partisan warfare is now often seen as characteristic of twentieth-century conflict, but we need to ask if there were medieval or early-modern equivalents to guerrilla or irregular warfare conceived in this privateering spirit? If so, were these initiatives organised, encouraged, or supported; or must they be seen as the spontaneous resistance of desperate peasants?[75]

The War of the League of Cambrai (1509–17) brought an impressive but cumbersome and ultimately fragile alliance of Habsburg Empire, France, the Papacy, Florence, Mantua, and Ferrara against the republic of Venice. Venice was defeated at Agnadello (14 May 1509), after which nearly all of the republic's mainland territory and towns were swiftly occupied by the League. However, Venice succeeded in re-taking Padua in a *coup de main* and holding the city in a celebrated siege from August to October 1509. While many of the patricians in formerly subject cities sided with the occupying forces, the peasants of the *terraferma* generally supported Venice and served in many ways in the long struggle that lasted until 1517 to win back the mainland provinces. For the lower orders the republic was seen as guarantor of rights only recently won from former feudal lords, and the provider of legal redress often effectively closed to them by the regional urban entities. Support was strong in the eastern frontier province of Friuli, where a particularly harsh feudal regime had been removed only recently and its restoration was feared.[76] Peasants were issued with arms and

---

[72] Satterfield, *Princes, Posts and Partisans*, 9.
[73] See Sicking, Chapter 11, below.
[74] Rodger, *Command*, 157–8, noting Vauban's *Mémoire sur la caprérie*, which argued the case for a privateer-based naval strategy for France, in place of an unequal struggle against Dutch and English naval strength. See also David Parrott's chapter in this volume.
[75] Symcox, 'Popular Resistance'.
[76] See Muir, *Mad Blood*, for the background to these events.

bore them in areas around Padua and in the delta zones of the Po and the Brenta. Urban resistance, not surprisingly, was mostly reported in connection with the defiant last words of resisters.

Peasant resistance here was both spontaneous and to some extent centrally supported, and provided a valuable supplement to the diplomacy that eventually allowed the Venetians to divide the alliance against them, and the conventional warfare waged with soldiers hired on the military market or imported from the republic's overseas territories.[77] In other sixteenth-century Italian wars the irregulars provided a principal component of the armed struggle.

The attacks launched on the supply lines feeding the siege camps around Florence in 1529–30 contributed significantly to the lengthy resistance of the last Florentine republic.[78] Early in the siege a raid deprived the imperial–papal alliance of its artillery en route from Siena to Florence. The heavy guns on which the alliance was counting had been lost three years earlier in 1526, when the Florentines had unsuccessfully laid siege to Siena. Diplomatic pressure persuaded Siena in 1529 to assist the imperial–papal alliance with the captured guns, but the convoy dragging the artillery northward had been ambushed by Florentine republican raiders, and the guns destroyed. Although the siege of Florence formally opened on 29 October 1529, it was the end of December before replacement artillery could be hauled over the passes from Milan and Ferrara, much of it by then in poor condition. The last siege of Florence has to be seen as the centre-piece of operations waged throughout the extensive surrounding territories, with most of the towns occupied but much of the countryside and some key fortresses in the hands of irregular Florentine forces. Resistance was led by Francesco Ferruccio, a civilian commissary with only limited prior experience of war (operating in the south); Lorenzo Carnesecchi, commissary at Castrocaro (in the east); and Cecotto Tosinghi, another civil commissary at Pisa (operating near the coast). Essentially it was a war of small bodies of troops: Ferruccio took only 1,500 men with him on his final operation, which ended when he was cornered and killed at Gavinana in August 1530, just before Florence surrendered.[79]

Shortly after opening the siege of Siena (January 1554 to May 1555) the Marquis of Marignano complained about attacks on his lines of

---

[77] These aspects of the war are the subject of current research. For general coverage of the war, see Mallett and Hale, *Military Organisation*.
[78] Roth, *Last Florentine Republic*, is still the most readable account, but see Falletti, *L'assedio*, and Comitato per le ororanze a Francesco Ferruccio, *Francesco Ferruccio*.
[79] Pepper, 'Face of the Siege', 48–9.

communication.[80] He called for mobile artillery to deploy against 'certain little places where those peasants who raid the highways are based'.[81] The isolated medieval towers and castles would be evacuated on the approach of troops with a single medium-calibre gun; but there were so many towers and so few of the mobile guns that the campaign to flush out the raiders was protracted. Here, as elsewhere, the iron cannonballs for the half-culverins employed against the 'little places' ran out, causing further delays in the mopping-up operations.[82] Sienese sources shed no light on the extent – if any – of central control. However, those responsible for implementing the defensive scorched-earth policy were certainly protected by general central pronouncements listing the places that would be defended and – by inference – condemning other targets to be destroyed. Later, in what developed into one of the longest sieges of the Italian wars, peasant blockade-runners kept communications open between Siena and Montalcino, the French base about twenty miles to the south. Messages were easiest to smuggle, if also the most dangerous for those caught. However, some of the blockade-running involved substantial herds of cattle that were assembled beyond the heavily patrolled approaches and then escorted in at speed by cavalry, with diversions to draw off the imperial patrols – complex operations, in short, requiring a level of communication between those inside and outside the blockaded city that belies the commonly held impression of a hermetically sealed siege.[83]

To these examples could be added many others, including the Calvinist *bosgeuzen* (Wood-Beggars), ordinary Netherlanders, often artisans, who conducted a bitter, low-intensity campaign against the Spanish between 1568 and 1572, sacking churches and killing priests, government officials, and informers; the Irish rebels of the 1590s, who successfully waged a guerrilla war in Ulster, but were defeated when in 1601–2 they finally took on the English army at conventional warfare; and the Cossacks and Polish partisans who conducted a series of raids on the communications of the Turkish army besieging Hotin in 1621, and who completely

[80] Marignano (1497–1555), who confronted these difficulties in Sienese Tuscany in the service of Cosimo de' Medici and the Emperor, was the same Giangiacomo de' Medici (no relative of Cosimo) who, as a political refugee from his native Milan, led an effective guerrilla campaign against successive occupiers of the Milanese from his base at the north end of Lake Como.

[81] Situation report from Marignano to Cosimo, ASF, Carte Strozziane, I, 109, fos. 150–1, and despatch, 28 January 1554, ASF, Mediceo del Principato 1853.

[82] Pepper and Adams, *Firearms and Fortifications*, 123–6, 166, 222 n. 26.

[83] Names from this undercover war included Agnolo Callocci, taken at Christmas 1554; Carlotto, captured March 1555; and Tiranfallo Guidi (celebrated for his twenty-two return trips in and out of besieged Montalcino in 1553), who may have survived.

demoralised the superior besieging Ottoman force, compelling it to make the long and perilous retreat back to the Danube.[84]

There is therefore a substantial body of 'circumstantial evidence' for the effective use of both offensive and defensive *petite guerre* operations throughout our extended period, culminating in the adoption by Louis XIV's France of a formal strategy of attrition (Showalter's analysis). France was not alone here. The continued maintenance of Hussars, *Grenzer*, Cossacks, *stradiotti*, and other quasi-regular standing forces speaks to a broad measure of state support for a style of warfare demanding both experience and special skills (often not far removed from banditry) but which was generally not highly esteemed amongst the officer classes of early-modern Europe (witness Prince Louis of Baden). Irregulars, special forces, and resisters are never easy to control (or to research); and the ability (or, as frequently, inability) of commanders to exercise control over such forces and their operations may well explain their place in the margins of mainstream military history. Their operational methods are certainly no longer on the margins, however, and when caught in the media spotlight stir very mixed feelings in the late twentieth and early twenty-first centuries.[85]

Conclusion

The intention behind this chapter has been to sharpen the picture of post-medieval operational art by bringing into focus, however briefly, factors that are often overlooked. These include developments in the pattern of communications and mapping and, hence, in the way many commanders (and increasingly their political masters) conceptualised large-scale operations and their own ability to influence events. The development of mapping, it has been suggested, represents a key area of change in the post-medieval era, which gave commanders at all levels an essentially new operational tool. Military professionals today might well point to another very recent but equivalent step-change in this field with the development of satellite reconnaissance, location-finding, targeting, and communications systems, which have even more spectacularly transformed contemporary operations. The development of gunpowder artillery represented yet another key area of change with profound operational implications. This is, of course, well known; however it is important to understand the pace of change. If bastioned fortifications

---

[84] Schütz (ed. and trans.), *Armeno-Kipchak Chronicle*, 55, 75, 87 (references courtesy of Rhoads Murphey).

[85] Witness the operations of the late-twentieth-century Balkan wars and, more recently, in Iraq, Afghanistan, and the Caucasus.

represented a strikingly effective response to improved gunpowder artillery, we also need to recognise the serious constraints on the ability of commanders to deploy the latest and most powerful gunpowder weapons in their arsenals. More than any other post-medieval weapons-system, big guns depended on a developed manufacturing base and a supporting infrastructure capable of keeping them maintained, ammunitioned, and manned by trained personnel, which included the hauliers who moved them to where they were needed. Failure in any area was critical, and although the new technology was understood, widely disseminated, and effectively utilised in sieges by the fifteenth century, only late in our period were all of the conditions satisfied regularly enough for artillery to fulfil its potential on the battlefield.

The very different conditions of low-intensity 'small war' have also been explored. Operations by small parties of soldiers or civilians in arms were often highly mobile and, if only occasionally decisive, were frequently conducted on a scale that called for what today would be seen as counter-insurgency operations, activities that – then as now – potentially tie down large numbers of troops and provide the classical justification for guerrilla warfare. Although relatively under-researched, 'small war' was a constant factor in warfare throughout the lengthy period covered by this volume.

Whether any of these factors, considered in isolation, can be placed on an equal footing with the tendency of risk-averse commanders to avoid battle or the effectiveness of post-medieval fortifications as drivers of military change is doubtful. Taken together, however, their impact on the wider conduct of operations was often highly significant.

10   Tactics and the face of battle

Clifford J. Rogers

Prologue: high-medieval tactics

Although revisionist historians have lately argued otherwise, in the High Middle Ages (*c.* 1000–1300) cavalry was the dominant arm in battle.[1] Infantry was valued, and was present at most battles, but its role was often almost purely defensive, and it usually takes offensive action to win a true victory. As Jim Bradbury observed in concluding his study of Anglo-Norman battles (in which dismounted knights played a substantial role), the biggest threat on the battlefield was a cavalry charge, but the strongest defence against a head-on mounted attack was a steady line of spear-armed footmen supported by archery.[2] In other words, cavalry and footmen could work together like sword and shield. A swordsman surely values a sturdy shield, and even knows it can sometimes be used to strike important blows, but would sooner dispense with it than try fighting without his blade.

Battles in this period tended to follow one of a few basic patterns. Often the opposing armies would face off, infantry-line to infantry-line, each with its cavalry to the flanks or rear. Then the mounted forces would charge each other at a trot, while the footmen either held their ground or advanced to contact very slowly, so that they could keep their order. Since the former closed much more quickly, and since mounted combat was typically decided more rapidly than a contest between shield walls, the issue of the battle as a whole was likely to be determined by the cavalry fight. At least some of the victorious horsemen could be expected to come in on the flank and rear of the enemy footmen while the latter were still engaged by infantry in front; when attacked from all directions, infantry had little chance of escape, and less of victory.

I owe thanks for their comments and assistance to John F. Guilmartin, Jr., Michiel de Jong, Geoffrey Parker, John Stapleton, Jr., and the conference participants; and for financial assistance to the United States Military Academy.

[1] Verbruggen, 'Role of the Cavalry'.
[2] Bradbury, 'Battles in England and Normandy', 193.

The side that was weaker in cavalry therefore often avoided battle, but if constrained to fight might try dismounting most of its knights and fighting primarily on the defensive, ideally in a position where the terrain protected their flanks. The men on foot would seek to hold off the attacks of the enemy infantry and cavalry until the latter had been worn down and disordered to the point where they were vulnerable to attack by a cavalry reserve, or at least until they gave up attacking. Such tactics sometimes (though not often) brought victory to the footmen, but even then the force with superior cavalry was typically able to retire without heavy loss or great strategic disadvantage.

Over the course of the thirteenth century, increasing urbanisation, expanding wealth, and the growing power of royal governments all contributed to the rising importance of infantry. At the start of the fourteenth century this trend reached a tipping point. Already there were normally several times more infantrymen in an army than there were cavalrymen, and while the men-at-arms remained qualitatively superior soldiers, their margin of advantage declined as the foot-soldiers (especially urban militiamen) improved their equipment, and strengthened their cohesion and morale through the continued development of more martial civic cultures. In the last decades of the thirteenth century the bowmen of Edward I of England and the Catalan *almugavers* proved invaluable, though they did not yet surpass the horsemen in importance. In one battle, for example, Ramón Muntaner went with 1,000 foot and 250 horse to fight a large Muslim army composed almost entirely of infantry. The badly outnumbered Catalan footmen were routed by the opposing infantry, but then the small body of horse charged into their mass and won a complete victory.[3]

Late-medieval tactics: the Infantry Revolution

In the fourteenth century, this balance was reversed.[4] Cavalry remained very important in battle, and even more so in the broader conduct of war, but it was men fighting on foot who won the battles of Courtrai, Bannockburn, Morgarten, Dupplin Moor and Halidon Hill, Laupen, Crécy, Vottem, Canturino, Nájera, Cascina, Aljubarrota, etc. The early victories in this series were won through a combination of favourable terrain and enemy errors, but their outcome also owed a great deal to the willingness of the infantry commanders to undertake offensive actions on the battlefield. Yet it remained true that the defence had a

[3] Muntaner, *Chronicle*, 510–11; cf. 117–19.
[4] Rogers, 'Military Revolutions', 56–64.

huge advantage in infantry combat, especially when fighting from a prepared position. The key to victory was to keep a formation in good order, and it was extremely difficult for attackers to avoid disrupting their array as they advanced, especially if they had to march through effective missile fire, or if the defenders were fighting behind trenches, marshes, hedges, stake-barriers, or other obstacles – as they commonly did.[5] John Chandos' observation of 1368 that 'it goes ill with the side that attacks first'[6] was echoed by Jean de Bueil in the late fifteenth century: 'All those who advance on foot break their own array and put themselves out of breath, and ordinarily they suffer defeat.'[7] Thus, strategy often involved the use of devastation, manoeuvres, or sieges designed to push the enemy into accepting the burden of the tactical initiative. But it required skilful generalship or serious mistakes by the opposing commander to lure an enemy into attacking a ready army on its chosen ground; often when two armies faced off, there was a substantial delay while each waited for the enemy to attack.

Sometimes such stand-offs did not lead to battles at all, but usually political, strategic, or operational considerations pushed one side into taking action to initiate the fight. The side with greater missile power might use its shot to provoke or force the other side into attacking. If the side with superior firepower also had the advantage in cavalry, it could use the threat or the action of the horsemen to keep the enemy foot pinned in place, then wear it down with shot until it was sufficiently shaken to be broken by a shock attack. Rather than undertaking a risky offensive, or standing and suffering prolonged attrition, the opposing commander could of course choose to retreat from the field, but that too could lead easily to disaster. Another option was to launch a pinning attack in front, while sending an enveloping force to win the battle by attacking the enemy's flank or rear. Cavalry was of course the best arm for such a manoeuvre, and this is one reason it remained important on the battlefield despite the Infantry Revolution.

The early-modern period: pike-squares

When the Swiss fought Charles the Bold of Burgundy or Emperor Maximilian, they did not have superior firepower or superior cavalry, yet they still won, and in so doing added great impetus to the spread

---

[5] Even Swiss battles were often won by lightly defending an earthwork, then counter-attacking: Winkler, 'Swiss', 48.

[6] Cuvelier, *La chanson*, lines 5875–8.

[7] Bueil, *Jouvencel*, I, 189; see also I, 153.

of a new model for European infantry tactics, one founded on the pike-square, supplemented and eventually surpassed in importance by attached formations of handgunners.

Until the advent of the Swiss, medieval infantry (and cavalry) tactics were usually essentially 'linear,' meaning that the normal infantry formation was much broader in front than it was deep. Like the ancient Greeks, medieval footmen typically fought in four to eight ranks. The width of the array then depended on the strength of the army. The Swiss, by contrast, might draw up their formations in squares forty or more men deep. In the sixteenth century, squares as many as sixty or seventy-five ranks deep were sometimes seen. Although these blocks are conventionally referred to as 'pike-squares', they usually contained a core of men with shorter weapons such as halberds or bills surrounded by pikemen, in varying proportion. In the late fifteenth century, Philipp von Seldeneck called for an infantry force of 10,000 men to be drawn up in a square 100 men deep and 100 across. In the sixteenth century, this would have been termed a 'just square of men'; other common arrangements were the 'square of ground' (which was square in area but only three men deep for every seven in front, since files were more tightly closed than ranks) and the 'broad square' (at least twice as broad as deep).[8]

Square formations of this sort, like any other arrangement of soldiers, had advantages and disadvantages. On the negative side, they were particularly vulnerable to artillery, since a single cannonball could kill many men.[9] Like all very deep close-order infantry formations, they were also vulnerable to the greatest disaster that could strike a pre-modern army: if they became disordered, they could become compressed to the point where the soldiers could not fight effectively, and even to the point where they crushed and smothered each other to death, as happened for example to the unusually deep formations of the Scots at Dupplin Moor, the Flemings at Roosebeke, and the French at Agincourt. It took the Swiss 'daily exercise' (and a culture in which boys and youths engaged in war games that prepared them for the task)[10] to develop the ability to manoeuvre and fight in formation without fatally compromising the integrity of their array. Also, because of their greatly reduced frontage, squares were much harder to anchor on terrain obstacles such as woods or villages. But then, one of the main

---

[8] Eltis, *Military Revolution*, 52–3; Seldeneck, *Kriegsbuch*, 91; Barret, *Moderne Warres*, 52, 75–7, 94–5.
[9] E.g. Winkler, 'Swiss', 140.
[10] *Ibid.*, 123 n.; see also Garrard, *Arte of Warre*, 9, 89; Styward, *Pathwaie*, 21.

purposes of having a square formation was to make the sides of the block inherently almost as strong as the front,[11] so that the danger of an exposed flank was much reduced. And on the offence, the narrower front was an advantage. Any little hedge or ditch posed a significant problem for a block of footmen trying to advance in formation,[12] and it is much easier to find an unobstructed approach to the enemy 40 yards wide than to find one 300 or 1,000 yards across.

When a pike-square lumbered forward, its mass gave it tremendous momentum. If the attacking footmen were well armoured, they could usually drive through even heavy rains of arrows or bolts and come to grips with missile-firing infantry, which would then almost inevitably break. A thinner formation of footmen armed with pole-arms likewise had little hope of resisting the onslaught of such a powerful mass. Of course, a thinner line would also, for a given number of men, be wider, which theoretically created a possibility of enveloping the square on the flanks and defeating it there even as it broke through the line in one spot, but this possibility was largely illusory. As already noted, the square was not terribly vulnerable to flank attacks. More importantly, the leaders of the deep mass could slam it directly against the principal banners of the opposing force, usually found in the centre of the line. Banners were the principal means of tactical command and control, and once they went down, those who fought under them usually broke; even if they continued fighting, they were much less able to do so effect-ively. 'The standard', explained a fifteenth-century banner-bearer, 'is like a torch set in a room to give light to all men; if by some accident it is put out, all remain in darkness and unseeing and are beaten'.[13]

In the Italian wars at the turn of the sixteenth century, experience showed that a Swiss attack could be halted, at least temporarily, in vari-ous ways – by cavalry attacks against the column's flank; by the use of entrenchments, sunken roads, or water barriers; or by an opposing block of other pikemen. But none of these methods would serve, alone, to prevent the advance from resuming, or truly to defeat the attackers. To secure a genuine victory over these fearsome warriors (or others using their tactics, such as the *Landsknechte* examined in Chapter 8), it was necessary to hammer the square with shot while it advanced and while it was checked. But because of new developments in armour technology, the old missile weapons (crossbows and longbows) were

---

[11] Barret, *Moderne Warres*, 76–7.
[12] Bueil, *Jouvencel*, II, 63.
[13] Guttiere Diaz de Gamez, quoted in Rogers, *Soldiers' Lives*, 198; cf. Benedetti, *Bello carolino*, 101, 150–1.

not really up to this job. Handguns and field artillery *were*, and their growing importance in the first half of the fifteenth century was the other half of the tactical transformation that marks the shift from medieval to early-modern on the battlefield.

The rise of the handgunner

There is a striking degree of continuity in tactics from Ancient Greece through the early Renaissance, deriving from the essentially constant capabilities of the human body and the limited possibilities for variation in hand-held weapons of steel and wood. That fact lies at the core of one sixteenth-century observer's comment that tactics had been 'from the first creation of the world until now the very same, the disposition of the people only varying in the difference of weapons, engines, and instruments, which have been invented'.[14] But the gun was new and fundamentally different, and increasingly came to replace the bow and crossbow, and to reduce even the cavalryman's reliance on the ancient weapons of cold steel. 'The arms of our grandfathers', commented Jean de Saulx-Tavannes, 'were the lance, the axe, the mace and the sword. The last we still use, but the rest are considered of little value partly because of armour of proof, which they neither pierce nor penetrate easily, and partly because of the invention of better pistols.'[15] This change in weapons naturally demanded changes in fighting methods, both individual and collective: 'at this day we are constrained to varie our order [from classical forms]', wrote William Garrard in 1591, 'considering our armes be varied, which do now fetch and [w]ound much more and further off, and are more pearcing then those of antient time'.[16] Robert Barret, a few years later, had little patience for his compatriots who still thought the English bill and bow could win great victories, as they had done through the medieval period, and even into the early sixteenth century: 'Time altereth the order of warre, with many new inventions daily'; 'then was then, and now is now; the wars are much altered since the fierie weapons first came up.'[17]

The importance of the shift to gunpowder weapons has long been recognised – and was well appreciated even in the sixteenth century[18] – but

---

[14] Quoted in Webb, *Elizabethan Military Science*, 16.
[15] Tavannes, *Mémoires*, 191–2.
[16] Garrard, *Arte of Warre*, 64.
[17] Barret, *Moderne Warres*, 2m, 2.
[18] In addition to the last three citations: Rich, *Fruites*, 68; Williams, *Briefe discourse*, 37; and Cruso, *Militarie Instructions*, A3v, who views the changes made in response to 'later inventions of fire weapons' as the only thing 'in these modern warres, which is not borrowed from antiquitie'. But cf. Smythe, *Certain Discourses*, *2v.

it is important to note that this change was itself not simply caused by the 'push' of an inherently superior weapon,[19] but rather (or also) by demand-pull on two fronts. First, there was demand for weapons-systems that would allow exploitation of increases in population and revenue not matched by a corresponding increase in the martial classes. Pikes and guns required training to use well – particularly *group* training (drill) – but they did not require soldiers who were raised and trained to their use from early youth, as the longbow and (to an extent) the lance did. A mere fortnight's drill was considered sufficient to make a recruit into a pikeman or arquebusier 'mete to serve'.[20] Humphrey Barwick meant to emphasise the difficulty of mastering matchlocks when he wrote that pikemen and halberdiers 'are made perfect in six daies, better than the fierie weapons are in 60 days' – but even sixty days' training was a relatively small investment of time compared to the years of practice that could profitably be applied to perfect the older martial skills (and the muscular development) of the man-at-arms or the archer. Indeed, it was proverbially recognised that only someone who had trained from boyhood could serve respectably as a knight or a longbowman.[21]

The other factor creating a demand-pull that encouraged the adoption of firearms was – as Tavannes indicated – the problem posed to older weapons by new metallurgical developments. Around the turn of the fifteenth century, Milanese smiths developed new techniques that allowed for a radical improvement in the practical effectiveness of the steel used in plate armour. The key was quenching the armour pieces rather than allowing them to air-cool. The technique was very difficult to master, but made a tremendous difference in the practical protective value of the harness. Top-quality armour was, however, very expensive, and metallurgical analysis of surviving pieces shows that, for a long time after the new methods were developed, there were plenty of mediocre harnesses being produced, and even more remained in service on the battlefield.[22]

[19] Eltis, *Military Revolution*, 102; note also Smythe, *Certain Discourses*, A2v.
[20] Audley, 'Treatise', 69; Roberts, *Gustavus Adolphus*, II, 239; and cf. Webb, *Elizabethan Military Science*, 35.
[21] Barwick, *Discourse*, 24 (and cf. 11, where he claimed he shot as well with an arquebus after five months as with a bow after many years). Knight: Bloch, *Feudal Society*, II, 293–4; cf. Cruso, *Militarie Instructions*, 30. The Dutch believed a lancer could be trained in three years (Puype, 'Victory', 82); in contrast, Tavannes believed only three months' training was needed for a pistoleer who would not be required to duel on horseback (Tavannes, *Mémoires*, 194). Longbowman: Strickland and Hardy, *Great Warbow* (New York edn), 30; Smythe, *Certain Discourses*, 26v–27; Pisan, 'Livre des fais d'armes', Bodleian, MS 824, fo. 27v.
[22] Hall, *Weapons*, 147; Williams, *Knight, passim*.

Even mediocre plate armour was very tough to overcome with weapons powered by human muscle. Normal bows and light crossbows were practically unable to do it; in fact, the very definition of a quality suit of plate was that it had been tested with an arrow or a bolt and found to be 'proof' against it.[23] Still, heavy crossbows and arrows loosed from the extraordinarily powerful English warbow *could* penetrate mild-steel plate – thin pieces like gauntlets, greaves, or visors fairly easily; thick breastplates or bascinet-tops only at close range and with an ideal angle of impact. Properly quenched high-carbon steel, with a Vickers hardness of around 350 (as opposed to around 150 for air-cooled medium-carbon steel) was another matter. It could successfully resist a weapon striking with *double* the kinetic energy required to defeat an old-style harness.[24] It was nearly impossible for even the strongest longbow or windlass-drawn crossbow to cause serious injury through a breastplate of that sort, and only a lucky shot from a strong bowman would even be able to cause a limb wound worth mentioning.[25] At Flodden in 1513, for example, English bowmen found that the Scottish pikemen were so well armoured that arrows 'did them no harm'.[26]

Handguns, on the other hand, were not limited by the energy-producing capability of the human body. Modern tests have demonstrated that the very strongest archers (who had 'hands and arms of iron' and 'bodies stronger than other men's')[27] could put a formidable 130 to 150 J of kinetic energy behind their armour-piercing shafts. A heavy steel-bowed crossbow produced somewhat more energy initially, perhaps up to around 200 J.[28] But a well-charged 1.5 oz (42.52 g) musket-ball could leave its barrel with around 3,100 J, a 1 oz (28.3 g) arquebus-ball with around 2,700 J; even a cavalryman's pistol could deliver over 1,000 J.[29] It is not simple to interpret the implications of these numbers for practical effectiveness, because ballistics is a complicated subject. For example, round bullets in their flight rapidly lose energy to friction with the air, unlike streamlined arrows or modern bullets; and

---

[23] Williams, *Knight*, 924.

[24] *Ibid.*, 62–4, 693–4. The Vickers test produces an objective measure of hardness, derived from a material's ability to resist plastic deformation from a standard source; the higher the Vickers number, the harder the material.

[25] Rogers, 'Agincourt', Appendix I; note also Fourquevaux, *Instructions*, I, 12, 38r–v.

[26] Strickland and Hardy, *Great Warbow*, 397–9.

[27] Mancini, *Usurpation*, 99.

[28] Arrows: Rogers, 'Agincourt', Appendix I. Crossbow: Williams, *Knight*, 919–20, but cf. Grancsay, 'Armor', 90 for just 31 J from a 740 lb crannequin crossbow with a 35 g bolt.

[29] Kalaus, 'Schiessversuche': (musket) 52, 56, 59; (28 g ball) 57; (18 g ball, 988 J) 53; (pistols) 55, 61; note also Grancsay, 'Armor', 91.

hardened steel arrowheads are far better suited for penetrating armour than are soft lead spheres.[30] Hence, a pistol ball at 200 yards (182.88 m) could easily be stopped by even the cheapest vambrace, whereas a strong archer's war-shaft could still punch through the armour like a cobbler's awl.[31] But if fired from just outside the reach of an enemy's lance, a pistol stood a fair chance of killing a well-armoured sixteenth-century man-at-arms, which an arrow or bolt did not.[32] A musket-ball could penetrate a high-quality corselet at 200 yards (182.88 m), defeat an average one at 400 yards (365.76 m), and ruin an unarmoured horse or man even at 600 yards (548.64 m),[33] a distance far outside the range at which even the best bowman could return fire.[34] Moreover, the wounds inflicted by early-modern bullets were generally much worse than those caused by arrows. A bodkin arrowhead that pierced through its target might create a wound cavity of around 45 cm³; by contrast, modern testing suggests that at close range an arquebus-ball might blast a hole in a human body three times that size at 100 m, or eight times at 9 m.[35] It was common for men wearing good fifteenth-century armour to suffer multiple wounds from arrows or crossbow-bolts and still to be able to fight. By contrast, Bayard was killed by a ball from a musket that struck him in the side, apparently penetrated his armour, and continued on to break his spine.[36]

To be sure, firearms had their disadvantages. Even a skilled hand-gunner with a well-made weapon and a tight-fitting ball could not hope to match the long-range accuracy of a good bowman. In Tudor times, the *minimum* range allowed for longbow practice by full-grown men was 220 yards (201.17 m), aiming at round targets 18 in (45.72 cm) in diameter! When the married men of Calais challenged the bachelors of the town to a shooting match in 1478, the distance between the targets

---

[30] Hall, *Weapons*, 137, 145–6; Williams, *Knight*, 646.

[31] Stretton, 'Medieval Arrowheads', 55; Williams, *Knight*, 928–9, 942; Hall, *Weapons*, 137, but cf. Barwick, *Discourse*, 20v.

[32] Tavannes, *Mémoires*, 191–2, 336; La Noue, *Discourses*, 199.

[33] Barwick, *Discourse*, 10v; Williams, *Knight*, 947–8; see also Williams, *Briefe discourse*, 40–1; Barret, *Moderne Warres*, 2–3; Monluc, *Memoirs*, 186; Smythe, *Certain Discourses*, 14r–v. Hall's lower assessment (*Weapons*, 146) contradicts these contemporaries and is not borne out by the modern tests. See also Eltis, *Military Revolution*, 13–15.

[34] Strickland and Hardy, *Great Warbow*, 409; cf. also Barret, *Moderne Warres*, 2–3; Monluc, *Memoirs*, 129; Barwick, *Discourse*, 20v.

[35] Barwick, *Discourse*, 14v–15: 'nowe … the weakest of us are able to give greater wounds, then the greatest and strongest archer'. Arquebus (28 g ball into soap block): Kalaus, 'Schiessversuche', 77, cf. 57; Hall, *Weapons*, 146. Arrow: based on 1.5 cm diameter head and 25 cm penetration; cf. Karger *et al.*, 'Wounds', 497–9.

[36] Berville, *Histoire*, 379; Similarly: Monluc, *Commentaires et lettres*, I, 71, 75, 203–4; see also Barwick, *Discourse*, 3.

was set at 260 yards (237.74 m).[37] By contrast, arquebusiers in 1560 were provided with butts 20 *feet* (6.10 m) wide by 16 feet (4.88 m) high, with target circles 54 in (1.37 m) in diameter, for shooting at just 120 yards (109.73 m).[38] Barwick's claim that with an arquebus he could hit a man standing at that distance was thus a boast,[39] and modern tests give reason to doubt that even an excellent gunner could manage that feat consistently. Owing to the Magnus effect, the unpredictable spin of a smooth-bore musket's ball causes it to curve unpredictably from its target line.[40] The inaccuracy of the weapon would have been seriously worsened by the normal battlefield practice of using balls significantly smaller than the gun bore.[41] Of course, there was no great need for precision on an early-modern battlefield, where the target would normally be an enemy pike formation, dozens of yards wide. But even against such a target, effective range was quite limited. Digges considered that a 'trained shot' ought to be able to deliver his ball between foot-height and head-height at 133 or 166 yards (121.62 to 151.79 m), but he admitted that 'our common shot, if they discharge not within an hundred pace [83 yards (75.90 m)], they wil wast their powder, and do little or no hurt at all to their Enimies'.[42]

An even bigger disadvantage was the time-consuming complexity of the reloading process, well described by Bert Hall:

The soldier first had to dismount and secure his match; then to blow any sparks from his firing pan; then to prime the pan with special fine gunpowder, remembering to shake any excess from the pan and to tamp the pan with his finger; then to recharge his piece with regular gunpowder and to reload it with wadding and shot, drawing out his ramrod and tamping the powder and ball with just the right amount of pressure. He was then ready to cock his mechanism, blow his match to life, fix it in the matchlock's jaws, present his piece, and give fire.[43]

---

[37] Strickland and Hardy, *Great Warbow*, 381; Soar, *Secrets*, 194; see also Smythe, *Certain Discourses*, 27v; Fourquevaux, *Instructions*, I, 12.

[38] Soar, *Secrets*, 194–5.

[39] Webb, *Elizabethan Military Science*, 94; cf. Barwick, *Discourse*, 17v–18.

[40] Hall, *Weapons*, 141–2. As a spinning ball flies, it creates a band of rotating air around it. Unless the spin is perpendicular to the flight (as with a rifle), this air is accelerated by the 'windstream' on one side of the ball, and decelerated by it on the other, creating a pressure differential that sucks the ball towards the faster-moving (lower-pressure) air. Modern tests: Hall, *Weapons*, 138–40, 142–3; Strickland and Hardy, *Great Warbow*, 31.

[41] Smythe, *Certain Discourses*, 17v–18.

[42] Digges and Digges, *Stratioticos*, 108, 122; Smythe, *Certain Discourses*, 5v (spelling modernised): 'arquebuses (considering their inaccuracy) are [not] to be used ... in the field, above three or four scores [50 to 66 yards (45.72 to 60.35 m)] at the farthest'; cf. *ibid.*, 14v [muskets 133 to 166 yards (121.62 to 151.79 m)]; 15v [17 to 42 yards (15.54 to 38.40 m)]; 17, 28v; Monluc, *Memoirs*, 105 [83 to 100 yards (75.90 to 91.44 m)].

[43] Hall, *Weapons*, 149; see also the words of command in Gheyn, *Wapenhandelinghe*.

In Gheyn's precisely scripted exercise of arms, this all required forty-two motions, not counting the movements of coming forward to the front of a formation to deliver fire, or retiring to its rear to reload.[44] Hence, some sixteenth-century captains considered that arquebusiers could not be expected to fire more than ten shots in an hour. True, Humphrey Barwick suggested a much higher rate of forty shots per hour – for an individual of unusual skill, on a practice ground. But for a common arquebusier acting in formation under combat conditions, one shot per two or three minutes is probably realistic.[45] The larger-calibre musket, because of its great weight, required a rest. The need to manage that as well as the match and the weapon itself made its rate of fire even slower.[46] An archer, by contrast, could certainly loose as many as nine or ten arrows a minute.[47] But then, it was better to deliver one ball that even against armoured men 'carries death and fear with it', than to loose numerous arrows or bolts that collectively posed 'little hazard of life'.[48]

Hence firearms became, by the mid sixteenth century, the predominant shot weapon for European soldiers. To be sure, there were also many other reasons for the replacement of man-powered missile weapons by gunpowder weapons, ranging from cultural and dietary changes in England, to the accelerating urbanisation and monetisation of the European economy, to the declining price of saltpetre and the rising price of yew staves.[49] Indeed, although rarely noted in the modern literature, the technical improvements of the weapons themselves (particularly lengthening barrels) contributed significantly to this development.[50] But superior armour-piercing capability was integral to the replacement of traditional weapons by firearms. Moreover, the importance of missile-firing troops relative to close-combat infantry rose dramatically in most armies, the exceptions being the

---

[44] Gheyn, *Wapenhandelinghe*.
[45] Barwick, *Discourse*, 4v; Mork, 'Flint and Steel', 27; Frost, *Northern Wars*, 105; cf. Eltis, *Military Revolution*, 15. Digges and Digges, *Stratioticos*, 124, claimed it would take over 15 minutes for 10,000 handgunners in formation each to deliver one shot. The fact that around 20 to 50 per cent of shots were like to be misfires reduced the effective rate further: Tallett, *War and Society*, 23; Smythe, *Certain Discourses*, 21r–v.
[46] Williams, *Briefe discourse*, 41 (probably overstated; cf. Gheyn, *Wapenhandelinghe*.)
[47] Strickland and Hardy, *Great Warbow*, 31; Rogers, 'Agincourt,' n. 132; Stretton in Soar, *Secrets*, 142–3; note also Sutcliffe, *Practice*, 190. However, Smythe, though an archery advocate, only claimed that bowmen could loose four or five shots to a gunner's one; Smythe, *Certain Discourses*, 20v.
[48] Tavannes, *Mémoires*, 192; Barret, *Moderne Warres*, 3–4. See also Barwick, *Discourse*, 18v, 8v, 10v, 15v.
[49] Hall, *Weapons*, 58; Strickland and Hardy, *Great Warbow* 450.
[50] Williams, *Knight*, 854–5 (noting mislabelling of columns, 854); Barwick, *Discourse*, B1; Tavannes, *Mémoires*, 191.

ones in which the shot already played a key role, as in England or Bohemia. But even in those places, it was something new in the sixteenth century to be able to say that 'many Tymes it hath bene sene that Battail hathe been [won] by shott onlie, without pushe or strocke stricken'.[51]

Pike and shot

As the handgun replaced the crossbow and longbow, the sword, mace, and axe – weapons that had played important parts in hand-to-hand combat literally for millennia – were largely replaced in infantry formations by the pike (supplemented by shorter weapons like the halberd). Why did this occur? For many reasons:

- Plate armour was generally too strong to be penetrated by one-handed edged weapons such as axes and swords, and distributed the force of impacts well enough to make maces largely ineffectual. (Swords were retained because they were useful for defence as well as attack, being well suited to parrying; because although they could not hack or punch through armour, they could be precisely thrust through joints or eye-slits; and because they could also be used to beat an enemy down.[52] And they remained excellent weapons for use against unarmoured or nearly-so soldiers, such as handgunners.) Weapons that put the full force of both arms behind a single point did better against sheet steel. Jean de Waurin, late in the fifteenth century, wrote of Flemish pikes that 'there is no armour so good that they cannot penetrate or break it'.[53]
- Pikes were by far the best weapons for defence against cavalry. The Swiss learned at Arbedo in 1422 what Barret affirmed much later: 'Against horse ... farre better is the Pike, then either Bill, or Halbard.'[54] A pike outreached a cavalryman's lance, and 'any [charging] horse struck in the breast by a pike must invariably die'.[55] Moreover, the great length of the weapon allowed pikemen to put not one or two, but five or six rows of pike points between the mass of a speeding horse and the relatively frail flesh of the front-line footman. Even if a skilled rider could

---

[51] Audley, 'Treatise', 68. Similarly Barret, *Moderne Warres*, 75; Barwick, *Discourse*, Bv; Rich, *Fruites*, 68; Mendoza, *Theoretique and Practise*, 109.

[52] Mailles, *History of Bayard*, 58, 60, 79; Tavannes, *Mémoires*, 192.

[53] Waurin, *Anchiennes cronicques*, III, 74; for halberds and bills, Boardman, *Medieval Soldier*, 175; Oman, *History Middle Ages*, II, 251 n.

[54] Winkler, 'Swiss', 49–53; note also 31–2; Barret, *Moderne Warres*, 4; Montecuccoli, *Sulle battaglia*, 88.

[55] Waurin, *Anchiennes cronicques*, III, 74.

get a war-trained mount to make a suicidal charge into the serried front of a pike phalanx, as long as the men stood their ground it was 'as hard to be pierced' by the horse 'as an angry porcupine or hedgehog with the end of a bare finger'.[56] This defensive strength was particularly important because, by the late fifteenth century, heavy cavalry had experienced something of resurgence on the battlefield, thanks to the improvements in armour already discussed and also because of the reduced volume of shot the horses had to pass through, owing to the rising predominance of slow-firing matchlocks.[57]

- Footmen too, unless they were also arrayed and armed in the same way, would find attacking a resolute stand of pikes as profitless as assailing 'a wall of bronze'. It is true that at the battles of Stoke Field (1487) and Flodden (1513) English billmen did very well against pikes. Nevertheless, in the late sixteenth century, Barret was categorical: 'for the plaine field, neither blacke bill, Halbard, nor Partizan [is] comparable to the Pike'.[58] As Montecuccoli, the great seventeenth-century Italian general and military commentator, observed: 'It may be taken as axiomatic that no battalion of pikemen can ever be ruptured in a head-on attack.'[59]

- The impressive successes of the Swiss, particularly from their defeats of Charles the Bold through the early Italian wars (and also those of Flemish pikemen, particularly at the battle of Guinegate in 1479), naturally evoked emulation.[60] The reasons for the Swiss victories were much broader than their use of the pike, but their tactics and weapons could easily be copied, unlike the social underpinnings of their exceptional cohesion.

- The pike, unlike any other hand-to-hand weapon, allowed a formation to protect not only itself, but a significant number of shot troops attached to it. When threatened by an enemy advance (particularly by enemy cavalry), arquebusiers could kneel, roll, or dive under the pike-hedge. A short file of gunners could even stand and deliver ready shots while squeezed between two stacks of pikes presented by the men behind them, though reloading in such conditions would be very difficult.[61] On the battlefields of the late fifteenth through the seventeenth centuries, shot troops badly needed

---

[56] Garrard, *Arte of Warre*, 229 (modernised).
[57] Vale, *War and Chivalry*, 128.
[58] Barret, *Moderne Warres*, 47, 4.
[59] Montecuccoli, *Sulle battaglia*, 104.
[60] Styward, *Pathwaie*, 156; Fourquevaux, *Instructions*, I, 12r–v; Stewart, 'Army', 135-40.
[61] Cf. Barret, *Moderne Warres*, 48, 96–8; Garrard, *Arte of Warre*, 106; or kneeling under the pikes: Smythe, *Certain Discourses*, 16v.

that protection. At Agincourt, the English and Welsh archers had been able to defend themselves largely by their own arrows, with just a little help from a rapidly set-up hedge of stakes.[62] Fifty years later, that was impractical, thanks to the improvements in armour already mentioned, and also to the declining number of really good bowmen.[63] Less fearsome archers than England's had never really been expected to play that role. Handgunners in the open could not hope to stand their ground against a determined attack by armoured cavalry or pikemen.[64] This simple fact rose in significance in tandem with the proportion of shot in the army, and that figure generally climbed in most nations over the sixteenth and seventeenth centuries, until two-thirds of all infantrymen were armed with firearms.

One solution to this tactical problem was a long, thin pike-wall with the shot stationed either behind the line or in alternating files. This tactic was employed, for example, by the Burgundians in the late fifteenth century.[65] It was better suited, however, to bowmen (who often arced their fire, and who could provide enough volume of shot to help defend the thin pike-line from a denser attack-column) than to fireshot. In particular, such formations proved unable to halt the steamroller charge of a deep Swiss-style square.

Another response to the vulnerability of handgunners (and other missile troops) that enjoyed substantial success in the fifteenth century was the use of *Wagenburgen* (wagon-fortresses). These, however, were normally only practical for an army on the defence. The Hussites scored very impressive successes by employing the *Wagenburg*, but their opponents lacked effective field artillery. An army that had enough mobile guns could concentrate them against one segment of the 'wall', and then storm the 'breach', enjoying the classic benefit of a massed attack against the divided forces of a static perimeter.[66]

Deep blocks of pike could resist other pike, had enough manpower to pay the cost of closing with and defeating unprotected shot, and were especially effective at defending themselves (and attached shot) against cavalry attacks, from front or flank. In some ways a square of men thirty or more ranks deep was very wasteful (only the first six or seven

[62] Rogers, 'Agincourt'.
[63] Barwick, *Discourse*, Bv, 20v, 21; Monluc, *Memoirs*, 129–30; Barret, *Moderne Warres*, 3; Smythe, *Certain Discourses*, 26v, but cf. 31v.
[64] Barret, *Moderne Warres*, 69; Webb, *Elizabethan Military Science*, 118–19; La Noue, *Discourses*, 203; Smythe, *Certain Discourses*, 19r–v; Garrard, *Arte of Warre*, 117.
[65] Vaughan, *Valois Burgundy*, 128, 125.
[66] Hall, *Weapons*, 130; cf. also Frost, *Northern Wars*, 63.

ranks could use their weapons to the front),[67] but the men further back could assist by providing weight to a push of pike, and replacements for the fallen when charging shot.[68] This is one principal line of explanation for the universal adoption in the sixteenth century of infantry formations composed basically of a core of pike encircled or flanked (or both) by shot.

It is crucial to realise, however, that the purpose of this pairing of pike and shot was as much for the protection of the former as for the safety of the latter. Pike-blocks were very vulnerable to fire if they could not simply overrun the enemy shot, which they might not be able to do if the latter were protected by formidable entrenchments, or shielded by obstacles like streams or sunken roads, or even if the gunners simply had room to manoeuvre away from the more cumbersome pike-block. Hence, thought Barret, 'by every man's judgment' an unsupported stand of pikemen, 'though never so well armed,' could be defeated by an equal number of arquebusiers. Moreover, enemy lancers through repeated charges (or sometimes even by mere threat of charges) could force a pike-column to halt and form for defence, thereby preventing it from closing with its target.[69] Finally, pikemen on their own had no really effective response to fire delivered by cavalry squadrons. As will be discussed in more detail below, pistoleers could ride up by ranks to just a few yards beyond the pike-points, discharge their pieces, then wheel and retire. The damage a squadron could do in an iteration of this 'caracole' technique was not negligible, and against a pike-block unsupported by shot it was almost entirely *one-sided*, and could be continued indefinitely.[70] Thus, pike and shot existed in a kind of tactical symbiosis. On the one hand, shot needed to be able to 'retyre safely' to the protection of pikemen 'whensoever they shall happen to be charged with Lances', or by pike. On the other, the shot were needed 'to … succour their Pykes, whensoever any attempt shalbe made by Argoletiers [dragoons] or Pistols to breake their array'.[71] 'The one without the other,' wrote Barret in 1591, 'is weakened the better halfe of their strength. Therefore of necessitie (according to the course of the warres in these dayes) the one is to be coupled & matched with the other, in such convenient proportion, that the advantage of the one may helpe the disavantage of the other.'[72]

---

[67] Montecuccoli, *Sulle battaglia*, 88; cf. Barret, *Moderne Warres*, 75.
[68] Eltis, *Military Revolution*, 54.
[69] Barret, *Moderne Warres*, 69; Sutcliffe, *Practice*, 181, 186, 189; but cf. La Noue, *Discourses*, 199.
[70] Barriffe, quoted in Mork, 'Flint and Steel', 27.
[71] Digges and Digges, *Stratiaticos*, 110.
[72] Barret, *Moderne Warres*, 69; Sutcliffe, *Practice*, 182–6; Audley, 'Treatise', 66.

The mutual protection of pike and shot did not extend a long distance. As already noted, an arquebus volley was relatively ineffectual past 100 yards (91.44 m) – this was especially true under battlefield conditions when, because of time, pressure, and stress, the weapons would often not be optimally loaded.[73] In the medieval tactical style it had been common to build a central battle of heavy infantry and have it flanked by two wings of shot; the central battle might have around 250 or 300 yards (228.6 to 274.32 m) of frontage, or more, and the wings would stretch further out. But if arquebusiers on the far flanks of the formation were 250 yards away from the edge of the pike-block in the centre, their fire could not reach far enough with any accuracy to provide much assistance even to the pikemen on the very edge of their mass, much less those in the centre. Even those gunners immediately adjacent to the heavy foot would have been hard-pressed to do much against pistoleers making a caracole against the centre of the line (Figure 10.1). Moreover, horsemen charging the shot at the far flank would be able to overrun them long before they could reach the shelter of the supporting pike.

The basic solution to this problem was to attach sleeves of shot to multiple smaller battalions of pike, rather than one single great block. But this array posed another problem. Placing shot units in the front line made it virtually impossible to prevent an enemy force of pike from breaking the line where the gunners stood. In late-medieval infantry tactics, the line was always contiguous, and if broken at any point was likely to collapse into rout.

A more segmented line, where each unit was physically separated from the ones to either side of it, had greater capacity to resist such a catastrophic rupture, especially if the soldiers knew that their side had a reserve line, with units that could be individually sent forward to respond to breakthroughs in the first line.

Already by the time of the Wars of Religion, French infantry was often arrayed in a formation similar to that used by the Romans' manipular legions, with battalions of pike arranged in two or three staggered lines, in which each formation was separated from the next by a space equal to or a bit greater than its own frontage, and where each such void space was faced by a unit in the next line back.[74] This was at that time more the exception than the rule; the Spanish and their many emulators preferred

---

[73] Proper loading made a huge difference in effectiveness; Smythe, *Certain Discourses*, 18v; Eltis, *Military Revolution*, 15; Tavannes, *Mémoires*, 191; La Noue, *Discourses*, 202; Williams, *Briefe discourse*, 38–9; Fourquevaux, *Instructions*, I, 38v; Bland, *Treatise*, 142.

[74] Lynn, 'Tactical Evolution, 178–9.

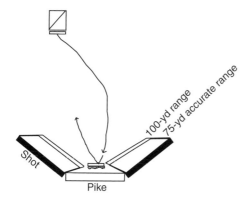

Figure 10.1 A caracole.

more solid fronts in single lines (with smaller reserves behind). But even those who argued that the use of many small battalions separated by intervals made for a weaker main battle-line recognised that a Roman-style checkerboard arrangement was suitable for the advanced shot troops of the forlorn hope, and tactics of this sort became more common over time. There were many variations on the theme, but the general trend in the early-modern period was increasingly to view the battle-line not as a single entity, or as the combination of just three elements (left, centre, and right) as in medieval tactics, but rather as a larger team of cooperating but essentially *tactically independent* troops, battalions, or brigades. Whether these smaller units were separated by broad intervals or only by narrow gaps, the battle-front was no longer a solid, contiguous front, a difference that would have been striking to any medieval commander viewing an early-modern army's deployment. The implications for tactics, and for the nature of officership, were enormous.

Intervals between units: infantry

In the 1590s, Barret described the advantage of dividing battalions of pike from one another by broad intervals (equal to the frontage of the units) as follows:

The voide spaces may serve for the troupes of shot to sallie out [to] skirmish with the enemy, and to retire againe, and also for the ... battallions of the second front, to march up and pass betwixt them, [as] the battallions of the first front having encountred the enemy, and feeling themselves distressed, are warily and orderly to retire with their faces and weapon point bent upon the enemie [... and similarly, eventually, with a third line, advancing on the flanks.] By which order it should seeme, fortune [would have] to abandon them thrice before that they should be quighte vanquished.[75]

In this passage we see identified the two main advantages of tactics based on independent small units: the ability to employ manoeuvre, including rotating fresh troops in to replace worn-down forces, and the possibility of suffering a partial defeat without losing the ability to withdraw gracefully from combat. When a single battalion collapsed, the presence of two friendly formations immediately behind and to each side of it made it practically impossible for the victorious unit opposing it to pursue, and the interval to its rear allowed it to escape without disordering the troops behind it. Moreover, the separation of the units made it much more likely that panic could be contained to one unit, without infecting its neighbours. They would of course be disadvantaged, but if necessary could withdraw in good order as their supports came up. As the very successful Italian general Montecuccoli put it, in praise of such a deployment, 'If a smaller troop is overturned, the disorder is not so great; nor is it as difficult to repair the breach which is not as wide.'[76]

A unit operating as an independent battalion in this manner was more likely to break than one that was part of a contiguous front, since its flanks were more vulnerable and since the individual soldiers had better prospects of escape (for the reasons just noted), thus reducing their motivation to stand fast. But, to repeat, the consequences of its breaking would be much less.

This meant that the role of chance in determining the outcome of the battle was reduced. Moreover, the switch from a few large, linked combat elements to many smaller, independent ones gave the wing- or army-commander much more of a role in shaping the battle. He had, as Michael Roberts put it, more 'tactical small change',[77] allowing him more opportunities to intervene effectively over the course of the combat. He had a whole hand of cards to play, rather than staking his fate on one roll of the dice. For Montecuccoli, this was a point of crucial importance:

the science of being a general consists ... [in] understanding how to make [troops] fight in an opportune fashion, i.e., successively and not simultaneously.

---

[75] Barret, *Moderne Warres*, 85; similarly Digges and Digges, *Stratioticos* (1579 edn), 103; Rohan, *Parfaict capitaine*, 263.
[76] Montecuccoli, *Sulle battaglia*, 90.
[77] Roberts, 'Gustav Adolf', 60.

The military leader must bear in mind that his troops will not obey him well after they have been called into combat; all the entreaties in the world will not make them stand firm once they have begun to flee. Conversely, troops in good order will execute a command properly, will affront the enemy, and will force him to desist from pursuit so that their fugitive comrades will have both time and space to pull themselves together.[78]

Another advantage of dividing an army into small units – especially if they had empty space on each side of them – was their greater ability to deal with difficult ground when on the tactical offensive. A battalion could swing to the side and pass around a farmhouse or bush in its path; by contrast, 'large bodies of men are inconvenient because they require a very level battlefield; without the latter they cannot maintain good order'.[79]

Nonetheless, Barret in 1598 recommended to his contemporaries that they continue to draw up their main forces in one or a few large squares – as they usually did – rather than many smaller units. He recognised the superiority of the latter arrangement in theory, for soldiers who were 'perfect and ready', but he thought that in practice it would not work out well, since the soldiers of his day were not as disciplined as the ancient Romans. It is 'daungerous to frame many batallions', he concluded, 'except men be very skilfull and well practised therein, by reason of the difficultie in seconding one another'.[80] Hence, it was better to rely on the square, which 'common reason and experience hath made most men confesse and agree … is the most assured, most strong, and most apt to bee reduced into any other forme'.[81]

What Barret had in mind here was the ad hoc dividing of a large army into separate fighting battalions. But even as he wrote, armies were coming more and more to be organised with permanent battalions of around 500 men (pike and shot) that drilled together more frequently, and that in battle fought in intervalled array. Eric XIV (1533–77) of Sweden and Maurice of Orange (1567–1625) had led the way in this change, and Gustavus Adolphus (1594–1632) dramatically demonstrated the potential value of the new structures.[82] True, they required a larger complement of officers – but officers were, as Montecuccoli

---

[78] Montecuccoli, *Sulle battaglia*, 84, apparently based on Rohan, *Parfaict capitaine*, 260–2.

[79] Montecuccoli, *Sulle battaglia*, 90.

[80] Barret, *Moderne Warres*, 82, 75. Cf. Sutcliffe, *Practice*, 175; Digges and Digges, *Stratioticos* (1579 edn), 103.

[81] Barret, *Moderne Warres*, 45; see also 76–7, 94–5. Bérault Stuart, in his 1508 military treatise (*Traité*, 7), gives no hint of the idea of intervals and advises against intermixing cavalry and infantry.

[82] Roberts, *Gustavus Adolphus*, II, 192–4, 182–5, 219–21, 247–51.

wrote, worth at least what they cost, expensive though they were.[83] Officers had always been important for maintaining morale and control, on the battlefield and off, but as units became more capable of independent action at a smaller level – and not just independent action, but complicated combined-arms action, requiring coordination at least of pike and shot, and perhaps of fully- and light-armed pike, musketeers and arquebusiers, and halberdiers or billmen – they became to a much greater extent decision-makers, as well as retaining their importance for supervision and inspiration. The resultant creation of a tactical hierarchy helped to create officers, in the modern sense, as opposed to leaders, and ultimately to give rise to professionalisation.[84]

As already noted above, the use of more numerous independent units compartmentalised by intervals served to increase greatly the chance that a breach in a battle-line could be repaired without causing a broader collapse. This tended to make battles last longer, a tendency already inherent in the use of slow-firing shot and deep, tough blocks of pike. This in turn had an unintended consequence of great import for soldiers and commanders alike: there was a marked tendency for battlefield casualties to be more evenly distributed between winners and losers than in the Middle Ages. In the earlier period, much of the fighting was done by well-armoured combatants who were very tough to kill, so long as they stayed in their formations. When one side broke, the slaughter could be horrendous, but it was nearly all on one side. In an early-modern battle involving many units, it was typical for each side to suffer localised, partial defeats before the overall outcome of the combat was decided, and so to suffer significant losses. Even if this did not occur, the attritional nature of exchanges of arquebus fire meant many were killed on both sides before the balance of victory tipped in one direction or the other.[85] A main impetus for the creation of battle-arrays with mutually supporting lines was to ensure that a battle would not be 'lost in the twinkling of an eye at the first joining';[86] thus, these tactics extended the period of mutual loss before the one-sided pursuit began. The depth of the pike-square had a similar effect. When pikemen fighting in the Swiss style clashed, it typically meant a relatively large number of killed on both sides, a phenomenon already observable in battles where handguns played little role.[87]

---

[83] Montecuccoli, *Mémoires*, 37; but cf. Parrott, 'Strategy', 229, 231.

[84] See Trim, *Chivalric Ethos*.

[85] Montecuccoli, *Sulle battaglia*, 162: 'during the fray, there are just as many victims on one side as there are on another'.

[86] Webb, *Elizabethan Military Science*, 47; cf. Mendoza, *Theoretique and Practise*, 107.

[87] Winkler, 'Swiss', 66–8, 45, 42–3, 92, 96; Barret, *Moderne Warres*, 85.

The combined effect of these factors meant a major change. There are plenty of medieval battles where the winner's losses amounted only to dozens of killed – or even fewer. The ratio of victors killed to defeated killed might be as low as 1:50 or even 1:100.[88] In the early-modern period, the victor's dead were almost certain to number in the hundreds, if not the thousands, and the ratio of killed was much more likely to be on the order of between 1:2 and 1:6. Indeed, an army that went on the offensive, in the somewhat unlikely event that it won a battle, might even suffer *more* killed than the 'loser' of the engagement.[89] 'Many of these sanguinary triumphs', as Montecuccoli rightly observed, 'are simply defeats in disguise'.[90]

For the strategist, the main significance of this trend was that it further reduced the already limited ability of a battlefield victory to bring decisive strategic or even operational results. Although that is an important effect, it is beyond the scope of this essay. But this was also of great significance to the individual soldier. The risks he faced in battle were significantly changed, and so therefore were the demands placed on his courage. Before, an armoured soldier could go into combat with a reasonably high confidence that he would survive, at least if his side won the day. But in the new military era, that was unrealistic. Humphrey Barwick recognised how things had changed: 'now by reason of the force of weapons, neither horse nor man is able to bear armour sufficient to defend their bodies from death, whereas in the former times ... wounds was the worst to have been [feared]'.[91] The soldier's odds of survival were worse, and the moral impact of this fact was redoubled by the fact that death was not only more likely, but also more random. An enemy's sword or lance could be parried; even an arrow or javelin could be spotted on its way in and dodged or blocked. But there was nothing the soldier could do to escape or deflect a musket-ball or cannonball. When engaged in hand-to-hand combat, a soldier's attention is typically absorbed by the immediate needs of physical action in response to visible threats. But, as Montecuccoli observed in another context, soldiers can 'become greatly agitated [when] they recognize that the question of their escape or destruction will be decided by the *virtù* of others'.[92] This situation – the requirement for a soldier to

---

[88] Rogers, *Soldiers' Lives*, 214–6, 229–30.

[89] E.g. Nieuwpoort, about 3,000 to 4,000 vs. about 2,500: Puype, 'Victory', 106. Ravenna, approximately 4,000 vs. 9,000; Marignano, about equal losses: Oman, *History Sixteenth Century*, 147–8, 170.

[90] Montecuccoli, *Sulle battaglia*, 162.

[91] Barwick, *Discourse*, 2bv, spelling modernised; note also 10v; Tavannes, *Mémoires*, 191.

[92] Montecuccoli, *Sulle battaglia*, 154.

overcome the particular sort of fear tinted by the knowledge that one's fate was not in one's own hands – was the norm on the early-modern battlefield, where 'every moment you felt cannon balls and arquebus shot whistling past your ears, and every hour you saw the ground sown with the minute pieces of the shattered bodies of your companions'.[93]

Tactical formations and drills are designed – whether through the conscious decisions of military leaders, or through the gradual moulding of the abstract forces of survival-of-the-fittest mechanisms – to support soldiers in facing moral challenges, as well as to facilitate their application of physical force to the enemy. The deeper formations and dance-like[94] movement-in-unison characteristic of early-modern combat were developed partly in response to the moral challenges of the new risk-environment. This was explicitly recognised by some early-modern observers, but particularly in the context of cavalry rather than infantry formations. This essay has so far focused on how new formations and weapons affected infantry combat, but horsemen too had their way of fighting transformed and transformed again in this period, in similar ways and for similar reasons. And the cavalry of the sixteenth century remained of very great importance on the battlefield despite (indeed, partly because of) the rise of firearms. A good case could be made – though many contemporary observers held the opposite opinion – that the cavalry in the sixteenth century returned to its pre-fourteenth-century position as the most important arm in determining victory or defeat.[95] In early-modern battles, if one side had clearly greater strength in infantry, and the other had a strong advantage in horsemen, the latter was more likely to win the fight overall, as arguably at the battle of Agnadello (1509) and indubitably at Ravenna (1512), Ceresole (1544), and St Quentin (1557).[96]

Cavalry tactics

The sources are usually laconic when it comes to the details of medieval cavalry tactics, but it seems that horsemen usually fought in thin

---

[93] Collado, quoted in Eltis, *Military Revolution*, 31.

[94] Digges and Digges, *Stratioticos* (1579 edn), 103.

[95] Compare Eltis, *Military Revolution*, 24; Fissel, *English Warfare*, 233–5; Audley, 'Treatise', 131; Oman, *History Sixteenth Century*, 32, 55, 93, 266; Parrott, 'Strategy', 236–8; Frost, *Northern Wars*, 63–9, and Montecuccoli, *Sulle battaglia*, 151, with Mendoza, *Theoretique and Practise*, 54; Styward, *Pathwaie*, 156–7; and Garrard, *Arte of Warre*, 139.

[96] Oman, *History Sixteenth Century*, 241–2, 93. The reverse was true at Guinegate in 1479, where the French cavalry won its fight, but the French infantry were defeated and lost the battle as a whole.

linear formations just one or two ranks deep. They sometimes employed open order (with each horse separated by an empty space roughly equal to its own width), sometimes closed order (stirrup to stirrup). When two opposing formations were both in open order, they would normally pass through each other when charging, each man attacking his opposite number in passing. When in closed order, if neither side shied away from contact then both would at the last moment slow to a walk, since otherwise the result would be an ugly pile-up. In this case the units would fight it out with hand-strokes until one or the other was penetrated, and broke.[97]

If attacking infantry, medieval cavalry sometimes used a tactic similar to the early-modern manoeuvre usually known as the caracole,[98] riding up in open order at a gallop, throwing javelins (which would carry further and hit harder because the velocity of the projectile would be enhanced by the speed of the horse), and then wheeling back before coming into range of the footmen's weapons. Alternatively, the cavalry might try simply to ride down the infantry. In this case the horsemen would normally advance in close order at the trot, in a small unit, while other units waited to follow up on the first unit's attack if it proved successful, or to charge any footmen foolish enough to break formation in pursuit if it did not. If the charging horsemen detected wavering in their target (as they likely would unless the foot-soldiers were of good quality), they would charge home and try to shatter the defending formation, for 'upon any smal disorder, they carrie with them victory'.[99] If there was no sign of such an opportunity, they might try charging in anyway, a manoeuvre that required excellent horsemanship and very well-trained horses, and was very dangerous for themselves and even more so for their horses. Such a shock action could potentially smash a hole in the enemy line for the next troop to exploit, though particularly against footmen armed with pike the attackers were more likely to be forced to 'retire with losse and disadvantage'.[100]

By the 1480s, cavalry was sometimes being formed in much deeper formations analogous to pike-squares.[101] It may be that at first these columnar arrays were not for fighting in, but rather deployed with the intent that individual ranks would step off from the front, charge, then

---

[97] Rogers, *Soldiers' Lives*, 191–6.
[98] Though that word in the early-modern sources often refers to various other manoeuvres.
[99] Garrard, *Arte of Warre*, 228–9.
[100] Barret, *Moderne Warres*, 76, 139; Sutcliffe, *Practice*, 182–3, 163; Styward, *Pathwaie*, 157. On the possibility of cavalry shock against infantry formations, see Rogers, *Soldiers' Lives*, 183–4; Frost, *Northern Wars*, 64.
[101] Seldeneck, *Kriegsbuch*, 107–9.

wheel and retire to the rear of the formation as the next rank charged in turn.[102] As is explicitly recognised in the early-modern treatises, only one or at most two or three ranks of lancers could effectively be employed simultaneously.[103]

The introduction of the wheel-lock pistol was the main influence on the drastic changes in cavalry tactics that took place in the sixteenth century. The pistol had three basic advantages over the lance, which, between the 1560s and the 1590s, caused it to become the principal arm of the horseman.

First was its penetrative capacity. La Noue considered it a 'miracle' if anyone in full sixteenth-century plate armour was killed by a lance, and although this is somewhat of an exaggeration (a charging horse put a great deal of kinetic energy and a massive amount of momentum behind a lance-point) it is true that we read of far fewer prominent individuals killed by cold steel than by bullets or cannonballs.[104] Tavannes, indeed, considered that firearms had increased the risk of death for military leaders a hundredfold.[105] Second, although a pistol was effective only at very short ranges, even if the horseman reserved fire until 'he could see the white in the eyes of the enemy', he would have the advantage in range over a lancer.[106]

Third, and perhaps most important, the pistol could be used effectively by horsemen attacking in a deep column,[107] who had many of the same advantages relative to thinner formations as did pike-squares. When a column of pistoleers passed through a line of horse, they could fire their pistols to the side, in such a way that they enfiladed the enemy line. And, if a mêlée ensued, their pistols and secondary weapons (swords) were generally preferable to lances, which were unwieldy and so not very effective unless employed in the charge.[108] Because of these three advantages, experience proved that pistol-armed German *Reiter*, and those who emulated them with sufficient skill, had a clear-cut advantage over lancers[109] – even aside from the facts that the pistoleers took less training and did not require such

---

[102] As much later described in Cruso, *Militarie Instructions*, 97.

[103] *Ibid.*, 30; Montecuccoli, *Sulle battaglia*, 106; Rohan, *Parfaict capitaine*, 230.

[104] La Noue, *Discourses*, 201, 199; similarly Tavannes, *Mémoires*, 192; but cf. Williams, *Briefe discourse*, 38–9; Benedetti, *Bello carolino*, 108, 146; Mailles, *History of Bayard*, 107, 185–6.

[105] Tavannes, *Mémoires*, 336, 191–2; note also Barwick, *Discourse*, 21v.

[106] Puype, 'Victory', 85.

[107] Eltis, *Military Revolution*, 63; Monluc, *Commentaires*, III, 484–5; La Noue, *Discourses*, 201–2; Rohan, *Parfaict capitaine*, 230.

[108] Montecuccoli, *Sulle battaglia*, 91; Tavannes, *Mémoires*, 192; Puype, 'Victory', 86 n.

[109] Love, 'Equestrian Army', 514–20, 531–2. However, Mook (1574) showed lancers could defeat pistoleers in the right circumstances, and some commentators thought

expensive mounts.[110] As Montecuccoli explained it (paraphrasing the much earlier La Noue), it might be true that only the first rank of a column could use its weapons to full advantage, but, in arraying a troop of horse,

one does not pay attention merely to the fact that each reiter fires one pistol shot and delivers a thrust of his sword. Rather, one should take care that the formation be able to rout whatever it confronts. This is the sole objective of whoever commits himself to battle, and it is accomplished much more readily when cavalry is disposed in [deep] squadrons [rather than in line] ... Even if that portion of the [line] which has not yet clicked its hoofs were to rush the flanks of the assailant, the squadrons that supported the latter would block the maneuver ... If three or four troops thus arrayed [in line] were to attack successively, a sole opposing squadron could overturn them as easily as a bowling ball can be used to knock down one row of pins after another.[111]

Montecuccoli recognised another key advantage for deep squadrons, a moral rather than physical one:

One may add that if several ranks are formed into a squadron, it is probable that the troopers who are stationed in front will be choice material and that those of the next row will second them in valor ... As for the remainder, whom we may regard as considerably more hesitant, they will be protected by those posted in front ... The valor of those in front will cause them to move ahead, and the assurance of security should make the others follow. Conversely, when a troop is formed [in line], even though the brave soldiers (who are normally in the minority) proceed resolutely to the fray, the others (who have no desire to take the bit into their mouth) remain behind. And so, over a distance of 200 paces, one sees this long rank thin out and dissolve.[112]

When formations of fully armoured lancers clashed, most soldiers derived from their armour the 'assurance of security' that emboldened them to stick with their comrades in the assault. But, as we have already remarked in our discussion of infantry combat, in the age of firearms 'neither horse nor man [was] able to beare armours sufficient to defend their bodies from death'; no longer could one's own skill shield against the random strike of a lead ball; no longer were 'woundes ... the worst to have been doubted'.[113] Hence, a new premium was put on the use of a tactical formation that did not rely on every man's courage being

---

them generally superior: Puype, 'Victory', 85; Mendoza, *Theoretique and Practise*, 51, 54–5; cf. Williams, *Briefe discourse*, 37–9; Frost, *Northern Wars*, 67–8.

[110] Puype, 'Victory', 82; Cruso, *Militarie Instructions*, 30; Tavannes, *Mémoires*, 191.

[111] Montecuccoli, *Sulle battaglia*, 91–2; La Noue, *Discourses*, 186–7.

[112] Montecuccoli, *Sulle battaglia*, 91–2 (paraphrasing La Noue); see also 110, and La Noue, *Discourses*, 188, 198–203.

[113] Barwick, *Discourse*, B2v.

sufficient to bear the risk of 'present death',[114] but rather helped to ameliorate the problem that 'large pistols have made [armour] useless, and made the melee so perilous that each person is eager to leave the fight'.[115]

Moreover, the pistol gave the horseman an effective way to attack a block of pike, provided that the latter had not been properly provided with attached shot, or after the latter had been detached or driven off. This was done through the caracole, the firearmed equivalent of the old javelin tactics, with ranks of horsemen riding to just outside the striking range of pikemen, loosing their pistols, and retiring to reload. Although this tactic has been much disparaged by modern historians, it was respected by the footmen who had to face it. As already noted above, Digges reckoned that one key role of arquebusiers was 'to … succour their Pykes, whensoever any attempt shalbe made by Argoletiers or Pistols to breake their array'.[116] The English cavalry at Turnhout in 1597 demonstrated what could be accomplished by horsemen using the caracole to create an opportunity for shock action: 'we charged their pikes,' reported Sir Francis Vere, 'not breaking through them at the first push, as was anciently used by the men-at-arms with their barded horses: but as the long pistols, delivered at hand [i.e. fired at very short range], had made the ranks thin, so thereupon, the rest of the horse got within them'.[117] Even if faced with a pike-square too determined and well-armoured to be shaken by this technique, the cavalrymen could use it gradually to wear down their enemies while simultaneously pinning them in place, or at least severely hindering their movement, through the constant threat of a charge with cold steel.

When forming up a wing of horsemen arrayed in deep squadrons, the commander essentially had no choice but to make use of intervals at least equal in width to the frontages of the units. In addition to the general advantages of having the line broken into individual units already discussed above, the intervals were necessary to allow the squadrons to employ the fire-and-retire technique of the caracole, and also allowed the squadrons of the second line the space they needed to protect those of the first line from threats to their flanks. Moreover, the empty spaces allowed room for other sorts of troops (particularly artillerymen or handgunners) to manoeuvre to aid the cavaliers, and vice versa.

---

[114] Barret, *Moderne Warres*, 3.
[115] Tavannes, *Mémoires*, 191; see also La Noue, *Discourses*, 202; Mendoza, *Theoretique and Practise*, 107.
[116] Digges and Digges, *Stratioticos*, 110.
[117] Quoted in Fissel, *English Warfare*, Figure 7.3; here modernised.

Combined arms

The caracole was especially effective if employed in combination with field artillery: an immobile pike-square was a big target, and each cannonball had the possibility of opening a lane down which the riders could charge into the midst of the pike and use their swords. If they got past the hedge of spear-points, they would be able to slaughter the foot-men like wolves inside a flock of sheep. Much the same could be said of the combination of *Reiter* and musketeers, whether used against a pike-square or against an all-cavalry force. Hence, noted François Billon in 1641, a mixed force of cavalry and infantry could expect to beat an all-infantry force two or three times as numerous.[118] When all three arms were employed together, the results could be even better. To quote the insightful veteran commander Raimondo Montecuccoli again:

Musketry and cavalry should be combined. The former makes the latter bolder. If the enemy is stronger in horsed troops, the musketry can establish an equilibrium; if he is weaker in this arm, the footmen will be able to rout him. It is incredible how much damage can be wreaked, how great a gap can be torn when musketry fires properly and when lances and cuirasses [*Reiter*] charge suddenly from behind this hail of bullets. It is quite certain that when a squadron sees nine or ten men felled from its front rank, the remainder thinks only of its own fate. Another favorable factor with regard to such musketry is that small cannon may be placed in its midst: this makes for a great slaughter of enemy horses.[119]

Or, he might have added, of enemy pikemen. To coordinate horsemen, pike, musketeers, and cannon successfully, however, was by no means easy. At Breitenfeld (1631), Gustavus Adolphus illustrated just how much could be achieved by these means, but it remained profoundly difficult to accomplish, whether at the small-unit level or for an army commander.

Complexity

At Agincourt, the English had only two types of soldier: archers and dismounted men-at-arms. Although the French had some other troops on the field, the only ones who played a significant role were men-at-arms (mostly dismounted) and a relatively small number of *gros valets* who were in tactical terms nearly equivalent to dismounted men-at-arms. The English army was divided into only five main units (two wings of

---

[118] Billon, *Principes*, 418 and the last (unnumbered) page of the table of materials.
[119] Montecuccoli, *Sulle battaglia*, 106.

archers and three nearly joined battles of men-at-arms) all arrayed in line, with the wings angled forward. The French, similarly, had two wings of cavalry, a body of crossbowmen and other shot, two lines of footmen, and a mounted reserve composed of *gros valets* and a few men-at-arms.[120]

By contrast, the infantry of an army of the sixteenth century would typically include around six types of footmen (armoured pikemen; part- or un-armoured pikemen; halberdiers or billmen; swordsmen with shields; arquebusiers; musketeers; possibly archers or crossbowmen, or men with musketoons;[121] and up to six types of horsemen (gendarmes, lancers, cuirassiers with pistols and swords, demi-cuirassed carabineers, dragoons with pikes, dragoons with muskets, and perhaps demi-lances or *stradiotti* or other eastern European light cavalry). In addition, field artillery, which only began to be of real significance by the mid fifteenth century, had by the mid sixteenth begun to play an integral and normal role as a major combat arm.[122]

All these men would be organised into far more independent tactical units: dozens of squadrons of *Reiter*, units of lancers, battalions of foot, and units of shot detached to support the cavalry. Rather than five or six or nine the total number might be as many as around 150, as for example in the battle-array of the Prince of Orange before Rees in 1614.[123] As noted above, each of these small units was truly independent: it was formed up with a distinct interval between it and the unit to its side, it could be committed to action and manoeuvre independently, and it could even break without automatically causing a disaster for its side. Moreover, even the individual battalions of foot were really composed of at least three distinct, articulated sections: a central body of pikemen and two wings or 'sleeves' of shot. And even these were not simple, uniform bodies. The pike-block had to be formed with the fully armoured men around the perimeter; the light-armed pike closer to the centre; and the ensign, musicians, and halberdiers or billmen in the centre.

---

[120] See Rogers, 'Agincourt'.

[121] For example Garrard, *Arte of Warre*, 57.

[122] Cf. Lynn, 'Tactical Evolution,' 184–6; Sutcliffe, *Practice*, 191; Mendoza, *Theoretique and Practise*, 107–9; Roberts, *Gustavus Adolphus*, 228–34. By Breitenfeld (1631), many imperial regiments were 'completely shattered by bombardment before they were able to enter action'. Montecuccoli, *Sulle battaglia*, 140; but cf. Parrott, 'Strategy', 238–39.

[123] Cruso, *Militarie Instructions*, Part IV, Chapter 8, Figure 12; cf. Benedetti, *Bello carolino*, 94–5. Such sketched battle-arrays became very common in the seventeenth century. They tended to be practical rather than theoretical, and hence are valuable sources for organisation of armies; see Roberts, 'Battle Plans'.

The complexity of the machine, with all its permutations and combinations, had increased a hundredfold. As a result, to quote Garrard, 'there be nowadays over many rules and reckonings of military discipline'.[124] The growth of tactical complexity had been stimulated by but was not solely due to the introduction of firearms.

Epilogue: from complexity to simplicity, 1670–1740

The combined-arms tactics based on intervalled lines and independently acting small units that the Swedes employed with such finesse in the 1630s were the norm by the later seventeenth century – but before the middle of the eighteenth century they had largely vanished, to be replaced with the simpler modes of 'linear tactics'. This change was not the result of a decline in the technical proficiency of European troops: on the contrary, mid-eighteenth-century units, now marching to a cadenced pace, were capable of executing tactical deployments with a precision that would have amazed Gustavus Adolphus.

Probably the single most important factor in driving tactical change over the turn of the eighteenth century was the near-universal rearming of European infantry with bayonet-equipped flintlock muskets (or 'fusils').[125] Eliminating the slow match and the fork (and using paper cartridges) simplified weapons use substantially, allowing a trained soldier to fire two to three times as quickly, with fewer misfires.[126] Increased firepower, in combination with the bayonet, allowed fusiliers to defend their own fronts effectively: 'if the infantry knows its own strength', commented Marshal Puységur, 'cavalry will not break it'.[127] The same troops could also now push forward and close with the enemy, as pikemen formerly had done. The proportion of pikemen had already been in decline, falling to under a third of the infantry by the 1650s, and a quarter by around 1680.[128] In 1687 Vauban noted that musketeers used their fire in every engagement, whereas pikemen might cross weapons with their adversaries in only three fights out of twenty.[129] The adoption of an effective socket bayonet finally convinced the conservatives that the pike had become obsolete.[130]

---

124 Garrard, *Arte of Warre*, 57.
125 Black, *European Warfare 1494–1660*, 39; Puységur, *Art de la guerre*, 57.
126 Puységur, *Art de la guerre*, 71, 67; Lynn, *Giant*, 460; Nosworthy, *Anatomy of Victory*, 39–41.
127 Puységur, *Art de la guerre*, 70–1; cf. Bland, *Treatise*, 91.
128 Puységur, *Art de la guerre*, 3, 36, 56; Lynn, *Giant*, 476.
129 Quoted in Lynn, *Giant*, 457.
130 Though cf. Saxe, *Mes Rêveries*, 32–3.

The rearming of the pikemen meant a given number of soldiers now had between a third and a half more shooters, each firing two or three times as fast, thus in total putting three or four times the amount of lead in the air. If cavalry charged the line, 'the Fire of one Platoon, given in due time, [was] sufficient to break any Squadron'; the bayonets behind the curtain of fire served mainly to ensure that the individual horsemen into which the squadron fragmented could not in turn break the infantry battalion.[131]

When, on the other hand, a battalion of fusiliers advanced to drive off an enemy, it was a 'receiv'd Maxim, that those who preserve their fire longest, will be sure to Conquer'.[132] Typically, the side that fired first might give its discharge at around sixty paces. A volley even at that distance, however, was 'less dreadful, and fewer lives are lost by it, than is generally imagined'.[133] The distinguished French field commander, Marshal Saxe, argued that not even the most efficacious blast of short-range fire could suffice to prevent the unit on the receiving end from giving its own volley at much closer range and then charging home with the bayonet. 'It is by this method only', he concluded, 'that numbers are to be destroyed, and victories obtained'.[134] Saxe's emphasis on the decisiveness of the final charge led him to write of 'the error of shooting' and to argue for a return to deeper formations, including pikemen, as more suited to shock action—but his opinion did not prevail.[135]

First, though it could be very effective to march through the enemy's fire without shooting back, it was very difficult to accomplish: in practice – whether the officers wished it or not – many advances devolved into firefights at relatively long range.[136] Second, armies often defended their fronts with entrenchments or natural obstacles. In such circumstances charges were often repulsed, in which case the casualties inflicted by the defenders' firepower (both during the attack and during the retreat) were of primary importance.[137] Third, when bayonet charges *were* successful, it was more by psychological than physical force. When the defending line delivered a close-range volley, the soldiers naturally expected their fire to have a devastating effect and

---

[131] Bland, *Treatise*, 91, 80; Puységur, *Art de la guerre*, 70–1.
[132] Bland, *Treatise*, 91; Saxe, *Reveries, or Memoirs*, 134; Quincy, *Maximes*, 67; Nosworthy, *Anatomy of Victory*, 104 (but cf. 108).
[133] Saxe, *Reveries, or Memoirs*, 20; cf. *Mes rêveries*, 40; but cf. Duffy, *Military Experience*, 204–6.
[134] Saxe, *Reveries, or Memoirs*, 20; cf. *Mes rêveries*, 40.
[135] Saxe, *Mes rêveries*, 38 (*l'abus de la tirerie*); cf. *Reveries, or Memoirs*, 19 ('insignificancy of small-arms'); see also Duffy, *Military Experience*, 205–14.
[136] Duffy, *Military Experience*, 207.
[137] Saxe, *Reveries, or Memoirs*, 71; *Mes rêveries*, 134–5.

stop the attackers in their tracks. The disappointment of these expectations inevitably shook the defenders' morale, and the subsequent bayonet charge often, even usually, caused them to break and run before a single bayonet was bloodied.[138] But in this case what really led to panic amongst the defenders was seeing 'their enemy advancing upon them through the smoke *with his fire reserved*';[139] 'it [is] certain, that when Troops see others Advance, and *going to pour in their Fire upon them, when theirs is gone*, they will immediately give way, or at least it happens seldom otherwise'.[140] Thus the real *cause* of the rout might be more the fear of suffering a volley at spitting distance than unwillingness to exchange blows with the bayonet.

The importance of the infantryman's increased firepower put a premium on formations that maximised the number of soldiers positioned where they could shoot effectively. This favoured thinner formations – three to four ranks deep – in solid, contiguous lines. Moreover, the increased speed of reloading made the counter-march unnecessary. This eliminated the need for open lanes between files and allowed infantrymen to form up much more densely, with one fusilier per 2 feet of battalion frontage, instead of one musketeer per 5 feet.[141] The empty space required to gain the manoeuvrability advantages of an intervalled line came to seem too costly in lost firepower to be justified, especially since new drills were developed that allowed battalions to manoeuvre effectively without needing empty space to turn through.[142]

The main reason given at the time for eliminating intervals between battalions, however, was that a unit not linked to friendly units on each side was vulnerable to enemy attacks on the flank, particularly by cavalry. To prevent the gaps that could create such vulnerabilities, 'the whole Line must act like one Battalion, both in Advancing, Attacking, and Pursuing the Enemy together'.[143] Such uniform action also much simplified command and control, obviating the need to send orders separately to each battalion.[144] Moreover, with the highly disciplined

---

[138] Saxe, *Reveries, or Memoirs*, 19, 71; *Mes rêveries*, 37–8, 134; Nosworthy, *Anatomy of Victory*, 111.

[139] Saxe, *Reveries, or Memoirs*, 19, emphasis added; the italicised text is not in the French edition (*Mes rêveries*, I, 37–8). Saxe certainly did, nonetheless, consider the retained potential of the charging soldiers to deliver shots at range close enough to burn the target's coat with the muzzle-flash (*à brûle-purpoint*) to be a key part of the threat they posed. *Mes rêveries*, 40.

[140] Bland, *Treatise*, 134, emphasis added; similarly, Nosworthy, *Anatomy of Victory*, 104 (Catinat), and Quincy, *Maximes*, 67.

[141] Puységur, *Art de la guerre*, 62–4; 36.

[142] *Ibid.*, 147–8.

[143] *Ibid.*, 3; Bland, *Treatise*, 134–5.

[144] Bland, *Treatise*, 139.

troops of the eighteenth century, the buffer against panic that intervals created was considered less necessary – especially since allowing a victorious battalion to push its advantage would expose its own flanks, particularly to the units of cavalry typically held ready for just that purpose.[145]

With intervals in the infantry-line minimised or eliminated, the prospects for combined-arms cooperation at the battalion level were much reduced. Moreover, the practical experience of battle in the later seventeenth century showed that the outcome of the engagement as a whole was often decided by a clash of sabre-charging horsemen on the armies' flanks.[146] For both these reasons, it became the norm (though not the universal practice) to push most of the horsemen to the wings of the army, thus reinstating an overall formation that had been common in the Middle Ages and antiquity, with two central lines of contiguous units of footmen, flanked by bodies of horse and backed up by a third line or reserve.[147]

Meanwhile, for reasons largely extraneous to tactical developments, armies were becoming much larger. Bigger armies, spread more thinly,[148] could make it difficult to find suitable battlefields: 'It is sometimes impossible', observed Marshal de Saxe, 'to find a piece of ground in a whole province, sufficient to contain a hundred thousand men, in order of battle'.[149] It took hours to form armies for battle, the duration of the deployment being roughly proportional to the length of the formation. The near-elimination of intervals between battalions helped bring the armies back closer into proportion with the landscape and the length of the day.[150]

Since the battle-line was basically just a set of march columns rotated 90 degrees, armies often formed for battle by having the lead units turn to march parallel to the enemy's front, with each unit facing left or right

---

[145] *Ibid.*, 134–5.

[146] D'Aurignac wrote in 1663 that 'it is the cavalry that ordinarily wins battles'; quoted in Lynn, *Giant*, 489. Note also Rohan, *Parfaict capitaine*, 263; Quincy, *Maximes*, 56.

[147] Anon., *The Art of War, in Four Parts*, 234; Saxe, *Reveries, or Memoirs*, 18, 63; Folard, *L'esprit*, 88; Frederick II of Prussia, *Instructions*, 342; Quincy, *Maximes*, 56.

[148] Lynn, 'Army Growth'; Puységur, *Art de la guerre*, 57–8, though cf. 52; Saxe, *Reveries*, 18–19; Montecuccoli, *Sulle Battaglia*, 90.

[149] Saxe, *Reveries*, 76.

[150] Puységur, *Art de la guerre*, 147–8, 123. Frederick the Great in 1747 prescribed that normally intervals for his infantry battalions should be only large enough to allow for the artillery, and that squadrons should be separated only by four paces; but on the other hand, he assumed that non-Prussian cavalry would operate with larger intervals, and that for some tactical purposes attack should be made with battalions in 'checkerboard' (i.e. with full intervals) – which Quincy still took as the norm in 1726: Frederick II of Prussia, *Instructions*, 383–5, 395; Quincy, *Maximes*, 57, 105.

once in position. This could involve a march of several miles and most of a day, which meant that battles generally took place only when both sides were willing.[151] An army not desiring battle could position itself on broken ground and entrench, thus deterring an attack, or it could simply move off while the enemy conducted his slow preparations for offensive action. When general engagements did take place, they often began only in the afternoon, and lasted until near dusk. For this reason, and because linear formations were ill suited to rapid movement, an effective pursuit became very difficult to effect. Since the firepower of the flintlock and the increasing number and effectiveness of artillery pieces deployed on eighteenth-century battlefields only increased the advantage of the defence and the costliness of the attrition phase of battle, the problem of pyrrhic victories grew significantly worse. Frederick the Great tellingly noted that the superior discipline and training of his Prussian infantry would have enabled him to conquer 'the entire universe, were it not for the fact *that their victories were as fatal to them as to their enemies*'.[152] His 'oblique order' attacks aimed to fix, or at least ameliorate, that problem, by holding the majority of his army back from the meat-grinder while the advanced wing won the battle. But with that observation, we pass beyond the chronological scope of this book.

Looking over the period as a whole, there is no question that, truly, tactics were 'much altered since the fierie weapons first came up'.[153] However, the reasons for changes in tactics and the soldier's experience of battle, and thus the art of command, were, as we have seen, broader and more complex than simply the invention of firearms.

[151] Nosworthy, *Anatomy of Victory*, 69–77.
[152] Frederick II of Prussia, *Principes*, 8 (emphasis added); cf. Puységur, *Art de la guerre*, 6–7.
[153] Barret, *Moderne Warres*, 2.

11   Naval warfare in Europe, *c.* 1330–*c.* 1680

Louis Sicking

Introduction

This chapter considers the question of how war at sea changed during the late-medieval and early-modern periods, and whether these changes constitute a 'naval revolution'. It is now recognised by historians such as Carlo M. Cipolla, Jan Glete, John F. Guilmartin, and Geoffrey Parker that, during the period roughly between 1500 and 1650, war at sea underwent a fundamental technological transformation.[1] This transformation was of great importance both for warfare at sea and for its organisation. Thanks to the fiscal means of the modern state, permanent, professional, and complex naval organisations became a general phenomenon in Europe. However, at the beginning of the early-modern period, permanent war fleets in most cases did not yet represent anything more than a small core of ships, in itself of limited military importance.[2]

All the same, many of the characteristic features of naval organisation, such as arsenals, admiralties, and standing navies, had come into existence in the Middle Ages. Both the arsenals of Venice and Aragon–Catalonia dated from the beginning of the thirteenth century. Admiralties appeared as institutions around the office of admiral, which originated in Sicily in the twelfth century and became permanent there in 1239. In the fifteenth century Admiralty Courts appeared in Brittany, Normandy, and Guyenne, to mention but a few. Sicily possessed a permanent war fleet in the thirteenth century; Venice established one in

I am indebted to Jan Glete, Jaap Bruijn, Michiel de Jong, Ruthy Gertwagen, and my colleagues of the medieval history section at the History Department at the University of Leiden for their comments on earlier versions of this paper. The author is fully responsible, however, for this final version and for any remaining inconsistencies.

[1] Cipolla, *Guns*; Glete, *Navies and Nations*; Glete, *Warfare at Sea*; Guilmartin, *Gunpowder* (citations are to the 1974 edn throughout the chapter); Guilmartin, *Galleons*; Parker, *Military Revolution*, 82–114.

[2] Glete, *Navies and Nations*, 1, 102, 125–7, 129–31, 146. Venice represents one of the major exceptions: see the next paragraph.

1301. England may have had a permanent squadron during the reign of Richard I, 'the Lionheart' (1189–99) but it was Henry V (1413–22) who actually developed something like a royal navy in the modern sense.[3] The question is, then, to what extent a divide exists between medieval and early-modern European naval warfare.

Because most of the typical institutions of naval warfare, or naval organisation, originated in the Middle Ages, it seems appropriate to look at how technological change influenced the conduct of naval warfare. As the introduction of heavy guns at sea or, more specifically, the introduction of gun-ports happens to have taken place around the year 1500, it will be possible to examine whether a divide exists between 'medieval' and 'early-modern' naval warfare. This is not to imply that naval institutions like arsenals, admiralties, or standing navies were immune to change, or that they would not influence the conduct of warfare. It seems however that the influence of technological change on naval warfare is more visible and perhaps more relevant to the question as to whether a divide exists between medieval and early-modern naval warfare than the influence of organisational change.

Naval historiography has had a tendency to focus on major battles such as that of Lepanto in 1571,[4] major fleets such as the 'Invincible Armada' of 1588,[5] or certain ships such as the *Mary Rose* (built in 1510–11, rebuilt in 1528 or 1536). The *Mary Rose* was not exceptional but has drawn a lot of attention because of her chance survival and her excavation.[6] This is not only understandable because of human interest in the exceptional or in the exceptional survival of evidence; it also reflects the fact that technological change reveals itself most clearly on those occasions, such as the attempted French invasion of England in 1545, when all the stops are pulled out.

J. F. Guilmartin has argued that 'changes in technology generally had their most significant impact upon the conduct of warfare at sea as a result of quantitative, not qualitative, factors'.[7] In other words, it is not the introduction, but the extent of the application of new

---

[3] Doumerc, 'Republic', 153, 155; Mott, 'Power', 107–8; Gertwagen, 'Contribution', 144; Rodger, *Safeguard*, 51, 53, 116; Rose, *Warfare*.

[4] E.g. Lesure, *Lépante*; Pigaillem, *Bataille*.

[5] E.g. Martin and Parker, *Armada*.

[6] Mollat du Jourdin, 'Mer', 300. In recent years much of the archaeological evidence of the *Mary Rose* has been reassessed. Conclusions have been revised often in a more cautious way, and so are open to more than one interpretation (e.g. Vine and Hildred, 'Evidence', 15–20). The older literature on the *Mary Rose* and references to it should therefore be used with caution: McKee, *Mary Rose*; Rule, *Mary Rose*; Loades, *Tudor Navy*, 49–50.

[7] Guilmartin, *Gunpowder*, 254.

technology that is decisive for the effectiveness of the changes in the conduct of warfare at sea. From this perspective the present paper will focus on the consequences of the introduction of heavy guns at sea and of the innovations in sailing-ship technology related to this introduction. Two important, successive changes will be considered: the introduction of heavy guns on galleys[8] and their introduction on sailing vessels, and their respective consequences for war at sea in Europe. This means that the focus will be more on ships rather than on naval organisation.

Emphasis in this chapter will be put on the continued importance of galleys in the Mediterranean on the one hand and of merchantmen for naval warfare in northern waters on the other. It should be noted that galleys also had sails to save human power whenever possible, but they were generally poor sailers unless in light breeze.[9] The 'return' of the galley in north-western and northern European naval warfare in the sixteenth century has received relatively little attention in the existing historiography, but may be considered as one of the most striking features of sixteenth-century naval warfare. The medieval north-western European way of naval warfare – that is, transforming merchantmen temporarily into warships – continued to be common practice into the seventeenth century. It will be argued that the introduction of the gun-port and heavy guns on board did not necessarily entail the development of specialised or purpose-built warships. It will also be argued that improvements in sailing-ship technology made possible the rise of the sailing ship in naval warfare in the Mediterranean.

The introduction of heavy guns at sea and of the innovations in sailing-ship technology had tremendous consequences for all European maritime powers, whether public or private, large or small. Space does not allow systematic discussion of these consequences to their full extent for all those involved; three important limitations have been made. First, references to individual powers will only be made in an exemplary way. If a certain prominence is given to the Low Countries in the selection of these references, it is merely a consequence of the author's familiarity. Second, European expansion overseas will only be considered tangentially.[10] Finally, this chapter will focus on warfare at sea determined and paid for by a public authority; hence 'naval

---

[8] Gertwagen, 'Characteristics', 547.

[9] Pryor, *Geography*, 71–2.

[10] This is not to deny of course the tremendous impact of gunpowder for power projection overseas. See for example Glete, *Warfare at Sea*; Trim and Fissel, *Amphibious Warfare*.

warfare', which means that privateering, filibustering, and piracy will largely be excluded.[11]

This last limitation needs some further explanation, as medieval and early-modern naval warfare until at least 1600 – and to a great extent until around 1650 – was largely fought with means bought or hired from the market, either voluntarily or by force: that is by arrest or requisition. War fleets directed and paid for by public authorities consisted for the majority of merchant vessels that had been transformed for the occasion.[12] This is not to say that kings or countries could not possess warships of their own or that they could not have been built or transformed for war purposes only. Several countries, like France and England, did create permanent war fleets, although even these often consisted of converted merchant vessels, like the standing fleet of Emperor Charles V at Veere in the Netherlands between 1550 and 1561.[13] However, the ships making up these permanent forces represented only a minority or nucleus of the entire naval forces in wartime. Therefore public authorities depended for naval expeditions on the owners of merchant vessels. As a sea-going ship could be easily transformed into a warship – by putting superstructures called 'castles' fore and aft[14] and, after the introduction of the heavy gun, by temporarily adding gun-ports and strengthening the hull and masts[15] – merchant fleets were of great military importance and crucial for the execution of sea power. The merchant fleet of a town, a region, or a country thus represented a military interest of great importance. A merchant fleet had maritime or naval potential; indeed, it is more accurate to consider a merchant fleet in a military context as a versatile or flexible fleet, a multi-purpose fleet useful both in times of war and peace.

Contemporaries were very well aware of this reality. In 1522 Margaret of Austria, regent of the Netherlands, received an instruction from Emperor Charles V that mentions the intention to make the Netherlandish towns equip ships '... to be used in war when the

---

[11] In reality all kinds of mixed forms of state and non-state violence existed. Thomson, *Mercenaries* offers an applicable theoretical framework that is useful to make at least some distinctions.

[12] Hutchinson, *Ships*, 149, 153; Unger, 'Conclusion', 257; Stradling, *Armada*, 165; Phillips, 'Galleon', 104; Fritze and Krause, *Seekriege*, 37–8, 54, 223. Kowaleski, 'Warfare', 235 has recently argued that this could be a profitable enterprise for medieval ship-owners.

[13] Hutchinson, *Ships*, 149, 153–6; Sicking, *Neptune*, Chapter 6.

[14] See for example Runyan, 'Cog', 47–58.

[15] Friel, *Ship*, 156; Sicking, *Neptune*, 381–4. Archaeologists excavating the wreck of a sixteenth-century ship, possibly used for warfare, that was recently discovered at the bottom of the Westerschelde near Flushing, found its hull had been strengthened; Vos, *Standaardrapport*.

opportunity arises; and in times of peace they will be able to serve the same towns to transport their merchandise ...'.[16] The examples could be multiplied.[17] The point is clear: any study of European naval warfare in the medieval and early-modern periods has to take into account the continued importance of the merchant fleet for naval warfare.

Only by choosing a long-term approach, starting in the Middle Ages, is it possible to assess continuities and changes in European warfare at sea while gunpowder was introduced. The first explicit evidence of a gunpowder weapon used for the defence of ships dates from 1337, although many scholars believe that those weapons appeared aboard ships even earlier, that is shortly after they began to be used on land. Throughout the fourteenth and fifteenth centuries the use of gunpowder weapons at sea increased. By 1450 they were commonplace on ships both in the Mediterranean and in the Atlantic.[18] Thus when the gunport was introduced by 1500, gunpowder had been used in maritime warfare for more than one-and-a-half centuries. The rising interest in medieval naval history in recent years will help to bridge the divide between medieval and early-modern naval history.[19] For reasons of clarity the dividing line between the medieval and early-modern periods will be drawn in the year 1500, which is somewhat arbitrary but fits well with the already mentioned introduction of the gun-port, usually dated around that year.[20] Thus 'medieval' in this chapter means pre-1500 and 'early-modern' indicates post-1500.

Rowing for war

Until the twelfth century, warships were mostly oared vessels both in northern waters and in the Mediterranean, but from then on, oars were gradually replaced by sails – initially along the Atlantic coast.[21] Galleys nevertheless remained popular as warships for a long time, not only in the Mediterranean. In 1120, for instance, the bishop of Santiago de Compostella hired a Genoese shipwright to build two bireme galleys for service against Muslim pirates. The galley remained the preferred warship in the Atlantic well into the fourteenth century, and it was the

---

[16] Sicking, *Neptune*, 206.
[17] E.g. Elias, *Vlootbouw*, 5. For examples from the fifteenth century, see Jongkees, 'Armement', 71–87; Bakker, 'Het bijeenbrengen', 3–20; Sicking, 'Les transports'.
[18] DeVries, 'Effectiveness', 389–90. Compare Cipolla, *Guns*, 75–6.
[19] E.g. Rose, *Warfare*; Hattendorf and Unger, *War at Sea*.
[20] Cipolla, *Guns*, 81–2.
[21] Fernández-Armesto, 'Warfare', 235–6.

primary combat vessel in all of the naval battles fought between Castile and Portugal during the 1300s.[22]

Height was a crucial factor in naval encounters. The naval experts of Aragon–Catalonia were well aware of this. In the late thirteenth century they designed galleys with particularly high forecastles and poops to accommodate and protect the 'deadly accurate' Catalan crossbowmen. This enabled the Catalan–Aragonese fleet to defeat the Angevin fleet, which used galleys with low bulwarks, in the battle of Malta (1283) during the War of the Sicilian Vespers (1282–1302).[23]

The introduction of the heavy gun on board: the advantage of the galley

Galleys were the first ships to take advantage of the use of heavy artillery; from the start of the sixteenth century all major galley fleets were so armed. Galleys mounted a single large gun forward in the bow of the vessel. Originally iron breech-loaders were used, but soon Mediterranean galleys were armed with more formidable bronze muzzle-loaders, which could fire either stone shot, or the heavier iron balls of 30 to 50 lb or more, with hull-smashing capacity. The Venetians were able to shoot at a distance of more than 450 m. By the beginning of the sixteenth century sliding carriages were used to absorb the shock of the recoil and thus to avoid damage to the hull of the ship. With the heavy gun the low galley could inflict serious damage on the high-sided hull of a large sailing ship, whereas before the higher sailing ship had held the advantage when attacked by galleys with infantry weapons. The galley was also vulnerable to gunfire, but with its low hull it was more difficult to hit than a high sailing ship.[24]

The galley with a heavy gun mounted in its bow could thus fire forward and be used in the standard line-abreast formation, which was practically the most frequently used tactic of warfare at sea as well as on land. The fact that only one heavy gun could be mounted in the bow of each galley was not an important disadvantage as long as heavy guns were scarce and sailing ships were unable to mount such a gun in their bow.[25] The only firearms that could be used from sailing ships in the same formation were small arms.[26] The fact that galleys, thanks to their

---

[22] Mott, 'Power', 105–6, 111.

[23] Hutchinson, *Ships*, 147; Mott, 'Power', 107.

[24] Rodger, *Safeguard*, 207–8; Guilmartin, *Galleons*, 114; Glete, *Warfare at Sea*, 22, 27–8.

[25] Glete, *Warfare*, 28.

[26] Rodger, *Safeguard*, 208.

oars, could be manoeuvred independently from the wind enabled them to fire with more precision than sailing ships. Unlike sixteenth-century sailing fleets, galleys could also manoeuvre in large formations where fleet and squadron commanders might exercise control and command. At Lepanto, the greatest naval battle of the age, more than 200 galleys fought on each side. Both as gun-carriers and as units of large fleets they were eminently suited to contemporary disciplined warfare with formalised tactics.[27]

There were certainly disadvantages to galleys mounting heavy artillery. They had a tendency to dig their bow into the slightest head sea, but shipwrights – those from the Venetian arsenal were probably the first – compensated for the weight of the artillery by designing hulls that were fuller at the bow and finer at the stern, resulting in a fish-like shape below the water surface.[28] They also became much heavier and thus needed more oarsmen.

But in spite of these inconveniences, from around 1500 until around 1580 galleys had gained a major advantage relative to sailing ships.[29] For centuries, galleys had been vulnerable to the high sides and decks of ships, but thanks to the heavy gun they could now stand off and sink them with impunity. As a result the galley gained importance for warfare at sea in the Mediterranean, in the waters of north-western Europe, and in the Baltic. In the Mediterranean there had been few permanent galley forces before 1500, but now the number of galleys increased dramatically. Thanks to the introduction of the heavy gun, the cannon-armed galley became the basis of a Mediterranean system of warfare that reached its apogee between 1520 and 1580 and was to dominate the middle sea until the 1630s.[30]

Although the galleys of the Mediterranean powers varied according to differences in strategic goals, resource availability, organisation, and social structure, differences in design and construction were marginal. They mainly involved fighting superstructures that could be quickly added or removed.[31] This was not only the case for the ordinary (war) galleys, which by 1290 had adopted the optimal rowing system – with three men per bench each having an oar – that was to remain dominant for two-and-a-half centuries. Next to these ordinary triremes the heavier merchant galley could be converted for war, thus becoming a

---

[27] Glete, *Warfare*, 28, 35.
[28] Guilmartin, *Galleons*, 115.
[29] Glete, *Warfare*, 27.
[30] Rodger, *Safeguard*, 208; Guilmartin, *Gunpowder*, 59; Guilmartin, *Galleons*, 118; Glete, *Warfare*, 27.
[31] Guilmartin, *Galleons*, 119–20.

gallee grosse, or great galley. These great galleys (which were sometimes purpose-built for military transports) were the tactical backbone of late-medieval galley fleets.[32] They could 'with astonishing agility' be turned into a warship in an emergency. In this way Genoa, Venice, and Aragon–Catalonia were able to use their merchant fleet for military purposes.[33] Their flexible galley fleets had enabled both Italian city-states to build maritime Empires stretching across the Mediterranean, the Black Sea, and the Sea of Azov, controlling the major sea-lanes.

The introduction of the heavy gun, however, reduced the importance of the heavy merchant galley for war. For two centuries merchant galleys had been the perfect solution for the transport of high-value commodities and for their protection against piracy. By 1520 the small fleets of four to five great galleys, which had assured the overseas trading connections of Venice, no longer offered effective protection. The speedy war galley had become the favourite galley for battle, and the war fleets of the large states in the Mediterranean – the Ottoman Empire, Spain, and France – outsized the small fleets of Venetian merchant galleys. The first line of Venice's trading network to feel the effects was the fleet trading with Romania and the Black Sea, partly as a consequence of the threat of Turkish guns both on the heights of the Golden Horn, near Constantinople, and on galleys at sea before the end of the fifteenth century. Fear that the English king Henry VIII might requisition Venetian merchant galleys to use them against France in the Channel contributed to the end of these 'galleys of Flanders' in 1533.[34] As a consequence the overseas trading network of Venice declined.

Both Venice and Genoa had established their maritime Empires thanks to their flexible fleets of convertible galleys that could be used for both commerce and warfare. Now they had to spend extra money for purpose-built galleys, which became more and more expensive for reasons that will be explained below. This separation of Mars and Mercury[35] in the Mediterranean gave an advantage to great powers like the Ottoman Empire and Spain, which could eventually concentrate more purpose-built war galleys than Genoa or Venice, although Venice showed a remarkable ability to enhance its fleet of war galleys. In response to rising sea power, mainly of the Ottoman Empire, Venice built up a reserve fleet rising from 50 galleys in the late fifteenth century to more than 100 after 1540. For the campaign of Lepanto in 1571 the Venetian arsenal turned

---

[32] *Ibid.*, 112–13; Rodger, *Safeguard*, 66.
[33] Balard, 'Genoese Naval Forces', 145; Rose, *Warfare*, 10–11.
[34] Lane, *Venice: A Maritime Republic*, 348–52.
[35] This expression was used in connection with Dutch naval warfare by Bruijn, 'Mars en Mercurius'.

out 100 galleys within two months, which represented about half of the Christian galley fleet.[36]

When the merchant galley disappeared as a cargo carrier around the middle of the sixteenth century it was redesigned into a hybrid warship, the galleass, with auxiliary oars, being able to carry much more heavy armament fore and aft than a regular war galley. Although these vessels greatly impressed contemporaries they would prove to be ineffective against the oarless 'ship-of-the-line'.[37]

The return of the galley in northern waters

The advantage galleys acquired over sailing ships resulted in what could be called the export of the 'Mediterranean system of armed conflict at sea'[38] or the return of the galleys to northern waters, between roughly 1520 and 1580. France and England began to use galleys and galleasses in the Channel, while Sweden (1540) and Denmark–Norway (1565) introduced galleys in the Baltic.[39] France seems to have been first in using war galleys with heavy centre-line bow-guns in northern waters. In 1513 off Brest, a French galley fleet under the command of Prégent de Bidoux, which had been built by the Genoese and the Venetians, shot its way through an English war fleet sinking one ship. The English, who tried to retrieve the situation with a bold attack that failed, were shocked by the superior firepower of the French guns – almost certainly bronze 'basiliks' – from Bidoux's galleys. This was 'an entirely new way of waging war at sea'.[40]

From 1517, the French king Francis I (1515–47) and his successor, Henry II (1547–59), used galleys in the Channel from their newly built naval base, Le Havre.[41] They represented the cream of the crop of French naval forces along the Atlantic. Thirty-seven galleys were intended to play an essential role in the maritime tactics envisaged by France in the Channel in 1545. The French armada of 1545, the greatest invasion force ever seen in north-western Europe until then, which posed the most serious threat to England since 1066, contained in addition to the galley force of, according to various estimates, between 125 and 300 sailing ships, which made it comparable in size to the Spanish

[36] Lane, *Venice: A Maritime Republic*, 362–4.
[37] Glete, *Warfare*, 31; Lane, *Venice: A Maritime Republic*, 357–8, 373–4; Oudendijk, *Ridder*, 77.
[38] Guilmartin, *Gunpowder*, 265.
[39] Glete, *Warfare*, 27; Guilmartin, *Gunpowder*, 59.
[40] Guilmartin, *Galleons*, 116 citing Rodger, *Safeguard*, 170–1.
[41] Knecht, *Renaissance Warrior*, 367. On the origin of Le Havre see most recently Lardin, *Tradition*.

Armada of 1588.[42] French expertise provided the way for Henry VIII of England to build new types of oared vessels, after he had begun construction of the *Galley Subtle* and tried in vain to obtain ten galleys from Charles V. The result was the construction of galleasses, and of eighteen light, fast, and very manoeuvrable rowing barges that proved highly effective during the sea combats between the French and the English near the Isle of Wight in 1545. When the English admiral Lord Lisle met his French counterpart Claude d'Annebaut in 1546, he told him that England was now well equipped 'having made 8 or 10 new galleasses … besides sundry light vessels, as swift with oars as their galleys'.[43] The French, however, were far more troublesome to England than the other way around.[44]

Unlike sailing ships in this period, galleys could safely operate close to the coast, enabling them to disembark troops and artillery or to serve as floating siege batteries close to the walls of seaside fortresses and towns. Heavy guns could smash their thin medieval walls.[45] When French galleys entered the estuaries of the River Scheldt and harboured in the roadstead of the island of Walcheren in Zeeland – outport of the Antwerp metropolis – in 1546, they caused great panic and fear amongst the inhabitants. A year later, the coastal fortress of Rammekens, the first fortress built in the Netherlands with bastions, had been completed. French galleys, seeking to use the natural harbour of Walcheren only as a temporary anchorage, had caused the island to become the 'bulwark of the Netherlands', in the words of contemporaries.[46]

Other examples of serious invasion efforts – in which galley fleets were considered essential – include, in the Mediterranean, the Turkish campaign in Apulia in 1537; and, in the Baltic, the Swedish effort in 1555 to take the Russian fortress of Nöteborg, on the River Neva, by an amphibious attack with a fleet of around twenty galleys and numerous other vessels.[47] In 1588 Spanish commanders involved in the preparation of the 'Invincible Armada' felt they needed at least twelve galleys because of the

---

[42] Mollat du Jourdin, 'Mer', 289; Loades, *Tudor Navy*, 131. Williamson, *Channel*, 175 mentions 150 ships; Roncière, *Histoire*, III, 416 mentions 150 sailing vessels and 25 galleys. According to the eyewitness du Bellay, the French armada of 1545 included 235 ships in total; Bellay, *Mémoires*, 553. Brewer *et al.*, *Letters and Papers*, XX, Part I, lvii suggest that 300 ships, 25 galleys, and 5 galleasses were involved.

[43] Bennell, 'Oared Vessels', 37.

[44] Brewer *et al.*, *Letters and Papers*, XX, Part I, lx.

[45] Guilmartin, *Gunpowder*, 265; Guilmartin, *Galleons*, 118; Trim and Fissel, *Amphibious Warfare*, 442–3.

[46] Sicking, *Neptune*, 303 n. 58, 304–6.

[47] Glete, 'Naval Power', 226; Glete, 'Amphibious Warfare', 128; Guilmartin, *Gunpowder*, 264.

amphibious nature of the operation.[48] Although none of the four galleys that eventually sailed with the Armada actually reached the Channel, it is clear that the galley gained importance in warfare at the northern seas during most of the sixteenth century.

The continued importance of galleys in the Mediterranean and the Baltic

The tactical logic of galley warfare dictated a constant increase in the amount of forward-firing ordnance. Flanking pieces were put alongside the main centre-line gun. By the 1530s a second, smaller pair of guns was put at the bow. The weight of artillery aboard Mediterranean galleys grew steadily, and with it the displacement of the ships: up to 200 tonnes for an ordinary war galley around 1550, and 300 tonnes around 1650. In order to keep up speed under oars, the increased weight entailed disproportionate numbers of additional oarsmen. Venetian experiments in the 1520s with a quinquereme, having five men and five oars to each bench, showed that a 50 per cent increase in displacement required a 100 per cent increase in oarsmen if speed was not to be compromised. In a period of rising prices and salaries it became more and more difficult to fulfil the growing demand of skilled and motivated oarsmen. This resulted in a change in the galley rowing system. Alongside and instead of free, professional oarsmen, slaves and convicts began to be used. Individual oars gave way to a single large oar for each bench. A single oar was less efficient than individual oars pulled by skilled oarsmen: four men – one skilled oarsman and three slaves and/or convicts to an oar – were needed to equal the speed of a trireme with three professional oarsmen per bench, each with an oar of their own. Contrary to the former free oarsmen, slaves could not engage in fighting. Therefore additional men were needed to fight and to guard the slaves under oars. Besides this reduced efficiency, the advantage was that only one skilled oarsman per oar was needed, which reduced the dependence on skilled oarsmen and enhanced the flexibility to add or remove oarsmen according to the tactical situation.[49] Spain, whose galleys seem to have carried a greater weight of ordnance than any other Mediterranean power, introduced the new rowing system first, in the 1550s. Venice, whose maritime artillery was relatively light, was the last to abandon the old system, at the end of

---

[48] Martin and Parker, *Armada*, 121–2.
[49] Guilmartin, *Galleons*, 120–1. For further details: Alertsz, 'Architecture'; Bondioli, Burlet, and Zysberg, 'Mechanics'. On the Venetian quinquereme, built on the initiative of a professor of Greek: Lehmann, *Queeste*, 40–4.

the sixteenth century.[50] As a result of the increase in manning density caused by the new rowing system the strategic radius of action of galleys decreased because they had to land more frequently to recharge water and food.

Galleys continued to grow larger and more powerful in the seventeenth century, but the number of galley fleets declined, as well as the number of galleys per fleet.[51] However, galleys retained their tactical utility and remained in use, first of all in the Mediterranean. Inspired by Colbert, according to whom 'There is no power which marks better the greatness of a prince than that of galleys' (1665), Louis XIV built the greatest galley fleet of the Mediterranean, counting 40 ships at the end of the seventeenth century on which 12,000 oarsmen, 3,000 officers and 4,000 soldiers served. Galleys played a significant role in the Venetian–Ottoman wars for Crete (1654–69) and the Morea (the Peloponnesus) (1694–8), albeit in conjunction with, and usually secondary to, sailing warships.[52] Spain and France operated small galley squadrons in the Channel around 1600 and at the time of Louis XIV respectively; the Dutch built some galleys to counter the Spanish ones.[53] When the latter were destroyed in 1603 they were not replaced. In the Baltic both Sweden and Russia used galleys in the Great Northern War of 1700–21.[54] Inspired by the Turks, the Russians built more than 400 galleys during the eighteenth century.[55] In sum, galleys remained important for warfare at sea mainly in the Mediterranean and in the Baltic during the early-modern era.

Sailing for war

From the twelfth century onwards, sailing vessels gradually became more important for warfare. Thanks to more masts and sails and the application of rudders 'fitted to stern-posts rising from the keel' instead of 'tillers dangled from the starboard towards the keel', the manoeuvrability of sailing vessels increased. These now became an alternative to oared vessels. Ships were thus freed from the economic and logistic burden of great numbers of oarsmen. Oar-powered vessels dominated Baltic warfare until 1210, when the crusading order of the Sword Brothers switched to cogs.

---

[50] Guilmartin, *Gunpowder*, 268.
[51] Guilmartin, *Galleons*, 125, 211.
[52] Zysberg, 'Galères', 123; Zysberg and Burlet, *Gloire*, 82–3; Rowlands, 'French Amphibious Warfare', 265, 268, 276–7. 'Il n'y a point de puissance qui marque mieux la grandeur d'un prince que celle des galères' (Zysberg and Burlet).
[53] Lehmann, *Galeien*, 95–103.
[54] Guilmartin, *Galleons*, 212; Lehmann, *Galeien*.
[55] Zysberg and Burlet, *Gloire*, 127.

The French at the battle of Sluys in 1340 used both the royal galleys and 170 sailing ships, of which many were certainly intended for the fray. In England, not until around 1400 did the fighting vanguard become almost entirely sail-driven, oared craft forming only a small part of its navy.[56]

Ships that did not need to be propelled by oars could have higher freeboards, offering them an important advantage in a time when height was a crucial tactical criterion. As a result, oarless craft played a growing – albeit slowly growing – role in Mediterranean warfare too.[57] The raids carried out by cogs from Bayonne in the Mediterranean in 1304 impressed the Genoese, Venetians, and Catalans who had started to build *coches* or cogs themselves.[58] Medieval sailing ships were equipped with superstructures fore and aft – castles – which allowed for attacking the enemy. In time these castles became higher and higher, making the ships top-heavy and causing them to look like floating fortresses. As a result it was almost impossible for a galley crew successfully to board and enter a sailing ship.[59] The attack on the Venetian Levant convoy by a Genoese fleet of eighteen galleys in 1264 offers a good illustration. The Venetian convoy, consisting of twelve single-decked sailing vessels of about 150 tons' displacement; half-a-dozen smaller craft; and a single large, round ship of 750 tons (the *Roccaforte*), although outnumbered by the Genoese, managed to resist for hours. When the Venetians finally retreated aboard the *Roccaforte*, the Genoese were unable successfully to assail the vessel.[60] Almost 200 years later, in 1453 during the Turkish siege of Constantinople, 150 Turkish boats gathered around four sailing vessels in the Bosporus but were unable to capture them. By the 1420s the Genoese were building carracks of 600 to 900 tons' displacement. Such vessels, prestige state warships, were 'essentially immune to attack by galleys'.[61] In the fifteenth century the Venetian state, too, commissioned large sailing warships for operations against corsair galleys.[62]

The introduction of the heavy gun on board: the slowly developed advantage of the sailing vessel.

From a medieval perspective, the introduction of the heavy gun at sea was yet another, but important, phase in the development of gunpowder

---

[56] Fernández-Armesto, 'Warfare', 236. Rodger, *Safeguard*, 473. Friel, *Ship*, 147–150.
[57] Fernández-Armesto, 'Warfare', 236.
[58] Runyan, 'Naval Power', 60–1; Gertwagen, 'Characteristics', 554; Runyan, 'Cog', 47–58.
[59] Fernández-Armesto, 'Warfare', 236.
[60] Guilmartin, *Galleons*, 114.
[61] Fernández-Armesto, 'Warfare', 236.
[62] Lane, *Venice: A Maritime Republic*, 412.

weapons in naval warfare. Originally used as anti-personnel weapons, gunpowder weapons increased in size and numbers on warships in the fifteenth century. Three technological innovations in the fifteenth century encouraged the rise of gunpowder weapons in naval warfare and remained of importance in the sixteenth century. The first was the addition of a swivel to the base of a small gun that could be used from the side of the hull or castle, or from the bow or stern of a galley. The second was the hand-held gunpowder weapon, allowing for more mobile gunfire, which began to be used on ships. The third was the large shipboard gun, which could be loaded with both the ball and the powder from the rear.[63]

Whereas the first two weapons could only be directed against opposing personnel, the third allowed for larger guns with hull-smashing capacity to be mounted on the sides of ships. The latter is confirmed by Philip of Cleves' treatise, *Instruction de toutes manières de guerroyer tant par terre que par mer*, which he wrote around 1516, and which is one of the few sixteenth-century treatises to deal with the fitting out of warships in a more or less systematic way. Philip states that two cannon and a big culverin on wheels should be placed between the mast and the forecastle on each side.[64]

The gun-port offered an alternative means to mount heavier guns as it enabled cannon to be placed below the deck. Ships could thus carry more and heavier artillery without becoming unstable. Traditionally dated to 1501, when a French shipwright is supposed to have invented the gun-port, there is evidence that gun-ports had already appeared in the late fifteenth century.[65] It is not well known, however, how exactly the broadside location of guns in the hull of sailing vessels developed. Philip of Cleves' treatise explicitly refers to the use of watertight gun-ports. The fact that the gun-ports needed 'hatches that can be raised by ropes when necessary in order to fire the cannons' indicates that they were located low down near the waterline. Philip added that these hatches could only be opened and the cannon behind them used if the weather permitted.[66] New technology is one thing; the successful application of it is another. This was to be dramatically illustrated thirty years later when the *Mary Rose*, the vice-admiralship of Henry VIII, overloaded with men and guns, heeled over with the wind and was flooded by

---

[63] DeVries, 'Effectiveness', 394–5; Hutchinson, *Ships*, 149.

[64] Oudendijk, *Ridder*, 122. The Warwick Roll (*c.* 1485) offers an example of this location; DeVries, 'Effectiveness', 394.

[65] Cipolla, *Guns*, 82; Friel, *Ship*, 154; Hutchinson, *Ships*, 160–1; DeVries, 'Effectiveness', 396.

[66] Oudendijk, *Ridder*, 122; Paviot, *Philippe*, 43.

water entering through the lowest gun-ports, which had been left open after firing.[67] Clearly, in spite of all the risks that gun-ports close to the waterline entailed, they were considered of great importance in order to optimise the chance of hitting the hulls of the enemy ships.

The challenge sailing ships were facing was that they could not fire forward to the same extent as galleys. Sailing vessels could fire nothing but small arms when they were attacked by a galley fleet in standard line-abreast formation.[68] A solution to this major tactical problem was only gradually found. Initially, there seems to have been a tendency to put the heavy artillery in the aft of sailing ships. Amongst the above-mentioned cannon behind hatches, Philip of Cleves explicitly included two cannon aft, one on either side of the rudder. Philip goes on to mention that on the first floor of the aftercastle – that is, one level higher than the above-mentioned cannon behind gun-ports with hatches – 'two great culverins should be put, one on either side of the mast, which shoot forward as they cannot be turned to be used on broadside because of their length'.[69] At the same level in the aftercastle two great cannon (*bastons*) should be placed, again one on each side of the rudder, to shoot from behind. Thus at least four great cannon were put in the aftercastle protruding from the stern of the ship. It seems that the largest guns were used aft originally, and the broadside guns below deck soon after.[70]

As the size (and number) of gunpowder weapons on ships increased, it became necessary to strengthen the ship's hull both to enable it to withstand the increased recoil of its own weapons and to protect it against hull-smashing balls from the enemy.[71] The introduction of the heavy gun at sea thus stimulated the development of purpose-built sailing warships. King James IV of Scotland's *Great Michael*, built between 1506 and 1512, was about 1,000 tons and revolutionary in design, as she was designed from the first to carry a main armament of heavy artillery.[72] King Hans of Denmark (1481–1513) built some of the largest warships in the world, like *Engelen* (*c.* 1510), whose size was probably around 1,500 to 2,000 tonnes' displacement.[73] The English king Henry VIII launched his *Henry Grace à Dieu* or *Great Harry*, carrying 186 guns, in 1514 in the presence of the court and the papal and

---

[67] McKee, *Mary Rose*, 65–8; Parker, *Military Revolution*, 91.
[68] Rodger, 'Development', 303.
[69] Oudendijk, *Ridder*, 122.
[70] Rodger, *Safeguard*, 207–9. Compare Sicking, 'Philip', 129.
[71] DeVries, 'Effectiveness', 394–5.
[72] Rodger, *Safeguard*, 168–9. See Macdougall, 'Greatiest scheip' for further details.
[73] Glete, 'Naval Power', 221.

imperial ambassadors. Francis I of France followed in 1521 with the *Grande Françoise*. This 1,500-ton ship, equipped with a chapel, a tennis court, and a windmill, was 'the most triumphant thing that any sailor ever saw'.[74] The Portuguese and Swedish kings respectively launched the *Sao João*, which is said to have carried no fewer than 366 guns, in 1534, and the *Elefanten* in 1555.[75]

'Great ships' like these were but a small minority of all ships available for naval warfare; they were also built as much for reasons of prestige and reputation as for their tactical value. They seem to have been lost more often through accidents, lack of money, or simple inability to sail, than through the effects of gunfire. The *Engelen* accidentally burnt at Santander in 1518 after the ship had been loaned by Hans' successor, Christian II, to his brother-in-law, Charles of Habsburg, to serve as flagship for his coronation voyage to Spain.[76] In the war of 1512–14, the *Great Michael* was sold to France because Scoland could not afford to maintain such a large ship.[77] The *Grande Françoise* proved to be what a Venetian visitor predicted: 'so magnificent that it looks as though she will be incapable of putting to sea'. Her draft was so deep that she could not leave the harbour.[78] And as already noted, the loss of the *Mary Rose* was due to instability, rather than to French fire.

These ships probably all carried heavy guns behind gun-ports. In order to mount as many guns as possible they were floating fortresses rather than manoeuvrable weapons of war.[79] However, the ability of ships to carry heavy guns behind gun-ports did not originate only in the above-mentioned ships of royal prestige. Sailing ships from Genoa and Lübeck, and privately owned English ships, which had been bought for the English navy around 1512–14, all carried heavy guns.[80] In the Netherlands, too, ships mounted heavy guns below deck in the 1510s and 1520s.[81] These examples represent different European traditions of the same ability to carry heavy guns.

New ship designs were developed to utilise heavy guns as effectively as galleys. One of these designs was the aforementioned galleass. The galleass had the bow of a galley able to mount a heavy gun, and carried guns on the broadside on a deck under which banks for oarsmen were located. Another, more frequently used ship type that developed was

---

[74] Rodger, *Safeguard*, 204, 547 n. 3.
[75] Cipolla, *Guns*, 82.
[76] Glete, 'Naval Power', 221.
[77] Rodger, *Safeguard*, 172; Macdougall, 'Greatiest scheip', 56–7.
[78] Rodger, *Safeguard*, 204 (citation). Knecht, *Renaissance Warrior*, 367.
[79] Cipolla, *Guns*, 83
[80] Carr Laughton, 'Ship-Guns', 242–85.
[81] Sicking, 'Philip'.

the galleon, which combined the fore-part of a galley with the after-part of a sailing ship. It connected the military advantage of the galley with the sea-worthiness of sails. The importance of the galleon and its focus on heavy gunnery in the bow until the end of the sixteenth century are explained by the fact that the galley remained the galleon's most important enemy. Although the word 'galleon' indicated a kind of ship, its precise meaning varied from country to country. Whereas the Portuguese *galeão* was practically a purpose-built warship, the Spanish *galleón* designated both warship and armed merchantman.[82] As the Spanish galleon had to be fit for war and trade, it will be discussed in the section on converted merchant vessels. The events of 1588 had shown that English galleons had an advantage over their slower Spanish counterparts thanks to a distinctive design technique of 'whole-moulding', which produced fast and weatherly hulls.[83] The superiority of the English galleons continued to be acknowledged in early–seventeenth-century Spain.[84]

The introduction of cast-iron guns around the middle of the sixteenth century made it economically possible to arm ships on an unprecedented scale, as guns of cast iron were much cheaper than bronze. At the same time important improvements were made in truck-carriage design and foundry practice. Cast-iron guns were considerably heavier than bronze pieces, which threw the same weight of ball, but cost only about a third or a quarter as much. The disparity increased in time until the cost of iron ordnance had fallen to an eighth of that of bronze in England in the 1670s.

A massive international trade in cast-iron guns developed, in which the Dutch played a particularly important role. In the words of contemporaries, the United Provinces became 'the arsenal of the world' thanks to the development of an important arms industry, which managed to assure and regulate the supply of raw materials, like iron from Sweden and saltpetre from the Indies, and which produced not only for the Dutch market but also for export. By 1650, cast-iron ordnance had become the standard means of defence afloat, although bronze ordnance did not entirely disappear.[85]

Thanks to broadside gun-ports and cast-iron guns a ship could carry far more guns. Depending on its size, the gun-armed sailing ship that developed in the seventeenth century had one, two, or – exceptionally – three complete battery decks. Besides, guns continued to be mounted under the quarterdeck and in the forecastle. When guns became

[82] Guilmartin, *Galleons*, 158–9; Phillips, 'Galleon', 103; Domingues, 'Forces', 195.
[83] Rodger, *Safeguard*, 212–13, 217–20; Phillips, 'Galleon', 104, 106.
[84] Martin and Parker, *Armada*, 11–12; Goodman, *Spanish Naval Power*, 114.
[85] Guilmartin, 'Guns', 149–50; De Jong, *'Staat'*.

cheaper, gun-ports were placed closer to each other so that even more artillery could be mounted on sailing ships. This stimulated the trend towards big and heavy ships.

At the same time initiatives were taken to build faster and more manoeuvrable ships. In Portugal, the caravel of between 150 and 180 tons with two covered decks, four masts, and narrow hull (to be distinguished from its smaller namesake, which had been used for discoveries in the fifteenth century), was probably mainly developed for naval purposes in the sixteenth century.[86] In England in the 1570s the so-called 'race-built' ship was introduced. This new design involved a reduction in the castles, sleeker lines, and a longer gun-deck. The reduction of the castles meant that less priority was given to optimising the use of anti-personnel weapons, the majority of which were traditionally used from these castles. The sleeker lines led to a faster and more manoeuvrable ship, whereas the longer gun-deck permitted an increase in the weight of the guns' broadside. Several English warships were built and rebuilt according to this race-built design.[87]

Developments in Flanders around 1600 led to a ship design that was to have a broader and longer-lasting influence on European warships: the frigate. Although the origins of this ship design are still being debated, it combined speed and manoeuvrability with hitting power thanks to a fine, shallow hull and a great spread of sail. Frigates had a low and almost even outline, into which the former castles had more or less been integrated; continuous decks allowed the placing of most guns amidships.[88] They were faster than any English ship and could '[run] rings round them', as English captains reported in the 1620s.[89] It has been suggested that the Flemish frigate represented 'the first generation of specialist fighting-ships in the West outside the Mediterranean'.[90] In the 1620s the Dutch also started to build and use frigates against their opponents.[91] England, and from the 1660s France too, used these mobile, purpose-built warships. Typically the shift that entailed the introduction of frigates was indicated in France as a shift in the warship from a *forteresse flottante* to a *forteresse mobile*.[92]

The development of ship design, concentrating on the strength of the hull, speed, and manoeuvrability, contributed to several ship types or, more precisely, broad categories of ship: a clear indication that

[86] Domingues, 'Forces', 194–5.
[87] Parker, 'Dreadnought Revolution', 270–2, 281.
[88] Stradling, *Armada*, 165–9.
[89] Rodger, *Safeguard*, 390.
[90] Stradling, *Armada*, 168.
[91] Bruijn, *Verleden*, 82–3.
[92] Parker, *Military Revolution*, 100, 102, 215.

early-modern European states were keen on optimising the effective use of the heavy gun at sea on sailing vessels in order to withstand and surpass the galley, which had originally held the advantage. The purpose-built sailing warship was developed along various lines and forms; its design and specification differed 'from country to country, from shipyard to shipyard and even from ship to ship'.[93] Moreover, it should not be forgotten that, simultaneously with the introduction of heavy guns with hull-smashing capacity, boarding remained an important tactic in maritime warfare well into the seventeenth century. As a consequence, ships with both a fore- and aftercastle, and equipped with anti-personnel weapons and anti-boarding netting, continued to be much desired.[94]

The return of the sailing vessel in the Mediterranean

Perhaps the most spectacular consequence of the slow and difficult but eventually successful adoption of broadside artillery on sailing ships was the return of the sailing vessel for warfare in the galley-dominated Mediterranean. Venice well represents this development. In 1499 the government-owned war fleet of Venice, which was maintained by the state in times of peace, had included a few very large sailing ships designed for war by shipwrights of the Venetian arsenal. But in the sixteenth century the building of such vessels had stopped; the arsenal then built only galleys. Next to its own galleys the Venetians also hired converted merchantmen. In 1618 they hired them for the first time from the Dutch and the English, who since the end of the sixteenth century had entered the Mediterranean for commercial ends.[95] It soon became routine for both Venice and the Ottoman Empire to lease Dutch and English ships for their wars – a clear indication that these ships were now considered sufficiently effective for warfare next to galleys in the Mediterranean. In 1667 the Venetian arsenal built its first ship-of-the-line using an English warship as a model. During the next fifty years, sixty-eight ships-of-the-line issued from the arsenal. Even so, the republic's Captain General of the Sea was still obliged to use a galley for his flagship as late as 1695, when the Turkish admiral used a ship-of-the-line.[96]

---

[93] Stradling, *Armada*, 164.
[94] Glete, *Warfare at Sea*, 30; Friel, *Ship*, 150, 156.
[95] Bruijn, *Verleden*, 31; Geyl, *Christofforo*, 224–69. On the Dutch and English presence in the Mediterranean see Braudel, *Méditerranée*, II, 315–20, 325–9, 341, and more recently for the Netherlands, Engels, *Merchants*.
[96] Lane, *Venice: A Maritime Republic*, 412, 414.

The continued importance of flexible fleets of merchantmen converted for war

In spite of the development of purpose-built sailing warships, the practice of converting merchant vessels for war, which had been an important characteristic of medieval naval warfare, remained important until around the middle of the seventeenth century.[97] The introduction of the heavy gun at sea did not end the phenomenon of the flexible fleet in the case of sailing vessels as it had in the case of galleys. On the contrary, the development of the sailing ship from the full-rigged ship of the fifteenth century – the three-master, which combined the Atlantic and northern square sail with the triangular lateen sail of the Mediterranean – to the 'relatively homogeneous type of seventeenth century sailing gun-armed ship', gave new opportunities for combinations of cargo-carrying and fighting power.[98] The maritime potential of Spain and the Netherlands was a major tool for naval warfare to these powers.

Spain had to support large galley fleets to counter Turkish incursions in the western Mediterranean from 1479 – when Castile and Aragon were joined in a personal union under Ferdinand and Isabella – until the truce with the Ottoman Empire in 1580. However, while these fleets absorbed the bulk of Spanish funds for naval warfare, Spain continued to lease armed merchantmen for the protection of the New World trade and for naval operations against French and English privateers in the Caribbean. Because it was in the government's interest that merchant ships be suitable for naval warfare, it tried to influence the merchant community to build larger ships by giving loading preferences at ports to larger ships from 1511, and by direct royal subsidies from the 1560s. The merchant community, however, preferred smaller vessels, because they were easier to unload and they handled better in the shoal waters of the Netherlands and the North Sea.[99]

After the truce with the Sublime Porte in 1580 the Spanish Monarchy could invest more money in building galleons suitable for Atlantic naval warfare. The reforms of Philip II after the disaster with the Armada of 1588 were designed to standardise the construction of galleons to ensure that they could serve for war at sea. The result was a revitalised fleet consisting of huge galleons in the beginning of the seventeenth century.

---

[97] E.g. Stradling, *Armada*, 165; Fritze and Krause, *Seekriege*, 54. It is revealing in this connection that in the late Middle Ages the French word *naveye* referred to a body of ships. Depending on the context it might mean the whole merchant fleet of a country; Rodger, *Safeguard*, 117.

[98] For a description of this development see Glete, *Warfare at Sea*, 28–31.

[99] Mott, 'Power', 111–14, 117. Phillips, 'Galleon', 104.

Until the 1630s it was a formidable force that repelled, for instance, an attack on Cadiz by a combined Anglo-Dutch fleet in 1625.[100] Yet these ships still had to be fit for trade as well. In 1601 King Philip III gave instructions to his superintendent of construction to build ships 'suitable for both commerce and the armada'.[101] A certain amount of speed and agility continued to be sacrificed for carrying capacity to meet the needs of the Spanish Empire for multi-purpose vessels.

Like Spain, the Habsburg Netherlands also continued the medieval tradition of providing war fleets by using merchantmen. This tradition remained common practice during the Habsburg–Valois wars, fought between 1521 and 1559. The placing of heavy artillery on board began to determine the choice of the ships as well as the way in which they were rebuilt. Hired merchant ships were modified to make them fit for war: gun-ports were added, the castles were modified, the hulls were strengthened as well as the masts to enable ships to use more sail. A comparison between Spanish and Netherlandish ships by a contemporary witness writing in 1552 reveals the emphasis put on the ability to carry heavy artillery: 'The ships from here [i.e. the Netherlands], especially the hulks, are sturdier and can carry larger and heavier artillery than the Spanish ones.'[102] Several initiatives were taken in the Dutch republic to develop new ship types suitable for naval warfare in the shoal-filled home waters – essential during the Dutch Revolt – as well as for the open sea, which resulted in a nucleus of specialised warships around 1621;[103] the majority of ships in Dutch war fleets continued to be transformed merchant vessels until shortly after the middle of the seventeenth century.[104]

In 1536 the States of Holland claimed explicitly that it was thanks to the large merchant fleet of Holland that Emperor Charles V had more ships than the kings of Portugal, France, and England put together.[105] Holland's fleet expanded rapidly in the remainder of the sixteenth century to become the largest merchant fleet in Europe and possibly in the world in the seventeenth century, surpassing that of Spain. Thanks to this enormous 'naval potential' and to the establishment of an inland arms industry, the Dutch were not only able to equip war fleets for the defence of their territory, their maritime commerce, and their fisheries

---

[100] Phillips, 'Galleon', 104; Mott, 'Power', 114–15.
[101] Goodman, *Spanish Naval Power*, 115.
[102] Sicking, 'Naval Power', 203. For more details see Sicking, *Neptune*, 370–3, 378–81; citation on p. 379.
[103] Jong, 'Staat', 64–70.
[104] Bruijn, 'Mars en Mercurius', 97–106; Bruijn, *Verleden*, 97; Snapper, *Oorlogsinvloeden*, 38.
[105] Sicking, *Neptune*, 359–60.

in Europe, but also to effect overseas expansion despite having to compete with larger powers such as Spain, England, and France. Besides this, the Dutch potential for turning merchant ships into warships had not reached its limits, for it was not only used for Dutch naval warfare but also for the naval warfare of foreign powers. Between the 1610s and the 1660s the Dutch and the English hired out armed merchantmen with guns and crews to Venice, France, Portugal, Denmark–Norway, and Sweden. This happened mostly in periods of war when it was crucial to mobilise as much naval power as possible. Thus, converted merchantmen continued to be of importance for these states. They were often used as a temporary extra force in combination with permanent navies.[106]

From a Dutch perspective the first half of the seventeenth century seems to have been the apogee of the converted merchantman for naval warfare. The Admiralties sold many of their purpose-built 'frigate-styled' warships during the peace negotiations with Spain in the 1640s. It is revealing in this connection that a plan developed by the Dutch admiral Maarten Harpertszoon Tromp in 1648, to build a strong war fleet to be maintained in peacetime, came to nothing. It was thought that in case of need the Dutch republic could always fall back on the old practice of hiring armed merchantmen.[107]

As England lacked any major long-distance trade in the sixteenth century,[108] the country could not rely on merchantmen for war at sea to the same extent as Spain and the Netherlands, but this rapidly changed in the first half of the seventeenth century when both the English and Dutch navies 'were run by merchants, for merchants, and largely made up of armed merchant ships'.[109] Denmark–Norway and Sweden did not have a large merchant marine.[110] Nevertheless, both Scandinavian countries gave customs preferences to armed merchantmen in order to create reserve fleets that might augment the permanent navy in time of war.[111]

In sum, European governments generally tried to use the merchant fleets of their own citizens or, if possible, of others, for war at sea and to enhance their effect to that end.[112] Sailing merchant vessels armed

---

[106] Glete, *Warfare at Sea*, 31; Bruijn, *Verleden*, 31.

[107] Bruijn, *Verleden*, 83–4.

[108] 'Lacking any major long-distance trade, the English had no need of the carrying capacity the Spanish needed, and could afford to sacrifice it to make a more effective, more specialized man-of-war.' England 'came late to oceanic voyaging, late to gunfounding, and late to carrying heavy guns at sea'. Rodger, *Safeguard*, 220.

[109] Rodger, *Command*, 12.

[110] Guilmartin, *Galleons*, 100.

[111] Glete, *Warfare*, 31–2.

[112] Phillips, 'Galleon', 104.

for the occasion remained, in numbers at least, of prime importance – along with the introduction of the heavy gun at sea – for naval warfare in Europe, as soon as the sailing vessel was capable of fighting the gun-armed galley. Like their purpose-built counterparts, armed merchantmen carried more and more heavy guns. As long as specialised or purpose-built sailing warships represented a minority within the naval forces of a state, the size of a state's merchant fleet, or its ability to hire or capture those fleets from others, remained of crucial importance for its sea power. Even when purpose-built warships came to dominate the naval forces of the European powers in the seventeenth century, merchant ships continued to be of military importance, albeit in an auxiliary and diminishing way.

The adoption of the line-ahead: a tactical revolution?

The flexible use of sailing merchantmen for war was gradually reduced, as it became clear around 1650 that merchantmen were no longer fit to fight wars. The three Anglo-Dutch wars (1652–4, 1665–7, 1672–4) induced its participants to naval reorganisations. These resulted in the universal application of the most effective use of the heavy gun at sea, thanks to continuous broadsides fired from ships-of-the-line formed in line-ahead.[113] This tactic was the best practical solution to the problem that the ship-of-the-line moved along one axis captive to the wind, but discharged its cannon along another. Its adoption has been called a 'Military Revolution afloat'.[114] The line-ahead formation was, however, neither sudden nor systematically adopted by the European maritime powers. Boarding and entering were the tactics of preference, and the line-ahead was considered a defensive expedient until halfway through the first Anglo-Dutch war.[115] Moreover, the adoption of the line-ahead did not exclude converted merchantmen from war fleets, at least not immediately.

This became apparent when the Dutch were probably the first to apply line-ahead tactics against the Spanish at the Downs off the English coast in 1639. The Dutch admiral Tromp led his squadron, consisting of purpose-built warships and converted merchantmen, in amongst the Spaniards (despite the presence of the English fleet, trying to keep the combatants apart) and sank forty of their fifty-three ships, which were mostly galleons and merchant vessels. Tromp had used the formation,

---

[113] Glete, *Warfare at Sea*, 39.
[114] Palmer, 'Revolution', 123–49.
[115] Guilmartin, *Galleons*, 210.

however, in a defensive way in difficult circumstances. For the *coup de grâce* he used fire ships and mêlée tactics: that is, fighting ship against ship. In 1645, when a Dutch squadron closed in on the Portuguese off the coast of Brazil, they chose a line of battle combining warships and converted merchantmen.[116]

The English were the first to adopt the line-ahead tactics *more systematically* during the first Anglo-Dutch war. Thanks to a successful adoption of line-ahead, the English, with 100 ships, defeated the Dutch, with about the same number under the command of Admiral Tromp, who stuck to the traditional boarding tactics. Off Gabbard Shoal at the mouth of the Thames in June 1653 the English sank twenty Dutch ships. The result was disastrous for the Dutch republic, as the barely damaged English fleet blockaded the coasts of Holland and Zeeland within a week. On 10 August at the battle of Ter Heide, in which Tromp was killed, the English sank another thirty Dutch warships. They were victorious thanks to their successful adoption of the line-ahead formation, which had made the fighting power of their fleet more effective.[117]

The first lesson the Dutch learned from their defeats was the ineffectiveness not of their tactics, but of their ships. They now realised that they could no longer continue to fight wars at sea with converted merchantmen. The result was that before the war was over two building programmes were launched for sixty purpose-built warships in total. In January 1654 the States-General took the unprecedented decision that none of these new warships were to be sold 'without unanimous consent' of the United Provinces.[118] Merchant vessels were no longer rented from private ship-owners; Mars and Mercury were separated. The merchant fleet now practically lost its military importance, although the Dutch East India Company (VOC) would for one last time deliver ships for the Dutch naval forces during the second Anglo-Dutch war. The possibility of using merchantmen as a flexible force in warfare at sea was gone, in European waters at least.[119]

It was not until after the first naval encounter of the second Anglo-Dutch war, off Lowestoft on 2 June 1665, that the Dutch embraced line-ahead and the three-squadron order, albeit in a somewhat modified

[116] Boer, *Tromp*, 2, 72, 75, 91–2, 132; Rodger, *Command*, 13; Parker, *Military Revolution*, 100–1. The painting of Willem van de Velde the Elder on p. 101 is revealing. See also Braunius, 'Oorlogsvaart', 330; Guilmartin, *Galleons*, 199, 203.
[117] Bruijn, *Verleden*, 94; Palmer, 'Revolution', 134–5, 143 where the battle is indicated as the battle of Scheveningen and is dated, according to the English (Julian) calendar, on 31 July. Rodger, *Command*, 17–18.
[118] Quoted in Bruijn, *Verleden*, 97.
[119] See Bruijn, *Verleden*, 97; Enthoven, 'Mars en Mercurius', 40; Snapper, *Oorlogsinvloeden*, 114; Nurmohamed, 'VOC'.

form. At Lowestoft the Dutch lost 32 of 100 ships but their tactics were partially linear; they still had not fully embraced the line-ahead formation. The new tactics were issued by Johan de Witt in August 1665. During the third Anglo-Dutch war, when both sides used line-ahead tactics, the more numerous Anglo-French fleet proved unable to achieve major successes against the Dutch.[120]

The great nineteenth-century naval historian Julian Corbett characterised the tactical orders issued by the English in 1653 as 'nothing less than revolutionary'.[121] If that is correct, and if the Dutch (and the French) were slow to follow, then it must be borne in mind that the English had also been slow to adopt the tactics that dependence on broadsides logically entailed – the larger English warships, in particular, had been functionally ships-of-the-line from the 1630s onwards.[122] In comparison, the successive formation of a standing fleet of purpose-built warships by the Dutch in 1654, and their adoption of line-ahead tactics in 1665, seems to be a process as gradual as the English creation of a fleet of ships-of-the-line, and its adoption of the line-ahead tactics.

Although eventually line-ahead tactics would be most effectively executed by purpose-built ships-of-the-line, this was not the result of a sudden introduction but of a gradual process. Not only the Dutch example illustrates this. In fact, the English, having adopted line-ahead tactics during the first Anglo-Dutch war, were using converted merchantmen during the second Anglo-Dutch war in 1665, more than a decade after the Dutch had decided to build a major standing navy.[123]

As line-ahead tactics remained a central element in the operations of European navies for a period of almost 150 years – that is, until the Industrial Revolution and the development of steam-driven ships with turreted guns – they can be considered as the last of a series of major changes in European naval warfare. Perhaps because they represented a last major change in warfare at sea, and because they occurred at the same time as linear tactics were adopted on land, line-ahead tactics have been accorded a prominent status in representing the 'naval dimension' of the military revolution.[124]

---

[120] Palmer, 'Revolution', 139, 146.
[121] Corbett cited in Harding, *Evolution*, 75.
[122] Guilmartin, *Galleons*, 210.
[123] Palmer, 'Revolution', 128, 138; Rodger, *Command*, 69.
[124] Palmer, 'Revolution', 128, 145, 148–9.

Conclusion

The introduction of gunpowder weapons at sea, the full-rigged ship, the heavy gun, the galley mounting a heavy gun in its prow, the gun-port, the galleon combining the prow of a galley with the sailing capacities of the full-rigged ship, the cast-iron gun, the broadside placement of guns, the frigate, the ship-of-the-line, and finally the adoption of line-ahead tactics – all represent important technological and tactical changes. Most of these changes have been designated as revolutions in their own right.[125] Their adoption occurred in a period ranging from the 1330s to the 1660s. None of these technological changes was adopted immediately or systematically across Europe. Their adoption depended generally on pragmatic considerations by different powers with different interests in different areas in different periods of time. This resulted in these technological changes being combined in a wide range of ways, which allowed for several continuities, bridging the divide that humanists – and historians following in their wake ever since – have constructed between the Middle Ages and the early-modern era. These include the continued importance of war galleys, armed merchantmen temporarily converted for war, and the traditional tactics of boarding and entering. It also allowed for 'reappearances', such as the return of the galley for war in northern waters and the return of the sailing vessel for war in the Mediterranean.

This wide variety of continuity and change related to naval warfare has influenced the different destinies of Europe's maritime powers. It is impossible to analyse this complex process in its entirety here but some remarks can nevertheless be made. First, the slow adoption of the heavy gun at sea should be emphasised again. If the years around 1500 can be considered as a turning point in this perspective, with galleys mounting a heavy gun in their bow and with the introduction of the gun-port, it had taken more than one-and-a-half centuries since gunpowder weaponry had first been used afloat.

Second, it took another one-and-a-half centuries for permanent navies consisting of purpose-built warships entirely to dominate European naval warfare. In spite of what has sometimes been suggested by scholars, the introduction of the heavy gun aboard ships did not immediately necessitate new types of purpose-built warships. On the contrary, the medieval warship *par excellence* – the galley – reached its apogee in the Mediterranean in the early-modern era. Equally, the sailing merchant vessel remained important for naval warfare. In the short run, the

---

[125] E.g. Guilmartin, 'Revolution'.

sailing vessel temporarily declined in military importance; the effective application of the heavy gun aboard sailing vessels, including the development of the optimal tactics for broadside gunnery, took much longer than the effective application of the heavy gun aboard galleys. In the long run, however, the sailing merchant vessel regained the precedence it had temporarily lost to galleys to become an important instrument in the execution of the naval policies of states until around 1650.

The sailing merchant vessel kept its military importance much longer than the merchant galley. When the war galley began to dominate Mediterranean warfare at sea around 1520, the merchant galley, which for over two centuries had served to create and maintain the sea-lanes of the overseas Empires of Genoa and Venice, survived for a few more decades in the military role, but only in the redesigned form of the galleass with its formidable armament. The fact that the war galley superseded the merchant galley in the Mediterranean in its original, flexible form, which had made it useful for both commerce and warfare, represented a first separation between Mars and Mercury, which presaged the end of the overseas Empires of Genoa and Venice.

The *return of the galley* in northern waters, in which France went ahead spectacularly in 1513, was, with hindsight, short-lived, except in the Baltic; but it was impressive, not least in the eyes of contemporary eyewitnesses. During the short period that galleys and galleasses were considered advantageous for warfare in northern European waters, they never constituted the bulk of war fleets. As a result, they could not have the same impact upon the conduct of northern maritime warfare as upon the conduct of Mediterranean maritime warfare.

The adoption of broadside gunnery by sailing vessels eventually made possible the *return of the sailing vessel* for war in the Mediterranean. Venice showed that it could effectively operate against the Turks when it enhanced its galley fleet with hired merchantmen converted for war during the first two-thirds of the seventeenth century, and subsequently by building ships-of-the line.

The continued (on the Atlantic side) or renewed (in the Mediterranean) use of transformed merchant vessels for war was not a simple sign of conservatism; rather, many simply continued to consider it as the optimal combination of effectiveness and cost-efficiency for power-projection at sea. The Dutch pushed the cost-efficient use of flexible merchant fleets to the ultimate limits of military effectiveness in an era when the English were to teach them the tough lesson that the future of naval warfare would be determined by purpose-built ships-of-the-line – more expensive than converted merchantmen, but more effective. The first Anglo-Dutch war announced a second separation of Mars and Mercury, although even during the next Anglo-Dutch war Indiamen and armed merchantmen still represented a minority of the Dutch and English fleets respectively. By then money, in the form of state fiscal means, and not technology became the critical element of change in European naval warfare.

It thus took a long time before expensive permanent navies consisting of purpose-built warships entirely replaced the cost-efficient flexible fleets. One of the implications of this conclusion is that the tendency of some early-modern naval historians to measure naval power by counting purpose-built warships does not make much sense before *c.* 1650 if they do not include merchant fleets in their calculations.[126] Another implication is that continuities – such as the Dutch and English use of merchant ships, and the Venetian and Turkish use of galleys – in European warfare at sea in the seventeenth century should not too easily be overlooked, or dismissed as historical anomalies. In warfare at sea in the period from 1330 to 1660 there is as much continuity as there is change.

When one contrasts the European navies of the late seventeenth century with those of the fourteenth century there are very great differences. These were, however, the product of many bigger and smaller changes that took place next to and in interaction with existing continuities. In light of the duration of more than three centuries between the appearance of gunpowder weapons at sea and the domination of warfare at sea by permanent navies of purpose-built warships, it seems more accurate to speak of a naval transformation, rather than a 'naval revolution' or 'military revolution afloat'.

---

[126] See for instance Modelski and Thompson, *Seapower*; and Glete, *Navies and Nations.*

12 Legality and legitimacy in war and its conduct, 1350–1650

Matthew Bennett

Introduction

This chapter considers the circumstances in which war was held to be legitimate and what was permissible in its conduct. It is a time-honoured premise that 'in times of war the law sleeps', yet this has only ever been true in part. There has always been a requirement for the protection of individuals or groups, both military and civilian, and for the regulation of combat. The variety of experiences at what has been called the 'sharp end' of war can mislead commentators when they come to assess how far such regulation achieved its aims. Especially in the case of chivalry there has been criticism for its failure to realise its high ideals, as if this somehow undermines the credibility of practitioners' intentions. This might be considered unreasonable in the context of modern attempts to restrict or control violence in warfare through the Geneva Conventions, which can still often be more honoured in the breach than the observance. A further issue for discussion is whether attitudes towards the legitimacy of violence changed across the divide between medieval and early-modern – in particular, in the period *c.* 1350 to *c.* 1650. In simple terms, did things get worse in the sixteenth and seventeenth centuries, perhaps as a result of the wars of religion in western Europe? Were there more unfortunate victims of warfare in the Thirty Years' War than 300 years earlier in the even-longer-running Anglo-French conflict, the so-called Hundred Years' War? What were the roots of atrocity and what attempts were made to tame the Horseman of the Apocalypse whose devastation was readily identified across the period in question?[1]

It seems to me that people's experience of warfare was entirely dependent upon what category they fell into at any particular moment, especially a moment of extreme danger. This might be experienced by a fighting man on the battlefield, but could equally be the fate of a non-combatant in a wide variety of circumstances. This is not to pretend

[1] Cf. Cunningham and Grell, *Four Horsemen.*

264

that an armed man, perhaps frightened for his life or subject to the red mist of combat, is always going to respond with the cool injunctions of the legal mind. What may seem reasonable to a lawyer, be he a canonist or a chivalric author, an innovator or compiler of precedents, may not always seem practicable in the heat of action.

Lawyers operate using categories that may or may not be appropriate for the situation in which the practitioners find themselves. The fact that many legal cases resulted in the fourteenth through seventeenth centuries from the issues of the regulation of violence, or abuse of military might, proves that the matter was a very complex one. In what follows I intend to suggest that any type of people could find themselves in the dehumanising category that meant they might be rightfully killed. Essentially, the category was that of traitor to an earthly lord, or to the heavenly one. The latter category was clearly a wider and more generic one than the former, more personal contract, so that a much greater number of people could fall prey to its exactions, many quite unintentionally. If there is a broad area of continuity across the period, then, it is found here, although the following analysis will need to nuance this statement if the complexities of varying situations are to be properly understood. I have divided my study into three main areas. First, I examine the concepts of Just War (especially those relating to *jus in bello*), as practised before the rise of the nation-state in the fifteenth century. Then I explore the impact of crusading ideology and of the later confessional division between Catholic and Protestant upon behaviours on campaign, towards combatants but especially towards non-combatants. The last section examines the idea of treason – against a ruler, or the state, or God – and how this may have resulted in a much wider application of unrestricted violence, particularly against prisoners, in the era of wars of religion.

Just War theory

It is of primary concern to learn whether wars and battles, deeds of arms and of chivalry ... are to be considered just matters or not, for in the exercise of arms many great wrongs, extortions, and grievous deeds are committed, as well as rapine, killings, forced execution and arson; all of these may well seem to some detestable and improper. For this reason ... it seems manifest that wars undertaken for just cause are permitted by God. (Christine de Pisan, *c.* 1410)[2]

Just War theory was devised by St Augustine of Hippo in the fifth century and refined by St Thomas Aquinas in the thirteenth century.

---

[2] Pisan, *Book of Deeds*, 14.

It can be divided into two main areas: *jus ad bellum*, which identified justifications for war; and *jus in bello*, which regulated its conduct.[3] In the former case, legitimate war required a just cause, proper authority, the right intention, appropriate means, and a just outcome. Although other factors could be added to this list, effectively these requirements were sufficient justification throughout the period in question. The regulation of the conduct of warfare, however, proved to be more mutable. This was largely because, on the one hand, there was a broadening of the categories of those who were considered to be legitimate combatants, while, on the other hand, a greater number of people found themselves at the mercy of arms-bearers on account of their religious practices. Those condemned as infidels or heretics were likely to be killed out of hand. The central issue was immunity from violence. This might be as narrowly focused as the moment of surrender by a warrior in combat, or as broadly as the treatment of non-combatants in general in a war zone. Crucial to developments across the period as a whole are, to my mind, crusading ideology and its implications for anyone decreed to be outside the proper community.[4] This could override the protection that the laws of war sought to provide for warriors and civilians alike.

In his study of *The Just War in the Middle Ages* Frederick Russell has provided an essential backdrop, which is worth quoting at length:

In Christian thought two types of war have been seen as permissible, the holy war and the just war. The holy war is fought for the goals or ideals of the faith and is waged by divine authority or on the authority of some religious leader. When the latter is an ecclesiastical official, the holy war becomes a crusade. The ... just war is usually fought on public authority for more mundane goals such as the defence of territory, persons and rights. Content with the achievement of more concrete political objectives, the just war stops short of countenancing the utter destruction of the adversaries and tends to limit the incidence of violence by codes of right conduct, of non-combatant immunity and by other humanitarian restraints lacking in holy war. In the holy war Christian participation is a positive duty, while in just wars participation is licit but restricted. In the Middle Ages the distinctions between holy war, crusade and just war were difficult to draw in theory and were glossed over by those concerned to justify a particular war ... At the moment a just war was deemed necessary, it easily became a holy war that pursued the supreme goals of the belligerents. The concept of a crusade encompassed both religious motivations for bellicosity and juridical institutions designed to punish those

---

[3] Still the categories used to justify military action today: see Guthrie and Quinlan, *Just War.*

[4] On the role of the Church and Christianity in shaping European attitudes to war, see Bachrach, *Religion.*

who offended the Christian religion. Hence the crusade became a strange hybrid of holy war and just war marked by an increasingly explicit chain of command.[5]

Through his analysis of the medieval laws of war, Maurice Keen explains the essentially personal nature of a warrior's responsibility for appropriate behaviours in wartime: 'Soldiering in the age of chivalry was regarded as a Christian profession, not a public service. Though he took up arms in a public quarrel, a soldier still fought as an individual, and rights were acquired by and against the side for which he fought.'[6]

It is for this reason, as Keen stresses throughout his seminal work, that chivalric regulation of warfare was not the same as international law determining relationships between states. However, he also proposes that 'War did not mean an exceptional period of international strife; it was the endemic condition of West European society'; and that the law of arms applied 'wherever there was war'.[7] Since issues of the just nature of war, of chivalry, and of the regulation of military profiteering all contributed to the law of arms, 'their combined influence contributed to the development of the concept of international law'.[8] Of course, these three categories did not encompass the entirety of wartime experience since they are restricted to the fighting elite. The treatment of non-combatants is largely excluded although there were accepted customs of behaviour towards them stemming from pre-crusade and crusading restrictions. It is immediately apparent that many of the preoccupations of modern attempts to legislate on warfare, such as those found in the Geneva Conventions of the late nineteenth century onwards, are absent, and they continued to be so throughout the period under discussion. So the concept of international law, even as it developed later in the period, in the sixteenth and seventeenth centuries, has to be understood as a limited one.

Jus in bello issues focused on the relationship between warring parties where each recognised the other as legitimate Christians. This was a self-referential system, for 'Christendom [was] a supra-national society of which Christian kingdoms were dependent members ... The only obligations which were universal were those which bound all Christian men alike, such as rules of chivalrous conduct, for allegiance to the honour of knighthood was not limited by place or time.'[9]

---

[5] Russell, *Just War*, 2.
[6] Keen, *Laws of War*, 24.
[7] *Ibid.*, 64, 4 in reference to 'the verdict of a court martial held in the Black Prince's army after the battle of Najera' in Spain (1367), n. 2.
[8] *Ibid.*, 4.
[9] *Ibid.*, 240.

Also, all war-worthy men were knights or esquires, be they simple tenants or great princes, and held the same responsibilities towards one another. King John II of France, in the midst of defeat at Poitiers in 1356, eagerly sought out a knight to take his surrender, because he knew that he could expect chivalrous treatment at his hands. In the following victory feast, Edward, Prince of Wales (the 'Black Prince'), was careful to show respect to the monarch by serving him personally; but essentially the relationship was that of equal members of a brotherhood of arms.[10]

An important difference from the later period of nation-states was the division of war into public and private zones. By right of their knighthood the warrior classes were entitled to pursue private quarrels or legal affronts through military action. This was known as *guerre couverte* – private war – in contrast to public or open war.[11] There were customary restrictions upon what was permissible in *guerre couverte* that differentiated it from the war of princes: there was to be no burning, no taking of prisoners, and no collection of booty. Needless to say, such activities often took place; but they were not licit and a perpetrator might have to answer at law for committing them. The defendant in a mid-fourteenth-century legal case over just such an issue protested that he had stuck to the restrictions and so had no case to answer.[12]

In contrast, public war entitled the prince who authorised it and his followers to engage in just such activities. Burning was a key factor in this type of warfare. To Henry V of England is attributed the aphorism: 'War without fire is like beef without mustard'! The burning of enemy territory was a statement of intent, often associated with military technique known as the *chevauchée*. A classic example of this is the English king Edward III's devastation along the River Somme in France in 1339, in which dozens of villages were destroyed for several miles' width along his army's line of march.[13] In contrast, anyone burning without princely authority was considered an incendiary or arsonist, and hence a criminal.[14] Similarly, the taking of booty or spoils of war and ransoms were limited to public war.

To a modern observer ransoming can seem an alien concept, commonly considered as the behaviour of terrorists or criminals; yet it had its own internal logic for the chivalric classes. It reduced the effusion of

---

[10] Froissart, *Chronicles*, 175 (Book I, Chapter 167).
[11] Keen, *Laws of War*, 104.
[12] *Ibid.*, 80.
[13] See Hooper and Bennett, *Cambridge Atlas of Warfare*, 118, for a map of this campaign, based upon Contamine, *War in the Middle Ages*.
[14] Keen, *Laws of War*, 64–5, 104, 106.

Christian blood, and another important justification was that it allowed licit warriors to support themselves from their 'trade': that is, war. It was considered more honourable than taking wages like a mercenary, for to fight *only* for pay was considered demeaning. Of course, men who considered themselves chivalrous, and their retinues, were paid by the state prior to 1500 as well as in the sixteenth and seventeenth centuries, and on large scale; but such payments could be represented as appropriate recompense for service to the prince, while the true *profits* of war came from booty and ransoms.[15] Once a man gave himself up to another he had effectively entered into a contract that he was required to fulfil at risk of dishonour or even legal proceedings.

The danger of ransom being exploited by unscrupulous participants was well understood at the time. Not all knights were chivalrous and some did stoop to torture and coercion to squeeze greater ransoms out of unlucky prisoners. Such practices were, of course, condemned, both in theory and (sometimes) in practice.[16] There was also the issue of entire communities being required to pay ransoms, or *pâtis*, to support alien lords.[17] This was especially the case in late-fourteenth-century France when English garrison commanders demanded payments from the surrounding territories (for example Brittany). This *appâtisation* was seen as an abuse by the unwilling subjects and was open to wider abuse by mercenary captains. Here, the issue was not necessarily a criticism of mercenaries per se, since they were seen as a useful tool for princes: rather it was the issue of *unpaid* mercenaries. Hence the problem in late-fourteenth-century France of the 'Free Companies', bands of soldiers whose contracts had permanently or sometimes temporarily ceased and who needed to support themselves in the interim.

This brings us to the issues of immunity from warfare. Knights were protected in war by chivalric behaviours, but what of non-combatants? There had long been injunctions by the Church against despoiling them, promulgated from the late tenth century by local bishops through the ideals of the Peace of God.[18] Such restrictions had been strengthened around 1100 by the development of crusading, for which an important justification was that it distracted the military classes from internecine

---

[15] E.g., Trim, 'Fighting', 77–88.

[16] Keen, *Laws of War*, 180, cites the legal case of a knight whose captor knocked some of his teeth out in order to expedite payment of the ransom.

[17] See Bouvet, *Tree of Battles*. This French vernacular treatise contains guidance on correct behaviour towards prisoners and non-combatants at the mercy of soldiers: e.g. Part IV, Chapters 46–8 (violence and extortion from prisoners), 55–61 (parole and military safe conducts), 86–96 (imprisonment of the vulnerable or infirm), 97–102 (civil safe-conducts); 152–89 *passim*.

[18] Head and Landes, *Peace of God*.

conflict. Theoretically, at least, the religious members of society were protected by virtue of their cloth, while pilgrims received the same exemption. Itinerant traders and merchants might also claim protection; but what if in their dealings they aided the enemy? Then clearly their goods and persons were forfeit. The peasantry, tied to their fields, suffered from the same double bind. Their very industry served to support the state that a prince was attacking, so they were to that extent complicit in the enemy war effort. It is striking that the greatest medieval commentator on war, the Dominican monk St Thomas Aquinas, provided 'no clear doctrine of non-combatant immunity', although his close associate, Vincent of Beauvais, urged 'a knight who waged a just war to refrain from punishing those subjects of his enemy who had refused aid, counsel or favour to their rulers'.[19] Yet this made them contumacious vassals or subjects of their natural lords, which left them in a very delicate situation, and so, despite Vincent's plea, they frequently were preyed on by both sides.

The impact of crusading ideology

Although the religious military movement that became known as the crusades had a specific context, the roots of its justification lay in St Augustine's analysis of licit war. When Pope Urban II preached at Clermont in November 1095, he spoke (as far as we can tell) about the oppression of the Christians of the east, specifically in the Holy Land, who required liberation by holy warriors. Saint Augustine had not distinguished between defensive and offensive wars, and it was his desire to defeat the Donatist heresy that spurred him to legitimise conflict in a Christian cause (a point to which I shall return later). The reforming Popes of the eleventh century, desperate to find a temporal force that could free them of dependence upon the German Emperor on the one hand or the free-booting Normans on the other, had developed the idea of sanctified warriors. Pope Gregory VII's *militia Christi* (literally soldiers of Christ) anticipated the eastern expedition that Urban delivered.[20] By the mid twelfth century the inspirational Cistercian monk St Bernard of Clairvaux had developed the idea further to the *equites Christi*, military monks whose purpose was holy war. When the Holy Land was lost in the late thirteenth century, so, to a large extent, was this purpose, which accounts for the destruction of the Templars; although the Knights Hospitaller reinvented themselves as

---

[19] Russell, *Just War*, 275.   [20] Robinson, 'Gregory VII'.

border warriors against Islam. Military orders similarly survived in the Iberian Peninsular and in eastern Europe although again they lost their purpose with the Christianisation of those regions. Nor did they fit in with the development of national monarchies across Europe from the fifteenth century onwards. The Teutonic Knights, for example, possessed an *Ordenstaat* that threatened to compromise the role of secular monarchy, which rendered them effectively obsolete by around 1500.

If it was easy to identify what the crusaders were fighting *for*, it was often more difficult to determine whom they should be fighting *against*. Initially, the target was the 'Saracen' oppressors of the Holy Land, those who had stolen Christ's patrimony (as it was conceived in feudal and legal terms).[21] This theory could be extended to recovering lands that had previously been Christian, for example in the Iberian Peninsula and the islands of the Mediterranean. So, theoretically at least, crusades were justified as being defensive actions, protecting or regaining Christian lands from the infidel. This was less credible when applied to the Baltic crusades, for the lands targeted by the Teutonic Knights had never been Christian; and it was decidedly awkward when applied to the Byzantine Empire.

It was to be the rise of the Ottoman Turks that effectively snuffed out Byzantium in all but name by 1400, and that posed the greatest threat to Christian rulers. Although Turkish defeats at Vienna (1529), Malta (1565), and Lepanto (1571) effectively determined Christendom's border with the largest Islamic regime for the next 200 years, this was not always apparent to western powers at the time. Clearly this threat required a holy war response, although during the fifteenth century these campaigns were more often identified with failure than success (with the honourable exception of János Hunyadi's Hungarians, already discussed in Chapters 2 and 5). The victorious Christian fleet at Lepanto was a crusading force; but matters had changed in western Europe as a result of the Reformation. Crusades required a degree of unity in Latin Christianity and indeed had been levied against heterodox groups within Christendom since the early twelfth century. The use of the crusade within Christendom was not just a way of confronting heresy; it was also a political tool.[22] Most of the later crusades against the Turks were noticeably unsuccessful, and the Nicopolis crusade of 1396 stands out in this respect. Latin crusaders, mostly French and Burgundian,

---

[21] Morris, 'Propaganda'.
[22] For example, against the Angevins in Italy, France against England in 1340, and England into Flanders in 1383.

advanced along the Danube into what is now Bulgaria and, despite the advice of their Hungarian allies, impetuously attacked the Ottoman army under its sultan, Bayezid II. Almost all the crusaders, including a great many noblemen, fell into captivity. They were released but only after paying huge ransoms. It is worth remembering that ransom operated across religious boundaries and had done so for centuries.[23]

One of the notable captives at Nicopolis was the French Marshal Jean de Boucicaut. His career and behaviours are instructive in understanding relationships across the religious divide. This epitome of chivalry was determined to seek out the infidel in order to do battle against them and to slay them. Yet, as a military tourist in the Balkans eight years earlier, he had spent time at the court of the Ottoman sultan Murad I and had even offered to fight for the Turks as long as they had Muslim opponents![24] Here there was a sense of brotherhood in arms transcending the barriers of *gens* and *lex*.

Yet this ran alongside a demonisation of the 'Turk' as the enemy of Christendom. He could be seen as the *Flagellum Dei*, the divine instrument for punishing sinners, and as a bestial opponent in his own right.[25] Indeed, it was possible for Christians to take on his characteristics – a *turkification* – which could then justify brutal behaviours by 'just' Christian warriors. So it was that Charles the Bold was considered the 'Turk of Burgundy' by his Swiss opponents in 1474–7.[26] Similarly, Hungarian lords who failed to defend their tenants against Ottoman raids were viewed as worse than Turks. There developed the idea that there were, within Christendom, 'internal Turks' seeking the breakdown of the Christian faith and the entire social order.[27] With the growth of reformist movements it became possible to characterise non-Catholics as barbarous enemies, too. During the crusades against the Hussites (discussed in Chapter 13), 'The crusaders were uncommonly brutal; as in the Albigensian Crusades two centuries earlier, the Catholic's demonisation of the enemy meant that customary laws of war were ignored or suspended.'[28]

With the arrival of the Reformation proper in the second quarter of the sixteenth century, the potential for all war to turn into religious warfare was exacerbated. While it was still possible for a philosopher of pacifist leanings like Erasmus to prefer to 'hate the sin and not the sinner', majority opinion did not make this distinction.[29] In

---

23 Friedman, *Encounter*.
24 Housley, *Religious Warfare*, 19.
25 *Ibid.*, 103.
26 *Ibid.*, 122. The Swiss wore white crosses to emphasise the rightness of their cause.
27 *Ibid.*, 137–9.
28 *Ibid.*, 35 and n. 27. As Erasmus actually put it: 'kill the Turk and not the man'.
29 *Ibid.*, 165.

addition, messianistic nationalism, which Norman Housley identifies in Anglo-French conflict in the era of Henry V and Joan of Arc, became more widespread.[30] Protestant states and nations, by their very essence, combined the defence of the faith and nationalism. Martin Luther, while opposed to the Catholic crusade ideology, in effect continued its ideals under the Protestant banner.[31] The result was that the ordinary peasant population suffered even more drastically than they had under chivalric laws:

The labouring people is stripped of everything, downtrodden, oppressed, beaten, robbed, so many are driven by want and hunger to leave their land. Some must even pay their dues to castle or town thrice over, even four times, now to one side, now to the other. For otherwise they would be driven from house and fields. And what is not taken from them by the castle in dues is eaten up by the armies … that prey upon the land.[32]

In the case of the Hussites, defence of *lingua*, *patria*, and *regnum* became tied up with defence of the reformed faith, and to its opponents the helpless civilian population was fair game:

Our simple country folk they seized in their hovels and on the roads, making off with their belongings and killing them without mercy out of raw hatred for the tongue they spoke. They burnt them alive in houses and grabbed little children from the arms of their grieving mothers. They spared nobody they could get near, be they unwarlike, young, old or suckling women. All they subjected to cruel death and blood-red massacre.[33]

As will be seen in Chapter 13, religious warfare increased awareness of difference, and led to demonisation of any adherents to an opposing cause. That this could be just as much evident in civil wars, where both sides shared a common language and culture, is apparent from the sixteenth-century French Wars of Religion. Although headline massacres, such as that of St Bartholomew's in Paris in 1572, were exceptional, they could set the scene for reprisals and revenge attacks. These were not unknown under the chivalric code, but as confessional warfare became more widespread so did the potential for the killing and brutalising of dissident populations. The result was that while professional soldiers might observe the rituals punctiliously amongst themselves, the non-combatant population had little or no protection from the Law of Arms. The massacres in Ireland by the Catholics in 1641, inspired

[30] *Ibid.*, 55–6. Both of these Christian nationalists protested their desire to crusade against the Turk and the Hussites in an internationalist way.
[31] *Ibid.*, 85.
[32] Quoted in *ibid.*, 174.
[33] Quoted in *ibid.*, 41–2.

by hatred of the Protestant planters' language, religion, and national affiliation, are an example of what might result. Of course, the relationship between the native Irish and the servants of the English crown had been extremely brutal from the very first, and the addition of a religious justification enhanced the ferocity. As a recent study has pointed out, Cromwell's response in 1649, despite its reputation, was actually in keeping with the existing laws of war.[34]

The question remains as to whether the situation improved after the Peace of Westphalia in 1648 effectively ended the era of confessional warfare.[35] There was indeed a reduction in the number of religiously inspired massacres; however, the creation of professional, state-maintained and standing armies in western Europe brought only marginal benefits. The impact of warfare upon a peasant population, or the civilian citizenry of a town under siege, remained the same. As long as armies were manoeuvring and fighting, backed up by supplies from magazines, then war could seem to be much better regulated. But as soon as soldiers needed to live off the land (and engaged in the 'small war' discussed in Chapter 9), then terror returned to the equation. Goya's depiction of *Los desastres de la guerra* (*The Horrors of War*) in the early nineteenth century could have come from France in the mid fourteenth, Hungary in the mid sixteenth, or Germany in the mid seventeenth centuries.

Prisoners, treason and heresy

It was not, however, only non-combatants who might face the ultimate sanction, even after combat was over. There were two issues that affected the survival of defeated combatants. The first was that non-armorial soldiers had always been subject to massacre rather than the protection of ransom. In return, when such non-noble soldiers, for example the Flemish and the Swiss, had the advantage, they gave the knights no quarter.[36] Second, the intensity of feeling in religious disputes led to the ignoring of the Law of Arms.

There is, however, a third strand, to which I wish to draw attention: the increasing significance of the idea of treason.[37] Maurice Keen examined the topic particularly in relation to the fifteenth-century civil wars in England. What began as summary trials after rebellions in the fourteenth century became instant execution after battle during

[34] Reilly, *Cromwell*.
[35] Cf. Trim, Chapter 13, above.
[36] Stacey, 'Age of Chivalry', 36.
[37] Keen, 'Treason Trials'.

the Wars of the Roses. After Tewkesbury in 1471 even an heir to the throne was despatched. Now, there always had been severe penalties for opposing one's legal lord in open field; but this could be moderated by the idea of *diffidatio*, a vassal's right to rebellion when wronged by a superior. As monarchy drew to itself a greater authority, and as the ruler's priorities became that of the nation-state, such mitigation was no longer allowable. The fifteenth century is notable for the number of executions of nobles and of heretics, and I suggest that the two are linked. When Henry V sent his former tutor Sir John Oldcastle to the stake for Lollard heresy and rebellion in 1417, he was behaving (in his own mind) as a loyal son of the Church. This is the same Henry V who approved the Council of Constance and proclaimed himself ready to lead a crusade against the Hussites. Heresy was treason against God's order, for which there could be nothing but the severest penalties overriding any privilege of nobility. When heresy became a wider European issue in the early sixteenth century it is hardly surprising that behaviour towards soldiers of an unacceptable faith took on the colour of punishing a capital crime.

Any atrocities committed in the sixteenth- and seventeenth-century European Wars of Religion are often attributed to confessional differences. Clearly, there is some validity in this view. Yet, as we have seen, in wars between Christians of a unified Church, oppression and massacre were often still the fate of those not protected by the Law of Arms. Since it was possible to do business with the infidel why was it not with 'heretics'? I believe that the answer lies in the changing relationship between the ruler and the ruled, and medieval monarchies becoming nation-states. As the old international order, under which the chivalric laws of war had been developed, broke down, there came about a different attitude to enemy combatants (and non-combatants) defined in the category of traitor and dissident. If every prince was allowed to determine his polity's religion, and if the polity was threatened by the treachery of enemies (both internal and external), then they might expect the punishment for treason. Geoffrey Parker has characterised the situation as *keine Kameraden* (the absence of a brotherhood in arms).[38] The Spanish *Requerimiento* is instructive in understanding such post-Reformation attitudes. New World peoples who did not accept the instruction of Mother Church found themselves stigmatised as only worthy of extermination. Such treatment was dished out to the Irish by their English conquerors in the sixteenth and seventeenth centuries, as it had been since the original invasion period of the late twelfth century.

---

[38] Parker, 'Early Modern Europe', esp. 56–7.

However, one aspect of the fate of prisoners that may have led to a misunderstanding of how far the laws of war actually applied in practice concerns siege warfare. Sieges were the most significant military operations from 1350 to 1650 and the most often cited as examples of failure to adhere to civilised conduct. Many examples of atrocities are from the resolution of a siege. From Limoges (1370), to Constantinople (1453), to Magdeburg (1631) or Drogheda (1649), it is possible to identify occasions when the garrisons and even non-combatant citizens of fortified towns were apparently given no quarter.[39]

In the period of the Wars of Religion historians have often attributed such brutality to religious hatred; but that was not the only explanation. The laws of war had always provided for different treatment of garrisons and citizens depending on the circumstances, particularly the timing, of their capture. Under the chivalric laws of war:

> detailed conditions for the surrender would be laid down in a solemn legal instrument, of which each party would have a copy signed by the other, and which established what some writers call the *lex deditionis*. Such an agreement was likely to be to the advantage of all parties. It guaranteed the lives of the citizens and of the garrison, saved the town from plunder, and the besiegers from the expense of a laborious and costly operation.[40]

Geoffrey Parker points out that during Spanish operations in the Netherlands during the 1570s, the duke of Alba identified six categories under which a town held against his forces would be treated when taken:

> First those that had been taken by the enemy after a siege; second those that had held out until the enemy brought up its artillery and could therefore resist with impunity no longer; third, those that had admitted the enemy because they had no alternative; and fourth, those that had requested a royalist garrison but had been threatened by the enemy before help could arrive. All such towns, according to Alba, deserved leniency when recaptured. Quite different were his fifth category – those that surrendered before the need arose – and his sixth – those that had refused government troops when offered them, choosing instead to admit the enemy.[41]

There were also generic regulations concerning when a defended place was at the mercy of the besiegers, usually as a result of their being obliged to launch an assault that risked the life and limb of the attackers. If a town was 'unreasonably' held against a besieger, then the garrison lost

---

[39] Cf. Reilly, *Cromwell*, on Oliver Cromwell's behaviour at Drogheda and Wexford in 1649.
[40] Keen, *Laws of War*, 128.
[41] Parker, 'Early Modern Europe', 49. Alba 'adhered meticulously to his own formula'.

any right to clemency and inhabitants were subject to the law of sack. Traditionally this lasted three days and was, on occasions, preceded by a celebratory service in church by the conquerors before the troops were let loose on the hapless population.

Such customs continued well into the nineteenth century and were observed (albeit reluctantly) by the duke of Wellington at the celebrated sieges of Ciudad Rodrigo and Badajoz in 1812. 'I believe that it has always been understood that defenders of a fortress stormed have no claim to quarter', he later wrote.[42] He was right – the laws of war had consistently classified some defenders of fortresses or towns as acting legitimately, but others (defined not so much by the nature of their behaviour as by its timing) as acting illegitimately, which left them at the victors' mercy (or lack thereof).

This brings me back to my original idea of categories. Combatants and non-combatants alike, finding themselves in the category of deserving death, were most likely to be killed under that dispensation. So, in conclusion, there is as much continuity as change over the period 1350–1650. The laws of war did not change significantly throughout the three centuries; what did change were the categories into which combatants and non-combatants might fall as a result of circumstances. People regarded as being engaged in licit combat or opposition to a supposed higher authority were protected under customary codes of behaviour. Those categorised as treasonable, infidel, or heretic, however, were frequently given no quarter. This has often been misrepresented by modern historians, who take headline accounts of 'atrocities' (often the product of contemporary propaganda) as somehow representing the totality of experience, when really they represented the exception, or even a rule misunderstood.

---

[42] Quoted in *ibid.*, 48 and n. 32.

13   Conflict, religion, and ideology

D. J. B. Trim

This chapter examines how religion influenced the ways in which polities and commanders conducted war and how the influence of religion changed over the period 1350–1750. This epoch witnessed both the greatest penetration by Islamic powers into Europe, and the Protestant Reformation. However, it must not be assumed either that religion was an unimportant factor in warfare *before* the Ottoman expansion into central Europe of the mid-to-late fifteenth century or the conflicts between Catholic and Protestant of the mid sixteenth to mid seventeenth centuries, or that it ceased to be influential after the Peace of Westphalia (1648), traditionally regarded as the terminal date of 'wars of religion'. In fact, religion was far from being unimportant at any point up to the mid eighteenth century – but its influence on conflict changed over the period.

Up to the mid seventeenth century, religion influenced the conduct of military operations, being one of several factors that led generals actively to *avoid* battles; but from the late seventeenth century on, this was no longer the case. Up to the 1520s, then, religion was important primarily as an influence on how warfare was conducted, rather than as a cause of warfare. It generated wars only on Europe's north-eastern, south-eastern, and south-western margins, and was a factor in mobilising men and resources from across Christendom for those wars. However, things changed and, in the 130-odd years from the 1530s to the middle of the seventeenth century, religion was an important and determining influence on conflict right across Christendom, not just in its borderlands. Later, in the second half of the seventeenth century and in the eighteenth century, religion influenced but did not determine the making of foreign and military policy, and remained an important factor in resource mobilisation.

This chapter was completed while the author was Walter C. Utt Visiting Professor in History, at Pacific Union College. The author is grateful to the Utt Endowment for appointment to the Utt Chair, and to Frank Tallett, Jan Willem Honig, and participants at the *Crossing the Divide* conference for comments and suggestions.

It was thus from the 1520s until *c.* 1650 that religion was *most* important in warfare. Not all major wars in this period were 'wars of religion'. But in these decades, in contrast to the two centuries that had preceded and the century that followed them, religious beliefs were a primary cause of wars, and they could determine, too, how and where military operations were conducted and how soldiers behaved while on campaign. The ideological clash between Christian and Muslim and between Protestant and Catholic Christians produced bitter, long-lasting conflicts, internationalised civil wars and rebellions, and turned bi-partisan conflicts into multi-faceted coalition wars. Indeed, the irre-solvable nature of war in the period *c.*1530–1650 (the subject of much historiographical debate) stemmed not only from tactical and techno-logical developments, but also to a great extent from the fact that par-ties to holy war were reluctant to concede victory to ideological, cosmic enemies, and from the ability of belligerents to draw support from ideo-logical allies from across Christendom. The focus on eternity eternal-ised warfare.

This chapter is divided into five sections: the influence on operational art and strategy of theology and theodicy; the influence of religion and the enduring concept of crusade on wars at Christendom's borders, from *c.* 1350 to the 1520s; wars between Christian and Muslim from the 1520s to 1683; 'wars of religion' between Catholic and Protestant from the 1520s to 1648; and the final, briefest, section, on the influ-ence of religion on war and international relations in western Europe, *c.* 1650 to 1750.

God as judge of battles

Throughout the period, religion, through the ethics of chivalry, affected concepts of what was legal and legitimate in warfare (as discussed in the previous chapter), but in addition theology also influenced war-making more broadly, especially in the attitude it produced towards battles.

Throughout the Middle Ages it was generally believed, in both east-ern (Greek) and western (Latin) Christendom, that, in words attrib-uted to St Augustine, 'when there is a battle, God looks down ... and [to] the side which he sees to be just he gives victory'.[1] The presump-tion that war was a juridical process before the court of heaven was not altered by the Reformation. In 1585, for example, one of the leaders of the Dutch Revolt, Filips Marnix van St Aldegonde, observed (with

---

[1] Quoted in DeVries, 'God and Defeat', 87; see *ibid.*, 87–9; Hare, 'Apparitions and War'; Lewis, 'War, Propaganda and Historiography', 9; Arthurson, 'King's Voyage', 5–6.

some resignation) that 'what occurs in battles is not in the hands of men'; and in 1624 the statesman turned philosopher-scientist, Francis Bacon, was categorical in his assertion that wars 'are suits of Appeale to the Tribunall of Gods Justice, where there are no Superiours on earth to determine the Cause'.[2]

However, Christians and Muslims alike believed that God sometimes chose to judge the worth not of the *cause*, but of those who maintained it, so that defeat could be a divine punishment for sinful behaviour or pride. For example, the Hungarian János Hunyadi attributed the Christian defeat by the Turks at Varna in 1444 to 'divine justice ... the barbarians won the day because of our sins'. Turkish chroniclers blamed the failure of the Ottoman siege of Oradea in Transylvania in 1598 (discussed in Chapter 7) on the Ottoman commander, Saturcu Mehmed Pasha, for presumptuously relying on God's miraculous intervention for victory, instead of making proper preparations. And in 1644 a Puritan chaplain contemplating a disastrous Parliamentary defeat in the English Civil War declared: 'God ... hath frowned upon not onely our Armies ... All have sinned: and our sinnes have an influence into this calamity.'[3] Christian soldiers commonly reflected on Hebrews 12.6, with its observation that 'whom the Lord loves He chastises'.[4]

Doubts about whom and what God might choose to punish were added to all the uncertainties a general had anyway, about the relative strengths and weaknesses of armies in men, material, and morale. Medieval soldiers were also keenly aware that, even if God did not intervene, *Fortuna* (luck), rather than men's virtue or ingenuity, could influence or even decide the result of a battle.[5] In consequence, until the seventeenth century, pitched battle was widely regarded as virtually a throw of the dice. As an experienced French commander, the Sieur de Tavannes, observed in 1569, to fight a battle could be 'to gamble a whole kingdom'.[6] Campaigns were therefore largely a matter of manoeuvre, of plundering the enemy's lands, of careful sieges, which could be managed. Battle was a risk that prudent commanders avoided. King Sebastian of Portugal, who lost his life and his army at the battle of Alcazarquivir in 1578, was condemned, even by those sympathetic to him, 'because he wilfully took upon him ... to give

---

[2] Marnix, *Bref recit*, sig. E4r; Bacon, *Considerations touching a warre with Spain*, 3.
[3] Hunyadi to Pope Eugenius IV, 1544, in Bannan and Edelenyi, *Documentary History*, 71–4; Selaniki Mustafa, *Tarih-i Selaniki*, II, 787–8 (I owe this reference to Rhoads Murphey); Newcomen, *Sermon*, 24.
[4] E.g. Rich, *Allarme*, B4v–C1r; Holles, *Letters*, 85.
[5] Patch, *Goddess Fortuna*, 66, 89, 107–10, esp. 107–8.
[6] BN, MS Fr. 18587, 501.

Battle ... in the Hour, the Day and Place, that ... was not thought fit for his Advantage'.[7] Such attitudes partly reflected the practical experience of warfare, including awareness of how significant luck, rather than good management, was in combat; but they also reflected theology and, indeed, theodicy.

By the late sixteenth and early seventeenth centuries, the imperatives of holy war could increasingly drive armies into battle, despite their reservations about how God might dispose of victory. Battle often could not be avoided, since the forces of Antichrist (the Protestant perspective) or heretics (the Catholic perspective) could not be allowed to flourish without invoking divine wrath, and so reservations over battle, while still present, were more readily overcome. Later, by the end of the seventeenth century, while God was still thanked for granting victory, we find that He *and* the victorious commanders and their troops *shared* the credit, and this represents a very significant shift.[8] After the 1670s, the changes in tactics discussed in Chapter 10 gave generals greater control over the battlefield; thus, although luck could still play an unwontedly large part in the result, battles were seen to be far less chancy and more likely to be won by good management. While generals often still decided to manoeuvre rather than engage in battle, they did so because of a rational calculation of the odds, rather than out of foreboding about divine favour.

Crusades, 1350–1525

For much of the same era, from the middle of the fourteenth century up to the 1520s, the concept of crusade remained influential. Western Christians retained possession of islands in the eastern Mediterranean basin, while the notion of crusade encompassed both the *Reconquista* of the Iberian Peninsula – which in the fifteenth century expanded to the Maghrib (modern Morocco) – and the wars of the Teutonic Order and others in the Baltic region; then in the 1420s there were crusades against the Hussites in Bohemia. Furthermore, from the mid fourteenth century the Ottoman Turks drove into Europe, and although, for the 175 years before the Turkish victories at Rhodes and Mohács in the 1520s, crusading was something done on the fringes of Europe, it *was* done. Campaigns against pagans and Muslims on the southern and eastern marches of Latin Christendom attracted interest, sympathy, donations, and troops. And though they no longer attracted Europe's

---

[7] Anon., *Continuation*, 445.
[8] McLay, 'Blessed Trinity'.

greatest monarchs, as the eleventh- and twelfth-century crusades had done, they still drew important princes and distinguished soldiers. The visceral emotional appeal of crusade was very long lasting.

Crusading in the eastern Mediterranean, the Iberian Peninsula, the Baltic, and Bohemia

Although no great trans-national expeditionary force was despatched to the Holy Land in the period covered by this book, a number of expeditionary forces and a steady stream of men and money still went east from Latin Christendom. Cyprus remained in Christian hands until the late sixteenth century; the Knights Hospitaller of St John, who relied on recruits and funds from northern Spain, France, Italy, Germany, and England, held a number of islands in the Aegean into the late fifteenth century, and their headquarters of Rhodes until 1522. Mediterranean campaigns attracted nobles and princes as well as landless younger sons seeking their fortune. In 1365 King Peter I of Cyprus launched the so-called Crusade of Alexandria, in which knights from across Latin Christendom participated.[9] In 1366 Amadeus VI of Savoy, with a force of French and Italian knights, captured Gallipoli from the Turks. In the 1370s and 1380s multi-national Christian forces campaigned on the mainland of what is now Turkey.[10] In 1390, English and French knights joined together in an expedition to Tunis – the 'Barbary Crusade'– which was led by the duke of Bourbon and included the earl of Devon and a grandson of Edward III of England.[11] Meanwhile, the Knights Hospitaller regularly raided Ottoman and Muslim maritime commerce, and conducted forays and participated in campaigns on the mainland. They also repelled major attacks on Rhodes by the sultan of Egypt in 1444 and by the Ottoman Sultan Mehmed II in 1480.

Wider Christian participation in the *Reconquista* was probably at its height in the thirteenth century, but parts of the Iberian Peninsula remained under Moorish rule until the late fifteenth century, and wars between Christians and Muslims continued to attract foreign Christian volunteers. For example, Bertrand du Guescelin, one of the most celebrated commanders of the Middle Ages, led a multi-national force against Granada in 1366, while Englishmen crusaded against the Moors for the Spanish in the 1370s and for the Portuguese in the 1470s. Spanish and Portuguese forces, including foreign volunteers,

---

[9] Kingsford, Review; Bell, *War*, 208, and 'Fourteenth-Century Soldier'.
[10] Savage, 'Enguerrand de Coucy', 427; Bell, 'Fourteenth-Century Soldier'.
[11] Bell, *War*, 28.

periodically campaigned in the Maghrib from the late fourteenth century until well into the sixteenth century.[12]

Meanwhile, in the second half of the fourteenth century there was an almost permanent crusade in the lands bordering the eastern Baltic, conducted by the Teutonic Order of Knights against the pagan inhabitants of Prussia, Lithuania, and Livonia. As noted in the previous chapter, the justification of their campaigns as 'crusading' was dubious, yet the Teutonic Knights obtained recruits from across Latin Christendom. Amongst those who crusaded in Prussia and Lithuania were many 'Frenchmen, Englishmen, Scots, Czechs, Hungarians, Poles, and a few Italians'. The English included Henry of Grosmont, one of Edward III's most trusted counsellors and generals; and Henry Bolingbroke, later King Henry IV.[13] But around 1400, the Lithuanians converted en masse to Christianity, and the crowns of Lithuania and Poland were united in marriage. Although the Teutonic Knights remained a significant secular political force for another century, the era of Baltic 'crusades' was at an end.

Germans were still able to crusade close to home in the fifteenth century, however, against the Hussites in Bohemia in the 1420s. In the four years after the martyrdom of John Huss in 1415, his followers in Bohemia organised themselves, and they rose in revolt in 1419. Pope Martin V called on all Christians to take up arms against the Hussites, but in fact the crusades that followed were mounted solely from the Empire and Poland. The Emperor Sigismund was three times defeated in crusading campaigns in Bohemia, but eventually the German Catholic forces used their superior numbers to obtain some successes, the Hussites split into factions, and in 1434 a compromise peace was negotiated.

The Ottoman threat

From the mid fourteenth century, the Ottoman Turks pushed into Europe. After their victory at the epic battle of Kosovo in 1389 the Ottomans expanded through south-eastern Europe, gradually conquering the region's Orthodox principalities but being steadfastly defied, as Chapter 5 shows, by the important (and Catholic) Hungarian kingdom. However, western Europe was not seriously threatened by the

---

[12] See O'Callaghan, *Reconquest and Crusade*; Bell, 'Fourteenth-Century Soldier'; Trim, 'Campaign of Alcazarquivir', 6, 8–9, 22.

[13] Urban, *Teutonic Knights*, 151, 174–5 (at 174) 182, 187, 189; Bell, *War*, 28, 92, and 'Fourteenth-Century Soldier', Table 4; Tipton, 'English at Nicopolis', 537; Smith, *Expeditions*.

Turks before the 1520s, and while campaigns against the Ottomans stimulated a significant response in the West in the late fourteenth century, they drew only a sporadic response in the 125 years after the disastrous denouement of the Crusade of Nicopolis in September 1396.

The Crusade of Nicopolis was reminiscent of the original crusades, in its pan-European appeal (which transcended even the Great Schism), the trans-national composition of the Christian forces, and its ability to attract illustrious nobles. The crusading army included contingents from France, Burgundy, Germany, England, Spain, Venice, and the Knights Hospitaller. Frederick of Hohenzollern led the Germans. The duke of Burgundy's son and heir, John, Count of Nevers, and Philip of Artois, High Constable of France, commanded the large numbers of French and Burgundians; including the *Maréchal* Boucicaut and Enguerrand de Coucy, Count of Soissons, who were amongst the most celebrated captains of the age.[14] The comprehensive Ottoman victory over the multi-national army was a decisive blow to the Christian cause in the Balkans.

Although Burgundians were again to see service outside the walls of Nicopolis, aiding the Wallachians in 1445,[15] the Polish and Hungarian armies in the Crusade of Varna (1544), which ended in a defeat more disastrous than that at Nicopolis, were joined by just a few Czech, German, and Italian troops. Only a small force of Italian troops and ships went to aid Constantinople during its final siege by Sultan Mehmed II in 1453. Three years later there was a very limited response to Pope Callistus III's efforts to raise troops to relieve Mehmed II's siege of Nandorfehervár (modern Belgrade), despite a papal pronouncement that its fall would endanger the whole Christian world. The remarkable Christian victory was celebrated by the ringing of church bells all over Christendom, but owed little to western aid.[16] Several subsequent fifteenth-century Popes, including Pius II, a veteran of Varna, attempted to organise a united Christian coalition, but although the Ottomans briefly occupied Otranto, on the Italian peninsula itself, in 1480, papal efforts received a lukewarm response until the sixteenth century.[17]

The muted western reaction in the fifteenth century has been attributed to the shock of the defeat at Nicopolis. Yet it is also the case that, for most of the fifteenth century, Hungary (albeit not the south-eastern

[14] Tipton, 'English at Nicopolis', 535, 539, *passim*; Oman, *History Middle Ages*, 348; Bell, *War*, 29, 106–7; Savage, 'Enguerrand de Coucy', 434.
[15] Savage, 'Enguerrand de Coucy', 436.
[16] Callistus III to a Burgundian bishop, 14 August 1456, in Bannan and Edelenyi, *Documentary History*, 78–80; Nisbet Bain, 'Siege'; Walsh, *Lives of the Popes*, 191–2.
[17] Currin, 'Play at Peace', esp. 209–10; Walsh, *Lives of the Popes*, 195–6.

European polities) succeeded reasonably well in its wars with the Turks, despite some defeats.[18] Thanks to the exploits of Hungarian soldiers like Hunyadi and Matthias Corvinus (which have been considered in Chapters 2 and 5), the Turks were kept at bay but, as a result, the princes of western Europe seem to have regarded the Turks as a very distant threat – and therefore a low priority.

Summing up the period from 1350 to the 1520s

Nevertheless, the ideal of crusade had an enduring emotional and intellectual power. Well into the sixteenth century, many western monarchs and statesmen contemplated in perfectly serious terms taking the cross and waging holy war; many nobles hoped and planned to join them when they did. Although a *general* crusade to the Holy Land had ceased to be a realistic possibility by the mid fourteenth century, this 'was not fatal to the crusading spirit. Once the general crusade was impossible, smaller enterprises flourished.'[19] As late as the 1490s Charles VIII of France made serious plans to crusade personally against the Turks. A major reason for his attempt to conquer Naples in 1494, a confidant explained, was to use it 'as a bridge for the transportation of his forces to Greece; he will not shed any more blood, nor expend his treasure [on Italy] … until he has overturned the Empire of the Ottomans or taken the road to paradise.'[20] Even princes unwilling to take up arms themselves against the Turk often sympathised with and helped those who did. In the summer of 1502, for example, Henry VII of England paid £10,000 to Maximilian, Archduke of Austria and King of the Romans, to help him in campaigns against the Ottomans.[21] However, that such attitudes were far from widespread is evident in the behaviour of Henry's son. In 1515 and probably at other times Henry VIII talked of going on crusade; but when, in the early 1520s, he received appeals for help from Louis II of Hungary, who was then facing an enormous Turkish invasion, Henry did nothing.[22] By the early sixteenth century, then, religious wars were not at the top of the agenda of most important western European statesmen.

---

[18] See Atiya, *Crusade*, 116–17; DeVries, 'Lack of Response'.

[19] Tyerman, 'Philip VI', 52.

[20] Quoted in Labande-Mailfert, *Charles VIII*, 180.

[21] Treaty of alliance, Antwerp, 20 June 1502, and undertaking to pay £10,000, same date, NAUK, E 30/689, 30/691; Maximilian's acquittance for the £10,000, Augsburg, 28 July 1502, E 30/690.

[22] Bapaume to Louise de Savoy, 6 November 1515, Louis II to Henry VIII, 30 June 1521, Brewer *et al.*, *Letters and Papers*, II, i, 294, no. 1113; III, i, 550, no. 1376.

In sum, for almost the first half of the period, religious divisions helped to generate conflicts on Europe's fringes. They had little effect on the patterns of either the great wars of the period, or indeed of nascent state development in England, France, Germany, and northern Italy, but wars in Christendom's borderlands consistently attracted men whose own countries were at peace, providing opportunities for employment and experience, although probably there was greater enthusiasm for taking advantage of these in the late fourteenth century than for most of the fifteenth century.

The European wars of religion, 1520s–1648

Starting in the 1520s, international warfare was to be dominated by wars that were primarily or significantly religious in character. The confessional division between Protestant and Catholic caused, intensified, expanded, and prolonged internal and international conflicts. The great European powers – France, Spain, Portugal, Austria, Sweden, the Dutch republic, and Britain – were all caught up in wars that were, either in part or in whole, the fruit of the fragmentation of Christendom, and that were some of the longest-lasting, bloodiest, and most bitterly contested and destructive conflicts of the period. Many historians writing on the military revolution and allied debates have highlighted the irresolvable nature of war in this period. It has been variously attributed to changes in technology, in governmental power, and in the art of war, or to resource deficiency. No doubt all were factors, but one of the chief causes of what we might call the 'Age of Indecision' in warfare has been overlooked – the Reformation.

Religious influences on wars in Germany and Switzerland, 1525–1555

In 1524–5 peasants rose in revolt across southern, western, and central Germany, inflamed by the version of the Lutheran Reformation preached by the firebrand radical Thomas Müntzer. The Peasants' War was unusual in that Luther condemned the peasants and the war ended with their slaughter by both Lutheran and Catholic forces. There was another outbreak of radical, lower-order Protestant violence in Münster in 1534–5. In general, however, in religious civil wars in the Holy Roman Empire there was fighting within and amongst both the second and third estates, rather than nobles fighting commoners; societies and international society were polarised along confessional lines.

The post-Reformation European religious wars started with the Knights' Revolt or Knights' War in the Rhineland in 1522–3. The Swiss Confederation was split by civil war in 1529 and 1531 and, while the Protestants had the worst of this conflict, later in the century the survival of the Reformation in Protestant cantons such as Bern and Zürich was ensured by their military strength, which was also used to impose or preserve the Reformation in other cities and cantons, notably Geneva, Lausanne, the pays de Vaud, and Mulhouse.[23] In Germany, meanwhile, Lutheran princes and cities established the League of Schmalkalden in 1531 to protect individual territories from attack by the Emperor, Charles V. In practice, the League helped to spread Lutheranism by force throughout northern Germany and eventually, in 1546, open war between the Emperor and the League broke out. The First Schmalkaldic War ended in 1547, with Charles V's celebrated victory at Mühlberg, but Lutheranism was too strongly entrenched for one victory to make a decisive difference. Hostilities eventually resumed in 1552 (the Princes' Revolt, or Second Schmalkaldic War) and continued until 1555.[24] The confessional nature of these wars is clouded, because the political relationship of the princes and free cities of the Empire vis-à-vis the Emperor was one of the issues at stake, and the Lutheran Maurice of Saxony fought for the Emperor. However, confessional division was a major factor in both causing and perpetuating the Schmalkaldic wars. In the end an uneasy peace returned to the Empire thanks to a compromise agreed at Augsburg in 1555, which accepted a principle of ecclesiastical territoriality summed up in the Latin tag *cuius regio, eius religio* ('whose realm, his religion'). This provided that the confessional allegiance of all polities in the Empire was to be determined by their rulers, and that this choice was to be respected by all other princes and free cities.

The Reformed Churches: militant Protestantism

A new strain of Protestantism was to make the European wars of religion more widespread and more bitterly fought. Calvinism emerged in Geneva in the 1540s, safeguarded from its Catholic neighbours by Bern's military strength. Calvinism fused with the Zwinglian reformation of Zürich and northern Switzerland to produce what became known as Reformed Protestantism. Often described simply as 'Calvinism', it is

---

[23] See Gordon, *Swiss Reformation*.
[24] Tracy, *Emperor Charles V*, Chapters 10–11.

increasingly clear that this underestimates other Swiss influences on Reformed thought and practice.[25]

Reformed theology and ecclesiology came together to produce a confession that was in some ways made for war. The distinctively Reformed doctrine of predestination and the Reformed version of the doctrine of the Church meant that, wherever there were members of God's Elect, predestined to salvation, there also must be the Reformed Church, an institution and organisation. Unlike Lutherans, therefore, the Reformed could have no truck with the ecclesiastical territoriality that had ended religious war in Germany. They also, collectively, had a formidable sense of group identity that transcended earthly ethnic and national identities. One endangered branch of the Reformed Church would call upon, and probably receive, financial and military help from the other branches, thus internationalising wars in which the Reformed were engaged. In addition, even more than other Protestants, the Reformed viewed the world through an apocalyptic lens. The Papacy did not merely have the characteristics of Antichrist: it literally *was* the Antichrist. Further, like most exegetes of Daniel and Revelation, they believed Christ's second coming would follow, rather than precede, the Millennium, which might therefore be inaugurated partly by the actions of God's Elect on earth. This in particular helped to produce an extraordinary boldness and defiance in the face of adversity, both because God could turn the darkest situation into triumph, and because those whom the Reformed were fighting were enemies in a cosmic, not merely a human, sense. Finally, the distinctive Reformed organisational structure lent itself to mobilisation: individual congregations were readily turned into companies, and regional synods or *classes* into regiments.[26]

All this must be borne in mind when considering, first, the extraordinary extent, duration, and bitterness of the wars that were to follow in France, the Low Countries and the British Isles, and, second, the disaster commonly known as the Thirty Years' War.

Wars of religion: France, the Low Countries, Germany and the British Isles, 1559–1651

Disputes about the place of an organised and powerful Reformed minority (the Huguenots) in what was a Catholic state resulted in France

---

[25] See Benedict, *Christ's Churches*, Chapters 1–3.
[26] See *ibid.*, 124–5, 135–6, 283–90; Walzer, *Revolution*, Chapters 2, 8; Murdock, *Beyond Calvin*, Chapters 2–3; Mattingly, *Renaissance Diplomacy*, Chapter 20; Trim, 'Calvinist Internationalism', 1029–35, and 'Huguenot Soldiering', 12–13.

being racked by forty years of confessional conflict from 1559: there were nine nationwide *guerres de religion* and twenty-one years of formal warfare between March 1562 and April 1598, and informal violence was endemic even in years of nominal peace. In the seventeenth century, further localised but serious wars followed periodically from 1612 to 1629.[27] From 1559 to 1573 religious divisions in Scotland were significant causal factors in two civil wars; a coup that overthrew Mary, Queen of Scots; and three English invasions, initially to ensure liberty of conscience for Protestants, later to maintain a Protestant government.[28]

In the Netherlands, an unsuccessful revolt in 1567–8 against the plans of the Habsburg ruler, Philip II, for governmental and ecclesiastical reform, gave way to guerrilla warfare on land and sea by Calvinist die-hards, before a further revolt in the spring of 1572 triggered thirty-seven years of constant warfare, followed by a twelve-year truce with Spain, then by renewed hostilities from 1621 to 1648: what the Dutch, slightly misleadingly, later called the Eighty Years' War. Not all the Dutch rebels against Spain were Reformed – they included Lutherans, Anabaptists, and members of smaller radical Protestant sects, as well as some Roman Catholics and Jews; and the Revolt of the Netherlands had political and economic, as well as confessional, objectives. But it was the Calvinists who, by their willingness to defy the military logic of their situation in the 1570s, provided the motor for the Revolt; and by the seventeenth century, the Reformed Church was effectively the Dutch state church and exercised considerable influence on government policy.[29]

The Thirty Years' War was triggered by resistance from the Reformed of Bohemia to religious persecution and their invitation to the Elector Palatine, perhaps the most important Reformed German prince, to take the Bohemian crown from its Habsburg incumbent. The war involved more than Calvinist–Catholic religious differences, for the peace established at Augsburg had become increasingly uneasy. By 1618 the Holy Roman Emperor Ferdinand II seems sincerely to have believed that by force of arms he could overturn the Lutheran Reformation. Spread by the imperial armies, the war became general across Germany in the 1620s, encompassed the Lutheran kingdoms of Denmark–Norway and then Sweden, and subsumed the second half of the Eighty Years'

---

[27] The best overview is Holt, *French Wars of Religion*; also useful is Knecht, *French Religious Wars*.
[28] Dawson, *Politics of Religion*, Chapters 3, 6; Trim, 'Seeking a Protestant Alliance', 147–8, 165–6.
[29] For authoritative accounts, see Parker, *Dutch Revolt*; Israel, *Dutch Republic*, Chapters 8–12, 16–17, 21–2.

War between Spain and the Dutch republic. Ferdinand provoked the Bohemian Revolt by reversing policies of limited toleration, and did much to spread and prolong the Thirty Years' War by his 1629 Edict of Restitution, which aimed to turn the religious clock back to 1552 (rather than to 1555, when the Peace of Augsburg was agreed).[30]

The religious character of the Thirty Years' War was eventually diminished, particularly by the entrance of Catholic France on the Protestant side in 1635, so that for much of its second half the war was as much about French–Habsburg rivalry and the politics of the Empire as about the Protestant–Catholic divide. However, the war was both started and prolonged by confessional rivalry; and confessional hatred helped make it unusually destructive of both human life and property. The Peace of Westphalia, which ended the war in 1648, endorsed the *cuius regio, eius religio* principle of Augsburg, and effectively tried to apply it not only to the Empire but also to international relations in general.

Meanwhile the new British monarchy had fought Catholic Spain from 1585 to 1603 and again in 1625. It then stayed out of the Thirty Years' War, but royal religious policy provoked resentment amongst the Reformed of both England and Scotland, and amongst Ireland's majority Catholic population. Confessional divisions eventually helped to create civil wars and revolution in England, Ireland, and Scotland (what some historians characterise as the 'British Wars of Religion'); the associated wars lasted almost uninterruptedly from 1641 to 1651, causing great destruction in much of the British Isles.[31]

Three clear conclusions emerge from this brief overview of the European wars of religion from the 1520s to 1648. First, parties to holy war were reluctant to concede victory to ideological enemies. They might fight on when, humanly speaking, there was no point. This was partly because of a natural dislike for making peace with (depending on the point of view) bloody persecutors, idolatrous agents of Antichrist, or blasphemous heretics who had evoked the wrath of God. It was also because of the belief that God could and would intervene.

At various points in the first, third, fourth, fifth, and eighth wars of religion in France, the Huguenot position seemed hopeless. The Huguenots each time assumed that God could work a miracle – and, fortified by their inner confidence and by foreign military assistance, they fought on, and obtained peace settlements that included substantial

---

[30] For good surveys in English, see Asch, *Thirty Years' War*; Parker, *Thirty Years' War*; Bonney, *Thirty Years' War*.

[31] See Morrill, *Nature of the English Revolution*; Scott, *England's Troubles*; Woolrych, *Britain in Revolution*; Braddick, *God's Fury*; Gaunt, *English Civil Wars*; Porter, *Destruction*.

concessions. Gaspard de Coligny's successful counter-offensive in Normandy in early 1563 and his celebrated march across France in the autumn of 1569 are examples of how a 'holy boldness', arising from belief in divine favour, could affect the conduct of operations, as well as general attitudes to making peace.

By 1574 the Dutch Revolt was confined to a few towns and islands in the provinces of Holland and Zeeland, and seemed over. William of Orange wrote in May that year to his younger brother John, in the aftermath of a disastrous defeat in which two more of their brothers had been killed. William was so 'perplexed', both 'by grief and melancholy' and by 'the state of affairs here', he wrote, 'that I hardly know what I do', but 'since this has been the will of God we have to bear it patiently'. He recalled how 'I told you some time ago, that we could defend this country against all the forces of the King of Spain for two years ... But I speak in human terms', he continued; and drew 'hope that the Lord God whose arm stretches far, may use His power and pity on us', declaring:

We always have to conform to the will of God and respect his divine providence and trust, that He who spilled the blood of His only son to maintain His church, will do only what will redound to the progress of His glory and maintenance of His church, though it seems impossible. And even if all of us should die ... God will never forsake His flock.[32]

Almost identical sentiments inspired Philip II of Spain. As I. A. A. Thompson puts it:

Whatever the outcome, Philip had to go on. The heretics must not be allowed to believe that it was God's will that they go unpunished. The obstacles that sprang up on every side were sent to try him for God's greater glory, maybe to punish him for his sins. If vengeance was to be the Lord's, he yet had an obligation to serve God in accordance with his conscience, if need be to sacrifice himself.[33]

Ferdinand II shared this 'God can do' attitude and hence attempted to reverse the results of almost 100 years of history with the sword. With God, all things were possible, if only his followers were faithful. Compromise was less an option in confessional conflict than in other wars; and often, as in the French Wars of Religion, compromise was merely a device to gain time to rest and regroup.[34]

Second, ideology meant there was a tendency to dehumanise enemies – whether Protestants seeing Catholics as agents of Antichrist

---

[32] Kossmann and Mellink, *Revolt*, 113–15.
[33] Thompson, 'Appointment', 203.
[34] Cf. Trim, 'Edict of Nantes'.

or Satan (literally demonising them), or Catholics seeing Protestants as sources of heretical pollution that provoked the judgement of God.[35] This meant that at the tactical level religious warfare was frequently waged with few restraints. To take but a few well-known examples: the French crown killed or sent to the galleys prisoners taken at Rouen in 1562; the Spanish executed at least 2,000 prisoners in cold blood after the surrender of Haarlem in 1573; and the English slaughtered some 600 Spanish and Italian prisoners at Smerwick in Ireland in 1580. The Thirty Years' War was notorious for its massacres, and although Cromwell's campaign in Ireland was not as vicious as depicted in traditional historiography, it was brutal enough. The bitterness engendered by such bloody-handed methods helped to make the resolution of conflict more difficult. So too, of course, did the knowledge that victory by one's enemies could mean death for one's families, regardless of whether they were in a war zone. The divisions between Catholic and Protestant were often so entrenched that peace-making was very difficult.

Third, because of the ideological component to wars between Protestant and Catholic – and ideology was present and important even when not the sole cause of conflict – wars were *internationalised*. The 'Protestant Cause' motivated sovereigns as diverse as Queen Elizabeth I of England; King Frederick II of Denmark and Norway; Frederick III and Frederick V, Electors Palatine; Frederick Henry, prince of Orange; and King Gustavus Adolphus of Sweden to send armies and fleets to aid foreign Protestants. It also motivated many Protestants (German, Swiss, Dutch, French, Scottish and English) to fight for co-religionists or donate money to help them, even when princes did not act. Reformed Protestants were particularly good at mobilising transnationally, whether with, without, or in parallel to, state action, to aid their brethren. Catholic solidarity moved Philip II of Spain to aid the Valois kings of France in the 1560s and 1570s, and helped produce a coordinated offensive by Spain and the Empire in the 1620s. It also motivated numerous Irish and Scottish volunteers to serve in Catholic armies in the Low Countries and the Empire.

This international dimension to national wars was the chief reason why the Peace of Westphalia established a policy of non-intervention as a necessary concomitant to the principle of national sovereignty. It was only practically possible because, by 1648, after nearly a century of very bitter fighting, ideological attachment had inevitably been somewhat diluted.

---

[35] E.g. Lake, 'Significance'; Hill, *Antichrist*, and *English Bible*, 56–65, 302; Crouzet, *Guerriers de Dieu*; Davis, 'Rites of Violence'; Racaut, 'Propaganda'; Cunningham and Grell, *Four Horsemen*.

The renaissance of crusade: Christian versus Muslim from the 1520s to 1662

The wars between Roman Catholic and Protestant were not the only religious wars that began in the early sixteenth century and lasted to the middle years of the seventeenth century. Alongside them, particularly in the sixteenth century, were renewed wars between Christian and Muslim that led to a renaissance of the ethos of crusade.

Islam on the offensive

In the late fourteenth and throughout the fifteenth century, the Ottoman threat was real, but localised in the Balkans. In the sixteenth century the extraordinary westward expansion of the Ottoman Empire under Selim I and Süleyman 'the Magnificent' meant that Ottoman armies were encamped on the eastern frontier of the Holy Roman Empire, while Ottoman fleets ranged from a new series of bases across the Mediterranean and even into the Atlantic, attacking the coastal regions of Italy, France, and Spain. These campaigns were described and analysed in Chapters 2, 6, and 7. As those chapters also showed, in the seventeenth century the Sublime Porte was troubled by Janissary revolts and other internal problems, and was distracted by the threat to its eastern borders from Safavid Persia. Nevertheless, Ottoman military capability remained potent. The Poles, for example, were given a drubbing in the early 1620s. The greatest extent of Ottoman control of the former Hungarian kingdom was actually reached in 1662, after Turkish victory against a briefly resurgent Transylvania.

Meanwhile, there had been a renewed threat to Portugal and the Spanish Monarchy from North Africa. Even after the conquest of Granada in 1492 there was still a good deal of contact between the Muslims of Africa and those under Spanish rule – when the Turks were at Spain's throat in the 1560s, the Moriscos rebelled in southern Spain, and they were aided by volunteers from across the Straits of Gibraltar, including from the kingdom of Fez, which was not under Ottoman rule. The Ottoman expansion into the Barbary States, and the naval threat they posed, led the Habsburgs to conduct a series of operations against the Mediterranean North African littoral. In the Maghrib, the powerful kingdom of Fez, which had been ruled by the Berber Wattasids, was conquered in the 1540s by the Arab Saadians from Marrakech, who were committed to ongoing holy war against Christians and pagans. The result was conflict with Portugal, which had been gradually expanding into what is now Morocco since 1415, a conflict in which both sides regarded the enemy as religious as well as economic and political rivals. When Sebastian I invaded Morocco in 1578, he and his nobles believed they were going on crusade.[36]

Consequences and responses

For much of the sixteenth century, there was an immediate and dangerous Muslim threat to the Habsburg rulers of Austria and the Holy Roman Empire; the Spanish monarchy; the German princes; the Papacy; the Serene Republic of Venice and the other Italian states; and the kings of Portugal and of Poland. What was in danger was more than just the loss of some territory; Ottoman aspirations and ambitions seemed limitless and, after the dramatic collapse of Hungary in the 1520s, the ravages of the Ottoman fleet, and the loss of Cyprus, there seemed a real prospect of an Ottoman conquest of Germany, Italy, and perhaps parts of Spain. Thus, unlike in the fifteenth century, the great powers of Europe had much at stake in the Turkish wars. Equally, the conflict between Portugal and Fez was a contest between a global power and a rising regional power; but because religious as well as geo-political factors were involved, a peaceful settlement to Luso-Saadian hostilities was impossible. The end result was that a major power, Portugal, was reduced to a possession of Spain because of the effects of waging war beyond its means – but Sebastian I had done only what he believed was required in war with the infidel.

The potency of the Muslim threat, and that from the Ottomans in particular, was recognised all over Europe and attracted a correspondingly broad response. Geo-political rivalries and even Catholic–Protestant confessional hostilities were periodically disregarded. This is not to say that Christendom was united. The rivalries of the western powers made it difficult to create effective, lasting alliances; and some, particularly the French, were prepared to ally with the Turks. One reason for Ottoman success in the sixteenth century, then, is that it faced a disunited enemy. However, when it did occur, cooperation between Christian states often proved effective. For example, because Malta was a base of the Knights Hospitaller, its siege by the Turks in 1565 prompted Italian and Spanish cooperation, which ultimately raised the siege.[37] The grand alliance that resulted in the Crusade of Lepanto brought a famous victory and one that was, in the long run, decisive.

---

[36] Trim, 'Campaign of Alcazarquivir', 9–12, 21–3 and sources cited there.
[37] Guilmartin, 'Siege'.

However, the lack of a united Christian front in response to the Islamic challenge was, to many people in western Europe, a shame and reproach. The refusal of the French crown in the sixteenth to act against the Turks proved unpopular in France. Hopes were raised in 1571 when the government considered a proposal to join the Crusade of Lepanto, before rejecting it.[38] It was therefore left to French nobles and their affinities to serve as volunteers in campaigns in the Mediterranean, including in the Lepanto campaign. After peace was restored in France in 1598, war having resumed between the Habsburgs and Ottomans, a French brigade served in the Emperor's army in Hungary.[39]

Furthermore, although the Reformation had created a confessional divide that left all in eastern and southern Europe on the Catholic side, many Protestants still regarded fighting Muslims as a Christian duty and were keenly interested in the wars against the Turks. Lutheran propaganda in Germany was vehemently anti-Turkish as well as anti-papal, and there was an avid market in England and the Netherlands for histories of the Ottomans and of Christian resistance to them, as well as for news reports of Christian victories (and defeats) in battle with the Turk.

Protestants were not just *interested* in the struggles of Catholic Christians with Muslims; they joined them. Lutheran troops were part of the successful defence of Vienna in 1529, and Lutheran and Calvinist soldiers and generals made important contributions to imperial armies in wars against the Ottomans for the rest of the sixteenth century.[40] Likewise, English volunteers, both Protestant and Catholic, served as volunteers in the Holy Roman Emperor's army in Hungary in the mid 1560s and again in the 1590s; they also served in papal and Spanish fleets in the Mediterranean in the 1560s and in the Crusade of Lepanto. French Calvinists served against the Turks: probably for the Venetians in the Lepanto campaign and in Hungary in the 1590s, and definitely for the Venetians in the 1620s and early 1630s. Although William of Orange, leader of the Dutch Revolt, made overtures to the Sublime Porte to make common cause against Spain, he sent troops to aid Sebastian's crusade to Africa in 1578, because the Muslims were still regarded as the enemies of all Christians, Protestant as well as Catholic. Walloon, Dutch, German, English, and Italian soldiers served the Portuguese in the Maghrib, though many had been hired

---

[38] BN, MS Fr. 18587, 29–53.
[39] BN, MS Fr. 20787, fo. 2; Braudel, *Mediterranean*, II, 1105; Finkel, 'French Mercenaries'.
[40] Fischer-Galati, *Ottoman Imperialism*; Tracy, 'Clash of Civilizations'.

as mercenaries rather than volunteering for a religious war.[41] Later, Maurice of Nassau, William's successor, was interested in aiding the rulers of the Turks' Christian vassal states in the Balkans, which were struggling to obtain independence. And in 1621 England engaged the Ottomans in a brief naval war in the Mediterranean, which met with much satisfaction even amongst those Englishmen discontented that their country had not joined in the Thirty Years' War – their hostility to Catholics did not include those who were oppressed by Islam.[42]

War and religion after Westphalia

Finally, in the century after *c.* 1650, although religion was no longer the primary cause of conflict, in the East there was still some willingness to ignore national rivalries in order to fight the Turks, albeit that they were no longer as dangerous. And in the West, the religious resentments and hatred engendered by confessional antagonism between Catholic and Protestant provided a powerful aid to mobilising populations for wars, because confessional elements would be emphasised in propaganda by increasingly powerful nation-states.

If the desire of sixteenth-century French nobility to crusade had been largely frustrated by their kings' policy of alliance with the Sublime Porte, the seventeenth century witnessed a new era of French crusading against Islam. In 1664 Louis XIV sent a French expedition to Djidjelli in North Africa. In May 1669, he 'contributed 16 warships, 13 galleys, over 30 auxiliary vessels, and around 6,000 troops ... to a relief armada', despatched 'under the Papal banner' to help save Venetian-governed Crete from Ottoman attack; this followed up 'an unofficial French expedition [to Crete] paid for privately in 1668'.[43] Insular Christian possessions in the eastern Mediterranean still retained some capacity to evoke enthusiasm for crusade! However, even though the Ottomans were victorious in Crete, and still fielded huge armies against Christian powers in Europe, from the mid 1660s onwards the Ottomans were no longer a threat to the whole of Christendom, there was no longer any prospect of Muslim armies descending into Germany and Italy, and while religion was still an important factor in motivating combatants, by this stage the causes of the wars involving the Ottomans were far more geo-political than religious.

---

[41] E.g. Trim, 'Fighting', 98, 376, 414, 'Campaign of Alcazarquivir', 14–15, 21–2, and 'Huguenot Soldiering', 14, 19, 24, 26; Davies, *Elizabethans Errant*; Braudel, *Mediterranean*, II, 1105.

[42] Stephen Bogdan to Maurice, 14 July 1610, NAN, Collectie van Hardenbroek 12. E.g. Christopher Heydon to Nathaniel Bacon, 27 October 1621, Folger Shakespeare Library, MS X.d.502.

[43] Rowlands, 'French Amphibious Warfare', 267–9 (quotation at 268).

Meanwhile, in western and central Europe, the Thirty Years' War was finally ended by the peace treaties of Westphalia (or of Münster) in 1648. The Peace of Westphalia has often been described as having 'put an end to the European wars of religion'.[44] In fact, it did not end confessional conflicts, which endured. However, their intensity was ameliorated by the Westphalian settlement; moreover, from the 1660s onwards, they were rarely the *cause* of war, as opposed to an influence on policy-making and a factor used to generate support for wars.

Confessional differences were still the chief cause of some rebellions and civil wars. When Louis XIV ended toleration of France's Reformed Church in 1685, the bloody persecution that was commenced led to a sustained, if limited, Huguenot rebellion in southern France, which lasted until 1715. The Catholic dukes of Savoy used troops to carry out bloody massacres of their Vaudois subjects in 1655 and again in the late 1680s, the latter prompting armed Vaudois resistance until limited toleration was restored. The Williamite War in Ireland (1689–91) was essentially a struggle between Catholic and Protestant. Similarly, armed support for the Jacobite rebellions in Scotland and northern England in 1689, 1715, and 1745 came almost entirely from Catholics. On the other hand, when Frederick the Great, for propaganda purposes, portrayed the War of the Austrian Succession and the Seven Years' War as being fought for the Protestant interest, there were terrible consequences for Austrian Protestants, as the Habsburgs took no chances of disloyalty. In any case, while foreign powers regularly encouraged the internal confessional opponents of their enemies, there was in no case a major military intervention on those rebels' behalf, of the sort regularly carried out by governments in aid of foreign co-religionists in the late sixteenth and early seventeenth centuries. It is true that persecution of Protestants in the Palatinate in the 1710s led to such marked tension that there were widespread fears of another general German religious war.[45] However, the fact is that, in sharp contrast to the analogous situation almost a century earlier, one did not occur. Although policy-makers in Britain and Prussia, in particular, were still influenced by concern for 'the Protestant interest', eighteenth-century efforts to ease the plight of oppressed Protestant minorities were diplomatic, rather than military.[46]

At the international level, religious animosity was still a factor in conflict, as historians increasingly recognise.[47] However, rather than

---

[44] Coady, *Ethics*, 21; cf. Holsti, *Peace and War*, 38.
[45] Ward, *Protestant Evangelical Awakening*, Chapter 1.
[46] See for example Thompson, *Britain, Hanover and the Protestant Interest*.
[47] E.g. Onnekink, *War and Religion*.

'causing wars in this period', confessional divisions were 'more likely to be resorted to in order to encourage support for and to explain a conflict that had already begun'. This was recognised by contemporaries, at least to some extent. In 1665, 'during the second Anglo-Dutch War', an English 'polemicist ... insisted that "wars for religion" were "but a speculation, an imaginary thing ... which wise or rather cunning men make use of to abuse fools"'.[48] This is symptomatic of the shift in attitudes, although it was unduly cynical, because even sophisticated people in the late seventeenth and eighteenth centuries were still interested in the plight of co-religionists and could be moved thereby to greater support for a national war effort that aided fellow believers. To many citizens (and indeed statesmen) of Brandenburg-Prussia, Denmark, the Dutch republic, and Great Britain, Louis XIV's France seemed the embodiment of Catholic aggression. Dutch, British, Danish, and Prussian and other German statesmen played on these feelings to obtain recruits and extra taxation domestically, and support internationally, for the Nine Years' War (1689–97) and the War of the Spanish Succession (1701–14). However, that British soldiers fought in the latter conflict to defend the territory of the Holy Roman Emperor is indicative of the change in European international relations, as is the fact that their allies at one time included the Papacy. 'The Seven Years' War was widely portrayed in propaganda as a religious conflict, a development that was in keeping with the stress on religious animosity in the domestic publications of several states.'[49] The causes of the war, however, can hardly be characterised as essentially confessional.

Conclusions

In sum, although the nature of religion's influence on conflict was not the same across the period or across the continent, it was almost always and everywhere an important factor, whether in the policy-making of princes, parties, and statesmen; or in the attitudes of soldiers; or in their conduct of operations. Additionally, however, the unwillingness of religiously motivated parties to accept defeat, the difficulties in making peace between ideological opponents, and the internationalisation of warfare because of ideology made it consistently difficult for initial operational successes to be converted into outright victory. Thus, warfare was effectively eternalised in sixteenth- and early-seventeenth-century Europe, not only because of limits to state power and of changes

---

[48] Black, 'Introduction' to *Origins of War*, 6; Pincus, *Protestantism*, 449.
[49] Black, 'Introduction' to *Origins of War*, 6 .

in military technology and tactics, but also because the conflicts that predominated in this period were ideological. Earlier and later, religion was a factor in warfare; from the 1520s to roughly 1650, it was the most important factor in most of the wars waged by the greatest powers in Europe.

14   Warfare, entrepreneurship, and the fiscal-military state

Jan Glete

Warfare, economy, and state formation

When historians write about warfare and economy they usually discuss economic causes of war, economic consequences of war, and the importance of economic resources to wage wars.[1] In a medieval and early-modern context, economic forces behind warfare are normally conflicts about trade and colonies. Conflicts between states and the relations between state and society in Europe are themes for political history or historical sociology. Economists and economic historians have normally not been interested in warfare, except its destructive consequences and financial impact on states and societies. Recently, economic historians have become interested in early-modern war finance and state formation, but the military and naval organisations are seldom parts of economic studies.[2]

This lack of interest in military affairs probably has its origin in the fact that economic historians have seen the state and its organisations as central to political history. State formation and war are also central problems for sociologists and political scientists, but they lack the theoretical tools to analyse efficient use of resources. Economics is the social science that is focused on how societies utilise scarce resources, and on causes for economic growth and stagnation. Continuity and change in warfare and organisation of states are important parts of how society utilises resources. As resources are essential in warfare, discussions about war, state, and society require some understanding of concepts used by economists, not as an alternative to political science or sociology but in order to provide balanced explanations.

The research for this chapter was supported by the Bank of Sweden Tercentenary Foundation.

[1] References are restricted to recent works. For detailed references see Glete, *Navies and Nations, Warfare at Sea*, and *War and the State*.
[2] For example Bowen and González Enciso, *Mobilising Resources*; Torres Sánchez, *Fiscal-Military States*.

State formation is a result of human capacity to create new structures. The growth of such structures may also reflect changes in human behaviour. The structures are in practice large and complex organisations with new administrative, military, and technical competencies. Theories developed in political science and sociology about war and state formation are normally not concerned with organisational and technical innovations, changing rules of human interaction, and their consequences for economic growth.[3] Neither is mainstream neoclassical economy interested in this interaction. Most economists regard rules of human interaction as a constant and show only limited interest in entrepreneurship and the governance of large organisations.

Historians have more use for theories from social sciences that are less mainstream and more focused on long-term development. Within economics, traditions labelled dynamic, evolutionary, or institutional provide theories in which human capacity to achieve innovations (entrepreneurship) and change and stability in rules of human interaction (institutions) are essential explanations of change and continuity. This chapter argues that such a combination of theories and objects of studies are useful for explanations of change and continuity in European warfare. It may also make it easier to understand motives and incentives for individuals and groups to participate in warfare or support it with taxes and loans.

Amongst historians, there is a broad consensus about the importance of money, men, and material resources for warfare. To emphasise that resources are essential is however not the same as using economic explanations. Historians studying wars often inadequately distinguish between the total resource endowments of a society and the resources available to a state to wage war. In medieval and early-modern Europe a state never ceased to wage war because the resources for war in the society were exhausted in a literal sense. It was the societies' and the elite groups' willingness to supply the state with resources, and the rulers' political and administrative competence to extract resources from society that put limits to war. Consequently, explanations emphasising 'lack of resources' as limits of medieval and early-modern warfare are political rather than economic.

Sixteenth- and seventeenth-century European states had very uneven abilities to mobilise resources for war. In medieval Europe the size of the population under a single ruler was seldom important in warfare. Large

---

[3] Tilly, *Coercion*; Downing, *Military Revolution*; Ertman, *Birth of the Leviathan*. An important exception, although written by an historian, is McNeill, *Pursuit of Power*. The military revolution debate has only tangentially been concerned with state formation; Rogers, *Military Revolution Debate*.

resources were rarely concentrated and large armed forces could not be deployed on long-distance operations. In modern Europe (say, 1789 to 1989) populations have been very important in warfare. Soldiers have been raised by general conscription and large numbers of men could be transferred far from their homes, even to other continents. During the early-modern transformation, organisation, rather than population, mattered. Small states that achieved large flows of resources from local society for war earlier than others could fight powers with considerably larger population- and resource-bases.

Absence of centralised states did not mean absence of warfare, but medieval wars were not typically fought between sovereign states. They were often conflicts between rulers and local elites or between local power-holders. The distinctions between 'civil' and 'international' wars were not sharp. The cause of wars was often the extent to which rulers should control violence in local society and extract resources from it for centrally determined purposes. Organisation of resources was inherently difficult, and warfare was often intermittent because resources for sustained operations were lacking. Medieval economic and political power was essentially local. Control over large territories depended on alliances between local power and central rulers, rather than on power exercised from a strong centre. When such alliances broke down, local power-holders – feudal lords, bishops, and cities – frequently allied themselves with foreign or alternative rulers, formed mutual alliances, or achieved independence.[4]

During the late-medieval and early-modern period several conflicts about the power of the state and its relation to local power intensified into decisive struggles about state formation. This period saw several Italian wars that, by 1454, had markedly reduced the number of small states in northern Italy; the fifteenth-century wars in France, England, and Spain, which ended with more centralised, dynastic states; and the break-up of the Nordic Union and the formation of Denmark–Norway and Sweden as centralised states in the early sixteenth century. After a period of relative stability from the 1480s, several domestic conflicts with international consequences erupted: French civil wars from 1562 to 1653, the Dutch Revolt and the formation of the Dutch republic (1568–1648), the civil war in early seventeenth-century Russia, the Thirty Years' War, the revolts of Portugal and Catalonia in 1640, the British Civil Wars in the 1640s, and the inconclusive conflicts in

---

[4] European state formation, 1200–1800: Bonney, *Economic Systems*; Reinhard, *Power Elites*; Blickle, *Resistance*; Bonney, *Fiscal State*; Contamine, *War and Competition between States*.

Poland–Lithuania which ended in a powerless state. However, from around 1660 wars in Europe were almost entirely conflicts between sovereign states whose control of their territories was undisputed.[5]

The fiscal-military state

An economic definition of the state is that it is an organisation with a *comparative advantage* in violence on a territory whose boundaries are determined by its power to raise taxes.[6] Most medieval European rulers had only small comparative advantages in violence in relation to other power-holders in society. It was often not enough to control society if several power-holders allied themselves against the ruler. By 1750 this advantage had grown to a practical monopoly of violence in well-defined territories, the classical Weberian definition of a state. A major transformation had occurred and spread to most parts of Europe, including the seas around the European peninsula. The operational ability to use violence in political power-struggles had been transferred from many groups in the society – feudal lords, peasant militias, autonomous cities, and private entrepreneurs in warfare and armed trade – to states with permanent and specialised organisations for war: armies and navies. The monopoly of violence was not only a result of new rules of human interaction. It was also the result of the appearance of a new type of organisation of resources for protection and violence.

In order to support armies and navies, states had developed fiscal organisations that raised taxes and custom duties. Individuals, groups, and local power-holders expected that the armed forces that they paid for should protect them from foreign threats and domestic violence. Central power-holders were able to control even hundreds of thousands of armed men by their power to pay and feed them. This power came from the fiscal organisations that could operate with low transaction costs (low risk of tax revolts), ultimately because armed force was available to the political authorities. Tax raising was however usually non-violent because central states had achieved sufficient legitimacy. The fiscal and military organisations and the central and local power-holders were interconnected differently from those in medieval Europe, where local society formed closed units of fiscal and military power over local resources.[7]

The new type of European state has in different historiographical traditions been termed the nation-state, the power-state (German

---

[5] Glete, *War and the State*, 10–41.
[6] North, *Structure and Change*, 21.
[7] Glete, *War and the State*, esp. 1–9.

Machtstaat), the fiscal or tax-state (German *Steuerstaat*), the military state (common in Swedish historiography) or the fiscal-military state.[8] The latter term is at present the most pertinent for generalisations, especially with economic theories. It puts equal emphasis on the income and expenditure parts of the resource flow through the state, and on the two main organisational parts of the state: the fiscal apparatus and the permanent armed forces. It was a crucial part of the European state formation that the fiscal and military organisations form separate chains of control and patronage, only connected at the central, political level of the state. Military men could not tax society and fiscal agents could not use the resources they raised for privately controlled armed forces. The central state gained a new importance by its ability to coordinate large resources through complex organisations. Politically and administratively (not necessarily physically), resources flowed from the local level to the central state before it was distributed to military units spread around the society or waging wars abroad.

In medieval society, most resources for war were raised and administrated locally. Power over the resources never left local society, even if they were physically centralised into armies, navies, and logistical support of operations. This centralisation was temporary and conditional. Local power-holders contributed to war efforts with armed forces under their own administrative control: feudal levies, militias, and armed merchantmen. They also invested in a multitude of local fortifications, which still are picturesque proof of the importance of local power in medieval Europe. Locally administered armed forces could be used against the ruler as much as they could serve him. Concentration of resources through political alliances was inherently unstable as long as the administrative control of most resources for war remained under local control. Economically, this can be explained in that the transaction costs of raising large resources and making them flow to the central state was prohibitively high. The prevailing rules of human behaviour favoured the legitimate use of resources for war by those who raised them, rather than their being sent to distant power-holders.

Economically, state formation from 1350 to 1750 was the establishment of mechanisms for major resource flows from local society to the central state, and the development of specialised and mobile organisations for armed force that could defend and control wide territories and long lines of maritime communications. Such organisations could

---

[8] Terminology: Jespersen, *Power State*, 27–30; Sweden as a military state: Nilsson, *Krigens tid*. The term fiscal-military state was introduced in Brewer, *Sinews of Power*. State formation in several sectors at the same time: Braddick, *State Formation*.

also project power at long distance, even to other continents. This new type of state was broadly accepted in the sense that rebellions and political resistance against it ceased. Especially after 1750, resistance was replaced by growing demand from below for control of the central state through formal constitutions and representative institutions. Domestic political upheavals in the late eighteenth and nineteenth centuries were mainly driven by demands for increased control of the state from below and for further concentration of states, primarily in Germany and Italy. Small, autonomous principalities and city-states were increasingly seen as anachronisms.

This was a major transformation of important rules of human interaction. It shows that broad groups of Europeans accepted the fact that impersonal organisations raised taxes, controlled violence, and provided protection. They demanded more of it, not less, but they also demanded control from below. Something important had happened that markedly reduced the transaction cost of concentrating resources. Why had it become so much easier politically to aggregate interests behind a centralised state? Why had European fiscal-military states gained a decisive comparative advantage in violence-control over practically all Europe?

Protection-selling, complex organisations, entrepreneurship, and institutions

In political science and sociology state formation is normally defined as extraction of resources from local society for the development of new, or stronger, centralised structures.[9] This places the focus on *resource flows* and the result, *centralised organisations*. Combined with an economic definition of the state as an organisation with a comparative advantage in violence, this makes it possible to study state formation with economic theory. Why did resources flow and why did the resource flow result in centralised, permanent organisations? Are there any economic theories and concepts that may explain this?

From an economic perspective the fiscal-military state was a new, large-scale actor on an old market: the market for *protection and control of violence*. It sold protection against violence to society by raising taxes through the fiscal organisation, and delivered the service through the military organisation. The theory of protection-selling and violence-control as economic activities, and early states as economic enterprises

---

[9] Almond and Powell, *Comparative Politics*, 35. In Tilly, *Coercion*, bargaining about resources between rulers and local elites is the essence of state formation.

in production of a utility – protection – was developed by the American economic historian Frederic C. Lane.[10] It is centred on protection cost and the possibility of reaping profit from cost-efficient use of violence for more sophisticated purposes than mere plunder. Lane used it in analyses of maritime trade, but he also suggested that state formation began when men skilled in the use of violence ceased to make profit from plunder and began to protect local society. Profit from violence-wielding increased if a society was forced to pay regularly for protection rather than being plundered. Those who received payment had a vested interest in providing protection from other predators as they otherwise would lose their incomes. In Europe, that transformation took place in the early- and high-medieval periods.

In a state formation perspective profit from protection-selling is the same as increased access to resources by efficient control of violence. These resources seldom appeared as surplus in state budgets, as they usually were invested in larger armed forces or spent on warfare. Economically, profits from the supply of protection were used for expansion, a normal behaviour in corporate growth. This expansion could be peaceful if efficient protectors could offer more territories and cities a service they required, or it could take the form of violent wars of conquest. Pre-modern European local societies often had a choice when they negotiated with protection-sellers. They might organise their own protection (militia, city wall, convoy system, hired mercenaries), choose local or central protectors (feudal lords, different rulers), or bargain about how much protection they should pay for.[11]

Whatever the circumstances, protection-selling is an effective instrument of power over society, used by men and groups with a comparative advantage in violence. Protectors normally form an elite group in society and political power is often derived from the ability to protect. Societies need protection, and skills to organise it are scarce. Agricultural societies are vulnerable to invasion, and trade with valuable goods is easy to plunder. In this period it was those who were most efficient in organising protection as a large-scale enterprise who gained power over local society. They gained that power in competition with other protection-selling enterprises and with traditional, local forms of protection. The organisations for protecting society did first of all protect those who controlled the organisation. Rulers protected their own interests (their share of the market) when they protected a society.

---

[10] Lane, *Profits from Power*.
[11] Alliances between local elites: Dollinger, *German Hansa*; Brady, *Turning Swiss*. For a comparative study of states and local societies in the early state formation process, see Gunn, Grummitt, and Cools, *War, State, and Society*.

The European fiscal-military states were early examples of *complex organisations*; multi-functional organisations with a potential for growth. They operated at a radically higher level of administrative, military, and technical sophistication in the eighteenth century compared to the fifteenth century, and they could achieve goals that were far beyond what local society could reach in temporary alliances. For historians it is essential to understand what a complex organisation is and what makes it different from human interaction based on personal contacts and eye-to-eye relationships. Theories about complex organisations are central in sociology and business administration rather than in mainstream economics, but organisational behaviour can be analysed with economic theory. Theories related to transaction costs, organisational growth, and path dependence are especially relevant.[12]

A complex organisation controls widely different types of human and capital resources. It reduces transaction cost by dividing labour, processing large amounts of information, and providing social containers for capital assets, skills, teamwork, and coherence, which would otherwise be unavailable. Scarce resources can be more rationally used if they are converted into a complex organisation rather than only temporarily coordinated. Usually, however, a complex organisation is also hierarchical, and its resources are coordinated and administrated in the interest of those who hold power at the top of the hierarchy. In early-modern Europe, permanent regiments of infantry and cavalry, heavy ordnance, navies with specialised warships, advanced fortifications located according to a national defence system, and logistical organisations able to support major operations were the most important complex organisations. These military organisations were hierarchical and their organisational pattern has often been the model of later large-scale corporations. Early-modern fiscal organisations were less homogeneous and often parts of local power structures. They did, however, transfer administrative control of resources from local society to the power of the central state, and local participation in that process might make it less costly. Local elite participation usually meant that the burden was shifted to non-elite groups.

Complex organisations do not emerge spontaneously and they are not mere agglomerations of resources. They are the result of the human ability to achieve both coordination and change: that is, to act according to a conscious strategy. This makes theories about innovation and entrepreneurs

---

[12] Perrow, *Complex Organizations*; Scott, *Organizations*; Pitelis, *Growth*; Dosi, Nelson, and Winter, *Nature and Dynamics*; Williamson, *Mechanisms of Governance*; O'Brien, 'Path Dependency'. Organisation and state formation: Glete, *War and the State*, 51–66.

central to explaining state formation. The theory about *entrepreneurship* was introduced by Joseph Schumpeter, the Austrian-American economist who formulated several seminal ideas in the border zone between economy, sociology, and history. The Schumpeterian entrepreneur is the individual or team that implements new combinations (innovations) in society with the aim of reaping profit from early and more efficient use of these combinations. Entrepreneurship may be political as well as economic. Schumpeter compared the modern businessman, aiming at creating a private enterprise by innovative behaviour, with medieval and early-modern princes, who wished to found their own kingdom.[13]

This is not only a rhetorical metaphor. European rulers, ministers, and military leaders in the period from 1350 to 1750 were often innovators. They had to be if they were to survive in a competitive environment. They worked with the problems of controlling subjects, raising taxes, and waging wars in more systematic and well-organised forms than earlier. In order to do that, they developed technology, administrative processes, and political links to the buyers of protection. In this they were not radically different from those who in modern society create a company around a new product by combining technology, business administration, and marketing. All have had to create new types of organisation, master the high technology of their age, and create confidence amongst a broad group of consumers that the innovation is better than earlier products on the market.

Rulers in our period, as well as modern business leaders, must find men and groups with the various skills they need, and they must have sufficient social competence and judgement to make their enterprise accepted by other social actors. If they do not, they fail. Rulers and those who became rulers were participants in an often desperate and brutal competition for power where their openness to innovations and ability to implement them really mattered for success and survival. Like the modern corporation, the fiscal-military state also favoured the social rise of skilled and ambitious individuals who were loyal to it. These states absorbed parts of the old elites but they also gave opportunities to new men.

Human beings are social animals and our interaction with other human beings is guided and restricted by *institutions*: rules of human interaction. These rules may change, however, and historical experience shows that they have changed during the last centuries of economic, social, and political transformation. Important theories about economic institutions have been developed by the economic historian

---

[13] Schumpeter, *Theory*; Schumpeter, *Capitalism*.

Douglass C. North, who puts special emphasis on how institutions since the late-medieval period have changed in interaction with organisations and innovations. With ideas derived from evolutionary psychology, North asserts that we prefer to cooperate and make exchanges on a personal level with individuals who we at least occasionally meet eye-to-eye. The development of impersonal markets, division of labour, and centralised mass production of goods and services (the growth of complex organisations) requires new rules of human interaction that are in conflict with our genetic heritage. This may also explain why only parts of the world have achieved this transformation, in spite of the fact that it has continued for several generations.[14]

Our genetic heritage evidently also allows human beings to think strategically and achieve new combinations (Schumpeterian entrepreneurship). If they prove successful they may favour new stable rules of human interaction on the political and economic markets. At least in societies with many complex organisations, we have learned how to act in a contractual manner and combine our interests with those of other individuals, most of whom we don't know and will never meet. The importance of stable rules in society and of kinship, friendship, and personal contacts in political and economic interaction is obvious to historians, but so probably is the existence of more adventurous individuals and groups who use innovations before others. If they gain in power and access to resources others may follow.

This interaction between innovators and society was at work in the European development of fiscal-military states and complex organisations for warfare. Protection from violence is a serious problem for all individuals, but to give up direct control of it in exchange for protection from a distant and impersonal state is a radical innovation. It will only be credible if locally exercised protection proves manifestly inferior to protection from a central state. Wars and political crisis may create threats and opportunities that make it possible for entrepreneurial individuals and groups to achieve changes that last, if their innovations in protection prove superior to other solutions.

Entrepreneurship and the rise of the fiscal-military states

The rise of the European fiscal-military state was the result of *lasting* changes in the *flow of resources* for protection and warfare in society.

---

[14] North, *Structure and Change, Understanding Economic Change*. There are similarities in North's thinking to Norbert Elias' earlier sociological studies of the civilisation process.

The resources were directed from local society to a centre of political and administrative power, which channelled them into complex organisations, used as instruments of centrally determined policy. Innovative entrepreneurship in that process is the ability markedly to increase the extraction of resources from society to the central state and transform the resources into permanent organisations that achieve a marked comparative advantage in violence and capacity to protect.

This entrepreneurship was organisational, technological, and political. Much of it consisted of raising resources with greater continuity and administrating them into growing social containers (organisations) of scarce financial, military, and technical competencies under the ruler's control. Administrative entrepreneurship included the search for men with key competencies and development of incentives to make them loyal to the aims of a hierarchical organisation. Political entrepreneurship in state formation was primarily the ability to negotiate about resources with existing elites, and to create links and lasting alliances with groups that might benefit from protection by the new type of state and the economic and social opportunities it created. There was a vast difference in cost of resource extraction depending on whether existing elites cooperated, remained passive, or resisted the new state. Lasting alliances require capacity for initiative, bargaining, and diplomacy. Links to society could be formal representative bodies or informal networks, but negotiations or some kind of tacit consent was necessary if resources were to flow from society to state without prohibitive transaction costs.

Political entrepreneurship might also involve actively changing the rules of human interaction. This could be achieved by control of the flow of information about threats, opportunities, and events, and ideological and religious indoctrination about the importance of the central state for protection and social order.[15] This type of entrepreneurship, comparable to the marketing function in a business enterprise, was important in at least some states, but its lasting value was small if a state failed to live up to the role of an efficient protector which it claimed to fulfil.

The foundation and growth of the fiscal-military states did not take place in a stable and homogeneous Europe. Arguably it was rather instability and variety that created threats and opportunities for enterprising individuals and groups to achieve new combinations. These combinations took root from the fifteenth to the early eighteenth centuries. They often had slow starts and several states experienced long

---

[15] Swedish domestic propaganda: Forssberg, *Informationsspridning.*

periods of political crisis before the innovations matured and achieved stability. State formation passes a critical threshold when a state controls resources sufficient to make it militarily stronger than any conceivable alternative combination of domestic power-holders. When that threshold is passed, state formation may rapidly accelerate, because the transaction costs of resource extraction diminish.

The threshold is easier to reach the better the resources are organised compared to larger but less well-structured resources controlled by several power-holders. This creates strong entrepreneurial incentives to develop organisation. In an unstable and varying world, more resources may also suddenly be available for a central state. Intense wars, political or religious upheavals resulting in crises for earlier elites and confiscation of property, or customs from rapidly increased trade may give political entrepreneurs opportunities to combine resources into new organisations.

Studies of entrepreneurship frequently encounter the problem of identifying the individuals and groups who actually achieve new combinations. In modern society they are found amongst managers, financiers, and politicians with an active will to achieve change, but most individuals in these categories are not innovators. Many of them are primarily concerned with conserving existing structures. The classical Schumpeterian entrepreneur was the founder of a new business corporation, but later in his life Schumpeter saw managers of already existing corporations as the most important entrepreneurs, as profitable corporations often grew and diversified by channelling resources into new enterprises. In the period from 1350 to 1750, European entrepreneurs in fiscal-military state formation are to be found amongst rulers and political, military, and administrative leaders of organisations governed by the state. Some republican leaders were important but the rise of the European fiscal-military state was intertwined with the rise of strong dynastic, hereditary power. This is not very different from many modern business enterprises where families and kinship are important.

The role of kings and individuals in political history is not always a fashionable theme amongst historians. Rulers who rise to power or markedly increase their power by innovative behaviour are, however, important in studies of change. If redefined as the entrepreneur, which some of these rulers actually were, we may study them in action and in context. Some entrepreneurial European rulers had inherited their power, but the rise of a fiscal-military state was often connected with a new dynasty, which had to compete or fight for power. Dynastic power often resulted when ambitious rulers and their followers seized the opportunity to do something different to achieve power. Some of them succeeded.

The earliest new dynasty to begin the process of change to a fiscal-military state may be the house of Aviz in Portugal. It gained power with João I in 1385 after a revolt and a war against Castilian ambitions to create a union. In the fifteenth and early sixteenth centuries the dynasty was central to the pioneering development of Portuguese naval power and the growth of a maritime Empire in trade and protection-selling around the coasts of Africa and the Indian Ocean. Its entrepreneurial and business-orientated character has been regarded as rather unusual in European history. It was, however, the maritime environment and Portugal's geographic position, rather than the dynasty's behaviour, that were special.[16]

A branch of the German house of Oldenburg appeared from 1448 as state-builder in the Nordic Union. The Oldenburgers were elected monarchs with limited power in loosely connected states with powerful aristocratic elites, but they had ambitions of their own. Although the majority of the Swedish elite after many conflicts eventually went its own way, the Oldenburgers could form a Danish–Norwegian–Holsteinian conglomerate state with unified armed forces under their control. This state was also protection-seller to shipping between the Baltic Sea and western Europe. The Sound Toll became a major source of income from protection-selling, largely channelled to naval power.

In England, decades of conflict and civil wars between factions of aristocrats and princes ended in 1485 with the victory of a new dynasty, the Tudors. It was followed by the development of new fiscal and, especially, naval structures during three generations of rulers, of whom Henry VII and Elizabeth I had serious problems because of questions over their legitimacy. This made them, however, aware of the importance of political entrepreneurship and well-organised armed forces for increasing the advantage in violence with which they had started their regimes. The Oldenburg and Tudor states had a similarity, in that royal power was closely connected to naval power. Both states had a maritime character, and technical competence and control of the sea gave the central ruler a marked advantage in political control of territory.

In Sweden, the aristocrat Gustav (I) Vasa founded a new dynasty in 1523 as a result of a rebellion against the Oldenburgs. In a personal manner he developed a new dynastic state with a fiscal apparatus penetrating into the society; a permanent army; a permanent navy; and state enterprises in mining, arms, and trade. Politically, he created

---

[16] A recent study: Domingues, *Os navios.*

alliances with peasant communities and aristocrats, and integrated their traditional capacity to use armed force with the new state-administrated army. Just like the Tudor and Oldenburg states, the Vasa dynasty gained much financial strength from the Reformation and the confiscation of Church property. In Sweden the Church also became an administrative and ideological backbone in resource mobilisation for the central state.[17]

In Russia, the Romanovs rose to power in the early seventeenth century after a chaotic period of civil wars. They began to recreate a strong Russian state, increasingly using western European fiscal-military states as their model. The obvious entrepreneur in the dynasty, the radical moderniser Tsar Peter I, appeared only in the third generation, but his ancestors had also tried to achieve change. Peter gained power as the younger brother to a mentally ill tsar, and in the brutal political environment that prevailed in Russia he had to fight and innovate in order to rule. The success of the fiscal-military state in a society with widely different rules of human interactions from those in western Europe is interesting for a comparative study.

Dynastic entrepreneurship in state formation was not limited to the senior branches of the ruling European royal families. Junior members might be even more ambitious because they were junior. The Burgundian dukes, who in the fifteenth century appeared as prominent territorial princes and leaders of strong armed forces, were members of the French royal family. For a time they appeared to be able to create a new powerful state between France and the German Empire, in fierce competition with the French kings. Isabella of Castile, together with her husband, Ferdinand of Aragon, the late fifteenth-century founder of a strong Spanish state and its permanent armed forces, gained power in Castile after revolts and wars against the senior branch of the Trastámara dynasty. Ferdinand and Isabella's successors in Spain, the Austrian Habsburgs (also descendants of the Burgundian dukes), were formally legitimate heirs. However, as a foreigner, the king and Emperor Charles V had strong incentives to be innovative and to secure control from above with superior organisation.[18]

This was even more obvious in Italy, where Charles and his son Philip II represented a foreign, partially conquering dynasty that had to prove reliable as the organiser of protection against the Ottomans, France, and regional Italian conflicts. After repeated wars up to 1559 the Habsburgs were rulers in large parts of Italy. As such they could claim

---

[17] Ihse, *Präst*; Holm, *Konstruktionen.*
[18] Tracy, *Emperor Charles V.*

hegemony over minor Italian princes, but formal control and claims of hegemony had to be supported by effective power. The result was the development of permanent Habsburg armed forces in Italy: army *tercios* and galley squadrons.[19] They had a regional origin but were controlled from above in a unified organisation.

At the same time, the Habsburgs failed (or hardly tried) to achieve any kind of fiscal-military state in their inherited lands in Austria. They made progress in that direction in the Netherlands, where they had ruled since the late fifteenth century, but the Dutch Revolt eliminated this in the northern Netherlands. The degree of success of Habsburg state formation was negatively related to the period of time they had ruled a territory, but positively related to the intensity of struggle for control over the resources. The comparison is relevant as it was the same rulers in action under different circumstances. Struggles over resources rather than inherited legitimacy created windows of opportunity for state formation. Austrian Habsburg state formation and German state formation in general only gained momentum after the upheavals from 1618 to 1648.[20]

In Denmark, Norway, and Holstein, a junior branch of the Oldenburgers ousted the senior branch in 1523. It had, by 1536, after two civil wars and confiscation of Church property, achieved a stronger and more centralised state than earlier members of the family. However, until 1660 the Oldenburg kings had to share control of that state with an aristocratic Council with limited ambitions to innovate. This delayed state formation in comparison with the dynamic process in Sweden. In that country, two of Gustav I's sons, Johan III in 1568 and Karl IX in 1598–9 gained power after rebellions against other Vasa kings. In particular the rebellion of Karl against his nephew Sigismund, who was also the elected king of Poland–Lithuania, created a situation of uncertainty and fierce dynastic and international competition. It led to an even stronger Swedish fiscal-military state under Karl's son Gustavus Adolphus. In contrast to Denmark, the Swedish aristocracy participated in the development of a fiscal-military state and contributed to administrative and military innovations in exchange for shared power over this state.[21]

Republican state formation is normally less easy to connect with individuals and families. Most European republics were mercantile,

[19] *Tercios*: Gunn, Chapter 3; galley squadrons: Sicking, Chapter 11; both in this volume.
[20] Glete, *War and the State*, 67–139. Recent studies: Aranda Pérez, *Declinación*; García Hernán and Maffi, *Guerra y sociedad*; Fenicia, *Regno di Napoli*.
[21] Glete, *War and the State*, 174–212; Jespersen, *Power State*; Lockhart, *Frederik II*; Bellamy, *Christian IV*.

and business entrepreneurship was a normal path to both economic and political power. Merchants were also personally involved in protection of cities, trade, and shipping. In one famous case, the Medicis in Florence, economic power led to political power and ultimately to dynastic power as grand dukes of Tuscany, a new state formed by the family. Late-medieval Venice was a pioneer in the creation of permanent armed forces, primarily a large galley navy, often regarded as a model of administrative efficiency. That, as well as the creation of an Italian–Greek territorial state, was achieved in a markedly republican fashion without any dominating individuals or families as entrepreneurs.

Switzerland was a late-medieval centre of military innovation – coherent, well-trained infantry – but local power-holders showed little interest in using this for territorial expansion or the creation of a strong central state. Their entrepreneurial activities remained private and some of them specialised in the supply of mercenary forces and financial services to territorial rulers, primarily France. The once powerful city-state of Genoa gave up major territorial ambitions but its leading entrepreneurial families, Doria, Spinola, Lomellini, and Centurione, became important naval and military contractors and financiers in French and, from 1528, Spanish service. In both Switzerland and Genoa, local political power, financial resources, and military competence were combined within entrepreneurial families, but they preferred to stay local and make entrepreneurial and financial profits from the major powers.[22]

The Dutch republic was different. It was the fiscal-military state that in the seventeenth century could mobilise the largest military and naval forces in relation to its population. The republic was from the late sixteenth and during most of the seventeenth century a hothouse of economic entrepreneurship and innovations. These activities also involved the financial, military, and naval sectors, and here it is possible to identify some innovative republican state-builders, primarily Johan van Oldenbarnevelt in the formative decades around 1600, and Johan de Witt, who in the 1650s and 1660s was a key person in the rapid expansion of Dutch naval power. Dutch military innovations are otherwise primarily associated with the princes of Orange and other members of the Nassau family who, from the late sixteenth century, provided military leadership and were important for the growth of a large, permanent Dutch army.[23]

[22] A recent study: Kirk, *Genoa*.
[23] Recent studies: Jong, *'Staat van oorlog'*; Nimwegen, *'Deser landen crijchsvolck': Het Staatse leger*; Vermesch, *Oorlog*; and Nimwegen, Chapter 8 in this volume.

The historiography of Dutch state formation has been dominated by supposed weaknesses created by powerful provinces and rivalry between republican leaders and the Nassaus and their supporters. The actual achievements strongly indicate that provincial elites raised resources more efficiently and took more responsibility for the external power of the central state than elites in monarchical states. Successive princes of Orange must, by their position as elected leaders rather than hereditary sovereign rulers, have had especially strong incentives to show military efficiency as political motivation for power. As political and organisational entrepreneurs, provincial elites and princes interacted with Europe's most dynamic society. They used this interaction to create armed forces able to fight the Spanish Monarchy and France, powers with ten times as many subjects.[24]

The last stadholder of the senior branch of the Nassau–Orange family, William III, ultimately also became king of England, Scotland, and Ireland. It was partially a result of his family's successful dynastic entrepreneurship (his mother was a Stuart), but his ability to combine strong Dutch armed forces with a political reputation as an efficient but constitutional (and Protestant) prince was more important. His brief period as king (1689–1702) was important for British state formation. It had taken a major step forward from 1642 to 1660 during the Civil Wars and the republican rule. The republican leaders had created both a powerful army and Europe's largest navy and both were markedly efficient. They eventually failed to create political and fiscal support for these organisations, and by 1660 domestic crisis led to the Stuart Restoration. Charles II and his brother James, abolished the (republican and unreliable) army but were able to create financial and political support for the navy, which they personally administered. In a remarkable combination of international entrepreneurship, the English opposition, powerful groups in the Dutch republic, and William III personally did in 1688–9 achieve an English revolution, followed by a financial revolution, a standing British army, and an enlarged navy with much increased scale and operational reach.[25]

As this brief survey shows, most European fiscal-military states were formed or increased by new dynasties, revolt by junior members of established dynasties, or republican leaders who depended on achievements rather than inherited power. It was often obvious that the survival of the new ruler and elite was uncertain if they remained passive and unenterprising. They had to create something new in order to gain

[24] Glete, *War and the State*, 140–73.
[25] Recent studies: Wheeler, *Making of a Power*; Rodger, *Safeguard, Command*.

a permanent advantage in violence against domestic rivals, pretenders, and foreign powers. It was arguably their insecurity and limited legitimacy that made them especially anxious to develop hierarchical fiscal and military structures under their personal control. The entrepreneurial agenda was shaped by the urgency to raise more resources and channel them into more efficient structures for violence-wielding and protection. If they were persistent and successful they created lasting links between society and state for resource mobilisation, and social containers where resources turned into specialised military know-how, advanced technology, and coherence between men who should fight for the state. This was entrepreneurship creating fiscal-military states.

From this perspective France provides an interesting contrast. French kings succeeded to the throne according to hereditary principles throughout this period until 1792. France is often seen as a leading military power and the size of the armed forces under certain rulers is often identified with a strong state. Much of France's strength as a great power was, however, the result of having Europe's largest population under a single ruler, rather than a high degree of resource mobilisation. French rulers could be innovative under periods of intense competition. The foundation of a permanent army in 1445 (actually a number of cavalry units) and the development of modern artillery in the following decades were the result of central initiatives. They came, however, in a period when the French kings Charles VII and Louis XI were involved in serious conflicts about French territory with England and the Burgundian dukes. France was also early with the creation of permanent sailing naval forces in the late fifteenth century, but an important part of that navy was actually run by the dukes of Brittany, who tried to remain autonomous of French royal power.

From the 1560s much of French state power disappeared in long civil wars. They ended with a compromise in the 1590s where the French king lost his monopoly of violence, as the Huguenots were allowed to defend their interests on their own. The monopoly was only regained in the late 1620s when a new French army and navy were able to suppress Huguenot autonomy. Richelieu appeared in this period as an efficient political entrepreneur, who achieved some centralised structure and a certain stability in a situation where few resources were available for royal power. After a new period of upheavals from 1648–1653 the young Louis XIV was able in the 1660s to achieve a more lasting solution. He was supported by entrepreneurial ministerial families with ambitions to achieve social rise: the army ministers Le Tellier and Louvois (father and son) and the minister of finance, navy, and trade, Colbert, who also founded an administrative dynasty. In a decade, they radically rearranged the flow of resources in French society and created Europe's largest army and largest navy. Compared to several other states, however, France still suffered from severe structural limits when it developed financial-military power. In the eighteenth century, the Bourbon state was increasingly unable to tap the vast French resources for war. It required a revolution to break these limits on French state formation and military expansion.[26]

Individuals, groups, and the fiscal-military states

The organisational similarities of the eighteenth century European armies and navies, even in societies with widely different constitutional, economic, and social structures, are striking. This makes it probable that the complex organisation gave a marked comparative advantage in violence-control to central states. The states did not gain control of resources only because they used violence or raised resources with oppression. Other power-holders had done so for many centuries. Fiscal-military states prevailed because they used and controlled violence in a more *rational* way than competitive social forms of protection.[27]

Whether the fiscal-military state on average offered its subjects better or worse economic and social conditions compared to earlier systems is a contrafactual question. The earlier systems of protection cannot easily be taken out of their context and placed in eighteenth-century Europe, with its more complex and integrated economies. To regard the new armed forces only as an increased burden is erroneous. The fiscal-military states made costs for protection and warfare more visible in budgets and public accounts, but these costs had earlier been embedded in society. Before the fiscal-military state, society had to absorb both the costs of local defence and the destructive effects of local violence and foreign attacks.

However, when the power of the state increased, the importance of power over the state also increased. Centralised states gave Europeans strong incentives to consider how subjects and groups should be protected against arbitrary power from far above. They also gave the societies new economic opportunities offered by increased protection of territory and long-distance trade, and more predictable conditions for investments. The ultimate Euro-American response was not to resist and dismantle the states as complex organisations but to develop

---

[26] Recent studies: Parker, *Class and State*; Dessert, *La Royale*; Lynn, *Giant*; Parrott, *Richelieu's Army*; Rowlands, *Dynastic State*, 'French Amphibious Warfare'; James, *Navy and Government*.

[27] This section is partly based on Glete, 'Local Elites'.

political institutions to control them. Parts of these solutions operated already in the formative periods of several fiscal-military states. The high degree of resource mobilisation shown by the Dutch, Swedish, and later the British state is difficult to imagine without the existence of representative institutions. Even in the early Spanish Monarchy and in parts of France, regional representative institutions were important for centralising resources.

The fiscal-military organisations were hierarchical power-structures, controlled from above, but they were not alien bodies in European societies; they were integrated parts of it. The organisations required skills and rewarded loyalty, and they offered new opportunities for social mobility. Parts of the traditional elite groups found employment in them as officers and bureaucrats, and could from these positions continue to exercise patronage and power in the interest of families and friends. Men outside the elites could channel their ambitions into careers as professionals in the new military and financial organisations. Young men without opportunities to inherit a farm could find employment as soldiers and seamen. The more ambitious of them could make a career as non-commissioned officers or skilled artisans. A disciplined regiment might be a valuable local market for those who provided it with housing and food. Merchants and industrialists could develop their enterprises with the armed forces as buyers of food, weapons, uniforms, and naval supplies. For financiers the states were large-scale customers, especially during wars. The growth of markets to supply the armed forces with resources was a part of the diversification and sophistication of European economic and social structures. Europeans had by 1750 learned to live with centralised states, fiscal demands from that type of state, and a practical monopoly of violence exercised by its armed forces.

Was it the result of changing institutions and a developing opinion that powerful states offering better protection and increased predictability might favour economic growth? Or was it resignation to an oppressive form of government that society had become too inferior in capacity for violence to resist? Both interpretations exist within various historical explanations of early-modern Europe. By 1750, most European states had arrived at surprisingly uniform organisational results, but the societies had during centuries travelled along different paths to reach it. It is plausible that opportunities and threats had been mixed in different proportions in different periods and in different parts of Europe. It is also plausible that the rules of human interaction had changed in different ways. Modern European history offers dramatic contrasts in the political and economic rules of human interaction that make it probable that the changes in earlier centuries had not been homogeneous.

It is less difficult to reach general conclusions about the increased legitimacy of centralised states and complex organisations. The rise of complex organisations, replacing the manor, the guild, the town, and the village, as the central building blocks of society, is one of the fundamental changes that characterise the modernisation of Europe from the late-medieval period to the twentieth century. In the early-modern period complex organisations were primarily rising fiscal-military states. The nineteenth century saw the rise of large, often state-controlled infrastructural organisations such as the railways. From the late nineteenth century we have experienced the rise of private corporations as large, complex, hierarchical organisations. Today, we daily entrust our lives to such organisations in the confidence that they will work and fulfil their parts of the complex contractual relationships we as individuals have with the rest of the world. We may still like to make certain types of exchange with individuals whom we meet eye-to-eye, but in the developed and developing parts of the world, trust in secular, anonymous organisations is decisive.

Conclusion

The growth of fiscal and military organisations was a marked change in a Europe that otherwise showed many continuities. Historians have often debated whether state formation was primarily driven by war or whether it was the result of more complex changes in political, social, and economic relations in Europe. It is perhaps more fruitful if empirical studies and theoretical explanations of state formation are related to violence-control and protection rather than to war, as that word is closely associated with international politics. The transformation of Europe from 1350 to 1750 was not a growth of a number of centralised states in societies with well-defined borders. It was rather a process where a number of enterprises in protection-selling developed in competition with each other and in interaction with a multitude of societies that demanded protection but that also were able to negotiate with the protection-selling enterprises. The enterprises fought each other but they also struggled to gain support and resources from the societies. The decisive phase of state formation was often a period of intense domestic power-struggle where the victors achieved stability by creating organisations with marked comparative advantage in violence-control within the society. Geo-political competition between states was also important but its role in state formation has frequently been overstated or studied out of its context of rising and competing fiscal-military states primarily created by domestic power-struggles.

The rise of the state as a complex and efficient organisation and the increased trust in anonymous and distant power for protection of large territories cannot be explained as two separate processes; they were interconnected phenomena. A state with a practical monopoly of violence was a powerful actor. Concentrated armed forces gave much power to those who controlled them but also gave them the ability to provide protection, and get support and loyalty. Europeans gradually learned that societies controlled and protected by such forces were predictable and promoted economic growth. Local elites became interested in cooperation and integration with central authorities because the complex organisation offered them new options to protect and increase their power and wealth. Central authorities developed new types of military and fiscal structures, not only for geo-political contests with other states but also to be in a better bargaining position for domestic power. Historians who study these processes will always find conflicts, compromises, or consensus around extraction and redistribution of resources from society to state. It is, however, also important to study how individuals, societies, and states in the long run developed new forms of interaction to increase security, promote predictability, and take advantage of the opportunities created by redistribution of resources for protection against violence.

15   War and state-building

Ronald G. Asch

Traditional accounts of the period with which this volume is concerned assume that state-building and war interacted almost permanently in ways that shaped both the structure of the late-medieval and early-modern state, and the framework and scope of warfare. The pressure warfare exerted on monarchies and republics alike to mobilise new resources has often been seen as one of the driving forces of the process of state-building. However, a number of chapters voice reservations about this, and in fact recent research in Britain, Germany, and elsewhere has called into question the entire process of state-building in its traditional sense. Indeed, any approach that subscribes to some sort of theory of modernisation has become widely unpopular in early-modern studies, and merely talking about state-building implies that in one way or another a process of modernisation did take place.[1] Of course, military history as opposed to cultural history, for example, which tends to see the past more as a system of self-referential symbols and meanings, would probably find it quite difficult to abandon the idea of modernisation entirely, if only in the technical sense of a move towards greater efficiency, greater firepower, greater degrees of 'Vickers hardness' and so on. Moreover, it is difficult to tell a coherent story about long-term changes in military history without some sort of teleological approach, as many historians would argue.

What we should bear in mind is that the notion of modernity has become more ambiguous and contradictory than in the past. Some historians have even argued that the most important thing about modernity was the fact that so many people actually thought that their age *was* modern and could therefore safely discard older traditions. However, if, even in this perspective, 'it is surely not quite enough to say that something was the case only because people in the past thought it was',[2] this is even more true for those historians who write books about warfare

---

[1] For recent criticism of this approach, see for example Meumann and Pröve, *Herrschaft in der Frühen Neuzeit*, in particular their 'Faszination'. Cf. Asch and Freist, *Staatsbildung*, and, for Britain, Braddick, *State Formation*.

[2] Bayly, *Birth*, 11.

and military history. Nevertheless there may be 'multiple modernities', not only with regard to present-day economic organisation but also with regard to military progress and state-building.[3] Are we looking at developments that led to the unified homogeneous and sovereign national states of the nineteenth century, as Otto Hintze and Max Weber did when they developed their theories of state-building and rational organisation; or are we looking at changes that ultimately led to the much more fragmented, post-national political systems of the twenty-first century, which for fighting out-of-area wars put some reliance on military contractors and certainly not on national conscript armies?

Even within the more limited period of late-medieval and early-modern history, competing concepts of modernity can be applied. As Rhoads Murphy points out, the military organisation of the Ottoman Empire was probably the most powerful and most efficient in Europe until the end of the seventeenth century, being controlled from the centre and lacking those elements of profit-orientated entrepreneurial warfare, which was so widespread elsewhere; but at the same time a political system organised on totally different lines, such as that of the Dutch republic, could also deploy considerable military power, notably at sea but, in times of crisis, also on land.[4] Whatever the Dutch republic was, it was certainly not a stronghold of absolutism. Indeed, recent research on early-modern Europe has often rejected the notion of absolutism altogether even for countries such as France, Spain, or the Habsburg monarchy, and has instead emphasised processes of negotiation and bargaining between rulers and ruled, even seeking to identify elements of state-building from below, at the local level: a sort of state-building that was much more than just the implementation of a political agenda set by central institutions.[5] Can this approach also be applied to military history? Some historians have certainly done so, concentrating on recruitment, billeting, and on the raising of contributions in occupied provinces,[6] and certainly it remains true in a wider perspective as well that the 'state's ability to make war depended on a range of negotiated relationships'.[7]

In any case, the state – or the great dynasties or sometimes the urban communities that managed to create states – were initially not more

---

[3] For the notion of multiple modernities see Eisenstadt, *Comparative Civilizations*.
[4] See above, Chapters 7 and 8.
[5] Brakensiek and Wunder, *Ergebene Diener*; Braddick and Walter, *Negotiating Power*; Duchhardt, *Barock und Aufklärung*, 169–77; Asch, 'Absolutism'; see also above, n. 1.
[6] See Kroll, 'Aushandeln'; cf. Kroll and Krüger, *Militär und ländliche Gesellschaft*; and Meumann and Rogge, *Besetzte res publica*.
[7] Gunn, above, 64.

than one amongst many competitors on a market for armed force. As Jan Glete has put it, 'From an economic perspective the fiscal-military state was a new, large-scale actor on an old market: the market for *protection and control of violence*. It sold protection against violence to society by raising taxes through the fiscal organisation, and delivered the service through the military organisation.'[8]

This is an approach that also underlies one of the more important recent works on early-modern state formation, Wolfgang Reinhard's *Geschichte der Staatsgewalt*.[9] For Reinhard, states seem at times to be no more than *magna latrocinia* – great robber bands, as Saint Augustine put it – although Reinhard is of course aware of the fact that religion and law were of crucial importance in giving a ruler legitimate authority. In fact, even the normal procedures of government required a certain amount of consent to work efficiently: perhaps not universal and express consent, but at least the tacit consent of relevant sections of the social and political elite. If this held true in peace it was even more true when a state was at war, and such consent could only be achieved when the ruler of a state managed to persuade his subjects that he was in the end more than just the chief of a band of robbers, and could rely on dynastic loyalty, religious allegiances, or outright patriotism. The same held true for local warlords and magnates involved in armed conflict or pursuing a feud. They could only maintain their power-base by appealing to ties of patronage, kinship, and friendship amongst their clients and allies. If they wanted to overcome rivals in conflicts they had to rely on morality as much as on force. 'Force without morality, or the semblance of morality, was nearly as ineffective as morality without the capacity and will to use force.'[10]

Thus political culture was certainly of crucial importance as a framework for waging war. This is not to deny that there was a strong economic element in warfare, in particular if we look at the role of military entrepreneurs. In the later sixteenth and early seventeenth centuries most states relied to a greater or lesser extent on 'enterprisers' to recruit troops and finance warfare. Military entrepreneurs could sometimes develop dangerous tendencies to act on their own. Moreover, in certain cases the military entrepreneurs were the very same noblemen who at the local level were typical *Gewaltunternehmer*, that is, men who were in the business of selling

---

[8] Glete, above, 305.
[9] Reinhard, *Geschichte der Staatsgewalt*, 20–5.
[10] Zmora, 'Values and Violence', 157. I am grateful to Hilay Zmora for drawing my attention to this essay.

their ability to organise violence and apply military force, and who ran local protection rackets.[11] Some of the Scottish magnates and clan chiefs of the late sixteenth and early seventeenth centuries, in particular in the Borders and Highlands, who recruited soldiers for foreign armies would be an example of this.[12] Some of the greatest of these regional warlords were, as Steven Gunn has pointed out, 'able to operate across cultural and political frontiers more effectively than were the more institutionalised forms of princely power', making the most prominent amongst them 'a factor to be reckoned with in the politics of more than one polity'.[13]

Certainly an army whose soldiers were recruited either from amongst the clients of noble magnates who themselves held royal commissions, or by military entrepreneurs, remained fragile in more than one way, especially in a civil war as in France after 1562.[14] The solution for this problem seemed to be a process whereby military administration became a more bureaucratic process, which to some extent abolished the need for relying on military entrepreneurs and also ensured that regimental and company commanders were subjected to a tighter control with regard to their financial practices. France is the prime example for such a process of growing bureaucratic control in the seventeenth century, but as Olaf van Nimwegen has pointed out the young Dutch republic was the first state to perfect this system of civilian control. The Dutch were able to achieve this control because the central provinces of the republic, Holland and Zeeland, had a flourishing commercial economy and the most modern tax-system of the time, but also because there were wealthy civilians who were prepared to act as financial brokers and to provide interim funds for pay and provisions, the *solliciteurs militaires*.[15]

However, we should be wary of viewing the road that led to the creation of reliably financed standing armies as a highway of military and administrative progress. Steven Gunn has rightly warned us that 'the potential for dysfunction was high' in bureaucracies that were created to raise the financial means necessary to supply and maintain standing armies and that were 'embedded in court-based patronage systems'.[16] David Parrott chooses a similar approach in his chapter on war, state, and society in

---

[11] For this phenomenon see Zmora, *State and Nobility*; cf. Jendorff and Krieb, 'Adel im Konflikt', 179–206.
[12] Lynch, 'James VI'; Murdoch, 'House of Stuart'.
[13] Gunn, above, 66.
[14] Wood, *King's Army*.
[15] See Chapter 8.
[16] Gunn, above, 66.

326 Ronald G. Asch

western Europe after 1600.[17] He rightly argues out that for a long time military contracting in its various forms worked well enough for most countries, and that for every Wallenstein or Mansfeld there were dozens of less powerful military commanders, who served their various masters faithfully and without developing undue political ambitions, and who might have claimed, like Blackwater USA today, that 'we meet or exceed all professional and contractual expectations and obligations', whatever the persuasiveness of such an assertion in the latter case.[18]

Moreover, in a modified form military entrepreneurship did survive after the mid seventeenth century, for example in the form of the Prussian *Kompaniewirtschaft* (the system whereby captains could make money from administering the finances of a company of soldiers) or in France itself in the form of venality for military commissions. In small-scale warfare (the so-called *kleine Krieg*, 'small war') that Simon Pepper mentions in Chapter 9 there was also a strong element of entrepreneurship as late as the eighteenth century, as special units of irregular troops such as *Freibataillone* (free battalions) or light cavalry were employed for this purpose.[19] Commanders of regular units, however, were now much more reluctant to make money by looting enemy property. Johann Friedrich August von der Marwitz, commander of an elite cavalry regiment, allegedly refused to plunder the castle of Hubertusburg during the Seven Years' War, arguing that this would be a fit task for the commanding officer of a *Freibataillon* but not for a colonel of the *Gens d'armes*.[20] It is inconceivable that a commander in the Thirty Years' War would have acted in a similar way, not to mention late-medieval military leaders. On the contrary, to live merely from wages paid by the prince was seen as demeaning. So some change had taken place.

But was this a change for the better in the sense that greater military efficiency was achieved while new administrative structures gave rulers greater control over their armed forces? David Parrott raises serious doubts about this widespread assumption, and one has to admit that the process whereby the army became a state, or at least a dynastic institution, and ceased to be a mere assembly of more or less privately owned regiments was a laborious one. The attempt to suppress traditions of military entrepreneurship was extremely costly and was

---

[17] Parrott, above, Chapter 4.
[18] www.blackwaterusa.com/company_profile/core_values.html (last accessed 10 June 2008).
[19] See Pepper, above, 195–201; see also Kunisch, *Kleine Krieg*; Rink, *Vom 'Partheygänger' zum Partisan*; cf. Carl, *Okkupation*, 232–8: Starkey, *War*, 53, cf. 95–6.
[20] Marwitz, *Nachrichten*, 11. The honour, however, to have refused the king's orders was also claimed by the family von Saldern for one of their members.

often undertaken with insufficient fiscal resources, as in the Habsburg monarchy after 1634 (the year when Wallenstein was killed), where its seeming success remained in many ways superficial for decades, if not indeed for more than a century, and was anyhow only achieved at the price of a structural financial crisis.[21] Nevertheless, this leaves us with a question: why did rulers try to reduce the entrepreneurial element in warfare in the first place? David Parrott suggests ideology as the main motivation.[22] Another reason may be that both contractors and mercenaries had often come from areas under the indirect control, though not the direct rule, of a monarch. Thus Spain had raised many of its regiments in northern and central Italy and in Germany, where she maintained a network of pensioners prepared to supply her with troops.[23] After 1640, Spanish influence declined in Germany and to a lesser extent in northern Italy. Moreover, states were more reluctant than in the past to let foreign princes recruit entire regiments amongst their subjects – although the Swiss, whose urban elites continued to derive a large share of their income from military contracts, remained an exception, not to mention the *Soldatenhandel*: the sale of soldiers by smaller German states such as Hessen-Kassel or Württemberg.[24] National or dynastic armies of some description became the only option available because the extensive extraterritorial recruiting networks maintained by states like Spain or Sweden until the mid seventeenth century were no longer viable, though the Emperor's influence in some areas of the Holy Roman Empire constitutes a partial exception to this generalisation.

Nevertheless, we should remember that there was considerable continuity between the older entrepreneurial system and the new standing armies, as David Parrott highlights. What is less clear is whether the French army, whose higher ranks of the officer-corps were dominated by the court nobility, was typical for European armies in general after 1660. In Brandenburg-Prussia, for example, there were no native magnates who could have dominated the higher echelons of the army, just a lower nobility of mostly modest financial means. In Austria, on the other hand, provincial noblemen – far less numerous in many provinces

---

[21] Hochedlinger, 'Gewaffnete Doppeladler', 234: 'Die "Monarchisierung" des Heeres war also zunächst ein Oberflächenphänomen, das fast eineinhalb Jahrhunderte brauchte, um sich nach unten hin durchzusetzen.' ('Rendering the armed forces more "monarchical" was at first a superficial process, which took a century-and-a-half to permeate all aspects of military life.')

[22] See Parrot, above, 88–89.

[23] Edelmayer, *Söldner und Pensionäre*.

[24] See for example Ingrao, *Hessian Mercenary State*.

than in Pomerania or Brandenburg anyhow – were more reluctant to send their sons to the army than in Prussia. In the imperial army a position as a low-ranking officer was less attractive than for example in Prussia where the *Kompaniewirtschaft* offered the prospect of a substantial income even to captains. Moreover, the prestige of a family depended more on the rank it held in the regional Diets or – in the case of the wealthier noble magnates – at court and in the Church, than on military honours.[25] If French nobles thought that it was 'sexy' to be an officer, Bohemian nobles seem to have thought that it was a much more attractive idea to become a canon in a cathedral chapter, or a bishop. Furthermore, it remained an option to stay at home and to lord it over one's own rural subjects. Thus in many ways the structure of an army was determined by the social structure and mentality of the nobility from amongst whose ranks the officer-corps was recruited.[26]

Having a comparatively numerous nobility could be an advantage for military recruitment but it might also be a grave obstacle to reform. In countries where the lesser nobility made up 6 per cent, 7 per cent, or even 8 per cent of the population, as in Hungary or Poland, and where nobles saw themselves as warriors, not as members of an urban elite, as they did to some extent in Castile (where the number of hidalgos was also comparatively high), it was obvious that an army of mercenaries or a standing army would not be large enough to provide every nobleman with a commission as an officer. Rather than serving as a common soldier in the royal army – perhaps even as a foot-soldier – nobles preferred to serve in the traditional feudal levy or as armed retainers of aristocratic magnates, who also acted as their patrons in civilian life. Military reforms would have threatened both the established political system and the traditional social structure. The battle of Mohács and much later the decline of Poland from the late seventeenth century showed that this resistance against any sort of modernisation entailed a high price: in the Hungarian case a national defeat of catastrophic proportions, and in the Polish instance the dissolution of the state itself.[27] The 'lateral-aristocratic ethnie' (or 'Adelsnation') in arms, perhaps a reasonably successful model in the late Middle Ages, clearly became an obsolete approach to warfare in the early-modern period.[28]

Of course, there were states and Empires taking part in European warfare that lacked a hereditary nobility to provide officers for their armies.

---

[25] Göse, 'Verhältnis'; Hochedlinger, 'Gewaffnete Doppeladler', 249–50, 235.

[26] For this problem see also Asch, *Europäischer Adel*, 193–218.

[27] See Chapters 5 and 6, above.

[28] For the notion of a 'lateral' as opposed to a 'vertical' ethnie, see Smith, *Ethnic Origins*, 75–83.

The Ottoman Empire is the best example for this. As Rhoads Murphey points out, 'the Ottomans surpassed their central European contemporaries in their ability to mobilise and support large armies in the field' until the beginning of the eighteenth century.[29] Not having a hereditary feudal nobility – and the timariots were no the equivalent of such a nobility – clearly had its advantages. The Janissaries as the elite corps of the Ottoman army played an important role in giving this army a special fighting power. In a way they were similar to the foreign elite regiments maintained by European rulers with an even stronger feeling of collective identity. The soldiers' conversion to Islam ensured their loyalty to the Empire though not necessarily to the sultan: from the early seventeenth century, interventions by the Janissaries and other units in politics became frequent. Rulers were deposed and candidates favoured by the elite troops installed until they too fell out of favour and were murdered.[30] The Ottoman Empire proves to some extent the point made by Steven Gunn: 'the capacity to fight external wars did not correspond in any uncomplicated sense to the ability to coerce internal dissidents ... even parts of standing armies might prove unreliable, mercenaries unpopular, and the greatest armies in Europe incapable of winning civil wars'.[31]

Interestingly, there were few countries in Europe where such a direct intervention of the military in political affairs occurred. Eighteenth-century Russia, perhaps, where the guards' regiments considered they had the right to depose unsuitable rulers, would provide an example for this. Otherwise one would have to go back to the Italian *condottiere* of the fourteenth and fifteenth centuries to find other examples of military rule or the direct intervention of soldiers in politics. If Wallenstein ever had such plans (and this is by no means clear[32]) he did not get very far; and Cromwell as a military and political leader and a sort of substitute monarch is very much an exceptional case in early-modern Europe. Although the Habsburg monarchy may have been less than efficient in mobilising its resources until the 1750s, as Rhoads Murphey argues in Chapter 7, the Emperor was not in danger of deposition by his soldiers or aristocratic magnates once the crisis of 1618–20 had been overcome and a lasting settlement had been achieved in 1648. The provincial estates may have pursued a policy of obstruction against plans for reform, but they were unlikely to engage in open rebellion, with the exception of the Hungarian nobility before *c.* 1720. Moreover, the precarious state of the imperial finances did improve considerably after

---

[29] See Murphey, above, 000.
[30] Shaw, *History*, 193–233.
[31] Gunn, above, 70.   [32] See above, 326.

about 1690. The alliance with Britain and, perhaps even more importantly, with the Dutch republic gave the Habsburg monarchy access to
the Amsterdam and London credit markets, while the foundation of the
Vienna city bank in 1706 was also an important step towards raising
loans at lower rates of interest than hitherto. Indeed, for the Habsburgs
and other rulers, a reliable system of state credit was perhaps as important as sufficient tax revenues for waging war, though we should not
forget that Joseph I and Charles VI managed to raise the necessary
revenues from taxes and monopolies.[33] Thus, despite the efficiency in
military administration documented by Rhoads Murphey, the military
and financial superiority of the Ottoman Empire, and even of France,
in comparison to the Austrian Habsburgs, was far less pronounced in
1700 than previously; and, as Gábor Ágoston shows in Chapter 6, in
the case of the Ottomans was disappearing altogether.[34]

Clearly one of the central problems for armies in the early-modern
period, as it is today, was to mobilise sufficient human resources, and
this was not just a financial issue but also one of motivation. This held
true for the officers as much as for the common soldiers. Of course,
for many noble elites some kind of military service had always been
part of their way of life, even if this constituted a brief rite of passage.[35]
However, this traditional military spirit was not necessarily compatible
with the qualities a standing army expected its officers to possess. Deep
cultural changes were necessary to transform individualistic warriors
inspired by the ideals of chivalry into professional officers.[36] Traditional
notions of military heroism were also transformed by the increasing
tendency, evident especially in the later eighteenth century but detect-
able earlier, to see acts of courage and bravery in a psychological perspective, and to consider not just the bodily actions but also the mental
and emotional torments a soldier faced as an essential part of his potentially heroic achievement. Mere subalterns of non-noble origin and
common soldiers could now be depicted as heroes since they shared the
inner experience of warfare as a kind of psychological self-revelation
with their aristocratic leaders, as Yuval Harari has recently argued.[37]
The glorification of a romanticised battle experience and the appeal to

---

[33] Winkelbauer, 'Finanzgeschichte', 213.
[34] Cf. Hochedlinger, 'Gewaffnete Doppeladler', and *Austria's Wars*.
[35] Cf. Parrott, *Richelieu's Army*. 313–65, in particular 317, 364.
[36] Drévillon, *L'impôt du sang*, 338; Trim, 'Introduction' to *Chivalric Ethos*, 24–30, 35.
[37] Harari, *Ultimate Experience*, 127–96, 265. For the rise of the common soldier as a
    potential hero see also Smith, *Nobility Reimagined*, 146–50, and Jones, *Great Nation*,
    259–61.

a patriotism based on a strong sense of national identity went hand in hand with the mass recruitment of conscript armies in the nineteenth and twentieth centuries; the latter would have been impossible without the former.

To appeal to such sentiments was much more difficult before the late eighteenth century; indeed, common soldiers in the two preceding centuries had often been mercenaries who may have lacked patriotism but nonetheless possessed a strong *esprit de corps*. In fact, the units with the greatest fighting power were often those that consisted of foreign soldiers, such as the Swiss, the Irish in the Spanish army of Flanders, the Anglo-Welsh units in the army of the Dutch republic, German units in the French army in the Thirty Years' War, or the Scots in Danish or Swedish service, and many other foreign regiments serving other states.[38] Fighting in a hostile environment, they developed a particularly strong sense of collective identity. Mercenaries would often have been unable to survive in a hostile environment without such an *esprit de corps*, given the very feeble logistic structures they had to rely on. This made them formidable opponents for their enemies, but often they were as great a menace for the civilian population that they were supposed to defend, but that, in the fog of war, was difficult to distinguish from enemy troops and often treated in a similar way. In this respect the well-organised Ottoman army seems, at least at times, to have been superior to many European armies, for the Ottoman High Command, as Rhoads Murphey shows, was able to impose strict standards of discipline on its troops when it felt like it – it clearly did not always do so – as in the war against Venice in 1715.

The alternative to hiring mercenaries was to arm one's own citizens or subjects. Machiavelli had already proposed such a solution, and subsequent military theoreticians who regarded the Roman legions as the prime example of a well-organised army followed him down this road, even when writing for princes and monarchs rather than urban republics. The ideal proved difficult to implement in practice. Sweden was alone in creating an efficient system of conscription in the seventeenth century, her example being followed by Prussia after 1730. It is interesting to look at the arguments that led the Dutch republic to reject such a system in the later eighteenth century. One was the fear that local authorities, which had a strong position in the Dutch political system, would interfere too much with army organisation so

---

[38] E.g. Burschel, *Söldner*; McCormack, *Mercenaries*; Stradling, *Wild Geese*; Trim, 'Fighting'; Baumann, *Landsknechte*; and Murdoch, *Scotland*.

that instead of having a single army there would be dozens of small provincial and urban militias. A second argument against the Prussian system was that the Hohenzollern kingdom treated its soldiers like sub-human robots, a state of affairs that a free republic could not tolerate.[39]

This view of the Prussian army was widely accepted, although it failed to distinguish between the foreign soldiers often forced into Prussian service by devious means, and the native recruits, who may not have been volunteers, but who nevertheless in peacetime were allowed to spend at least half the year and often longer in their home village. Native soldiers were not always as submissive in civilian life, as one might suspect. Although subjected to a harsh discipline they could be more self-assured than mere peasants, and their military service may even have had an emancipating effect.[40] Conscription certainly had a deep impact on local society, and next to the tax-collector the recruiting sergeant was probably the most important agent of the centralising state in countries where there was some form of general conscription at least for the rural population; the examples of Prussia after about 1730, and of Austria after 1770, show this clearly.[41]

If the end of the entrepreneurial system in its classical form made warfare more expensive while reducing the social costs of warfare, such as looting, the same also held good for the changes in sea warfare that took place at about the same time. Up to the mid seventeenth century, small naval forces that had been designed for warfare at sea could easily be supplemented by merchant vessels with some additional guns on board. After this point, such a solution no longer worked; indeed, with regard to galleys the change had taken place even earlier, as Louis Sicking demonstrates in Chapter 11. This made naval warfare more expensive than in the past, and smaller commercial states such as the Dutch republic, which had a vast merchant fleet, now found it much more difficult to compete with larger states with a stronger coercive element in their military organisation.

It has always been recognised that technical innovations in land warfare had an impact both on the way armies were organised and on the structure of society itself. It has often been assumed that from the fifteenth century battlefields were dominated by foot-soldiers and

---

[39] Discussed in Chapter 8, above.
[40] Hagen, *Ordinary Prussians*, 471; Kloosterhuis, 'Zwischen Aufruhr'; Kaak, 'Soldaten'; Winter, *Untertanengeist durch Militärpflicht?*; see also Wilson, 'Social Militarisation'.
[41] Hochedlinger, *Austria's Wars*, 295.

that cavalry, though important for pursuing a defeated enemy, played only a minor role henceforth. However, as Clifford Rogers points out in Chapter 10, horsemen learned to use firepower as well as foot-soldiers, and the caracole, the preferred cavalry form of attack in western Europe from the later sixteenth century, was by no means as inefficient as has often been claimed.[42] Yet this sort of technique required a different sort of horsemanship from the one practised by late-medieval knights. If it is true that notions of horsemanship were closely linked to concepts of nobility,[43] then the new riding techniques employed in warfare and taught at riding academies and similar institutions that became so important for noble education in this period created a new noble *habitus*, both physical and mental. This transformed noble behaviour, not only on the battlefield but also in society and politics. Thus changes in warfare once more interacted with more general changes in noble culture.

Cultural changes engendering the rise of new legal concepts were also important in shaping the rules of warfare. In Christian Europe, as Matthew Bennett points out in Chapter 12, restraints on warfare applied initially in the Middle Ages only to opponents who were members of the elite and who could pay a ransom when captured; common soldiers enjoyed no such privileges and were more likely to be killed when their army was defeated. Select groups of civilians, including clerics and women, also enjoyed some protection, at least in theory. But during a siege, and in particular when a besieged town had to surrender or was taken by assault, these rules were not always respected; and in the latter case, they were not even held to apply. Fighting against an enemy who was seen as a heretic or as a traitor, or as a rebel against his lord, could considerably exacerbate the conflict, as it did initially in the Netherlands after 1570 and in France in the Wars of Religion. However, it is important to remember that soldiers have committed violent acts against civilians in wartime throughout history. Religious war is thus not a necessary precondition for military violence against civilians, although confessional hatred could intensify and aggravate the tendency towards it, even when not a primary cause – this seems to have been in the case in the Thirty Years' War, for example.[44] The slaughter of Catholic clergy or Protestant ministers, both frequent occurrences in the French Wars of Religion, was largely absent from the Thirty Years' War, despite incidents like the notorious Sack of

---

[42] Cf. Love, 'Equestrian Army'.
[43] Tucker, 'French Noble Identity', 274; cf. Roche, *Le cheval*.
[44] Cf. Asch, 'Military Violence'.

Magdeburg in 1631, which was exceptional. What really got atrocities going in the seventeenth century (and in the twenty-first) were certain notions of religious purity. Calvinists in France saw priests not just as theologians subscribing to the wrong religious ideas, but as agents of the Whore of Babylon spreading idolatry amongst the people; while hard-line Catholics believed that Protestantism was not just schismatic but an infection that had to be purged from the diseased body politic through rituals of violence.[45] In Ireland similar attitudes prevailed in the mid seventeenth century, combined with the idea that the war was a cultural and ethnic conflict, leading the Irish who rose against Protestant rule in Ulster in 1641 to slaughter even English cattle, whereas their enemies saw their own religious and ethnic purity tainted by mere contact with the allegedly savage Irish.[46]

Ultimately the effect of the religious wars of the century between 1560 and 1660 was ambivalent. Kelly deVries points out in Chapter 2 that regional or local conflicts became more internationalised after Cateau-Cambrésis; that the greater powers at least learned to think in European dimensions. It is difficult not to see this greater unity of Europe as a stage for fighting out and settling conflicts, as a result of the confessional antagonism. Once every war, whether interdynastic or domestic, acquired a confessional dimension, all of Europe was in some way involved in it. Thus, the triumph of Protestants in France was seen by many co-religionists in Germany, in particular by Calvinists, as something that affected their own political fate, and the same held true for the Dutch Revolt. On the other side, Catholics from Ireland to Bohemia saw Spain as their natural protector in the later sixteenth century. Through its religious disputes Europe became a *Konfliktgemeinschaft*, a community united by the conflict itself. The greater coherence of the European states system created by religious conflict was certainly not a harmonious one but in the end it did foster a heightened awareness of belonging to the same political community, as the Peace of Westphalia was to prove: a tendency Friedrich Schiller emphasised 200 years ago in his history of the Thirty Years' War.[47] Admittedly it took a long time before a peace treaty signed by representatives of both great confessional groups proved to be stable. Before 1648, as David Trim has reminded us, the principle of *haereticis fides*

---

[45] Crouzet, *Guerriers de Dieu*. Cf. Davis, 'Rites of Violence'; Brendle and Schindling, *Religionskriege*.

[46] Simms, 'Violence'; cf. Clifton, 'Massacre'; Volmer, 'Comparative Study of Massacres'.

[47] Schiller, *Geschichte*, 30–1.

non servanda est often undermined peace treaties.[48] Even the Peace of
Augsburg of 1555, which for a number of decades proved reasonably
successful, was finally destabilised by the tendency of both Catholics
and Protestants to define the central concepts of the treaty in terms
compatible only with their own theological and legal ideals, or even
to engage in outright dissimulation, using one definition of a term for
external discussions and another for internal debate (a common tendency in current cultural and religious conflicts as well).[49] Only the rise
of a confessionally neutral law of nations and a secularised *jus publicum*
for the Empire created a vocabulary that allowed diplomats to overcome such problems.[50]

What changed in warfare between 1350 and 1750 and what remained
the same? To answer this question it may be useful to look more
closely at the eighteenth century, the last period under discussion here.
Eighteenth-century states had finally achieved the monopoly of military force that had eluded their predecessors despite enduring elements of military entrepreneurship such as the *Kompaniewirtschaft*. They
had managed to create a well-policed society in which crime may still
have been a problem, but where feuds and routine acts of violence, and
legal self-help by local warlords and nobles had largely disappeared.
Nevertheless, these peaceful, rather unwarlike societies financed and
sustained armies that were greater and more formidable than ever.
However, a price had to be paid for this achievement. The bureaucratic and disciplinary controls to which commanders were subjected
in the age of Enlightenment had clearly some drawbacks. When troops
occupied a foreign territory or province they became more dependent
on local administrative institutions, for example; without the cooperation of local officials the sophisticated system of logistic support and
war finance on which they relied could not be maintained. This meant
that some sort of compromise with local authorities had to be negotiated, unless one decided to lay waste a province entirely as the French
had done in the Palatinate and elsewhere in 1688–90. But such a pro-
cedure became quite unusual in the eighteenth century, and warfare
therefore in many ways more restrained than in the past. Indeed, some
Enlightenment writers such as Emer de Vattel, an important specialist
on international law, could declare that for the civilians it ought to
make no difference whether their towns and villages were occupied by

<hr />

[48] Trim, above, 290–91.
[49] Asch, *Thirty Years' War*, 16–23; Heckel, 'Krise der Religionsverfassung'.
[50] Tuck, 'Modern Theory'.

foreign troops or not; normal life could go on regardless.[51] There may have been some wishful thinking about this, but most states waging war agreed for example in the eighteenth century that small groups of soldiers – say 15 to 20 men – who looted and plundered were to be treated as criminals, not as soldiers, and refused quarter when captured.[52] This reduced the scope for the small-scale partisan warfare that had been widespread before 1700, as Simon Pepper shows in Chapter 9; indeed, governments often discouraged their own civilians from actively resisting foreign troops.

However, if warfare became more restrained and more humane it also became more difficult to wage a war in which the objective was total victory rather than some limited military superiority. The classical *ancien régime* armies could be used for defensive purposes and to achieve limited political objectives, but that was the extent of it, at least in Europe, though colonial wars were a different matter.[53] In Europe these armies were not really suitable for destroying an entire state unless this state had lost the capacity to defend itself entirely, as Poland had in the late eighteenth century. There was a further problem because military and civilian life had been more successfully separated in the eighteenth century than in the past. Accordingly, most European societies had become peaceful and unwarlike. This may have made life more pleasant but it made it difficult to mobilise military and economic resources fully in a crisis, as the Revolutionary Wars after 1792 were to demonstrate.

Today, we in the West, and certainly in continental Europe, live in societies that have been thoroughly demilitarised,[54] even more successfully than in the age of Enlightenment, which left war mostly to professionals. After 1789 the answer to this problem – deeply un-military societies having to fight a war for survival – was patriotism and an ideology of unbridled nationalism. Today, when the West is fighting a series of wars in Asia that some observers might call neo-colonial, this answer is no longer available. Perhaps the answer of the future will be once again, as in the Thirty Years' War, the large-scale military entrepreneur, whose demise in the late seventeenth century may have owed more to monarchs' desire to reassert their domestic authority than to strictly military considerations. To outsource warfare to another state or a private company may not always be the wisest political option

---

[51] Vattel, *Droit de Gens*, III.viii.147 (p. 438).
[52] Corvisier, 'Au seuil', 542; Carl, *Okkupation*, 14.
[53] For the character of warfare in the eighteenth century see Chagniot, *Guerre et société*, 164–71; cf. Showalter, 'Hubertusburg to Auerstedt'.
[54] Sheehan, *Soldiers*.

but it was and is often the cheapest one, and if modern law courts allow private citizens to claim reparations for war crimes from foreign governments regardless of treaties their own governments have signed, as Italian courts recently did, then the making of war and peace may indeed once again be 'privatised' much more thoroughly than we can imagine at the moment.

Bibliography

PRIMARY SOURCES

Agha, M. *Nusretname*, ed. I. Parmaksızoğlu, 2 vols. Istanbul, 1962–9.

Anon. *Der bussen meesterije*. Amsterdam 1588.

Continuation of the Adventures of Don Sebastian. London, 1603.

Anon. (trans.). *The Art of War, in Four Parts*. London, 1707.

Audley, T. 'A Treatise on the Art of War', ed. W. St P. Bunbury, *Journal of the Society for Army Historical Research*, **6** (1927).

Bacon, F. *Considerations touching a warre with Spain* [1624], in *Certaine Miscellany Works of The Right Honourable, Francis Lo. Verulam, Viscount S. Alban. Published by William Rawley* (London, 1629), 1–76.

Bannan, A. J., and A. Edelenyi (eds.). *Documentary History of Eastern Europe* (New York, 1970), 71–80, repr. at the University of Calgary website, *The End of Europe's Middle Ages*, www.ucalgary.ca/applied_history/tutor/endmiddle/bluedot/hunyadi.html.

Barret, R. *The Theoretike and Practicke of Moderne Warres*. London, 1598.

Barwick, H. *A Breefe Discourse, Concerning the force and effect of all manuall weapons of fire*. London, [1594].

Bellay, M. du. *Les mémoires de messire Martin du Bellay, contenant le discours de plusieurs choses advenues au royaume de France, depuis l'an 1513, jusques au trespas du roy François Ier*, in [J. F.] Michaud, and [J. J. F.] Poujoulat (eds.), *Nouvelle collection des mémoires pour servir à l'histoire de France depuis le XIIIe siècle jusqu'à la fin du XVIIIe*, series 1, 32 vols. (Paris, 1836–9), V, 95–568.

Benedetti, A. *De bello carolino*, ed. and trans. D. Schullian. New York, 1967.

Berville, G. de. *Histoire du Pierre de Terrail, dit Chevalier Bayard*. Lyon, 1809.

Billon, J. de. *Principes de l'art militaire*. Rouen, 1641.

Bland, H. *A Treatise of Military Discipline*. 2nd edn. London, 1727.

Bouvet, H. *The Tree of Battles of Honore Bonet [recte Bouvet]*, ed. G. W. Coopland. Liverpool, 1949.

Braun, G., and F. Hogenberg, *Civitates orbis terrarum*, 6 vols. Cologne, 1572–1618.

Brewer, J. S. *et al.* (eds.). *Letters and Papers, Foreign and Domestic, of the Reign of Henry VIII*, 23 vols. in 38. London, 1862–1932.

Brue, B. *Journal de la campagne que le grand vesir Ali Pacha a faite en 1715 pour la conquete de la Morée*. Paris, 1870.

Bueil, J. de. *Le Jouvencel*, ed. L. Lecestre, 2 vols. Paris, 1887–9.

Cechová, G., J. Janácek, and J. Kocí (eds.). *Documenta Bohemia bellum tricennale illustrantia*, 7 vols. (Prague, 1871–7), V: *Der schwedische Krieg und Wallensteins Ende, 1630–35*.

Cellini, B. *The Autobiography of Benvenuto Cellini*, trans. G. Bull. Harmondsworth, 1956.

Commynes, P. de. *Memoirs: The Reign of Louis XI 1461–83*, ed. M. C. E. Jones. Harmondsworth, 1972.

Cruso, J. *Militarie Instructions for the Cavallrie*. Cambridge, 1632.

Cuvelier, J. *La chanson de Bertrand du Guesclin*, ed. J.-C. Faucon, 3 vols. Toulouse, 1990–1.

Dibbetz, J. *Het groot militair woordenboek*. Den Haag, 1740.

Digges, L. and T. *An arithmeticall warlike treatise named Stratioticos*. London, 1579, 1590. (Unless otherwise noted, citations are to the 1590 edn.)

Fer, N. de. *Les forces de l'Europe*, 8 vols. Paris, 1693–7.

Folard, J. C. de. *L'esprit de Chevalier Folard*, ed. Frederick II of Prussia. Leipzig, 1761.

Fourquevaux, R. de B. de P., sieur de. *Instructions sur la faict de la guerre*, 2 vols. Paris, 1548.

Frederick II of Prussia. *Die Werke Friedrichs des Großen*, ed. A. Ritter, 2 vols. Berlin, n.d.

  Instructions to His Generals, in T. R. Phillips (ed.), *Roots of Strategy*, 177–301.

  Les principes généraux de la guerre, in J. D. E. Preuss (ed.), *Oeuvres de Frédéric le Grand*, 31 vols. in 33 (Berlin, 1846–57), XXVIII.

Froissart, J. *Froissart's Chronicles*, trans. and ed. J. Jolliffe. London, 1977.

Frontinus, S. Julius. *Strategemata* [first century AD], trans. C. E. Bennett. London and Cambridge, MA, 2003.

Garrard, W. *The Arte of Warre*. London, 1591.

Gheyn J. de. *Wapenhandelinghe van roers, musquetten ende spiessen*. The Hague, 1607.

Guicciardini, F. *The History of Italy*, ed. and trans. S. Alexander. Princeton, NJ, 1969.

Henderson, E. F. (ed. and trans.). *Select Historical Documents of the Middle Ages*. London, 1910.

Hildbrandt, R. (ed.). *Quellen und Regesten zu den Augsburger Handelshäusern Paler und Rehlinger, 1539–1642*, 2 vols. Stuttgart, 2004.

Holles, Sir J. *Letters of John Holles 1587–1637*, ed. P. R. Seddon, 3 vols., I, Thoroton Records Society 31. Nottingham, 1975.

Imber, C. (ed.). *The Crusade of Varna, 1443–45*. Aldershot, 2006.

Kemal Paşazade. *Tarih*, ed. S. Turan. Facsimile edn, 10 vols. Ankara, 1954.

Knolles, R. *The generall historie of the Turkes*. 5th edn. London, 1638.

Kossman, E. H., and A. F. Mellink (eds.). *Texts Concerning the Revolt of the Netherlands*. Cambridge, 1974.

La Noue, F. de. *Politike and Militarie Discourses*. London, 1587.

Lipsius, J. *Politica: Six Books of Politics or Political Instruction*, ed. and trans. J. Waszink. Assen, 2004.

  Politica van Iustus Lipsius, dat is van de regeeringhe van landen ende steden in ses boecken begrepen. Franeker, 1590.

Politicorum sive civilis doctrinae libri sex. 1589.

Louis XIV. *Memoirs for the Dauphin,* ed. and trans. P. Sonnino. New York, 1970.

Machiavelli, N. *Art of War,* ed. and trans. C. Lynch. Chicago, 2003.

The Art of War. ed. and trans. N. Wood. New York, 1965.

The Prince (with Related Documents), ed. and trans. W. J. Connell. Boston, 2005.

Mailles, J. de. *History of Bayard.* London, 1883.

Marnix, van St Aldegonde, F. *Bref recit de l'estat de la ville d'Anvers, du temps de l'assiegement & rendition d'icelle.* 1585.

Marwitz. F. A. L. von der. *Nachrichten aus meinem Leben, 1777–1808,* ed. G. de Bruyn and G. Wolf. Berlin, 1989.

Mendoza, B. de. *Theoretique and Practise of Warre,* trans. E. Hoby. London, 1598.

Michaud, [J. F.] and [J. J. F.] Poujoulat (eds.), *Nouvelle collection des mémoires pour servir à l'histoire de France depuis le XIIIe siècle jusqu'à la fin du XVIIIe,* series 1, 32 vols. Paris, 1836–9.

Monluc, B. de. *Commentaires et lettres,* ed. A. de Ruble, 5 vols. Paris, 1864–72.

Military Memoirs, ed. I. Roy. Hamden, CT, 1972.

Montecuccoli, R. *Mémoires.* Paris, 1712.

Sulle battaglia, trans. in T. M. Barker, *The Military Intellectual and Battle.* Albany, N.Y., 1975.

Muntaner, R. *The Chronicle of Muntaner,* trans. H. Goodenough. Cambridge, ON, 2000.

Müteferrika, I. *Milletlerin Düzeninde İlmî Usüller.* Istanbul, 1990.

Netherlands, States-General of the. *Recueil van verscheide placaaten, ordonnantiën, resolutiën, instructiën, ordres en lijsten &c. betreffende de saaken van den oorlog te water en te lande,* 7 vols. [1750–78], I. Den Haag, n.d.

Newcomen, M. *A Sermon, tending To set forth the Right Use of the Disasters that befall our Armies.* London, 1644.

Petrosian, I. E. (ed.). *Mebde-i kanun-i yeniçeri ocağı tarihi.* Facsimile edn. Moscow, 1987.

Phillips, T. R. (ed. and trans.). *Roots of Strategy: The 5 Greatest Military Classics of All Time.* Mechanicsburg, PA, 1985.

Pizan [Pisan], C. de. *Livre des fais d'armes,* Bodleian MS 824.

The Book of Deeds of Arms and Chivalry, ed. C. C. Willard, trans. S. Willard. Philadelphia, 1999.

Puységur, J. F. de Chastenet, marquis de. *Art de la guerre.* Paris, 1743.

Art de la guerre, par principes et par règles, 2 vols. Paris, 1749.

Quincy, C., marquis de. *Histoire militaire du règne de Louis le Grand,* 7 vols. in 8 (Paris, 1726), VII, Part II: *Maximes et instructions sur l'art militaire.*

Raşid, M. *Tarih-i Raşid,* 3 vols. Istanbul, 1740.

Rich, B. *Allarme to England.* London, 1578.

Fruites of Long Experience. London, 1604.

Rohan, H., duc de. *La parfaict capitaine.* Paris, 1636.

Salignac, B. de. *Le siège de Metz,* Collection complète des mémoirs relatifs à l'histoire de France, ed. M. Petitot, XXXII. Paris, 1823.

Le siège de Metz par l'Empereur Charles V en l'an 1552, in Michaud and Poujoulat (eds.), *Nouvelle collection,* series 1, VIII. Paris, 1850.

Saxe, M., comte de. *Mes rêveries*, 2 vols., I. Paris, 1757.
Reveries, or Memoirs upon the Art of War. London, 1757.
Schütz, E. (ed. and trans.). *An Armeno-Kipchak Chronicle on the Polish–Turkish Wars in 1620–1621.* Budapest, 1968.
Schwendi, L. von. *Der erste deutsche Verkünder der allgemeinen Wehrpflicht*, ed. E. von Frauenholz. Hamburg, 1939.
Selaniki Mustafa, *Tarih-i Selaniki*, ed. M. Mehmed Ipşirli, 2 vols. Istanbul, 1989.
Seldeneck, P. von. *Kriegsbuch*, ed. K. Neubauer, dissertation, Heidelberg, 1963.
Smith, L. T. (ed.). *Expeditions to Prussia and the Holy Land Made by Henry, Earl of Derby, in the Years 1390–1 and 1392–3*, Camden Society, n.s. 52. London, 1894.
Smythe, J. *Certain Discourses.* London, 1590.
Soranzo, L. *The Ottoman History of Loranzo Soranzo.* London, 1603. (English trans. of Italian original (1598)).
Stuart, B. *Traité sur l'art de la guerre*, ed. E. de Comminges. The Hague, 1976.
Styward, T. *Pathwaie to Martiall Discipline.* London, 1582.
Sutcliffe, M. *The Practice, Proceedings, and Law of Armes.* London, 1593.
Tavannes, J. de Saulx-. *Mémoires de Gaspard et Guillaume de Saulx-Tavannes*, in Michaud et Poujolat (eds.), *Nouvelle collection des mémoires pour servir à l'histoire de France*, VIII. Paris, 1854.
Tursun Beg. *The History of Mehmed the Conqueror by Tursun Beg*, ed. and trans. H. İnalcık and R. Murphey. Minneapolis and Chicago, 1978.
Tyaerda van Rinsumageest, W. *Vierde boek der Kronyken van Friesland bevattende de geschiedenis van de vijftiende eeuw.* Leeuwarden, 1850.
Vattel, E. de. *Le Droit de Gens ou Principes de la loi naturelle*, German trans. W. Euler, as *Klassiker des Völkerrechts in modernen deutschen Übersetzungen*, ed. W. Schätzel, 4 vols. (Tübingen, 1950–65), III.
Vegetius Renatus, F. *De re militari* [fourth century AD], in T. R. Phillips (ed. and trans.), *Roots of strategy: The 5 greatest military classics of all time* (Harrisburg, PA, 1985), 65–175.
Waurin, J. de. *Anchiennes cronicques*, ed. E. Dupont, 3 vols. Paris, 1858–63.
Williams, R. *A briefe discourse of warre.* London, 1590.
Zeiller, M. *Topographia Galliae.* Paris, 1655–7.

SECONDARY SOURCES

Abulafia, D. (ed.). *The French Descent into Renaissance Italy, 1494–95.* Aldershot, 1995.
Adams, S. L. 'A Puritan Crusade? The Composition of the Earl of Leicester's Expedition to the Netherlands, 1585–86', in Adams, *Leicester and the Court: Essays on Elizabethan Politics* (Manchester, 2002), 176–95.
'Tactics or Politics? "Military Revolution" and the Hapsburg Hegemony, 1525–1648', in C. J. Rogers (ed.), *The Military Revolution Debate: Readings on the Military Transformation of Early Modern Europe* (Boulder, CO, San Francisco and Oxford, 1995), 253–72.
Ágoston, G. 'Behind the Turkish War Machine: Gunpowder Technology and War Industry in the Ottoman Empire, 1450–1700', in B. Steele and

T. Dorland (eds.), *The Heirs of Archimedes: Science and the Art of War through the Age of Enlightenment* (Cambridge, MA, 2005), 101–33.

'Disjointed Historiography and Islamic Military Technology: The European Military Revolution Debate and the Ottomans', in M. Kaçar and Z. Durukal (eds.), *Essays in Honour of Ekmeleddin İhsanoğlu* (Istanbul, 2006), 567–82.

'A Flexible Empire: Authority and Its Limits on the Ottoman Frontiers', *International Journal of Turkish Studies* **9** (2003), 15–31.

Guns for the Sultan: Military Power and the Weapons Industry in the Ottoman Empire. Cambridge, 2005.

'Habsburgs and Ottomans: Defense, Military Change and Shifts in Power', *Turkish Studies Association Bulletin* **22** (1998), 126–41.

'Information, Ideology, and Limits of Imperial Policy: Ottoman Grand Strategy in the Context of Ottoman–Habsburg Rivalry', in V. H. Aksan and D. Goffman (eds.), *The Early Modern Ottomans: Remapping the Empire* (New York and Cambridge, 2007), 75–103.

'Ottoman Artillery and European Military Technology in the Fifteenth and Seventeenth Centuries', *AoH* **47** (1994), 15–48.

'Ottoman Warfare in Europe 1453–1826', in J. Black (ed.), *European Warfare 1453–1815* (New York and Basingstoke, 1999), 118–44, 262–3.

Aksan V. 'Locating the Ottomans among Early Modern Empires', *Journal of Early Modern History* **3** (1999), 103–34.

Ottoman Wars 1700–1870: An Empire Besieged. Harlow and New York, 2007.

Alertsz, U. 'The Naval Architecture and Oar Systems of Medieval and Later Galleys', in R. Gardiner and J. Morrison (eds.), *The Age of the Galley: Mediterranean Oared Vessels since Pre-Classical Times* (London, 2004), 142–162.

Almond, G., and Powell, G. B., Jr. *Comparative Politics: A Developmental Approach*. Boston, 1966.

Amersfoort, H. 'Voor vaderland en Oranje', in *Mededelingen van de Sectie Militaire Geschiedenis Landmachtstaf* **7** (1984), 5–35.

André, L. *Michel Le Tellier et Louvois*. Paris, 1942.

Andrews, K. R. *Trade, Plunder and Settlement*. Cambridge, 1984.

Anglo, S. *Aproximación a la historia militar de España*, 3 vols. Madrid, 2006.

Machiavelli: The First Century. Studies in Enthusiasm, Hostility and Irrelevance. Oxford, 2005.

Aranda Pérez, F. J. (ed.). *La declinación de la Monarquía Hispánica en el siglo XVII: Actas de la VIIa Reunión Científica de la Fundación Española de la Historia Moderna*. Cuenca, 2004.

Archer, C. I., J. R. Ferris, H. H. Herwig, and T. H. E. Travers. *World History of Warfare*. Lincoln, NE, 2002.

Arnold, T. F. 'Fortifications and the Military Revolution: The Gonzaga Experience, 1530–1630', in Rogers (ed.), *Military Revolution Debate*, 201–26.

Arthurson, I. 'The King's Voyage into Scotland: The War that Never Was', in D. Williams (ed.), *England in the Fifteenth Century: Proceedings of the 1986 Harlaxton Symposium* (Woodbridge, 1987), 1–22.

Asch, R. G. 'Absolutism and Royal Government', in P. H. Wilson (ed.), *A Companion to Eighteenth-Century Europe* (Oxford, 2008), 451–63.

Europäischer Adel in der Frühen Neuzeit. Cologne, 2008.

The Thirty Years' War: The Holy Roman Empire and Europe, 1618–1648. Basingstoke, 1997.

'Warfare in the Age of the Thirty Years' War 1598–1648', in Black (ed.), *European Warfare 1453–1815*, 45–68, 250–6.

' "Wo der soldat hinkömbt, da ist alles sein": Military Violence and Atrocities in the Thirty Years War Re-examined', *German History* **18** (2000), 291–309.

Asch, R. G., and D. Freist (eds.). *Staatsbildung als kultureller Prozeß: Strukturwandel und Legitimation von Herrschaft in der Frühen Neuzeit.* Cologne, 2005.

Atiya, A. S. *The Crusade of Nicopolis.* London, 1934.

Awty, B. G. 'The Continental Origins of Wealden Ironworkers 1451–1544', *Economic History Review*, n.s. 34 (1981), 524–39.

'Parson Levett and English Cannon Founding', *Sussex Archaeological Collections* **127** (1989), 133–45.

Ayton, A. 'The Battle of Crécy: Context and Significance', in A. Ayton and P. Preston (eds.), *The Battle of Crécy, 1346* (Woodbridge, 2005), 1–34.

'English Armies in the Fourteenth Century', in Curry and Hughes (eds.), *Arms, Armies and Fortifications*, 21–38.

Bachrach, D. *Religion and the Conduct of War c. 300–c. 1215.* Woodbridge, 2003.

Bak, J. M. 'Hungary and Crusading in the Fifteenth Century', in N. Housley (ed.), *Crusading in the Fifteenth Century: Message and Impact* (Basingstoke and New York, 2004), 116–27.

Bak, J. M., and B. K. Király (eds.). *From Hunyadi to Rákóczi. War and Society in Late Medieval and Early Modern Hungary*, Brooklyn College Studies on Society in Change 12, East European Monographs 104. New York, 1982.

Bakker, F. J. 'Het bijeenbrengen van een vrachtvloot in Holland en Zeeland. Van charter tot requisitie (april–juni 1475)', *Tijdschrift voor zeegeschiedenis* **24** (2005), 3–20.

Balard, M. 'Genoese Naval Forces in the Mediterranean during the Fifteenth and Sixteenth Centuries', in J. B. Hattendorf and R. W. Unger (eds.), *War at Sea in the Middle Ages and the Renaissance* (Woodbridge and Rochester, NY, 2003), 137–49.

Balsamo, J. (ed.). *Passer les monts: Français en Italie–l'Italie en France (1494–1525). Xe colloque de la Société française d'étude du seizième siècle.* Paris, 1998.

Barkan, Ö. L. 'H 1079–1080 (1669–1670) Mali Yılına ait Bir Osmanlı Bütçesi ve ekleri', in *Osmanlı devletinin sosyal ve ekonomik tarihi*, **II**, 759–837.

'1070–1071 (1660–1661) Tarihli Osmanlı Bütçesi ve Bir Mukayese', in *Osmanlı devletinin sosyal ve ekonomik tarihi*, **II**, 838–81.

'Osmanlı İmparatorluğu Bütçelerine Dair Notlar', in Ö. L. Barkan, *Osmanlı devletinin sosyal ve ekonomik tarihi: Tetkikler-makaleler*, ed. H. Özdeğer, 2 vols. (Istanbul, 2000), II, 727–58.

Barker, J. *Agincourt: The King, the Campaign, the Battle.* London, 2005.

Barkey, K. *Bandits and Bureaucrats. The Ottoman Route to State Centralization.* Ithaca, NY, and London, 1994.

Barnett, C. *Marlborough.* London, 1974.

Baumann, R. *Georg von Frundsberg. Der Vater der Landsknechte und Feld-hauptmann von Tirol. Eine gesellschaftsgeschichtliche Biographie.* Munich, 1984.

Landsknechte: Ihre Geschichte und Kultur vom späten Mittelalter bis zum Dreißigjährigen Krieg. Munich, 1994.

Bayly, C. A. *The Birth of the Modern World, 1780–1914.* Oxford, 2004.

Behnen, M. 'Der Gerechte und der Notwendige Krieg: 'necessitas' und 'utilitas republicae' in der Kriegstheorie des 16. und 17. Jahrhunderts', in B. Stollberg-Rilinger and J. Kunisch (eds.), *Staatsverfassung und Heeresverfassung in der europäischen Geschichte der frühen Neuzeit* (Berlin, 1986), 43–106.

Bell, A. R. 'The Fourteenth-Century Soldier: More Chaucer's Knight or Medieval Career?', in J. R. France (ed.), *Mercenaries and Paid Men: The Mercenary Identity in the Middle Ages* (Leiden and Boston, MA, 2008), 301–16.

War and the Soldier in the Fourteenth Century. Woodbridge, 2004.

Bellamy, M. *Christian IV and his Navy: A Political and Administrative History of the Danish Navy, 1596–1618.* Leiden, 2006.

Benedict, P. *Christ's Churches Purely Reformed: A Social History of Calvinism.* New Haven, CT and London, 2002.

Bennell, J. 'The Oared Vessels', in C. S. Knighton and D. Loades (eds.), *The Anthony Roll of Henry VIII's Navy. Pepys Library 2991 and British Library Additional MS 22047 with Related Documents,* Naval Records Society, Occasional Publications, 2 (Aldershot and Cambridge, 2000), 37.

Berckmans, O. 'Mariembourg et Philippeville, villes neuves et fortes de la Renaissance. II: Philippeville', *Bulletin de la Commission Royale des Monuments et Sites,* n.s. **8** (1979), 107–38.

Bethencourt, F., and K. Chaudhuri (eds.). *História da expansão Portuguesa. Vol. I: A formação da imperio (1415–1570).* Lisbon, 1998.

Biskup, M. 'Das Problem der Söldner in den Streitkräften des Deut-schordenstaates vom Ende des 14. Jhs. bis 1525', *Ordines militares: Colloquia torunensia historica* **6** (Torun, 1991), 49–74.

Black, J., *The Cambridge Illustrated Atlas of Warfare: Renaissance to Revolution, 1492–1792.* Cambridge, 1996.

(ed.). *European Warfare 1453–1815.* New York, 1999.

European Warfare 1494–1660. London and New York, 2002.

European Warfare 1660–1815. London and New York, 1994.

'Introduction' to J. Black (ed.), *War in the Early Modern World, 1450–1815* (London, 1995), 1–23.

A Military Revolution? Military Change and European Society, 1550–1800. London, 1991.

'Military Revolutions and Early Modern Europe: The Case of Spain', in E. García Hernán and D. Maffi (eds.), *Guerra y sociedad en la monarquía hispánica,* 2 vols. (Madrid, 2006), I, 17–30.

'On Diversity and Military History', in 'Military Revolutions: A Forum', *Historically Speaking* 4:4 (April 2003), 7–9.

(ed.). *The Origins of War in Early Modern Europe.* Edinburgh, 1987.

War and the World: Military Power and the Fate of Continents 1450–2000. New Haven, CT and London, 2000.

(ed.). *War in the Early Modern World, 1450–1815.* London, 1995.

'Was There a Military Revolution in Early Modern Europe?', *History Today* **58**:7 (July 2008), 34–41.

Blickle, P. (ed.). *Resistance, Representation and Community.* Oxford, 1997.

Bloch, M. *Feudal Society,* trans. L. A. Manyon, 2 vols. Chicago, 1961.

Boardman, A. W. *The Medieval Soldier in the Wars of the Roses.* Stroud, 1998.

Boer, M. G. de. *Tromp en de armada van 1639,* Werken uitgegeven door de Commissie voor zeegeschiedenis 6. Amsterdam, 1941.

Böhme, K.-R. 'Geld für die Schwedischen Armeen nach 1640', *Scandia* **33** (1967), 54–95.

Bohna, M. 'Armed Force and Civic Legitimacy in Jack Cade's Revolt, 1450', *EHR* **118** (2003), 563–82.

Boillet, D., and M. F. Piejus (eds.). *Les guerres d'Italie: Histoires, pratiques, représentations.* Paris, 2002.

Bondioli, M., R. Burlet, and A. Zysberg. 'Oar Mechanics and Oar Power in Medieval and Later Galleys', in Gardiner and Morrison (eds.), *The Age of the Galley,* 172–205.

Bonney, R. (ed.). *Economic Systems and State Finance.* Oxford, 1995.

'Introduction', in Bonney (ed.), *Fiscal State,* 1–17.

'Revenue', in Bonney (ed.), *Economic Systems and State Finance,* 423–505.

(ed.). *The Rise of the Fiscal State in Europe, c. 1200–1815.* Oxford, 1999.

The Thirty Years' War, 1618–1648. Botley and New York, 2002.

Börekçi, G. 'A Contribution to the Military Revolution Debate: The Janissaries' Use of Volley Fire during the Long Ottoman–Habsburg War of 1593–1606 and the Problem of Origins', *AoH* **59** (2006) [2007], 407–38

Boulton, D'A. J. D. *The Knights of the Crown: The Monarchical Orders of Knighthood in Later Medieval Europe 1325–1520.* Woodbridge, 1987.

Bovill, E. W. *The Battle of Alcazar: An Account of the Defeat of Don Sebastian of Portugal at El-Ksar el-Kebir.* London, 1952.

Bowen, H. V., and A. González Enciso (eds.). *Mobilising Resources for War: Britain and Spain at Work during the Early Modern Period.* Barañaín, 2006.

Boynton, L. *The Elizabethan Militia 1558–1638.* London: Routledge, 1967.

Bradbury, J. 'Battles in England and Normandy, 1066–1154', in M. Strickland (ed.), *Anglo-Norman Warfare* (Woodbridge, 1992), 182–93.

Braddick, M. *God's Fury, England's Fire. A New History of the English Civil Wars.* London, 2008.

State Formation in Early Modern England, c. 1550–1700. Cambridge, 2000.

Braddick, M., and J. Walter (eds.). *Negotiating Power in Early Modern Society: Order, Hierarchy and Subordination in Britain and Ireland.* Cambridge, 2001.

Brady, C. 'The Captains' Games: Army and Society in Elizabethan Ireland', in T. Bartlett and K. Jeffery (eds.), *A Military History of Ireland* (Cambridge, 1996), 136–59.

The Chief Governors: The Rise and Fall of Reform Government in Tudor Ireland, 1536–1588. Cambridge, 1994.

Brady, T. A. *Turning Swiss: Cities and Empire, 1450–1550.* Cambridge, 1985.

Brakensiek, S., and H. Wunder (eds.). *Ergebene Diener ihrer Herren? Herrschaftsvermittlung im alten Europa.* Cologne, 2005.

Braudel, F. *La Méditerranée et le monde méditerranéen à l'époque de Philippe II.* 9th edn, 3 vols. Paris, 1990.

The Mediterranean and the Mediterranean World in the Age of Philip II, trans. Siân Reynolds, 2 vols. London, 1973.

Braunius, S. W. P. C. 'Oorlogsvaart', in L. M. Akveld, S. Hart, and W. J. van Hoboken (eds.), *Maritieme geschiedenis der Nederlanden*, 4 vols. (Bussum, 1976–8), II, 316–54.

Brendle, F., and A. Schindling (eds.). *Religionskriege im Alten Reich und in Alteuropa.* Münster, 2006.

Brewer, J. *The Sinews of Power: War, Money and the English State, 1688–1783.* London, 1989.

Brockman, E. *The Two Sieges of Rhodes: The Knights of St John at War, 1480–1522.* New York, 1969.

Bruijn, J. R. 'Mars en Mercurius uiteen. De uitrusting van de oorlogsvloot in de zeventiende eeuw', in S. Groenveld *et al.* (eds.), *Bestuurders en geleerden. Opstellen over onderwerpen uit de Nederlandse geschiedenis van de 16de, 17de en 18de eeuw, aangeboden aan prof. dr J. J. Woltjer bij zijn afscheid als hoogleraar aan de Rijksuniversiteit Leiden* (Amsterdam, 1985), 97–106.

Varend verleden. De Nederlandse oorlogsvloot in de zeventiende en achttiende eeuw. Amsterdam, 1998.

Buisseret, D. *The Mapmaker's Quest: Depicting New Worlds in Renaissance Europe.* Oxford, 2003.

(ed.). *Monarchs, Ministers and Maps: The Emergence of Cartography as a Tool of Government in Early Modern Europe.* Chicago, 1992.

Burin de Roziers, M. *Les capitulations militaires entre la Suisse et la France*, thèse de doctorat, Paris, 1902.

Burne, A. H. *The Agincourt War: A Military History of the Latter Part of the Hundred Years War from 1369 to 1453.* London, 1956.

'The Battle of Castillon, 1453', *History Today* **3** (1953), 249–56.

Burschel, P. *Söldner im Nordwestdeutschland des 16. und 17. Jahrhunderts.* Göttingen, 1994.

Bush, M. L. *The Pilgrimage of Grace: A Study of the Rebel Armies of October 1536.* Manchester, 1996.

Calabria, A. *The Cost of Empire: The Finances of the Kingdom of Naples in the Time of Spanish Rule.* Cambridge, 1991.

Campbell, C., and A. Chong (eds.). *Bellini and the East.* London, 2005.

Carl, H. *Okkupation und Regionalismus. Die preußischen Westprovinzen im Siebenjährigen Krieg.* Mainz, 1993.

Carr Laughton, L. G. 'Early Tudor Ship-Guns', *Mariner's Mirror* **46** (1960), 242–85.

Carroll, S. *Noble Power during the French Wars of Religion: The Guise Affinity and the Catholic Cause in Normandy.* Cambridge, 1998.

Chagniot, J. *Guerre et société à l'époque moderne.* Paris, 2001.

'La rationalisation de l'armée française après 1660', in *Armées et diplomatie dans l'Europe du XVIIe siècle: Actes du colloque des associations des historiens modernistes* (Paris, 1991), 97–108.

Paris et l'armée au xviiie siècle: Étude politique et sociale. Paris, 1985.

Chandler, D. *The Art of Warfare in the Age of Marlborough.* London, 1976.

Chase, K. *Firearms: A Global History to 1700.* Cambridge, 2003.

Chastel, A. *The Sack of Rome, 1527,* trans. B. Archer. Princeton, NJ, 1983.

Checa Cremades, F. *Carlos V: La imagen del poder en el renacimiento.* Madrid, 1999.

'Monarchic Liturgies and the "Hidden King": The Function and Meaning of Spanish Royal Portraiture in the Sixteenth and Seventeenth Centuries', in A. Ellenius (ed.), *Iconography, Propaganda and Legitimation* (Oxford, 1998).

Chéruel, A. *Histoire de France sous le ministère de Mazarin (1651–1661),* 3 vols. Paris, 1882.

Cigány, I. *Reform vagy kudarc? Kísérletek a magyarországi katonaság beillesztésére a Habsburg Birodalom haderejébe 1660–1700.* Budapest, 2004.

Cipolla, C. M. *Guns, Sails and Empires: Technological Innovation and the Early Phases of European Expansion, 1400–1700.* 3rd edn. Manhattan, KS, 1988.

Citino, R. M. 'Military Histories Old and New: A Reintroduction', *AHR* **112** (2007), 1070–90.

Clifton, R. ' "An indiscriminate blackness": Massacre, Counter-massacre and Ethnic Cleansing in Ireland, 1640–1660', *War and Genocide* **1** (1999), 107–26.

Coady, C. A. J. *The Ethics of Armed Humanitarian Intervention,* Peaceworks 45. Washington, DC, 2002.

Collins, J. B. *Fiscal Limits of Absolutism: Direct Taxation in Early Seventeenth-Century France.* Berkeley and Los Angeles, 1988.

Comitato per le ororanze a Francesco Ferruccio. *Francesco Ferruccio e la guerra di Firenze.* Firenze, 1889.

Concina, E. *La macchina territoriale: La progettazione della difesa nel Cinquecento Veneto.* Bari, 1983.

Contamine, P. *Guerre, état et société à la fin du moyen âge: Études sur les armées des rois de France, 1337–1494.* Paris, 1972.

Histoire militaire de la France, 4 vols. (Paris, 1992–4), I: *Des origines à 1715.*

(ed.). *La guerre au Moyen Age.* Paris, 1980.

'Structures militaires de la France et de l'Angleterre au milieu du XVe siècle', in R. Schneider (ed.), *Das spätmittelalterliche Königtum im europäischen Vergleich,* Vorträge und Forschungen 32 (Sigmaringen, 1987), 319–35.

(ed.). *War and Competition between States.* Oxford, 2000.

War in the Middle Ages, trans. M. Jones. Oxford, 1984.

Cook, W. F. 'The Cannon Conquest of Nasrid Spain and the end of the Reconquista', *JMH* **57** (1993), 43–70.

The Hundred Years War for Morocco: Gunpowder and the Military Revolution in the Early Modern Muslim World. Boulder, CO, 1994.

Cornette, J. *Le Roi de Guerre. Essai sur la souveraineté dans la France du Grand Siècle.* Paris, 1993.

Corvisier, A. 'Au seuil d'une époque nouvelle: L'épreuve de la guerre de succession d'Espagne, guerre reglée et guerre nationale', in Contamine (ed.), *Histoire militaire*, 527–50.

Louvois. Paris, 1983.

Covini, M. N. 'Liens politiques et militaires dans le système des Etats italiens (XIIIe–XVIe siècle)', in P. Contamine (ed.), *Guerre et concurrence entre les Etats européens du XIVe au XVIIIe siècle* (Paris, 1998), 9–42.

'Political and Military Bonds in the Italian State System, Thirteenth to Sixteenth Centuries', in Contamine (ed.), *War and Competition between States*, 9–36.

Craeybeckx, J. *Un grand commerce d'importation: Les vins de France aux anciens Pays-Bas (XIIIe–XVIe siècles)*. Paris, 1958.

Crouzet, D. *Les Guerriers de Dieu. La violence au temps des troubles de religion*, 2 vols. Seyssel, 1990.

Crowley, R. *Constantinople: The Last Great Siege, 1453*. London, 2005.

Croxton, D. 'A Territorial Imperative? The Military evolution, Strategy and Peacemaking in the Thirty Years' War', *War in History* **5** (1998), 253–79.

Cunningham, A., and O. P. Grell. *The Four Horsemen of the Apocalypse: Religion, War, Famine and Death in Reformation Europe*. Cambridge, 2000.

Currin, J. M. 'To Play at Peace: Henry VII, War against France, and the Chieregato–Flores Mediation of 1490,' *Albion* **31** (1999), 207–37.

Curry, A. *Agincourt: A New History*. Stroud: Tempus, 2005.

'English Armies in the Fifteenth Century', in Curry and Hughes (eds.), *Arms, Armies and Fortifications*, 48–68.

Curry, A., and M. Hughes (eds.). *Arms, Armies and Fortifications in the Hundred Years War*. Woodbridge, 1994.

Czamanska, I. 'Poland and Turkey in the First Half of the Sixteenth Century: Turning Points', in I. Zombori (ed.), *Fight against the Turk in Central-Europe in the First Half of the Sixteenth Century* (Budapest, 2004), 91–102.

Dávid, G., and P. Fodor (eds.). *Ottomans, Hungarians and Habsburgs in Central Europe: The Military Confines in the Era of Ottoman Conquest*. Leiden and Boston, 2000.

Davies, B. 'The Development of Russian Military Power 1453–1815', in Black (ed.), *European Warfare 1453–1815*, 145–79, 264–68.

Davies, D. W. *Elizabethans Errant: The Strange Fortunes of Sir Thomas Sherley and His Three Sons as Well in the Dutch Wars as in Muscovy, Morocco, Persia, Spain and the Indies*. Ithaca, NY, 1967.

Davis, N. Z. 'The Rites of Violence: Religious Riot in Sixteenth-Century France', *Past and Present* **59** (1973), 51–91.

Dawson, J. E. A. *The Politics of Religion in the Age of Mary, Queen of Scots: The Earl of Argyll and the Struggle for Britain and Ireland*. Cambridge, 2002.

Delbrück, H. *Geschichte der Kriegskunst im Rahmen der politischen Geschichte*, 5 vols. (Berlin, 1920–8), IV: *Neuzeit*.

Dessert, D. *La Royale. Vaisseaux et marins du Roi-Soleil*. Paris, 1996.

DeVries, K. 'Catapults Are Not Atomic Bombs: Towards a Redefinition of "Effectiveness" in Premodern Military Technology', *War in History* **4** (1997), 454–70.

'The Effectiveness of Fifteenth-Century Shipboard Artillery', *Mariner's Mirror* **84** (1998), 389–99.

'Fortifications and the Cost of Premodern Occupation', in *Aspects économiques de la défense à travers les grands conflits mondiaux/The Economic Aspects of Defence through Major World Conflicts: Actes/Acta, XXXth Congrès International d'Histoire Militaire* (Rabat, 2005), 97–112.

'God and Defeat in Medieval Warfare: Some Preliminary Thoughts', in D. J. Kagay and L. J. A. Villalon (eds.), *The Circle of War in the Middle Ages: Essays on Medieval Military and Naval History* (Woodbridge, 1999), 87–97.

'Gunpowder Weaponry and the Rise of the Early Modern State', *War in History* **5** (1998), 127–45.

'Gunpowder Weaponry at the Siege of Constantinople, 1453', in Y. Lev (ed.), *War, Army and Society in the Eastern Mediterranean, 7th–16th Centuries* (Leiden, 1996), 343–62.

Guns and Men in Medieval Europe, 1200–1500: Studies in Military History and Technology. Aldershot, 2002.

'The Lack of a Western European Military Response to the Ottoman Invasions of Eastern Europe from Nicopolis (1396) to Mohács (1526)', *JMH* **63** (1999), 539–60.

'Sites of Military Science and Technology', in K. Park and L. Daston (eds.), *The Cambridge History of Science*, 5 vols. to date (Cambridge, 2003–), III: *Early Modern Europe*, 306–19.

Devyver, A. *Le sang épurée: Les préjugés de race chez les gentilshommes français de l'Ancien Régime, 1560–1720.* Brussels, 1973.

Dewald, J. *Aristocratic Experience and the Origins of Modern Culture: France, 1570–1715.* Berkeley and Los Angeles, 1993.

Diffie, B. W., and G. D. Winius. *Foundations of Portuguese Empire, 1415–1850.* Minneapolis, 1978.

Disney, A. 'Portuguese Expansion, 1400–1800: Encounters, Negotiations, and Interactions', in F. Bethencourt and D. Ramada Curto (eds.), *Portuguese Oceanic Expansion, 1400–1800* (Cambridge, 2007), 283–313.

Dollinger, Philippe. *The German Hansa.* London, 1999 (repr. of 1970 edn).

Domingues, F. C. *Os navios do Mar Oceano: Teoria e empiria na arquitectura naval portuguesa dos séculos XVI e XVII.* Lisbon, 2004.

'The State of Portuguese Naval Forces in the Sixteenth Century', in Hattendorf and Unger (eds.), *War at Sea*, 187–197.

Doran, Susan. *Elizabeth I and Foreign Policy, 1558–1603.* London, 2000.

Dorman, A., M. Smith, and M. Uttley (eds.). *The Changing Face of Military Power: Joint Warfare in an Expeditionary Age.* Basingstoke, 2002.

Dosi, G., Nelson, R. R., and Winter, S. G. (eds.). *The Nature and Dynamics of Organizational Capabilities*, Oxford, 2000.

Doumerc, B. 'An Exemplary Maritime Republic: Venice at the End of the Middle Ages', in Hattendorf and Unger (eds.), *War at Sea*, 151–165.

Downing, B. M. *The Military Revolution and Political Change: Origins of Democracy and Autocracy in Early Modern Europe*, Princeton, 1992.

Drévillon, H. *L'impôt du sang: Le métier des armes sous Louis XIV.* Paris, 2005.

Duchhardt, H. *Barock und Aufklärung.* Munich, 2007.

Duffy, C. *The Army of Frederick the Great*. Newton Abbot, London, and Vancouver, 1974.

The Army of Maria Theresa: The Armed Forces of Imperial Austria, 1740–1780. London, 1977.

Frederick the Great: A Military Life. London, 1985.

The Military Experience in the Age of Reason. New York, 1987.

Siege Warfare: The Fortress in the Early Modern World 1494–1660. London, 1979.

Durdík, J. *Hussitisches Heerwesen.* Berlin, 1961.

Edelmayer, F. *Söldner und Pensionäre: Das Netzwerk Phillipps II. im Heiligen Römischen Reich.* Vienna: Verlag für Geschichte und Politik, 2002.

Edelmayer, F., M. Lanzinner, and P. Rauscher (eds.). *Finanzen und Herrschaft: Materielle Grundlagen fürstlicher Politik in den habsburgischen Ländern und im Heiligen Römischen Reich im 16. Jahrhundert.* Munich and Vienna, 2003.

Eisenstadt, S. N. *Comparative Civilizations and Multiple Modernities,* 2 vols. Leiden, 2003.

Ekdahl, S. 'Das Pferd und seine Rolle im Kriegswesen des Deutschen Ordens', in *Ordines militares: Colloquia torunensia historica* **6** (Torun, 1991), 29–47.

'Der Krieg zwischen dem deutschen Orden und Polen–Litauen im Jahre 1422', *ZfO* **13** (1964), 614–51.

'Die Flucht der Litauer in der Schlacht bei Tannenberg', *ZfO* **12** (1963), 11–19.

'Horse and Crossbows: Two Important Warfare Advantages of the Teutonic Order in Prussia', in H. Nicholson (ed.), *The Military Orders, II: Welfare and Warfare,* (Aldershot: Ashgate, 1998), 119–51.

Elbl, M. M. 'Portuguese Urban Fortifications in Morocco: Borrowing, Adaptation, and Innovation along a Military Frontier', in J. D. Tracy (ed.), *City Walls: The Urban Enceinte in Global Perspective* (Cambridge, 2000), 349–85.

Elias, J. E. *De vlootbouw in Nederland in de eerste helft van de 17e eeuw, 1596–1655.* Amsterdam, 1933.

Elias, N. *The Civilising Process.* Oxford: Blackwell, 1994.

Elliott, J. H. *Europe Divided, 1559–1598.* London, 1968.

'A Europe of Composite Monarchies', *Past and Present* **137** (1992), 48–71.

Imperial Spain, 1469–1716. New York, 1963.

'A Question of Reputation? Spanish Foreign Policy in the Seventeenth Century', *Journal of Modern History* **55** (1983), 475–83.

Ellis, S. G. *Tudor Frontiers and Noble Power: The Making of the British State.* Oxford, 1995.

Eltis, D. *The Military Revolution in Sixteenth-Century Europe.* London, 1995.

Emberton, J. W. *'Love Loyalty': The Close and Perilous Siege of Basing House, 1643–1645.* London, 1972.

Encyclopaedia of Islam, New Edition, 12 vols. Leiden , 1960–2004.

Engel, P. 'János Hunyadi: The Decisive Years of His Career 1440–1444', in Bak and Király (eds.), *From Hunyadi to Rákóczi,* 103–24.

The Realm of St Stephen: A History of Medieval Hungary, 895–1526. London and New York, 2005

Engels, M.C. *Merchants, Interlopers, Seamen and Corsairs: The 'Flemish' Community in Livorno and Genoa (1615–1635)*. Hilversum, 1997.

Enthoven, V. 'Mars en Mercurius bijeen: De smalle marges van het Nederlandse maritieme veiligheidsbeleid rond 1650', in L. Akveld *et al.* (eds.), *In het kielzog: Maritiem-historische studies aangeboden aan Jaap R. Bruijn bij zijn vertrek als hoogleraar zeegeschiedenis aan de Universiteit Leiden* (Amsterdam, 2003), 40–60.

Ernstberger, A. *Hans de Witte, Finanzmann Wallensteins*. Wiesbaden, 1954.

'Wallenstein als Volkswirt', in *Franken – Böhmen – Europa. Gesammelte Aufsätze*, 2 vols. (Kallmünz, 1959), I, 269–85.

Ertman, T. *Birth of the Leviathan: Building States and Regimes in Medieval and Early Modern Europe*. Cambridge, 1997.

Estríngana, A.E. *Guerra y finanzas en los Países Bajos católicos: De Farnesio a Spínola (1592–1630)*. Madrid, 2002.

Falletti, P.C. *L'assedio di Firenze*, 2 vols. Palermo, 1885.

Fantoni, M. 'Il "perfetto capitano": storia e mitografia', in M. Fantoni (ed.), *Il 'perfetto capitano': immagini e realtà (secoli XV–XVII)* (Rome, 2001), 15–66.

Fenicia, G. *Il regno di Napoli e la difesa del Mediterraneo nell'età di Filippo II (1556–1598): Organizzazione e finanziamento*. Bari, 2003.

Fernández-Armesto, F. 'Naval Warfare after the Viking Age, *c.* 1100–1500', in M. Keen (ed.), *Medieval Warfare: A History* (Oxford, 1999), 230–52.

Fichtner, P. *The Habsburg Monarchy, 1490–1848*. Basingstoke, 2003.

Fiedler, S. *Kriegswesen und Kriegführung im Zeitalter der Landsknechte*. Koblenz, 1985.

Finkel, C. *The Administration of Warfare: The Ottoman Military Campaigns in Hungary, 1593–1606*. Vienna, 1988.

'French Mercenaries in the Habsburg–Ottoman War of 1593–1606: The Desertion of the Papa Garrison to the Ottomans in 1600', *Bulletin of the School of Oriental and African Studies, University of London* **55** (1992), 451–71.

Osman's Dream: The History of the Ottoman Empire 1300–1923. London and New York, 2005.

Finlay, R. 'The Immortal Republic: The Myth of Venice during the Italian Wars (1494–1530)', *SCJ* 30 (1999), 931–944.

Fiorani, F. *The Marvel of Maps: Art, Cartography and Politics in Renaissance Italy*. New Haven, CT, and London, 2005.

Fischer, W. (ed.). *Handbuch der europäischen Wirtschafts- und Sozialgeschichte, III: Europäische Wirtschafts- und Sozialgeschichte vom ausgehenden Mittelalter bis zur Mitte des 17. Jhs*, ed. H. Kellenbenz. Stuttgart, 1986.

Fischer-Galati, S.A. *Ottoman Imperialism and German Protestantism 1521–1555*, Harvard Historical Monographs 43. Cambridge, MA, 1959.

Fissel, M.C. *English Warfare, 1511–1642*. London and New York, 2001.

Fleischer C. 'The Lawgiver as Messiah: The Making of the Imperial Image in the Reign of Süleyman', in G. Veinstein (ed.), *Soliman le Magnifique et son temps* (Paris, 1992), 159–77.

Fodor, P. 'Ottoman Policy towards Hungary, 1520–1541', *AoH* **45** (1991), 271–345.

'The Simburg and the Dragon: The Ottoman Empire and Hungary (1390–1533)', in Zombori (ed.), *Fight against the Turk*, 9–36.

Válallkozásra kényszerítve: Az oszmán pénzügyigazgatás és hatalmi elit változásai a 16–17. század fordulóján. Budapest, 2006.

Forssberg, A.M. *Att hålla folket på gott humör: Informationsspridning, krigspropaganda och mobilisering i Sverige, 1655–1680.* Stockholm, 2005.

Freedman, L. 'Britain and the Revolution in Military Affairs', in Dorman, Smith and Uttley (eds.), *Changing Face of Military Power*, 111–28.

Freely, J. *Jem Sultan: The Adventures of a Captive Turkish Prince in Renaissance Europe.* London, 2004.

Friedman, Y. *Encounter between Enemies: Captivity and Ransom in the Latin Kingdom of Jerusalem*, Cultures, Beliefs and Traditions, Medieval and Early Modern Periods 10. Leiden and Boston, 2002.

Friel, I. *The Good Ship: Ships, Shipbuilding and Technology in England, 1200–1520.* London, 1995.

Fritze, K., and G. Krause, *Seekriege der Hanse.* Berlin, 1989.

Frost, R.I. *The Northern Wars, 1558–1721.* Harlow, 2000.

Galasso, G. *Il regno di Napoli: Il Mezziogorno spagnolo (1494–1622)*, Storia d'Italia 15:2. Turin, 2005.

Gallagher, P., and D.W. Cruickshank (eds.). *God's Obvious Design: Papers from the Spanish Armada Symposium, Sligo, 1988.* London, 1990.

Gambi, L., and A. Pinelli (eds.). *La galleria delle carte geografiche in Vaticano*, 3 vols. Rome, 1994.

García Hernán, E., and D. Maffi (eds.). *Guerra y sociedad en la monarquía hispánica: Política, estrategia y cultura en la Europa moderna (1500–1700)*, 2 vols. Madrid, 2006.

Gardiner, R., and J. Morrison (eds.). *The Age of the Galley: Mediterranean Oared Vessels since Pre-Classical Times.* London, 2004.

Gardiner, R., and R.W. Unger (eds.). *Cogs, Caravels and Galleons: The Sailing Ship 1000–1650.* Edison, NJ, 2000.

Gaunt, P. *The English Civil Wars 1642–1651.* Botley and New York, 2003.

Gecsényi, L. 'Ungarische Städte im Vorfeld der Türkenabwehr Österreichs: Zur Problematik der ungarischen Städteentwicklung', in E. Springer and L. Kammerhofer (eds.), *Archiv und Forschung: Das Haus-, Hof- und Staatsarchiv in seiner Bedeutung für die Geschichte Österreichs und Europas* (Vienna, 1993), 57–77.

Gembruch, W. 'Zum Verhältnis von Staat und Heer im Zeitalter der Großen Französischen Revolution', in B. Stollberg-Rilinger and J. Kunisch (eds.), *Staatsverfassung und Heeresverfassung in der europäischen Geschichte der frühen Neuzeit* (Berlin, 1986), 377–395.

Genç, M. 'L'économie ottomane et la guerre au XVIIIe siècle', *Turcica* 27 (1995), 177–196.

Genç, M., and E. Özvar (eds.). *Osmanlı maliyesi: Kurumlar ve bütçeler*, 2 vols. Istanbul, 2006.

Genet, J.-P. 'Which State Rises?', *Historical Research* 65 (1992), 119–33.

Geőcze, I. 'Hadi tanácskozások az 1577-ik évben', *Hk* 7 (1894), Part 1, 502–37, Part 2, 647–73.

Gerola, G. 'I plastici delle fortezze venete al Museo storico navale di Venezia', *Atti dell'istituto veneto di scienze, lettere ed arti* 90:2 (1930–1), 217–21.

Gertwagen, R. 'Characteristics of Mediterranean Sea Going Ships of the 13th–15th Centuries', in Gertwagen, *Mediterraneum. Splendour of the Medieval Mediterranean, 13th-15th Centuries* (Barcelona, 2004), 543–61.

'The Contribution of Venice's Colonies to Its Naval Warfare in the Eastern Mediterranean in the Fifteenth Century', in R. Cancila (ed.), *Mediterraneo in armi (secc. XV–XVIII)*, Quaderni mediterranea 4 (Palermo, 2007), 113–78.

Geyl, P. *Christofforo Suriano: Resident van de Serenissime Republiek van Venetië in Den Haag, 1616–1623.* The Hague, 1913.

The Revolt of the Netherlands, 1555–1609. 2nd edn. London, 1958.

Giono, J. *The Battle of Pavia, 24th February 1525*, trans. A. E. Murch. London, 1965.

Glete, J. 'Amphibious Warfare in the Baltic, 1550–1700', in Trim and Fissel (eds.), *Amphibious Warfare*, 123–147.

'Local Elites and Complex Organizations: Interaction, Innovations and the Emergence of the Early Modern Fiscal-Military States', unpublished conference paper, *War and the Golden Age: The Netherlands in Comparative Perspective, c. 1550–1700*, Rijswijk, 2005.

(ed.). *Naval History, 1500–1680.* Aldershot, 2005.

'Naval Power and Control of the Sea in the Baltic in the Sixteenth Century', in Hattendorf and Unger (eds.), *War at Sea*, 217–32.

Navies and Nations: Warships, Navies and State Building in Europe and America, 1500–1860, Acta universitatis stockholmiensis/Stockholm Studies in History 48, 2 vols. Stockholm, 1993.

War and the State in Early Modern Europe: Spain, the Dutch Republic and Sweden as Fiscal-Military States, 1500–1660. London, 2002.

Warfare at Sea, 1500–1650: Maritime Conflicts and the Transformation of Europe. London and New York, 2000.

Godwin, G. N. *The Civil War in Hampshire, 1642–45, and the story of Basing House.* London, 1882.

González de León, F. 'Spanish Military Power and the Military Revolution', in G. Mortimer (ed.), *Early Modern Military History, 1450–1815* (Basingstoke, 2004), 25–42.

Goodman, A. *The Wars of the Roses: Military Activity and English Society, 1452–97.* London: Routledge, 1981.

Goodman, D. C. *Power and Penury: Government, Technology and Science in Philip II's Spain.* Cambridge, 1988.

Spanish Naval Power, 1589–1665: Reconstruction and Defeat. Cambridge, 1997.

Gordon, B. *The Swiss Reformation.* Manchester, 2002.

Goring, J. 'Social change and military decline in mid-Tudor England', *History* 60 (1975), 185–97.

Göse, F. 'Zum Verhältnis von landadliger Sozialisation zu adliger Militärkarriere: Das Beispiel Preußen und Österreich im ausgehenden 17. und 18. Jahrhundert', *Mitteilungen des Instituts für Österreichische Geschichtsforschung* 109 (2000), 118–53.

Grancsay, S. 'Just How Good Was Armor?', *True* (April 1954).

Griffiths, R. A. 'Local Rivalries and National Politics: The Percies, the Nevilles and the Duke of Exeter, 1452–1454', in Griffiths, *King and Country: England and Wales in the Fifteenth Century* (London, 1991), 322–64.

Griswold, W.J. *The Great Anatolian Rebellion, 1000–1020/1591–1611*. Berlin, 1983.

Grummitt, D. *The Calais Garrison 1436–1558: War and Military Service in England, 1436–1558*. Woodbridge, 2008.

'The Defence of Calais and the Development of Gunpowder Weaponry in England in the Late Fifteenth Century', *War in History* 7 (2000), 253–72.

Guddat, M. *Grenadiere – Musketiere – Füseliere. Die Infanterie Friedrichs des Großen*. Herford, 1986.

Guenée, B. *States and Rulers in Later Medieval Europe*. Oxford, 1985.

Guilmartin, J.F. *Galleons and Galleys*. London, 2002.

Gunpowder and Galleys: Changing Technology and Mediterranean Warfare at Sea in the Sixteenth Century. 2nd edn. London, 2003.

Gunpowder and Galleys: Changing Technology and War at Sea in the Sixteenth Century. New York and Cambridge, 1974.

'Guns and Gunnery', in R. Gardiner (ed.), *Cogs, Caravels and Galleons*, 139–50.

'The Military Revolution: Origins and First Tests Abroad', in Rogers (ed.), *Military Revolution Debate*, 299–333.

'The Siege of Malta (1565) and the Habsburg–Ottoman Struggle for Domination of the Mediterranean', in Trim and Fissel (eds.), *Amphibious Warfare*, 149–80.

Gunn, S., D. Grummitt, and H. Cools. 'War and the State in Early Modern Europe: Widening the Debate', *War in History* 15 (2008), 371–88.

War, State, and Society in England and the Netherlands, 1477–1559. Oxford, 2007.

Guthrie, C., and M. Quinlan. *Just War: The Just War Tradition in Modern Warfare*. London, 2007.

Guy, A.J. *Oeconomy and Discipline: Officership and Administration in the British Army 1714–63*. Manchester, 1985.

Hagen, W. *Ordinary Prussians: Brandenburg Junkers and Villagers 1500–1800*. Cambridge, 2002.

Hahlweg, W. *Die Heeresreform der Oranier und die Antike: Studien zur Geschichte des Kriegswesens der Niederlande, Deutschlands, Frankreichs, Englands, Italiens, Spaniens und der Schweiz vom Jahre 1589 bis zum Dreißigjährigen Kriege*. Berlin, 1941.

Haigh, C.A. *English Reformations: Religion, Politics and Society under the Tudors*. Oxford, 1993.

Hale, J.R. 'The Early Development of the Bastion, 1440–1534', in J.R. Hale, R. Highfield, and B. Smalley (eds.), *Europe in the Late Middle Ages* (London, 1965), 466–94.

Renaissance War Studies. London, 1983.

War and Society in Renaissance Europe 1450–1620. London, 1985.

Hall, B. *Weapons and Warfare in Renaissance Europe*. Baltimore, 1997.

Hamilton, E.J. 'Imports of American Gold and Silver into Spain, 1503–1660', *Quarterly Journal of Economy* 43 (1929), 436–72.

Hanlon, G. *The Twilight of a Military Tradition: Italian Aristocrats and European Conflicts, 1560–1800*. London, 1998.

Hanson, V.D. *Carnage and Culture: Landmark Battles in the Rise of Western Power*. New York, 2001.

Harari, Y. N. *Special Operations in the Age of Chivalry, 1100–1550*. Woodbridge, 2007.

The Ultimate Experience: Battlefield Revelations and the Making of Modern Culture, 1450–2000. Basingstoke, 2008.

Harding, R. *The Evolution of the Sailing Navy, 1509–1815*. New York, 1995.

'Naval Warfare 1453–1815', in Black (ed.), *European Warfare 1453–1815*, 96–117, 258–61.

Harding, R. R. *Anatomy of a Power Elite: The Provincial Governors of Early Modern France*. New Haven, CT and London, 1978.

Hare, K. G. 'Apparitions and War in Anglo-Saxon England', in Kagay and Villalon (eds.), *Circle of War*, 76–86.

Hattendorf, J. B., and R. W. Unger (eds.). *War at Sea in the Middle Ages and the Renaissance*. Woodbridge and Rochester, NY, 2003.

Head, T., and R. Landes (eds.). *The Peace of God: Social Violence and Religious Response in France around the Year 1000*. London, 1992.

Headley, J. M. 'The Conflict between Nobles and Magistrates in Franche-Comté, 1508–18', *Journal of Medieval and Renaissance Studies* **9** (1979), 49–80.

Heckel, M. 'Die Krise der Religionsverfassung des Reiches und die Anfänge des Dreißigjährigen Krieges', in Heckel, *Gesammelte Schriften: Staat, Kirche, Recht, Geschichte*, ed. K. Schlaich, 2 vols. (Tübingen, 1989), II, 970–98.

Hegyi, K. *A török hódoltság várai és várkatonái*, 3 vols. Budapest, 2007.

Held, J. 'The Defense of Belgrade in 1456: A Discussion of Controversial Issues', in S. B. Vardy, and A. J. Vardy (eds.), *Society in Change: Studies in Honor of Béla K. Király*, East European Monographs 132 (New York, 1983), 25–37.

Henderson, N. *Prince Eugene of Savoy*. London, 1964.

Henneman, J. B. 'France in the Middle Ages', in Bonney (ed.), *Fiscal State*, 101–22.

Hess, A. C. 'The Evolution of the Ottoman Seaborne Empire in the Age of the Oceanic Discoveries, 1453–1525', *AHR* **75** (1970), 1892–1919.

'The Ottoman Conquest of Egypt (1517) and the Beginning of the Sixteenth-Century World War', *International Journal of Middle Eastern Studies* **4** (1973), 55–76.

Hill, C. *Antichrist in Seventeenth-Century England*. Newcastle-upon-Tyne and London, 1971.

The English Bible and the Seventeenth-Century Revolution. London, 1993; paperback edn, Harmondsworth, 1994.

Hillgarth, J. *The Spanish Kingdoms, 1250–1516*, 2 vols. Oxford, 1976–8.

Hintze, O. 'The Formation of States and Constitutional Development: A Study in History and Politics', in *The Historical Essays of Otto Hintze*, ed. F. Gilbert (New York, 1975), 157–77.

The Historical Essays of Otto Hintze, ed. F. Gilbert (New York, 1975).

'Military Organisation and the Organisation of the State', in *Historical Essays*, 178–215.

Hochedlinger, M. *Austria's Wars of Emergence: War, State and Society in the Habsburg Monarchy, 1683–1797*. Harlow and London, 2003.

'Der gewaffnete Doppeladler: Ständische Landesdefension, Stehendes Heer und "Staatsverdichtung" in der frühneuzeitlichen Habsburgermonarchie', in P. Mat'a and T. Winkelbauer (eds.), *Die Habsburgermonarchie 1620 bis*

1740: Leistungen und Grenzen des Absolutismusparadigmas (Stuttgart, 2006), 217–50.

Hocquet, J.-C. 'Venice and the Turks', in S. Carboni (ed.), *Venice and the Islamic World, 828–1797*, trans. D. Dusinbere (New Haven, CT, 2007), 36–51.

Höfer, E. *Das Ende des Dreißigjährigen Krieges: Strategie und Kriegsbild.* Cologne, 1997.

Holm, J. *Konstruktionen av en stormakt: Kungamakt, skattebönder och statsbildning, 1595–1640.* Stockholm, 2007.

Holmes, R. *Marlborough: England's Fragile Genius.* London and New York, 2008.

Holsti, K. J. *Peace and War: Armed Conflicts and International Order 1648–1989,* Studies in International Relations 14. Cambridge, 1991.

Holt, M. P. *The French Wars of Religion 1562–1629.* Cambridge, 1995.

Hook, J. 'Fortifications and the End of the Sienese State', *History* **62** (1977), 372–87.

The Sack of Rome, 1527. London, 1972.

Hooper, N., and M. Bennett. *The Cambridge Illustrated Atlas of Warfare: The Middle Ages.* Cambridge and New York, 1996.

Housley, N. (ed.). *Crusading in the Fifteenth Century: Message and Impact.* Basingstoke and New York, 2004.

'Giovanni da Capistrano and the Crusade of 1456', in Housley (ed.), *Crusading in the Fifteenth Century,* 94–115.

Religious Warfare in Europe 1400–1536. Oxford, 2002.

Howard, M. *War in European History.* Oxford, 1976.

Howard, M., G. J. Andreopoulos, and M. R. Schulman (eds.). *The Laws of War: Constraints on Warfare in the Western World.* New Haven, CT and London, 1994.

Hutchinson, G. *Medieval Ships and Shipping.* London and Washington, 1994.

Hüther, M. 'Der Dreißigjährige Krieg als fiskalisches Problem: Lösungsversuche und ihre Konsequenzen', *Scripta Mercaturae* **21** (1987), 52–81.

Ihse, C. *Präst, stånd och stat: Kung och kyrka i förhandling.* Stockholm, 2005.

Imber, C. *The Ottoman Empire, 1300–1650: The Structure of Power.* Basingstoke, 2002.

İnalcık, H. 'The Crusade of Varna', in K. M. Setton (gen. ed.), *A History of the Crusades,* 8 vols. (Madison, WI, 1855–89), VI: *The Impact of the Crusades on Europe,* ed. H. W. Hazard and N. P. Zacour.

'Military and Fiscal Transformation in the Ottoman Empire', *Archivum Ottomanicum* **6** (1980), 283–37.

The Ottoman Empire: The Classical Age, 1300–1600, trans. N. Itzkowitz and C. Imber. New York, 1973.

'The Socio-Political Effects of the Diffusion of Fire-Arms in the Middle East', in V. J. Parry and M. E. Yapp (eds.), *War, Technology and Society in the Middle East* (London, 1975), 195–217.

İnalcık, H., and D. Quataert (eds.). *An Economic and Social History of the Ottoman Empire, 1300–1914.* Cambridge, 1994.

Inglis-Jones, J. *The Grand Condé in Exile: Power Politics in France, Spain and the Spanish Netherlands,* unpublished D.Phil. thesis, Oxford, 1994.

Ingrao, C. W. *The Hessian Mercenary State: Ideas, Institutions and Reforms under Frederick II 1760–1785.* Cambridge, 1987.

İpşirli, M. 'Hasan Kâfî el-Akhisarî ve Devlet Düzenine ait Eseri Usûlü'l-hikem fi Nizâmi'l-âlem', *Tarih Enstitüsü Dergisi* **10**–11 (1979–80), 239–78.

Israel, J. 'The Courts of the House of Orange, *c.* 1580–1795', in J. Adamson (ed.), *The Princely Courts of Europe* (London, 1999), 119–39.

The Dutch Republic: Its Rise, Greatness, and Fall, 1477–1806. Oxford, 1995.

James, A. *The Navy and Government in Early Modern France, 1572–1661.* Woodbridge, 2004.

Jardine, L. *The Awful End of Prince William the Silent: The First Assassination of a Head of State with a Handgun.* London, 2005.

Jendorff, A., and S. Krieb. 'Adel im Konflikt: Beobachtungen zu den Austragungsformen der Fehde im Spätmittelalter', *Zeitschrift für historische forschung* **30** (2003), 179–206

Jensen, De L. 'The Ottoman Turks in Sixteenth-Century French Diplomacy', *SCJ* **16** (1985), 451–70.

Jespersen, L. *A Revolution from Above? The Power State of 16th and 17th Century Scandinavia.* Odense, 2000.

Jones, A. *The Art of War in the Western World.* Urbana, IL, 1987.

Jones, C. *The Great Nation: France from Louis XIV to Napoleon.* New York, 2002.

Jones, M. K. 'Somerset, York and the Wars of the Roses', *EHR* **104** (1989), 285–307.

Jones, W. R. 'The English church and propaganda during the Hundred Years War', *Journal of British Studies* **19** (1979), 18–30.

Jong, M. de. '*Staat van oorlog': Wapenbedrijf en militaire hervorming in de Republiek der Verenigde Nederlanden, 1585–1621.* Hilversum, 2005.

Jongkees, A. G. 'Armement et action d'une flotte de guerre: la contribution des comtés maritimes à l'armée générale des pays de par-deçà en 1477', *Publications du Centre européen d'études bourguignonnes* **26** (1986), 71–87.

Jouanna, A. 'La noblesse et les valeurs guerrières au XVIe siècle', in G.-A. Pérousse, A. Thierry, and A Tournon (eds.), *L'homme de guerre au XVIe siècle* (Saint-Etienne, 1992), 205–17.

Kaak, H. 'Soldaten aus dem Dorf, Soldaten im Dorf, Soldaten gegen das Dorf: Militär in den Augen der brandenburgischen Landbevölkerung, 1725–1780', in S. Kroll and K. Krüger (eds.), *Militär und ländliche Gesellschaft in der frühen Neuzeit* (Münster, 2000), 297–326.

Kagay, D. J., and L. J. A. Villalon (eds.). *The Circle of War in the Middle Ages: Essays on Medieval Military and Naval History.* Woodbridge, 1999.

Kaiser, M. *Politik und Kriegführung: Maximilian von Bayern, Tilly und die Katholische Liga im Dreißigjährigen Krieg.* Münster, 1999.

Káldy-Nagy, G. 'The First Centuries of the Ottoman Military Organization,' *AoH* **31** (1977), 147–62.

Kalaus, P. 'Schiessversuche mit historischen Feuerwaffen', in *Von alten Handfeuerwaffen.* Graz, 1989.

Kalous, A. 'Elfeledett források a mohácsi csatáról: Antonio Burgio pápai nuncius jelentései és azok hadtörténeti jelentősége' ['Forgotten Sources on the

Battle of Mohács: The Reports of Papal Legate Antonio Burgio and Their Military Historical Significance'], *Hk* **120** (2007), 603–22.

Kamen, H. *Philip of Spain*. New Haven: Yale University Press, 1997.

Kampmann, C. *Reichsrebellion und Kaiserliche Acht: Politische Strafjustiz im Dreißigjährigen Krieg und das Verfahren gegen Wallenstein 1634*. Münster, 1992.

Kapser, C. *Die bayerische Kriegsorganisation in der zweiten Hälfte des Dreißigjährigen Krieges, 1635–1648/49*. Münster, 1997.

Karger, B., H. Sudhues, B. P. Kneubuehl, and B. Brinkmann. 'Experimental Arrow Wounds: Ballistics and Traumatology', *Journal of Trauma* **45** (1998), 495–501.

Keen, M. *Chivalry*. Oxford, 1984.

The Laws of War. London, 1975.

'Treason Trials under the Law of Arms', *TRHS*, 5th series, **12** (1962), 85–102.

Kelenik, J. 'The Military Revolution in Hungary,' in G. Dávid and P. Fodor (eds.), *Ottomans, Hungarians, and Habsburgs in Central Europe: The Military Confines in the Era of Ottoman Conquest* (Leiden and Boston, 2000), 117–59.

Kelsey, H. *Sir John Hawkins: Queen Elizabeth's Slave Trader*. New Haven and London, 2003.

Kennedy, P. 'Grand Strategy in War and Peace: Toward a Broader Definition', in *Grand Strategies in War and Peace* (New Haven and London, 1991), 1–10.

The Rise and Fall of the Great Powers: Economic Change and Military Conflict from 1500 to 2000. London, 1998.

Kennett, L. *The French Armies in the Seven Years' War: A Study in Military Organization and Administration*. Durham, NC, 1967.

Kenyeres, I. 'Die Einkünfte und Reformen der Finanzverwaltung Ferdinands I. in Ungarn', in M. Fuchs, T. Oborni, and G. Újváry (eds.), *Kaiser Ferdinand I: Ein mitteleuropäischer Herrscher* (Münster, 2005), 111–46.

'Die Finanzen des Königreichs Ungarn in der zweiten Hälfte des 16. Jahrhunderts', in Edelmayer, Lanzinner, and Rauscher (eds.), *Finanzen und Herrschaft*, 84–122.

Kerkhoff, A. H. M. *Over de geneeskundige verzorging in het Staatse leger*. Nijmegen, 1976.

Kiernan, V. G. 'Foreign Mercenaries and Absolute Monarchy', *Past and Present* **11** (April 1957), 66–86.

Kingsford, C. L. Review of N. Jorga, *Philippe de Mézières, 1327–1405, et la Croisade au XIVe siècle* (Paris, 1896), in *EHR* 13 (1898), 159–61.

Király, B., and L. Veszprémy (eds.). *A Millennium of Hungarian Military History*, trans. E. Arató, East European Monographs 621. Boulder, CO, 2002.

Kirk, T. A. *Genoa and the Sea: Policy and Power in an Early Modern Maritime Republic, 1559–1684*. Baltimore, 2005.

Klein, S. *Patriots republikanisme. Politieke cultuur in Nederland (1766–1787)*. Amsterdam, 1995.

Kloosterhuis, J. 'Zwischen Aufruhr und Akzeptanz: Zur Ausformung und Einbettung des Kantonssytems in den Wirtschafts- und Sozialstrukturen des preußischen Westfalen', in B.R. Kroener and R. Pröve (eds.), *Krieg und Frieden, Militär und Gesellschaft in der frühen Neuzeit* (Paderborn, 1996), 167–90.

Knecht, R.J. *The French Civil Wars, 1562–1598.* Harlow, 2000.

The French Religious Wars, 1562–1598. Botley and New York, 2002.

Renaissance Warrior and Patron: The Reign of Francis I. Cambridge, 1994.

Knevel, P. *Burgers in het geweer: De schutterijen in Holland, 1550–1700.* Hilversum, 1994.

Knighton, C.S., and D. Loades (eds.). *The Anthony Roll of Henry VIII's Navy: Pepys Library 2991 and British Library Additional MS 22047 with Related Documents,* Naval Records Society, Occasional Publications 2, Aldershot and Cambridge, 2000.

Knox, M., and Murray, W. (eds.). *The Dynamics of Military Revolution, 1300–2050.* Cambridge and New York, 2001.

Knox, M., and Murray, W. 'Thinking about revolutions in warfare', in Knox and Murray (eds.), *Dynamics of Military Revolution,* 1–14.

Kokken, H. *Steden en staten: Dagvaarten van steden en staten van Holland onder Maria van Bourgondië en het eerste regentschap van Maximiliaan van Oostenrijk (1477–1494).* The Hague, 1991.

Kolodziejczyk, D. 'Inner Lake or Frontier? The Ottoman Black Sea in the Sixteenth and Seventeenth Centuries', in F. Bilici, I. Candea, and A. Popescu (eds.), *Enjeux politiques, économoques et militaires en Mer Noire (XIVe–XXIe siècles: Etudes à la mémoire de Mahail Guboglu)* (Braïla, 2007), 125–39.

Konstam, A. *Pavia, 1525: The Climax of the Italian Wars.* London, 1996.

Spanish Galleon, 1530–1690. London, 2004.

Konstam, R.A. '16th Century Naval Tactics and Gunnery', *International Journal of Nautical Archaeology and Underwater Exploration* 17 (1988), 17–23.

Konze, F. *Die Stärke, Zusammensetzung und Verteilung der Wallensteinischen Armee während des Jahres 1633: Ein Beitrag zur Heeresgeschichte des 30 Jährigen Krieges,* dissertation, Frankfurt-am-Main, 1906.

Körner, M. 'Expenditure', in Bonney (ed.), *Economic Systems and State Finance,* 393–422.

Kovács, P.E. *Mattia Corvino.* Coscenza, 2000.

Kowaleski, M. 'Warfare, Shipping, and Crown Patronage: The Economic Impact of the Hundred Years War on the English Port Towns', in L. Armstrong, I. Elbl, and M.M. Elbl (eds.), *Money, Markets and Trade in Late Medieval Europe: Essays in Honour of John H. A. Munro* (Leiden and Boston, 2007), 233–54.

Kroener, B. 'Soldat oder Soldateska? Programmatischer Aufriß einer Sozialgeschichte militärischer Unterschichten in der ersten Hälfte des 17. Jahrhunderts', in M. Messerschmidt (ed.), *Militärgeschichte: Probleme, Thesen, Wege* (Stuttgart, 1982), 100–23.

Kroener, B.R., and R. Pröve (eds.). *Krieg und Frieden: Militär und Gesellschaft in der frühen Neuzeit.* Paderborn, 1996.

Kroll, S. 'Aushandeln von Herrschaft am Beispiel der Landrekrutenstellung in Kursachsen im 18. Jahrhundert', in M. Meumann and R. Pröve (eds.),

Herrschaft in der Frühen Neuzei:. Umrisse eines dynamisch-kommunikativen Prozesses (Münster, 2004), 161–94.

Kroll, S., and K. Krüger (eds.). *Militär und ländliche Gesellschaft in der frühen Neuzeit.* Münster, 2000.

Krüger, K. 'Dänische und schwedische Kriegsfinanzierung im Dreissigjährigen Krieg bis 1635', in K. Repgen (ed.), *Krieg und Politik, 1618–1648: Europäische Probleme und Perspektiven.* Munich: Oldenbourg, 1988.

Kubinyi, A. 'The Battle of Szávaszentdemeter-Nagyolaszi (1523). Ottoman Advance and Hungarian Defence on the Eve of Mohacs', in Dávid and Fodor (eds.), *Ottomans, Hungarians and Habsburgs*, 71–116.

'Hungary's Power Factions and the Turkish Threat in the Jagellonian Period, 1490–1526', in Zombori (ed.), *Fight against the Turk*, 130–45.

Matthias Rex. Budapest, 2008.

'The Road to Defeat: Hungarian Politics and Defense in the Jagellonian Period', in Bak and Király (eds.), *From Hunyadi to Rákóczi*, 159–78.

Kunisch, J. *Der kleine Krieg: Studien zum Heerwesen des Absolutismus.* Wiesbaden 1973

Fürst – Gesellschaft – Krieg. Studien zur bellizistischen Disposition des absoluten Fürstenstaates. Cologne, 1992.

'Wallenstein als Kriegsunternehmer', in U. Schultz, *Mit dem Zehnten fing es an: Eine Kulturgeschichte der Steuer.* Munich, 1986.

Kunt, M., and C. Woodhead (eds.). *Süleyman the Magnificent and His Age: The Ottoman Empire in the Early Modern World.* London, 1995.

Labande-Mailfert, Y. *Charles VIII et son milieu: La jeunesse au pouvoir.* Paris, 1975.

Lake, P. 'The Significance of the Elizabethan Identification of the Pope as Antichrist', *Journal of Ecclesiastical History* 31 (1980), 161–7.

Lane, F. C. *Profits from Power: Readings in Protection Rent and Violence-Controlling Enterprises.* Albany, 1979.

Venice: A Maritime Republic. Baltimore and London, 1973.

Venice and History: The Collected Papers of Frederic C. Lane. Baltimore, 1966.

Lardin, P. *Entre tradition et modernité: Les premières années du Havre (1517–1541).* Rouen, 2003.

Lassalmonie, J. F. 'L'abbé Le Grand et le compte du trésorier des guerres pour 1464: Les compagnies d'ordonnance à la veille du Bien public', *Journal des savants* (2001).

Law, J. E. 'The Significance of Citadels in North Italian Cities in the Late Middle Ages and Renaissance', in M. Boone and P. Stabel (eds.), *Shaping Urban Identity in Late Medieval Europe* (Leuven, 2000), 169–81.

Lehmann, L. T. *De galeien: Een bijdrage aan de kennis der zeegeschiedenis.* Amsterdam, 1987.

De queeste naar de multireme: Theorieën uit Renaissance en Barok over antieke oorlogschepen. Amsterdam, 1995.

Lenman, B. *England's Colonial Wars 1550–1688: Conflict, Empire and National Identity.* Harlow, 2001.

Lesure, M. *Lépante: La crise de l'Empire ottomane.* Paris, 1972.

Lewis, P. S. 'War, Propaganda and Historiography in Fifteenth-Century France', *TRHS*, 5th series, 15 (1965), 1–21.

Liddell Hart, B. H. *Strategy*. 2nd edn. New York, 1991.

Loades, D. *The Tudor Navy. An Administrative, Political and Military History*. Aldershot, 1992.

Lockhart, P. D. *Frederik II and the Protestant Cause: Denmark in the Wars of Religion, 1559–1596*. Leiden and Boston, 2004.

Lomax, D. W. *The Reconquest of Spain*. London: Longman, 1978.

Lombarès, M. de. 'Castillon (17 juillet 1453), dernière bataille de la guerre de Cent Ans, première victoire de l'artillerie', *Revue historique des armées* (1976), 7–31.

Lorentzen, T. *Die Schwedische Armee im Dreißigjährigen Kriege und ihre Abdankung*. Leipzig, 1894.

Love, R. S. ' "All the King's Horsemen": The Equestrian Army of Henri IV, 1585–1598', *SCJ* 22 (1991), 511–33.

Löwe, V. *Die Organisation und Verwaltung der Wallensteinischen Heere*, dissertation, Freiburg, 1895.

Lund, E. *War for the Every Day: Generals, Knowledge, and Warfare in Early Modern Europe, 1680–1740*. Westport, CT and London, 1999.

Luttwak, E. N. *The Grand Strategy of the Roman Empire: From the First Century AD to the Third*. Baltimore, 1976.

Lynch, M. 'James VI and the "Highland Problem"', in J. Goodare and M. Lynch (eds.), *The Reign of James VI* (East Linton, 2000), 208–27.

Lynn, J. A. 'The Embattled Future of Academic Military History', *JMH* **61** (1997), 777–89.

Giant of the Grand siècle: The French Army, 1610–1715. Cambridge, 1997.

'Recalculating French Army Growth in the *Grand siècle*, 1610–1715', in Rogers (ed.), *Military Revolution Debate*, 117–148.

'Tactical Evolution in the French Army, 1560–1660', *French Historical Studies* **14** (1985), 176–91.

The Wars of Louis XIV, 1667–1714. London and New York, 1999.

McConachy, B. 'The Roots of Artillery Doctrine: Napoleonic Artillery Tactics Reconsidered', *JMH* **65** (July 2001), 617–40.

McCormack, J. *One Million Mercenaries: Swiss Soldiers in the Armies of the World*. London, 1993.

McCullough, R. L. *Coercion, Conversion, and Counterinsurgency in Louis XIV's France*. Leiden and Boston, 2007.

Macdougall, N. ' "The greatiest scheip that ewer saillit in Ingland or France": James IV's *Great Michael*', in N. MacDougall (ed.), *Scotland and War AD 79–1918* (Edinburgh, 1991), 36–60.

McKay, D. *Prince Eugene of Savoy*. London, 1977.

McKee, A. *King Henry VIII's Mary Rose*. New York, 1974.

McLay, K. A. J. 'The Blessed Trinity: The Army, the Navy and Providence in the Conduct of Warfare, 1688–1713', in D. Onnekink (ed.), *War and Religion after Westphalia, 1648–1713* (Aldershot, 2009), 103–20.

McNeill, W. H. *The Pursuit of Power: Technology, Armed Force, and Society since AD 1000*. Oxford, 1982.

Maffi, D. *Il baluardo della corona: Guerra, esercito, finanze e società nella Lombardia seicentesca (1630–1660)*. Florence, 2007.

Magocsi, P. R. *Historical Atlas of Central Europe*. Rev. edn. Washington, 2002.

Majer, H.J. '17. yüzyılın sonlarında Avusturya ve Osmanlı ordularının seferl-erdeki lojıstik sorunları', *Journal of Ottoman Studies* **2** (1981), 185–194.

Mallett, M. *The Borgias: The Rise and Fall of a Renaissance Dynasty*. London, 1981.

Mercenaries and Their Masters: Warfare in Renaissance Italy. London and Totowa, NJ, 1974.

Mallett, M.E., and J.R. Hale. *The Military Organisation of a Renaissance State: Venice, c. 1400 to 1617*. Cambridge, 1984.

Mancini, D. *The Usurpation of Richard the Third*, trans. C.A.J. Armstrong. London, 1989.

Mann, G. *Wallenstein: Sein Leben erzählt*. 2nd edn. Frankfurt-am-Main, 1971.

Mann, M. *The Sources of Social Power*, 2 vols. Cambridge, 1986.

Manz, B.F. *Power, Politics and Religion in Timurid Iran*. Cambridge, 2007.

The Rise and Rule of Tamerlane. Cambridge, 1989.

Marosi, E. *XVI. századi váraink (521–1606)*. Budapest and Miskolc, 1991.

Marozzi, J. *Tamerlane: Sword of Islam, Conqueror of the World*. London, 2004.

Martin C., and G. Parker, *The Spanish Armada*. London, 1988.

Martin, R. 'The Army of Louis XIV', in P. Sonnino (ed.), *The Reign of Louis XIV* (Totowa, NJ and London, 1991), 111–26.

Mat'a, P., and T. Winkelbauer (eds.). *Die Habsburgermonarchie 1620 bis 1740: Leistungen und Grenzen des Absolutismusparadigmas*. Stuttgart, 2006.

Matthew, D. *Atlas of Medieval Europe*. London, 1983.

Mattingly, G. *The Defeat of the Spanish Armada*. London, 1959.

'The First Resident Embassies: Mediaeval Italian Origins of Modern Diplomacy', *Speculum* **12** (1937), 423–39.

Renaissance Diplomacy. Harmondsworth, 1965.

Mears, J.A. 'The Thirty Years War, the "General Crisis" and the Origins of a Standing Professional Army in the Habsburg Monarchy', *Central European History* **21** (1988), 122–41.

Melville-Jones, J.R. (ed.). *The Siege of Constantinople 1453*. Amsterdam, 1972.

Meumann, M., and R. Pröve. 'Die Faszination des Staates und die histor-ische Praxis: Zur Beschreibung von Herrschaftsbeziehungen jenseits tel-eologischer und dualistischer Begriffsbildungen', in Meumann and Pröve (eds.), *Herrschaft in der Frühen Neuzeit*, 11–50.

(eds.). *Herrschaft in der Frühen Neuzeit: Umrisse eines dynamisch-kommunika-tiven Prozesses*. Münster, 2004.

Meumann, M., and J. Rogge (eds.). *Die Besetzte res publica: Zum Verhältnis von ziviler Obrigkeit und militärischer Herrschaft in besetzten Gebieten vom Spätmittelalter bis zum 18. Jahrhundert*. Münster, 2006.

Modelski, G., and W.R. Thompson. *Seapower in Global Politics, 1494–1993*. London, 1988.

Mollat du Jourdin, M. ' "Etre roi sur la mer": Naissance d'une ambition', in Contamine (ed.), *Histoire militaire*, I : *Des origines à 1715*, 279–301.

Möller, H.-M. *Das Regiment der Landsknechte: Untersuchungen zu Verfassung, Recht und Selbstverständnis in deutschen Söldnerheeren des 16. Jahrhunderts*. Wiesbaden, 1976.

Mork, G.R. 'Flint and Steel: A Study in Military Technology and Tactics in 17th-Century Europe', *Smithsonian Journal of History* **2** (1967).

Morrill, J. *The Nature of the English Revolution*. London and New York, 1993.

Morris, C. 'Propaganda for War: The Dissemination of the Crusading Ideal in the Twelfth Century', in W. J. Sheils (ed.), *The Church in War*, Studies in Church History 20 (Oxford, 1983), 79–101.

Motley, J. L. *The History of the United Netherlands: From the Death of William the Silent to the Twelve Years' Truce, 1609*. New York: Harper and Brothers, 1876.

Mott, L. V. 'Iberian Naval Power, 1000–1650', in Hattendorf and Unger, *War at Sea*, 105–118.

Mueller, C. *Fragmenta historicorum graecorum*, 5 vols., I. Paris, 1851.

Muir, E. *Mad Blood Stirring: Vendetta and Factions in Friuli during the Renaissance*. Baltimore, 1993.

Tactics and the Experience of Battle in the Age of Napoleon. New Haven and London, 1998.

Murdoch, S. 'The House of Stuart and the Scottish Professional Soldier 1618–40: A Conflict of Nationality and Identities', in B. Taithe and T. Thornton (eds.), *War: Identities in Conflict 1300–2000* (Stroud, 1998), 37–56.

(ed.) *Scotland and the Thirty Years' War 1618–1648*. Leiden, 2001.

Murdock, G. *Beyond Calvin: The Intellectual, Political and Cultural World of Europe's Reformed Churches, c. 1540–1620*. Basingstoke and New York, 2004.

Murphey, R. *Ottoman Warfare 1500–1700*. London and New Brunswick, NJ, 1999.

'Yeni-Çeri', in *Encyclopaedia of Islam*, XI.

Muto, G. 'The Spanish System: Centre and Periphery', in Bonney (ed.), *Economic Systems and State Finance*, 231–59.

Nadolski, A. *Uzbrojenie w Polsce sredniowiecznej 1350–1450*. Lódz, 1990.

Nagy, L. *Hajdúvitézek, 1591–1699*. Budapest, 1986.

"Megint fölszánt magyar világ van ..." Társadalom és hadsereg a XVII század első felének Habsburg-ellenes küzdelmeiben. Budapest, 1985.

Nef, J. U. 'War and the Rise of Industrial Civilization, 1640–1740', *Canadian Journal of Economics and Political Science* **10** (1944), 36–78.

Newitt, M. 'Portuguese Amphibious Warfare in the East in the Sixteenth Century (1500–1520)', in Trim and Fissel (eds.), *Amphibious Warfare*, 103–21.

Nicholson, H. *Medieval Warfare: Theory and Practice of War in Europe 300–1500*. Basingstoke and New York, 2004.

Nicolle, D. C. *Fornovo, 1495: France's Bloody Fighting Retreat*. London, 1999.

Nilsson, S. A. *De stora krigens tid: Om Sveriges som militärstat och bondesamhälle*. Uppsala, 1990.

Nimwegen, O. van. *'Deser landen crijchsvolck': Het Staatse leger en de militaire revoluties, 1588–1688*. Amsterdam, 2006.

'Het Staatse leger en de militaire revolutie van de vroegmoderne tijd', *Bijdragen en Mededelingen betreffende de Geschiedenis der Nederlanden* **118** (2003), 494–518.

De subsistentie van het leger: Logistiek en strategie van het Geallieerde en met name het Staatse leger tijdens de Spaanse Successieoorlog in de Nederlanden en het Heilige Roomse Rijk (1701–1712). Amsterdam, 1995.

Nisbet Bain, R. 'The Siege of Belgrade by Muhammad II, July 1–23, 1456', *EHR* 7 (1892), 235–252.

Noailles, A. M. R. A., vicomte de. *Bernhard de Saxe Weimar, 1604–1639*. Paris, 1908.

North, D. C. *Structure and Change in Economic History*. New York, 1981.

Understanding the Process of Economic Change. Princeton, 2005.

Norwich, J. J. *A History of Venice*. New York, 1989.

Nosworthy, B. *The Anatomy of Victory: Battle Tactics 1689–1763*. New York, 1990.

Nowakowska, N. 'Poland and the Crusade in the Reign of King Jan Olbracht, 1492–1501', in Housley (ed.), *Crusading in the Fifteenth Century*, 128–147.

Nurmohamed, A. 'De VOC, de admiraliteiten en hun schepen in de 17e eeuw', unpublished paper, Instituut voor Maritieme Historie, The Hague, 1999.

Oborni, T. 'Die Herrschaft Ferdinands I. in Ungarn', in M. Fuchs and A. Kohler (eds.), *Kaiser Ferdinand I: Aspekte eines Herrscherlebens* (Münster, 2003), 147–65.

O'Brien, P. K. 'Path Dependency, or Why Britain Became an Industrialised and Urbanised Economy Long before France', *Economic History Review*, n.s. **49** (1996), 213–49.

O'Brien, P. K., and P. A. Hunt. 'England, 1485–1815', in Bonney (ed.), *Fiscal State*, 53–101.

O'Callaghan, J. F. *Reconquest and Crusade in Medieval Spain*. Philadelphia, 2003.

Oestreich, G. *Antiker Geist und moderner Staat bei Justus Lipsius (1547–1606): Der Neustoizismus als politische Bewegung* (Habilitationsschrift 1954), ed. N. Mout. Göttingen, 1989.

'Justus Lipsius als Theoretiker des neuzeitlichen Machtstaates', *HZ* **181** (1956), 31–78

Neostoicism and the Early Modern State. Cambridge, 1982.

Oman, C. *A History of the Art of War in the Middle Ages*, 2 vols., II. London, 1924.

A History of the Art of War in the Sixteenth Century. London, 1987 (repr.)

Onnekink, D. (ed.). *War and Religion after Westphalia, 1648–1713*. Aldershot, 2009.

Opel, J. O. 'Deutsche Finanznoth beim Beginn des Dreißigjährigen Krieges', *HZ* **16** (1886), 213–68.

Orhonlu, C. *Osmanlı tarihine aid belgeler: telhisler (1597–1607)*. Istanbul, 1970.

Ormrod, W. M. 'England in the Middle Ages', in Bonney (ed.), *Fiscal State*, 19–52.

Political Life in Medieval England, 1300–1450. Basingstoke, 1995.

Oschmann, A. *Der Nürnberger Executionstag 1649–50: Das Ende des Dreißigjährigen Krieges in Deutschland*. Münster, 1991.

Ostapchuk, V. 'The Human Landscape of the Ottoman Black Sea in the Face of the Cossack Naval Raids,' *Oriente moderno* **81** (2001), 23–95.

Ostwald, J. *Vauban under Siege: Engineering Efficiency and Martial Vigor in the War of the Spanish Succession*. Leiden and Boston, 2007.

Oudendijk, J. K. *Een Bourgondisch ridder over den oorlog ter zee: Philips van Kleef als leermeester van Karel V*. Amsterdam, 1941.

Özvar, E. 'Osmanlı devletinin bütçe harcamaları (1509–1788),' in Genç and Özvar (eds.), *Osmanlı maliyesi: Kurumları ve bütçeler*, I, 197–238.

Pablo, J. de. 'Contribution à l'étude de l'histoire des institutions militaires huguenotes, II: L'armée huguenote entre 1562 et 1573', *Archiv für Reformationsgeschichte* **48** (1957), 192–216.

Pálffy, G. 'The Origins and Development of the Border Defence System against the Ottoman Empire in Hungary (up to the Early Eighteenth Century)', in Dávid and Fodor (eds.), *Ottomans, Hungarians and Habsburgs*, 3–70.

'Der Preis für die Verteidigung der Habsburgermonarchie. Die Kosten der Türkenabwehr in der zweiten Hälfte des 16. Jahrhunderts', in Edelmayer, Lanzinner and Rauscher (eds.), *Finanzen und Herrschaft*, 20–44.

Palmer, M.A.J. 'The "Military Revolution" Afloat: The Era of the Anglo-Dutch Wars and the Transition to Modern Warfare at Sea', *War in History* **4** (1997), 123–49.

Papke, G. *Von der Miliz zum stehenden Heer: Wehrwesen im Absolutismus*, in Militärgeschichtliches Forschungsamt (ed.), Handbuch zum deutschen Militärgeschichte, 6 vols. (Munich, 1979), I.

Papp, S. 'Hungary and the Ottoman Empire (from the Beginnings to 1540)', in Zombori (ed.), *Fight against the Turk*, 37–90.

Parker, D. *Class and State in* Ancien Régime *France: The Road to Modernity?* London, 1996.

Parker, G. *The Army of Flanders and the Spanish Road, 1567–1659*. Cambridge, 1972; revd impression, 1990.

'The Dreadnought Revolution of Tudor England', *Mariner's Mirror* **82** (1996), 269–300.

The Dutch Revolt. 2nd edn. London, 1985.

'Early Modern Europe', in Howard, Andreopoulis, and Schulman (eds.), *Laws of War*, 40–58.

Empire, War and Faith in Early Modern Europe. London, 2002. (US edn: *Success is Never Final: Empire, War and Faith in Early Modern Europe*. New York, 2002.)

The Grand Strategy of Philip II. New Haven: Yale University Press, 1998.

'The Gunpowder Revolution 1300–1500', in Parker (ed.), *The Cambridge History of Warfare* (Cambridge, 2005), 101–14.

'The "Military Revolution", 1955–2005: From Belfast to Barcelona and The Hague', *JMH* **69** (2005), 205–10.

The Military Revolution: Military Innovation and the Rise of the West, 1500–1800. Cambridge, 1988; 2nd edn, Cambridge, 1996; revd. 1999.

'Military Revolutions, Past and Present', in 'Military Revolutions: A Forum', *Historically Speaking* **4**:4 (April 2003), 2–7.

Philip II. London, 1979.

'Philip II, Maps and Power', in Parker, *Empire, War and Faith in Early Modern Europe*, 96–121.

(ed.). *The Thirty Years' War*. 2nd edn. London and New York, 1997.

'The Treaty of Lyon (1601) and the Spanish Road', in Parker, *Empire, War and Faith in Early Modern Europe*, 126–42.

The World Is Not Enough: The Imperial Vision of Philip II of Spain. Waco, TX, 2001.

Parrott, D. *Richelieu's Army: War, Government and Society in France, 1624–1642.* Cambridge, 2001.

'Strategy and Tactics in the Thirty Years' War', in Rogers (ed.), *Military Revolution Debate*, 227–52.

Parry, V.J. 'La manière de combattre,' in V.J. Parry and M.E. Yapp (eds.), *War, Technology and Society in the Middle East* (London and New York, 1975), 218–56.

Paschalidou, E. 'The Walls of Constantinople: An Obstacle to the New Power of Artillery', in *XXII. Kongress der Internationalen Kommission für Militärgeschichte* (Vienna, 1997), 172–8.

Patch, H.R. *The Goddess Fortuna in Medieval Literature.* Cambridge, MA, 1927.

Paviot, J. (ed.). *Philippe de Clèves seigneur de Ravestein: L'instruction de toutes manières de guerroyer ... sur mer. Edition critique du manuscrit français 1244 de la Bibliothèque nationale de France*, Bibliothèque de l'Ecole des hautes études: Sciences historiques et philosophiques, 333. Paris 1997.

La politique navale des ducs de Bourgogne, 1384–1482. Lille 1995.

Pearson, M.N. 'The Indian Ocean and the Portuguese in the Sixteenth Century', in L. de Albuquerque and I. Guerreiro (eds.), *Il seminário internacional de história indo-portuguesa, actas* (Lisbon, 1985), 102–17.

Pedani, M.P. 'Turkish Raids in Friuli at the End of the Fifteenth Century', in *Acta viennensia ottomanica* (Vienna, 1999), 287–91.

Pepper, S. 'Castles and Cannon in the Naples Campaign of 1494–95', in Abulafia (ed.), *The French Descent*, 263–93.

'The Face of the Siege: Fortification, Tactics and Strategy in the Early Italian Wars', in C. Shaw (ed.), *Italy and the European Powers: The Impact of War, 1500–1530* (Leiden and Boston, 2006), 33–56.

Pepper, S., and N. Adams, *Firearms and Fortifications: Military Architecture and Siege Warfare in Sixteenth-Century Siena.* Chicago, 1986.

Perjés, G. *The Fall of the Medieval Kingdom of Hungary: Mohács 1526–Buda 1541.* Boulder, CO, 1989.

Perrow, C. *Complex Organizations: A Critical Essay.* 3rd edn. New York, 1993.

Peterson, L. 'Defence, War and Finance: Christian IV and the Council of the Realm, 1596–1629', *Scandinavian Journal of History* 7 (1982), 277–313.

Petrin, S. *Der österreichische Hussitenkrieg 1420–1434*, Militärhistorische Schriftenreihe 44. Vienna, 1983.

Phillips, C.R. 'The Galleon', in Gardiner and Unger (eds.), *Cogs, Caravels and Galleons*, 98–114.

Six Galleons for the King of Spain: Imperial Defense in the Seventeenth Century. Baltimore, 1986.

Phillips, G. *The Anglo-Scots Wars 1513–50.* Woodbridge, 1999.

Phillips, J.R.S. *The Medieval Expansion of Europe.* 2nd edn. Oxford, 1998.

Pigaillem, H. *La bataille de Lépante, 1571.* Paris 2003.

Pincus, S.C.A. *Protestantism and Patriotism: Ideologies and the Making of English Foreign Policy, 1650–1668.* Cambridge, 1996.

Pitelis, C. (ed.). *The Growth of the Firm: The Legacy of Edith Penrose.* Oxford, 2002.

Pohl, J. '*Die Profiantirung der keyserlichen Armaden ahnbelangendt*': *Studien zur Versorgung der kaiserlichen Armee, 1634*–35. Vienna, 1994.

Porter, B. *War and the Rise of the State: The Military Foundations of Modern Politics.* New York, 1994.

Porter, S. *Destruction in the English Civil Wars.* Stroud, 1994.

Potter, D. 'Chivalry and Professionalism in the French Armies of the Renaissance', in D. J. B. Trim (ed.), *Chivalric Ethos*, 149–82.

'The International Mercenary Market in the Sixteenth Century: Anglo-French Competition in Germany, 1543–50', *EHR* **111** (1996), 24–58.

' "Rigueur de justice": Crime, Murder and the Law in Picardy, Fifteenth to Sixteenth centuries', *French History* **11** (1997), 265–309.

War and Government in the French Provinces: Picardy 1470–1560. Cambridge, 1993.

Potter, M. *Corps and Clienteles: Public Finance and Political Change in France, 1688–1715.* Aldershot, 2003.

Powell, E. *Kingship, Law and Society: Criminal Justice in the Reign of Henry V.* Oxford, 1989.

Pryor, J. H. *Geography, Technology, and War: Studies in the Maritime History of the Mediterranean, 649–1571.* Cambridge, 1988.

Puype, J. P. 'Victory at Nieuwpoort', in M. van der Hoeven (ed.), *Exercise of Arms: Warfare in the Netherlands, 1568–1648* (Leiden, 1997), 69–112.

Quaas, G. *Das Handwerk der Landsknechte: Waffen und Bewaffnung zwischen 1500 und 1600.* Osnabrück, 1997.

Quataert, D. *The Ottoman Empire, 1700–1922.* 2nd edn. Cambridge, 2005.

Queller, D. E. *The Office of Ambassador in the Middle Ages.* Princeton, 1967.

Racaut, L. 'Persecution or Pluralism? Propaganda and Opinion-Forming during the French Wars of Religion', in R. Bonney and D. J. B. Trim (eds.), *Persecution and Pluralism: Calvinists and Religious Minorities in Early Modern Europe, 1550–1700* (Oxford, Bern and New York, 2006), 65–87.

Rácz, I. *Hajdúk a XVII. században.* Debrecen, 1969.

Rady, M. 'Rethinking Jagiello Hungary (1490–1526)', *Central Europe* **3** (2005), 3–18.

Rapp, R. T. *Industry and Economic Decline in Seventeenth-Century Venice.* Cambridge, 1976.

Rázsó, G. 'Hungarian Strategy against the Ottomans, 1365–1526', in *XXII. Kongress der Internationalen Kommission für Militärgeschichte. Acta 22* (Vienna, 1997), 226–37.

'The Mercenary Army of King Matthias Corvinus', in Bak and Király (eds.), *From Hunyadi to Rákóczi*, 125–40.

'Military Reforms in the Fifteenth Century', in Király and Veszprémy (eds.), *Millennium of Hungarian Military History*, 54–84.

Redlich, F. 'Contributions in the Thirty Years' War', *Economic History* Review, n.s. **12** (1959–60), 247–54.

The German Military Enterpriser and his Work Force: A Study in European Economic and Social History, 2 vols., Vierteljahrschrift für Sozial- und Wirtschaftsgeschichte, Beihefte 47–48. Wiesbaden, 1964–65.

De Praede Militare. Looting and Booty, 1500–1815, Vierteljahrschrift für Sozial- und Wirtschaftsgeschichte, Beihefte 39. Wiesbaden, 1956.

Reilly, B. F. *The Contest of Christian and Muslim Spain, 1031–1157.* Oxford, 1992.

Reilly, T. *Cromwell: An Honourable Enemy.* London, 2000.

Reinhard, W. *Geschichte der Staatsgewalt: Eine vergleichende Verfassungsgeschichte Europas von den Anfängen bis zur Gegenwart.* Munich, 1999.

(ed.). *Power Elites and State Building.* Oxford, 1996.

Rink, M. *Vom 'Partheygänger' zum Partisan: Die Konzeption des kleinen Krieges in Preußen 1740–1813.* Frankfurt-am-Main, 1999.

Ritter, M. 'Das Kontributionssystem Wallensteins', *HZ* **54** (1902–3), 193–249.

Roberts, K. 'Battle Plans: The Practical Use of Battlefield Plans in the English Civil War', *Cromwelliana* (1997).

Roberts, M. *Essays in Swedish History.* London, 1967.

From Oxenstierna to Charles XII: Four Studies. Cambridge, 1991.

'Gustav Adolf and the Art of War', in Roberts, *Essays in Swedish History.*

Gustavus Adolphus, 2 vols. London, 1958.

'The Military Revolution, 1560–1660', in Roberts, *Essays in Swedish History,* 195–225; repr. in Rogers (ed.), *Military Revolution Debate,* 13–36.

Robinson, I. S. 'Gregory VII and the Soldiers of Christ', *History* **58** (1973), 169–92.

Robisheaux, T. W. *Rural Society and the Search for Order in Early Modern Germany.* Cambridge, 1987.

Roche, D. (ed.). *Le cheval et la guerre du XVe au XXe siècle.* Paris, 2002.

Rodger, N. A. M. *The Command of the Ocean: A Naval History of Britain, 1649–1815.* London, 2004.

'The Development of Broadside Gunnery, 1450–1650', *Mariner's Mirror* **82** (1996), 301–24.

The Safeguard of the Sea: A Naval History of Britain, 660–1649. London, 1997.

Rodríguez-Salgado, M. J. (ed.). *Armada, 1588–1988: An International Exhibition to Commemorate the Spanish Armada.* Harmondsworth, 1988.

Rogers, C. J. 'The Battle of Agincourt', in L. J. A. Villalon and D. J. Kagay (eds.), *The Hundred Years War,* 2 vols., II: *Different Vistas* (Leiden and Boston, 2008), Chapter 2.

(ed.). *The Military Revolution Debate: Readings on the Military Transformation of Early Modern Europe.* Boulder, CO, San Francisco and Oxford, 1995.

'The Military Revolutions of the Hundred Years' War', in Rogers (ed.), *Military Revolution Debate,* 55–94.

Soldiers' Lives through History: The Middle Ages. Westport, CT, 2007.

Roncière, C. de la. *Histoire de la marine française,* 6 vols., III. Paris, 1906.

Roosens, B. 'De keizerlijke artillerie op het einde van de regering van Karel V', *Belgisch tijdschrift voor militaire geschiedenis* **33** (1979), 117–36.

'Het arsenaal van Mechelen en de wapenhandel (1551–1567)', *Bijdragen tot de geschiedenis* **60** (1970), 175–247.

Ropp, T. *War in the Modern World.* 2nd edn. New York, 1962.

Rose, S. *Medieval Naval Warfare, 1000–1500.* London and New York 2002.

Roth, C. *The Last Florentine Republic, 1527–1530.* London, 1925.

Rousset, C. *Louvois,* 4 vols. Paris, 1879.

Roux, A. de, N. Faucherre, and G. Monsaingeon. *Les plans en relief des places du roi*. Paris, 1989.

Rowell, S. C. *Lithuania Ascending: A Pagan Empire within East Central Europe, 1295–1345*. Cambridge, 1994.

Rowlands, G. *The Dynastic State and the Army under Louis XIV: Royal Service and Private Interest, 1661–1701*. Cambridge, 2002.

'The King's Two Arms: French Amphibious Warfare in the Mediterranean under Louis XIV, 1664 to 1697', in Trim and Fissel (eds.), *Amphibious Warfare*, 263–314.

'Louis XIV, Aristocratic Power and the Elite Units of the French Army', *French History* **13** (1999), 303–31.

'Louis XIV, Vittorio Amadeo II and French Military Failures in Italy, 1688–96', *EHR* **115** (2000), 534–69.

'The Monopolisation of Military Power in France, 1515 to 1715', in R. G. Asch, W. E. Voß, and M. Wrede (eds.), *Frieden und Krieg in der Frühen Neuzeit: Die europäische Staatenordnung und die außereuropäische Welt* (Munich, 2001), 139–60.

Rule, M. *The Mary Rose: The Excavation and Raising of Henry VIII's Flagship*. London, 1982.

Runciman, Steven. *The Fall of Constantinople, 1453*. Cambridge, 1965.

Runyan, T. J. 'The Cog as Warship', in Gardiner and Unger (eds.), *Cogs, Caravels and Galleons*, 47–58.

'Naval Power and Maritime Technology during the Hundred Years War', in Hattendorf and Unger (eds.), *War at Sea*, 53–67.

Ruppert, K. *Die kaiserliche Politik auf dem Westfälischen Friedenskongreß (1643–1648)*. Münster, 1979.

Russell, F. H. *The Just War in the Middle Ages*. Cambridge, 1975.

Russell, J. G. *Peacemaking in the Renaissance*. London, 1996.

Russell, P. *Prince Henry 'the Navigator': A Life*. New Haven, CT, 2001.

Russell-Wood, A. J. B. *A World on the Move: The Portuguese in Africa, Asia, and America, 1415–1808*. Baltimore, 1998.

Russocki, S. 'Zwischen Monarchie, Oligarchie und Adelsdemokratie: Das polnische Königtum im 15. Jahrhundert', in Schneider (ed.), *Das spätmittelalterliche Königtum*, 398–402.

Salm, H. *Armeefinanzierung im Dreißigjährigen Krieg: Der Niederrheinisch-Westfälische Reichskreis, 1635–50*. Münster, 1990.

Satterfield, G. *Princes, Posts and Partisans: The Army of Louis XIV and Partisan Warfare in the Netherlands 1673–1678*. Leiden and Boston, 2003.

Savage, H. L. 'Enguerrand de Coucy VII and the Campaign of Nicopolis', *Speculum* **14** (1939), 423–42.

Scammel, G. V. *Seafaring, Sailors and Trade, 1450–1750: Studies in British and European Maritime and Imperial History*. Aldershot, 2003.

Ships, Oceans, and Empire: Studies in European Maritime and Colonial History, 1400–1750. Aldershot, 1995.

Schiller, F. *Geschichte des Dreißigjährigen Krieges*. Zürich, 1985.

Schmidtchen, V. 'Karrenbüchse und Wagenburg: Hussitische Innovationen zur Technik und Taktik im Kriegswesen des späten Mittelalters', in V. Schmidtchen and E. Jäger (eds.), *Wirtschaft, Technik und Geschichte: Beiträge zur Erforschung der Kulturbeziehungen in Deutschland und Osteuropa. Festschrift Albrecht Timm* (Berlin, 1980), 83–108.

Schneider, R. (ed.). *Das spätmittelalterliche Königtum im europäischen Vergleich*, Vorträge und Forschungen 32. Sigmaringen, 1987.

Schnitter, H. *Volk und Landesdefension: Volksaufgebote, Defensionswerke, Landmilizien in den deutschen Territorien vom 15. bis zum 18. Jahrhundert.* Berlin, 1977.

Schofield, R. 'Taxation and the Political Limits of the Tudor State', in C. Cross *et al.* (eds.), *Law and Government under the Tudors: Essays Presented to Sir Geoffrey Elton on his Retirement* (Cambridge, 1988), 227–55.

Schöningh, F. J. *Die Rehlinger von Augsburg: Ein Beitrag zur deutschen Wirtschaftsgeschichte des 16. und 17. Jahrhunderts*, dissertation, Paderborn, 1927.

Schubert, H. 'The First Cast-Iron Cannon Made in England', *Journal of the Iron and Steel Institute*, **146**:2 (1942), 131–40.

'The Superiority of English Cast-Iron Cannon at the Close of the Sixteenth Century', *Journal of the Iron and Steel Institute*, **161**:1 (1949), 85–6.

Schulten, C. 'Une nouvelle approche de Maurice de Nassau (1567–1625)', in P. Chaunu (ed.), *Le soldat, la stratégie, la mort: Mélanges André Corvisier* (Paris, 1989), 42–53.

Schulze, W. 'Die deutsche Landesdefensionen im 16. und 17. Jahrhundert', in Stollberg-Rilinger and Kunisch (eds.), *Staatsverfassung*, 129–49.

'The Emergence and Consolidation of the "Tax State". I: The Sixteenth Century', in Bonney (ed.), *Economic Systems and State Finance*, 261–79.

Schumpeter, J. A. *Capitalism, Socialism and Democracy.* London, 1992 [1942].

The Theory of Economic Development: An Inquiry into Profits, Capital, Credit, Interest, and the Business Cycle. New Brunswick, 1983 [1911].

Scott, J. *England's Troubles: Seventeenth-Century English Political Instability in European Context.* Cambridge, 2000.

Scott, W. R. *Organizations: Rational, Natural and Open Systems.* 5th edn. Upper Saddle River, 2003.

Sedlar, J. W. (ed.). *East Central Europe in the Middle Ages, 1000–1500.* Seattle, 1994.

Seed, P. 'Conquest of the Americas, 1500–1650', in G. Parker (ed.), *The Cambridge Illustrated History of Warfare: The Triumph of the West* (Cambridge, 1995), 132–45.

Seguin, J.-P. *L'information en France, de Louis XII à Henri II.* Geneva, 1961.

Setton, K. M. *The Papacy and the Levant (1204–1571)*, 4 vols. Philadelphia, 1976–84.

Venice, Austria, and the Turks in the Seventeenth Century. Philadelphia, 1991.

Shaïk, R. van. 'Taxation, Public Finances and the State-Making Process in the Late Middle Ages: The Case of the Duchy of Guelders', *Journal of Medieval History* **19** (1993), 251–71.

Shaw, C. (ed.). *Italy and the European Powers: The Impact of War, 1500–1530.* Leiden, 2006.

Shaw, S. J. *History of the Ottoman Empire and Modern Turkey*, 2 vols. Cambridge, 1976–7, I: *Empire of the Gazis: The Rise and Decline of the Ottoman Empire 1280–1808.*

Sheehan, J.J. *Where Have All the Soldiers Gone? The Transformation of Modern Europe.* Boston, 2008.

Sherborne, J. *War, Politics and Culture in Fourteenth-Century England.* London and Rio Grande, OH, 1994.

Showalter, D.E. 'Hubertusburg to Auerstedt: The Prussian Army in Decline?', *German History* **12** (1994), 308–33.

The Wars of Frederick the Great. London and New York, 1996.

Sicken, B. 'Der Dreißigjährige Krieg als Wendepunkt: Kriegsführung und Heeresstruktur im Übergang zum *miles perpetuus*', in H. Duchhardt (ed.), *Der Westfälische Friede: Diplomatie, politische Zäsur, kulturelles Umfeld, Rezeptionsgeschichte* (Munich, 1998), 581–98.

Sicking, L. 'Les transports militaires par mer: L'importance des Pays-Bas aux XVe siècle', in S. Curveiller *et al.* (eds.), *Se déplacer du Moyen Age à nos jours* (Calais, 2008).

'Naval Power in the Netherlands before the Dutch Revolt', in Hattendorf and Unger (eds.), *War at Sea*, 199–216.

Neptune and the Netherlands. State, Economy, and War at Sea in the Renaissance. Leiden and Boston 2004.

'Philip of Cleves' *Instruction de toutes manières de guerroyer* and the Fitting Out of Warships in the Netherlands during the Habsburg–Valois Wars', in J. Haemers, C. van Hoorebeeck, and H. Wijsman (eds.), *Entre la ville, la noblesse et l'Etat: Philippe de Clèves (1456–1528), homme politique et bibliophile* (Turnhout, 2007), 117–42.

Zeemacht en onmacht: Maritieme politiek in de Nederlanden, 1488–1558. Amsterdam, 1998.

Sikora, M. 'Verzweiflung oder "Leichtsinn"? Militärstand und Desertion im 18. Jahrhundert', in Kroener and Pröve (eds.), *Krieg und Frieden*, 237–64.

Simms, H. 'Violence in County Armagh', in B. MacCuarta (ed.), *Ulster 1641: Aspects of the Rising* (Belfast, 1993), 123–38.

Smith, A.D. *The Ethnic Origins of Nations.* Oxford, 1986.

Smith, J.M. *Nobility Reimagined: The Patriotic Nation in Eighteenth-Century France.* Ithaca, NY, 2005.

Smith, M., and M. Uttley. 'Military Power in a Multipolar World', in Dorman, Smith, and Uttley (eds.), *Changing Face of Military Power*, 1–14.

Smith, R.D., and K. DeVries. *The Sieges of Rhodes: A Story of Cannon, Stone and Men, 1480–1521* (forthcoming).

Snapper, F. *Oorlogsinvloeden op de overzeese handel van Holland, 1551–1719.* Amsterdam, 1959.

Soar, H. *Secrets of the English War Bow.* Yardley, PA, 2006.

Sörensson, P. 'Das Kriegswesen während der letzten Periode des Dreißigjährigen Krieges', in H. Rudolf (ed.), *Der Dreißigjährige Krieg: Perspektiven und Strukturen* (Darmstadt, 1977), 431–57.

Srbik, H. von. *Wallenstein's Ende: Ursachen, Verlauf and Folgen der Katastrophe.* Salzburg, 1952.

Stacey, R.C. 'The Age of Chivalry', in Howard, Andreopoulis, and Schulman (eds.), *Laws of War*, 27–39.

Stapleton, J.M. 'Forging a Coalition Army: William III, the Grand Alliance, and the Confederate Army in the Spanish Netherlands, 1688–1697', unpublished Ph.D. dissertation, Ohio State, 2003.

Starkey, A. *War in the Age of the Enlightenment, 1700–1789*. Westport, CT, 2003.

Stewart, P. J. 'The Army of the Catholic Kings: Spanish Military Organization and Administration in the Reign of Ferdinand and Isabella, 1474-1516', unpublished Ph.D. dissertation, Illinois, 1961.

Stollberg-Rilinger, B., and J. Kunisch (eds.). *Staatsverfassung und Heeresverfassung in der europäischen Geschichte der frühen Neuzeit*. Berlin, 1986.

Stone, D. *The Polish–Lithuanian State, 1386–1765*. Seattle, 2001.

Stone, J. 'Technology, Society, and the Infantry Revolution of the Fourteenth Century', *JMH* **68** (2004), 361–80.

Storrs, C., and H. M. Scott. 'The Military Revolution and the European Nobility, c. 1600–1800', *War in History* **3** (1996), 1–41.

Strachan, H. Letter to Editor, *Journal of the Royal United Services Institute*, **152**:4 (August 2007), 4.

Stradling, R. A. *The Armada of Flanders: Spanish Maritime Policy and European War, 1568–1668*. Cambridge and New York, 1992.

The Spanish Monarchy and Irish Mercenaries: The Wild Geese in Spain, 1618–1668. Dublin, 1994.

Stretton, M. 'Medieval Arrowheads: Practical Tests, Part Two', *The Glade* **108** (2005).

Strickland, M., and R. Hardy. *The Great Warbow: From Hastings to the Mary Rose*. Stroud, 2005.

The Great Warbow: A History of the Military Archer. New York, 2005.

Sumption, J. *The Hundred Years War*, 3 vols, II: *Trial by Fire*. London, 1992.

Swart, E. *Krijgsvolk: Militaire professionalisering en het ontstaan van het Staatse leger, 1568–1590*. Amsterdam, 2006.

Symcox, G. *The Crisis of French Sea Power, 1688–1697: From the guerre d'escadre to the guerre de course*. The Hague, 1974.

'Two Forms of Popular Resistance in the Savoyard State of the 1680s: The Rebels of the Mondovi and the Vaudois', in G. Lombardi (ed.), *La guerra del sale (1680–1699): Rivolte e frontiere del Piemonte barocco*, 3 vols., I (Milan, 1986), 275–90.

Szabó, J. B., *Mohács (1526): Soliman le Magnifique prend pied en Europe centrale*. Paris, 2009.

A Mohácsi csata. Budapest, 2006; French trans., Paris, 2008.

'A mohácsi csata és a "hadügyi forradalom"', Parts I–II; *Hk* **117** (2004), 443–80 and 118 (2005), 573–632 (in Hungarian, with English summaries).

Szakály, F. 'The Hungarian–Croatian Border Defense System and Its Collapse', in Bak and Király (eds.), *From Hunyadi to Rákóczi*, 141–58.

'Phases in Turco-Hungarian Warfare before the Battle of Mohács', *AoH* **23** (1979), 65–111.

Szymczak, J. 'Les coûts de la construction des murailles en Pologne jusqu'au XVIe siècle', *Acta Universitatis lodziensis, folia archeologica* **14** (1991), 3–13.

Tallett, F. *War and Society in Early Modern Europe, 1495–1715*. London, 1992.

Tanner, M. *The Last Descendant of Aeneas: The Hapsburgs and the Mythic Image of the Emperor*. New Haven, CT: Yale University Press, 1993.

Taylor, F. L. *The Art of War in Italy, 1494–1529*. Cambridge, 1921.

Tenenti, A. *Piracy and the Decline of Venice, 1580–1615*, trans. J. and B. Pullan. Los Angeles and Berkeley, 1967.

Thiriot, J. *Portes, tours et murailles de la cité de Metz*. Metz, 1970.

Thompson, A. C. *Britain, Hanover and the Protestant Interest*. Woodbridge, 2006.

Thompson, I. A. A. 'The Appointment of the Duke of Medina Sidonia to the Command of the Spanish Armada', *Historical Journal* **12** (1969), 197–216.

'Aspects of Spanish Military and Naval Organization during the Ministry of Olivares', in I. A. A. Thompson, *War and Society in Habsburg Spain* (Aldershot, 1992), Chapter 4, 1–26.

' "Money, money and yet more money!" Finance, the Fiscal-State, and the Military Revolution: Spain 1500–1650', in Rogers (ed.), *Military Revolution Debate*, 273–98.

War and Government in Habsburg Spain 1560–1620. London, 1976.

Thomson, J. E. *Mercenaries, Pirates, and Sovereign:. State-Building and Extraterritorial Violence in Early Modern Europe*. Princeton, NJ, 1994.

Tighe, W. J. 'The Gentlemen Pensioners in Elizabethan Politics and Government', unpublished Ph.D. thesis, Cambridge, 1983.

Tilly, C. *Coercion, Capital and European States, AD 990–1990*. Oxford, 1990.

(ed.). *The Formation of National States in Western Europe*. Princeton, NJ, 1975.

Tipton, C. L. 'The English at Nicopolis', *Speculum* **37** (1962), 528–40.

Topping, P. 'Venice's Last Imperial Venture', *Proceedings of the American Philosophical Society* **120**:3 (June 1976), 159–65.

Torres Sánchez, R. *War State and Development: Fiscal-Military States in the Eighteenth Century*. Barañáin, 2007.

Tracy, J. D. 'A Clash of Civilizations: Habsburg Lands, the Ottoman Empire, and the Struggle for the Middle Danube Basin, 1522–1592', unpublished conference paper, *Sixteenth Century Studies Conference*, St Louis, 24 October 2008.

Emperor Charles V, Impresario of War: Campaign Strategy, International Finance, and Domestic Politics. Cambridge, 2002.

Emperor Charles V's Crusades against Tunis and Algiers: Appearance and Reality. Minneapolis, 2001.

Holland under Habsburg rule, 1505–1566: The Formation of a Body Politic. Berkeley and Los Angeles, CA, 1990.

Tresp, U. *Söldner aus Böhmen. Im Dienst deutscher Fürsten: Krieggeschäft und Heeresorganisation im 15. Jh.* Paderborn, Munich, Vienna and Zürich, 2004.

Trim, D. J. B. 'Army, Society and Military Professionalism in the Netherlands during the Eighty Years' War', in Trim (ed.), *Chivalric Ethos*, 269–89.

'Calvinist Internationalism and the English Officer Corps, 1562–1642', *History Compass* **4** (2006), 1024–48.

(ed.). *The Chivalric Ethos and the Development of Military Professionalism*. Leiden and Boston, 2003.

'Early Modern Colonial Warfare and the Campaign of Alcazarquivir 1578', *Small Wars and Insurgencies*, 8:1 (1997), 1–34; repr. in P. E. J. Hammer (ed.), *Warfare in Early Modern Europe 1450–1660* (Aldershot, 2007), 323–56.

'Edict of Nantes: Product of Military Success or Failure?', in K. Cameron, M. Greengrass, and P. Roberts (eds.), *The Adventure of Religious Pluralism in Early Modern France* (Oxford, Bern and New York, 2000), 85–99.

'Fighting "Jacob's Wars". The Employment of English and Welsh Mercenaries in the European Wars of Religion: France and the Netherlands, 1562–1610', unpublished Ph.D. thesis, London, 2002.

'Huguenot Soldiering *c.* 1560–1685: The Origins of a Tradition', in M. Glozier and D. Onnekink (eds.), *War, Religion and Service: Huguenot Soldiering, 1685–1713* (Aldershot, 2007), 9–30.

'Seeking a Protestant Alliance and Liberty of Conscience on the Continent, 1558–85', in S. Doran and G. Richardson (eds.), *Tudor England and Its Neighbours* (Basingstoke and New York, 2005), 139–77.

Trim, D. J. B., and M. C. Fissel (eds.). *Amphibious Warfare 1000–1700: Commerce, State Formation and European Expansion.* Leiden and Boston, 2006.

Troeyer, B. de. *Lamoraal van Egmont: Een critische studie over zijn rol in de jaren 1559–64 in verband met het schuldvraagstuk,* Verhandelingen van de Koninklijke Vlaamsche Academie voor Wetenschappen, Letteren en Schone Kunsten van België, Klasse der Letteren 40. Brussels, 1961.

Troso, M. *Italia! Italia! 1526–1530: La prima guerra d'indipendenza Italiana con gli assedi di Milano, Napoli, Firenze, il sacco di Roma e le battaglia di Capo d'Orso e Gavinana.* Parma, 2001.

Tuck, R. 'The Modern Theory of Natural Law', in A. Pagden (ed.), *The Languages of Political Theory in Early-Modern Europe* (Cambridge, 1987), 99–119.

Tucker, T. J. 'Early Modern French Noble Identity and the Equestrian "Airs above the Ground" ', in K. Raber and T. J. Tucker (eds.), *The Culture of the Horse: Status, Discipline and Identity in the Early Modern World* (Basingstoke, 2005), 273–310.

Turnbull, S. *The Ottoman Empire, 1326–1699.* London, 2003.

Turrel, C. *Metz, deux mille ans d'architecture militaire.* Metz, 1986.

Tyerman, C. J. 'Philip VI and the Recovery of the Holy Land', *EHR* **100** (1985), 25–52.

Unger, R. W. 'Conclusion: Towards a History of Medieval Sea Power', in Hattendorf and Unger (eds.), *War at Sea*, 249–61.

Urban, M. *Generals: Ten British Commanders who Shaped the World.* London, 2005.

Urban, W. *The Teutonic Knights: A Military History.* London, 2003.

Vale, M. G. A. *War and Chivalry: Warfare and Aristocratic Culture in England, France and Burgundy at the End of the Middle Ages.* London, 1981.

Vatin, N. *Sultan Djem. Un prince Ottoman dans l'Europe du XVe siècle d'après deux sources contemporaines: Vâki'ât-i Sultân Cem/Oeuvres de Guillaume Caoursin,* Publications de la Société Turque d'Histoire, series 18:14. Ankara, 1994.

Vaughan, R. *Valois Burgundy.* Hamden, CT, 1975.

Veinstein. G. 'Some Views on Provisioning in the Hungarian Campaigns of Suleyman the Magnificent', in G. Veinstein, *Etat et société dans l'Empire ottoman, XVIe-XVIIIe siècles* (Aldershot, 1994), 177–85.

Verbruggen, J. F. *De krijgskunst in West-Europa in de middeleeuwen (IXe tot begin XIVe eeuw).* Brussels, 1954.

'The Role of the Cavalry in Medieval Warfare', *Journal of Medieval Military History* **3** (2005), 46–71.

Vermesch, G. *Oorlog, steden en staatsvorming: De grenssteden Gorinchem en Doesburg tijdens de geboorte-eeuw van de Republiek (1570–1680)*. Amsterdam, 2006.

Veszprémy, L. 'The Birth of Military Science in Hungary: The Period of the Angevin and Luxemburg Kings', in Király and Veszprémy (eds.), *Millennium of Hungarian Military History*, 26–53.

'Bombardes, arquebuses et manuscrits de l'art militaire: L'apparition des armes à feu en Hongrie jusqu'en 1526', *Cahiers d'études et de recherches du Musée de l'Armée* (forthcoming).

'Innovations techniques et manuscrits d'art militaire autour de Sigismond de Luxembourg', in I. Takács (ed.), *Sigismundus, rex et imperator: Art et culture à l'époque de Sigismond de Luxembourg, 1387–1437* (Budapest and Luxembourg, 2006), 287–91.

'Some Remarks on Recent Historiography of the Crusade of Nicopolis (1396)', in Z. Hunyadi and J. Laszlovszky (eds.), *The Crusades and the Military Orders: Expanding the Frontiers of Medieval Latin Christianity* (Budapest, 2001), 223–30.

Villiger, V., J. Steinauer, and D. Bitterli. *Les chevauchées du colonel Koenig: Un aventurier dans l'Europe en guerre*. Fribourg, 2006.

Vine, S., and A. Hildred, 'The Evidence of the Mary Rose Excavation', in C. S. Knighton and D. Loades (eds.), *The Anthony Roll*, 15–20.

Volmer, I. 'A Comparative Study of Massacres during the Wars of the Three Kingdoms, 1642–1653', unpublished Ph.D. thesis, Cambridge, 2007.

Vos, A. *Standaardrapport inventarisatie scheepswrak Ritthem*. Amersfoort, 2008.

Wagner, J. V. *Graf Wilhelm von Fürstenberg (1491–1549) und die politisch-geistigen Mächte seiner Zeit*. Stuttgart, 1966.

Walker, S. K. 'Janico Dartasso: Chivalry, Nationality and the Man-at-Arms', *History* **84** (1999), 31–51.

Walsh, M. J. (ed.). *Lives of the Popes*. London, 1998.

Walzer, M. *The Revolution of the Saints: A Study in the Origins of Radical Politics*. Cambridge, MA, 1965; London, 1966.

Ward, W. R. *The Protestant Evangelical Awakening*. Cambridge, 1992.

Warren, W. T. *The Story of the Great Siege of Basing House, 1642–1645*. London, 1908.

Webb, H. J. *Elizabethan Military Science*. Madison, WI, 1965.

Weber, M. *Economy and Society*, ed. G. Roth and C. Wittich, 2 vols. Berkeley, CA, 1978.

Weigley, R. *The Age of Battles: The Quest for Decisive Warfare from Breitenfeld to Waterloo*. London, 1993.

Weise, E. 'Der Heidenkampf des deutschen Ordens', Parts 1–3, *ZfO* **12** (1963), 420–73, 622–72; 13 (1964), 400–40.

Wellens, R. 'Le procès de Philibert de Marigny, gouverneur de Mariembourg (1550–1552)', *Namurcum* **31** (1957).

Wernham, R. B. 'Amphibious Operations and the Elizabethan Assault on Spain's Atlantic Economy', in Trim and Fissel (eds.), *Amphibious Warfare*, 181–215.

Wheeler, E. L. 'Methodological Limits and the Mirage of Roman Strategy', *JMH* **57** (1993), 7–41, 215–40.

Wheeler, J. S. *The Making of a World Power: War and the Military Revolution in Seventeenth-Century England*. Stroud, 1999.

Wiesflecker, H. *Kaiser Maximilian I: Das Reich, Österreich und Europa an der Wende zur Neuzeit*, 5 vols. Munich, 1971–86.

Wijn, J. W. 'Het Noordhollandse regiment in de eerste jaren van de Opstand tegen Spanje', *Tijdschrift voor Geschiedenis* **62** (1949), 235–61.

Williams, A. R. *The Knight and the Blast Furnace: A History of the Metallurgy of Armour in the Middle Ages and the Early Modern Period*. Leiden and Boston, 2003.

Williams, P. *The Tudor Regime*. Oxford, 1979.

Williamson, J. A. *The English Channel: A History*. London 1959.

Williamson, O. E. *The Mechanisms of Governance*. Oxford, 1996.

Wills, G. *Venice: Lion City. The Religion of Empire*. New York, 2001.

Wills, J. E. 'Maritime Asia, 1500–1800: The Interactive Emergence of European Domination', *AHR* **98** (1993), 83–105.

Wilson, P. *Absolutism in Central Europe*. London, 2000.

German Armies: War and German Politics, 1648–1806. London, 1998.

'Social Militarisation in Eighteenth-Century Germany', *German History* **18** (2000), 1–39.

Winkelbauer, T. '*Nervus rerum Austriacarum*: Zur Finanzgeschichte der Habsburgermonarchie um 1700', in Mat'a and Winkelbauer (eds.), *Die Habsburgermonarchie*, 179–216.

Winkler, A. L. 'The Swiss and War: The Impact of Society on the Swiss Military in the Fourteenth and Fifteenth Centuries', unpublished Ph.D. dissertation, Brigham Young, 1982.

Winter, M. *Untertanengeist durch Militärpflicht? Das preußische Kantonssystem in brandenburgischen Städten im 18. Jahrhundert*. Bielefeld, 2005.

Wohlfeil, R. 'Adel und neues Heerwesen', in H. Rössler (ed.), *Deutscher Adel, 1430–1555* (Darmstadt, 1965), 203–33.

Wolf, J. B. 'Commentary,' in M. D. Wright and L. J. Paszek (eds.), *Science, Technology, and Warfare: The Proceedings of the Third Military History Symposium, United States Air Force Academy, 8–9 May 1969* (Washington, DC, 1969), 33–43.

Wolfe, M. *The Conversion of Henri IV: Politics, Power, and Religious Belief in Early Modern France*. Cambridge, MA, 1993.

Wood, J. B. *The King's Army: Warfare, Soldiers and Society during the Wars of Religion in France, 1562–1576*. Cambridge, 1996.

Woolrych, A. H. *Britain in Revolution, 1625–1660*. Oxford, 2002.

Yıldız, H. *Haydi Osmanlı sefere: Prut seferinde lojistik ve organizasyon*. Istanbul, 2006.

Yurdusev, A. N. (ed.). *Ottoman Diplomacy: Conventional or Unconventional?* London, 2004.

Zakythinos, D. *La despotat grec de la Moreé*, 2 vols. London, 1975.

Zay, F. *Az lándorfejírvár elveszésének oka e vót*, ed. I. Kovács. Budapest, 1980.

Zeller, G. 'Le siège de Metz par Charles-Quint (Octobre–Décembre 1552)', *Annales de l'Est* **13** (1943), 1–270.

Zmora, H. *Monarchy, Aristocracy, and the State in Europe, 1300–1800*. London, 2001.

State and Nobility in Early Modern Germany: The Knightly Feud in Franconia, 1440–1567. Cambridge, 1997.

'Values and Violence: The Morals of Feuding in Late Medieval Germany', in J. Büchert Netterstrom and B. Poulsen (eds.), *Feud in Medieval and Early Modern Europe* (Aarhus, 2007), 145–58.

Zombori, I. (ed.) *Fight against the Turk in Central-Europe in the First Half of the Sixteenth Century.* Budapest, 2004.

Zünckel, J. *Rüstungsgeschäfte im Dreißigjährigen Krieg.* Berlin, 1997.

'Rüstungshandel im Zeitalter des Dreißigjährigen Krieges: "militärisches Revolution", internationale Strategien und Hamburger Perspektiven', in B. von Krusenstjern and H. Medick (eds.), *Zwischen Alltag und Katastrophe: Der Dreißigjährige Krieg aus der Nähe* (Göttingen, 2001), 83–11.

Zysberg, A. 'Les galères de France entre 1661–1748: Restauration, apogée et survivance d'une flotte de guerre en Méditerranée', in M. Vergé-Franceschi (ed.), *Guerre et commerce en Méditerranée IXe–XXe siècles* (Paris 1991), 123–60.

Zysberg, A., and R. Burlet. *Gloire et misère des galères.* Paris, 1987.

Index